Via Santa
Chiara
Italy hotel 21.
com/
roma/
santa_
chiara

TimeOut

Rome

timeout.com/rome

Penguin Books

PENGUIN BOOKS

Published by the Penguin Group
Penguin Books Ltd, 27 Wrights Lane, London W8 5TZ, England
Penguin Books USA Inc., 375 Hudson Street, New York, New York 10014, USA
Penguin Books Australia Ltd, Ringwood, Victoria, Australia
Penguin Books Canada Ltd, 10 Alcorn Avenue, Toronto, Ontario, Canada M4V 3B2
Penguin Books (NZ) Ltd, 182-190 Wairau Road, Auckland 10, New Zealand

Penguin Books Ltd, Registered Offices: Harmondsworth, Middlesex, England

First published 1994
Second edition 1996
Third edition 1998
Fourth edition 1999
Fifth edition 2001
10 9 8 7 6 5 4 3 2 1

Colour reprographics by Icon, Crown House, 56-58 Southwark Street, London SE1
and Precise Litho, 34-35 Great Sutton Street, London EC1
Printed and bound by Cayfosa-Quebecor, Ctra. de Caldes, Km 3 08 130 Sta, Perpètua de Mogoda, Barcelona, Spain

Edited and designed by
Time Out Guides Limited
Universal House
251 Tottenham Court Road
London W1T 7AB
Tel + 44 (020) 7813 3000
Fax + 44 (020) 7813 6001
Email guides@timeout.com
www.timeout.com

Editorial

Editor Anne Hanley
Deputy Editor Rosamund Sales
Listings Editor Fulvia Angelini
Proofreader Marion Moisy
Indexer Jackie Brind

Editorial Director Peter Fiennes
Series Editor Ruth Jarvis
Deputy Series Editor Jonathan Cox
Guides Co-ordinator Jenny Noden

Design

Art Director John Oakey
Art Editor Mandy Martin
Senior Designer Scott Moore
Designers Benjamin de Lotz, Lucy Grant,
Kate Vincent-Smith
Scanning/Imaging Dan Conway
Picture Editor Kerri Miles
Deputy Picture Editor Olivia Duncan-Jones
Ad Make-up Glen Impey

Advertising

Group Commercial Director Lesley Gill
Sales Director/Sponsorship Mark Phillips
International Sales Co-ordinator Ross Canadé
Advertisement Sales Manager (Rome)
Margherita Tedone
Advertising Assistant Catherine Shepherd

Administration

Publisher Tony Elliott
Managing Director Mike Hardwick
Group Financial Director Kevin Ellis
Marketing Director Christine Cort
Marketing Manager Mandy Martinez
Group General Manager Nichola Coulthard
Production Manager Mark Lamond
Production Controller Samantha Furniss
Accountant Sarah Bostock

Features in this guide were written and researched by:
Introduction Anne Hanley. **History** Anne Hanley, Ferdie McDonald, *Lust, Murder and Incest* Lee Marshall. **Rome Today** Lee Marshall, Anne Hanley. **Architecture** Anne Hanley, Paul Duncan. **Art in Rome** Frederick Ilchman. **Accommodation** Michelle Hough. **Sightseeing** Anne Hanley, William Ward, Ros Belford, *Roma Felix* Peter Douglas, *Big Nose* Katia Gizzi, *Conclave Capers* Philippa Hitchen. **Eating Out** Lee Marshall. **Cafés, Pubs & Gelaterie** Sarah Delaney, Anne Hanley. **Shops & Services** Mari Beth Bittan, *Runway Success* Peter Douglas. **By Season** Anne Hanley. **Children** Anne Hanley. **Contemporary Art** Michelle Rogers. **Film** Lee Marshall. **Gay & Lesbian** Peter Douglas. **Music: Classical & Opera** Linda Bordoni, Robert Adams. **Nightlife** Katia Gizzi, Paul Toohill. **Sport & Fitness** Sylvie Hogg, Chris Endean. **Theatre & Dance** Sarah Delaney, Linda Bordoni. **Trips Out of Town** Anne Hanley. **Directory** Fabrizio Giusto.

The Editor would like to thank:
Fulvia Angelini and Ros Sales for their untiring efforts. Special thanks to Lee and Clara Marshall. Margherita Tedone would like to thank Ilaria Sinibaldi.

Maps by LS International, via Sanremo 17, 20133 Milan, Italy. Map on page 140 by Mapworld.

Photography by Adam Eastland except: page 113 Guido Fuà; pages 28, 123, 127, 128 and 129 Anne Hanley; pages 7, 8, 12, 13, 18, 25, 31, 32, 82-83, 95, 104, 105 and 159 AKG; page 238 British Film Institute; page 19 Associated Press; pages 246 and 247 Performing Arts Library; pages 269, 271, 272, 273, 274, 276, 278 and 281 Corbis Images.

The following picture was supplied by the featured establishments/organisations: page 234.

Contents

Introduction

In 1931, Mussolini asserted the superiority of his regime – even over ancient Rome – by bulldozing a multi-laned traffic artery through one of the densest patches of remains in the city. Down came the medieval and Renaissance *palazzi* that had grown out of the foundations of the Fori Imperiali over the centuries, and down went tarmac over what remained. Ancient temples, law courts and meeting houses – built by Rome's emperors to commemorate their real military triumphs – gave way to a sweep of road conceived as a parade ground, where Mussolini's troops would mark their hollow ones.

For decades, via dei Fori Imperiali epitomised the quandary in which Rome still finds itself. Here was the most visible symbol of the less-than-reverent way that Romans have treated their ancient heritage (not to mention a reminder of an era that, with time, grew to seem ever more preposterous). On the other hand, it was useful: as the city's traffic chaos grew, the via dei Fori Imperiali ferried vehicles swiftly away from piazza Venezia and out towards the southern and eastern suburbs.

And, for decades, the powers that be squabbled about it. Archaeologists wanted the road demolished; town planners and traffic engineers threw up their hands in horror, imagining the resulting logjam; and politicians sat back and let them fight it out among themselves, happy to have an excuse for their usual complacent inactivity.

The wind of change that has been blowing over Rome since the mid-1990s – coinciding more or less with the arrival at City Hall of the Green mayor, Francesco Rutelli – has had profound effects on the Fori Imperiali. Depending on whom you ask, you'll be told that the solution devised for the future of this incomparable heap of ancient masonry is either fence-sitting or ingenious. But the fact remains that the fora – not exactly in their entirety, but large sections – are reopening to the public and the traffic is continuing to flow. How? Raised walkways, underpasses, carefully plotted itineraries that don't impinge on the internal combustion engines thundering by. Think what you may of the compromise, it puts the fora back on the map.

It's not the only thing that is on view again. Scaffolding has been taken down from buildings that had long been under wraps; masterpieces of the ancient world have had their dust sheets removed and been put in brand new museums; and another affront to the classical world – the stretch of ring road that sliced right through the Appian Way – has been buried in a tunnel and the *regina viarium* (Queen of Roads) is intact again.

Which isn't to say that all's right with the Eternal City. The confusion that is so much a part of its character for the visitor, and so infuriating for its residents, still reigns. What has changed is the assumption that the most eternal thing about Rome is its problems. The apathy that had gripped the city since World War II has been eroded. Granted, Rome throws up obstacles to progress like few other cities: medieval streets and sewage systems, and Renaissance thoroughfares that were fine when the widest thing to barrel down them was a horse and cart. But what has dawned on the city over the past decade is that, by directing a little of the ingenuity for which Romans are famous into finding ways round these obstacles, there is some hope of dragging this frustrating but lovely city into the 21st century. The onus is now on Rome's leaders to capitalise on this change in Roman mentality and provide the city with the infrastructure it so sorely needs.

ABOUT THE TIME OUT CITY GUIDES

The *Time Out Rome Guide* is one of an expanding series of *Time Out* City Guides, now numbering over 30, produced by the people behind London and New York's successful listings magazines. Our guides are written and updated by resident experts who have striven to provide you with all the most up-to-date information you'll need to explore the city or read up on its background, whether you're a local or a first-time visitor.

THE LOWDOWN ON THE LISTINGS

Above all, we've tried to make this book as useful as possible. Addresses, telephone numbers, websites, transport information, opening times, admission prices and credit card details are all included in our listings, which

> There is an online version of this guide, as well as weekly events listings for over 30 international cities, at www.timeout.com.

were all checked and correct as we went to press. However, in Rome, opening hours – both of small shops and major tourist sights – are subject to abrupt changes, the former by personal and the latter by official whim. Before you go out of your way, we'd advise you to phone ahead and check opening times and so on. While every effort has been made to ensure the accuracy of the information in this guide, the publishers cannot accept responsibility for any errors it may contain.

PRICES AND PAYMENT
We have noted where venues such as shops, hotels and restaurants accept the following credit cards: American Express (**AmEx**), Diners Club (**DC**), MasterCard (**MC**), and Visa (**V**). Many businesses also accept other cards, including Switch, Delta and JCB. In addition, some shops, restaurants and attractions take travellers' cheques issued by major financial institutions.

THE LIE OF THE LAND AND MAPS
We have divided the city into areas that correspond to the coloured zones of the street maps on page 320 to page 327. In those chapters where listings are *not* divided by area, the area name has been added to the end of the address: note that this is there to help you locate the area on the map more easily; it is *not* part of the official address. There's also a map reference, indicating the page and square on which an address will be found on our maps.

TELEPHONE NUMBERS
You must dial area codes with all numbers in Italy, even for local calls. Hence all Rome numbers begin with 06, whether or not you're calling from outside the city. From abroad, you must dial 39 (the international dialling code for Italy) followed by the number given in this book – including the initial 0. Mobile phone prefixes begin with 3; until mid-2001 they began 03 and you'll still find many written that way. Drop the zero, whether you're calling from inside or outside Italy.

ESSENTIAL INFORMATION
For all the practical information you might need for visiting the city, including emergency phone numbers and details of local transport, turn to the **Directory** chapter at the back of the guide. It starts on page 283.

LET US KNOW WHAT YOU THINK
We hope you enjoy the *Time Out Rome Guide*, and we'd like to know what you think of it. We welcome tips for places you consider we should include in future editions and take note of your criticism of our choices. There's a reader's reply card at the back of this book, or email us on romeguide@timeout.com.

The Euro

As of 28 February 2002, the lira will cease to be legal tender, its place taken by the Euro.

As this guide went to press, €1 was worth around 62 British pence and 88 US cents, though these rates are subject to fluctuation. Currencies of Euro zone countries are pegged to the Euro. €1 equals:

1,936.27 Italian lire
6.55957 French francs
1.95583 German marks
166.386 Spanish pesetas
0.787564 Irish punts

Sponsors & Advertisers

We would like to stress that no establishment has been included in this guide because it has advertised in any of our publications and no payment of any kind has influenced any review. The opinions given in this book are those of *Time Out* writers and entirely independent.

Targasys.

A world of services.

Targasys is always with you, ready to assure you all the tranquillity and serenity that you desire for your journeys, 24 hours a day 365 days a year.

Roadside assistance always and everywhere, infomobility so not to have surprises, insurance... and lots more.

To get to know us better contact us at the toll-free number **00-800-55555555**.

...and to discover Targa Connect's exclusive and innovative integrated infotelematic services onboard system visit us at:

www.targaconnect.com

In Context

History

Rome's might stemmed from a fratricide, a mass abduction and some superb military organisation.

ROMULUS AND REMUS

There are few cities that can claim an exact beginning. But, out of the legend of Romulus and Remus, ancient Roman historians created a self-glorifying chronicle, complete with exact dates, for the foundation of the city and its earliest rulers. According to them, Rome was founded by Romulus on 21 April 753 BC. This date is still celebrated as the city's official 'birthday' (*see p224*).

Romulus and Remus were the fruits of a rape by the god of war, Mars, of a local princess, called Rhea Silvia. Cast adrift as babies on the Tiber and washed up in the marshy area below the Palatine Hill, the twins were suckled by a she-wolf until found by a shepherd. Romulus rose to be leader of his tribe, quarrelled with and killed his brother, founded the city and, deciding his community was short on females, abducted all the women of the neighbouring Sabine tribe (*see p11* **Tribes on their hills**).

The true origins of Rome are lost, but ninth-century BC huts have been excavated on the Palatine – proof there was a primitive village there, at least. The first historically documented king of Rome was an Etruscan (*see p11* **Tribes on their hills**), Tarquinius Priscus, who reigned from 616 BC. It was probably Etruscans who drained the marshy area between the seven hills to create the Forum, hub of the city's political, economic and religious life.

According to Roman historians, in 509 BC the son of King Tarquinius Superbus raped Lucretia, the wife of a Roman, Collatinus. The next day, before killing herself, she told her husband and his friend Brutus what happened, and in revenge they led a rebellion against the Tarquins. The Etruscan dynasty was expelled and the Roman Republic was founded, with Brutus and Collatinus as its first consuls.

This is doubtless a romanticised account of what happened, but in time Etruscan influence

Sabine women fall prey to their testosterone-driven Roman neighbours. *See p11.*

over the region did wane and authority passed to Rome's magistrates. And chief among these were the two annually elected consuls, guided by a council of elders called the Senate. The number of people who could participate in the political life of the Republic was limited to a few ancient families or clans who formed the patrician class. Only they could vote, be appointed to the Senate or hold the more important public and religious offices.

The lower classes, or plebeians, struggled for a greater say in their own affairs. In 494 BC, the office of Tribune of the Plebeians was created to represent their interests, and by 367 BC a plebeian could hold the office of consul. The class system, however, was maintained – rich or successful plebeians were simply designated patricians.

All the Romans of the Republic were united by a belief in their right to conquer other tribes. Their superb military organisation, and an agile policy of divide and rule in making alliances, allowed them to pick off the neighbouring peoples of central and southern Italy, and bring the other communities – including the Etruscans – under Roman control. To ensure the spread of Roman power, new cities were established in conquered territories, and an extensive infrastructure was created to support the many conquests. The first great Roman road, the via Appia (Appian Way), was begun

in 312 BC, and shortly afterwards work started on the Acqua Appia, the first aqueduct to bring fresh water to the city. The port of Ostia (*see p270* **Ostia Antica**), founded at the mouth of the Tiber in 380 BC, expanded rapidly, as streams of barges plied the river, bringing corn, wine, oil and building materials to Rome.

Rome's expansion brought her into conflict with two equally powerful peoples, the Carthaginians of North Africa and Spain, and the Greeks, who had colonised southern Italy and Sicily. The latter were expelled from mainland Italy in 272 BC, but the Punic Wars against the Carthaginians lasted for almost 120 years, and Rome was more than once in danger of annihilation. In 219 BC Hannibal made his historic crossing of the Alps, gaining control of much of Italy, but was too cautious to press home his advantage with an assault on Rome. Carthage was finally destroyed in 146 BC, leaving Rome in control of the western Mediterranean.

In the early days of the Republic most Romans, rich or poor, had been farmers, tending to their own land or livestock in the surrounding countryside. Wars like those against Carthage, however, required huge standing armies. At the same time, much of the land in Italy had been been laid waste, either by Hannibal or the Roman armies. Wealthy Romans bought huge estates at knock-

down prices, while landless peasants flocked to the capital. By the end of the second century BC, the Romans were a race of soldiers, engineers, administrators and merchants, supported by tribute in the form of money and goods from defeated enemies and the slave labour of prisoners taken in battle. Keeping the mass of the Roman poor content required the exaction of still more tribute money from the conquered territories. A parasitic relationship was thus established, in which all classes in Rome lived off the rest of the Empire.

The political situation in the first century BC became more and more anarchic. Vast armies were required to fight distant wars on the boundaries of the Empire, and soldiers came to owe greater loyalty to their general, who rewarded them with the fruits of conquest, than to the government back in Rome. The result was a succession of civil wars between rival generals.

Julius Caesar and Pompey, the two greatest generals of the first century BC, tried to bury their differences in a three-man triumvirate with Crassus, but in 49 BC Caesar, then governor of Gaul, defied the Senate by bringing his army into Italy ('crossing the Rubicon', the muddy stream that marked the border). All opposition was swept aside, and for the last six years of his life Julius Caesar ruled Rome as a dictator. The Republican spirit was not quite

dead, though, and in 44 BC he was assassinated. His death did not lead to the restoration of the Republic but to a power struggle between Mark Antony and Caesar's nephew, Octavian, which escalated into a full-blown civil war.

PAX ROMANA

Octavian eventually defeated Mark Antony and Cleopatra at the Battle of Actium, in 31 BC. The Empire now stretched from Gaul and Spain in the west to Egypt and Asia Minor in the east, and to hold it together a single central power was needed. Octavian naturally felt the person to embody such authority was himself, and took the name Augustus (meaning 'favoured by the gods'). The transformation from Republic to Empire was not declared immediately, but he quickly acquired permanent power over the Roman state.

To give greater authority to his assumption of absolute power, Augustus encouraged the cult of his uncle Julius Caesar as a god, building a temple to him in the Forum. The Ara Pacis, decorated with a frieze showing Augustus and his family, was a reminder that it was he who had brought peace to the Roman world. Later in his reign, statues of Augustus sprang up all over the Empire, and he was more than happy to be worshipped as a god himself.

Augustus lived on the Palatine hill (*see p66*) in a relatively modest house, but later emperors indulged their apparently limitless wealth and power to the full, building a series of extravagant palaces. The last member of Augustus's family to inherit the Empire was the megalomaniac Nero, who built himself the biggest palace Rome had ever seen, the Domus Aurea or 'Golden House' (*see p130*).

When Nero died in AD 68, with no heir, the Empire was up for grabs, and generals converged from across the Empire to claim the throne. The eventual winner of this struggle was a bluff soldier called Vespasian, founder of the Flavian dynasty.

ROME AT THE TOP

Over the next 100 years Rome enjoyed an era of unparalleled stability. The Empire reached its greatest extent during the reign of Trajan (AD 98-117). Thereafter it was a matter of protecting the existing boundaries, and making sure civil war did not threaten the Empire from within.

Peace throughout the Mediterranean encouraged trade and brought even greater prosperity to Rome. At the same time, however, the power and influence of the capital and its inhabitants declined. Many talented imperial officials, generals and even emperors were Greeks, North Africans or Spaniards. Trajan and Hadrian, for example, were both born in Spain.

To keep an increasingly disparate mass of people content, emperors relied on the policy neatly summed up in the poet Juvenal's phrase 'bread and circuses'. From the first century AD a regular hand-out of grain was given to the poor, ostensibly to maintain a supply of fit young men for the army, but also to ensure that unrest in the city was kept to a minimum. Such a degree of generosity to the poor of Rome necessitated still further exploitation of the outlying provinces of the Empire. Even in years of famine, Spain and Egypt were required to send grain to Rome.

The other means used to keep over a million fairly idle souls quiet and loyal to their emperor was the staging of lavish public entertainments. The most famous venue for such spectacles was the Colosseum (see p66), built by the emperors Vespasian and Domitian and completed in AD 96.

> **'Christianity, with its promise of personal salvation in the afterlife, had great appeal among the oppressed – slaves, freedmen, women.'**

Imperial Rome was the most populous metropolis the world had ever seen. In Augustus's day its population was about one million. By the reign of Trajan a century later it had risen to 1,500,000. No other city even approached this size until the 19th century. It was superbly equipped in its public areas, with eight bridges across the Tiber, magnificent major buildings and 18 large squares.

The golden age of Rome ended with the death of Emperor Marcus Aurelius in AD 180. Defending the eastern provinces and fortifying the borders along the Danube and the Rhine placed a huge strain on the imperial purse and the manpower of the legions. Moreover, the exploitative relationship between the Roman state and its distant provinces meant that the latter were unable – and at times unwilling – to defend themselves.

The threat from barbarian invaders and civil wars became so serious that in the third century the Emperor Aurelius was obliged to fortify the city of Rome with massive defences. The Aurelian Wall, which was later reinforced by medieval popes, still surrounds much of the city. It is a splendid – but misleading – monument to the engineering skills of the ancient Romans. In its heyday, the city needed no defences. Its protection lay in the vastness of its Empire and the guaranteed security of the *pax romana*.

A NEW RELIGION

The end of the third century AD was a turning point in the history of Rome. Radical decisions taken by two powerful emperors, Diocletian (284-305) and Constantine (306-37), ensured that the city's days as head of a great empire were numbered. Diocletian established new capital cities at Mediolanum (Milan) and Nicomedia (in present-day Turkey) and also divided the Empire into four sectors, sharing power with a second 'Augustus', Maximian, and two 'Caesars', Constantius and Galerius. The priorities of the over-extended Empire were now to defend the Rhine and Danube borders against invading Germanic tribes, and the eastern provinces from the Persians. Rome was abandoned to itself.

The reign of Diocletian is also remembered as one of the periods of most intense persecution of Christians in the Empire. Christian communities had been established in Rome very soon after the death of Christ, centred in clandestine meeting-houses called *tituli*. Christianity, though, was just one of many mystical cults that had spread from the Middle East through the Roman Empire. Its followers were probably fewer than the devotees of Mithraism, a Persian religion open only to men. Christianity, with its promise of personal salvation in the afterlife, had great appeal among the oppressed – slaves, freedmen, women. Within two decades of the persecutions of Diocletian, Emperor Constantine would first tolerate and then recognise Christianity as the official religion of the Roman Empire.

When Constantius, Constantine's father and commander of the western provinces, died at York in 306, his army acclaimed young Constantine as 'Augustus' in his place. The early part of his reign was taken up with campaigns against rival emperors, the most powerful being Maxentius, who commanded Italy and North Africa.

The decisive battle was fought just to the north of Rome at the Milvian Bridge (Ponte Milvio) in 312. Before the battle a flaming cross is said to have appeared in the sky, bearing the words 'by this sign shall you conquer'. As the legend goes, Constantine's cavalry then swept Maxentius's superior forces into the Tiber. The following year, in the Edict of Milan, Constantine decreed that Christianity be tolerated throughout the Empire. Later in his reign, when he had gained control of the Eastern Empire and started to build his new capital city at Constantinople (now Istanbul), it became the state religion.

Christianity was much stronger in the east than in the west, and its effect on Roman life was at first limited, the new faith simply coexisting with the other religions.

Tribes on their hills

The **Latins** – of whom the earliest settlers on the Palatine hill were an offshoot – probably swept in from central Europe sometime during the Iron Age, to pitch their camps in the Alban Hills (*see p274*). They were stock-raisers and, gradually, field-tillers. But they were not the only tribe in the rolling hills and lush flatlands of central Italy.

Just to the north-east were the **Sabines** who sent an advance party to settle the Quirinale Hill, only to have their women – legend says – toted off by their testosterone-driven neighbours on the Palatine. Beyond them, in the sparser peaks, shepherds of the **Umbrian** and **Abruzzan** tribes scratched out a living in regions that still bear their names.

Further south towards Naples, the war-like **Samnites** derived a certain finesse, and much military nonce, from their friendly relations with the sophisticated Greeks who settled along the coast from the ninth century BC; centuries later, they would give the Romans a run for their money when the latter were battling to expand their control southward. Until the first century BC it was their language – Oscan – and not Latin which was the *lingua franca* of south-central Italy.

But even as Romulus was ploughing his wiggly furrow with his prehistoric plough, Rome's neighbours to the immediate north were probably giggling at his primitive efforts. By that time, the **Etruscans** were already a highly developed, worldly nation, mining their rich copper and iron deposits, trading with much of the Mediterranean, making exquisite silver and gold jewellery and producing art (displayed in the **Museo di Villa Giulia**, *see p83*) to rival that of the Greeks.

With Etruscan writing still largely an unsolved puzzle, we have only bitter Roman accounts of the neighbours whom they vanquished in the late fourth century BC. These dwell contemptuously on the Etruscans' cruelty, effeteness, epicurian lifestyle and obsession with the supernatural. They neglect, on the whole, to give the Etruscans their probable due for building the **Cloaca Maxima** (*see p109*) to drain the soggy area that were to become the Foro Romano (*see p71*); they downplay the fact that the chief Roman gods – Jupiter, Juno and Apollo – were introduced to them by Etruscans, as was the art of divination; they forget to mention that the Capitoline wolf (*see p62*) is a work of Etruscan art. But even Roman chroniclers were not able to overlook the fact that at least two of Rome's first kings were Etruscan.

While the mild Tarquinius Priscus is credited with nothing worse than having dreamt up the *Ludi romani* (Roman games), the reign of terror instituted by his grandson Tarquinius Superbus put Romans off monarchs – and Etruscans – definitely.

Constantine's reign saw the building of three great basilicas, but these were situated on the outskirts of the city. St Peter's (*see p139*) and St Paul's without the Walls (San Paolo fuori le Mura; *see p153*) were built over existing shrines, while the Bishop of Rome was given land to build a basilica beside the Aurelian Wall – San Giovanni in Laterano (*see p129*). To give Rome credibility as a centre of its new religion, fragments alleged to be of the 'True Cross' were brought from the Holy Land by Constantine's mother, St Helena. Meanwhile, life in fourth-century Rome went on much as before. The departure of part of the imperial court to Constantinople was a heavy blow to a city accustomed to considering itself *caput mundi*, the capital of the world, but the old pagan holidays were still observed, games were staged, and bread was doled out to the poor.

All around, however, the Roman world was falling apart. Constantine learned nothing from the conflicts created by Diocletian's division of power, and on his death left the Empire to be split between his three sons. From this point on, the Western Empire and the Byzantine Empire were two separate entities, united for the last time under Theodosius in the late fourth century. Byzantium would stand for another thousand years, while Rome's glorious palaces, temples, aqueducts, statues and fountains would be destroyed by successive waves of Germanic invaders (*see p16* **Barbarians 'r' Us**).

The first great shock came in 410, when Alaric's Visigoths marched into Italy and sacked Rome. Even more significant was the conquest of North Africa by the Vandals in 435, which cut Rome off from its main source of grain. In 455 the Vandals, too, sacked Rome, removing everything of value they could carry. After this, the Western Empire survived in name alone. The great aqueducts supplying water to Rome ceased to function, while much of the Italian countryside was laid waste. The emperors in Rome had become nothing more

Lust, murder and incest (or, naming and shaming the Borgias)

The name 'Borgia' evokes daggers in dark alleyways, smouldering, incestuous passions and chalices of poisoned wine. For most modern historians, though, the family has been grossly misrepresented.

True, the Borgias were no saints – except, of course, for Francisco de Borja, a Spanish General of the Jesuit order who was canonised by Clement X in 1572. But neither were they any worse than most of the other wealthy families who mixed religion and politics in early Renaissance Rome. The difference was that they were foreigners – so naturally, the local media had it in for them.

When the 75-year-old Cardinal Alonso Borja was elected to the papacy as Calixtus III in 1455, he was a dark horse, emerging victorious from the conclave after a stalemate between the candidates of the powerful Roman Orsini and Colonna families. The bishop lost no time in calling his family over from Jativa, near Valencia, to share in his good fortune. Two nephews were made cardinals – though the younger, Rodrigo, was only twenty-five.

A strong, smart, good-looking, sexually active youth, Rodrigo set to work consolidating the Roman powerbase of the family, which had by this time Italianised its name to Borgia. By the time he became Pope Alexander VI in 1492, Rodrigo had already fathered seven children, four of them with his long-term mistress, the formidable Vanozza Catanei.

Which is where Cesare and Lucrezia (both pictured) come into the picture. The latter – Catanei's eldest son – soon made a mark as a determined, ambitious, unscrupulous power broker. His sister Lucrezia was beautiful and cultured, which made her a useful pawn in the

than the puppets of the assorted Germanic invaders who controlled the Italian peninsula. The last emperor, Romulus, was given the diminutive nickname Augustulus, since he was such a feeble shadow of the Empire's founder. In 476 he was deposed by the German chieftain Odoacer, who styled himself King of Italy. He was in turn deposed by Theodoric the Ostrogoth, who invaded Italy with the support of Byzantium and established an urbane court in Ravenna that ruled with stability for the next 30 years.

In the sixth century much of Italy was reconquered by the Eastern Empire. Then, in around 567, yet another Germanic tribe swept in. The Lombards overran much of the centre of the peninsula, but when they threatened to besiege Rome they met their match in Pope

Gregory the Great (590-604), who bought them off with tribute. Gregory was a tireless organiser, overseeing the running of the estates that had been acquired by the church throughout western Europe, encouraging the establishment of new monasteries and convents, and sending missionaries as far afield as pagan Britain.

He also did a great deal to build up the prestige of the papacy. Rome had been merely one of the centres of the early Church, the others – Byzantium, Jerusalem, Antioch and Alexandria – all being in the east. Disputes were sometimes referred to the Bishop of Rome, but many Christians, particularly in the eastern Churches, did not accord him overall primacy. The collapse of all secular government in the west, however, and above all in Italy, meant that

straddles via San Francesco di Paola – a dark flight of steps leading up from via Cavour to piazza San Pietro in Vincoli, *see p131*.) There is even less evidence to support the claim that Cesare was carrying on an incestuous relationship with Lucrezia; the rumour, it seems, was put about by her disgruntled first husband, Giovanni Sforza, a reserved *milanese* who was shocked by the family's ostentatious displays of affection.

Cesare went on to prove his worth – and to confirm his military and administrative skills – when he carved out a fiefdom for himself in north-eastern Italy in 1502-3. In doing so he earned the admiration of Niccolò Macchiavelli, who took Cesare as the model of the soldier-prince in his how-to-win-towns-and-execute-people manual, *Il principe*. Lucrezia ended her life as the Duchess of Ferrara, a respected patroness of poets, musicians and humanist scholars such as Pietro Bembo.

family's dynastic games. All three of the marriages forced on Lucrezia by her father were designed to seal territorial alliances. When the first two alliances fell through, so – on the pope's orders – did the marriages: the first ended in divorce; Cesare drew a line under the second by having the unfortunate Alfonso of Aragon strangled in his sleep.

There is, on the other hand, nothing but circumstancial evidence to connect Cesare with the murder of his brother Juan, who was stabbed nine times by an unknown assassin when leaving a party at Catanei's house. (Legend has it that his palazzo is the one that

But by then, the damage had been done. It was considered bad form for foreign popes – and their offspring – to attempt to outdo the natives in dynastic ambition, underhand methods and love of *la dolce vita*. A huge campaign of vilification, orchestrated to a large extent by clans like the Orsini and the Colonnas, proved extremely effective in blackening the name of Borgia. Romantics such as Byron or Victor Hugo would later swallow the lust-and-incest line, painting the Borgias as rebel angels.

the papacy emerged almost by default as the sole centre of authority, with the pope a political leader as well as head of the Roman Church.

ROME IN THE BADLANDS
The Dark Ages must have been particularly galling for the inhabitants of Rome, living among the magnificent ruins of a vanished golden age. There was no fresh water, as the aqueducts cut during the invasions of the fifth century had never been repaired. Disease was rife. Formerly built-up areas reverted to grazing land, or were planted as vegetable gardens by land-owning religious orders. Fear of attack meant that the countryside around the city was practically deserted. Having reached over a million at the height of the Empire, Rome's population could be counted in no more than

hundreds by the sixth century. Ancient ruins became convenient quarries for builders. Marble and other limestone was burned to make cement, most of which was used to repair fortifications.

For several centuries the city still owed nominal allegiance to the emperor in Byzantium and his representative in Italy, the exarch, whose court was at Ravenna. However, the exarch's troops were normally too busy defending their own cities in north-east Italy to be of much help to Rome. The city did have a military commander, a *dux*, and a *comune* (city council) that met, as the *Comune di Roma* still does, on the Capitoline Hill, but the papacy also had its parallel courts and administration. In the end the power of the Church prevailed. In time, this would lead to a permanent rift with Byzantium and the eastern Orthodox Churches.

A NEW EMPIRE

During the Dark Ages, the Roman nobles who controlled the papacy and the city set out to re-establish something akin to the old Empire. When the Lombards seized Ravenna in 751 and threatened to do the same to Rome, Pope Stephen II enlisted Pepin, King of the Franks, as defender of the Church. The papacy's alliance with the Franks grew with the victories of Pepin's son, Charlemagne, over the Lombards, and was sealed on Christmas Day 800, when the pope caught Charlemagne unawares in St Peter's and crowned him Holy Roman Emperor.

Rome appeared to have recovered much of its long-lost power and prestige. It had the protection of an emperor, and was blessed by the pope, who in return was rewarded by the gift of large areas of land in central Italy. As things turned out, this arrangement caused nothing but trouble for the next 500 years, as popes, emperors and other monarchs vied to determine whose power was greatest. Roman nobles took sides in these disputes, seizing every occasion to promote members of their own families to the papacy and frequently reducing the city to a state of anarchy. At regular intervals one faction or another would idealistically declare Rome to be a republic once more, to no real effect.

The prestige of the papacy reached a low ebb in the tenth century, when the Frankish Empire collapsed and the papal crown was passed around between a series of dissipated Roman nobles. One of these, John XII (955-64), was obliged to call on the Saxon King Otto for assistance and crowned him Holy Roman Emperor, but then immediately thought better of it. He began to plot against Otto, who rushed to Rome and commanded the clergy and people never again to elect a pope without the consent of himself or his successors.

Papal independence was reasserted in the second half of the 11th century by Pope Gregory VII (1073-85), who also established many of the distinctive institutions of the Church. It was Gregory who first made celibacy obligatory for priests, and he set up the College of Cardinals, giving it sole authority to elect all future popes. He also insisted that no bishop or abbot could be invested by a lay ruler such as a king or emperor, which led to a cataclysmic struggle for power with the Emperor Henry IV.

When Henry marched on Rome in 1084, bringing with him a new papal candidate, Gregory demanded help from Robert Guiscard, leader of the Normans who had established a strong power base in southern Italy. By the time Robert arrived, Rome had already capitulated to Henry's army; in protest, the Normans indulged in a three-day orgy of looting, then set fire to the little that was still standing. From the Palatine to San Giovanni in Laterano, nothing remained but the blackened hulks of once-great *palazzi* and the smoking ruins of churches. Gregory slunk out of his hiding place in Castel Sant'Angelo (*see p144*) and left Rome a broken man; he died the following year.

Despite never-ending conflict between rival factions, usually headed by the powerful Colonna and Orsini families, the 12th and 13th centuries were a time of great architectural innovation in Rome. The creative spirit of the Middle Ages is preserved in beautiful cloisters like those of San Giovanni (*see p129*) and San Lorenzo fuori le Mura (*see p151*), and in Romanesque churches with graceful brick bell-towers and floors of fine mosaic.

Rome's prestige, however, suffered a severe blow in 1309, when the French overruled the College of Cardinals and imposed their own candidate as pope, who promptly decamped to Avignon. A pope returned to Rome in 1378, but the situation became farcical, with three separate pontiffs laying claim to St Peter's throne. Stability was only restored in 1417, when Oddo Colonna was elected as Pope Martin V at the Council of Constance, marking the end of the Great Schism. He returned to Rome in 1420, to find the city and the surrounding Papal States in a ruinous condition.

RENAISSANCE ROME

With the reign of Martin V (1417-31) some semblance of dignity was restored to the office of Christ's Vicar on Earth. It was at this time that the perennial uncertainty as to who ruled the city was solved: henceforth, the city councillors would be nominees of the pope. At the same time, the popes chose to make the Vatican their principal residence, as it offered greater security than their traditional seat in the Lateran Palace.

Successive popes took advantage of this new sense of authority, and Rome became an international city once more. Meanwhile, the renewed prestige of the papacy enabled it to draw funds from all over Catholic Europe in the form of tithes and taxes. The papacy also developed the money-spinning idea of the Holy Year, first instituted in 1300 and repeated in 1423, 1450 and 1475. Such measures enabled the Church to finance the lavish artistic patronage of Renaissance Rome.

Nicholas V (1447-55) is remembered as the pope who brought the spirit of the Renaissance to Rome. A lover of philosophy, science and the arts, he founded the Vatican Library and had many ancient Greek texts translated into Latin.

He also made plans to rebuild St Peter's, the structure of which was perilously unstable. The Venetian Pope Paul II (1464-71) built the city's first great Renaissance palazzo, the massive Palazzo Venezia (*see p63*), and his successor, Sixtus IV, invited leading artists from Tuscany and Umbria – Botticelli, Perugino, Ghirlandaio and Pinturicchio – to fresco the walls of his new Sistine Chapel in the Vatican.

> **'If Catholicism was to hold its own against austere Protestantism, lavish ecclesiastical lifestyles had to be restrained.'**

Since the papacy had become such a fat prize, the great families of Italy redoubled their efforts to secure it, and always had younger sons groomed and ready as potential popes. The French and Spanish kings, too, usually had their own candidates. Political clout, rather than spirituality, was the prime concern of Renaissance popes. Sixtus IV and his successors Innocent VIII and Alexander VI (the infamous Rodrigo Borgia; *see p12* **Lust, murder & incest**) devoted far more of their energies to politics and war than spiritual matters, and papal armies were continually in the field, carving out an ever-increasing area of central Italy for themselves.

The epitome of the worldly Renaissance pope, Julius II (1503-13), made the idea of a strong papal state a reality, at the same time reviving the dream of restoring Rome to its former greatness as spiritual capital of the world. He began the magnificent collection of classical sculpture that is the nucleus of today's Vatican Museums, and invited the greatest architects, sculptors and painters of the day to Rome, including Bramante, Michelangelo and Raphael. Julius's rule was not as enlightened as he liked to think, but he did issue a bull forbidding simony (the buying or selling of church offices) in the election of a pope. In his own financial dealings, he depended on the advice and loans of the fabulously wealthy Sienese banker Agostino Chigi, whose beautiful villa beside the Tiber, now known as the Villa Farnesina (*see p115*), still gives a vivid impression of the luxurious way of life of the papal court.

Julius's successors were less successful. Some were simply *bons viveurs*, like Giovanni de' Medici who, on being made Pope Leo X in 1513, said to his brother, 'God has given us the papacy. Let us enjoy it.' Enjoy it he did. A great patron of the arts, his other passions were hunting, music, theatre and throwing spectacular dinner parties. He plunged the papacy into debt, spending huge sums on French hounds, Icelandic falcons, and banquets of nightingale pies, peacock's tongues and lampreys cooked in Cretan wine.

Future popes had to face two great threats to the status quo of Catholic Europe: the protests of Martin Luther against the Catholic Church – and Roman extravagance in particular – and the growing rivalry between Francis I of France and Spanish King and Holy Roman Emperor Charles V, who were establishing themselves as the dominant powers in Europe.

The year 1523 saw the death of Pope Adrian VI, a Flemish protégé of Charles V and the last non-Italian pope until 1978. He was succeeded by Clement VII, formerly Giulio de' Medici, who rather unwisely backed France against the all-powerful emperor. Charles captured the Duchy of Milan in 1525, and threatened to take over the whole of Italy in retaliation for the pope's disloyalty. In 1527 a large, ill-disciplined imperial army, many of whom were Germans with Lutheran condemnations of Rome ringing in their ears, sacked the city. The looters were chiefly interested in gold and ready money, but they also destroyed churches and thousands of houses, burnt or stole countless precious relics and works of art, looted tombs, and killed indiscriminately. The dead lay unburied in the streets for months.

Pope Clement held out for seven months in Castel Sant'Angelo, but eventually slunk away in disguise. He returned the following year, and shortly afterwards crowned Charles as Holy Roman Emperor in Bologna. In return, Charles grudgingly confirmed Clement VII's sovereignty over the Papal States.

COUNTER-REFORMATION

The sacking of Rome put an end to the Renaissance popes' dream of making Rome a great political power. The primary concerns now were to rebuild the city and push forward the Counter-Reformation, the Catholic Church's response to Protestantism.

The first great Counter-Reformation pope was Alessandro Farnese, Paul III (1534-49), who had produced four illegitimate children during his riotous youth. He realised that if Catholicism was to hold its own against austere Protestantism, lavish ecclesiastical lifestyles had to be restrained. Paul summoned the Council of Trent to redefine Catholicism, and encouraged new religious groups such as the Jesuits – founded by the Spaniard Ignatius of Loyola and approved in 1540 – over older, discredited orders. From their mother church in Rome, the Gesù (*see p103*), the Jesuits led the fight against heresy and set out to convert the world.

Barbarians 'r' Us

A who's who of marauding hordes.

Franks: in the mid-fourth century, the Germanic Franks emerged from their huts on the lower Rhine to occupy small areas on the fringes of Roman-controlled Gaul. Alternately allies and foes of the Romans, they took advantage of the Vandals' rampage through Gaul to grab what is now Belgium and north-eastern France, moving southwards under King Clovis to rout the Visigoths in the early sixth century. Converting to Roman Catholicism (unlike other Germanic peoples who espoused the Arian heresy), Clovis endeared himself and his people to authorities in ex-Roman Europe. The Frankish leader Charlemagne reunified the former Roman territories, for which the pope crowned him Holy Roman Emperor in 800.

Germans: Franks, Lombards, Vandals and Goths of all descriptions (not to mention Angles and Saxons) were branches of the Germanic or Teutonic people, speakers of Germanic Indo-European languages who drifted out of southern Sweden and the

Danish peninsula during the Bronze Age, displacing the Celts.

Goths: drove their cousins the Vandals from the southern shores of the Baltic before expanding southwards towards the Balkans, to harry the eastern fringes of the Roman Empire from the second century AD. *See also* Ostrogoths and Visigoths.

Huns: no one could beat an arrow-armed Hun on horseback, a fact which allowed this eastern people to subjugate the terrified Germanic tribes of south-eastern Europe in the fourth century, before turning its attention to the Eastern Roman Empire in the fifth. Under brilliant strategist Attila, the Huns came within a hair's breadth of taking Constantinople in 447, then turned their attention to Gaul and Italy, where famine and plague halted their Rome-bound pillaging in 453. Squabbling between heirs after Attila's death left the Huns a spent force.

Lombards: the pastoral *longobardi* (long beards) left their farms in north-western Germany in the fourth century, to occupy

Pope Paul IV (1555-9), the next major reformer, was a firm believer in the Inquisition, the burning of heretics and homosexuals, and the strictest censorship. He expelled all Jews from the Papal States, except for those in Rome itself, whom he confined to the Ghetto in 1556 (*see pp104-6*).

By the end of the 16th century, the authority of the papacy was on the wane outside Rome, and the papal treasury was increasingly dependent on loans. Nevertheless, in the following century, popes continued to spend money as if the Vatican's wealth was inexhaustible, commissioning architects of the stature of Bernini and Borromini to design the churches, *palazzi* and fountains that would transform the face of the Eternal City forever (*see chapter* **Architecture**). Inevitably, the economy of the Papal States became chronically depressed.

If two centuries of papal opulence had turned monumental Rome into a spectacular sight, squalor and poverty were still the norm for most of its people: the streets of Trastevere and the Monti district (earlier the Suburra or great slum quarter of ancient Rome) were filthy and dangerous, and the Jewish population lived in even more insanitary conditions in the Ghetto. The city was, however, a more peaceful place to live. The rich no longer shut themselves up in

fortress-like *palazzi*, but built delightful villas in landscaped parks, such as Villa Borghese (*see pp79-81*) and Villa Pamphili (*see p155*). Rome had many attractions, in spite of the waning prestige of the popes. A Europe-wide resurgence of interest in the classical past was also under way, and shortly the city would discover the joys – and earning power – of tourism. Rome was about to be invaded again.

GRAND TOURISTS

By the 18th century a visit to Rome as part of a 'Grand Tour' was near-obligatory for any European gentleman who aspired to be cultured, and Romans responded eagerly to this new influx. The city produced little great art or architecture at this time, due in part to the poor state of papal finances. The two great Roman sights that date from this period, the Spanish Steps (*see p86*) and the Fontana di Trevi (*see p74*), are a late flowering of earlier Roman baroque. The few big building projects undertaken were for the benefit of tourists, notably Giuseppe Valadier's splendid park on the Pincio (*see p80*) and the neo-classical facelift he gave to piazza del Popolo (*see p89*).

Although on the surface Rome was a cultured city, there were many customs that reeked of medieval superstition. Smollett, Gibbon and Goethe, forgetting the full brutality of ancient today's Austria by the end of the fifth. When Byzantium overthrew Italy's Ostrogothic rulers (*see below*), the Lombards continued their south-bound progress virtually unimpeded, crossing the Alps in 568 and occupying all the major towns of northern Italy by 572. Conversion to Christianity during the late seventh century failed to endear them to the Church, which called in Charlemagne's Frankish forces when the Lombards attacked the Papal States in 773. Victorious, Charlemagne added 'King of the Lombards' to his list of titles.

Ostrogoths: the 'eastern Germans' quit the shores of the Baltic to create an empire that stretched from the River Don to modern-day Belarus, only to be subjugated by the Huns around 370 AD. When Hun rule collapsed, the Ostrogoths were on the move once more: their leader, Theodoric the Great established his urbane court in Ravenna, Italy, from 493 to 526. His death in that year plunged Italy into crisis, and the Ostrogoths into oblivion.

Vandals: fleeing Hun harassment in the early fifth century, the Germanic Vandals left a trail of devastation across Gaul and Spain before setting up a kingdom (429-534) led by Gaiseric in what is now Tunisia and north-eastern Algeria. After crushing Carthage, Vandals dominated the western Mediterranean, annexing Corsica, Sardinia and Sicily and occupying Rome for a two-week rape 'n' pillage fest in 455. They were crushed by Byzantine forces in 533.

Visigoths: the 'western Germans' separated from the Ostrogoths (eastern Germans) around 376 AD when Hun attackers drove them across the Danube into Roman territory. After a spot of plundering in the Balkans, they registered their displeasure at their on/off confederacy with the Romans by sacking Rome in 410, under the leadership of Alaric. With the bit between their teeth, they continued to rampage across Europe, to create vast kingdoms in France, and in Spain where they remained until Muslim forces routed them in 711.

Rome, all remarked on the contrast between the sophistication of vanished civilisation and the barbarism lurking beneath the surface of papal Rome. Some executions were still carried out by means of the *martello*, in which the condemned man was beaten about the temples with a hammer before having his throat cut and his stomach ripped open. This humane method remained in use until the 1820s.

> **'The Risorgimento was a movement for the unification of Italy, but in itself it was very diverse.'**

Executions were traditionally staged in the piazza del Popolo, and often timed to coincide with the *carnevale*, a period of frantic merrymaking before Lent. For a few days via del Corso was one long masked ball, as bands played and people showered each other with confetti, flour, water and more dangerous missiles. The centrepiece was the race of riderless horses along the Corso. They had heavy balls filled with spikes dangling at their sides, and boiling pitch pumped into their *recta* to get them moving. Rome was a city of spectacle for much of the rest of the year, as well.

In summer, piazza Navona was flooded by blocking the outlets of the fountains, and the nobility sploshed around the piazza in their carriages. The only time the city fell quiet was in late summer, when everyone who could left for their villas in the Alban Hills, to escape the stifling heat and the threat of malaria.

ROMANTIC REBELLIONS
In 1798 everything changed. French troops under Napoleon occupied the city, and Rome became a republic once more. Pope Pius VI, a feeble old man, was exiled from the city and died in France.

Like most attempts to restore the Roman Republic, this one was short-lived. The next pope, Pius VII, elected in Venice, signed a concordat with Napoleon in 1801, which allowed him to return to Rome. The papacy was expelled for a second time when French troops returned in 1808. Napoleon promised the city a modernising, reforming administration, but Romans were not keen to be conscripted into his armies. When the pope finally reclaimed Rome after the fall of Napoleon in 1814, its noble families and many of the people welcomed his return.

The patchwork of duchies, principalities and kingdoms that had existed in Italy before Napoleon's invasions was restored after 1815.

The Papal States were handed back to Pius VII. Nevertheless, the brief taste of liberty under the French had helped inspire a movement for unification, modernisation and independence from the domination of foreign rulers.

The Risorgimento was a movement for the unification of the country, but in itself it was very diverse. Its supporters ranged from liberals who believed in unification for economic reasons, to conservatives who looked to the papacy itself to unify Italy. Initially, the most prominent members were the idealistic republicans of the Giovine Italia (Young Italy) movement, headed by Giuseppe Mazzini. They were flanked by more extreme groups and secret societies such as the Carbonari.

Two reactionary popes, Leo XII (1823-9) and Gregory XVI (1831-46), used a network of police spies and censorship to put down opposition of any kind. Most of the unrest in the Papal States, though, was in the north; in Rome life went on much as before. Travellers continued to visit, and Shelley, Dickens and Lord Macaulay all passed through, only to be horrified at the repressive regime.

The election of a new pope in 1846 aroused great optimism. Pius IX came to the throne with a liberal reputation, and immediately announced an amnesty for over 400 political prisoners. However, the spate of revolutions that spread through Europe in 1848 radically altered his attitude. In November that year his chief minister was assassinated, and Pius fled in panic. In his absence, a popular assembly declared Rome a republic. Seizing the chance to make his dream reality, Mazzini rushed to the city, where he was chosen as one of a triumvirate of rulers. Meanwhile, another idealist arrived in Rome to defend the Republic, at the head of 500 armed followers. He was Giuseppe Garibaldi, a former sailor who had gained his military experience fighting in wars of liberation in South America.

Giuseppe Garibaldi, hero of the Risorgimento.

Ironically, it was republican France, with Napoleon I's nephew Louis Napoleon as president, which decided it was her duty to restore the pope to Rome. Louis Napoleon's motivation was simple, and not especially religious: he wanted to stop Austrian power spreading further within Italy. A French force marched on Rome, but was repelled by the *garibaldini* (followers of Garibaldi) – a ragbag mixture of former papal troops, young volunteers and enthusiastic citizens. The French attacked again in greater numbers, mounting their assault from the gardens of Villa Pamphili. For the whole of June 1849 the defenders fought valiantly from their positions on the Gianicolo, but the end of the Republic was by now inevitable.

For the next 20 years, while the rest of Italy was being united under King Vittorio Emanuele of Piedmont, a garrison of French troops protected Pope Pius from invasion. Garibaldi protested vainly to the politicians of the new state – it was, he said, a question of *Roma o morte* ('Rome or death') – but the Kingdom of Italy, established in 1860, was not prepared to take on Napoleon III's France. Meanwhile, the policies of the former liberal Pius IX were increasingly reactionary. In 1869 he convened the first Vatican Council in order to set down the Catholic Church's response to the upheavals of the industrial age. It did so with intransigence, making the doctrine of papal infallibility an official dogma of the Church for the first time.

ROME, ITALY

Even though it was still under papal rule, Rome had been chosen as the capital of the newly unified kingdom. In 1870, with the defeat of Napoleon III in the Franco-Prussian war, the French withdrew from Rome, and Italian troops occupied the city. Pius IX withdrew into the Vatican, refusing to hand over the keys of the Quirinale, the future residence of the Italian royal family: troops had to break in.

There followed the most rapid period of change Rome had experienced since the fall of the Empire. The new capital needed government buildings and housing for the civil servants who worked in them. Church properties were confiscated, and for a time government officials worked in converted monasteries and convents. Two aristocratic *palazzi* were adapted to house the Italian parliament: Palazzo di Montecitorio (*see p86*) became the Chamber of Deputies, and Palazzo Madama (*see p96*) the Senate.

The city's great building boom lasted for over 30 years (*see chapter* **Architecture**). Entirely new avenues appeared: via Nazionale and via Cavour linked the old city with the new Stazione Termini in the east, and corso Vittorio Emanuele was driven through the historic centre. The new ministries were often massive piles quite out of keeping with their surroundings; still more extravagant was the monstrous Vittoriale, the marble monument to Vittorio Emanuele erected in piazza Venezia.

Rome was little affected by World War I, social unrest broke out following the war, with the fear of socialism encouraging the rise of fascism. Benito Mussolini was a radical journalist who, having become alienated from the far left, shifted to the extreme right. Like so many before him, he turned to ancient Rome to find an emblem to embody his idea of a totalitarian state: *fasces* were the bundles of rods tied round an axe carried by the Roman

Benito Mussolini, scourge of late trains.

lictors (marshals) as they walked in front of the city's consuls. In 1922 Mussolini sent his blackshirt squads on their 'March on Rome', demanding, and winning, full power in government. He had been prepared to back out at the first sign of real resistance by the constitutional parties, and himself made the 'March' by train.

Mussolini's ambition was to transform the country into a dynamic, aggressive society. Among other things, he wanted to put Italians in uniform and stop them eating pasta, which he thought made them lazy and un-warlike. His ideas for changing the face of Rome were equally far-fetched. He planned to rebuild Rome in gleaming marble, with fora, obelisks, and heroic statues proclaiming the *Duce* (Leader) as a modern Augustus at the head of a new Roman Empire. The most prominent surviving monuments to his megalomania are the suburb of EUR (*see p152*), which was planned as the site for an international exhibition of fascism, and the Foro Italico sports complex (*see p150*).

When put to the test in World War II, fascist Italy rapidly foundered. Mussolini was ousted from power in 1943, and the citizens of Rome had no difficulty in switching their allegiance from the Axis to the Allies. During the period of German occupation that followed, Italian partisans showed themselves capable of acts of great courage. Rome was declared an open city – the *Roma città aperta* of Rossellini's great film – meaning that the Germans agreed not to defend it, pitching their defence south of the city around Frascati (*see p274*). While other Italian cities and towns were pounded by shells and bombs, Rome suffered only one serious bombing raid during the war.

After the war Italy voted to become a republic, and Rome quickly adapted to the new political structures. *Partitocrazia* – government by a group of political parties sharing power and dividing up lucrative government jobs and contracts between them – suited the Roman approach to life well. The political unrest of the 1970s affected Rome less than it did Milan or Turin, and the Romans simply swam with the political tide, voting in their first Communist mayor in 1976.

The city has benefited greatly from Italy's post-war economic boom. It has spread radially along its major arterial roads. The problem of the city authorities since the war has been how to preserve the old city and yet encourage development. Rome's main industry is still being itself, whether as capital of Italy or historical relic, and the city continues to thrive, trading as it has done for the last 1,500 years on its unforgettable past.

Key events

* = Dates according to ancient Roman historians, and based on legend.
*753 BC Romulus kills Remus and founds the city of Rome.
*750 BC Rape of the Sabine Women.
*616 BC Tarquin elected king. Forum drained.
*509 BC Tarquins are ousted after rape of Lucretia.
*507-6 BC Roman Republic founded. The Latins and Etruscans declare war.
*494 BC Plebeians revolt. Tribunate founded.
*450 BC Roman Law is codified into Twelve Tables.
434 BC War against the Etruscans.
390 BC Gauls sack Rome.
264-146 BC Punic Wars against Carthage. In 212 Rome conquers Sicily; in 146 Carthage is destroyed.
200-168 BC Rome conquers Greece. Greek gods introduced to Rome.
60-50 BC First triumvirate: Julius Caesar, Pompey, Crassus.
55 BC Caesar invades Britain.
51-50 BC Caesar conquers Gaul and crosses the Rubicon.
48 BC Caesar defeats Pompey and meets Cleopatra.
45 BC Caesar declared *imperator* (emperor).
44 BC Caesar is assassinated by Brutus and Cassius.
43-32 BC Second triumvirate: Octavian, Mark Antony and Lepidus.

PAX ROMANA
31 BC Battle of Actium. Antony and Cleopatra defeated and Octavian (Augustus) becomes sole ruler.
41 Caligula assassinated. Claudius accedes.
64 City slums cleared in great fire; Nero in command.
67 Saints Peter and Paul are martyred.
80 Construction of Colosseum begun.
125 Pantheon rebuilt to designs by Hadrian.
164-180 Great Plague throughout the Empire.
284-305 Diocletian splits Empire into East and West.

A NEW RELIGION
313 Constantine proclaims Edict of Milan, allowing toleration of Christianity.
382 Severe persecution of pagans.
410 Alaric the Goth sacks Rome.
475-6 Byzantium becomes seat of Empire. Goths rule Rome.
567 Lombards overrun much of Italy.

778 Charlemagne defeats last Lombard king.
800 Pope crowns Charlemagne Holy Roman Emperor.
1084 Holy Roman Emperor Henry IV sacks Rome. Robert Guiscard and the Normans sack Rome again.
1097 First Crusade begins.
1300 First Holy Year. Thousands of pilgrims flock to Rome – the city's first tourists.
1309 Pope Clement V moves the papacy to Avignon.
1347 Cola di Rienzo sets up Roman republic.
1417 End of Great Schism in the papacy.

RENAISSANCE ROME
1494 Charles VIII of France invades Italy.
1508 Michelangelo begins the Sistine ceiling.
1527 Sacking of Rome by Spanish-led imperial army.
1556 Roman Jews confined to the Ghetto.
1563 Council of Trent launches the Counter-Reformation.
1585 Sixtus V begins to change city's layout.
1626 The new St Peter's is consecrated.
1721 Bonnie Prince Charlie born in Rome.
1773 Jesuits expelled from Rome.
1798 French exile pope and declare Rome a republic.
1806 End of Holy Roman Empire.
1808 Rome made a 'free city' in Napoleon's empire.
1821 Death of Keats in Rome.
1848 Revolutionaries declare Roman Republic; they are put down by French troops, who occupy the city until 1870.

ROME, ITALY
1870 Italian army enters Rome, which becomes capital of a united Italy.
1922 Mussolini marches on Rome.
1929 Lateran Treaty creates the Vatican State.
1944 Rome liberated.
1946 A national referendum makes Italy a republic.
1957 Common Market Treaty signed in Rome.
1960 Olympic Games held in Rome.
1962 Second Vatican Council: Church reform.
1981 John Paul II shot in St Peter's Square.
1993 Tangentopoli corruption investigations begin: political parties crumble; summer Mafia bombs kill 11 in Rome, Florence, Milan; in December Francesco Rutelli becomes Rome's first Green mayor.
1997 Rutelli wins second term as mayor.
2000 Jubilee Holy Year.

Rome Today

Can Rome, with its ancient heritage, be a modern city?

There is a wide gap between the Rome of tourist cliché and the city as experienced by most of its present-day inhabitants. Sure, there are still long lunches, hopeful gigolos, shady politicians, window-shopping nuns and Fiat 500s hurtling the wrong way down one-way streets.

But in the age of globalisation, these are increasingly endangered species. Most teenage *romani* have the same compass points as their peers in Seattle or Tokyo: mobile phones, Coca Cola, Britney Spears, Nike and the Internet. And if you look a little further up the age range, there are still more parallels than differences: a steady job and a nice house are added to the previous list. Oh, and being within easy walking distance of *mamma*'s house (complete with its free food/babysitting/laundry facilities), which is – it must be admitted – more distinctly Italian (other societies have Indian takeaways, nurseries and launderettes).

And yet there is a distinctly Roman character, and a distinctly Roman take on the universe. To a certain extent, this has been moulded by history.

For the many centuries that the Western world was ruled from here, only a tiny minority actually did the ruling; the rest were spoon-fed bread and circuses to keep them docile and pliable, a historical precedent that may explain why today's Romans-on-the-street sit back and do little to improve their own backyard. Instead, they wait for the powers that be to do it for them, grumbling when they don't, but grumbling equally loudly if any work to improve the city causes them the least personal discomfort. Then they'll slip, in self-satisfied fashion, into possession of the end result, as if it were nothing more than they deserved.

Through the Middle Ages, Rome slid further and further into decline, a decline made all the more poignant by the crumbling architectural reminders of the power it once was. Renaissance Romans wreaked their schizoid revenge by using those ruins as building materials. Even into the 20th century the havoc was further compounded when, during the economic boom of the 1960s and '70s, Rome's citizens surrounded their ancient relics with apartment blocks of astounding ugliness,

gobbling up countryside that had long been lauded by writers and poets. Yet modern Romans are neither ignorant about nor insensitive towards their cultural heritage. Rather, this devil-may-care attitude towards ruins, art and the beauties that surround them is caused by their being so totally steeped in their history that it is an integral part of modern life: part of its beauty, and part of its frustrations. Old buildings are not pickled in nostalgia: they are part of the surroundings and accepted as such. Kids kick footballs around the pillars of the Pantheon, girls totter across centuries-old cobblestones in chunky platforms, and drivers barrel down medieval alleys, squeezing their cars into parking places too small for an ancient handcart.

When Rome became capital of Italy in 1870 the city, and the papacy that had ruled it, were a political irrelevance residing in a provincial backwater. Romans let rip with a gleeful binge of the anticlericism that such close contact with the Vatican had made part of their DNA: they erected statues to 'heretics' burnt at the stake and named streets after heroes of the Risorgimento struggle that had toppled the pope and made Italy a united country. Beyond this snook-cocking, however, the city was unsure of what to do with its new-found position as capital of the nation: even today, it is still struggling to find a role it can be proud of.

In 1993 – after generations of stasis at best, blatant pocket-lining at worst – a wind of change began blowing through City Hall on the Capitoline hill. In two terms in the mayor's office, prominent Green Francesco Rutelli and his centre-left team brought about palpable changes.

Rutelli's administration faced its greatest challenge in the year 2000. Designated a Jubilee Holy Year by the Vatican, Rome's wobbly infrastructure was declared to be on the verge of irreversible collapse by the world's press, and the Eternal City's residents – never slow to take advantage of an opportunity for whinging – declared their home unliveable-in as City Hall rushed to prepare for the predicted onslaught of 30 million pilgrims.

In the event, the extra visitors were comfortably lodged, fed and ferried about without putting too much strain on a city built on ancient foundations, its waste flowing through ancient or medieval drains, its traffic clogging medieval and Renaissance streets.

What those pilgrims – and the brave souls who ignored media panic-mongering – found was a glowing, freshly painted city, its streets spruced up, its parks and gardens blooming, its revamped museums open long, long hours, and its public transport… well, you can't have everything. But even in this field, there have been immense leaps forward. Anyone who had visited a decade ago would notice the change: shining new trams plying brand new lines, and a system of residents' parking that has brought some of the traditional excesses of triple- and quadruple-parking to a halt.

But even this successful handling of a major event such as a Holy Year could not hide the fact that much of Rutelli's makeover was confined to the highly visible, tourist-trail centre. Inhabitants of the sprawling, high-rise, down-at-heel outskirts of town lament that their lot has remained largely unchanged, give or take a park with a swing or two. They gave eloquent voice to their disapproval at the ballot box in 2000, electing Francesco Storace, from the extreme right *Alleanza nazionale* party, as president of the Lazio regional council, thus placing the capital and its surrounding area at political loggerheads.

'Even today, Rome is struggling to find a role it can be proud of.'

In 2001, Rutelli left the mayor's office to run for prime minister. As this guide went to press, city council elections were due and Walter Veltroni, a leading light in the post-Communist Democratici di sinistra (DS) party, looked set to step into Rutelli's shoes. He promised to continue with the previous administration's improvement programme, extending its benefits to the suburbs.

But any mayor of any political persuasion who pledges to turn Rome into a streamlined modern city, with the kind of clout enjoyed by Italy's economic powerhouse in Milan or the miraculous north-east, is kidding themselves and/or the electorate. For the problems each administration inherits go far beyond medieval sewers and Renaissance topography. Rome has some tough cultural, psychological and image barriers to get over.

The capital was traditionally lumbered with the massive machinery of state industry and banking, which, until recently, provided jobs for the highly unqualified boys, and lost money hand over fist.

More recently, new, young, go-getting managers have presided over the dismantling of great parts of this state conglomerate and its sale to the private sector. The under-achieving jobs-for-life mentality of lower-level employees remains, however: a recent move to ban local council employees from clocking off at 2pm to go on to their more lucrative – and frequently black-economy – afternoon jobs raised a near-riot.

And naturally, Rome is home to central government, a dubious honour given the mistrust with which politics are regarded in Italy. The corrupt old guard may have collapsed in a welter of anti-graft investigations in the mid-1990s, but the new political generation has yet to convince voters it is any better; the bitterly fought 2001 general election didn't dispel any doubts. This nationally felt scepticism *vis à vis* things parliamentary spills over on to the capital as a whole, and there is still a tendency elsewhere in the country to regard all Romans as pen-pushing parasites of an ineffective state.

Romans, equally naturally, reject this, and do so by doing what they do best: simply being Roman. They may be brusque and stroppy, but they manage to be so with sunny gusto. It's hard not to fall in love with the exuberant play they act out against their glorious city backdrop.

Behind the play-acting is a wheeler-dealing determination that used ꞏ employed (as the rest of the country suspected) in getting as much as possible for as little as possible out of the state and its trappings. Those opportunities are fast drying up, but Roman ingenuity remains.

What they will make of that ingenuity in the future remains to be seen. For the time being, Romans seem to be taking stock, getting to grips with a city that is fast becoming multi-cultural, multi-confessional, and multi-faceted. They've shown that they can put on a good show for the world. Now they have to show that they can capitalise on these first steps forward, in time extending the benefits, and extending them to areas that are still waiting for the breakthrough. Rome may never be a 'modern' city... and indeed, who would want this capital of the ancient world to be that? But it can be a functioning city within the magnificent, breathtaking limits of its glorious past.

Roman numbers

Population: 2.7 million
Non-EU immigrant population (Interior Ministry): 222,500
Non-EU immigrant population (Caritas): 270,400
Pilgrims who came to Rome for 2000 Holy Year festivities: 25 million
Number of official Holy Year events: 3,400
Hotel beds in Rome in 1996: 62,000
Hotel beds in Rome in 1999: 70,000
Hailstorms in Rome in 1999: 13
Hailstorms in Rome in 2000: 2
Unauthorised posters removed from walls daily in 2001 election campaign: 6,000

Best of Sabina

Historical Homes and Country Estates

Untouched by the mass tourism, less than fifty Kilometers North of Rome, lies the territory of Sabina. Its landscape of gentle hills where agriculture is in perfect harmony with the surrounding nature, is scattered with roman villas, medieval castles, churches and abbeys. In this rural paradise "Best of Sabina" has selected quality accomodation for their guest. In these charming and historically rich locations, the warm hospitality of our hosts will make your stay in Sabina absolutely memorable.

Villa Vallerosa
*Self catering apartments
Club house, Cooking
course, Walking tours,
Landscape painting
course*

Villa Vallerosa

Corlando Tre
*Self catering apartments,
Walking tours,
Cooking course*

Corlando Tre

Il paese delle Meraviglie
*Self catering apartments,
Bed and breakfast,
Cooking course*

Il paese delle Meraviglie

La Torretta
*Bed and breakfast,
Walking tours,
Culture tours,
Activity tours*

La Torretta

Il Casale di Max
*Self catering apartments,
Bed and breakfast,
Club house,
Cooking course*

Il Casale di Max

Montepiano
*Self catering apartments,
Club house, Cooking course,
Walking tours,
Landscape painting course*

Montepiano

Cjase me
*Bed and breakfast,
Cooking course,
Walking tours*

Cjase me

I Vignacci
*Self catering apartments,
Walking tours*

I Vignacci

Colle Cesoni

Colle Cesoni
*Self catering apartments,
Walking tours*

Le Fattorie Caracciolo

Le Fattorie Caracciolo
*Self catering apartments
Club house, Cooking course,
Walking tours*

Casale Tancia

Casale Tancia
*Self catering apartments,
Bed and breakfast, Club house,
Walking tours, Small restaurant*

Piazza Garibaldi, 13 - 02040 Selci Sabino (Ri) - ITALY
Tel. +0039 765.519154 - www.bestofsabina.it - bestofsabina@tiscalinet.it

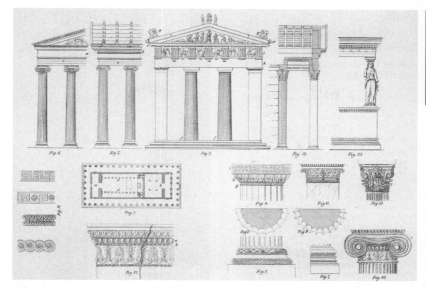

Fig.6   Fig.5   Fig.7   Fig.14   Fig.12

Fig.4   Fig.9   Fig.11   Fig.13

Fig.1   Fig.2   Fig.3

Fig.12   Fig.5   Fig.7   Fig.10

Architecture

Ancient clout, Renaissance propaganda, baroque
exuberance... and now revolutionary design

Perhaps the most striking thing about Rome's
architecture is not how much lies in ruin, but
how much has survived. The Eternal City was
sacked by Gauls (390 BC), Visigoths (AD 410),
Vandals (445), Normans (1084), and the forces of
the Holy Roman Emperor (1527), who destroyed
some 1,000 churches on their rampage. Then
there was fire (including the devastating one
during Nero's reign in AD 64), earthquake,
pestilence, and the advent of high-handed
post-Unification planners, determined to stop
at nothing to transform Rome into a 'fitting'
capital for the newly united nation in the 1870s.

THE ANCIENT CITY
The major buildings of ancient Rome were
designed to express the glamour, sophistication
and clout of the city. But it was a while before
the Romans developed much in the way of
architectural styles for themselves.

If the Romans had the Etruscans to thank for
insights into hydraulics and town planning, it

was the Greek system of orders – sequences
of columns of different proportions based on
their width – that was followed for important
façades. The main Greek orders were Doric,
plain and sturdy; Ionic, more slender and
ornate; and Corinthian, the most delicate and
ornate of all. The **Colosseum** (*see p66*) is a
good example of how they were used: hefty
Doric at the bottom to support the construction;
lighter, more elegant Ionic in the middle; and
the decorative Corinthian top layer.

It wasn't only columns that were copied from
Greece: whole genres of building were based on
Greek models. Temples were colonnaded, and
either rectangular, like the **temples of Saturn**
(*see p71*) or **Portunus** (*see p109*), or circular
like the **temples of Vesta** (*see p71*) and
Hercules Victor (*see p109*). Theatres (*see
p104*) were derived from Greek models, too.

Eventually, the Romans did come up with
their own ideas: elliptical arenas – known as
amphitheatres – designed for blood sports;

Top five Baroque

Gian Lorenzo Bernini (1598-1680)

Poet, playwright, sculptor and painter; the artistic dictator of Rome for over 20 years, he decorated much of St Peter's (*see p139*), made the Fontane dei Quattro Fiumi in piazza Navona (*see p96*), and is an inescapable presence in the city.

Francesco Borromini (1598-1667)

An eccentric genius and manic depressive, Borromini lived in Bernini's shadow. His dizzying designs (San Carlino alle Quattro Fontane, *see p77*; Sant'Ivo alla Sapienza, *see p97*; Sant'Agnese in Agone, *see p96*) mix passion and maths in a way that broke all the rules.

Pietro da Cortona (1598-1669)

Primarily a painter, Pietro's architectural record puts him up with the masters: the church of Santi Luca e Martina in the Foro Romano (*see p71*, closed to the public) is stunningly simple, that of Santa Maria della Pace (*see p93*) is stunningly theatrical.

Domenico Fontana (1543-1607)

Pet architect of the town-planning Pope Sixtus V, designed the (less famous) Sistine Chapel at Santa Maria Maggiore (*see p132*), and helped Della Porta (*below*) on the dome of St Peter's.

Giacomo della Porta (c1535-1602)

A student of Michelangelo, he finished off some of his designs (the dome of St Peter's, *see p139*; the Palazzo dei Conservatori, *see p62*), altering them along the way. Also worked on Sant' Andrea della Valle (*see p104*) and the façade of the Gesù (*see p103*).

The Pantheon: impossible without concrete.

developed, made of *pozzolana* (a volcanic ash), lime and *tufa* rubble. This, however, was not aesthetically pleasing, so buildings were faced with veneers of coloured marble or travertine (a calcareous limestone).

Without concrete, constructing the **Pantheon** (*see p98*) would have been impossible. The huge hemispherical dome is the largest cast-concrete construction made before the 20th century. Other feats of cast-concrete engineering include the **Terme di Diocleziano** (*see p135*) and **Terme di Caracalla** (*see p126*). The ruined domes of the latter reveal how the building was put together: layered brick, concrete and marble are still visible.

Brick, the other fundamental Roman building material, was used to face buildings, to lend internal support to concrete walls, and as a material in its own right. The most impressive example is the **Mercati di Traiano** (*see p70*).

EARLY CHRISTIAN ROME

There are traces of the early Christians everywhere in Rome – and they're not confined to dank catacombs or the scant, buried remains of *tituli* (the earliest meeting houses; *see p125* **Inconspicuous early church**). Scores of early churches survive too, though in many cases the original building is hidden beneath later accretions. The tell-tale signs are there if you know what to look for.

rectangular meeting houses flanked by columns, known as basilicas; and efficient plumbing and heating systems, complete with piping hot running water. Perhaps most importantly, the Romans took the arch to unprecedented heights of perfection, and gave the world its first large-scale, free-standing masonry.

The commonest stone found around Rome was soft, volcanic *tufa*. This was not an ideal building material, and as early as the third century BC a form of concrete had been

Early Christian basilical churches are the ghosts of ancient Roman basilicas. Churches founded in the fourth and fifth centuries such as **San Paolo fuori le Mura** (*see p153*), **San Giovanni in Laterano** (*see p129*), **Santi Quattro Coronati** (*see p126*), **Santa Maria in Trastevere** (*see p117*), and **San Pietro in Vincoli** (*see p131*) are the most tangible connection we have with the interiors of ancient civic Rome: go into any of them and imagine them shorn of their later decoration. The construction is generally simple and stately. Most are rectangular, with a flat roof and a colonnade separating a tall nave from lower aisles. Natural light enters the nave from high windows. Behind the altar, opposite the entrance, is an apse topped by a conch (domed roof). Perhaps the best example of all is **Santa Sabina** (*see p119*), which was shorn of later additions in a no-holds-barred restoration in the 1930s.

The fortunes of the Catholic Church are well reflected in architecture. When it was poor, as in the fifth century, buildings were plain and functional; when it was rich, in periods such as the eighth and 12th centuries, churches were adorned with brilliant mosaics. The most magnificent to have survived are in **Santa Maria Maggiore** (*see p132*), **Santa Prassede** (*see p133*) and **Santa Maria in Trastevere** (*see p115*). Many churches were decorated with Cosmati-work (*see p87* **Glossary**): exquisitely carved and inlaid pulpits, choirs, candlesticks, and floors. Very occasionally, circular churches were built, perhaps inspired by Roman tombs like Hadrian's

mausoleum (now **Castel Sant' Angelo**, *see p144*). The dazzling mosaic-caked **Santa Costanza** (*see p151*) was probably built in the fourth century as a mausoleum for the daughters of Emperor Constantine; its contemporary, **Santo Stefano Rotondo** (*see p126*) may have been inspired by the church of the Holy Sepulchre in Jerusalem.

> **'If Rome was to take on fully its role as focus of Christianity, it had to look the part.'**

During the Middle Ages, Rome's influential families were engaged in an almost constant battle for power, a fact that was reflected in the civic architecture of the city. Construction was unrestricted and unplanned: the tortuous warren of streets in the Monti district (*see chapter* **Monti & Esquilino**) is a result. Anyone who could, opted for a fortress-home with lookout towers. The Torre delle Milizie, behind the **Mercati di Traiano** (*see p70*), and Torre degli Anguillara in Trastevere are examples.

The quarrels between the families were to have long-lasting effects: with daggers constantly drawn, they failed to impose a Roman candidate on the throne of St Peter's. France stepped in, had Clement V elected, and helped him shift the papacy to Avignon in 1309, where it remained until 1377. The international funds that used to shore up the spendthrift papacy were diverted to the French city, and Rome was left bankrupt. The Gothic had already passed the city by (the one exception being the church of **Santa Maria sopra Minerva**, *see p98*). The early Renaissance, too, was lost on this shadow of its former self that Rome had become.

THE RENAISSANCE

In the late 14th century, a huge revolution in art, architecture and thought was under way in Tuscany. In crumbling, medieval Rome, it was not until the following century that the Renaissance began to gather momentum (the sole exception being the group of artists around genius Pietro Cavallini, *see also p32*).

In 1445 the Florentine architect Antonio Filarete created one of Rome's first significant Renaissance works: the magnificent central bronze doors of **St Peter's** (*see p139*).

Pope Nicholas V (1447-55), who knew the architectural theorist Leon Battista Alberti and other key protagonists of the early Renaissance, decided that if Rome was to take on fully its role as focus of Christianity, it had to look the part. After consultations with Alberti, Nicholas

The **Terme di Caracalla**. *See p26.*

commissioned extensive restoration work on St Peter's, which at the time was in imminent danger of collapse. Meanwhile, those with lucrative church connections built fabulous palaces: in 1508 papal banker Agostino Chigi commissioned a lavish villa, now the **Villa Farnesina** (*see p115*), and in 1515 work started on **Palazzo Farnese** (*see p103*) for Cardinal Alessandro Farnese.

Pope Pius II (1458-64), a cultured Tuscan steeped in classical literature, put a stop to the common practice of quarrying ancient buildings for construction materials. Sixtus IV (1471-84) had roads paved and widened, churches such as **Santa Maria della Pace** (*see p93*) and **Santa Maria del Popolo** (*see p89*) rebuilt, the Ponte Sisto begun and the **Sistine Chapel** (*see p143*) built and decorated by some of the foremost artists of the time, among them Ghirlandaio, Pinturicchio and Signorelli.

Rome's Renaissance reached its peak with Julius II (1503-13), who made Donato Bramante his chief architect. Bramante came to Rome from Milan in 1499, and in 1502 to mark the spot **Tempietto** (*see p117*) to mark the spot traditionally thought to be that of St Peter's execution. A domed cylinder surrounded by a Tuscan Doric colonnade, it came closer than any other building to the spirit of antiquity.

Julius also commissioned Michelangelo to sculpt his tomb and fresco the ceiling of the Sistine Chapel, and Raphael to decorate the *stanze* (rooms) in the Vatican palace. Not satisfied with the restoration of St Peter's initiated by his predecessors, Julius decided to scrap the old building and start again. The job was given to Bramante, and in 1506 the foundation stone was laid.

Work began on Bramante's Greek-cross design, but was halted after his death in 1514. In 1547 Michelangelo took over, keeping to the centralised design but increasing the scale tremendously. During the papacy of Sixtus V (1585-90) – an obsessive planner responsible for the layout of much of modern Rome – Giacomo del Duca erected the dome. The original Greek-cross design was scuppered by Paul V (1605-21), who commissioned Carlo Maderno to lengthen the nave, in accordance with Counter-Reformation dictates.

THE COUNTER-REFORMATION

The second half of the 16th century in Rome was dominated by the austere reforms of the Council of Trent (1545-63), designed to counter the ideas of Luther's Reformation, and by the establishment of heavy-handed new religious orders such as the Jesuits and Oratarians. Consequently, the earliest churches of the period, such as the **Chiesa Nuova** (*see p92*), were plain and provided with long naves, suitable for processions. The **Gesù** (*see p103*), with its wide

Basilica: **San Giovanni in Laterano**. *See p27.*

nave, was deemed ideal for the purposes of the Jesuits, as no architectural obstacles came between the preacher and his flock.

As the Counter-Reformation gathered pace, great cycles of decoration teaching the mysteries of the faith (such as the Cappella Sistina of **Santa Maria Maggiore**, *see p132*) or inspiring the onlooker to identify with the sufferings of martyrs (as in the bloodthirsty frescos of **Santo Stefano Rotondo**, *see p126*) began to appear.

THE BAROQUE

On their heels came an increasingly exuberant, theatrical style of art and architecture, the baroque. It is to a great extent the endlessly inventive confections of the baroque that make Rome what it is today. Architects such as Giacomo della Porta and Domenico Fontana (1543-1607) set the scene in which the real shapers of the baroque grew up: the architects Gian Lorenzo Bernini, Francesco Borromini and Pietro da Cortona (*see p26* **Top Five baroque**).

Bernini virtually made the baroque his own, with his imaginative use of marble, bronze and stucco, his combination of sensuality and mysticism. He was jealously guarded by his Barberini patrons, carrying out much of the decoration of the interior of St Peter's for the Barberini Pope Urban VIII. He so dominated the arts that the architect Borromini, Rome's other great genius of the era, was relatively neglected.

Bernini said that quarrelsome, neurotic Borromini 'had been sent to destroy architecture'. For centuries Borromini was vilified as a wild iconoclast. Today he is recognised as one of the great masters of the period, perhaps greatest of all in the inventive use of ground plan and the creation of spatial effects. The most startling examples of his work are **San Carlino alle Quattro Fontane** (*see p77*) and **Sant'Ivo alla Sapienza** (*see p97*), both of which broke all established rules. Perhaps because of his temperament (a manic depressive, he eventually committed suicide), he never attained anything like Bernini's status, but his lay patrons allowed him a freedom to develop his ideas that he might not have enjoyed had he worked for the popes-with-agendas.

Like Bernini, Pietro da Cortona created some of his greatest works for the Barberini popes. He was principally a painter; his most significant contribution to architecture was his three-dimensional treatment of walls. At **Santa Maria della Pace** (*see p93*) he combined opposing convex forms that, curving sharply at the ends, are nearly flat in the middle. The result is overwhelmingly theatrical.

Throughout the baroque period, it was the continuing patronage of the popes, their families and the religious orders that sustained the explosion of artistic and architectural fervour. Popes commissioned the decoration of St Peter's (Urban VIII, 1623-44); the colonnade in front of it (Alexander VII, 1655-67); the layout of **piazza Navona** (*see pp93-5*) and the redecoration of San Giovanni in Laterano (Innocent X, 1644-55). Their cardinal nephews inspired a many lesser building schemes: the redecoration or restoration of existing churches, and private villas, gardens, palaces and picture galleries.

The religious orders were no less profligate. The Gesù, for example, though begun in the 1560s, was not completed until the baroque period. It was originally intended to have bare interior walls; in the 1640s it began to acquire the alarming profusion of decoration we see today.

NEO-CLASSICISM & UNIFICATION

During the 18th century the baroque gained something of a rococo gloss, as seen in Francesco de Sanctis' **Spanish Steps** (*see p86*),

Neo-classical: **Piazza del Popolo**. *See p30.*

Nicola Salvi's **Fontana di Trevi** (*see p74*) and Fernando Fuga's hallucinatory **Palazzo della Consulta** on Piazza del Quirinale. Giovanni Battista Piranesi imposed his neo-classical theories on the city in the later

Top five ## Contemporary

Massimiliano Fuksas

His Centro Congressi Italia – a mega-fishtank containing a swirling cloud – is due to open its doors in EUR (*see p153*) in December 2004.

Zaha Hadid

The Anglo-Iranian responsible for the Cardiff Opera House has come up with a design looking much like molten, twisted train tracks for the new Centro delle Arti Contemporanee (*see p150*), to be concealed inside a former army barracks.

Richard Meier

An American, Meier won the privilege of being the first architect to direct post-war building work in the *centro storico* with his design for

a new 'container' to replace the fascist-era box around the Ara Pacis (*see p91*). Work is due to finish in spring 2002.

Renzo Piano

The Auditorium (*see p246*) – a striking concert venue whose three halls bear more than a passing resemblance to massive computer mice – has been dogged by delays, but was scheduled to be fully operational in April 2002.

Paolo Portoghesi

His visionary mosque (*see p150 and p300*) in the northern suburbs was opened in 1995, amid huge protests at the presence of an Islamic centre at the heart of Catholicism.

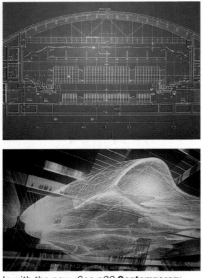

In with the new. *See p29* **Contemporary**.

part of the 18th century, creating striking tableaux such as the **piazza dei Cavalieri di Malta** (*see p118*).

The French occupation of the city (1809-14) brought a flurry of Gallic blueprints for changes both in town planning and sanitation. Some plans – such as Giuseppe Valadier's magnificent reorganisation of **piazza del Popolo** (*see p89*) and the **Pincio** (*see pp80-1*) – were carried out under French rule. Still others were adopted by the restored papacy after 1815, and claimed as its own.

In 1870, the city became capital of a united Italy, ruled by the northern Savoy dynasty, which sought to impose order on the chaotic cityscape, providing it with a road system and structures to house the burgeoning bureaucracy… even if this meant razing entire medieval and Renaissance quarters in the process. **Piazza Vittorio** (*see p135*), **Palazzo delle Esposizioni** (*see p78*) and the imperious, jingoistic **Vittoriano** (*see p62*) monument in piazza Venezia are fine examples. Occasional relief from the pomposity comes in the shape of lovely 'Liberty' (art nouveau) outcrops, such as the **Casina della Civetta** (*see p150*), the palazzo housing the **Museo Hendrik Christian Andersen** (*see p82*), the frescoed Galleria Sciarra arcade at via Minghetti 10 and the whole, extraordinary Coppedè district centring on piazza Mincio.

TWENTIETH-CENTURY ROME

The fascist era (1923-43) had a significant impact on Rome's architecture, much of it strikingly positive. **Stazione Termini** (*see p134*) is an example: its wide, overhanging entrance portal and huge foyer with wave-like ceiling are still stunning. North of the Tiber is the **Foro Italico** (*see p150*), a magnificent sports complex – though it's doubtful whether its builders intended the huge statues of naked male athletes to be quite as homoerotic as they are. The best buildings from the period are at EUR (*see p153*), south of the city, a surreal example of 1930s town planning, where structures such as the **Palazzo della Civiltà del Lavoro** and **Museo della Civiltà Romana** (*see p155*) look like something from a de Chirico cityscape.

Having transformed the suburbs, Mussolini intended to turn his attention to the *centro storico*. Addressing the city council, he said: 'Rome must appear wonderful to the whole world: immense, orderly and powerful. The approaches to the Theatre of Marcellus, the Campidoglio and the Pantheon must be cleared of everything that has grown up round them during the centuries of decadence. Within five years the hill of the Pantheon must be visible through an avenue leading from piazza Colonna.'

Fortunately, the advent of war stopped him wreaking too much havoc. But not before he had bludgeoned the via dei Fori Imperiali across the ruins of ancient fora from the **Colosseum** to piazza Venezia: a massive dig to undo his damage began in the 1990s, with the aim of creating a **Museo dei Fori Imperiali** (*see p70*).

From the 1950s to the 1970s, high-rise apartment and office blocks galloped across what had been unspoilt countryside, revealing little in the way of new or exciting architectural ideas. The flying saucer-like **Palazzo dello Sport** (*see p154*), built by Pier Luigi Nervi and Marcello Piacentini for the 1960 Olympics, is one exception. Its reinforced concrete dome, with a diameter of 100 metres (350 feet), took from the Pantheon the record for the world's largest free-standing concrete dome.

The city centre, luckily, remained largely untouched by post-war development: the first major post-war building project within the Aurelian Walls did not, in fact, begin until 2000.

Today, the decades-long slump in new architectural thinking is over, and Rome has become a hotbed of revolutionary design. Three futuristic new bridges are planned for the Tiber, whole areas – including the sweep of road from the Porta San Paolo to the Circo Massimo – are up for refurbishment, and top international names (*see p29* **Top five contemporary**) are breathing life into their unashamedly modern ideas in the inner suburbs.

Art in Rome

No other centre of art can boast a 3,000-year continuum.

On 3 December 1786, the German poet Johann Wolfgang von Goethe wrote from Rome about his latest fixations: 'the Pantheon, the Apollo Belvedere, one or two colossal heads and, recently, the Sistine Chapel have so obsessed me that I see almost nothing else.'

Goethe's list reflects not only his omnivorous curiosity, but also the range of art to be seen in Rome: intact temples, Roman marble copies of Greek bronze statues, fragments of larger sculptures, and Michelangelo frescos. Such diversity allows a sightseeing experience not found in any other city on earth. That the city displays art covering nearly 3,000 years is staggering enough in itself: that almost all of it was produced right here is even more amazing, and no other city – especially not those great art centres of London, Paris and New York – can boast as much.

Yet many visitors find Rome disorienting. After all, there is no Louvre to offer one-stop museum shopping, nor an Uffizi to present a complete survey of Italian painting. Moreover, the city's sprawling layout – with a dozen 'principal' squares – can frustrate the most intrepid traveller. Even those most closely involved with Rome's heritage experience a sense of bewilderment: 'Being minister of culture here is like being minister of oil in Saudi Arabia,' said Giovanna Melandri, who headed Italy's Culture Ministry until 2001.

With a little planning and sense of adventure, however, Rome offers a unique continuum of past and present: splendid monuments and intimate spaces, and the layered richness of a hundred generations of artists, patrons, and collectors who basked in the absolute certainty that Rome was the centre of the civilised world.

Although the art of Rome has furthered the needs of the Catholic Church for nearly two millennia, the single strongest influence has always been the weighty legacy of the ancient world. In few cities are the remains of the past so palpable. Ancient Rome, as *caput mundi*, harvested or created much of the best art of antiquity. Although successive sacks or occupations of the city – from Alaric in 410 to Napoleon in 1808 (*see chapter* **History**) – have pillaged much of this patrimony, but the fraction that has survived continues to astonish.

Egyptian obelisks transported across the Mediterranean still mark major squares. And while there are not many certain Greek originals in Rome today, the miracle of Greek art can be studied and appreciated in scores of important Roman copies. These marbles – often copies of bronze originals long since destroyed – display the Greek flair for endowing the human body with beauty, purpose, and sense of potential movement (especially the *contrapposto* pose, in which a figure's weight is borne on one leg). The classical ideal, combining striking naturalism with idealised body types, offered a standard of beauty that was hard to ignore.

Although the most famous Greek sculpture in Rome is the *Ludovisi Throne* – the centrepiece of the Ludovisi family collection housed in the Palazzo Altemps (*see p95*) – many works are transitional in nature, somewhere between Greek and Roman. An outstanding example in this category is the hulking *Belvedere Torso* – a superhuman physique from about 50 BC that inspired Michelangelo – now housed in the Pio Clementino Museum (*see p142*).

The Etruscans, the pre-Roman peoples who dominated central Italy from the sixth to the third century BC (*see p7*), produced an exuberant, violent, and sensuous art. The newly refurbished Museo di Villa Giulia (*see p83*) offers an extraordinary selection of Etruscan art, including life-sized terracotta sculptures from the temple of Apollo at Veio (*see p278*), and the tender terracotta sarcophagus of a married couple. Equally important is the Etruscan work known as the *Lupa Capitolina* (the Capitoline She-Wolf), a bronze treasure in the Musei Capitolini (*see p62*).

Beginning in the third century BC, the Romans literally built upon this Greek and Etruscan legacy with an unprecedented construction boom. New structural techniques – notably the arch and poured concrete technology (*see also chapter* **Architecture**) – gave birth to daring and spacious buildings (*see* the Pantheon *p98*; the Domus Aurea *p130*). The Romans were also responsible for monumental forms that blur the boundary between architecture and art, such as the triumphal arch ornamented with reliefs (particularly those of Septimus Severus and Titus in the Forum *see p71*, and that of Constantine near the Colosseum *see p66*) and the independent column ornamented with a spiral band (*see* Colonna di Trajano *p70*; colonna di Marco Aurelio *p86*). A further Roman innovation on a smaller scale was the portrait bust, which recorded facial features of the great and the average with an arresting honesty.

Much of the best classical art is now concentrated in a few major museums. The

Caravaggio's *Calling of Matthew. See p34.*

Palazzo Altemps (*see p95*), which contains the statue of the *Gaul's Suicide*, is an ideal first stop for the neophyte connoisseur. The Palazzo Massimo alle Terme (*see p93*) houses important works of Roman painting and sculpture, including a fine Augustus and two copies of the *Discus Thrower* of Myron. The Musei Capitolini (*see p62*) feature *The Dying Gaul* and beautiful centaurs in dark marble from Hadrian's Villa (*see p273*). And though the sheer size of the Vatican Museums' (*see pp141-143*) classical collection can be demoralising, one Hellenistic work there, however, never disappoints; the *Laocoön*, showing a powerful man and his two sons struggling for their lives against serpents, may be the most dynamic statue in the history of art.

> ## 'The classical ideal offered a standard of beauty that was hard to ignore.'

Christian art flourished in Rome after AD 313, when Emperor Constantine's Edict of Milan (*see p10*) legitimised the new religion. Rome was thus transformed from a city of temples to one of churches. Sadly, little portable early Christian art – the devotional apparatus of the newly recognised religion – survives. Stunning mosaics, however, decorate a number of churches: Santa Costanza (fourth century, *see p151*), Santa Maria Maggiore (fifth century, *see p132*), Santi Cosma e Damiano (sixth century, *see p73*), Santa Prassede (ninth century, *see p133*). Two of the most atmospheric early churches are the austere and lovely Santa Sabina (*see p119*) on the Aventine Hill, and San Clemente (*see p122*), with 12th-century mosaics and even earlier murals.

Later medieval art can be enjoyed in Santa Cecilia in Trastevere (*see p117*) which includes a ciborium (altar canopy; 1283) by Arnolfo di Cambio (best know as the architect of the

Duomo in Florence), and a pioneering fresco of the *Last Judgment* (1293) by Pietro Cavallini above the nun's choir. The little-known Cavallini – who perhaps deserves to rank with Giotto as an initiator of the dawn of the Renaissance – impresses as well with his narrative mosaics (1291) in nearby Santa Maria in Trastevere (*see p115*).

From 1305 to 1378, the Papacy was headquartered in Avignon; Rome withered, and only a fraction of the population remained Thus the Gothic period is largely absent in the Eternal City. The lack of late Medieval art, however, is richly compensated by the wealth of Renaissance, and particularly High Renaissance, art of the 15th and 16th centuries.

The definitive return of the Papacy in 1420 permitted the Renaissance and its doctrine of Humanism to take root and eventually flourish.

Humanism was preoccupied with reviving the language and art of the ancient Greeks and Romans, and reconciling this pagan heritage with Christianity. Renaissance ideas began to leave their mark on the city with architecture based on ancient examples, and sculpture and painting that assimilated the *contrapposto* grace and naturalism of the best classical statues. The Papacy concluded that patronage of this new art could extend the faith: on his deathbed in 1455, Pope Nicholas V informed his successors that 'noble edifices combining taste and beauty with imposing proportions would immensely conduce to the exaltation of the chair of St Peter'.

Nicholas's extant contribution to Vatican beatification – the little Chapel of Nicholas V (*see p142*) frescoed by **Fra Angelico** and **Benozzo Gozzoli** (1447-9) – may be modest in the light of his ambitions, but it remains an extraordinary jewel of the early Renaissance. Later popes undertook grander campaigns: Sixtus IV (1471-84) engaged the greatest painters of the day – **Perugino**, **Botticelli**, **Ghirlandaio**, and **Cosimo Rosselli** – to fresco the walls of his Sistine Chapel from 1481-2. Whatever you may of the morals of the Borgia Pope Alexander VI (*see p12* **Lust, murder & incest**), his taste in art was exquisite, as seen in the frescos (1493-5) by **Pinturicchio** that perpetuate Perugino's sweet style throughout the many rooms of the Borgia Apartments (*see p143*).

Outside the Vatican, the grace of 15th-century Florentine art can also be seen in the joyful and energetic frescos (1489-93) of **Filippino Lippi** in the Caraffa Chapel in the church of Santa Maria sopra Minerva (*see p99*).

In the 16th century, art and architecture took a monumental turn. In painting, the human figure grew in relation to the pictorial field: the busy backgrounds of 15th-century art were eliminated. Sculptors took their cue from ancient statues and made the human body newly heroic. **Michelangelo** (1475-1564) first worked in Rome from 1496-1501 for sophisticated clerics and businessmen. He carved his first *Pietà* (now in St Peter's, *see p139*) for a French cardinal; his 1498 contract challenged the supremacy of classical sculpture in promising to create a piece 'more beautiful than any work in marble to be seen in Rome today'. Michelangelo positioned the dead Christ gracefully in his mother's lap, achieving an eternal meditation on death, and fulfilling his boastful pledge.

Under Julius II (1503-1513), Papal patronage called ever-greater artists to work on ever-larger projects at the Vatican, shifting the centre of the Renaissance from Florence to Rome. Julius summoned Michelangelo back from Florence to begin work on the pope's own monumental tomb, a work full of over-life-size statues destined for the choir of the old St Peter's. The headstrong Julius soon changed his mind, insisting that the young sculptor paint the ceiling of the Sistine Chapel. Although bitterly complaining that he was 'no painter', Michelangelo rapidly frescoed the ceiling (1508-11), retelling the first nine chapters of Genesis with a grandeur and solidity previously associated with sculpture. If the recent cleaning of the frescos provoked controversy, the vivid colours we now see are far closer to Michelangelo's original intentions than the dark forms worshipped in the 19th and 20th centuries.

Although a later campaign to fresco the chapel's altar wall produced the triumphant and awe-inspiring *Last Judgment* (1534-41), the tomb for Julius limped to an unsatisfactory conclusion in the early 1540s in San Pietro in Vincoli (*see p131*), employing the powerful *Moses* (c1515) as its centrepiece.

Julius initiated his grandest plan of all when he called upon **Donato Bramante** (1444-1514) to design a new St Peter's. The grandeur of Bramante's style inspired painters as well as other architects. The most influential of the former was, **Raphael** (1483-1520).

Julius II would not deign to occupy the apartments of his dissolute Borgia predecessor; he insisted on a new suite of rooms – the so-called *stanze*, *see p142* – decorated by Raphael from 1508. The presence of Michelangelo working next door on the Sistine ceiling was a spur to the young painter: the elegant *School of Athens* (1510-1) exemplifies the notion of the High Renaissance with its animated re-creation of the great philosophers of ancient Greece, against a backdrop of imaginary architecture borrowed from Bramante.

If Michelangelo was unsurpassed in depicting the human body in complex poses, the *stanze* show Raphael's superiority in arranging poised compositions. The huge demand for this style forced Raphael to run an efficient workshop staffed with assistants. Raphael's success at delegation is most apparent in the delightful frescos in the Villa Farnesina (*see p115*); but one can measure the astonishingly swift development of the master himself in a single room of the Vatican Pinacoteca (*see p143*). There, three masterful altarpieces – *The Coronation of the Virgin* (1505), *The Madonna of Foligno* (c. 1511), and *The Transfiguration* (c1518-20) – chart the amazing shift from a sweetness reminiscent of Perugino to a brooding, dramatic late style. (This rapid evolution would be paralleled four centuries later in the career of another child prodigy, Picasso.) In the same room, note the lavish tapestries designed by Raphael to decorate the lower walls of the Sistine Chapel, far more costly than any painting.

The Sack of Rome in 1527 (*see p15*) halted the artistic boom of the High Renaissance. The simultaneous spread of the Protestant Reformation directly challenged the legitimacy of the pope and his worldly expenses. A more hardened, pessimistic spirit preferred the extraordinary forms of Mannerist art, a style of exaggerated proportions and contorted poses that developed out of the mature work of Raphael and Michelangelo. Frescos (c1545) by Raphael's assistant **Perino del Vaga** (1501-47) in the Castel Sant'Angelo (*see p144*) depict both hyper-elegant humans and statues, playing with levels of reality.

By the second half of the 16th century, Mannerist style had lost its wit and energy. Baroque rescue came through the works of **Annibale Carracci** (1560-1609) of Bologna and the shocking naturalism of Michelangelo Merisi, better known as **Caravaggio** (1571-1610). Although Carracci is now hard to appreciate in Rome (besides a lovely *Flight into Egypt* in the Galleria Doria Pamphili, *see p97*), his contemporary, Caravaggio, left paintings throughout the city during his stormy career. These works, with their extreme *chiaroscuro*, can be seen in the churches of Sant'Agostino (*see p97*) and Santa Maria del Popolo (*see p91*). His masterpiece may be the *Calling of St Matthew* (c1599-1602) in the church of San Luigi dei Francesi (*see p96*), where the beckoning finger of Christ recalls Michelangelo's *Creation of Adam* in the Sistine Chapel (*see p143*). Altercations with police and patrons marked Caravaggio's Roman years. After losing a tennis match and killing his opponent, Caravaggio fled south; yet his violent style persisted for a generation, as witnessed in the extraordinary room of baroque altarpieces and easel paintings by **Poussin**, **Reni**, and **Guercino** in the Vatican Pinacoteca.

The consummate artist of the Roman baroque, however, was primarily a sculptor, **Gian Lorenzo Bernini** (1598-1660). Bernini perhaps surpassed Michelangelo in the virtuosity of his marble carving. The confident energy inherent in baroque art is revealed by comparing Bernini's greatest religious sculpture, *The Ecstacy of St Theresa* (1647-52) in Santa Maria della Vittoria (*see p137*), with Michelangelo's *Pietà* (pictured on p31). Michelangelo's mild Virgin shows perpetual, placid bereavement; Bernini's Theresa captures a split second of sensual rapture.

> ## 'The confident energy of baroque art is revealed in Bernini's Ecstasy of St Theresa.'

Theatrical sculptures like Bernini's *Apollo and Daphne* (1622-5) in the Galleria Borghese (*see p81*) push back the boundaries of sculpture; Bernini tried to capture whole narratives in a frozen instant, and describe textures more vividly than any previous carver. The Galleria Borghese contains many other Bernini statues, plus superb paintings, providing a fine example of a patrician art collection.

Similarly, the Galleria Doria Pamphili (*see p97*) evokes the epoch with outstanding pictures in a magnificent setting; one small room forces a comparison of two portraits of the Pamphili Pope Innocent X (1644-55): a bust by Bernini and a canvas by **Diego Velazquez**.

The baroque style persisted well into the 18th century.

The final great artistic movement born in Rome was Neoclassicism, a nostalgic – some would say sentimental – celebration of ancient Greek art, in stark white statues and reliefs. **Antonio Canova** (1757-1822) created enormous, muscular statues like *Hercules and Lichas* in the Galleria Nazionale d'Arte Moderna (*see p82*) and dignified tombs in St Peter's.

Later movements of the 19th and 20th centuries can be seen at the Galleria Nazionale d'Arte Moderna and the new Galleria Communale d'Arte Moderna (*see p85*). Modern art, regularly exhibited at the Scuderie Papali and the Palazzo delle Esposizioni (for both, *see p78*), offers a respite to overwhelmed tourists and proves that the city isn't (entirely) trapped by its own past.

Accommodation

Accommodation   **37**

7:00 am 11:30 pm

12:00 pm

[Every moment is the right one]

The Ripa All Suites Hotel offers you a choice of 170
spacious and modern suites designed [suite ampie e moderne]
to provide our guests with the maximum amount
of space, light and comfort [il massimo dello spazio, della luce
e delle comodità]; 2 private conference rooms

[sale conferenze] with place for up to 180 persons
and another 5 meeting rooms [5 sale attrezzate]
equipped with all the latest technology
for business meetings, classes and conventions;
a high-quality restaurant, [ristorante di alta qualità]
Riparte Cafè, perfect for a business lunch, intimate
dinner or large party, noted for its creative
Mediterranean cuisine as well as its excellent sushi bar..
It is also now possible to meet up at the music
club Suite [ripa sound hotel] where premier live music and
a relaxing atmosphere await you for out-of-the-ordinary
after-dinner entertainment

RIPA
ALL SUITES
HOTEL

RIP*a*RTE

café

suite
ripa
sound
hotel

1 via degli orti di trastevere 00153 rome
t 0658611 f 065814550
t 065861857/835/861 f 065861832 reservations
e-mail: info@ripahotel.com
www.ripahotel.com

Accommodation

Whether you're finding your paradise lost or making pilgrim's progress, there's no need to sell your soul to find a decent hotel in Rome.

Although a lot of Romans looked down their noses at the hordes of marauding pilgrims invading the city for the 2000 Jubilee Holy Year, the long-term positive effect those visitors had on the city is undeniable. Historic buildings suddenly emerged from behind decades of accumulated muck and hoteliers finally cleaned up their acts (and their rooms) and stuck their hands out for a piece of the Jubilee pie.

Large amounts of money have been ploughed into revamping old hotels and opening new ones. Results have been impressive, ranging from the small, intimate and unspeakably exquisite (such as **Casa Howard** *p42*), to the enormous and jaw-droppingly opulent (such as **St Regis Grand** *p51*). Even hotels that didn't go so far as to completely transform themselves are at least making some kind of effort and, unless you wander into some of the dark corners around Termini station, you're a lot less likely to stumble across an expensive flea-pit where you'll find the previous guest's toenail clippings – and worse – in the bathroom sink.

A few things that haven't changed on the Rome hotel scene recently are the ever-increasing prices, the small size of hotel rooms and the lack of a view. EM Forster had to send his characters to Florence to find the latter, and you may have to follow in their footsteps if that's what you're looking for, because unless you're fortunate enough to get a room at **Abruzzi** (*see p49*), or can afford to pay a fortune to stay at **Hassler Villa Medici** (*see p39*), you'll be lucky if you see much more than the bare wall opposite until you step outside the hotel door.

STANDARDS & PRICES

Italian hotels are classified on a star system, from one to five. One star usually indicates *pensioni*, which are cheap but have very few facilities, and you may have to share a bathroom. The more stars, the more facilities a hotel will have; a higher rating, however, does not guarantee friendliness, cleanliness or decent service.

Pricewise, a double room in a one-star can set you back €26-€77/L50,000-L150,000; two-star, €36-€129/L70,000-L250,000; three-star, €62-€248/L120,000-L480,000; four-star, €207-€515/L400,000-L1,000,000. Five-star prices start at

about €310/L600,000, and don't stop until most people would need a second mortgage just for one night.

Prices generally rise by about 10 per cent each year. Many hotels do special weekend rates, and one-off deals for certain holidays. Hotel websites will have latest details. Groups, or people staying for longer periods, should ask about discounts.

If you're visiting with children, most hotels will be happy to squeeze a cot or camp bed into a room, but will probably charge 30 to 50 per cent extra for the privilege. Self-catering accommodation (*see p55*) could prove a cheaper alternative.

BOOKING A ROOM

Always reserve a room well in advance, especially at peak times, which now means most of the year, with lulls during winter (January to March) and in the dog days of August. If you're coming at the same time as a major religious holiday (Christmas or Easter) it's wise to book weeks, or even months, ahead.

It is standard practice among larger hotels to ask you to fax confirmation of a booking, with a credit card number in lieu of a deposit. Smaller hotels may ask you to send a money order to secure rooms in high season. The booking service at www.venere.com has a long list of hotels in an extensive price range.

If you arrive with nowhere to stay, the APT tourist office (*see p303*) provides a list of hotels but you must do the booking yourself. The tourist information agency Enjoy Rome (*see p304*) will book a hotel for you. The Hotel Reservation agency, with desks at Termini station and Fiumicino airport, has details on availability for numerous hotels at all prices and also offers a shuttle service to and from Fiumicino (€9.55/L18,000 one way). Staff speak English. Avoid the hotel touts that hang around Termini: you're likely to end up paying more than you should for a very grotty hotel.

Hotel Reservation

Fiumicino airport, arrivals halls Terminals A, B & C (06 699 1000/fax 06 678 1469 or 06 6994 0705/ www.hotelreservation.it). **Open** 7.30am-10.30pm daily. **No credit cards.**
Branches: *Apr-Nov* Ciampino airport; Termini station, at the head of platform 20 (06 699 1000).

Hotels

For Santa Claus

The sleigh's waiting for him in the foyer of the **Raphael** (*see p45*), but can he get a herd of reindeer past the ever-vigilant doorman?

For Sergei Eisenstein

The Spanish Steps may not be Odessa, and Rome may not have a branch of Mothercare. But what the hell, it's about time he stayed at the **Hassler Villa Medici** (*see p39*) and made *Battleship Potemkin Part II*.

For Cleopatra

She may not want to get her asp out in the **Valadier**'s (*see p42*) seductive piano bar, but she's bound to love the mirrors on the bedroom ceiling.

For Maximus the Gladiator

After a hard day fighting tigers at the Colosseum down the road, Max can come home to the **Celio** (*see p51*) and brush up on his technique using the hotel's extensive video collection. What would sir like tonight, *Spartacus* again – or a bit of *Ben Hur*?

For EM Forster

To show him how *Howard's End* (**Casa Howard**, *see p42*) can be recreated in the 21st century: Turkish bath, central location – and no nasty Anthony Hopkins trying to turf you out in the morning.

For Cinderella

After being waltzed around the **Plaza**'s (*see p42*) magnificent ballroom, Cinders can go out onto via del Corso, buy a decent pair of slippers and even find a taxi after midnight.

OUR CHOICE

Most of the hotels listed here are in a good location (*see also p53* **Location, location, location**), offer value for money or just have bags of character. In the luxury category the emphasis is on opulence. Those in mid to upper-price ranges are smaller, many in old *palazzi* with pretty, though often small, bedrooms. *Pensioni* are fairly basic, but those listed here are friendly and usually family-run.

Few Roman hotels have even heard of non-smoking areas, and not many have access for the disabled (*see p293*). Staff are generally very

willing to help guests with mobility problems, but most places have so many stairs there's not much they can do.

Unless stated, prices are for rooms with bathrooms, and include breakfast.

The Trevi Fountain & the Quirinale

Mid-range

Residenza Cellini

Via Modena 5 (06 4782 5204/fax 06 4788 1806/ residenzacellini@tin.it/www.residenzacellini.it). Metro Repubblica/bus to via Nazionale. **Rates** €129.11-€175.60/L250,000-L340,000 double room for single occupant; €144.61-€196.25/L280,000-L380,000 double room; €144.61-€196.25/L280,000-L380,000 junior suite for single occupant; €165.27-€216.91/L320,000-L420,000 junior suite. **Credit** AmEx, DC, MC, V. **Map** p323 2B.

Reopened in October 2000 after a complete renovation, this once-grubby *pensione* full of shoebox-sized rooms has been transformed into a delightfully luminous and spacious residence containing three double rooms and three junior suites. Rooms are huge, and decorated with simple elegance. Mattresses are orthopaedic and, for anyone who may be worried about spontaneous combustion, bed linen is anti-inflammable. Bathrooms have marble sinks and porcelain baths or jacuzzi.

Hotel services *Air-conditioning. Dry-cleaning. Fax. Laundry. Non-smoking rooms. Parking (€12.91-€20.66/L25,000-L40,000 per day).* **Room services** *Air-conditioning. Dataport. Hair dryer. Jacuzzi. Mini-bar. Radio. Safe. TV (satellite).*

Via Veneto & the Villa Borghese

Deluxe

Eden

Via Ludovisi 49 (06 478 121/fax 06 482 1584/ reservations@hotel-eden.it/www.hotel-eden.it). Metro Barberini/bus to via Veneto. **Rates** (exclusive of 10 per cent tax) €392.51-€408.00/L760,000-L790,000 single; €568.10-€661.06/L1,100,000-L1,280,000 double; from €826.33/L1,600,000 studio room; from €1,497.72/L2,900,000 suites; €2,324.05/L4,500,000 presidential suite; Ludovisi and penthouse suites on request; breakfast €21.70-€33.57/L42,000-L65,000 extra. **Credit** AmEx, DC, MC, V. **Map** p323 1C.

Beautifully understated, the hotel Eden manages to be stylish yet relaxed; offering the attentiveness and attention to detail of a top-notch hotel without the stuffiness. Just off via Veneto, the Eden has elegant reception rooms, tastefully decorated bedrooms and a roof terrace with a top-ranked restaurant (*see p164*) and truly spectacular views. The hotel was reopened in 1995 after a massive refurbishment by none other than Margaret Thatcher. So *that's* what happens to ex-prime ministers.

Hotel services *Air-conditioning. Babysitting. Bar. Business services. Conference facilities (70). Currency exchange. Dry-cleaning. Fax. Gym. Laundry. Lifts. Non-smoking rooms. Restaurant. Safe. Tours.* **Room services** *Fax. Hair dryer. Internet access. Air-conditioning. Bathrobe and slippers. Dataport. Hair dryer. Iron. Mini-bar. PC point. Radio. Room service (24-hour). Safe. Telephone (two lines). TV (satellite/pay). VCR (suites).*

Excelsior

Via V Veneto 125 (06 47 081/fax 06 482 6205/ res070.excelsior.rome@westin.com/www.westin.com/ excelsiorroma). Metro Barberini/bus to via Veneto. **Rates** €313-€375/L606,000-L726,000 single; €495-€560/L958,000-L1,084,000 double; €1,307-€1,591/L2,531,000-L3,081,000 suites; other suites on request. **Credit** AmEx, DC, MC, V. **Map** p323 1B.

The mind-boggling Villa La Cupola suite (two floors, 1,100sq m/11,820 sq ft, eight-seat cinema!) is one of the biggest in Europe, and this massive hotel is for those for whom size really does matter. The entrance is grand and lavish – and a bit gloomy if you arrive in the daytime. Rooms are a Hollywood-style fantasy. Staff are attentive in a slightly robot-like way.

Hotel services *Air-conditioning. Babysitting. Bar. Business services. Conference facilities (450). Currency exchange. Dry-cleaning. Fax. Laundry. Lifts. Multilingual staff. Non-smoking rooms. Parking (nearby). Restaurant. Safe.* **Room services** *Air-conditioning. Dataport. Fax point. Hair dryer. Mini-bar. Radio. Room service (24-hour). Telephone. TV (satellite/pay).*

Hassler Villa Medici

Piazza Trinità dei Monti 6 (06 699 340/fax 06 678 9991/hasslerroma@mclink.it/www.hotelhasslerroma. com). Metro Spagna/bus to piazza Barberini. **Rates** €366.68/L710,000 single; €495.80-€655.90/L960,000-L1,270,000 double; suites (15) on request; breakfast €22.72-€39.77/L44,000-L77,000 extra. **Credit** AmEx, DC, MC, V. **Map** p323 1C.

Looking imperiously down from the top of the Spanish steps, the Hassler is easy to spot by the long line of limousines parked out front. The Hassler is one Rome's classic hotels with all the trappings and trimmings you might expect: chandeliers and lots of wood and marble. Lesser mortals can only dream of staying there – and take comfort in the fact that the lovely rooftop bar probably doesn't do a decent pint anyway.

Hotel services *Air-conditioning. Babysitting. Bars. Beauty salon. Conference facilities (100). Currency exchange. Dry-cleaning. Fax. Garden. Laundry. Lifts. Limousine. Parking (€25.82/L50,000 per day). Restaurant. Safe.* **Room services** *Air-conditioning. Dataport. Fax point. Hair dryer. Laptop rent. Mini-bar. PC point. Radio. Room service (24-hour). Safe. Telephone. TV (satellite, cable).*

Majestic

Via V Veneto 50 (06 421 441/fax 06 488 5657/ hotel.majestic@flashnet.it/www.hotelmajestic.com). Metro Barberini/bus to via Veneto. **Rates** €302.12-€374.43/L585,000-L725,000 single; €408-€490.63/L790,000-L950,000 double; €568.10/ L1,100,000 junior suite; other suites on request; breakfast €19.63-€36.16/L38,000-L70,000 extra. **Credit** AmEx, DC, MC, V. **Map** p323 1B.

Former prime ministers do the honours at the **Eden**. *See p38.*

The first hotel to open its doors on via Veneto, the Majestic has been in business since 1889. With its peaceful but rather formal atmosphere, the Majestic lives up to its name: there are silk settees and frescos in the reception room and white Carrara marble in the bathrooms. Be warned though: in some of the rooms there's a startling clash of colours and designs, so you might want to keep your sunglasses on.
Hotel Services *Air-conditioning. Babysitting. Bar. Conference facilities (150). Currency exchange. Dry cleaning. Fax. Laptop (available on request). Laundry. Lifts. Parking. Restaurants (2). Safe.*
Room services *Air-conditioning. Dataport. Fax point. Hair dryer. Jacuzzi. Mini-bar. Radio. Room service. Safe. Telephone. TV (satellite). VCR.*

Expensive

Barocco
Via della Purificazione 4 (06 487 2001/fax 06 485 994/info@hotelbarocco.com/www.hotelbarocco.com/www.hotelbaroccco.it). Metro Barberini/bus to piazza Barberini. **Rates** €149.78-€196.25/L290,000-L380,000 single; €216.92-€284.05/L420,000-L550,000 double; €284.06-€361.52/L550,000-L700,000 triple; €309.88-€387.34/L600,000-L750,000 junior suite; €361.52-€490.63/L700,000-L950,000 suite. **Credit** AmEx, DC, MC, V. **Map** p323 1C.
On a tiny street off via Veneto, the Barocco manages to combine a central location with calm, and four-star quality with the intimacy of a small hotel. Completely refurbished at the beginning of 2001, the 42 rooms are stylish, with marble bathrooms, dark wood bureaus, sashed curtains and enormous mirrors.
Hotel services *Air-conditioning. Babysitting. Bar. Currency exchange. Dry-cleaning. Fax. Laundry. Lifts. Non-smoking rooms. Payphone. Safe. Sauna. TV room.* **Room services** *Air-conditioning. Iron. Mini-bar. Radio. Room service. Safe. TV (pay/cable).*

Eliseo
Via di Porta Pinciana 30 (06 487 0456/06 482 8658/fax 06 481 9629/leonardi@travel.it/ www.travel.it). Metro Spagna/bus to via Veneto. **Rates** €134.28-€196.26/L260,000-L380,000 single; €165.27-€284.05/L320,000-L550,000 double; €258.23-€387.34/L500,000-L750,000 suite. **Credit** AmEx, DC, MC, V. **Map** p323 1C.
On the edge of Villa Borghese, the Eliseo may not compete in terms of luxury with the big boys around the corner on via Veneto, but it does offer efficiency at affordable rates in a generally expensive area. The decor can sometimes verge on tackiness, what with a veritable army of gold cherubs flying about the walls, but is forgiven once you munch your *cornetti* in the sixth-floor breakfast room with its breathtaking view across Villa Borghese to St Peter's. The seventh-floor bedrooms also have fantastic views.
Hotel services *Air-conditioning. Bar. Business services. Conference facilities(15). Currency exchange. Dry-cleaning. Fax. Laundry. Lifts. Payphone. Safe. TV room.* **Room services** *Air-conditioning. Hair dryer. Iron. Mini-bar. Room service. Safe. Telephone. Trouser press. TV (satellite/pay).*

Scalinata di Spagna
Piazza Trinità dei Monti 17 (reservations 06 679 3006/06 6994 0806/fax 06 6994 0598/ info@hotelscalinata.com/www.hotelscalinata.com). Metro Spagna or Barberini/bus to piazza Barberini or via del Tritone. **Rates** €196.25-€309.87/L380,000-L600,000 single & double; €464.81-€619.75/L900,000-L1,200,000 suite. **Credit** AmEx, MC, V. **Map** p323 1C.
You could almost miss the Scalinata di Spagna, tucked romantically away into the corner of the piazza, a world away from the tourists and the constant stream of limousines to the Hassler (*see p39*) across the road. A quaint, intimate hotel that becomes its setting at the top of the Spanish steps, the Scalinata has 16 rooms decorated in a rather enthusiastic yellow. Some rooms have terraces looking down over the roof tops, including that of ex-neighbour, Keats.
Hotel services *Air-conditioning. Babysitting. Bar. Currency exchange. Dry cleaning. Fax. Laundry. Parking (€23.24/L45,000 per day). Safe.*
Room services *Air-conditioning. Hair dryer. Mini-bar. Radio. Room service. Safe. Telephone. TV.*

Mid-range

La Residenza
Via Emilia 22-24 (06 488 0789/fax 06 485 721/ hotel.la.residenza@venere.it/www.venere.it/roma/la_ residenza). Metro Barberini/bus to via Veneto. **Rates** €82.60-€92.90/L160,000-L180,000 single; €175.60-€185.90/L340,000-L360,000 double; €201.40-€211.70/L390,000-L410,000 suite. **Credit** MC, V. **Map** p323 1B.
La Residenza is located in a beautifully kept palazzo on a quiet street just behind via Veneto. The staff can be slightly formal, but the muted lighting creates a cosy atmosphere for anyone wanting to veg out on the comfortable settees in the lounge (although the brightly striped wallpaper may cause the odd migraine). The double rooms are large if unimaginatively decorated; singles, on the other hand, are quite small. Amazingly, the hotel is to become a smoke-free zone by the end of 2001.
Hotel services *Air-conditioning. Babysitting. Bar. Currency exchange. Dataport (in lounge). Dry-cleaning. Fax. Laundry. Lifts. Payphone. Safe.* **Room services** *Air-conditioning. Dataport. Hair dryer. Mini-bar. Radio. Room service. Safe. Telephone. TV (satellite).*

Villa Borghese
Via Pinciana 31 (06 8530 0919/06 854 9648/fax 06 841 4100/hotel.villaborghese@tiscalinet.it/ www.charmerelax.it/83.html). Bus to via Pinciana or piazza G Tartini. **Rates** €108.46-€139.44/L210,000-L270,000 single; €149.77-€180.76/L290,000-L350,000 double; €211.75-€237.57/L410,000-L460,000 suite. **Credit** AmEx, DC, MC, V. **Map** p322 2B.
A hotel since the 1950s, the Villa Borghese was once the family home of writer Alberto Moravia. It's a family-run establishment with a cosy, even old-fashioned feel to it; sometimes too much so, especially in bathrooms and bedrooms which verge on the

Accommodation

depressing. The hotel is separated from the Villa Borghese gardens and the Galleria Borghese by an incredibly noisy road; thankfully, the rooms are all double glazed.

Hotel services *Air-conditioning. Bar. Fax. Laundry. Non-smoking rooms. Parking (€20.66/L40,000 per day). Payphone. Safe. TV room.* **Room services** *Air-conditioning. Hair dryer. Mini-bar. Telephone. TV (satellite).*

Il Tridente

Deluxe

De Russie

Via del Babuino 9 (06 328 881/fax 06 3288 8888/ reservations@hotelderussie.it/www.rfhotels.it). Metro Flaminio/bus to via del Corso. **Rates** *€351.19-€387.34/L680,000-L750,000 single; €490.63-€645.57/ L950,000-L1,250,000 double; €877.98-€1,859.24/L1,700,000-L3,600,000 suites; breakfast €20.66-€30.99/L40,000-L60,000 extra.* **Credit** AmEx, DC, MC, V. **Map** p320 2A.

In its inspired attempt to bring the Rome luxury hotel scene into the 21st century, the Hotel de Russie wouldn't be caught dead with acres of extravagant chandeliers and fake gold. Instead, the refurbishment in the spring of 2000, saw Tommaso Ziffer go all out on the modern look. The minimalist grey reception area and rooms may not be to everyone's tastes and the corridors may remind you of a hospital but the gardens are gorgeous and the health centre with its array of treatments is probably the best in Rome. The hotel is a star magnet, with Cameron Diaz and Leonardo di Caprio staying there while filming *Gangs of New York*, and Tom and Nicole defecting from the Eden (*see p38*) to stay here (before they defected from each other).

Hotel services *Air-conditioning. Babysitting. Bar. Beauty salon. Business services. Concierge. Conference facilities (90). Currency exchange. Disabled rooms. Dry-cleaning. Fax. Garden. Gym. Laundry. Lifts. Limousine. Non-smoking rooms. Parking (€36.15/L70,000 per day). Restaurant. Safe. Sauna. Swimming pool.* **Room services** *Air-conditioning. Dataport. Fax machine on request. Hair dryer. Mini-bar. Radio. Room service (24-hour). Safe. Telephone (2 lines). TV (satellite/pay/cable). VCR.*

Plaza

Via del Corso 126 (06 6992 1111/fax 06 6994 1575/www.grandhotelplaza.com). Bus to piazza Augusto Imperatore or via Tomacelli. **Rates** *€201.42-€361.52/L390,000-L700,000 single; €289.22-€464.81/L560,000-L900,000 double; €516.46-€1,394.43/L1,000,000-L2,700,000 suite.* **Credit** AmEx, DC, MC, V. **Map** p321 1A.

A legendary hotel established around the time of Italy's unification, the Plaza has hosted more famous names than *Who's Who*. Although the lobby is showing signs of wear and tear, the hotel has managed to retain its *fin-de-siècle* atmosphere and the frescos and chandeliers in the 19th-century ballroom

have lost none of their magnificence. Rooms are generally large; if you're lucky enough to have a room on the sixth floor at the back, you'll be treated to a fantastic view of the Spanish Steps.

Hotel services *Air-conditioning. Babysitting. Bar. Beauty salon. Business centre. Bistro bar. Concierge. Conference facilities (700). Currency exchange. Disabled rooms. Dry-cleaning. Fax. Garden terrace. Laundry. Lifts. Non-smoking rooms. Payphone. Safe.* **Room services** *Air-conditioning. Dataport. Fax point. Hair dryer. Jacuzzi. Mini-bar. Radio. PC point. Room service. Safe. Telephone. TV (satellite). VCR.*

Expensive

Valadier

Via della Fontanella 15 (06 361 1998/06 361 2344/06 361 0559/fax 06 320 1558/ info@hotelvaladier.com/www.hotelvaladier.com). Bus to piazza del Popolo or piazza Augusto Imperatore. **Rates** *€149.77-€268.56/L290,000-L520,000 single; €201.42-€351.19/L390,000-L680,000 double; €232.41-€438.99/L450,000-L850,000 suite.* **Credit** AmEx, DC, MC, V. **Map** p320 2A.

Egyptian architect Sabah Hajar revamped the Valadier a number of years ago, lending it a musky, exotic feel. There are obelisks in the corridors and mirrored ceilings in the bedrooms, which aren't particularly spacious but most guests are probably too busy looking up at themselves to notice. The hotel's piano bar looks like something out of *Casablanca*. Guests have internal access to the Il Valentino restaurant next door, where breakfast is served.

Hotel services *Air-conditioning. Babysitting. Bar. Conference facilities (50). Currency exchange. Dry-cleaning. Fax. Laundry. Lift. Payphone. Restaurant. Safe. TV room.* **Room services** *Air-conditioning. Dataport. Hair dryer. Mini-bar. Phone. Radio. Room service (24hrs). Safe. Telephone. TV (satellite).*

Mid-range

Casa Howard

Via Capo le Case 18 (tel/fax 06 6794 6444/ www.casahoward.com). Metro Spagna/bus to via del Tritone. **Rates** *€118.79-€160.10/L230,000-L310,000 single; €149.77-€185.92/L290,000-L360,000 double; breakfast €7.75/L15,000 extra.* **Credit** MC, V. **Map** p323 1C.

Casa Howard (Howard's End) is a beautifully decorated residence near piazza di Spagna. Each of the five rooms has been individually designed with a strong emphasis on quality. Whether you're in the exotic Chinese room or the more serious blue room, the beds have been specially made and furniture designed by Ilaria Miani. Although only two bedrooms have bathrooms, kimonos are provided daily along with a pair of slippers so you can flip-flop to the Turkish bath down the hall.

Hotel services *Air-conditioning. Courtesy phone. Dry cleaning. Fax. Laundry. Lifts. Non-smoking rooms. Safe. Turkish bath.* **Room services** *Air-conditioning. Dataport. Hair dryer. TV (satellite).*

Film directors love the
Locarno. *See p45.*

HOTEL NAPOLEON

★★★★

The Quietest, in the heart of the Eternal City

As a result of its distinctive structure, the Hotel Napoleon can boast a tranquillity perhaps unmatched in the historical centre. Indeed all the rooms look out onto large sunny courtyards from which it is impossible to hear any of the irritating sounds of the city.

The Friendly Atmosphere

The Hotel Napoleon, run for 40 years by the Cioce-Duranti family, will welcome you in a friendly atmosphere, with a kind and attentive staff, together with the style and the glamour of a 4 star Hotel: the elegant lounges, rich with antiques, the intimate bar and the small restaurant.

The Napoleon's cosy Bar

The right place to start your Roman evening with a good cocktail well prepared by Giacomino (James)

Piazza Vittorio Emanuele II, 105 - 00185 Roma
Tel. 064467264 - Fax 064467282
email: infobook@napoleon.it
http://www.napoleon.it

Fontanella Borghese

*Largo Fontanella Borghese 84 (06 6880 9504/
06 6880 9624/fax 06 686 1295/
fontanellaborghese@libero.it/fontanellaborghese@int
erfree.it/www.fontanellaborghese.com). Bus to via del
Corso or piazza Augusto Imperatore.* **Rates**
€113.62/L220,000 single; €180.76/L350,000 double;
€222.08/L430,000 triple; €237.57/L460,000 quad.
Credit AmEx, DC, MC, V. **Map** pp321 1A.
The Fontanella Borghese offers family-run intimacy in the centre of Rome. On the second and third
floors of an old building, the hotel is elegantly done
out in relaxing cream and muted colours brightened
by a generous array of pot plants. You'll find via del
Corso and via Condotti just around the corner, making the Fontanella ideal for those who want to be in
the thick of things with somewhere to bolt to when
the crowds just get to be too much.
Hotel Services *Air-conditioning. Bar. Dry-cleaning.
Fax. Laundry. Lifts. Payphone. Safe.* **Room
services** *Fax point. Hair dryer. Mini bar. PC point.
Room service. Safe. Telephone. TV (satellite).*

Locarno

*Via della Penna 22 (06 361 0841/fax 06 321
5249/www.hotellocarno.com). Metro Flaminio/bus
to via di Ripetta.* **Rates** €111.04/L215,000 single;
€170.43-€185.92/L330,000-L360,000 double;
€201.42/L390,000 double superior; €216.91/
L420,000 junior suite; €232.41-€309.88/L450,000-
L600,000 double deluxe; €247.90/L480,000 triple
superior; €516.46/L1,000,000 suite. **Credit** AmEx,
DC, MC, V. **Map** p320 2A.
The Locarno, between the Tiber and piazza del
Popolo, was founded in the 1920s and the lobby looks
like a set for an Agatha Christie film. It retains some
original details: a Tiffany lamp, a grandfather clock,
a wrought-iron cage lift. The lounge has a fire in winter, and there's a pretty patio with fountain. The lovely suites in the new wing across the patio make the
rooms in the main body of the hotel look decidedly
dowdy. Regulars include director Peter Greenaway.
Hotel services *Air-conditioning. Bar. Bicycles (free
for guests). Disabled room. Laundry. Lifts.
Multilingual staff. Parking. Safe.* **Room services**
*Fax point. Hair dryer. Mini-bar. Radio. Safe.
Telephone. TV (satellite).*

Marcus

*Via del Clementino 94 (06 6830 0320/fax 06 6830
0312). Bus to via del Corso or via Tomacelli.* **Rates**
€72.30-€82.63/L140,000-L160,000 single; €103.29-
€134.28/L200,000-L260,000 double; €134.28-
€154.94/L260,000-L300,000 triple; €144.61-€165.27/
L280,000-L320,000 quad. **Credit** AmEx, MC, V.
Map p321 1A.
Descend the Spanish Steps and keep on walking to
get to the Marcus, a good bet for being in the heart
of Rome without paying top-of-the-range prices.
Peaceful and family-operated, it offers perks such as
cut-price entrance to a nearby gym and free airport
transfer in the low season; on the down side, it's a bit
shabby and the decor's an old-fashioned mix of bric-
a-brac and ill-matched furniture.

Hotel services *Air-conditioning. Bar. Currency
exchange. Fax. Lifts. Non-smoking rooms. Safe.*
Room services *Air-conditioning. Hair dryer. Mini-
bar. Room service. Safe. Telephone. TV (satellite).*

The Pantheon & Piazza Navona

Expensive

Raphael

*Largo Febo 2 (06 682 831/fax 06 687 8993/
info@raphaelhotel.com/www.raphaelhotel.com). Bus
to corso Rinascimento.* **Rates** €227.24-€268.56/
L440,000-L520,000 single; €335.70-
€438.98/L650,000-L850,000 double; €506.13-
€619.74/L980,000-L1,200,000 suite; breakfast
€12.91-€20.66/L25,000-L40,000 extra. **Credit**
AmEx, DC, MC, V. **Map** p321 2A.
This ivy-draped hotel behind piazza Navona is much
more eccentric than its exterior suggests. An antique
sleigh sits among other odd items in the reception;
around the corner are shelves full of original Picasso
ceramics; a 17th-century Russian icon sit in what
could easily be mistaken for the TV cabinet in the
lounge. Rooms are enthusiastically decorated in rich
colours and stripes, and some even have marble
pillars – or do they? If you knock on them you'll find
they're fake. Close to the Senate, the Raphael has long
been popular with politicians; Anthony Burgess men-
tions it in the Rome segment of *Earthly Powers.*

Politicians prefer the **Raphael**.

Existentialists liked the Sole al Pantheon.

Hotel services *Air-conditioning. Babysitting. Bars. Conference facilities (30). Currency exchange. Dry-cleaning. Fax. Gym. Laundry. Lifts. Non-smoking rooms. Restaurants. Safe. Sauna.* **Room services** *Air-conditioning. Dataport. Hair dryer. Mini-bar. Radio. Room service. Safe. Telephone. TV (satellite/pay).*

Sole al Pantheon
Piazza della Rotonda 63 (06 678 0441/fax 06 6994 0689/info@hotelsolealpantheon.com/ www.hotelsolealpantheon.com). Bus or tram to largo Argentina. **Rates** €206.58/L400,000 single; €247.90/L480,000 double for single occupant; €309.87/L600,000 double; €387.34-€438.99/ L750,000-L850,000 suite.* **Credit** AmEx, DC, MC, V. **Map** p321 2A.
The Sole dates back to the 15th century, making it – or so the management will tell you – the oldest hotel in Europe. Former guests range from the Renaissance poet Ariosto to existentialist Jean-Paul Sartre. It has recently been sensitively refurbished, with tiles and pretty frescos. Bedrooms are cool and have a fresh, Mediterranean feel. When booking, ask for one of the rooms at the front with superb views over the Pantheon. If they're not available, you'll have to console yourself by seeking out the glorious interior courtyard where breakfast is served in the warmer months.
Hotel services *Air-conditioning. Babysitting. Bar. Business services. Conference facilities (10). Currency exchange. Dry-cleaning. Fax. Laundry. Lifts.* **Room services** *Air-conditioning. Hair dryer. Jacuzzi in most rooms. Iron. Mini-bar. Radio. Room service. Safe. Telephone. TV (satellite/pay).*

Mid-range
Due Torri
Vicolo del Leonetto 23/25 (06 6880 6956/06 687 6983/fax 06 686 5442/www.hotelduetorriroma.com). Bus to corso Rinascimento. **Rates** €98.13-€154.93/L190,000-L200,000 single; €165.27-€180.72/L320,000-L350,000 double; €222.08-€258.23/L430,000-L500,000 suite for 3-4.* **Credit** AmEx, DC, MC, V. **Map** p321 2A.
Well hidden among the labyrinth of cobbled streets in the *centro storico*, the Due Torri has a warm, welcoming atmosphere and the 26 rooms – some of which have terraces that look over the roof tops – are cosy. Ask the friendly staff about the building's history: it's been the residence of cardinals, one of whom that became pope, as well as being home to some not-so-pious individuals.
Hotel services *Air-conditioning. Bar. Currency exchange. Fax. Laundry. Lifts. Parking (€25.83/L50,000 per day, nearby). TV room.* **Room services** *Air-conditioning. Hair dryer. Mini-bar. Radio. Room service. Safe. Telephone. TV (satellite).*

Residenza Zanardelli
Via G Zanardelli 7 (06 6821 1392/fax 06 6880 3802/info@hotelnavona.com/www.hotelnavona.com). Bus to via Zanardelli or lungotevere Tor di Nona. **Rates** €139.44/L270,000 double; €154.94/L300,000 suite.* **Credit** MC, V. **Map** p321 1B.
Run by the same family as the Navona (*see p49*), the Zanardelli is a quiet, pleasant place in the heart of the *centro storico*, just around the corner from piazza Navona and not far from St Peter's. With a total of

seven rooms, the residence is a little bit more up-market and intimate than its sister hotel. The owner has decorated the rooms with impeccable taste, right down to the silk and gold leaf Versace wallpaper.
Hotel Services *Air-conditioning. Fax. Lifts. Non-smoking rooms. Safe. TV room.* **Room services** *Air-conditioning. Hair dryer. Iron. Telephone. TV (satellite).*

Budget

Abruzzi

Piazza della Rotonda 69 (06 679 2021). Bus or tram to largo Argentina. **Rates** €59.39/L115,000 single; €87.80/L170,000 double. **No credit cards.** **Map** p321 2A.

You'll be hard-pushed to find anything more basic than this 25-room place: the rooms all have sinks, but there are only nine shared bathrooms. However, there are advantages: rooms are a good size and several have a view of the Pantheon which is right in front of the hotel in all its thunderous magnificence. It's an interesting old building, but ask for a room at the back if you want quiet at night.
Hotel services *Multilingual staff. Safe.*

Mimosa

Via di Santa Chiara 61 (06 6880 1753/fax 06 683 3557/hotelmimosa@tin.it/www.hotelmimosa.net). Bus or tram to largo Argentina. **Rates** €51.65-€61.97/L100,000-L120,000 single without bath; €72.30-€82.63/L140,000-L160,000 double without bath; €98.13/L190,000 double with bath; breakfast €3.87-€5.16/L7,500-L10,000 extra. **No credit cards. Map** p321 2A.

In medieval times this palazzo housed the Cavalieri della Croce, an order of crusading knights; for anyone wanting to go AWOL there was a handy escape tunnel to the Tiber. However, there's been little effort since to bring this second-floor *pensione* into the 21st century (there's no lift; don't even mention the Internet) so be prepared to rough it. The up side? It's incredibly central, located just around the corner from the Pantheon. Its other selling point is that the hotel is owned by Roman nobility, and all profits go to charity.
Hotel services *Fax. Non-smoking bedrooms. Telephone.* **Room services** *Telephone (2 rooms).*

Navona

Via dei Sediari 8 (06 686 4203/fax 06 6880 3802/www.hotelnavona.com). Bus to corso Rinascimento. **Rates** €82.63/L160,000 single; €108.46/L210,000 double; €136.86/L265,000 suite. **No credit cards. Map** p321 2A.

Just around the corner from piazza Navona, this hotel has a welcoming, communal atmosphere, which makes it a good choice for lone travellers. It is located on the second floor of a palazzo that stands on the site of the ancient baths of Agrippa (*see p135*); the ground floor of the building dates back to AD 1. At one time, this was the hotel of choice for literary stars: Keats and Shelley stayed on the top floor. The staff and owners are very helpful and friendly.
Hotel services *Air-conditioning. Car parking facilities. Currency exchange. Fax. Multilingual staff. Non-smoking rooms. Safe.* **Room services** *Air-conditioning (€15.49/L30,000 extra). Hair dryer (on request).*

Cardinals have kipped at the **Due Torri**. See p47.

The Ghetto & campo de' Fiori

Mid-range

Teatro di Pompeo

Largo del Pallaro 8 (06 687 2812/06 6830 0170/fax 06 6880 5531). Bus to corso Vittorio Emanuele. **Rates** €139.44/L270,000 double for single occupant; €180.76/L350,000 double. **Credit** AmEx, DC, MC, V. **Map** p321 2A.

A long-established hotel near campo de' Fiori, the Teatro di Pompeo can claim, at least in part, to be the oldest hotel in Rome. Breakfast is served in what was part of the first-century BC Teatro di Pompeo (*see p104*). The decor of the bar and 13 bedrooms is unfussy, verging on plain.

Hotel services *Air-conditioning. Bar. Fax. Laundry. Lift. Non-smoking rooms. Payphone. TV room.* **Room services** *Air-conditioning. Hair dryer. Mini-bar. Radio. Room service. Safe. Telephone. TV (satellite/pay).*

Budget

Della Lunetta

Piazza del Paradiso 68 (06 686 1080/06 687 7630/ fax 06 689 2028). Bus to corso Vittorio Emanuele. **Rates** €46.48/L90,000 single without bath; €56.81/ L110,000 single; €77.47/L150,000 double without bath; €103.29/L200,000 double; €108.46-€131.70/ L210,000-L255,000 triple; €134.28-€165.27/L260,000-L320,000 quad. **Credit** MC, V. **Map** p321 2B.

Built on the foundations of the Teatro di Pompeo (*see p104*), you could be forgiven for hoping that the Lunetta would live up to its former glory. But no, it's been allowed to fall into neglect: rooms are best described as functional. However, it's slap bang between campo de' Fiori and piazza Navona, and it's very cheap. Moreover, a 2,000-year-old stone trough found on the site is now being used as a rather large goldfish bowl (containing – surprise, surprise – rather large goldfish) in the TV room. The hotel doesn't do breakfast, but the area is full of bars for a delicious cappuccino and *cornetto*.

Hotel services *Fax. Safe. TV room.* **Room services** *Telephone.*

Pomezia

Via dei Chiavari 13 (06 686 1371/fax 06 686 1371/ hotel.pomezia@libero.it). Bus to corso Vittorio Emanuele. **Rates** €41.32-€67.14/L80,000-L130,000 single without bath; €51.65-€103.29/L100,000-L200,000 single; €67.14-€92.96/L130,000-L180,000 double without bath; €77.47-€123.95/L150,000-L240,000 double. **Credit** AmEx, MC, V. **Map** p321 2A.

Downstairs, the Pomezia's reception and breakfast room have been refurbished and a large disabled room added. Upstairs will soon follow with the addition of a lift, and bathrooms for the rooms without. Bedrooms are small and very basic but clean. The hotel is family-run, with friendly, helpful staff.

Hotel services *Bar. Currency exchange. Disabled room. Dry cleaning. Fax. Laundry. Multilingual staff.* **Room services** *Room service. Telephone.*

Smeraldo

Vicolo dei Chiodaroli 9 (06 687 5929/06 689 2121/fax 06 6880 5495/albergosmeraldoroma @tin.it/www.hotelsmeraldoroma.com). Bus or tram to largo Argentina. **Rates** €38.74-€49.07/L75,000-L95,000 single without bath; €51.65-€72.30/ L100,000-L140,000 single; €56.81-€72.30/ L110,000-L140,000 double without bath; €87.80-€103.29/L170,000-L200,000 double; breakfast €5.16/L10,000 extra. **Credit** AmEx, DC, MC, V. **Map** p321 2A.

Half of the Smeraldo's 50 bedrooms had been refurbished as this guide went to press; the other half was soon to follow. Although the decor isn't particularly adventurous, the owners are making a valid effort to bring the place up to date. Situated near campo de' Fiori, it's well connected transport-wise with the whole city, and its terrace offers a pretty view across Rome's rooftops.

Hotel services *Air-conditioning. Bar. Currency exchange. Disabled room. Fax. Payphone. Roof terrace. Safe. TV room.* **Room services** *Air-conditioning. Hair dryer. Room service. TV (satellite).*

Trastevere

Budget

Hotel Trastevere

Via Luciano Manara 24/25 (06 581 4713/fax 06 588 1016). Bus or tram to piazza Sonnino. **Rates** €77.47/L150,000 single; €98.13/L190,000 double; €123.95/L240,000 triple; €144.61/L280,000 quad. **Credit** AmEx, MC, V. **Map** p324 2B.

Completely refurbished in 1998, the Trastevere is a small hotel down a quiet street just across the road from the Vatican ministries. The staff are extremely friendly and helpful and although some of the nine rooms are small, they are all pleasant. Some look out on to the morning market in piazza San Cosimato.

Hotel services *Bar. Fax. Lifts. Safe. TV room.* **Room services** *Air-conditioning. Hair dryer. Radio. Room service. Telephone. TV.*

The Aventine

Mid-range

Villa San Pio, Sant'Anselmo & Aventino

Piazza Sant'Anselmo 2 (06 578 3214/06 574 8119/ fax 06 578 3604). Metro Circo Massimo/bus to viale Aventino or via di Santa Prisca. **Rates** €72.31-€108.46/L140,000-L210,000 single; €98.13-€165.27/ L190,000-L320,000 double; €113.63-€191.09/L220,000-L370,000 triple; €129.15-€206.59/L250,000-L400,000 quad. **Credit** AmEx, DC, MC, V. **Map** p325 1A.

The three hotels in this group are all within a stone's throw of each other in the leafy residential area on the Aventine hill. To complicate matters, the Villa Pio itself consists of three separate buildings (a total of 100 rooms) that share the same pretty landscaped gardens and an airy breakfast room. San Pio building B has recently been refurbished, giving it a light and airy feel and making it a very comfortable and pleasant place to stay; many rooms have terraces with views either of the surrounding greenery or of Testaccio (see p119) in the distance with fascist EUR (see p153) looming beyond. Its sister hotels the Sant'Anselmo and Aventino are less manicured and have yet to be refurbished. But the management is loath to let you specify which hotel you'd like to book in; where possible, go all out to stay in the Villa San Pio, as the quality of the rooms is far superior.

Hotel services *Air-conditioning. Babysitting. Bar. Currency exchange. Fax. Garden. Laundry. Lifts. Parking. Safe.* **Room services** *Air-conditioning. Hair dryer. Jacuzzi. Mini bar. Room service. Telephone. TV (satellite).*

The Celio

Expensive

Celio
Via Santi Quattro 35C (06 7049 5333/ fax 06 709 6377/info@hotelcelio.com/www.hotelcelio.sstefano.com). Metro Colosseo/bus to piazza del Colosseo or via Labicana. **Rates** €129.11-€185.92/L250,000-L360,000 single; €144.61-€232.41/L280,000-L450,000 double; €258.23-€464.81/L500,000-L900,000 Ambassador suite; €309.87-€619.75/L600,000-L1,200,000 Penthouse suite. **Credit** AmEx, DC, MC, V. **Map** p326 2B.

Down a street by the Colosseum, the Celio's quite ordinary exterior hides the riot of madcap colours and styles to be found inside. Mosaic floors, large sunray mirrors and sea scenes painted on the walls give the hotel an offbeat yet homely feel. With only 19 rooms, most with beautifully frescoed details, the hotel is intimate and welcoming.

Hotel Services *Air-conditioning. Babysitting. Currency exchange. Disabled room (though steps make access difficult). Dry-cleaning. Fax. Garage (€25.82/ L50,000). Laundry. Non-smoking rooms. Parking (€15.49/L30,000 per day). TV room.* **Room services** *Air-conditioning. Dataport. Hair dryer. Mini-bar. Radio. Room service. Safe. Telephone. TV (satellite/pay). VCR with large selection of English and Italian films.*

Mid-range

Lancelot
Via Capo d'Africa 47 (06 7045 0615/06 7045 0640/lancelot@italyhotel.com/www.lancelothotel.com). Metro Colosseo/bus to piazza del Colosseo. **Rates** €82.63/L160,000 single; €134.28/L260,000 double; €154.94/L300,000 triple. **Credit** AmEx, DC, MC, V. **Map** p326 2B.

This beautifully kept and attractive family-run hotel is close to the Colosseum. The place underwent a refurbishment in 1998, with the owners opting for a Mediterranean-style decor that used simple, elegant mixes of linen, wood and tiles for the bedrooms. Downstairs, the reception area has been given a distinctive, home-from-home feel by the sprinkling of various curious *objets*, along with some unusual knick-knacks.

Hotel services *Air-conditioning Babysitting. Currency exchange. Disabled rooms (4). Dry-cleaning. Fax. Laundry. Lifts. Non-smoking rooms. Parking (€7.75/L15,000 per day). Restaurant. Safe. TV room.* **Room services** *Air-conditioning. Dataport. Hair dryer. Telephone. TV (satellite).*

Monti & Esquilino

Deluxe

St Regis Grand
Via VE Orlando 3 (06 47 091/reservations 06 4708 2740/06 4708 2799/ fax 06 474 7307/res071stregisgrand.rome@stregis.com/ www.stregis.com/GrandRome). Metro Repubblica/ bus to piazza della Repubblica. **Rates** (exclusive of 10 per cent tax) €464.81-€542.28/L900,000-L1,050,00 double for single occupant; €516.45-€754/L1,000,000-L1.460,000 double; €1,007.09- €7,230.40/L1,950,000-L14,000,000 suites; breakfast €25.82-€36.15/ L50,000-L70,000 extra. **Credit** AmEx, DC, MC, V. **Map** p323 1B.

Nineteen hundred years or so after the Romans first stamped their mark on Europe, another Caesar came to Rome to get his own back. Caesar Ritz, the father of luxury, came into town and built the biggest and best hotel around: not only did this establishment have working toilets, but, in addition, each room had the previously unheard-of luxury of three electric light bulbs to penetrate the gloom of malaria-ridden Rome. In 1999 the St Regis underwent a $35 million makeover, with the aim of restoring it to its former glory. Today, the hotel's original Murano chandeliers hang in massive reception rooms that are decorated in luscious gold, beige and red. Rooms have been individually designed using rich fabrics, and are filled with silk-covered Empire and Regency-style furnishings. And, as a finishing touch, over every bed are frescos portraying little-known Roman archaeological sites.

Hotel services *Air-conditioning. Babysitting. Bar. Business services. Butler service. Concierge. Conference facilities (400). Currency exchange. Disabled rooms. Dry-cleaning. Fax. Gym. Laundry. Lifts. Limousine. Non-smoking rooms. Parking (€25.82/L50,000 per day). Restaurants (2). Safe. Sauna. Wine cellar.* **Room services** *Air-conditioning. Dataport. Hair dryer. Mini-bar. Radio. Room service (24-hour). Safe. Telephone. TV (satellite/pay). VCR.*

Location, location, location

When booking a room, it pays to think carefully about location.

Il Tridente

The chic shopping streets around the **piazza di Spagna** are home to elegant, traditional, well-refurbished hotels, mostly in the upper price ranges.

Via Veneto & Villa Borghese

Rome's top-end hotels have always clustered around the once-chic **via Veneto**, which is now a quiet, rather sad shadow of its *Dolce Vita* self.

The Pantheon & piazza Navona

Bursting with restaurants and buzzing with life, the area around **piazza Navona** has hotels in mid- to-upper-price brackets.

The Ghetto & campo de' Fiori

As lively as the piazza Navona area but slightly more affordable (even downmarket) on the hotel front, the **campo de' Fiori** abounds with low- to medium-priced hotels with bags of character.

Monti & Esquilino

Though this area is not without its pleasant hotels, single and female travellers should bear in mind that the area around **Termini** station can be seriously nasty after dark.

The Celio & San Giovanni

Though out on a limb from the frantic activity of the *centro storico*, the **Celio** offers quiet charm and quietly charming hotels.

Trastevere

There's strangely little choice in hotels in this very popular neighbourhood, although eateries and nightlife abound.

The Vatican & Prati

From spartan pilgrim hostels to comfy hotels; here bustling medieval lanes give on to busy shopping thoroughfares.

The Aventine

Mid- to high-price hotels grace this green, leafy and very peaceful area a stone's throw from the *centro*.

Expensive

Bailey's

Via Flavia 39 (06 4202 0486/fax 06 4202 0170/www.hotelbailey.com). Bus to via XX Settembre. **Rates** €129.11-€149.77/L250,000-L290,000 single; €185.92-€258.23/L360,000-L500,000 double; €237.57-€320.20/L460,000-L620,000 triple; €340.86-€469.98/L660,000-L910,000 suite. **Credit** AmEx, DC, MC, V. **Map** p323 1A.

Having only opened its doors in March 2001, Bailey's has yet to make its mark on the Rome hotel scene. So far, however, it looks very promising, with stucco ceilings and generous lashings of marble in the 29 rooms. **Hotel services** *Air-conditioning. Babysitting. Bar. Currency exchange. Disabled rooms. Dry-cleaning. Fax. Laundry. Lifts. Non-smoking rooms. Parking (€10.33/L20,000 per day). Payphone. Safe. TV room.* **Room services** *Air-conditioning. Dataport. Fax point. Hair dryer. Mini-bar. Radio. Room service. Safe. Telephone. TV (satellite/pay).*

Forum

Via Tor de' Conti 25-30 (06 679 2446/ fax 06 678 6479/info@hotelforum.com/ www.hotelforum.com). Metro Cavour/bus to via Cavour or via dei Fori Imperiali. **Rates** €144.66-€211.75/L280,000-L410,000 single; €216.91-€304.71/L420,000-L590,000 double; €284.05/L550,000 triple; €351.19/L680,000 suites. **Credit** AmEx, DC, MC, V. **Map** p326 1C.

As the name suggests, the Forum is perched on the edge of the Fori Imperiali (*see p70*), giving guests a stunning eyeful of ancient Rome from front rooms and the roof terrace. On the downside, an English country house look has been adopted for the reception area and corridors: oak-panelled walls, overstuffed chairs and acres of carpets. The bedrooms, too, leave something to be desired, and the threadbare velvet headboards are a bit off-putting. Staff tend to be abrupt.
Hotel services *Air-conditioning. Bar. Concierge. Conference facilities (100). Currency exchange. Fax. Laundry. Lifts. Non-smoking rooms. Parking (€20.66/L40,000 per day). Restaurant. Safe. TV room.* **Room services** *Air-conditioning. Hair dryer. Mini-bar. Radio. Room service. Safe. Telephone. TV (satellite).*

Nerva

Via Tor de' Conti 3 (06 678 1835/fax 06 6992 2204/info@hotelnerva.com/www.hotelnerva.com). Metro Cavour/bus to via Cavour or via dei Fori Imperiali. **Rates** €103.29-€154.94/L200,000-L300,000 single; €134.28-€216.91/L260,000-L420,000 double; €170.43-€258.23/L330,000-L500,000 triple; €232.41-€335.70/L450,000-L650,000 suite. **Credit** AmEx, DC, MC, V. **Map** p326 1C.

Small and very friendly, the Nerva is right next to the Forum, but unfortunately has no direct views as it faces onto a wall, albeit an ancient one and part of the Foro di Nerva (*see p70*). It's excellently located, however, with the Colosseum, piazza Venezia and via del Corso all within a five-minute walk. The rooms have been beautifully refurbished without losing their original features, and the hotel is run by a very chatty, lively family.

Hotel services *Air-conditioning. Bar. Currency exchange. Disabled rooms. Laundry. Non-smoking rooms. Safe. TV room.* **Room services** *Air-conditioning. Dataport. Hairdryer. Mini-bar. Safe. Telephone. TV (satellite/pay).*

Budget

Siracusa

Via Marsala 50 (06 490 191/fax 06 444 1377/www.sebraeli.it). Metro Termini/bus to piazza del Cinquecento. **Rates** €56.81/L110,000 single; €77.47/L150,000 double. **Credit** AmEx, DC, MC, V. **Map** p323 2A.

The area around Termini station is not Rome's most pleasant, and hotels there tend to be of the decidedly unsalubrious kind. This exception, right by the station, has been recently renovated. The 150 bedrooms are very pleasant for the price and there's also a large, luminous breakfast room.

Hotel services *Air-conditioning. Lifts. Safe.*
Room services *Mini-bar. Telephone. TV (satellite).*

YWCA

Via Cesare Balbo 4 (06 488 0460/06 488 3917/fax 06 487 1028). Metro Cavour/bus to piazza dell'Esquilino. **Rates** €36.15/L70,000 single without bath; €46.48/L90,000 single; €61.97/L120,000 double without bath; €72.30/L140,000 double; €25.82/L50,000 per person triple/quad; meals €10.33/L20,000. **No credit cards.** **Map** p323 2B.

Bedrooms for women with from one to four beds in each. A little too close to Termini station for comfort, but lone females may feel safer here than in mixed hostels or *pensioni*. Midnight curfew.

The Vatican & Prati

Mid-range

Amalia

Via Germanico 66 (06 3972 3354/fax 06 3972 3365/hotelamalia@iol.it/www.hotelamalia.com). Metro Ottaviano/bus or tram to piazza Risorgimento. **Rates** €51.65-€129.11/L100,000-L250,000 single; €77.47-€180.76/L150,000-L350,000 double. **Credit** AmEx, DC, MC, V. **Map** p320 2C.

This 40-room *pensione* is located between the Ottaviano metro station and St Peter's, strategically situated next door to the Castroni deli (*see p212*), one of the few places in Rome where the homesick can find vegemite and HP sauce. Rooms are very simple and clean; price varies according to room size. **Hotel services** *Air-conditioning. Fax. Laundry. Lifts. Non-smoking rooms. Payphone. Safe.* **Room services** *Air-conditioning (most rooms) Hair dryer. Mini-bar. Phone. Safe. TV (satellite).*

Bramante

Vicolo delle Palline 24 (06 6880 6426/fax 06 687 9881/bramante@excalha.it/www.hotelbramante.com). Metro Ottaviano/bus to piazza Pia. **Rates** €103.29-€129.11/L200,000-L250,000 single; €144.61-€191.09/L280,000-L370,000 double; €154.94-€216.91/L300,000-L420,000 suite. **Credit** AmEx, DC, MC, V. **Map** p321 1C.

A romantic hotel, hidden down a cobbled street a couple of hundred metres from St Peter's, the Bramante would be easy to miss. Home to architect Domenico Fontana in the 16th century, the building became an inn in 1873. It has since lost the horses and ale-swilling occupants and gained a large pleasant reception and a little patio for the summer. Refurbished in 1999, the 16 rooms of varying sizes – some powder blue, others lemon – are simple yet elegant; most have high-beamed ceilings, some have wrought-iron beds.

Hotel services *Air-conditioning. Babysitting. Currency exchange. Dry-cleaning. Fax. Laundry. Non-smoking rooms. Payphone. Safe. TV room.* **Room services** *Air-conditioning. Dataport. Fax point. Internet. Hair dryer. Iron. Mini-bar. Telephone. TV (satellite).*

Sant'Anna

Borgo Pio 133-134 (06 6880 1602/fax 06 6830 8717/santanna@travel.it/www.travel.it/roma/santanna. Metro Ottaviano/bus to piazza Pia. **Rates** €103.29-€139.44/L200,000-L270,000 single; €154.94-€191.09/L300,000-L370,000 double; €180.76-€206.58/L350,000-L400,000 triple. **Credit** AmEx, DC, MC, V. **Map** p321 1C.

Just 200m (700ft) from the Vatican wall, the Sant'Anna is a quiet hotel with 20 rooms pleasantly decorated in pastel shades. In summer you can have drinks in the small courtyard at the back; in winter, you can sip your cocktail under the stern gaze of Cardinal Borromeo in the reception.

Hotel services *Air-conditioning. Babysitting. Currency exchange. Disabled room. Fax. Laundry. Lifts.* **Room services** *Fax point. Hair dryer. Mini-bar. PC point. Radio. Safe. Telephone. TV (satellite).*

Budget

Colors Hotel & Hostel

Via Boezio 31 (06 687 4030/fax 06 686 7947/info@enjoyrome.com/www.colorshotel.com). Metro Ottaviano/bus to piazza Risorgimento. **Rates** €18.08/L35,000 per person in dorm; €61.97/L120,000 double without bath; €72.30-€77.47/L140,000-L150,000 double with bath; €72.30/L140,000 triple without bath; €77.47-€92.96/L150,000-L180,000 triple with bath. **No credit cards.** **Map** pp320 2C.

A five-minute walk from St Peter's and the Vatican museums, Colors has bright, clean dorm and hotel accommodation, plus self-catering facilities. Run by the ever-reliable Enjoy Rome agency (*see p304*), the helpful staff are multilingual.

Hotel services *Kitchen. Laundry facilities. Lounge with satellite TV. Terrace.*

The Suburbs

Expensive

Turner

Via Nomentana 29 (06 4425 0077/fax 06 4425 0165/info@hotelturner.com/www.hotelturner.com). Bus to porta Pia/tram to viale Regina Margherita. **Rates** €108.45-€191.09/L210,000-L370,000 single; €139.45-€276.30/L270,000-L535,000 double; €152.36-€363.07/L295,000-L703,000 triple; €309.88-€610.46/L600,000-L1,182,000 suite; breakfast €12.91/L25,000 extra. **Credit** AmEx, DC, MC, V. **Map** p322 2A.

Named after the British artist and a favourite with footballers and Italian TV and film stars, the Turner has been beautifully refurbished with the emphasis on luxury. The 47 rooms contain tapestries and elegant *bois de rose* and *boule* furniture; some of the wardrobes are imitations of pieces in the Louvre. Bathrooms have jacuzzis and showers; some have Turkish baths. The owner is passionate about golf, and has a deal with a nearby club allowing guests to use facilities. Guided tours are also arranged. **Hotel services** *Air-conditioning. Babysitting. Bar. Business services. Conference facilities (40). Car park (€12.39/L24,000 per day). Currency exchange. Disabled rooms. Dry-cleaning. Fax. Laundry. Lifts. Non-smoking rooms. Safe. TV room.* **Room services** *Dataport. Hair dryer. Mini-bar. Radio. Room service. Safe. Telephone. TV (satellite/pay).*

Budget

Ostello della Gioventù Foro Italico

Via delle Olimpiadi 61 (06 324 2571/06 323 6267/fax 06 324 2613/www.hostels-aig.org). Bus to lungotevere Maresciallo Cadorna. **Rates** €15.46/L28,000 bed & breakfast; meals €7.75/L15,000. **No credit cards.**

There are 400 beds in dormitories at this neobrutalist building near the Stadio Olimpico. This is the IYHF's main Rome hostel (standard category), and open to members only, although you can join here. There's a garden, restaurant and bar. It's well adapted for wheelchairs.

Self-catering

If you're staying in Rome for more than a couple of weeks, especially if there are more than two of you, it's worth considering renting a flat or staying in a residential hotel. They are cheaper than normal hotels, and offer similar services.

Aldovrandi Residence

Via U Aldovrandi 11 (06 322 1430/fax 06 322 2181/www.aldovrandiresidence.it). Bus or tram to piazza Pitagora. **Rates** (exclusive of 10 per cent tax) €1,032.91-€1,446.08/L2,000,000-L2,800,000 one-bed apartment per week; €1,446.08-€1,807.60/L2,800,000-L3,500,000 two-bed apartment per week; €1,807.60-€2,324.06/ L3,500,000-L4,500,000 one person studio flat per month; €2,582.28-€3,615.20/L5,000,000-L7,000,000 one-bed apartment per month. **Credit** AmEx. **Map** p322 1C.

Flanked by the exclusive Parioli area on one side and the Villa Borghese and its zoo on the other (although not so close that you get woken up by the grunts and snuffles of wildebeasts at 5am) the Aldovrandi residence offers apartments from one week up to months. All apartments have a kitchen/ette and daily maid service. The terrace offers incredible views over the countryside. There's also a swimming pool. **Hotel services** *Air-conditioning. Bar. Garden. Lift. Multilingual staff. Parking (nearby). Restaurant. Swimming pool.* **Apartment services** *Radio. Telephone. TV (satellite).*

IDEC

Via Poliziano 27 (06 7045 4074/fax 06 7045 4455/info@flatinrome.com/www.idecroma.com/www.flatinrome.com). **Rates** €361.52-€929.62/L700,000-L1,800,000 weekly; €877.98-€2,065.83/L1,700,000-L4,000,000 monthly. **No credit cards.**

This reliable agency rents out apartments – from small studio flats to four-bed accommodation – all over central Rome. Prices, naturally, depend on size and location.

Residence Ripetta

Via di Ripetta 231 (06 323 1144/fax 06 320 3959/info@ripetta.it). Bus to ponte Cavour or piazza Risorgimento. **Rates** (exclusive of 10 per cent tax) 1- and 2-bed studio flats from €852.15/L1,650,000 weekly; €1,394.43/L2,700,000 fortnightly; €2,143.30/L4,150,000 monthly; 2-bed flats from €877.98/L1,700,000 weekly; €1,497.73/L2,900,000 fortnightly; €2,334.39/L4,520,000 monthly; 4-bed flats from €1,342.79/L2,600,000 weekly; €2,334.39/L4,520,000 fortnightly; €3,641.02/L7,050,000 monthly. **Credit** AmEx, MC, V. **Map** p320 2A.

In a central location close to via del Corso, the Ripetta consists of 69 self-catering flats that were refurbished in 2000. Kitchens are fully equipped, and the flats are cleaned daily. Some look over the Tiber. **Apartment services** *Air-conditioning. Fax. Lift. Parking. Radio. Safe. Telephone. TV (satellite).*

Bed & breakfast

B&Bs were virtually unknown until the 2000 Holy Year, when authorities – anxious about the numbers of pilgrims expected – set up a fairly efficient operation for vetting would-be hosts. Visitors stay as guests in private homes: it's pot-luck, but the accommodation can be very good. By law, breakfast has to consist of pre-packaged fare – meaning there are no fry-ups. The APT (*see p303*) provides a comprehensive list of all B&Bs in Rome, with prices. Alternatively, the Rome Chamber of Commerce provides a free booking service for those B&Bs it has awarded its stamp of quality. For booking and information contact 06 679 5937/06 678 9222/fax 06 678 6521/www.hotelreservation.it.

Sightseeing

Introduction

Post-2000 Rome is cleaner, brighter and indescribably lovelier.

As the Vatican's massive 2000 Holy Year shindig approached, and the Eternal City preened itself for the onslaught of pilgrim-tourists, Romans were constantly up in arms: roadworks abounded; there was hardly a palazzo in the *centro storico* not shrouded in scaffolding; buildings galore were being converted into hostels; archeological digs sprang from nowhere. The city, locals lamented loudly, was one big building site. But even whinging Romans were impressed at the results. The city centre emerged from the makeover in a coat of many, dazzling colours, with a host of new and restored museums and galleries.

The Eternal City's magnificent piazzas, palaces, churches and ancient monuments, that are the legacy of over 2,000 years of history, many of them at the centre of the western stage, were looking more beautiful than ever. Moreover, even a wash-and-brush-up of these dimensions failed to turn Rome into a sterile open-air museum. This remains one of Europe's most vivacious capitals, and its accumulated glories form the backdrop for the chaotic exuberance of everyday Roman life.

So overwhelming can this be, that it's perhaps best to take the first impact sitting down. Choose a seat at any café and take time just to breathe in car fumes, as Rome rushes compulsively by. This done, you can proceed to outdoor sights, and there are enough of these to keep you busy for weeks. When you've absorbed a place by day, go back at night. Many sites are floodlit, and even those that aren't look spectacular in a blend of moonlight and the soft glow of street lamps. After that, it's time to start in on the museums, galleries, *palazzi* and churches, which are – and contain – Rome's seemingly inexhaustible artistic treasures.

It's rare to have to queue for a Roman attraction, with the exception of the **Colosseum** (*see p66*) or the **Musei Vaticani** (*see p141*) in high season. If you want to be absolutely sure of getting into your chosen museum or monument, many can be pre-booked (*see p60*).

ANCIENT SITES

The most concentrated cluster of ancient remains lies in the area bound by the Capitoline, Palatine, Esquiline and Quirinale hills. This was the official heart of the ancient city. Here, too, was the most desirable residential area in Rome, the **Palatine** (*see p66*), where – if ancient historians are to be believed – the sexual excesses of emperors, empresses, politicians and poets were matched only by the passion with which they plotted against and poisoned one another.

CHURCHES

Central Rome has over 400 churches – excessive, perhaps, even for the headquarters of the Catholic Church. Across the centuries popes, princes and aristocrats commissioned artists and architects to build, rebuild, adorn, fresco and paint their preferred places of worship. Motives were not wholly pious. For many, it was a cynical means of assuring a place in heaven, securing temporal power, increasing prestige, or a combination of all three. Whatever the reasons, the results of all this munificence now form some of Rome's most spectacular sights.

Churches are places of worship. Though only the **Vatican** (*see p138*) imposes its dress code strictly, respect is appreciated. Very short skirts or shorts are frowned upon. Many

Closing days

Monday

Casina delle Civette & Villa Torlonia (*see p274*); Castel Sant'Angelo (*see p144*); Catacombe di Priscilla (*see p150*); Centrale Montemartini (*see p153*); Chiostro dei Genovesi (*see p116*); Cimitero Acattolico (*see p121*); Circo di Massenzio & Mausoleo di Romolo (*see p147*); Colosseum (*see p66*); Complesso del Vittoriano (*see p62*); Galleria Borghese (*see p81*); Galleria Comunale d'Arte Moderna e Contemporanea (*see p85*); Galleria Comunale d'Arte Moderna e Contemporanea (ex-Birreria Peroni) (*see p151*); Galleria Nazionale d'Arte Antica – Palazzo Corsini (*see p113*); Galleria Nazionale d'Arte Moderna e Contemporanea (p82). Galleria Spada (*see p101*); Mercati di Traiano (*see p70*); Musei Capitolini (*see p62*); Museo dell'Alto Medioevo (*see p155*); Museo Barracco di Scultura Antica (*see p100*); Museo della Civiltà Romana (*see p155*); Museo del Corso (*see p98*); Museo Hendrik Christian Andersen (*see p82*); Museo delle Mura (*see p148*); Museo Napoleonico (*see p95*); Museo Nazionale delle Arti e Tradizioni Popolari (*see p155*); Museo Nazionale Romano – Crypta Balbi (*see p103*); Museo Nazionale Romano – Palazzo Altemps (*see p95*); Museo Nazionale Romano – Palazzo Massimo alle Terme (*see p135*); Museo Nazionale degli Strumenti Musicali (*see p129*); Museo Nazionale di Villa Giulia (*see p82*); Museo Nazionale di Zoologia (*see p82*); Museo di Palazzo Venezia (*see p63*); Museo di Roma in Trastevere (*see p113*); Museo Storico della Liberazione di Roma (*see p129*); Orto Botanico (*see p115*); Palazzo Barberini – Galeria Nazionale d'Arte Antica (*see p76*); Sant'Agnese in Agone (*see p96*); Santa Maria della Pace (*see p93*); Terme di Diocleziano (*see p135*); Tomba di Cecilia Metella (*see p148*); Villa dei Quintili (*see p148*).

Tuesday

Catacombe di Domitilla (*see p148*); Domus Aurea (*see p130*); Galleria dell'Accademia di San Luca (*see p74*); Museo Storico Nazionale dell'Arte Sanitaria (*see p145*); Palazzo delle Esposizioni (*see p78*); Sant'Andrea al Quirinale (*see p78*).

Wednesday

Catacombe di San Callisto (*see p148*); Chiostro dei Genovesi (*see p116*).

Thursday

Galleria dell'Accademia di San Luca (*see p74*); Galleria Doria Pamphili (*see p97*); Museo Storico Nazionale dell'Arte Sanitaria (*see p145*).

Friday

Chiostro dei Genovesi (*see p116*).

Saturday

Chiostro dei Genovesi (*see p116*); Galleria dell'Accademia di San Luca (*see p74*); Museo d'Arte Ebraica (*see p106*); Museo Storico Nazionale dell'Arte Sanitaria (*see p145*); San Paolo entro le Mura (*see p137*).

Sunday

Catacombe di San Sebastiano (*see p148*); Chiostro dei Genovesi (*see p116*); Galleria dell'Accademia di San Luca (*see p74*); Keats-Shelley Memorial House (*see p85*); Musei Vaticani (open last Sunday of the month, *see p141*); Museo Storico Nazionale dell'Arte Sanitaria (*see p145*); Santo Stefano Rotondo (*see p126*); St Peter's Basilica: Necropolis and Vatican Gardens (for both, *see p141*); Villa Farnesina (*see p115*).

churches ask tourists to refrain from visiting during services; if you are admitted, you will be expected not to take photos, talk loudly or wander around. A supply of coins for the meters to light up the most interesting art works is always handy.

MUSEUMS AND GALLERIES

The days of closed doors, wildcat strikes and endless restoration programmes seem to have receded. Opening hours are refreshingly longer, though still subject to seasonal changes that can vary at the last moment.

Opening hours

Winter (roughly October-May) hours are given in the listings in the following chapters. Summer hours can vary significantly, especially at major museums and archaeological sites. Some keep doors open until 11pm. Check for current times at information kiosks (*see p303*).

Ticket offices at many museums, galleries and ancient sites stop issuing tickets an hour or more before closing time; where the gap is more than half an hour, this has been indicated.

Church opening times should be taken as rough guidelines: most open and close an hour later in summer (May-October). In many, whether doors are open depends on the whims of military service-dodging youths assigned to lend a hand to the diocese of Rome.

Tickets

Entrance to all publicly owned museums and sites is free to EU citizens (and those of other countries with bi-lateral agreements) under 18 and over 65. Under-25s in full-time education may also be eligible for discounts, as may teachers, journalists and various others. Make sure you carry a range of ID. No Roman sights accept credit cards, though one reservation service (*see below*) grudgingly does.

One week each year is designated *Settimana dei beni culturali* (cultural heritage week), when all publicly owned museums and sites are open long hours and free of charge (*see p224*).

Booking and cumulative tickets

Booking is mandatory for the **Domus Aurea** (*see p130*) and the **Galleria Borghese** (*see p81*), though if you turn up mid-week in low season, there's little chance of being rejected.

Booking is possible for many other sites and museums, though the difficulties involved in getting through to the reservation phonelines can outweigh any benefits. A time and day for your visit is reserved through these services, listed below; tickets must be picked up and paid for at the museum or sight half an hour before your appointment. Expect to be charged *diritti di prevendita* (pre-sale tax) of €0.52-€1.03/L1,000-L2,000 on top of the ticket price if you do book.

Note that calls to all numbers beginning 06 3996 are put through to the same private call centre operating on behalf of the Sovrintendenza, Rome's heritage board.

Centro Servizi per L'Archeologia

Via G Amendola 2. Metro Termini/bus to piazza Cinquecento. **Open** 9am-1pm, 2-7pm Mon-Sat. **Credit** AmEx, DC, MC, V. **Map** p323 2A.
(06 3996 7700) 24hr recorded information in English on all its sights. Sat booking service 9am-6pm Mon-Fri, 9am-1pm Sat (to talk to an operator, *don't* press 2 for information).
(06 481 5576) Information and credit card booking service 9am-1pm, 2-5pm Mon-Sat.
This service handles the following sights: Colosseum (*see p66*), Crypta Balbi (*see p103*), Domus Aurea (*see p130*), Foro Romano (*see p71*), Palatine (*see p66*), Palazzo Altemps (*see p95*), Palazzo Massimo alle Terme (*see p135*), Terme di Caracalla (*see p126*), Terme di Diocleziano (*see p135*), Tomba

di Cecilia Metella (*see p148*) and Villa dei Quintili (*see p148*). As well as providing the phone services listed above, it dispenses information and takes bookings in person in its office, and organises guided tours. It offers the following cumulative tickets and services:
€15.49/L30,000 – five-day ticket for Colosseum, Crypta Balbi, Palatino, Palazzo Altemps, Palazzo Massimo alle Terme, Terme di Caracalla, Terme di Diocleziano.
€7.75/L15,000 – five-day ticket for Crypta Balbi, Palazzo Altemps, Palazzo Massimo alle Terme, Terme di Diocleziano.
€5.16/L10,000 – five-day pass for guided tours or rental of audio-guides in Colosseum, Crypta Balbi, Palatino, Palazzo Altemps, Palazzo Massimo alle Terme, Terme di Caracalla, Terme di Diocleziano.

Sistema Musei Capitolini

(06 3996 7800). **Open** *Recorded information* 24hrs daily. *Bookings & information* 9am-6pm Mon-Fri; 9am-1pm Sat.
This call-line handles the Musei Capitolini (*see p62*) and the Centrale Montemartini (*see p153*), dispensing information and organising bookings and guided tours. A cumulative ticket for the two museums, valid for one week and costing €9.81/L19,000 (€7.75/L15,000 concessions) can be purchased at the ticket office of either site.

Ticketeria

(06 32 810/fax 06 3265 1327/www.ticketeria.it). **Open** *Recorded information* 24hrs daily. *Bookings* 9am-6pm Mon-Fri; 9am-1pm Sat.
This service provides information on, and handles bookings for, Galleria Borghese (*see p81*), Palazzo Barberini (*see p76*), Palazzo Corsini (*see p113*), Palazzo Spada (*see p101*), and Villa Giulia (*see p83*), as well as the excavations at Ostia Antica (*see p269*), the Museo Nazionale at Tarquinia (*see p280*) and the Etruscan necropolis at Cerveteri (*see p280*).

Getting through locked gates

Many of Rome's minor archeological sites can only be visited with prior permission from what used to be known as Ripartizione X but now seems to have become a nameless section within the heritage department.

The tourist with a passion for mini-mithraeums and fragments of faded fresco can arrange access by sending a fax in any major western language to 06 689 2115. Remember to include a phone number (preferably in Rome) where you can be contacted to fix an appointment. Viewings are usually arranged within four or five days of application. If you are not contacted, phone 06 6710 3819 during office hours to chase up your request. Admission charges depend on sites requested.

From the Capitoline to the Palatine

At the heart and hub of ancient Rome is a shopping mall, a health-restoring Christ-child, and the world's biggest urban archaeological dig.

Castor, one of the twin saviours of Rome.

The most historically significant part of the city, the heart and hub of ancient Rome, lies beyond the Capitoline to the south-east. It was here that Rome was born, in the **Foro Romano** (Roman Forum) and the **Palatino** (Palatine), and it's here that you will find the city's best-recognised landmark: the **Colosseum**.

The Capitoline & piazza Venezia

The **Campidoglio** – Capitoline – was, politically speaking, the most important of ancient Rome's seven hills, and the site of the three major temples: to Jupiter, symbolic father of the city; Minerva, goddess of wisdom; and Juno Moneta, a vigilant goddess who was expected to sound the alarm in times of danger. The temple of Juno, the site of which is now occupied by the church of **Santa Maria in Aracoeli**, housed the sacred Capitoline geese, in commemoration of the gaggle that supposedly raised the alarm when the Gauls attacked Rome in 390 BC.

The elegant piazza we see today was designed in the 1530s by Michelangelo for Pope Paul III. It took about 100 years to complete, and some of Michelangelo's ideas were modified along the way, but it is still much as he envisaged it. The best approach is via the great ramp of steps called the *cordonata*, also by Michelangelo, that sweeps up from via del Teatro di Marcello. At the top they are flanked by two giant Roman statues of the mythical twins Castor and Pollux, placed here in 1583. The building opposite the top of the steps is the Palazzo Senatorio, Rome's city hall, completed by Giacomo della Porta and Girolamo Rainaldi to a design by Michelangelo. To the left is the Palazzo Nuovo and to the right the Palazzo dei Conservatori, together forming the **Musei Capitolini** (Capitoline Museums). For four centuries the piazza's central pedestal supported a magnificent second-century equestrian statue of Emperor Marcus Aurelius, placed here by Michelangelo. The statue now on the pedestal is a computer-generated copy; the original, after years of restoration, is behind glass in the Palazzo Nuovo.

To the north of the Capitoline, **piazza Venezia** is a dizzying roundabout where six busy roads converge. It emerged as an important focus of business and power in the 15th century when the Venetian Pope Paul II had **Palazzo Venezia** constructed on its western side. Now an art museum, the palace was one of the first Renaissance buildings in Rome. Centuries later Mussolini would make it his headquarters, delivering orations from the balcony overlooking the piazza, where pedestrians were prevented from standing still by security-obsessed guards. To the left of the palazzo stands San Marco, a church founded in the fourth century and remodelled for Paul II.

Dominating the square is the glacial **Vittoriano** (aka l'Altare della patria), a piece of nationalistic kitsch that outdoes anything dreamed up by the ancients. This vast pile, entirely out of proportion with anything around it and made of unsuitably dazzling marble brought specially and at great cost from Brescia, was constructed between 1885 and 1911 to honour the first king of united Italy, Vittorio Emanuele of Savoy. Centred on an equestrian statue of the king, who sports a moustache three metres (ten feet) long, it is also the home of the eternal flame, Italy's memorial to the unknown soldier. To the right of the monument are the miserable remains of the Roman and medieval houses razed to make way for the monstrosity.

Complesso del Vittoriano

Piazza Venezia/via di San Pietro in Carcere/piazza Aracoeli (06 699 1718). Bus to piazza Venezia. **Open** *Monument* 10.30am-4pm Tue-Sun. *Sagrario delle Bandiere* 9am-1pm Tue-Sun. *Other sections* varies depending on exhibitions. **Admission** *Monument, Sagrario* free. *Other sections* varies depending on exhibitions. **No credit cards. Map** p324 1A.

The **Vittoriano** is now a useful eyesore.

After many years of on-off restorations, the Vittoriano is finally firing on all pistons: an eyesore it remains, but at least it's now a useful eyesore. The climb to the top of the monument is worthwhile not only to appreciate the enormity of the thing, but also to see the charmingly kitsch art nouveau mosaic propaganda-extravaganzas in the colonnade and – more importantly – to savour the spectacular view from the only place where you can see the whole city without the panorama being disturbed by the bulk of the Vittoriano itself. In the bowels of the building are various spaces: two galleries (entrance in via San Pietro in Carcere) host temporary exhibitions; an exhibition space entered in piazza Aracoeli, from which there is access – sometimes, during selected exhibitions – to a maze of Roman and medieval tunnels extending deep beneath the monument; and the Sagrario delle Bandiere (entrance in via San Pietro in Carcere), which contains standards, and the ornate chests in which they were kept, from many Italian navy vessels. This last also has a couple of torpedo boats, including a manned *Maiale* (Pig) torpedo in this rather hushed 'don't-mention-the-war' collection.

Musei Capitolini

Piazza del Campidoglio 1 (06 6710 2071). Bus to piazza Venezia. **Open** 9.30am-7pm Tue-Fri, Sun; 9.30am-11pm Sat (ticket office closes 1hr earlier). **Admission** €6.19/L12,000; €4.13/L8,000 concessions; additional charge for special exhibitions; *see also p60* **Tickets. No credit cards. Map** p324 1A.

Standing on opposite sides of Michelangelo's piazza del Campidoglio (*see p61*) and housed in the twin palaces of Palazzo Nuovo and Palazzo dei Conservatori, the Capitoline Museums are the oldest public museums in the world. The collection they house was initiated in 1471, when Pope Sixtus IV presented the Roman people with a group of classical sculptures. Until the creation of the Vatican Museums (*see p141*), Sixtus's successors continued to enrich the collection with examples of ancient art, most of which was sculpture, and, at a later date, some important Renaissance and post-Renaissance paintings. The entire collection was finally opened to the public in 1734, by Pope Clement XII. The museums were overhauled in a massive restoration project that culminated in 2000. The most exciting innovation was the opening to the public of an artefact-lined tunnel passing beneath the square, joining the two *palazzi* but also allowing access to the **Tabularium** – ancient Rome's archive – from where the view over the Foro Romano (*see p71*) below is simply breathtaking. Entrance to the Musei Capitolini is by the **Palazzo dei Conservatori**, on the right as you come up Michelangelo's stairs. The courtyard contains what is left of a colossal statue of Constantine (the rest was made of wood) that originally stood in the Basilica of Maxentius in the Forum (*see p71*).

Upstairs, the huge Sala degli Orazi e Curiazi (Room I) is home to a statue (1635-40) by Bernini of his patron Urban VIII in which everything about the

(Room I) is home to a statue (1635-40) by Bernini of his patron Urban VIII in which everything about the pope seems to be in motion. There's also a second-century BC gilded bronze statue of Hercules. Room II (Sala dei Capitani) has late 16th-century frescos of great moments in ancient Roman history. In room III (Sala dei Trionfi), the first-century BC bronze of a boy removing a thorn from his foot, known as the *Spinario*, is probably an original Greek work. There's also a rare bronze portrait bust from the fourth or third century BC, popularly believed to be of Rome's first consul, Brutus. Room IV (Sala della Lupa) is home to the much-reproduced She-Wolf. This one is a fifth-century BC Etruscan bronze; the suckling twins were added during the Renaissance by, according to tradition, Antonio del Pollaiolo. In room V (Sala delle Oche) is Bernini's touchingly pained-looking Medusa, and an 18th-century bronze portrait of Michelangelo, believed to have been based on the great master's death mask. Room VI (Sala delle Aquile) is frescoed with 16th-century Roman scenes amid faux-ancient 'grotesque' decorations. In room X (Sala degli Arazzi), a marvellously well-preserved marble group shows the Emperor Commodus (of *Gladiator* fame) dressing up as Hercules, and being adored by two Tritons. Room XI (Sala di Annibale) still has its original, early 16th-century frescos that show, among other things, Hannibal riding on an elephant that Walt Disney would have been proud of.

On the second floor, the **Pinacoteca Capitolina** (Capitoline Art Gallery) contains a number of significant works. The most striking is Caravaggio's *St John the Baptist* (1596; in the Sala di Santa Petronilla), who has nothing even remotely saintly about him, but don't let it overshadow paintings by other greats: there's the weepiest of *Penitent Magdalenes* (c1598) by Tintoretto; a *Rape of Europa* by Veronese; and an early *Baptism of Christ* (c1512) by Titian in Room III. There are also some strangely impressionistic works by Guido Reni in Room VI, various busy scenes by Pietro da Cortona in the room named after him, and some luscious portraits by Van Dyck in the Galleria Cini, which also contains a self-portrait by Velázquez (1649-51) and some lovely early 18th-century scenes of Rome by Gaspare Vanvitelli.

At the other end of the passage which passes through the Tabularium beneath piazza del Campidoglio, the **Palazzo Nuovo** houses one of Europe's most significant collections of ancient sculpture. The three small ground-floor rooms contain endearing portrait busts of Roman citizens, and a huge sarcophagus with scenes from the life of Achilles, topped by two reclining second-century AD figures. Dominating the atrium and courtyard are the gilded bronze statue of Marcus Aurelius – which used to grace the square outside but has recently been replaced by a modern copy – and the first-century AD river god, known as Marforio, reclining above his little fountain.

The collection continues upstairs. In the long gallery (Room I), the wounded warrior, falling to the ground with his shield, is probably a third-century BC discus thrower's top half, turned on its side and given a new pair of legs in the 17th century. Room II (Sala delle Colombe) contains a statue of a little girl protecting a dove from a snake, a much-reworked drunken old woman clutching an urn of wine, and a dove mosaic from Hadrian's villa (*see p273*) at Tivoli. Room III (Gabinetto della Venere) is home to the coy first-century BC *Capitoline Venus*. This was probably based on Praxiteles' *Venus of Cnodis*, considered so erotic by the fourth-century BC inhabitants of Kos that one desperate citizen was caught *in flagrante* with it. In Room IV (Sala degli Imperatori), portrait busts of emperors, their consorts and children, are arranged chronologically, providing a good insight into changing fashions and hairstyles. Next door in Room V (Sala dei Filosofi) are ancient portraits of philosophers and poets. Larger statues of mythical figures grace the huge Salone (Room VI). Room VII (Sala del Fauno) is named after an inebriated faun in *rosso antico* marble, carved in the late second century BC. In Room VIII (Sala del Gladiatore) is the moving *Dying Gaul*, probably based on a third-century BC Greek original (but bearing a stunning resemblance to a '70s TV cop). Many ancient sculptures long hidden in the storerooms of the Musei Capitolini can now be seen at the **Centrale Montemartini**; *see p153*.

Museo di Palazzo Venezia

Via del Plebiscito 118 (06 6999 4319/06 6999 4243). Bus to piazza Venezia. **Open** 9am-7.30pm Tue-Sat. **Admission** €4.13/L8,000; €2.06/L4,000 concessions. **No credit cards. Map** p324 1A.
Palazzo Venezia contains a hotchpotch of everything from medieval decorative art to Bernini's terracotta models for major statues. In Room 1 are Venetian odds and ends, including a double portrait by Giorgione; Room 4 has a glorious zodiac motif on the ceiling. Amid the 17th- and 18th-century offerings in Room 6 is a touching group portrait of Duke Orsino's children, and a very sad *St Peter* by Guercino. Room 8 has pastel portraits of 18th-century aristos. In the long corridor are collections of Italian ceramics, and porcelain, including some Meissen. In Rooms 18-26 are Bernini's terracotta musings for the Fontana del Tritone, and one to link the angels on Ponte Sant'Angelo (built to link Castel Sant'Angelo with the centro storico). The huge Sala del Mappamondo, so called because of an early map of the world kept there in the 16th century, was Mussolini's office. The museum often hosts major-sounding exhibitions that do not always live up to expectations.

San Marco

Piazza San Marco (06 679 5205). Bus to piazza Venezia. **Open** 7.30am-1pm, 4-7pm daily. **Map** p324 1A.
There's a strong Venetian flavour to this church which, according to local lore, was founded in 336 on the site of the house where St Mark the Evangelist – the patron saint of Venice – stayed. There are medieval lions, the symbol of St Mark, by

Sightseeing

Maharajah

Indian Restaurant

Typical Indian cuisine in an elegant atmosphere,
located not far from the Colosseum. Special Indian dishes
include chicken tikka masala, lamb vindaloo, chicken maharaja
tandoori and makhani paneer. Attentive and courteous service.
Open every day

❖   ❖   ❖

Via dei Serpenti, 124 • 00184 Roma
Tel: 06/47.47.144 Fax: 06/47.88.53.93
In Venice: Maharani • Via G. Verdi, 97/99 • 30171 Mestre Venezia
Tel: 041/98.46.81 Fax: 041/95.86.98
http://mall4all.com/maharajah

the main entrance door; inside are graves of Venetians and paintings of Venetian saints. Rebuilt during the fifth century, the church was further reorganised by Pope Paul II in the 15th century when the neighbouring Palazzo Venezia (see p63) was built. It was given its baroque look in the mid-18th century. Remaining from its earlier manifestations are the 11th-century bell-tower, a portico attributed to Renaissance man Leon Battista Alberti, the 15th-century ceiling with Paul II's coat of arms, and the rigid, Byzantine-style, ninth-century mosaic of Christ in the apse. Among the figures below Christ is Gregory IV, who was pope when the mosaic was made: his square halo marks him out as bound for sainthood though still alive. In the portico is the gravestone of Vanozza Catanei, mistress of Rodrigo Borgia (see p12 **Lust, Murder and Incest**) – Pope Alexander VI – and mother of Cesare and Lucrezia. The chapel to the right at the end of the nave was designed by Pietro da Cortona and contains a funerary monument by neo-classical sculptor Antonio Canova.

Santa Maria in Aracoeli

Piazza del Campidoglio 4 (06 679 8155). Bus to piazza Venezia. **Open** 6.30am-5.30pm daily. **Map** p326 1C.

Rising behind the Vittoriano monument (see p62), at the head of a daunting flight of steps built in the 14th century in thanks for deliverance from a plague epidemic, the Romanesque Aracoeli (altar of heaven) stands on the site of an ancient temple to Juno Moneta. It was here, legend has it, that a sybil whispered to the Emperor Augustus *haec est ara primogeniti Dei* ('this is the altar of God's first-born'). Though there is an altar purporting to be the one erected by Augustus in the chapel of St Helena (to the left of the high altar) there's no record of a Christian church here until the sixth century. The current basilica-form church was designed – perhaps by Arnolfo di Cambio – for the Franciscan order in the late 13th century.

Dividing the church into a nave and two aisles are 22 columns purloined from Roman buildings. There's a cosmatesque (see p87 **Glossary**) floor punctuated by marble gravestones, and a very gilded ceiling commemorating the Christian victory over the Turks at the Battle of Lepanto in 1571. Just inside the main door, on a pilaster to the right, is the worn tombstone of one Giovanni Crivelli, carved and signed by Donatello (c1432). The first chapel on the right contains enchanting scenes from the life of St Francis's helpmate St Bernadino by Pinturicchio (1486).

Approaching the main altar in the right aisle, chapel of San Pasquale Baylon was decorated with dull 16th-century works until 2000, when parts were removed to reveal a huge fresco, probably by 13th-century genius Pietro Cavallini (see also p32); as this guide went to press, the fresco was behind scaffolding. The large chapel beside it, with scenes from the life of St Francis, contains a marvellous mosaic-encrusted 13th-century tomb: the upper section may

be by Arnolfo di Cambio; the lower part is a third-century BC Roman sarcophagus.

On the main altar is a tenth-century image of Mary. Apse paintings by Pietro Cavallini were demolished in the mid-16th century. To the left of the altar, eight *giallo antico* columns mark the round chapel of St Helena, where relics of this redoubtable lady – mother of the Emperor Constantine and finder of the 'true' cross – are kept in a porphyry urn. An ancient stone altar, said to be that erected by Augustus, can be seen behind and beneath the altar.

Beyond the chapel, at the back of the transept, is the Chapel of the Holy Child, which contains a much-venerated disease-healing *bambinello*, which is often whisked to the bedside of moribund Romans. The original – carved, it is said, in the 15th century from the wood of an olive tree from the Garden of Gethsemane – was stolen in 1994 and replaced by a copy. The *faux-bambinello* excites the same fervent devotion (note the baskets of letters asking for the Christ-child's help), especially around Christmas time when it is removed to the nativity scene in the second chapel from the main entrance on the left.

The occupant of the Gothic tomb opposite the Chapel of the Holy Child entrance – Matteo d'Acquasparta – was mentioned by Dante in his *Paradiso*. Above is a *Madonna and Child with Two Saints* attributed to Cavallini. Three chapels from the main door in the left aisle is a fresco (c1449) by Benozzo Gozzoli of St Anthony of Padua, over the altar. Rome's gypsy community flocks to this church on Christmas eve for a colourful, lively midnight mass.

The Palatine & the Colosseum

This was where it all started, atop an easily defended rise – the Palatine hill – overlooking the Tiber at the point where an island made the river crossing easier. Roman myth places the foundation of the city in the eighth century BC; in fact, proto-Romans were already settled here over a century before that, and maybe much earlier.

The presence of Rome's earliest temples on the Palatine hill made the area into desirable real estate, pushing commerce and bureaucracy down into the **Foro Romano** (see p71) as the Palatine became increasingly residential.

To the north-west of the Palatine, the valley where the **Colosseum** now stands was hemmed in by the Palatine, Celian and Oppian hills, and by the Velia, the saddle of land that joined the Oppian and Palatine hills: what was left of the Velia was bulldozed away by Mussolini when he drove his via dei Fori Imperiali through the **Imperial Fora** (see p70). The dwellings which had built up there from the seventh century BC were swept clean by the great fire of AD 64, leaving the area free to become the garden of Nero's **Domus Aurea** (see p130). To the south of the Palatine, the **Circo Massimo** opened for races in the fourth century BC, or maybe earlier.

Arco di Constantino

Piazza del Colosseo. Metro Colosseo/bus to piazza del Colosseo. **Map** p326 2C.

Standing beside the Colosseum, Constantine's triumphal arch was one of the last great Roman monuments, erected in AD 315, shortly before he abandoned the city for Byzantium (*see chapter* **History**). Although it appears magnificent enough at first glance, a close look reveals its splendours to be shallow – most of the carvings and statues were simply scavenged from other monuments around the city.

Circo Massimo

Via del Circo Massimo. Metro Circo Massimo/bus or tram to viale Aventino. **Map** p327 1C.

Ancient Rome's major chariot-racing venue, the Circus Maximus, is now ringed by several lanes of furious traffic. Nevertheless, it's still possible to visualise the flat base of the long, grassy basin as the racetrack, and the sloping sides as the stadium stands. At the southern end there are remains of the original seating, although the tower there is medieval. This was the oldest and largest of Rome's ancient arenas, and chariot races were held here from at least the fourth century BC. It was rebuilt by Julius Caesar, and by the days of the Empire could hold as many as 300,000 people. The circus was also used for mock sea battles (with the arena flooded with millions of gallons of water), the ever-popular fights with wild animals, and the occasional large-scale execution.

Colosseum

Piazza del Colosseo (06 700 5469/06 3996 7700). Metro Colosseo/bus to piazza del Colosseo. **Open** 9am-5pm Tue-Sun; ticket office closes 4pm. **Admission** €5.16/L10,000; €2.58/L5,000 concessions; *see also p60* **Tickets. No credit cards. Map** p326 2B.

Built in AD 72 by Vespasian on the newly drained site of a lake in the grounds of Nero's **Domus Aurea** (*see p130*), the Colosseum hosted gory battles between gladiators, slaves, prisoners and wild animals of all descriptions. As this guide went to press, work was under way that will revolutionise the Colosseum as we see it. In a project scheduled for completion in 2003, much larger areas of the arena will be opened up to the public, a section of the awnings which once protected the audience will be re-created, and – most strikingly – the sandy floor which had long disappeared, revealing subterranean tunnels through which animals were funnelled into the arena, will be rebuilt. Besides giving a more accurate picture of what the amphitheatre really looked like, this last will allow it to be used once again as a performance venue.

The top rows of the Colosseum are the best vantage point from which to appreciate the truly massive scale of the building. Properly called the Anfiteatro flavio (Flavian amphitheatre) but later known as the Colosseum not because it was big, but because of a gold-plated colossal statue, now lost, which stood alongside, the arena was a third of a mile in circumference, could seat over 50,000 people and could be filled or emptied in ten minutes through a network of *vomitoria* (exits) that remains the basic model for stadium design today.

Nowhere in the world was there a larger or more glorious setting for the mass slaughter so loved by the brutal Romans. If costly, highly trained professional gladiators were often spared at the end of their bloody bouts, not so the slaves, criminals and assorted unfortunates roped in to do battle against them. Fights were to the death: any combatant who disappointed the crowd by not showing enough grit was put to death anyway, and corpses were prodded with red-hot pokers to make sure no one tried to elude fate by playing dead. It was not only human life which was sacrificed to Roman blood-lust: wildlife, too, was legitimate fodder. Animals fought animals; people fought animals. In the ten-day carnage held to inaugurate the amphitheatre in AD 80, 5,000 beasts perished. By the time wild-animal shows were finally banned in AD 523, the elephant and tiger were all but extinct in North Africa and Arabia.

Entrance to the Colosseum was free for all, although a membership card was necessary, and a rigid seating plan kept the sexes and social classes in their rightful places. The emperor and senators occupied marble seats in the front rows; on benches higher up came priests and magistrates, then foreign diplomats. Women were confined to the upper reaches – all, that is, except the Vestal Virgins: less addicted to blood-letting than their fellow Romans, these hapless females, Suetonius reports, were often carried out from their privileged seats near the emperor fainting in shock.

When gladiatorial blood sports went out of fashion in the sixth century, the Colosseum became one big quarry, where Romans turned for stone and marble to build and decorate their *palazzi*. This pillaging was not halted until the mid-18th century, when Pope Benedict XIV had stations of the cross built inside it, and consecrated it as a church. For another 100 years it was left to its own devices, becoming home to hundreds of species of flowers and plants. After Unification in 1870 that flora was yanked up, in what English writer Augustus Hare described as 'aimless excavations'. 'In dragging out the roots of its shrubs,' he moaned in his *Walks in Rome* (1883), 'more of the building was destroyed than would have fallen naturally in five centuries'.

Il Palatino

Via di San Gregorio 30/piazza di Santa Maria Nova 53 (06 699 0110/06 3996 7700). Metro Colosseo/ bus to via dei Fori Imperiali. **Open** 9am-5pm daily. *Museo Palatino* 9am-4.30pm daily; ticket office closes 4pm. **Admission** €6.20/L12,000; €3.10/L5,000 concessions; *see also p60* **Tickets. No credit cards. Map** p326 2C.

Numbers refer to the map on p67.

The Beverly Hills of ancient Rome, the Palatine hill

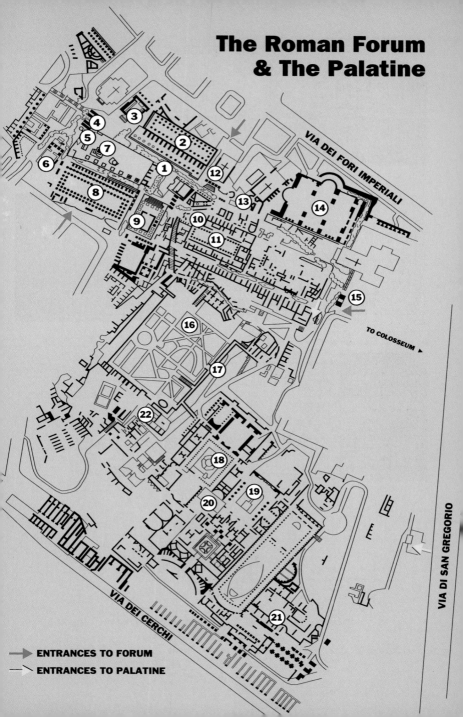

The Roman Forum
& The Palatine

VIA DEI FORI IMPERIALI

TO COLOSSEUM ▶

VIA DI SAN GREGORIO

VIA DEI CERCHI

➡ ENTRANCES TO FORUM

⟍ ENTRANCES TO PALATINE

American Bar - Piano Bar
An exclusive meeting place
for a cocktail or to listen
some good music after dinner.
From 11.00 a.m. to 02.00 p.m.

Restaurant - Piano Bar
An elegant restaurant with Italian
and international cuisine
and Grande Parte with selection of wines.
Sale Privèe for reservation dinner.
From 12.30 a.m. to 15.00 p.m.
and from 19.30 a.m. to 01.00 p.m.

Bistrot
Straight on Via Veneto
with a wonderful view
of Porta Pinciana.

Harry's Bar was established
in the early '60s: they were
the years of the best Italy.
The years of the famous
Italian "dolce vita".

Closed on Sunday - All credit cards accepted
For information and reservation:
Harry's Bar Roma - Via Vittorio Veneto, 150 - 00187 Roma
Tel. +39 06484643 - +39 06.4742103
Fax +39 06.4883117

was where the movers and shakers of both Republic and Empire built their palaces. The choice of location was understandable: the Palatine overlooks the Roman Forum, yet is a comfortable distance from the disturbances and riff-raff down in the valley.

Entering the Palatine from the Roman Forum, you pass the Hortus Farnese (**16**) on the right. Originally the Domus Tiberiana, these gardens full of orange trees and burbling fountains were laid out in the 16th century, making them one of the oldest botanical gardens in Europe. The gardens were created for a member of a papal family, Cardinal Alessandro Farnese, who used them for lavish garden parties. The pavilion at the top of the hill is 17th-century, with a good view over the Forum. Underneath the gardens, behind the pavilion, is the Cryptoporticus (**17**), a long semi-subterranean tunnel built by Nero for hot-weather promenades or as a secret route between the Palatine buildings and his palace, the Domus Aurea (Nero's Golden House, *see p130*), across the valley on the Oppian hill. Lit only by slits in the walls, the Cryptoporticus is welcomingly cool in summer, and at one end there are remnants of a stucco ceiling-frieze and floor mosaics.

South of the gardens are the remains of the imperial palaces built by Domitian at the end of the first century AD, which became the principal residence of the emperors for the next three centuries. The nearest section, the Domus Flavia (**18**), contained the public rooms. According to the biographer Suetonius, Domitian was so terrified of assassination that he had the walls faced with shiny black selenite so he could see anybody creeping up behind

him. It didn't work. The strange-looking room, with what appears to be a maze in the middle, was the courtyard; next to this was the dining room, where parts of the marble floor have survived, although it's usually covered for protection. The brick oval in the middle was probably a fountain. Next door is the emperor's private residence, the Domus Augustana (**19**). The oval building close to it may have been a garden, or a miniature stadium for Domitian's private entertainment.

Sandwiched between the Domus Flavia and Domus Augustana is a tall grey building that houses the Museo Palatino (Palatine Museum, **20**). Downstairs are human remains and artefacts from the earliest hut communities of Rome, founded in the Forum and Palatine areas from the ninth century BC: Room II has a model of an eighth-century village. Emerging from the floor are foundations of Domitian's dwelling. Upstairs are busts, Gods and some fascinating eave-edgings from the first to the fourth centuries AD.

To the south of the Domus Augustana lie the remains of the comparatively small palace and baths of Septimius Severus (**21**), some of the best-preserved buildings in the area. Back towards the Farnese gardens is the Domus Livia (**22**), named after Augustus's wife. The wall paintings here date from the late Republic, and include *trompe l'œil* marble panels and scenes from mythology.

The fora

The **Foro Romano**, the oldest of Rome's fora, began life as a swampy valley at the foot of the

Ancient emperors built the **Fori Imperiali** to mark military triumphs. *See p70.*

Sightseeing

Trajan's column tells of vanquished Dacians.

Palatine (*see p66*) used for burials. Drained, according to legend, in the late seventh century BC by Rome's Etruscan king, Tarquinius Priscus, who had the Cloaca Maxima (*see p109*) built, the Forum became the centre of commerce, law, and bureaucracy.

As the existing fora became too small to cope with the legal, social and commercial life of the city, the emperors combined philanthropy with propaganda, and created new ones of their own, the **Fori Imperiali** (Imperial Fora). All but one were built to celebrate military triumphs. Clearly visible from the main road – and with sections that, as this guide went to press, were to be made accessible to the public – there are five separate fora, each built by a different emperor. Mussolini thought fit to slice through the remains to build the via dei Fori Imperiali (he was planning to create a bigger, better empire of his own after all). Since the 1990s, work has been under way to reverse this situation, turning the Fori Imperiali into the world's biggest urban archaeological dig.

In his wisdom, Mussolini saved modern archaeologists the anguish of having to decide what to do with the medieval and early Renaissance buildings – including dozens of defence towers – which had grown up out of the Roman ruins: he bulldozed them. The recently-restored **Torre delle Milizie** tower behind **Trajan's Markets** is a picturesque memento.

Carcere Mamertino

Clivio Argentario 1 (06 679 2902). Bus to via dei Fori Imperiali or piazza Venezia. **Open** 9am-noon, 2-5pm daily. **Admission** donation expected. **Map** p326 1C.
Anyone thought to pose a threat to the security of the ancient Roman state was thrown into the Mamertine Prison, a dank, dark and oppressive little underground dungeon, squashed between the Roman Forum and via dei Fori Imperiali at the bottom of the steps up to the Capitoline. In those days, the only way down to the lower level (built in the fourth century BC) was through a hole in the floor. The numberless prisoners who starved to death here were tossed into the Cloaca Maxima, the city's main sewer. The most famous of the prison's residents, legend has it, were saints Peter and Paul (*see p132* **Peter and Paul**). Peter head-butted the wall in the ground-level room, leaving his features impressed on the rock (or so the plaque says). He also caused a miraculous well to bubble up downstairs in order to baptise his prison guards, whom he converted by his shining example.

Fori Imperiali & Mercati di Traiano

Fori: via dei Fori Imperiali (06 678 9487/ www.capitolium.org). Metro Colosseo/bus to piazza del Colosseo. **Map** p326 1C.
Mercati di Traiano: via IV Novembre 94 (06 679 0048). Bus to via Nazionale. **Open** 9am-5pm Tue-Sun. **Admission** €6.20/L12,000; €3.10/L6,000 concessions. **No credit cards**. **Map** p326 1C.
By the end of 2001, Rome's authorities hope to inaugurate the first phase of a Museo dei Fori Imperiali (Museum of the Imperial Fora). This will

consist of a museum, to be housed inside Mercati di Traiano (Trajan's Markets), with reconstructions, explanations and artefacts pertaining to ancient Rome's fora. In addition, there will be itineraries around the fora of Trajan, Augustus and Nerva, complete with explanatory panels and wheelchair-accessible walkways. Until then, Trajan's Markets and Forum can be visited. A second phase of the museum – to include itineraries through those parts of the fora excavated since 1998, joined by passageways beneath the via Fori Imperiali – will open at a later date.

On the Roman Forum side of the via dei Fori Imperiali and still being excavated as this guide went to press, the Forum of Caesar is the earliest of the imperial fora, begun by Julius Caesar in 51 BC, after he had conquered Gaul. Straddling the via dei Fori Imperiali, the Forum of Nerva was begun by Domitian but dedicated by Nerva in AD 97. It was dominated by a temple to Minerva; part of its original frieze survives.

Augustus decided to build his Forum (on the north side of via dei Fori Imperiali) around 42 BC after he had avenged Caesar's death; it was inaugurated in 2 BC. The high wall that separated it from the Suburra slum district is still visible, as are the

remains of a temple to Mars Ultore (the avenger). Next door stands the most ambitious of all the fora: Trajan's. Inaugurated in AD 112-3 after the emperor had annexed Dacia – roughly present-day Romania – Trajan's Forum was dominated by the Basilica Ulpia, the largest basilica ever built in ancient Rome and still clearly visible next to Trajan's column. The beautifully carved reliefs spiralling up the column tell the story of the emperor's campaign against the Dacians. The column is 38m (125ft) high, and has over 100 scenes carved up its sides. They were originally painted, and would have been easily visible from galleries on the nearby buildings. They are difficult to see today, but there are replicas in the Museo della Civiltà Romana in EUR (*see p155*). The statue of St Peter atop the column was added by Pope Sixtus V in 1587 to replace the original one of Trajan.

Towering above Trajan's Forum is the same emperor's markets, which he had built in the early second century AD, partly to shore up the Quirinale hill. Designed by Apollodorus of Damascus (who was later executed by Hadrian on suspicion of treachery), it is the ancient Roman equivalent of a shopping mall. The most distinctive feature is a multi-storey brick crescent or hemicycle. At the back of the crescent is a large hall, which may have been used for the distribution of the corn dole (*see chapter* **History**). In total there were five levels to the building, containing about 150 small shops. They were probably organised into areas – the ground floor for wine and oil, first floor for fruit and flowers, and so on. The shops are mostly intact, and you can still see some of the ridges into which shutters were dropped at closing time. Attached to the market are several medieval buildings, including the **Torre delle Milizie** (Militia Tower), part of a fortress built for Pope Gregory IX in the 13th century. For years it was erroneously believed to be the place from where Nero watched Rome burn, after he had supposedly set fire to it. Recently restored, it will be opened to the public in the first phase of the Museo dei Fori Imperiali.

Little remains of the Forum of Peace, built by Vespasian in AD 71-5, and destroyed by fire in 192. Its Temple of Peace contained treasures looted from the Temple of Jerusalem; the temple's library is now part of the church of **Cosma e Damiano**.

The best Ancient collections

Centrale Montemartini
Odds and ends from the city's collection, set strikingly against the restored machinery of a decommissioned power station. *See p153*.

Musei Capitolini
One of the world's most significant collections, in one of the world's oldest public museums. *See p62*.

Musei Vaticani
The Vatican's Museo Pio-Clementino contains a massive collection of exquisite pieces, including the *Belvedere Apollo*. *See p141*.

Palazzo Altemps
Ancient masterpieces, many of them patched up by Renaissance masters. *See p95*.

Palazzo Massimo alle Terme
The biggest and best from the Museo Nazionale Romano collection, including stunning frescos and a fascinating display on ancient money and commerce. *See p137*.

Foro Romano
Entrances from largo Romolo e Remo, via dei Fori Imperiali, piazza del Colosseo and via Foro Romano (06 699 0110). Metro Colosseo/bus to via dei Fori Imperiali. **Open** 9am-5pm daily. **Admission** free. **Map** p326 2B-C.
Numbers refer to the map on p67.
In the earliest days of the Republic, the Roman Forum was much like any Italian piazza today: an open space where people would shop, gossip, catch up on the latest news and perhaps visit a temple. In the second century BC, when Rome had become the capital of an empire that included Greece, Sicily and Carthage, it

The **arch of Titus** tells of Jerusalem sacked.

was decided the city needed a more dignified centre. The food stalls were moved out, and permanent law courts and offices were built. In time this centre was also deemed too small, and emperors began to build the new Imperial Fora (*see p70*). Nevertheless, the Foro Romano remained the symbolic heart of the Empire, and emperors continued to renovate and embellish it until the fourth century AD. (A recent decision to do away with the entry fee, 'returning' the Forum to the Romans, was warmly welcomed by locals who can be seen wandering through it on sunny weekends, looking very much at home.)

The area today consists of little more than the layouts of floors and a few columns, but with a bit of imagination a tour around the Forum can still give an accurate impression of what ancient Rome looked like. Before entering, look down over the Forum from behind the Capitoline for a view of its overall layout. Its central thoroughfare, the via Sacra (**1**), runs almost directly through the middle. Entering the Forum from the via dei Fori Imperiali entrance, the Basilica Emilia (**2**) is to the left. This was a large hall, originally built for business and moneylending in 179 BC, though what remains is mainly from later periods. The brown rusty marks dotted around the basilica at the end towards the Capitoline are bronze coins that fused into the floor during a fire in AD 410. The tall brick building at the coin end is a 1930s reconstruction of the Curia (**3**) or Senate House.

Standing out to the left of the Curia is the best-preserved monument in this part of the Forum, the massive Arch of Septimius Severus (**4**), built in AD 203 to celebrate a victory over the Parthians. Near here was the Golden Milestone (Millarium Aureum), from which all distances to and from Rome were measured.

Beyond the Arch of Septimius are the remains of Caesar's rostrum (**5**), a platform from which speeches and demonstrations of power were made, and from where Mark Antony supposedly asked the Roman populace to lend him its ears. Further back, the eight massive columns that formed part of the Temple of Saturn (**6**), built in the fifth century BC, stand out. The state treasury was housed underneath it. Also clearly visible is the solitary Column of Phocas (**7**), erected in AD 608 by Pope Boniface IV to thank the Byzantine Emperor for giving him the Pantheon as a church. Visible on the other side of the via Sacra are the foundations of the Basilica Giulia (**8**), built by Julius Caesar in 55 BC and once a major – and by all accounts very noisy – law court. Ancient board games are carved into the steps.

Further into the Forum are three elegant columns that formed part of the Temple of Castor and Pollux (**9**), the saviours of Rome. According to legend, these twin giants and their horses appeared to the Roman forces during a battle in 499 BC, and helped the Republic to victory.

Beyond the Temple are the remains of the round Temple of Vesta (**10**) and, within its garden, the Atrium Vestae), the rectangular House of the Vestal Virgins (**11**). On the via dei Fori Imperiali side of the via Sacra are the columns, atop a flight of steep steps, of the Temple of Antonius and Faustina (**12**), built to honour a second-century emperor and his wife and, since the 11th century, part of the church of San Lorenzo in Miranda. The oldest graves ever unearthed in Rome were found here; the bodies are now housed in the Palatine Museum (*see p67*). The circular building further up the slope is the Temple of Romulus (**13**), dating from the fourth century AD. It has nothing to do with the co-founder of Rome: this Romulus was a son of the Emperor Maxentius, who died in 309. The bronze door of his temple is still locked with the original ancient key.

Looming above these temples are giant vaults that were part of the Basilica of Maxentius (**14**), also known as the Basilica of Constantine, begun in AD 306 and studied by Michelangelo and Bramante when they were designing St Peter's. By the southern exit, which leads down to the Colosseum, stands the Arch of Titus (**15**), built in AD 81 to celebrate the sacking of Jerusalem; the event is depicted in the elaborate relic panels (note the sacred seven-branched candelabra). A path to the right of this arch leads to the Palatine; another beyond leads to the Colosseum.

Santi Cosma e Damiano

Via dei Fori Imperiali 1 (06 699 1540). Metro Colosseo/bus to via dei Fori Imperiali. **Open** 8am-12.45pm, 3-7pm daily. **Map** p326 2C.

This small church on the fringe of the Forum incorporates the library of Vespasian's Temple of Peace and the Temple of Romulus. It has a wonderful sixth-century mosaic in the apse, representing the Second Coming, with the figure of Christ appearing huge against a blue setting as he descends a staircase of

The Trevi Fountain & the Quirinale

Grand *palazzi*, exquisite churches and the inescapable splash of coins.

Said by local tradition to have been first settled by Sabines – who would later join with the Latins over on the Palatine to form the nucleus of Rome – the Quirinale has long been the *colle* (hill) *per eccellenza*. It was dotted with important temples in ancient times, and was the residence of popes centuries later. Today, an incumbent prime minister who *sale al Colle* ('climbs the hill' – there's no need to specify which) does so in desperation, to hand in his resignation to the head of state who occupies the **Palazzo del Quirinale** (*see p78*).

There has always been a sharp contrast between the hill and the area below: once a semi-rural seat of power towering above a densely built-up area around the Acqua Vergine, the Quirinale still retains its air of splendidly monumental isolation above the seething tourist mass drawn by the irresistible urge to throw coins in the Trevi Fountain.

Around the Trevi Fountain

The west-facing slopes of the hill towards the built-up area around the **Fontana di Trevi** (Trevi Fountain) were a rocky, vegetation-filled expanse until as late as the mid-18th century. Some street names nearby hark back to the days of papal rule, when the Holy See had its machinery of state around here: **via della Dataria** was home to the office of the same name that handed out perks to the clergy, while the papal printing works was in **via della Stamperia** (printing works street) where the august **Accademia di San Luca** has its headquarters and gallery. Close to the hub of power yet vibrantly alive with the craft community that had long been established here, this was an area where very different strata of society chose to dwell: some of the city's most powerful noble families – the Colonnas, the Odescalchis and the Grimaldis, for example – built their palaces in the thick of it, around piazza dei SS Apostoli. The **Galleria Colonna** still contains that family's art collection.

Nowadays, only the occasional office linked to the presidential palace has resisted the overwhelming force of mass tourism: there's barely a shop or eaterie in the area that is not very obviously there for the purpose of serving the coin-throwing hordes. The hard sell is interrupted by some interesting churches (including **Santi Vicenzo e Anastasio** with its papal innards, **Santa Maria in Via** with its miraculous spring, and tiny **Santa Maria dell'Archetto**) and a museum dedicated to Italy's national dish (the **Museo Nazionale delle Paste Alimentari**).

Fontana di Trevi

Piazza di Trevi. Bus to piazza San Silvestro or via del Tritone. **Map** p323 2C.

The Trevi Fountain is known the world over as the fountain where Anita Ekberg cooled off in *La Dolce Vita*, and into which you should throw a coin if you want to be drawn back to Rome. Although tucked away in a tiny piazza, it's almost impossible to miss: the alleys approaching it are glutted with souvenir shops and takeaway pizzerias, but full of the sound of water. Permanently surrounded by crowds, the fountain's creamy travertine gleams beneath powerful torrents of water and constant camera flashes. The attention is justified: it's a magnificent rococo extravaganza of rearing sea horses, conch-blowing tritons, craggy rocks and flimsy trees, cavorting below the wall of the Palazzo Poli. In a relief high on the palace wall is the virgin of legend showing three thirsty Roman soldiers to a handy spring (hence the Acqua Vergine, the name of the source that still feeds the fountain). According to one version of the story, the unfortunate maid was called Trivia; the fountain's name is more likely to come from its position at the meeting of three roads, *tre vie*. Designed by Nicolò Salvi for Pope Clement XII, the fountain was finished in 1762, although the aqueduct bringing the Acqua Vergine has been here since Roman times. Would-be Ekbergs should think twice before plunging in: not only are they likely to be arrested, but the water contains unpalatable quantities of bleach.

Galleria dell'Accademia di San Luca

Piazza dell'Accademia 77 (06 679 8850). Bus to piazza San Silvestro or via del Tritone. **Open** 10am-12.30pm Mon, Wed, Fri and last Sun of month. Closed July, Aug. Currently closed for renovations. **Admission** free. **Map** p323 2C.

Lire-lobbing at the **Trevi Fountain**. *See p74.*

The Great Hall has a dramatic frescoed ceiling depicting the *Apotheosis of Marcantonio Colonna*; next to it is the Hall of the Desks, so named because of two lavish writing desks, one decorated with *pietra dura* and bronze statuettes, the other covered in carved ivory. The ceiling is a fantasy of evil cherubs, endangered maidens and threatening Turks, by Sebastiano Ricci. Other highlights include the wonderfully sensuous *Venus and Cupid* by Bronzino, the nightmarish *Temptation of St Anthony* by a follower of Hieronymus Bosch, and Annibale Carracci's earthy *The Bean-Eater*, a familiar, much-reproduced face. A guided tour in English, included in the ticket price, starts at 11.45am. Groups of ten or more can arrange guided tours of the gallery and/or the private apartments during the week; call the number above to enquire about bookings and prices.

Museo Nazionale delle Paste Alimentari

Piazza Scanderbeg 117 (06 699 1119). Bus to via del Tritone. **Open** 9.30am-5.30pm daily. **Admission** €6.20/L12,000; €4.65/L9,000 concessions. **No credit cards.** Map p323 2C.

This grandly named tribute to pasta is one of the best-organised museums in Rome. Visitors are issued with a portable CD player, with commentary in six languages, to talk them through the collection of pasta-making equipment, labels, art inspired by Italy's national dish and prints and photos of famous – and not so famous – people slurping spaghetti. You hear more than strictly necessary on the techniques of pasta making, and some of the displays are a bit repetitive, but for anyone with a passing interest in the national dish, the museum is worth a visit.

Santa Maria dell'Archetto

Via San Marcello 41 (no phone). Bus to via del Tritone or piazza Venezia. **Open** 6.30-7.30pm daily. Map p323 2C.

One of Rome's tiniest churches and only open for the evening rosary, Santa Maria dell'Archetto is a miniature jewel-casket. Its little dome and main altar has frescos by Costantino Brumidi, a 19th-century Roman artist who decamped to the US soon after finishing here, to work on Capitol Hill and earn himself the (rather exaggerated) title of 'the Michelangelo of the United States'.

Santa Maria in Via

Via Santa Maria in Via (06 679 3841). Bus to piazza San Silvestro or via del Tritone. **Open** 7.30am-8pm daily. Map p323 2C.

An ornate baroque façade, completed in 1681 by Carlo Rainaldi, a pupil of Bernini, hides a little chapel containing a well where, in 1256, a stone bearing an image of the Virgin's face floated to the surface, or so the story goes. Shots of the water, which supposedly has the power to cure the sick, are handed out in little plastic cups from the altar rail in exchange for a donation.

This august institution, founded in 1577 to train artists in the grand Renaissance style, was closed for renovations as this guide went to press; it's due to reopen at the end of 2001. The highlight of the collection is a fragment of a Raphael fresco, but there are also works by Titian, Rubens, Reni and Van Dyck, and fascinating self-portraits by the few women members of the Academy, such as Lavinia Fontana (1552-1614) and Angelica Kauffman (1741-1807). It's a good place, too, to track the changing face of Rome through its collection of artistically forgettable but nonetheless endearing portrayals of the Eternal City. Note the curious elliptical staircase near the entrance, a typically original addition by Borromini.

Galleria Colonna

Via della Pilotta 17 (06 678 4350/www. galleriacolonna.it). Bus to piazza Venezia. **Open** 9am-1pm Sat. Closed Aug. **Admission** €5.16/L10,000; concessions €4.13/L8,000. **No credit cards.** Map p323 2C.

It's well worth making the effort one Saturday morning to see this lavish six-roomed gallery (completed in 1703), in the still family-owned Palazzo Colonna.

Santi Vincenzo ed Anastasio

*Piazza di Trevi (06 678 3098). Bus to piazza San
Silvestro or via del Tritone.* **Open** 7am-noon, 4-7pm
daily. **Map** p323 2C.

Your chance to stand in the presence of the livers,
spleens and pancreases of every pope from Sixtus V
(1585-90) to Leo XIII (1878-1903). After each pope's
death his innards were bottled, labelled and deposit-
ed here – but you cannot see them. Despite rumours
that they would be unveiled for Holy Year festivities in 2000, at the time of writing they remained
firmly under wraps. You'll have to settle for reading
the list of bits on a marble plaque by the altar.

Piazza Barberini &
the Quattro Fontane

Nestling north of the Quirinale, at the foot of
the once-glamorous via Veneto (*see p84*), is
piazza Barberini, overlooked by the huge
Palazzo Barberini gallery, with Bernini's
Fontana del Tritone as its centrepiece. In
ancient times, this site was occupied by the
Flora Circus, where erotic dances would mark
the coming of spring.

From piazza Barberini, via delle Quattro
Fontane – part of the via Felice sliced through
16th-century Rome by the town-planner Pope
Sixtus V (*see p28*) – shoots south-east to the
top of the Quirinale hill, where it bisects the
equally straight via del Quirinale at a busy
crossroads replete with statues of the
Quattro Fontane (four fountains) after
which the street is named. From the
crossroads here there are extraordinary
views of the obelisks in front of the Trinità
dei Monti church (*see p85*, Spanish Steps)
and the basilica of Santa Maria Maggiore
(*see p132*), plus one of Borromini's great
masterpieces, the church of **San Carlino
alle Quattro Fontane**.

The area north-east of the square was
mostly rebuilt in the fascist era, when **via
Barberini** and **via Bissolati** were
relentlessly bulldozed through the urban
fabric. These two streets are now the heart of
Rome's airline and travel business.

Fontana del Tritone

*Piazza Barberini. Metro Barberini/bus to piazza
Barberini.* **Map** p323 1B.

Like many Bernini figures, this cheerful Triton, now
stranded in freshly repaved isolation in the middle
of a hellish major traffic junction, has a well-
developed abdomen. Completed in 1642, he sits, his
two fish-tail legs tucked beneath him, on a shell
supported by four dolphins, and blows water
through a conch in his mouth. The bees on the coat
of arms on the fountain were a symbol of the
Barberini clan, the family of Bernini's great patron,
Pope Urban VIII.

Renaissance gem **Palazzo Barberini**.

Palazzo Barberini – Galleria
Nazionale d'Arte Antica

*Via delle Quattro Fontane 13/via Barberini 18 (06
481 4591/bookings 06 32 810/www.galleria
borghese.it). Metro Barberini/bus to piazza Barberini.*
Open 9am-7.30pm Tue-Sun. **Admission** €6.20/
L12,000; €1.03/L2,000-€5.61/L7,000 concessions. *See
also p60* **Tickets. No credit cards. Map** p323 1B.

Maderno, Bernini and Borromini all contributed to
the design of the Palazzo Barberini, built for the
Barberini Pope Urban VIII between 1627 and 1633.
Borromini's handiwork can be seen in the characteristic oval secondary staircase on the right, while
Bernini was responsible for the rectangular main
staircase – severely marred by the addition of a lift –
to the left. The most famous feature of the interior is
the Gran Salone, dramatically frescoed by Pietro da

Cortona in 1633-39 with *The Triumph of Divine Providence* (usually open for special exhibitions only).

The art collection tends to be rearranged from time to time, and will undergo further changes at some (frequently postponed) point in the future when Armed Forces officers are evicted from their club on the ground floor and the gallery expands. Highlights of the collection include: Filippo Lippi's *Madonna* (with possibly the ugliest Christ-child ever painted); a recently restored, enigmatic portrait of a courtesan – *La Fornarina* – traditionally (although probably wrongly) believed to represent Raphael's mistress (*see p111*, Casa della Fornarina); a portrait of Erasmus by Flemish artist Quentin Metsys; a *Nativity* and *Baptism of Christ* by El Greco; Tintoretto's dramatic *Christ and the Woman taken in Adultery*; Titian's *Venus and Adonis*; two Caravaggios, one of Judith rather gingerly cutting off Holofernes' head; a Holbein portrait, *Henry VIII Dressed for his Wedding to Anne of Cleves* (although it has been suggested this may be a copy); Bronzino's forceful portrait of Stefano Colonna; Guido Reni's portrait of incest-victim Beatrice Cenci (*see p107*, Palazzo Cenci); a Bernini bust and painted portrait of Pope Urban VIII, who commissioned the palace; works by Raphael's best-known follower, Sodoma (the nickname, apparently, was apt), including a *Rape of the Sabine Women* with predictably compliant subjects *The Mystic Marriage of Saint Catherine*; and a very self-assured self-portrait by Artemisia Gentileschi.

Visitors also have access to a suite of small private rooms, exquisitely painted and furnished for Princess Cornelia Costanza Barberini in the 18th century (note the charming natives in the room decorated with depictions of the discovery of America). Cornelia was the last of the Barberinis, and the name died out when she was married off to one of the Colonna family at the age of 12. These rooms also house some Barberini family clothes and furniture.

Le Quattro Fontane

Bus to piazza Barberini or via Nazionale. **Map** p323 2B. Standing at the fume-filled crossroads between via delle Quattro Fontane and via XX Settembre, these four charming baroque fountains date from 1593

and represent four gods. The river god accom... by the she-wolf is obviously the Tiber, althou... is unclear whether the other male figure is meant... represent the Nile or the Aniene. The females are probably Juno (with duck) and Diana.

San Carlino alle Quattro Fontane

Via del Quirinale 23 (06 488 3261). Bus to piazza Barberini or via Nazionale. **Open** 10am-1pm, 3-4pm Mon-Fri; 10am-1pm Sat; 11am-1pm Sun. **Map** p323 2B. This church was Borromini's first solo commission (1634-41), and is an ingenious building for a cramped site. The most remarkable feature is the dizzying oval dome. The geometrical coffers in its decoration decrease in size towards the lantern to give the illusion of additional height, and the illumination, through hidden windows, makes the dome appear to be floating in mid-air. Recently restored, this gem of a church – and the charming if somewhat austere courtyard in the adjoining monastery – opens very much at the whim of the monastery's residents.

From the Quirinale to via Nazionale

If you are impressed – and you will be – by the daytime view over Rome's rooftops and across to the dome of St Peter's from the terrace on the **piazza del Quirinale**, go back at sunset: on a good evening, it's simply stunning (*see also p78* **The best sunsets**).

One of the centres of official Rome, this expanse – also known as piazza di Monte Cavallo – is dominated by the huge, orange **Palazzo del Quirinale**. At the centre of the piazza is an obelisk originally from the Mausoleum of Augustus (*see p91*). The square is dominated by disproportionately large Roman statues of the heavenly twins Castor and Pollux, each 5.5 metres (19 feet) tall, atop a fountain that was moved here in the 1800s after – legend has it – centuries of use as a cattle trough in the Roman Forum (*see p71*). The Palazzo del Quirinale looks

Sightseeing

Renaissance highway, the **via Quattro Fontane**.

nsets

...that it's just the extraordinary ...ction of the sun's last rays through Rome's extraordinary pollution, but there's no denying that the Eternal City's sunsets have a very special quality about them. Seeing the apricots and terracotta hues of the city's *palazzi* reflected in and enhanced by a good *tramonto* (sunset) is a truly memorable experience. Pick your evening, then pick the right spot to go with your mood.

Bar La Terrazza, Hotel Eden

See the lights come up, dry Martini in hand. *See p50.*

Il Gianicolo

It faces the wrong way (due east) but don't let that worry you: nestling at your feet, embraced by distant mountains, Rome turns heart-stoppingly, knee-wobblingly red here anyway. *See p117.*

Parco Savello

Watch the palette's colour deepen amid the sylvan charm of this orange garden. *See p118.*

Piazza del Quirinale

Lowly Rome unfolds at the feet of the city's most powerful hill. *See p77.*

Spanish Steps

In Rome, even clichés will melt your heart: what could be more romantic than watching the sun go down from the top of the Spanish Steps. *See p85.*

across the piazza to the former papal stables, now transformed into an exhibition space, the **Scuderie Papali al Quirinale**; and it looks across via del Quirinale to Bernini's church of **Sant'Andrea al Quirinale**.

Post-Unification *palazzi* occupy the Quirinale's south-facing slope, which descends past police stations, court buildings, and ministry offshoots towards the high-street fashion shopping artery of **via Nazionale** and the **Palazzo delle Esposizioni**.

Palazzo delle Esposizioni

Via Nazionale 194 (06 474 5903/ www.palaexpo.com). Bus to via Nazionale. **Open** 10am-9pm Mon, Wed-Sun; ticket office closes 8.15pm. **Admission** €7.75/L15,000; €4.13/L8,000 concessions; extra charge for some exhibitions. **No credit cards. Map** p323 2B.

Dating from the late 19th century, this imposing palazzo on via Nazionale was one of Rome's first purpose-built exhibition halls. After years of neglect and restoration it reopened in 1990 to become the city's most prominent cultural centre, holding exhibitions, film screenings, conferences and many other events. Incorporated into the complex are a bookshop, design shop, bar and rooftop restaurant.

Palazzo del Quirinale

Piazza del Quirinale (06 46 991/www.quirinale.it). Bus to via Nazionale. **Open** 8.30am-12.30pm Sun. Closed July, Aug. **Admission** €5.16/L10,000. **No credit cards. Map** p323 2C.

The Quirinale was begun in 1574 as a papal summer residence, but it soon became more popular with pontiffs as a permanent base than the low-lying Vatican palace. So that they should not have to return to the other place for conclaves, the Cappella Paolina, a replica of the Sistine Chapel (in size and shape, not decoration), was built in the following century, and accommodation for the cardinals was provided in the Manica Lunga, the immensely long façade running the length of via del Quirinale. Popes Pius VI and VII were forcibly removed from the palace and deported by Napoleon, in 1799 and 1809 respectively; republican rebels forced Pius IX to sneak ignominiously out the back door in 1848. After his return to Rome, the disgruntled Pius refused to hand over the keys of the Quirinale to Italy's new king in 1870, and soldiers had to break into the palace before Vittorio Emanuele could take up residence there (*see chapter* **History**). Since the end of the monarchy in 1946 it has been home to the president of Italy. The graceful door in the main façade is by Bernini. The lofty public rooms and beautiful gardens open to the public on Sunday mornings.

Sant'Andrea al Quirinale

Via del Quirinale 29 (06 474 4801). Bus to via Nazionale. **Open** 9am-noon, 4-7pm Mon, Wed-Sun. **Map** p323 2C.

This oval church, decorated in pink marble, is a typically theatrical Bernini production, finished in 1670 and cleverly designed to create a sense of grandeur in a small space. Inside, every surface is lavishly decorated, but pride of place must go to a plaster St Andrew floating through a broken pediment on his way to heaven.

Scuderie Papali al Quirinale

Via XXIV Maggio 16 (06 696 270/www. scuderiepapali.it). Bus to via Nazionale. **Open** 10am-7pm Mon-Thur, Sun; 10am-11pm Fri, Sat; ticket office closes one hour earlier. **Admission** €7.75/ L15,000; €5.16/L10,000 concessions. **Credit** *phone bookings only* AmEx, DC, MC, V. **Map** p323 2C.

The former stables of the Palazzo del Quirinale have been magnificently restored to house high-standard temporary exhibitions featuring work ranging from post-Impressionism to Bellini's sketches to illustrate Dante's *Divine Comedy*. The view over Rome from the stairs on the way to the exit is breathtaking.

Via Veneto
& Villa Borghese

The *Dolce Vita* is a distant memory, but acres of green, canvas and marble remain.

Rollerbladers and romantics gather at the **Pincio.** *See p80.*

From ancient times until the building boom of the late 1800s, the area far to the north and north-east of the settlement by the Tiber, stretching from what is now the Pincio to Porta Pia, was one of gardens, villas and religious orders. In the first century BC, the **Horti Sallustiani** (*see p84*) were Rome's most extensive monumental gardens. From the Renaissance on, noble Roman families such as the Borgheses and Ludovisi-Boncompagnis embellished their sprawling estates here.

Of these, only the **Villa Borghese** was saved from the clutches of post-Unification property speculators. The rest of the greenery was carved up to build the kind of heavy, pompous *palazzi* (with the occasional art nouveau touch; *see chapter* **Architecture**) so beloved of the upper-middle-class pen-pushers of the newly united Italy.

Villa Borghese & the Pincio

In 1580 the wealthy and noble Borghese family bought a vineyard in a semi-rural area north of Rome. Two decades later, the plot of land caught the fancy of pleasure-loving Cardinal Scipione Borghese, the favourite nephew of Pope Paul V, who was seeking a location for a *giardino delle delizie*, a garden of earthly delights. In 1608 he began buying up land all around it, and hired architects Flaminio Ponzio and Jan van Santen (Italianised to Giovanni Vasanzio) to produce a worthy backdrop for his sybaritic leisure activities and matchless collection of art.

Work on the magnificent gardens went on until Scipione's death in 1633. The result was a baroque fun-park, complete with trick fountains that sprayed unwitting passers-by, automata and erotic paintings, aviaries, menageries of wild beasts, and an *al fresco* dining room (still visible, to the right as you look at the façade of the Galleria Borghese) where the cardinal entertained his guests with due magnificence on warm summer evenings. At the centre of the park, flanked by formal gardens with exotic plants and fruit trees, rose the Casino (now the **Galleria Borghese**, an elaborate construction intended not as a residence but as a permanent home for Scipione's mushrooming collection of canvas and marble.

Successive generations of the Borghese family altered Scipione's park according to changing fashions, and added to (or, tragically, partly sold off) his superlative art collection. When Rome became capital of a unified Italy, the clan looked set to sell off the estate to property speculators. In a rare example of civic far-sightedness, the state stepped in in 1901, wresting possession of the Villa from the family in a bitter court battle, and turning it into a public park.

Today the Borghese family's pleasure grounds are used for jogging, dog-walking, picnics and cruising. Wandering around it is a great way to recuperate from an overdose of sightseeing and carbon monoxide, although culture vultures can continue to sweat it out in three of Rome's greatest art depositories: the **Galleria Borghese** itself, the Etruscan museum at **Villa Giulia** and the **Galleria Nazionale d'Arte Moderna**. The park also houses the Dei Piccoli children's cinema, Rome's **Bioparco-Zoo** and **Museo Nazionale di Zoologia**. Other sights worth looking out for include the piazza di Siena, an elegantly shaped arena used for opera and show jumping, imitation ancient temples, and a lake with rowing boats (for hire from 9.30am to sunset daily). There is also a good view of the Moro Torto section of the Aurelian Wall from the bridge between the Pincio and Villa Borghese. Once a favourite suicide spot, this is now strung with nets to make sure that no depressed Romans can plunge onto the constant stream of traffic below.

Overlooking piazza del Popolo (*see p89*), and now an integral part of the Villa Borghese, is one of the oldest gardens in Rome, the **Pincio**. The Pinci family commissioned the first gardens here in the fourth century, although the present layout was designed by Giuseppe Valadier in 1814. The garden is best known for its view of the Vatican at sunset, with the dome of St Peter's silhouetted in gold. The paved area behind the viewpoint is popular with cyclists (bikes can be hired nearby) and skaters.

To the south-east is the Casino Valadier; once a tearoom, it was, after many years of inactivity, being revamped as super-cook Gianfranco Vissani's new restaurant as this

Galleria Borghese: a pleasure pavilion of canvas and marble. *See p81.*

The original paparazzo

'Here are your friends, on the attack again,' drawls a sultry Anouk Aimée from behind the wheel of her convertible as flash guns snap around her. 'It's the same old story, every evening. Don't they ever get sick of it?'

'Paparazzo, *basta*,' says journalist Marcello Mastroianni, climbing in beside her. The photographer Paparazzo is his inseparable companion; Marcello's brush-off is offhand and unconvincing. 'There's nothing you can do about it,' he says as the convertible makes its way down via Veneto. 'You're part of the news.'

Federico Fellini's epoch-making film *La Dolce Vita* (1959) gave the world the term *paparazzo* (lifted by Fellini's scriptwriter Ennio Flaiano from George Gissing's 1897 travelogue *By the Ionian Sea*, in which an importunous Calabrian hotel owner was called Coriolano Paparazzo).

But the craft of invasive photojournalism was already well established, and extensively practised in Rome. A film-production boom at Cinecittà (*see p234*) had brought a slew of American stars to the Eternal City; these, along with home-grown divas such as Sofia Loren, were the raw material for photo services craved by the western world's glamour-hungry public.

The unchallenged prince of Roman society photographers was Tazio Secchiaroli (1925-1998), model for the character Paparazzo. Born in the Rome suburbs, he began his photographic career by taking snapshots of American troops and tourists in 1944. By 1955, when he set up the legendary Roma Press Photo agency, he was a household name: he had an uncanny knack for being in the right celebrity-studded place at the right time; when he wasn't, he created his own highly photogenic 'incidents'.

Having led the way for future generations of aggressive, prying practitioners of photography for scandal's sake (no need even to be a hero or a star: 'You're as photogenic as a diva,' the character Paparazzo tells Aimée as justification for pursuing her) he went over to the other side. By 1958 Secchiaroli was working alongside Fellini, documenting the great director's every action in arresting black and white. And, for 20 years, he was Sofia Loren's official photographer, jealously guarding her image.

guide went to press. In the manicured green to the south-east sits the **Villa Medici**, the French academy in Rome, which opens to the public occasionally for high-profile art exhibitions; contact 06 67 711 or consult www.villamedici.it for programme information.

Between Villa Borghese and the river are two more museums which are well worth a visit if you have stamina and/or kids: a striking art nouveau villa houses the **Museo Hendrik Christian Andersen** and a former bus depot is home to the long-awaited children's museum, **Explora – Museo dei Bambini di Roma**.

Bioparco-Zoo

Piazzale del Giardino Zoologico 1 (06 360 8211). Bus to via Pinciana or via Mercadante/tram to via Aldrovandi. **Open** 9.30am-5pm daily; ticket office closes 4pm. **Admission** €7.23/L14,000; €5.16/L10,000 4-12s. **No credit cards.** **Map** p322 1B.

Rome's ropey old zoo, with morose animals in cramped cages, has been relabelled the Bioparco and is gradually being given an eco-friendly once-over. It has all the regular furry and feathered friends, a snazzy reptile house, and free organised games and face-painting for kids daily in school holidays, and at weekends at other times.

Explora – Museo dei Bambini di Roma

Via Flaminia 80 (06 361 3741/fax 06 3608 6803/info@mdbr.it/www.mdbr.it). Metro Flaminio/bus to via Flaminia. **Open** (visits of 1hr 45mins, beginning at following times) 9.30am, 11.30am Mon; 9.30am, 11.30am, 2pm, 4pm Tue-Fri; 10am, noon, 2.15pm, 4.15pm Sat, Sun & public holidays. **Admission** €5.16/L10,000; under-3s free. **Credit** MC, V. **Map** p320 1A.

Rome's long-awaited children's museum opened its gates in May 2001, in a glorious wrought-iron and glass former bus depot on the river side of the Villa Borghese. Inside is a whole city in miniature, where kids can follow letters through the postal system, cash in their lire for euros, visit (or staff) a hospital out-patients department, and make a film, complete with special effects. The whole complex is powered by one of Europe's biggest solar energy plants.

Galleria Borghese

Piazzale Scipione Borghese 5 (information and bookings 06 32 810/www.galleriaborghese.it). Bus to via Veneto, via Pinciana or corso d'Italia. **Open** 9am-7.30pm Tue-Sun; booking always advisable, essential in high season (phone 2wks in advance). **Admission** €7.23/L14,000; €1.03/L2,000-€4.13/L8,000 concessions. *See also p60* **Tickets. No credit cards. Map** p322 2B.

The Casino was designed in 1613 by Jan van Santen (Giovanni Vasanzio) to house Cardinal Scipione Borghese's art collection. One of Bernini's greatest patrons and also a collector of classical sculpture, the cardinal was a man with as good an eye for a bargain as for a masterpiece, and he picked up many works – even the odd Caravaggio – at bargain prices after they were rejected by the disappointed or shocked patrons who had commissioned them. After a 15-year closure, the gallery reopened in 1998 with decorations and art works fully restored. The imposing entrance salon has fourth-century AD floor mosaics showing gladiators fighting wild animals, and ancient Roman statuary; next to it in Room 1 is one of the Gallery's sculptural highlights, Canova's 1804 figure of Pauline, sister of Napoleon and wife of Prince Camillo Borghese. She is portrayed as a topless Venus; Prince Camillo thought the work so provocative that he forbade even the artist from seeing it after completion (asked by a shocked friend how she could bear to pose naked, the irascible Pauline is said to have snapped: 'the studio was heated').

Rooms 2-4 contain some spectacular sculptures by Bernini, made early in his career but already showing his genius: notice how Pluto's hand presses into Proserpine's marble thigh in *The Rape of Proserpine*. Room 3 houses perhaps his most famous work, *Apollo and Daphne*, showing the nymph fleeing the sun god, her desperate attempt at flight hampered as she turns, fingertips first, into a laurel tree.

Room 5 contains important pieces of classical sculpture, many of them Roman copies of Greek originals. Among the most renowned are a Roman copy of a Greek dancing faun, and a copy of a sleeping hermaphrodite, displayed with his/her back to the onlooker so that the breasts and genitals are invisible. Bernini's *Enea e Anchise* dominates Room 6, while Room 7 contains more classical statues.

In Room 8 are six works by Caravaggio, including *David Holding Aloft the Head of Goliath*, his luscious *Boy with a Basket of Fruit* and an uncanny *Madonna of the Serpent*. His *Sick Bacchus* is believed to be a self-portrait.

The first-floor picture gallery is packed with one masterpiece after another. Look out in particular for: Raphael's *Deposition* and Pinturicchio's *Crucifixion with Saints Jerome and Christopher* (Room 9); Correggio's *Danae*, commissioned as 16th-century soft porn for Charles V of Spain, and Lucas Cranach's *Venus and Cupid with Honeycomb* (Room 10); a dark, brooding *Pietà* by Raphael's follower Sodoma (Room 12); two self-portraits and two sculpted busts of Cardinal Scipione Borghese by Bernini (Room 14); Ruben's spectacular *Pietà* and *Susanna and the Elders* (Room 18); Titian's *Venus Blindfolding Cupid* and the recently restored *Sacred and Profane Love* are the centrepieces of Room 20, which also contains works by Veronese, Giorgione and Carpaccio, and a stunning *Portrait of a Man* by Antonello da Messina.

Galleria Nazionale d'Arte Moderna e Contemporanea

Viale delle Belle Arti 131 (06 323 4000/ www.beniculturali.it/gnam). Bus/tram to viale delle Belle Arti. **Open** 8.30am-7.30pm Tue-Sun; ticket office closes 6.40pm. **Admission** €6.20/L12,000; €3.10/L6,000 concessions. **No credit cards**. **Map** p322 1C.

Italy's national collection of modern art, housed in a massive neo-classical palace built in 1912, with a recently opened modern wing, covers the 19th and 20th centuries. Italian art of this period is relatively unknown outside the country. Most of what's on display here will make you understand why, but a few works (and the cool, quiet elegance of the gallery itself) make it worth crossing Villa Borghese to take a look. The 19th-century collection contains works by the *macchiaioli*, who used dots of colour to create their paintings. The 20th-century component is stronger, with many works by De Chirico, Carrà, Sironi, Morandi, Marini and others, as well as representatives of movements such as *Arte povera* and the *Transavanguardia*. There's an interesting assortment of works by international artists, among them Klimt, Kandinsky, Cézanne and Henry Moore. The museum has a well-stocked shop and a café-restaurant, the Caffè delle Arti.

Museo Hendrik Christian Andersen

Via Pasquale Stanislao Mancini 20 (06 321 9089/ www.beniculturali.it/gnam). Bus/tram to via Flaminia. **Open** 9am-8pm Tue-Sun; ticket office closes 7.15pm. **Admission** €4.13/L8,000; €2.06/L4,000 concessions. **No credit cards**. **Map** p320 1B.

Sightseeing

Titian's *Sacred and Profane Love* in the **Galleria Borghese.** *See p81*

In a striking art nouveau villa between Villa Giulia (*see p83*) and the river, this offshoot of the Museo Nazionale dell'Arte Moderna (*above*) was the studio-home of Norwegian-American Hendrik Christian Andersen, a man whose artistic ambitions were monumental but whose fans were few. (One notable exception was Henry James who, reportedly, had his eye on the man rather than his works.) Andersen's proto-fascist productions stride manfully across his studio. The terrace bar upstairs is wonderful, and accessible without visiting the museum.

Museo Nazionale di Villa Giulia

Piazzale di Villa Giulia 9 (06 322 6571). Bus/tram to via Flaminia or viale delle Belle Arti. **Open** 8.30am-7.30pm Tue-Sat; 9am-7.30pm Sun; ticket office closes 6.30pm. **Admission** €4.13/L8,000; €2.06/L4,000 concessions. **No credit cards.**
Map p320 1A.

Villa Giulia was built for pleasure-loving Pope Julius III in the mid-16th century and was, like the Borghese Casino across the park, intended for entertainment rather than living in. Extensive gardens and pavilions were laid out by Vignola and Vasari, while Ammannati and Michelangelo both had a hand in the creation of the fountains. The villa was transformed into a museum in 1889, and houses Italy's richest collection of Etruscan art and artefacts. Most of the exhibits here came from tombs: very few Etruscan buildings have survived (*see p280*). A fifth-century BC terracotta relief from a temple pediment from the port of Pyrgi depicts life-size episodes from the Theban cycle, indicating the

Greek presence in Etruscan art. The Faliscan crater, an urn from the fourth century BC, depicts Dawn rising in her chariot, while the Chigi vase features hunting tales from the sixth century BC. Even the jewellery is covered with carved animals, as are the hundreds of miniature vases, pieces of furniture and models of buildings made to accompany the dead to their eternal life. Red, black and white pottery shows scenes of dancing, hunting and more intimate pleasures. The sixth-century BC terracotta *Sarcofago degli Sposi*, presumably made as a tomb for a husband and wife, is adorned with a sculpture of the happy couple reclining on its lid.

In the garden there is a reconstruction of an Etruscan temple. Look out, too, for the frescos in the colonnaded loggia, and the sunken *nymphaeum* (water garden) in the courtyard, decorated with mosaics, fountains and statues. The Santa Cecilia academy presents breathtaking concerts here each summer (*see p248*).

Museo Nazionale di Zoologia

Via Aldrovandi 18 (06 321 6586/ www.comune.roma.it/museozoologia). Bus/tram to via Aldrovandi. **Open** 9am-5pm Tue-Sun.
Admission €2.58/L5,000; free under-18s. **No credit cards. Map** p322 1B.

On the north-east side of the zoo is the Museo di Zoologia, with spanking new sections on animal reproduction, biodiversity and extreme habitats, plus a vast and glorious collection of dusty and moth-eaten stuffed animals in its old wing. Access is possible from via Aldrovandi or from inside the Bioparco (*see p81*).

Via Veneto & the Quartiere Ludovisi

Rome's most famous modern street – officially via Vittorio Veneto – cuts through what was once the heart of the palace and gardens of the Villa Ludovisi, laid out in 1662. It was one of the largest of the princely villas that dotted Rome until the post-Unification Piedmontese influx in the 1870s and '80s, when most were sold off by their aristocratic owners to the new breed of building speculators. Fortunately for Rome, the Villa Borghese, just to the north, was taken over by the state and made into a public park (*see pp79-81*).

Prince Boncompagni Ludovisi (whose surnames have been given to major roads in the vicinity) sold off his glorious estate in 1885, and with the proceeds built a massive palazzo in part of the grounds. Crippled by running costs and the tax bill on the sale of the land, he sold it to Margherita, widow of King Umberto I. The renamed Villa Margherita, halfway down via Veneto, is now the US Embassy.

The area was swiftly built up, immediately acquiring the reputation for luxury that it retained right up until the late 1960s. The area on the hill, known as the Quartiere Ludovisi, largely consists of late 19th-century *palazzi* and villas, and is synonymous with the upper end of the finance and service industries.

Via Veneto itself is lined with major hotels and the headquarters of publishers, banks and insurance companies. With its impersonal expense-account restaurants and unenticing glass-fronted cafés, the broad sweep of via Veneto could be a street in any northern-European business district. The worldwide reputation it acquired in the 1950s was largely due to the enormous American presence at Cinecittà (*see chapter* **Film**). Fellini's 1959 film *La Dolce Vita*, starring the late and much lamented Marcello Mastroianni, consecrated the scene and originated the term *paparazzo*, the surname of a character in the film, who was modelled on the legendary photographer Tazio Secchiaroli (*see p81* **The original pararazzo**).

Nowadays, there is little *vita* on via Veneto, apart from droves of middle-aged visitors. The local tourist industry tries desperately to resurrect the corpse for them. What they get are bimbos on the doorsteps of wildly expensive nightclubs, enticing them in for atrocious floorshows, terrible food and sleazy company.

The lower reaches of via Veneto are home to the eerie church of the **Immacolata Concezione** and to the **Fontana delle Api** (bee fountain), by Bernini. Bees featured on the coat of arms of the Barberini family, from which Bernini's great patron Pope Urban VIII hailed.

L'Immacolata Concezione

Via Vittorio Veneto 27 (06 487 1185). Metro Barberini/bus to piazza Barberini. **Open** *Church* 7am-noon, 3.30-7pm daily. *Crypt* 9am-noon, 3-6pm daily. **Admission** *Crypt* donation expected. **Map** p323 1B.

Commonly known as I Cappuccini (the Capuchins) after the long-bearded, brown-clad Franciscan sub-order to which it belongs, this baroque church at the foot of via Veneto has a *St Michael* (1635) by Reni (first chapel on the right) that was a major hit with English Grand Tourists, and a fine rendition of *St Paul's Sight Being Restored* (1631) by Pietro da Cortona (first chapel on the left). Its real attraction, though, lies below in the crypt, where the dry bones of generations of monks have been removed from the order's short supply of soil from Jerusalem and attractively arranged in swirls, sunbursts and curlicues all over the walls, as a reminder (as a notice states) that 'you will be what we now are'.

Piazza Sallustio & Porta Pia

East of Villa Borghese, street after street of imposing late 19th-century *palazzi* cover what was ancient Rome's greatest garden, the Horti Sallustiani. Originally owned by Julius Caesar, this property, with its swathes of statues and huge villa that occupied the valley between the **Quirinale** (*see p77*) and the **Pincio** (*see p80*) hills, was home to the historian Sallust before passing once again into imperial hands, to be lived in by Nero, Vespasian and Nerva. The Goths rampaged through it as they invaded Rome in 410, but enough was left for Renaissance writers to dwell on its clumps of picturesque ruins. The only ruins visible now are in piazza Sallustio, where a hole in the middle of the square contains sufficient masonry to give an idea of lost grandeur (entry by appointment only; *see p60*). Statues found in the gardens include the *Dying Gaul* (*see p62*) and the *Ludovisi Throne* (*see p95*).

Further east, the internal façade of the **Porta Pia** (by the British embassy, a sadly out-of-place modern construction, was designed by Michelangelo.

If the breach which plagues British school children is the one Henry V urged his troops unto once more, Italian kids have the *breccia* (breach) *di Porta Pia* hammered into them: it was by this monumental entrance gate into Rome that a hole was blown, allowing Unification troops to flood through, march along what is now via XX Settembre, and evict the pope from his final stronghold in the Quirinale Palace.

The Tridente

Designer togs and high-street fashion, an ancient altar and an English village church, Caravaggio and bohemian daubers.

Via del Corso shoots down from **piazza del Popolo** (*see p89*) to **piazza Venezia** (*see p61*), jammed with traffic and hemmed in by clothes shops, shoe shops and banks. It forms the central prong of three streets (the others are **via del Babuino** and **via Ripetta**) known, for reasons that are obvious from any map, as Il Tridente.

In Rome's earliest days, this flat expanse – stretching all the way to the Capitoline (*see p61*) – was the Campus Martius, reserved for military training and horse races. Only thinly populated until the 15th century, it later housed communities of foreign traders. Its current three-pronged layout was commissioned under Pope Leo X in the early 16th century.

Via del Babuino & piazza di Spagna

The most famous piazza in the area, the **piazza di Spagna** (*see p86*), was at the centre of what 18th-century Romans called the *ghetto de l'inglesi* (the English ghetto), despite having its fair share of Grand Tourists from all over Europe (to Romans, all foreigners were English, and all equally fleeceable). The whole area was given over to sheep and ruins until Pope Sixtus V (1585-90) subjected it to a touch of his favourite hobby, town planning (*see p28*). Nowadays, the piazza has lost little of its charm, despite the fact that since its metro stop opened in the 1980s it has become a favourite hangout for suburban youths, who fill the square and the **Spanish Steps** above it, importuning foreign females.

The grid of streets below the piazza di Spagna is home to the latest creations of the best-known Italian designers, with **via Condotti** still unchallenged as the city's chic-est shopping thoroughfare: during the week well-heeled Romans browse in Armani, Gucci and Bulgari and crowds of Japanese visitors queue patiently to enter Prada and Louis Vuitton. The Spagna district also has relics of the Rome of the original Grand Tourists. You can still have coffee at the **Caffè Greco** (*see p194*) – where clients have included Casanova and mad King Ludwig of Bavaria – or a cuppa at Babington's Tea Rooms, set up by two

Victorian spinsters, or visit the **Keats-Shelley Memorial House**, where the poet died of consumption and a broken heart; the apartment right above Keats's can be rented.

Leading out of piazza di Spagna to the north-west is **via del Babuino**, once home to artists and composers such as Poussin and Wagner and now lined with serious antique and opulent interior design shops. The street is named after a statue that was considered so ugly it was named 'the baboon'. The statue is close to the incongruously neo-Gothic **All Saint's** church, designed by the English architect GE Street and looking for all the world like a stray from an English village – an impression confirmed by the tea and biscuits served in the garden at the back on sunny Sundays.

Tucked in beside via del Babuino is **via Margutta**, synonymous with the bohemian art boom of the 1950s and '60s and with Rome's great mythologist Federico Fellini, who lived here until his death in 1993. Some modern art can be seen at the **Galleria Comunale d'Arte Moderna e Contemporanea** (*see below*) south of piazza di Spagna.

Galleria Comunale d'Arte Moderna e Contemporanea

Via Francesco Crispi, 24 (06 474 2848). Metro Barberini or Spagna/bus to via del Tritone. **Open** 10am-1.30pm, 2.30-6pm Tue-Sat; 9.30am-1pm Sun. **Admission** €2.60/L5,000; €1.30/L3,000 concessions. **No credit cards. Map** p323 1C.
Somewhat directionless since the opening of the contemporary art centre in the old Peroni brewery (*see p151*), this small gallery continues to show part of the city's permanent collection, which contains works by Rodin, De Pisis, Morandi, Guttuso, Afro and Capogrossi.

Keats-Shelley Memorial House

Piazza di Spagna, 26 (06 678 4235). Metro Spagna/bus to piazza San Silvestro. **Open** 9am-1pm, 3-6pm Mon-Fri; 11am-2pm, 3-6pm Sat. **Admission** €2.60/L5,000. **No credit cards. Map** p323 1C.
The house at the bottom of the Spanish Steps where the 25-year-old John Keats died of tuberculosis in 1821 is crammed with mementos: a lock of Keats' hair and his death mask, a minuscule urn holding tiny pieces of Shelley's charred skeleton, copies of documents and letters, and a massive library make this a Romantic enthusiast's paradise. Devotees should also make the pilgrimage to the Cimitero Acattolico (Protestant

Sightseeing

Cemetery, *see p121*) in Testaccio, where both Keats and Shelley are buried. The apartment above the Keats-Shelley House can be rented for holidays, through the Landmark Trust (UK 0162 882 5925/ bookings@landmarktrust.co.uk).

Piazza di Spagna & Spanish Steps

Metro Spagna/bus to piazza San Silvestro.
Map p323 1C.

Piazza di Spagna has been a compulsory stop for visitors to Rome ever since the 18th century, when a host of poets and musicians stayed nearby. The square takes its name from the Spanish Embassy to the Vatican, which has been here for several centuries, but is better known for the Spanish Steps (Scalinata di Trinità dei Monti), the elegant staircase that cascades down from the church of Trinità dei Monti. In fact, the steps could more accurately be called 'French', having been funded by French diplomat Etienne Gueffier, who felt that the muddy slope leading up to the church – itself built with money provided by a French king – needed a revamp. The stairs were completed in 1725. At Christmas a crib is erected halfway up; in spring and summer, the steps are adorned with huge tubs of azaleas for the fashion shows held here (*see p225*). At the foot of the stairs is a delightful boat-shaped fountain, designed in 1627 by either Gian Lorenzo Bernini or perhaps his less famous father Pietro; it's ingeniously sunk below ground level to compensate for the low pressure of the delicious Acqua Vergine that feeds it.

Via del Corso & piazza del Popolo

Via del Corso is the last urban stretch of the ancient via Flaminia, which linked Rome with the north Adriatic coast. Over the past 2,000 years it has been successively a processional route for Roman legions, a country lane, a track for *carnevale* races and, from the late 19th century, a showcase principal street for the capital.

The street's liveliest period began in the mid-15th century, when Pope Paul II began to fret over the debauched goings-on at the pre-Lenten *carnevale* celebrations in Testaccio. He decided to transfer the races and processions to somewhere more central, where he and his troops could keep an eye on things. The obvious spot was the via Flaminia – then known simply as via Lata, or 'wide street' – at the end of which he built his new Palazzo Venezia (*see p63*). He had the street paved (using funds from a tax on prostitutes) and renamed Il Corso (the avenue). For over four centuries Romans flocked there at *carnevale* time to be entertained by such edifying spectacles as races between press-ganged Jews, hunchbacks, prostitutes, and horses with hot pitch up their recta to make them run faster.

In the footsteps of Keats and Shelley on the **Spanish Steps**.

These grotesqueries only stopped after Italian Unification in the 1870s, when the new national government set up shop halfway along via del Corso. The cheap shops and eateries that lined the street were shut down, to be replaced by pompous neo-classical offices for banks and insurance companies. This set the tone for what remains the country's political heart: the Lower House (Camera dei Deputati) is in **Palazzo di Montecitorio**, in the piazza of the same name, and **Palazzo Chigi**, home of the prime minister's office, is in piazza Colonna, so named for the magnificent second century AD **Colonna di Marco Aurelio** (Column of Marcus Aurelius) that graces it. Legends of Machiavellian wheeler-dealing cling to every restaurant and bar around the parliament building.

North from Palazzo Chigi, imposing edifices such as **Palazzo Ruspoli** give way to lower-end clothing outlets, which, at weekends, attract a seething mass of teenagers from the suburbs. The recently pedestrianised **piazza San Lorenzo in Lucina**, with the church of the same name, is a welcome retreat from the fumes and crowds.

Beyond the retail crush is the symmetrically elegant **piazza del Popolo**, once the papacy's favourite place for executions – graced by the Caravaggio-packed church of **Santa Maria del Popolo**; now, it's gloriously restored and virtually traffic-free. And though Federico Fellini no longer graces the **Bar Canova** (*see p195*), his spirit hovers above it and its equally famous rival across the way, **Rosati** (*see p196*).

Colonna di Marco Aurelio

Piazza Colonna. Bus to largo Chigi. **Map** p321 1A.
The 30m (100ft) Column of Marcus Aurelius was built between AD 180 and 196 to commemorate the victories on the battlefield of that most intellectual of Roman emperors. Author of the famous *Meditations*, he died while campaigning in 180 (to be replaced by his son Commodus, who was largely forgotten until Ridley Scott resurrected him for his 2000 film *Gladiator*). The reliefs on the column, modelled on the earlier ones on Trajan's Column (*see p71*) in the Imperial Fora, are vivid illustrations of Roman army life. A statue of Marcus Aurelius on top of the column was replaced by one of St Paul in 1589.

Glossary

Amphitheatre (*ancient*) oval open-air theatre
Apse large recess at the high-altar end of a church
Architrave a main beam resting across the top of columns
Atrium (*ancient*) courtyard
Baldacchino canopy supported by columns
Baroque artistic period from the 17th to the 18th century, in which the decorative element became increasingly florid, culminating in the Rococo (*qv*)
Basilica ancient Roman rectangular public building; rectangular Christian church
Campanile bell tower
Caryatid supporting pillar carved in the shape of a woman
Cavea semi-circular step-like seating area in an amphitheatre (*qv*) or theatre (*qv*)
Chiaroscuro painting or drawing technique using no colours, but shades of black, white and grey
Clivus (*ancient*) street on the side of a hill
Cloister exterior courtyard surrounded on all sides by a covered walkway
Confessio crypt beneath a raised altar
Cosmati, cosmatesque mosaic technique using coloured marble chips introduced in the 12th century by the Cosmati family
Cupola dome-shaped roof or ceiling
Cryptoporticus underground corridor
Decumanus (*ancient*) main road, usually running east–west
Domus (*ancient*) Roman city house
Entablature section above a column or row of columns including the frieze and cornice
Exedra (*ancient*) a semi-circular architectural space
Ex-voto an offering given to fulfil a vow; often a small model in silver of the limb/organ/loved one cured as a result of prayer
Gothic architectural and artistic style of the late Middle Ages (from the 12th century), of soaring, pointed arches

Greek cross (*church*) in the shape of a cross with arms of equal length
Insula (*ancient*) a multi-storey city apartment block
Latin cross (*church*) in the shape of a cross with one arm longer than the other
Loggia gallery open on one side
Maiolica fine earthenware with coloured decoration on an opaque white tin glaze
Mithraeum temple, usually underground, to the sun-deity Mithras, god of contracts and loyalty; this Persian cult was very strong in the early Christian era.
Narthex enclosed porch in front of a church
Nave main body of a church; the longest section of a Latin cross church (*qv*)
Necropolis (*ancient*) literally, city of the dead, graveyard
Nymphaeum (*ancient*) a niche containing a spring or pool, dedicated to a nymph; later, a monumental fountain
Palazzo large and/or important building (not necessarily a palace in the traditional English sense)
Pendentives four concave triangular sections on top of piers supporting a dome
Peristyle (*ancient*) temple or court surrounded by columns
Piazza (or *largo*) square
Romanesque architectural style of the early Middle Ages (c500 to 1200), drawing on Roman and Byzantine influences
Sarcophagus (*ancient*) stone or marble coffin
Theatre (*ancient*) semi-circular open-air theatre
Titulus early Christian meeting place (*see p125* **The inconspicuous early Church**)
Transept shorter arms of a Latin cross church (*qv*)
Triclinium (*ancient*) dining room
Triumphal arch arch in front of an apse (*qv*), usually over the high altar
Trompe l'oeil decorative painting effect to make surface appear three-dimensional

Sightseeing

CARMI & UBERTIS DESIGN

Laboratorio Pane Pasticceria *Utensili*

Taste Cioccolato Tè Caffè *Shop*

Abbigliamento

Panetteria Salsamenteria Vineria Ristorante

Tavola Fiori

Pescheria Vineria Ristorante

Scuola di cucina *Eventi*

Per dare più spazio al vostro piacere allarghiamo i nostri confini.

Siamo qui, nella piazza riprogettata, con nuove idee e nuovi luoghi
dove ritrovare sensazioni esclusive.
Gustare, leggere, ascoltare, indossare, ricercare e arredare.
Per dare più gusto ai tuoi desideri.

Piaceri eclusivi. *A Roma*

'*Gusto* Piazza Augusto Imperatore, Roma

Palazzo di Montecitorio

Piazza di Montecitorio (06 67 601/www.senato.it).
Bus to via del Corso or largo Chigi. **Open** 1st Sun of
every month; guided tours (in Italian) 10am-5pm.
Closed Aug. **Admission** free. **Map** p321 1A.

Since 1871 this has been the Lower House of Italy's
parliament, which is why police and barricades
sometimes prevent you from getting anywhere near
its elegantly curving façade. The building was
designed by Bernini in 1650 for Pope Innocent X,
and although much of it has been greatly altered
since, the clock tower, columns and window sills of
rough-hewn stone are his originals. In piazza di
Montecitorio, the tenth-century BC obelisk of
Psammeticus was brought from Heliopolis by
Augustus to act as the gnomon (projecting piece) for
the emperor's great sundial. In a recent refurbishment of the square a sundial of sorts was inlaid into
the cobblestones.

Palazzo Ruspoli –Fondazione Memmo

Via del Corso, 418 (06 6830 7344). Bus to largo
Chigi or piazza San Silvestro. **Open** exhibition
times vary. **Admission** varies with exhibition.
Map p321 1A.

The palace of one of Rome's old noble families is
today used for touring exhibitions of art, photography, archaeology and history. It stays open late
at least one or two nights a week. The basement
rooms often host photo exhibitions, and admission
is sometimes free.

Piazza del Popolo

Metro Flaminio/bus or train to piazzale Flaminio.
Map p320 2A.

For centuries piazza del Popolo was the first
glimpse most travellers got of Rome, for it lies at
the end of the ancient via Flaminia and directly
inside the city's northern gate, the Porta del Popolo.
If Grand Tourists arrived during *carnevale* time,
they were likely to witness condemned criminals
being tortured here for the edification or entertainment of the populace. The piazza was given its
present oval form by Rome's leading neo-classical
architect Giuseppe Valadier in the early 19th
century (*see chapter* **Architecture**); the obelisk in
the centre was brought from Egypt by Augustus
and stood in the Circo Massimo (Circus Maximus,
see p66) until 1589, when it was moved to its
present site by Pope Sixtus V. It appears to stand
at the apex of a perfect triangle formed by via di
Ripetta, via del Corso and via del Babuino, although
this is an illusion. The churches on either side of via
del Corso – **Santa Maria dei Miracoli** and **Santa
Maria di Monte Santo** – appear to be twins, but
are actually different sizes. Carlo Rainaldi, who
designed them in the 1660s, made them and the
angles of the adjacent streets appear symmetrical
by giving one an oval dome, and the other a round
one. The immense **Porta del Popolo** gate was
given a facelift by Bernini in 1655 to welcome
Sweden's Queen Christina, who had shocked her

Santa Maria del Popolo. *See p91.*

subjects by abdicating her throne to become a
Catholic. The plaque wishing *felice fausto ingressui*
(a happy and blessed arrival) was addressed to the
Church's illustrious new signing. The piazza's
greatest monument, though, is the church of **Santa
Maria del Popolo** (*see p91*). In the piazza itself
are the eternally fashionable meeting points, the
Rosati and **Canova** cafés (*see p196, p195*).

San Lorenzo in Lucina

Piazza San Lorenzo in Lucina, 16A (06 687 1494).
Bus to largo Chigi or piazza Augusto Imperatore.
Open *Church* 9am-noon, 4.30-7.30pm daily. *Roman*
remains guided tour 4.30pm last Sat of each month;
other Sats by appointment for groups of 15 or more.
Admission *Roman remains* €1.30/L3,000. **Map**
p321 1A.

This 12th-century church was built on the site of an
early Christian place of worship, which in turn is
believed to stand on the site of an ancient well
sacred to Juno. A guided tour of the lower levels
takes place on the last Saturday of the month. The
church's exterior incorporates Roman columns,
while the 17th-century interior contains a wealth of
treasures including Bernini portrait busts in the
Fonseca Chapel, a kitsch 17th-century *Crucifixion*
by Guido Reni, and a monument to French artist
Nicolas Poussin, who died in Rome in 1665. In the
first chapel on the right is an ancient grill, reputed
to be the one on which the martyr St Lawrence was
roasted to death.

**Piazza del
Popolo.**
See p89.

Santa Maria del Popolo

Piazza del Popolo, 12 (06 361 0836). Metro Flaminio/bus to piazzale Flaminio. **Open** 7am-noon, 4-7pm Mon-Sat; 8am-1.30pm, 4.30-7.30pm Sun. **Map** p320 2A.

According to legend, Santa Maria del Popolo occupies the site of a garden in which Nero's nurse and mistress secretly buried the hated emperor's corpse. A thousand years later the site was still believed to be haunted by demons, and in 1099 Pope Paschal II built a chapel there to dispel them. Nearly four centuries later, beginning in 1472, Pope Sixtus IV rebuilt the chapel as a church, financing it by taxing foreign churches and selling ecclesiastical jobs.

In the apse are Rome's first stained-glass windows, created by French artist Guillaume de Marcillat in 1509. The apse itself was designed by Bramante, the Chigi Chapel by Raphael, and the choir ceiling and two of the chapels in the right aisle (first and third) were frescoed by Pinturicchio, the favourite artist of the Borgias. In Pinturicchio's exquisite works, the Virgin and a host of saints keep company with some very pre-Christian sybils. Most intriguing is the Chigi Chapel, designed by Raphael for Agostino Chigi. The mosaics in the dome depict God creating the sun and the seven planets, and Agostino's personal horoscope: with binoculars, you can just about make out a crab, a bull, a lion and a pair of scales. The chapel was completed by Bernini, who, on the orders of Agostino's descendant Pope Alexander VII, added the two theatrical statues of Daniel and Habakkuk. The church's most-gawped-at possessions, however, are the two masterpieces by Caravaggio in the Cerasi Chapel, to the left of the main altar. On a vast scale, and suffused with lashings of the master's own particular light, they show the stories of St Peter and St Paul. Note, also, the bizarre memorial of 17th-century notable GB Gisleni, left of the main door: grisly skeletons, chrysalids and butterflies remind us of our brief passage through this life before we exit the other end.

Via Ripetta

Halfway down the third arm of the Tridente, via Ripetta, is the emphatic piazza Augusto Imperatore, built by Mussolini around the rather neglected **Mausoleo di Augusto** – the family funeral-mound of the Emperor Augustus – with the intention of having himself buried there with the Caesars. Above is the **Ara Pacis Augustae**, erected by Augustus to celebrate peace in the Mediterranean after his conquest of Gaul and Spain.

South of the square stand two fine churches: **San Girolamo degli Illirici**, serving Rome's Croatian community, and **San Rocco**, built for local innkeepers and Tiber boatmen by Alexander VI (1492-1503). Heading back towards via del Corso, the giant, curving walls of the **Palazzo Borghese** come into view;

acquired in 1506 by Camillo Borghese, the future pope Paul V, it was later the home of Napoleon's sister Pauline.

Ara Pacis Augustae

Via di Ripetta/lungotevere in Augusta (06 3600 3471/www.comune.roma.it/arapacis). Bus to piazza Augusto Imperatore. Closed for restoration until spring 2002. **Map** p320 2A.

Currently at the centre of whirlwind building activity, the Ara Pacis, or altar of peace, is one of the most artistically distinguished monuments of ancient Rome. It was inaugurated in 9 BC to celebrate the wealth and security that Augustus's victories in Spain and Gaul had brought to the Empire. Originally located near piazza San Lorenzo in Lucina, the altar was rebuilt on this site in the early 20th century, from ancient fragments amassed through a fiendishly long and difficult excavation and a trawl through various museums. The altar itself sits in an enclosure carved with delicately realistic reliefs. The lower band of the frieze is decorated with a relief of swirling acanthus leaves and swans with outstretched wings; the upper band shows a procession, thought to depict the ceremonies surrounding the dedication of the altar. The carved faces of Augustus and his family have all been identified.

At the time of writing the Ara Pacis had disappeared under scaffolding; it is due to re-emerge in spring 2002 with an enlarged pavilion and exhibition space for showing Ara-related artefacts. The enlarged space has been designed by American architect Richard Meier. The road outside will be pedestrianised, and a garden created to link the Ara Pacis museum with the Mausoleo di Augusto (*see below*).

Mausoleo di Augusto

Piazza Augusto Imperatore/via di Ripetta. Bus to piazza Augusto Imperatore. **Open** with prior permission only (*see p60*). **Map** p320 2A.

It's hard to believe this forlorn-looking brick cylinder was one of the most important monuments of ancient Rome – the Mausoleum of Augustus. It was originally covered with marble pillars and statues, all of which have long since been looted. Two obelisks that stood either side of the main entrance are now in the piazza del Quirinale (*see p77*) and piazza dell'Esquilino. The mausoleum was built in honour of Augustus, who had brought peace to the city and its Empire, and begun in 28 BC. The first person buried here was Augustus's nephew, favourite son-in-law and probable successor, Marcellus, also commemorated in the Teatro di Marcello (*see p109*). He died young in 23 BC. Augustus himself was laid to rest in the central chamber on his death in AD 14, and many more early Caesars went on to join him. In the Middle Ages the mausoleum was used as a fortress, and later hosted concerts, but Mussolini had it restored, reportedly because he thought it a fitting place for his own illustrious corpse. He also planted the cedars and built the Fascist-classical-style square that now surrounds the tomb.

The Pantheon & Piazza Navona

The teeming heart of the *centro storico* has grand squares, art-packed churches and a café scene second to none.

The tightly knit web of narrow streets and *piazze* on the right bank of the river Tiber forms the core of Rome's *centro storico* (historic centre). By day its small shops, markets, craft workshops; by night it's the turn of the clubs, bars – and the restaurants again.

There are sharp social and economic contrasts here. In ancient cobbled streets off **via dei Banchi Nuovi** and **via del Governo Vecchio**, dingy motorcycle repair shops spill out onto pavements shared with chic lunchtime cafés, and exclusive boutiques stand cheek-by-jowl with grubby-looking junk shops. The inhabitants are also a mixed bunch: down-at-heel pensioners still shuffle among the fur-coated occupants of smart apartments that have been carved out of patrician *palazzi*.

In ancient times, much of the area was quite thinly populated, and a large section of it to the north was kept empty as the Campus Martius, the training ground reserved for games and exercises to keep Romans ready for war. The area was built up from the Dark Ages onwards under papal rule.

From via de' Coronari to corso Vittorio

The inhabitants of the *centro* have been making a living out of tourists for centuries. **Via de' Coronari** is now home to some of the old centre's showiest antique shops, but it started out in the 15th century as the via Recta (straight street), designed to ferry pilgrims to the Vatican quickly with their money-bags intact. However, within a few years rosary-makers (*coronari*), ancestors of modern souvenir-sellers, had taken over the street and were making a killing out of the passing trade.

By the high Renaissance there were over two dozen banks, hundreds of hotels and numerous courtesans in the area, servicing the financial and physical needs of visiting ecclesiastics, pilgrims and merchants. Survivors of the era include the 16th-century Banco di Santo Spirito

in the street of the same name, which was originally home to the papal mint.

At night the whole area is chaotic, with obsessive to-ing and fro-ing between *pizzerie*, *trattorie*, *gelaterie* and bars. The most popular area for nightlife lies south of the eastern end of via de' Coronari, and is known as il *triangolo della Pace* after the eternally fashionable **Bar della Pace** (*see p196*) on via della Pace. Smartly dressed Romans gather to drink, meet or pose in and around the bars along these narrow cobbled streets leading to the exquisite church of **Santa Maria della Pace**. Others get bottles of beer from cheap bars and hang out on the fringes.

In the 1880s **corso Vittorio Emanuele** (more commonly known as corso Vittorio) was driven through the area, carving what is now a heavily trafficked and grimy fast-track to St Peter's past historic churches – including the **Chiesa Nuova** – and *palazzi* such as the grimy but stately **Palazzo Massimo alle Colonne**.

Chiesa Nuova/ Santa Maria in Vallicella

Piazza della Chiesa Nuova (06 687 5289). Bus to corso Vittorio Emanuele. **Open** 8am-noon, 4.30-7pm daily. **Map** p321 2B.

Filippo Neri (1515-1595) was a Florentine businessman who gave up his career to live and work among the poor in Rome. He was a personable character, who danced on church altars and played practical jokes on priests, and became one of the most popular figures in the city, his fame helped along by a miracle or two. He founded the Oratorian Order to continue his mission. Work began on the Chiesa Nuova, the order's headquarters, in 1575, with funds raised by his followers. Neri wanted a large and simple building, but after his death the whitewashed walls were covered with exuberant frescoes and multi-coloured marbles. Pietro da Cortona painted *Neri's Vision of the Virgin* (1664-5) in the vault, the *Trinity in Glory* (1647) in the cupola and the *Assumption of the Virgin* (1650) in the apse; Rubens contributed three paintings, the *Virgin and Child* (1607) over the altar, and *Sts Gregory* and *Domitilla*, right and left respectively of the main altar (1607-8). The result is one of the

Rome's great baroque theatre, **piazza Navona**.

most satisfying church interiors in Rome. The body of Neri, canonised in 1622, lies in a chapel ornately decorated with marble to the left of the main altar; his rooms are open to the public on 26 May, his feast day. Singing was an important part of Oratorian worship, and oratory as a musical form developed out of the order's services. Next to the church, Borromini designed the fine Oratorio dei Filippini, which is still used for concerts.

Palazzo Massimo alle Colonne

Corso Vittorio Emanuele 141 (06 6880 1545). Bus to corso Vittorio Emanuele. **Open** 8am-1pm, 16 March only. **Map** p321 2A-B.

The aristocratic Massimo family is one of the city's oldest, claiming to trace descent from ancient Rome. When its palace was built in the 1530s by Baldassare Peruzzi, the unique design – curved walls with a portico built into the bend of the road that follows the stands of the ancient Stadium of Domitian (*see* piazza Navona, *p96*) – aroused suitable admiration. The interior is only open to the public on one day each year, 16 March, in commemoration of the day in 1583 when a young Massimo was allegedly raised from the dead by St Filippo Neri. At the rear of the palace is the piazza de' Massimi, dominated by an ancient column originally from the circus.

Santa Maria della Pace

Vicolo del Arco della Pace 5 (06 686 1156). Bus to corso Rinascimento. **Open** 10am-noon, 4-6pm Tue-Sat; 9-11am Sun. **Map** p321 2B.

As the front door is usually locked, you're likely to enter this church via a simple, beautifully harmonious cloister by Bramante, his first work after arriving in Rome in the early 1500s. The church itself was built in 1482 for Pope Sixtus IV, while the theatrical baroque façade was added by Pietro da Cortona in 1656. The church's most famous artwork is Raphael's *Sybils*, just inside the door. It was painted in 1514 for Agostino Chigi, the playboy banker and first owner of the Villa Farnesina (*see p115*). Bramante's cloister, on the other hand, is likely to be filled with exhibitions of works by contemporary artists.

Piazza Navona

The *centro*'s squares may have venerable histories and architecture, but they share the area's endearingly self-deprecating character, providing magnificent sets for the less-than-grandiose happenings of everyday life. Pride of place has to go to the great theatre of baroque Rome, **piazza Navona**. For all its gracious sweep, with Bernini's fountains, Borromini's church of **Sant'Agnese in Agone** and salubrious pavement cafés, its denizens nevertheless range from soothsayers, caricature artists, buskers and suburban smoothies to tourists, nuns, businessmen, ladies of leisure and anyone who simply wants a gossip or an ice-cream.

At the south-western end of piazza Navona, in little **piazza Pasquino**, stands the patron of the city's scandalmongers, a severely truncated classical statue lodged against one wall. Placed here in 1501, it is known as Pasquino, supposedly after a tailor who had his shop in the piazza and did work for the Vatican. The loose-tongued Pasquino become famous for regaling his mates with insider gossip. He left some of his best stories and lampoons pinned to the statue, and when other people joined in,

The Drunken Ship

The Original American Bar
in the heart of Rome
P.zza Campo De Fiori 20/21
Tel. 06.68300535
www.drunkenship.com
Open 7 days a week
Hours 5:00 pm - 2:00 am

YOU NEVER KNOW WHAT CAN HAPPEN TO YOU AT THE SHIP

Happy Hours
EVERYDAY
from 5:00 pm to 9:00 pm

Outdoor seating

Student Discounts, free entrance
Surprise specials all week long

We accept all major credit cards

THE BEST DJs EVERY NIGHT GET A SHIP T-SHIRT SHOT GLASS or HAT

Sloppy Sam's Bar & Grill
Rome

American sports bar
P.zza Campo De Fiori 9/10 - Rome - Italy
Tel. 06.68802637 - www.sloppysams.com

Open 7 days a week - 365 days a year
Hours from 4:00 pm - 2:00 am

Outdoor seating, frozen cocktails smooth
& easy atmosphere in the afternoon, crazy partying
at night with fun people in the
historical center

Happy Hours
EVERYDAY
from 4:00 pm to 9:00 pm

We have chicken wings - nachos supreme - potate
vegetable platter with blue cheese dip - cheese
super sampler - jumbo sandw

Daily specials & student disc
starting from 9:00 pm - 2

Best Music in Rome

We show all m
sporting ev

Come and join us
for the fun!
We accept all major
credit cards

Velazquez's *Innocent X* in the **Galleria Doria Pamphili**. *See p97.*

it became the Renaissance equivalent of a satirical magazine. Scurrilous and libellous verses, called *pasquinate* and usually targeted at the aristocratic and ecclesiastical establishment, were attached to the statue anonymously to be read by all. In papal Rome, this was just about the only channel of free speech. In time, Pasquino gained correspondents, as the lampoons carried on the statue were 'answered' by others. He also engaged in dialogues with other 'talking statues' such as Madame Lucrezia (in piazza Venezia), Luigi Abate (next to Sant'Andrea della Valle, *see p104*) and Marforio (the river god in the Palazzo Nuovo courtyard of the Musei Capitolini (Capitoline Museums, *see p62*). Barbed prose is still to be found tacked there today.

In an attraction-packed area to the north of piazza Navona are **Palazzo Altemps**, with its spectacular collection of antique statuary, the church of **Sant'Agostino**, with its Caravaggio masterpiece, and the **Museo Napoleonico**. On via dell'Orso, a street that during the Renaissance was inhabited mainly by upmarket courtesans, the Osteria dell'Orso (due to reopen in 2001 as a very chic restaurant) has been an eaterie since the 15th century.

East from the piazza, the Senate building – **Palazzo Madama** – is flanked by the church of **San Luigi dei Francesi** with yet more Caravaggios, and Borromini's extraordinary **Sant'Ivo alla Sapienza**.

Museo Napoleonico

Piazza Ponte Umberto I° 1 (06 6880 6286). Bus to corso Rinascimento. **Open** 9am-7pm Tue-Sat; 9am-2pm Sun. **Admission** €2.58/L5,000; €1.55/L3,000 concessions. **No credit cards. Map** p321 1B.

Although Napoleon spent only a short time in Rome, other members of his family, including his mother Letizia and sister Pauline, settled here. This collection of art and memorabilia relating (sometimes tenuously) to the family was left to the city in 1927 by Napoleon's last descendants, the Counts Primoli. The museum has been restored and redecorated in keeping with an aristocratic palazzo of the early 19th century. You will find portraits of family members, including one by David of Napoleon's sister Charlotte, alongside uniforms, other clothes and some of Canova's studies for the infamous sculpture of Pauline (now on show at the Galleria Borghese, *see p81*), including a cast of her right breast.

Museo Nazionale Romano – Palazzo Altemps

Piazza Sant'Apollinare 46 (06 683 3566). Bus to corso Rinascimento. **Open** 9am-7.45pm Tue-Sun; ticket office closes 7pm. **Admission** €5.16/L10,000; €2.58/L5,000 concessions; *see also p60* **Tickets. No credit cards. Map** p321 1A-B.

The 15th- to 16th-century Palazzo Altemps, just north of piazza Navona, has been beautifully restored to house part of the state-owned stock of Roman treasures (the rest is spread between Palazzo Massimo alle Terme, *see p137,* and the Terme di Diocleziano, *see p135*). Here, in perfectly lit salons, loggias and courtyards, you can admire gems of classical statuary originally in the private Boncompagni-Ludovisi, Altemps and Mattei collections.

The Ludovisis were great ones for having contemporary artists re-do bits of statues that had dropped off over the ages, or simply didn't appeal to the tastes of the day, as copious notes (in English) by each work explain. In Room 9, for example, is a stately *Athena with Serpent*, revamped in the 17th century by Alessandro Algardi, who also had a hand in 'improving' the *Hermes Loghios* in Room 19 upstairs. In Room 20, the former dining room with pretty 15th-century frescoes on foody themes, is an *Ares* touched up by Bernini. Room 21 has the museum's greatest treasure – or greatest hoax, if you subscribe to the theory of the late, great art historian and polemicist Federico Zeri – the 'Ludovisi throne'. On what may or may not be a fifth century BC work from Magna Grecia (Zeri insisted it was a clumsy 19th-century copy of an original now in Boston), Aphrodite is being delicately and modestly lifted out of the sea spray from which she was born; on one side of her is a serious lady burning incense, and on the other is a naked one playing the flute. In Room 26 there is a Roman copy of a Greek *Gaul's Suicide*, which was commissioned, recent research has suggested, by Julius Caesar; also here is the Ludovisi sarcophagus, with some action-packed

Sightseeing

high-relief depictions of Roman soldiers thoroughly trouncing barbarians. Room 34 has a graceful *Bathing Aphrodite*, an Imperial Roman copy of a Greek bronze dating from the third century BC.

Piazza Navona

Bus to corso Vittorio Emanuele or corso Rinascimento. **Map** p321 2A-B.

This tremendous theatrical oval, dominated by the gleaming marble composition of Bernini's **Fontana dei Quattro Fiumi**, is the hub of the *centro storico*. The piazza owes its shape to an ancient stadium, built in AD 86 by the Emperor Domitian, which was the scene of at least one martyrdom (St Agnes was thrown to her death here for refusing to marry), as well as sporting events. Just north of the piazza at piazza di Tor Sanguigna 16, you can still see some remains of the original arena, sunk below street level. These remains are partially visible from the street; they can also be visited on guided tours on Saturday and Sunday from 10am-1pm; phone 06 6710 3819 for bookings and information.

The piazza acquired its current form in the mid-17th century. Its western side is dominated by Borromini's façade for the church of **Sant'Agnese in Agone** (*see p96*) and the adjacent Palazzo Pamphili, built for Pope Innocent X in 1644-50. The 'Fountain of the Four Rivers' at the centre of the piazza, finished in 1651, is one of the most extravagant masterpieces designed – though only partly sculpted – by Bernini. Its main figures represent the rivers Ganges, Nile, Danube and Plate, surrounded by geographically appropriate flora and fauna. The figure of the Nile is veiled, as its source was unknown, although for centuries the story went that Bernini designed it that way so the river god appeared to be recoiling in horror from the façade of Sant'Agnese, designed by his arch-rival Borromini. In fact, the church was built after the fountain was finished. The obelisk in its centre came from the Circus of Maxentius on the via Appia Antica (*see p146*). The less spectacular **Fontana del Moro** is at the southern end of the piazza. The central figure (called the Moor, although he looks more like a portly sea god wrestling with a dolphin) was the only part designed by Bernini himself.

Palazzo Madama

Corso Rinascimento (06 67 061/www.senato.it). Bus to corso Rinascimento. **Open** Guided tours only (in Italian) 10am-6pm 1st Sat of the month. **Admission** free. **Map** p321 2A.

Home to the Italian Senate since 1871, this palazzo was built by the Medici family in the 16th century as their Rome residence. Its rather twee façade, with a frieze of cherubs and bunches of fruit, was added a hundred years later. The Madama of its name was Margaret of Parma (1522-86), the illegitimate daughter of Emperor Charles V, who lived here in the 1560s before moving to the Netherlands, where she instigated some of the bloodiest excesses of the religious wars.

Borromini's **Sant'Agnese in Agone**.

San Luigi dei Francesi

Piazza San Luigi dei Francesi (06 688 271). Bus to corso Rinascimento. **Open** 8.30am-12.30pm, 3.30-7pm Mon-Wed, Fri-Sun; 8am-12.30pm Thur. **Map** p321 2A.

Completed in 1589, San Luigi is the church of Rome's French community. That the interior is lavish to the point of gaudiness goes unnoticed by the majority of visitors, who are here for one thing: Caravaggio's spectacular scenes from the life of St Matthew in the fifth chapel on the left. Painted in 1600-02, they depict Christ singling out Matthew (left), Matthew being dragged to his execution (right) and an angel briefing the evangelist about what he should write in his gospel (over the altar). Don't let Caravaggio's brooding brilliance and dramatic effects of light and shade blind you to the lovely frescoes of scenes from the life of St Cecilia by Domenichino (1615-7), in the second chapel on the right.

Sant'Agnese in Agone

Piazza Navona (no phone). Bus to corso Vittorio Emanuele or corso Rinascimento. **Open** 10am-7pm Tue-Sun. **Map** p321 2B.

The virgin martyr Saint Agnes was stripped in public when she refused to abjure Christ, who kindly caused a miraculous growth of hair to cover her embarrassment; the flames of her execution pyre then failed to consume her, so her pagan persecutors lopped her head off, supposedly on the exact spot where the church of Sant'Agnese, the grandest building on piazza Navona, now stands. Sant'Agnese was begun by Carlo and Girolamo Rainaldi for Pope Innocent X in 1652. It was intended to be their masterpiece, but they quarrelled with the pope, and Borromini was appointed in their place. He revised the design considerably, and added the concave façade that is one of his greatest achievements. The *trompe l'œil* interior is typically Borromini, with pillars distributed irregularly to create the illusion that the apses are the same size.

Sant'Agostino

Piazza di Sant'Agostino (06 6880 1962). Bus to corso Rinascimento. **Open** 8am-noon, 4-7.30pm daily. **Map** p321 1A.

This 15th-century church stands on the site of a ninth-century one, and has one of the earliest Renaissance façades in Rome, fashioned out of travertine rock filched from the Colosseum. The third column on the left bears a fresco of Isaiah by Raphael (when its commissioner complained that the artist had charged him too much for the work, Michelangelo is said to have snapped: 'the knee alone is worth that'). Near this is a beautiful sculpture of Mary, her mother Anne and Jesus by Andrea Sansovino. In the first chapel on the left is Caravaggio's depiction of the grubbiest, most threadbare pilgrims ever to present themselves at the feet of the startlingly beautiful *Madonna of the Pilgrims* (1604). So dirty were they, in fact, that the church that originally commissioned the picture refused point blank to have it. The main altar was designed by Bernini, who personally sculpted the two highest angels.

Sant'Ivo alla Sapienza

Corso Rinascimento 40 (06 686 4987). Bus to corso Rinascimento. **Open** 9am-noon Sun. **Map** p321 2A.

Perhaps the most imaginative geometrical design by tortured genius Francesco Borromini, with a concave façade countered by the convex bulk of the dome, which terminates in a bizarre corkscrew spire. The interior is based on a six-pointed star, but the opposition of convex and concave surfaces continues in the floor plan, on the walls and up into the dome, in a dizzying whirl that can bring on an attack of vertigo.

From the Pantheon to via del Corso

Piazza della Rotonda, home to the **Pantheon** (*see p98*), is adorned with a central fountain the steps of which provide an ever-popular hangout for hippies, punks and other counter-cultural varieties. All seem oblivious to the well-heeled tourists paying over the odds for coffee at tables in the square, and to the smell that pervades when the wind blows the wrong way over the square's hamburger joint. South of the Pantheon, piazza della Minerva is home to Rome's only Gothic church, **Santa Maria Sopra Minerva** (*see p99*).

Further east, piazza Collegio Romano contains one of Rome's finest art collections in the **Galleria Doria Pamphili** (*see p97*). The charmingly rococo piazza Sant'Ignazio has a severe Jesuit church, **Sant'Ignazio di Loyola**, while in piazza di Pietra the columns of the **Tempio di Adriano** (Hadrian's Temple) can be seen embedded in the walls of Rome's singularly inactive stock exchange.

The quieter lanes close to via del Corso contain outposts of the Lower House in piazza del Montecitorio; journalists, MPs and assorted hangers-on haunt the area's bars. On the lower reaches of via del Corso is the privately owned **Museo del Corso** exhibition space.

Galleria Doria Pamphili

Piazza del Collegio Romano 2 (06 679 7323/ www.doriapamphilj.it). Bus to piazza Venezia or via del Corso. **Open** 10am-5pm Mon-Wed, Fri-Sun; ticket office closes 4pm. **Admission** *Gallery* €7.23/L14,000; €5.68/L11,000 concessions. *Private apartments* closed indefinitely for restoration. **No credit cards. Map** p321 2A.

One of Rome's finest private art collections, housed in the rambling palace of the Doria Pamphili (also spelt Pamphilj) family, a pillar of Rome's aristocracy now headed by two half-British siblings. For many years the collection was crammed on to the walls of four corridors (Wings 1-4). It has now spilled into other areas of the palace, although the best is definitely still in the gallery proper. A complete overhaul of the palazzo in 1996 restored it, as closely as possible, to the way it was arranged in the 18th century. Among the works on show are a portrait by Raphael of two gentlemen (1500s room), Correggio's unfinished *Allegory of Virtue* (Wing Three), four Titians, including *Religion Succoured by Spain* (Aldobrandini room) and a self-possessed Salome holding the head of John the Baptist (1500s room). Caravaggio is represented by a *Penitent Magdalen* and the early *Rest During the Flight into Egypt* (both in the 1600s room). Of the paintings by Guercino, the martyred *St Agnes* (Wing 3), as she fails to catch light at the stake, stands out. There are also many works by the prolific Guido Reni, darling of the Victorians but rarely to third millennium tastes. The suite of rooms that leads off the far end of Wing 2 houses Italian and some Flemish works, arranged chronologically by century; Wing 4 contains a number of works by Dutch and Flemish artists, including Brueghel. The collection's greatest jewel is arguably the extraordinary portrait by Velázquez of the Pamphili pope Innocent X, displayed in a separate room of Wing 1, alongside a Bernini bust of the same pontiff. Landscapes by Carracci, Claude Lorraine and others are found in Wing 1. In the series of rooms en route to the gallery proper, a spectacular 18th-century ballroom leads into the Yellow Room, with its Gobelin tapestries, and then into a series of elegant rooms beyond. The chapel, by Carlo Fontana (1689), has been repeatedly altered, but has retained its original *trompe l'oeil* painted ceiling.

The private apartments, which also contain important pictures – such as a delicate *Annunciation* by Filippo Lippi, and Sebastiano del Piombo's portrait of the Genoese admiral and patriarch Andrea Doria as Neptune – were closed for restoration at the time of writing.

Still standing: conversion to a church saved the **Pantheon**.

Museo del Corso

Via del Corso 320 (06 678 6209/
www.museodelcorso.it). Bus to via del Corso. **Open**
10am-8pm Tue-Sun. **Admission** varies with
exhibition. **No credit cards. Map** p321 2A.
This privately owned space stages small exhibitions
on artistic, historical and literary themes; the pre-
sentation is often more impressive than the content.
There's also a handy café and internet access point.

Pantheon

Piazza della Rotonda (06 6830 0230). Bus to largo
Argentina or via del Corso/tram to largo Argentina.
Open 9am-7.30pm Mon-Sat; 9am-6pm Sun.
Admission free. **Map** p321 2A.
The Pantheon is the best preserved of the remains
of ancient Rome. It was built by Hadrian in AD 119-
128 as a temple to the 12 most important classical
deities; the inscription on the pediment records an

The **Pantheon**'s portico once held a market.

earlier Pantheon built a hundred years earlier by Augustus's General Marcus Agrippa, which confused historians for centuries. Its fine state of preservation is due to the building's conversion to a Christian church in 608, when it was presented to the Pope by the Byzantine Emperor Phocas. The Pantheon has nevertheless suffered over the years – notably when bronze cladding was stripped from the roof in 667, and when Pope Urban VIII allowed Bernini to remove the remaining bronze from the beams in the portico to melt it down for his *baldacchino* in St Peter's (*see p139*) in the 1620s. The simplicity of the building's exterior, though, remains largely unchanged, and it retains its original Roman bronze doors.

Inside, the key to the Pantheon's extraordinary harmony is its dimensions. The radius of the dome is exactly equal to its height, so it could potentially accommodate a perfect sphere. At the centre of the dome is a circular hole 9m (30ft) in diameter, the oculus, which is the only source of light and a symbolic link between the temple and the heavens. The building is still officially a church, but it's easy to overlook this, in spite of all the paraphernalia added over the years and the tombs of eminent Italians, including the Renaissance artist Raphael and the first king of united Italy, Vittorio Emanuele II. Until the 18th century the portico was used as a market: supports for the stalls were inserted into the notches that can be seen in the stonework of the columns.

Piazza della Minerva & Bernini's Elephant

Bus or tram to largo Argentina. **Map** p321 2A.
The otherwise unremarkable square-cum-car-park of piazza della Minerva is home to *Il Pulcino della Minerva*, aka Bernini's elephant. This cuddly marble animal, with wrinkled bottom and benign expression, has stood here since 1667. It was designed by Bernini as a tribute to Pope Alexander VII; elephants were both a symbol of wisdom and a model of sexual abstinence. They were believed to be monogamous and to mate only once every five years, which, the Church felt, was the way things

should be. The sixth-century BC Egyptian obelisk perched on its back was taken from an ancient temple to the goddess Isis.

Santa Maria sopra Minerva

Piazza della Minerva 42 (06 679 3926). Bus or tram to largo Argentina. **Open** 7am-7.30pm daily. **Map** p321 2A.
This is Rome's only Gothic church, built on the site of an ancient temple of Minerva. The best of its art works are Renaissance: on the right of the transept is the superb Carafa chapel, with late 15th-century frescoes by Filippino Lippi (1457-1504), commissioned by Cardinal Oliviero Carafa in honour of St Thomas Aquinas. Carafa took Renaissance self-assurance to extremes: the altar painting shows him being presented to the Virgin, right at the moment when Gabriel informs her she's going to give birth to Christ. The tomb of the Carafa Pope Paul IV (1555-59) is also in the chapel. He was one of the prime movers of the Counter-Reformation, chiefly remembered for persecuting the Jews and ordering Daniele da Volterra to paint loincloths on the nudes of Michelangelo's *Last Judgment*. A bronze loincloth was also ordered to cover Christ's genitals on a work by Michelangelo here: the statue was finished by Pietro Urbano (1514-21) and depicts a heroic Christ holding up a flimsy cross. An early Renaissance work is the *Madonna and Child*, believed by some to be by Fra Angelico, in the chapel to the left of the altar, close to the artistic monk's own tomb. The father of modern astronomy, Galileo Galilei, who dared suggest in the early 16th century that the earth revolved around the sun and not vice versa, was tried for heresy in the adjoining monastery.

Sant'Ignazio di Loyola

Piazza Sant'Ignazio (06 679 4406). Bus to via del Corso. **Open** 7.30am-12.15pm, 4-7.15pm daily. **Map** p321 2A.
Sant'Ignazio was built to commemorate the canonisation of St Ignatius, founder of the Jesuit order, in 1626. *Trompe l'œil* columns soar above the nave, and architraves by Andrea Pozzo open to a cloudy heaven in which figures are ascending. Trickery was also involved in creating the dome: the Dominican monks next door claimed that a real dome would rob them of light, so, rather than tussle with 17th-century planners, Pozzo simply painted a dome on the inside of the roof. The result is pretty convincing if you stand on the disc embedded in the floor of the nave. Walk away, however, and the illusion collapses.

Tempio di Adriano

Piazza di Pietra. Bus to via del Corso. **Map** p321 2A.
Along the south side of a building in the otherwise unremarkable piazza di Pietra are 11 15m (48ft) high Corinthian columns, now embedded in the grimy wall of Rome's inactive stock exchange. These originally formed part of a temple built to honour Emperor Hadrian (Adriano) by his adopted son, Antoninus Pius, in AD 145.

Sightseeing

The Ghetto & Campo de' Fiori

Homely and workaday, the southern *centro* has markets, schools, and theatrical foundations.

Like the area around the Pantheon and piazza Navona (*see chapter* **Pantheon & Piazza Navona**), much of the southern sector of the *centro storico* stretching from the Amedeo Savoia d'Aosta bridge to the church of **Santa Maria in Cosmedin** (*see p109*) was part of the sparsely populated Campus Martius, set aside for sporting events aimed at keeping Roman manhood war-ready. There was less bellicose entertainment here as well, in the ancient city's three major theatres (*see p104* **Theatres**).

Like the northern *centro*, this area was built up, with little thought for intelligent planning, from the Dark Ages. Here, however, the warren of streets rarely opens out into the kind of grandiose squares found on the other side of corso Vittorio Emanuele, the one notable exception being **piazza Farnese** (*see p103*): even **campo de' Fiori** (*see p101*), large as it is, is homely and workaday; any grandeur that **largo Argentina** (*see p103*) may once have had has succumbed to the onslaught of the internal combustion engine.

The southern *centro* has its abundant share of restaurants and clubs, especially around the campo de' Fiori. But here, the calm, echoing corners are more numerous and the everyday life quotient is higher: picturesque **via Giulia**, for example, with its art galleries and high, ivy-dripping walls, is predominantly a haphazard antechamber and moped-park for the school at its far end; and the **Ghetto** (*see pp105-7*), with its Roman ruins and exquisite fountain, remains a focal point for Rome's Jewish community.

North-west of campo de' Fiori

Between the western end of the traffic-choked corso Vittorio Emanuele and the river, a series of long streets each revel in their very own particular atmosphere: via dei Banchi Vecchi is lined with restaurants and bars; via Monserrato has seminaries; via dei Cappellari (once the haunt of hat – *cappello* – makers) is home to an endless succession of furniture restorers;

elegant via Giulia houses the top end of Rome's antique and gallery fraternity.

Just off corso Vittorio, the Vatican-owned **Palazzo della Cancelleria** is one of the area's most impressive examples of Renaissance architecture; nearby, the **Museo Barracco** has an eclectic collection of ancient bits and bobs.

Museo Barracco di Scultura Antica

Corso Vittorio Emanuele 166 (06 6880 6848). Bus to corso Vittorio Emanuele. **Open** 9am-7pm Tue-Sun. **Admission** €2.58/5,000; €1.55/L3,000 concessions. **No credit cards. Map** p321 2B.

This small collection of mainly pre-Roman art was amassed by Giovanni Barracco in the first half of the 20th century. His interests covered the gamut of ancient art; there are extraordinary Assyrian reliefs, Attic vases, sphinxes, bas-reliefs, and Babylonian stone lions, as well as Roman and Etruscan exhibits and Greek sculptures. Don't miss the copy of the *Wounded Bitch* by Lysippus, on the second floor.

Palazzo della Cancelleria

Piazza della Cancelleria. Bus to corso Vittorio Emanuele. Closed to the public. **Map** p321 2B.

One of the most refined examples of Renaissance architecture in Rome, the Palazzo della Cancelleria was built, possibly by Bramante, between 1483 and 1513 for Raffaele Riario. He was the great-nephew of Pope Sixtus IV, who made him a cardinal at the age of 17, though Raffaele didn't allow his ecclesiastical duties to cramp his style. He is said to have raised a third of the cost of this palace with the winnings of a single night's gambling. He also got involved in plotting against the powerful Florentine Medici family; in retaliation the palace was confiscated for the Church when Giovanni de' Medici became Pope Leo X in 1513. It later became the Papal Chancellery, and is still Vatican property. The fourth-century church of San Lorenzo in Damaso was incorporated into one side of the building.

Campo de' Fiori & largo Argentina

The busy bus stops and tram terminus of **largo Argentina** sit oddly against the expanse of Roman ruins that fills the hole in the centre of the square (complete with cat haven, *see p108*

Caravaggio played tennis, Giordano Bruno went up in smoke in **campo de' Fiori.**

Felix Roma). From here, buses go east along via del Plebiscito past the **Gesù** church or via delle Botteghe Oscure past the **Crypta Balbi**, on their way to piazza Venezia. **Sant' Andrea della Valle**, with Rome's second-tallest dome, is just to the west, on corso Vittorio.

Those traffic arteries are a far cry from what lies to the west of largo Argentina, where narrow, crooked streets carry the names of the trades carried on there in medieval times – via dei Baullari (chest-makers), via dei Barbieri (barbers), and via dei Giubbonari (jerkin-makers) – all of which converge on **campo de' Fiori**. Between the the campo and via Giulia is solemn, operatic **piazza Farnese**, with its twin fountains. Overlooking them is ponderous **Palazzo Farnese**, designed by Michelangelo and now home to the French Embassy. Nearby is pretty **palazzo Spada**, with its **Galleria**.

Campo de' Fiori
Bus to corso Vittorio Emanuele/tram to via Arenula.
Map p321 2B.
Home to Rome's most picturesque – although also most costly – food market in the mornings, campo de' Fiori, known to all simply as Il Campo, is surrounded by tall *palazzi*, many of whose once-worn walls and warped shutters have recently undergone colourful facelifts. The Campo has been a focus of Roman life since the 15th century. Lucrezia Borgia

(*see p12* **Lust, murder & incest**) was born nearby, her brother was murdered down the road, and Caravaggio played a game of tennis on the piazza, after which he murdered his opponent for having the temerity to beat him. The cowled statue in the centre is of Giordano Bruno, burned at the stake on this spot (*dove il rogo arse* 'where the pyre burned', as the inscription reads) in 1600 for reaching the conclusion that philosophy and magic were superior to religion. Any resemblance to Darth Vader is unintentional.

The market begins around 6am and packs up in the early afternoon, when people flow into the Campo's restaurants for lunch. Afternoons are quiet and slow, with things beginning to pick up around 6pm, when the ever-popular Vineria wine bar (*see p198*) opens up. Much to the annoyance of residents, *alternativi* types with flea-bitten dogs, bongo drums and – locals will tell you, bitterly – a flourishing sideline in drug dealing, gather beneath Giordano Bruno as the sun goes down. This, however, doesn't deter the diners who, by 10pm, have filled the restaurants again, nor the wine-sipping crowds that spill out from the bars to invade most of the square.

Galleria Spada
Piazza Capo di Ferro 3 (06 687 4896/www. galleriaborghese.it). Bus to largo Argentina/tram to via Arenula. **Open** 8.30am-7.30pm Tue-Sat; 8.30am-6.30pm Sun. **Admission** €5.16/L10,000; €2.58/L5,000 concessions. *See also p60* **Tickets. No credit cards. Map p324 1B.**

A ROMA
OLTRE 2500
VETTURE SPAZIOSE
MULTIPLE E WAGON
DA PIU' DI 30 ANNI
AL VOSTRO SERVIZIO

Radiotaxi 3570 counts over 2,400 cabs that guarantee quickness and efficiency in all Rome and suburbs.

You can ask, at no extra charge, station wagons, sedans, air conditionating, no smoking cabs or with certification UNI EN ISO 9002, payments POS (bancomat and credit cards).

You just need to dial 06.3570 and you'll be connected to one fo our operators.

Radiotaxi 3570. The town become more easy.
www.3570.it

One of Rome's prettiest palaces, built for Cardinal Girolamo Capo di Ferro in 1540, Palazzo Spada was acquired by Cardinal Bernardino Spada in 1632. Its most famous feature is Borromini's ingenious *trompe l'œil* colonnade in the garden, which is 9m (30ft) long but appears much longer. Today, the palace houses high court offices as well as the art collection of Cardinal Spada, displayed in its original setting. Spada's portrait by his protegé Guido Reni is on show in Room 1. More portraits follow in Room 2, including Titian's wonderful, unfinished *Musician*. Don't miss the wacky-hatted *Cleopatra* by Lavinia Fontana in the same room. Room 3 contains massive, gloomy paintings such as Guercino's *Death of Dido* and Jan Brueghel the Elder's very un-Roman *Landscape with Windmill*, plus a couple of Dutch 17th-century globes. Room 4 has two powerful works by Artemisia Gentileschi – *St Cecilia Playing a Lute* and *Madonna and Child* – along with *Martyrdom of a Saint* by Domenichino. Copious notes in many languages are provided for each room.

Il Gesù

Piazza del Gesù (06 697 001/Loyola's rooms 06 6920 5800). Bus to via del Plebiscito or piazza Venezia. **Open** *Church* 6.30am-12.30pm, 4-7.30pm daily. *Loyola's rooms* 4-6pm Mon-Sat; 10am-noon Sun. **Admission** free. **Map** p324 1A.

The huge Gesù is the principal church of the Jesuits, the order founded by Basque soldier Ignatius Loyola in the 1530s. Realising the power of appealing directly to the emotions, he devised a series of 'spiritual exercises' aimed at training devotees to experience the agony and ecstasy of the saints. The Gesù itself was designed to involve the congregation as closely as possible in the proceedings, with a nave unobstructed by aisles, offering a clear view of the main altar. Work began in 1568, and the façade by Giacomo della Porta was added in 1575. His design was repeated *ad nauseam* on Jesuit churches across Italy (and the world) for decades afterwards. A large, bright fresco by Il Baciccia (1676-79) – one of Rome's great baroque masterpieces – decorates the gilded ceiling of the nave, which seems to dissolve on either side as stucco figures, by Antonio Raggi, and other painted images are sucked up into the dazzling light of the heavens. The figures falling back to earth are presumably Protestants. On the left is another spectacular baroque achievement, the chapel of Sant'Ignazio (1696-1700) by Andrea Pozzo, which is adorned with gold, silver and coloured marble. The statue of St Ignatius is by Antonio Canova. Towering above the altar is what was long believed to be the biggest lump of lapis lazuli in the world. In fact, it's covered concrete. Outside the church, at piazza del Gesù 45, you can visit the rooms of St Ignatius, which contain a wonderful painted corridor with *trompe l'œil* special effects by Pozzo, and mementoes of the saint, including his death mask.

Largo Argentina

Bus or tram to largo Argentina. **Map** p324 1A.

Officially largo di Torre Argentina (nothing to do with the Latin American country; the name refers to a tower – *torre* – in a nearby street, plus the fact that the local diocese was called Argentoratum, a word derived from *argento* – silver), this huge open space is a busy bus and tram junction. Between waiting for one piece of public transport or another, cast an eye into the hole in the middle of the square: there lies Rome's largest expanse of fully excavated Republican-era remains. A narrow warren of streets that stood here was bulldozed in 1885, and then further obliterated in 1926-9, to reveal what is known as the Sacred Area (Area Sacra Argentina). Visible are columns, altars and foundations from one round and three rectangular temples dating from the mid third-century BC to c100 BC. The frescos on the taller brickwork are from the 12th-century church of San Nicola de' Cesarini, which was built into one of the temples here.

Museo Nazionale Romano – Crypta Balbi

Via delle Botteghe Oscure 31 (06 481 5576). Bus to via delle Botteghe Oscure or largo Argentina/tram to largo Argentina. **Open** 9am-7.45pm Tue-Sun; ticket office closes 6.45pm. **Admission** €4.13/L8,000; €2.06/L4,000 concessions. *See also p60* **Tickets**. **No credit cards**. **Map** p324 1A.

In 1981, digging began in a down-at-heel city block on the northern fringe of the Ghetto, on what had been the southern fringes of the ancient Campus Martius. What was found went on show in 2000, in one of the most fascinating of Rome's new archaeological offerings. As well as being a sight in itself, the *crypta* (a large lobby) of the ancient Teatro di Balbo (*see p104* **Theatres**) hosts displays documenting the changing faces of the palimpsest that is Rome: how accumulated detritus raised the street level, how the ancient fabric was incorporated into the medieval and modern city. There's a particularly rich section on Rome from the fall of the Empire in the fifth century until the tenth century.

Palazzo Farnese

Piazza Farnese (06 687 4834). Bus to corso Vittorio Emanuele. Closed to the public. **Map** p324 1B.

This palazzo has housed the French Embassy since the 1870s and is not generally open to the public, but guided tours can sometimes be arranged by appointment (preference is given to art historians). Considered by many to be the finest Renaissance palace in Rome, the huge building – recently and dramatically restored – was begun for Cardinal Alessandro Farnese (later Pope Paul III) in 1514 by Antonio da Sangallo the Younger. Sangallo died before it was completed, and in 1546 Michelangelo took over. He was responsible for most of the upper storeys and the grand cornice along the roof. After his death the building was completed by Giacomo della Porta. Inside it has superb frescos by Annibale Carracci.

Sightseeing

Theatres

Where entertainment was concerned, the ancient Romans were a crude lot, far preferring the blood and gore of gladiatorial games to the lofty erudition of Greek drama. Mime and buffoonery were the order of the day: so lowly were the spectacles on offer (and so difficult to exploit for political ends, unlike the bread-and-circuses fare on offer at the Colosseum, *see p66*, and other larger stadia) that the Senate banned the building of permanent theatres inside the city walls until the late Republic.

Temporary wooden stages were set up in the Campus Martius (*see p100*), which was also where Pompey opted to build the first permanent stone theatre in 55BC. The outlines of the **Teatro di Pompeo** can be seen in the streets around campo de' Fiori: via di Grottapinta follows the curve of the *cavea* (semi-circular seating area) while via dei Chiavari and piazza dei Satiri mark where the stage stood; beyond this, stretching to largo Argentina, was the theatre's huge portico, where the unfortunate Julius Caesar met his end – somewhere near via Monte della Farina – on 15 March, 44 BC.

It was Augustus who made theatres more respectable after coming to power in 31 BC. Not only did he have one built himself, dedicating it in 11 BC to his favourite nephew Marcellus (see p109, Teatro di Marcello), but he convinced his friend Lucius Cornelius

Balbus, a Spaniard from Cadiz, to construct another nearby, at Crypta Balbi (*see p103*). With a diametre of 90 metres (315 feet), the Teatro di Balbo was the smallest of Rome's theatres, but also the most richly decorated. It was inaugurated in AD 13.

Piazza Farnese
Bus to corso Vittorio Emanuele. **Map** p324 1B.
Serene, elegant and dominated by the refined façade of Michelangelo's Palazzo Farnese, this piazza is a world away from the bustle of adjacent campo de' Fiori. It's uncluttered save for its two fountains, created in the 17th century out of granite tubs from the Terme (Baths) of Caracalla (*see p126*) and topped with lilies – the Farnese family emblem. The square is most atmospheric at night, when the palace is lit up and chandeliers inside are switched on to reveal ceilings with sumptuous frescos.

Sant'Andrea della Valle
Corso Vittorio Emanuele 6 (06 686 1339). Bus to corso Vittorio Emanuele. **Open** 8am-noon, 4.30-7pm daily. **Map** p324 1B.
On corso Vittorio Emanuele between the Campo and largo Argentina, Sant'Andrea was originally designed by Giacomo della Porta for the Theatine order in 1524, but the church's façade and dizzyingly frescoed dome both date from about a century later, when the Church was in a far more flamboyant frame of mind. The dome, by Carlo Maderno, is the

second largest in Rome after St Peter's. Giovanni Lanfranco nearly died while painting the dome fresco – allegedly because his rival Domenichino had sabotaged the scaffolding on which he was working. Puccini set the opening act of *Tosca* in the first chapel on the left inside the church.

The Ghetto

Rome's Jews occupy a unique place in the history of the diaspora. They have maintained an uninterrupted presence in the city for over 2,000 years, making this Europe's longest-surviving Jewish community, and one that enjoyed a surprising degree of security, even at times (such as in the years following the Black Death) when waves of anti-Semitism were sweeping the rest of Europe. Some Italian Jews even applied a rather fanciful Hebrew etymology to 'Italia', deriving from it *I Tal Ya* – island of the dew of God.

It may seem odd that the city that was the great centre of power for the Christian Church

All three followed the basic Greek theatre plan: a semi-circular *cavea* consisting of seats rising in steps above an orchestra pit, with a stage occupying the straight end. The Greek chorus having been dispensed with in Roman drama, the pit became the most prestigious seating area, reserved for members of society's highest ranks. Unlike Greek theatres, where backdrops were painted to suit the action on stage, Roman theatres had fixed architectural backgrounds, intended to dazzle the easily impressed populace by their sheer majesty.

represented such a safe haven for Jews, but their security came at a price. The popes took on the double role of protectors (curbing popular violence against Jews) and oppressors, bringing Jews under their direct jurisdiction and making sure they paid for the privilege. The first documented tax on Roman Jews dates back to 1310, and set the pattern for the tradition of blackmail that characterised the Church's relations with the Jewish community until the 19th century. Payment of tax exempted Jews from the humiliating *carnevale* games, where they were liable to be packed into barrels and rolled from the top of Monte Testaccio (*see p121*).

The historic memory of this kind of exploitation was revived during World War II. In September 1943 the German occupiers demanded 50 kilograms of gold from the Jewish community, to be produced in 36 hours. After an appeal to which both Jews and non-Jews responded, the target was reached, but this time accepting blackmail did not bring security. On 16 October over a thousand Jews – mostly women and children – were rounded up and deported in cattle trucks to Auschwitz. A quarter of Rome's Jews died in the camps, a proportion that would have been higher had it not been for the help given by wide sections of Roman society, including the Catholic priesthood (but not, many believe, the Vatican).

Rome's Jews had originally settled in Trastevere (*see chapter* **Trastevere & Gianicolo**), but by the 13th century they had started to cross the river into the area that would become the Jewish Ghetto: a cramped quarter in one corner of the *centro storico*, immediately north of the Tiber island. Its chief landmark today is the imposing synagogue, begun in 1874. This incorporates the **Museo di Arte Ebraica**, a small museum of Roman Jewish life and ritual.

The Ghetto (the word is Venetian in origin) was definitively walled off from the rest of the city in 1556 after the bull *Cum nimis absurdam*, issued by the anti-Semitic Pope Paul IV, ordered a physical separation between Jewish and Christian parts of cities. Many Jews actually welcomed the protection the walls and curfews afforded, despite the fact that they were also obliged periodically to attend Mass in churches, to be lectured on their sinfulness. However, overcrowding, the loss of property rights and trade restrictions imposed on the community all took their toll, and the Ghetto experienced a long decline from the 16th to the 18th centuries.

By the time of Italian Unification in 1870, conditions for the more than 5,000 people who lived in the Ghetto had become desperately squalid. The new government ordered that the walls be destroyed, and large sections of the district rebuilt.

The via Portico d'Ottavia, an anarchic hotchpotch of ancient, medieval and Renaissance architecture, leading to the **Portico d'Ottavia** itself, used to mark the boundary of the Ghetto. This street is still the centre of Rome's Jewish life, even though many of the people you'll see sitting around chatting in the evening or on Saturdays have come in from the suburbs. It's also a good place to sample that unique hybrid, Roman Jewish food. Restaurants like **Sora Margherita** (*see p176*) specialise in such delicacies as artichokes fried Jewish-style, while at one end of the street, in a tiny unmarked corner shop (the **Forno del Ghetto**, *see chapter* **Shopping: Cakes and Confectionery**), a bakery turns out a *torta di ricotta e visciole* – ricotta and damson tart – that has achieved legendary status among Roman gourmets. The Ghetto's winding alleys also hide gems such as the delicate, elegant **Fontana delle Tartarughe** (turtle fountain), and the forbidding **Palazzo Cenci**.

Fontana delle Tartarughe

Piazza Mattei. Bus or tram to largo Argentina. **Map** p324 1A.

One of Rome's most beautiful fountains lies in the maze of streets of the old Ghetto. Four elegant boys cavort around its base, gently hoisting tortoises up to the waters above them. According to legend, Giacomo della Porta and Taddeo Landini built the fountain in a single night during the 1580s for the Duke of Mattei (whose family palazzo, packed with looted antiquities and now home to an American study centre, is also in the square). The Duke, the story goes, had lost all his money and hence his fiancée, and wanted to prove to her father that he could still achieve great things. The tortoises, possibly by Bernini, were added in the next century.

Museo d'Arte Ebraica

Lungotevere Cenci (06 684 0061). Bus to lungotevere Cenci or piazza di Monte Savello. **Open** *Sept-Apr* 9am-5pm Mon-Thur; 9.30am-2pm Fri; 9am-12.30pm Sun. *May-Aug* 9am-8pm Mon-Fri, Sun. Closed on Jewish holidays. **Admission** €5.16/L10,000; €3.10/ L6,000 concessions. **No credit cards**. **Map** p324 2A.

As well as luxurious crowns, Torah mantles and silverware, the museum presents vivid reminders of the persecution suffered by Rome's Jewish community at various times during its long history. Copies of 16th-century papal edicts banning Jews from an ever-growing list of activities are a disturbing foretaste of the horrors forced on them by the

The boat-shaped **Isola Tiberina**.

Nazis, which in turn are commemorated by stark photographs and heart-rending relics from the concentration camps. Admission includes a visit to the synagogue, built in the 1870s.

Palazzo Cenci

Vicolo dei Cenci. Bus to lungotevere dei Cenci/tram to via Arenula. Closed to the public. **Map p324 1A.**
Hidden in the middle of the Ghetto, this unassuming palazzo was home to the Cenci family, which gained notoriety in 1598 when Beatrice Cenci, her mother and two brothers were arrested for hiring thugs to murder her father. Popular opinion came to her defence when it was revealed that the father had forced Beatrice to commit incest; nevertheless, the Pope condemned her to death and she was beheaded outside Castel Sant'Angelo in 1599. Shelley used the story in his play *The Cenci*, banned in Britain until 1886 because of its subject matter.

Portico d'Ottavia

Via del Portico d'Ottavia. Bus to piazza di Monte Savello or via del Teatro di Marcello. **Map p324 2A.**
These remains have been nonchalantly built around and into over the centuries, and are now held together by rusting braces to form the porch of the church of Sant'Angelo in Pescheria. They originally formed the entrance to a massive colonnaded square containing shops, libraries and temples. Emperor Augustus rebuilt the portico in the first century BC and dedicated it to his sister Octavia; the isolated columns outside belong to a later (AD 213) restoration by Septimius Severus. For centuries the portico also formed part of Rome's main fish market,

hence the name of the church. At the time of writing, a dig in progress around the base of the portico has allowed fascinating glimpses of ancient urban infrastructure, but has also severely marred the attractiveness of this most Roman of quarters.

The Tiber island & the Bocca della Verità

When the last Etruscan king was driven from Rome, the Romans uprooted the wheat from his fields and threw it in baskets into the river. There the baskets lay, accumulating silt around them until an island formed. That, at least, is what legend says. The only island – known quite simply as **l'Isola Tiberina**, the Tiber island – to disturb the stately flow of Rome's river, it was transformed into a sanctuary dedicated to Esculapius, god of medicine, in 291 BC. In the first century BC the island was shored up and given its present boat shape: on the wide footpath at river level, the remains of the ancient 'boat' can still be seen, complete with Esculapius' rod and snakes symbol. The island's vocation to public health continues to this day: much of it is occupied by the Fatebenefratelli hospital.

At the southern end of the Tiber island stand the scant remains of Rome's oldest bridge, which is prosaically known as the **Ponte Rotto** (Broken Bridge). Nearby, in the embankment, is the mouth of the ancient **Cloaca Maxima** sewer.

Roma Felix

Rome may seem like a heaven for contented cats, but the popular postcard image of picturesque ruins providing attractive traffic-free havens for prowling and lounging felines is not the whole story. Each year Romans abandon hundreds of kittens, many of which end up in the Foro Romano (*see p71*), near the Pyramid of Caius Cestius (*see p121*) or among the ruins of largo Argentina (*see p103*). The odd *gattara* (cat lady) has always fed such strays. In recent years, however, a dedicated band of (mostly) women have taken matters into their much more organised hands.

At largo Argentina, where some 500 cats are dumped every year, the Cat Sanctuary has been saving, feeding, sterilising and vaccinating strays since 1993. Led by the charismatic Silvia Viviani, who is flanked by a 30-strong band of dedicated volunteers, the sanctuary cares for up to 250 cats at any one time. Many need immediate medical treatment, arriving at the centre's ER in a pitiful state: minus a leg, tail or ear. Some need an emergency amputation. As in any modern hospital, all patients have their own personal computer record, complete with name, ID photo and medical history.

Of late, the cat sanctuary has become a tourist attraction in its own right. Both the cat-lover and the curious can visit the centre, where, below the thundering traffic, the largo Argentina band battle to keep up with the influx of abandoned animals. At the time of writing, however, the whole operation was under threat of eviction by the city's archaeological department, not quite happy at a band of mangy moggies occupying this Sacred Area very near the spot where the divine Caesar met his nemesis.

There are financial problems, too, though special gala events and guided tours of the cats and the ruins (not to mention vital contributions from the London-based Anglo-Italian Society for the Protection of Animals) bring in much-needed funds. The cats that wander these ancient environs can also be legally adopted: over 300 felines find permanent homes in Italy and abroad each year. So if you're a cat lover who's looking for a furry reminder of your visit to the Eternal City, consider including a genuine Roman beast in your home-bound hand luggage. For the quarantine-challenged, *adozioni a distanza* (long-distance adoptions) are also available.

Torre Argentina Cat Sanctuary

Corner of via Florida and via di Torre Argentina (06 687 2133/ torreargentina@yahoo.com/ www.romancats.com). Bus or tram to largo Argentina. **Open** noon-6pm daily; guided tours 3pm Sun.

On the right bank, opposite the island's southern end, stood ancient Rome's *forum boarium* (cattle market) and *forum holitorium* (vegetable market). Besides the striking remains of the **Teatro di Marcello** (*see also p104* **Theatres**), it's now home to two delightful temples as well as a number of churches, including **Santa Maria in Cosmedin** with its Bocca della Verità (mouth of truth), **San Nicola in Carcere**, with market columns built into its walls, and **Santa Maria in Campitelli**.

Ponte Rotto & the Cloaca Maxima

Views from Ponte Palatino, Isola Tiberina and lungotevere Pierleoni. Bus to piazza Sonnino, piazza di Monte Savello, lungotevere Pierleoni, or lungotevere Ripa. **Map** p324 2A.

The 'broken bridge' was the first stone bridge in Rome, dating from 142 BC. Parts of it fell down at least twice before the bridge's final collapse in 1598. Near its west side there is a tunnel in the embankment, the gaping mouth of the Cloaca Maxima, the city's 'great sewer', first built under the Tarquins (Rome's Etruscan kings, *see p7*) in the sixth century BC to drain the area round the Forum, and given its final form in the first century BC.

San Nicola in Carcere

Via del Teatro di Marcello 46 (06 6830 7198). Bus to via del Teatro di Marcello. **Open** 7am-noon, 4-7pm Mon-Sat; 10am-1pm Sun. **Map** p324 2A.

This church was built in the 11th century, within the ruins of three Republican-era temples. These were dedicated to the two-faced god, Janus, the goddess Juno, and to Spes (Hope). They overlooked the city's fruit and veg market (*forum holitorium*), the columns of which can still be seen embedded in the wall.

Santa Maria in Campitelli

Piazza Campitelli 9 (06 6880 3978). Bus to via del Teatro di Marcello. **Open** 7.30am-noon, 4-7pm daily. **Map** p324 1A.

This church was commissioned in 1656 to house the medieval icon of the Madonna del Portico, to which the population had prayed (successfully) for a prompt release from a bout of the plague. Carlo Rainaldi completed his masterpiece in 1667: a solemn, austere exercise in mass and light. The floor plan is complex: Greek cross, plus (hidden) dome, plus apse, with a series of side chapels. Inside are some fine baroque paintings, and a spectacularly over-the-top gilt altar tabernacle by Giovanni Antonio de Rossi.

Santa Maria in Cosmedin

Piazza della Bocca della Verità 18 (06 678 1419). Bus to piazza Bocca della Verità. **Open** Apr-Sept 9am-6.30pm daily. Oct-Mar 9am-5pm daily. **Map** p324 2A.

Santa Maria in Cosmedin was first built in the sixth century. It was enlarged in the ninth century, and given a beautiful *campanile* in the 12th. Between the 11th and 13th centuries much of the original decoration was replaced with Cosmati work (*see p87*):

the spiralling floor, the throne, the choir, the 13th-century *baldacchino* (located over the ultimate example of recycling, a Roman bath-tub used as an altar). If you want to prove a point, stick your hand into the *Bocca della Verità* (the 'Mouth of Truth'), a worn stone face under the portico that was probably an ancient drain cover, and is said to bite the hands of liars. According to legend it was much used by husbands to test the faithfulness of their wives. The scene in *Roman Holiday* where Gregory Peck ad-libs getting his hand bitten, eliciting a (reportedly) unscripted shriek of genuine alarm from Audrey Hepburn, is one of the most delightful moments in cinema. In the sacristy is a fragment of an eighth-century mosaic of the Holy Family, brought here from the original St Peter's. On Sunday mornings at 10.30 a Byzantine rite mass is sung in the church.

Teatro di Marcello

Via del Teatro di Marcello. Bus to via del Teatro di Marcello. **Open** with prior permission only (*see p60*). **Map** p324 2A.

If you haven't had time to seek formal permission to enter the Theatre of Marcellus, don't give up: it is visible from the street outside. It's one of the strangest and most impressive sights in Rome – a Renaissance palace grafted on to an ancient, time-worn circular theatre. Julius Caesar began building a massive theatre here to rival Pompey's (*see p104* **Theatres**) in the Campus Martius, but it was finished in 11 BC by Augustus, who named it after his favourite nephew. At one time it was connected to the adjacent Portico of Octavia (*see p107*), and originally had three tiers in different styles (Ionic, Doric and Corinthian), but the top one has collapsed. After the theatre was abandoned in the fourth century AD it had various uses, including as a fortress, before Baldassare Peruzzi built a palace for the Savelli family on top of the crumbling remains in the 16th century. To the north of the theatre are three columns that were part of the Temple of Apollo, built in 433 BC.

'Tempio di Vesta' and 'Tempio di Fortuna Virilis' (Temples of Hercules Victor and Portunus)

Piazza della Bocca della Verità. Bus to piazza Bocca della Verità. **Map** p324 2A.

Like the Pantheon, both these diminutive Republican-era temples owe their fine state of preservation to their conversion into churches during the Middle Ages. The round one, which looks like an English folly, was built in the first century BC and dedicated to Hercules. Early archaeologists were confused by its round shape, which is similar to the Temple of Vesta in the Roman Forum, and mistakenly dubbed it the Temple of Vesta. Romans still tend to refer to it by this name. The second temple, square but similarly perfect in form, is a century older and was dedicated to Portunus, god of harbours, since this was the port area of ancient Rome. This was also misattributed as being dedicated to 'manly fortune'. Both temples were deconsecrated and designated as ancient monuments in the 1920s on orders from Mussolini.

Sightseeing

Trastevere & the Gianicolo

Pea-shelling ladies, whittling carpenters and floury bakers mix with tourist hordes and foreign residents in *er core de Roma*.

There has been a small colony on the west bank of the Tiber (across the Tiber – *trans Tiberim* – hence Trastevere) since the foundation of Rome, reached by a ford where the Ponte Palatino now crosses from piazza Bocca della Verità. During the Empire, Trastevere was sufficiently important to be included within the Aurelian Wall (*see p146*). The area consisted mainly of vegetable gardens, orchards and hunting forests owned by noble families, most famously the Caesars; Cleopatra is thought to have stayed here.

After the fall of the Empire, Trastevere was gradually colonised by Syrian and Jewish trading communities, and the remains of an early **synagogue** can still be seen in vicolo dell'Atleta. In the early Middle Ages the Jews moved out and across the Tiber to the Ghetto (*see pp104-6*), and in time Trastevere became established as the main working-class district of the papal capital.

In the two centuries prior to Italian Unification, and for a while afterwards, there was a strong tradition of violent rivalry between the *bulli trasteverini* (Trastevere toughs) and the *monticiani* (the boys from Monti, *see p130*). The gangs, their leaders, and their stone-throwing battles, knife-fights and frequent fatalities became enshrined in popular lore, a prototype *West Side Story* duly written down by dialect poet Giuseppe Gioacchino Belli (1791-1863) and illustrated by Hogarth-meets-Goya cartoonist Bartolomeo Pinelli (1781-1835). The 200-odd sonnets by the former (whose top-hatted statue now graces **piazza GG Belli**, the taxi-rank at the beginning of viale Trastevere) are still a useful way to make sense of the character and philosophy of the modern-day Roman. Despite the fact that Trastevere strove hard to prove itself a separate city, the good-humoured cynicism, proud independence and fun-loving vulgarity

Old ladies still shell peas on the streets of Trastevere.

Bohemians hang out in **piazza Santa Maria in Trastevere**. *See p115.*

that set it apart have now come to be regarded as quintessentially Roman traits.

Today, Trastevere contends with Testaccio (*see p119*) across the river for the title of *er core de Roma* – the heart of Rome. Trastevere still puts up a good fight. Although many of its apartments have fallen into the hands of assorted foreigners, the locals have not allowed this to throw them off their stride: old ladies sit outside their kitchen doors commenting on passers-by as they shell the peas; neighbours shout to one another across the street from high windows; and carpenters whittle and floury bakers bake in shops and workshops sandwiched between the numerous wine bars and restaurants.

Trastevere is divided into two sharply different sectors by the traffic-snarled avenue of the same name.

North of viale Trastevere

To the north of the *viale* lies the true tourist mecca: all streets seem to lead to the stunning **piazza Santa Maria in Trastevere**, with its church of the same name. The piazza still manages to preserve an aura of ancient calm, despite the impromptu football matches played against the walls of its church and the fiendish mandolin-strummers who serenade the diners at its two overpriced restaurants.

In some streets in this area, notably **vicolo del Cinque** and **via della Scala**, it seems that every ground-floor space is a restaurant, a 'piano bar', or a herbal bookshop with tearoom attached. When the bustle gets too much, get a taste of old Trastevere in the **Museo di Roma in Trastevere** or, better still, escape with a stroll along via della Lungara. Widened and paved by Pope Julius II to mirror his via Giulia on the other bank of the Tiber, it contains some of Rome's finest *palazzi*, including the Raphael-frescoed **Villa Farnesina**, and the **Palazzo Corsini**, backing on to the beautiful **Orto Botanico** (botanical garden). There is also the notorious Regina Coeli, a medieval prison still in use. En route to it is the **Casa della Fornarina** where Raphael's mistress is said to have lived.

Casa della Fornarina

Via di Santa Dorotea 20. Bus to lungotevere Sanzio or piazza Sonnino/tram to viale Trastevere. Closed to the public. **Map p324 2B.**

This unassuming house, with a pretty window high on the façade and a granite column embedded in its wall, is believed to have been that of Margherita, La Fornarina (the Baker's Girl), Raphael's model and lover for many years. Universally considered a fallen woman for her very publicly untoward conduct with the artist, poor Margherita was then rejected by Raphael on his deathbed, as he sought to atone for

his life of sin and debauchery. According to local lore, she took refuge in the convent of Sant'Apollonia in piazza Santa Margherita, just around the corner from her home.

Galleria Nazionale d'Arte Antica – Palazzo Corsini

Via della Lungara 10 (06 6880 2323/www. gallerianorghese.it). Bus to lungotevere della Farnesina or piazza Sonnino/tram to viale Trastevere. **Open** 8.30am-7.30pm Tue-Sun. **Admission** €4.13/L8,000; €2.06/L4,000 concessions; *see also p60* **Tickets**. **No credit cards. Map** p324 1C.

This palace, designed in stages by Ferdinando Fuga between 1738 and 1758, incorporated the Palazzo Riario of 1510, once the Roman residence of the 17th century's highest-profile convert to Catholicism, Queen Christina of Sweden. A plaque marks the room in which she died in 1689. Today, the palace houses part of the national art collection, the bulk of which is in the Palazzo Barberini (*see p76*). The galleries are beautifully painted with frescos and *trompe l'œils* and house paintings dating mainly

from the 16th and 17th centuries. There are the usual scores of Holy Families, and Madonnas and Children (the most memorable a *Madonna* by Van Dyck). Other works include a sensual pair of Annunciations by Guercino; two St Sebastians, one by Rubens, the other by Annibale Carracci; Caravaggio's unadorned *Narcissus*; and a triptych by Fra Angelico. The works by Guido Reni also stand out, notably the melancholy *Salome*. The original palace grounds behind the building are now Rome's botanical garden, the Orto Botanico (*see p115*).

Museo di Roma in Trastevere

Piazza Sant'Egidio 1B (06 581 6563). Bus to lungotevere Sanzio/tram to viale Trastevere. **Open** 10am-7.45pm Tue-Sun; ticket office closes 7pm. **Admission** €2.58/L5,000; €1.55/L3,000 concessions. **No credit cards. Map** p324 2B.

Rome's folklore museum is housed in a 17th-century convent formerly occupied by Carmelite nuns. Reopened in 2000 after a lengthy restoration, it still contains the same rather musty collection of period paintings and prints, along with a series of

Big-nose

The peoples of the Mediterranean basin have always had a real passion for water, perhaps because of the relative lack of it. Nobody was more passionate than the ancient Romans, who built mighty aqueducts – the first being the Acqua Appia in 312 BC – to ensure that the supply of spring water from surrounding mountains was adequate to feed their many baths and fountains.

Today there are more than 3,500 fountains in Rome. Many are purely ornamental, and use the enormous quantities of undrinkable water still carried by ancient aqueducts. But some 2,000 are *nasoni* (big nose) drinking fountains. These are found all over the city, spurting safe, fresh water, even through the long, hot summers.

The first 20 *nasoni* were produced in 1874, to a design that is still used today. A few of the originals are still around: one is in **piazza in Piscinula** on the southern side of viale Trastevere. Arguably the most popular item of Roman street furniture, the *nasoni*'s 'nose' may seem too low for the purpose of drinking, but block the end of the nose with your finger, and water will spout from a small hole halfway up the pipe at the perfect level.

The cultural importance of fountains to the Romans has made them into the stuff of legend and folk tales. When Queen Christina of Sweden visited the Eternal City for the first time in 1650, she thanked everybody for the

celebrations held in her honour, adding that they could turn the fountains off now that she had been well and truly welcomed. So astonished was she – the story goes – when told that they ran constantly, that she converted to Catholicism, abdicated, and moved to Rome for good, taking up residence in Palazzo Corsini (*see p113*).

Sightseeing

Wise and foolish virgins frequent **Santa Maria in Trastevere**. *See p115.*

waxwork tableaux relating to the life, work, pastimes and superstitions of the man in the street in 18th- and 19th-century Italy. Temporary exhibitions are held in the pretty cloister.

Orto Botanico

Largo Cristina di Svezia 24 (06 4991 7106/06 4991 7107). Bus to lungotevere Farnesina. **Open** 9am-5.30pm Tue-Sat. Closed Aug. **Admission** €2.06/L4,000; €1.02/L2,000 concessions. **Map** p324 2C.
Established in 1883, when part of the grounds of the Palazzo Corsini was donated to Rome University, the Orto Botanico contains some 7,000 species in wondrous green exuberance that is barely held in check: here there is none of the sterile order that can render botanical gardens in northern climes so cold. Plants tumble over steps and into fountains and fishponds, creating verdant hidden corners disturbed only by frolicking children, parked here by Trastevere mums.

Piazza Santa Maria in Trastevere

Bus to piazza Sonnino or lungotevere Sanzio/tram to piazza Sonnino. **Map** p324 2B.
This is the heart and soul of Trastevere, a traffic-free cobbled square. Overlooking the fountain, designed by Carlo Fontana in 1692, are the fantastic 13th-century mosaics on the façade of **Santa Maria in Trastevere** (*see below*), one of the oldest churches in Rome. Legend has it that a miraculous well of oil sprang from this spot when Christ was born, and flowed to the Tiber all day. A small street leading out of the piazza, via della Fonte dell'Olio ('Oil Well Street'), commemorates the miracle.

Santa Maria in Trastevere

Piazza Santa Maria in Trastevere (06 581 4802). Bus to viale Trastevere or lungotevere Sanzio/tram to viale Trastevere. **Open** 7.30am-9pm daily. **Map** p324 2B.
The first church on this site was begun in 337 by Pope Julius I, and was one of the first in Rome to be dedicated to the Virgin. The present building was erected for Pope Innocent II in the 12th century, and has wonderful mosaics. Those on the façade – from the 12th and 13th centuries – show Mary breast-feeding Christ, and ten women with crowns and lanterns on a gold background. Their significance is uncertain, as they have been altered over the years, but they may represent the parable of the wise and foolish virgins. Inside, the apse has a 12th-century mosaic of Jesus and his mother; the figure holding the church on the far left is Pope Innocent. Lower down, between the windows, there are beautiful 13th-century mosaics showing scenes from the life of the Virgin by Pietro Cavallini (*see also* **Santa Cecilia,** *p117*), whose relaxed, realistic figures represent the re-emergence of a Roman style after long years of the hegemony of Byzantine models. The *Madonna and Child* with rainbow overhead is also by Cavallini. Through the wooden door on the left, just before entering the transept, there are two tiny, exquisite fragments of first century AD mosaics

Smoke, from the cannon, white

In his poem *Amours de Voyage* (c1849), traveller, poet and classicist Arthur Hugh Clough described watching the French attack on the Gianicolo:

Twelve o'clock, on the Pincian Hill, with lots of English,
Germans, Americans, French, – the Frenchmen, too, are protected, –
So we stand in the sun, but afraid of a probable shower;
So we stand and stare, and see, to the left of St Peter's,
Smoke, from the cannon, white, – but that is at intervals only, –
Black, from a burning house, we suppose, by the Cavalleggieri;
And we believe we discern some lines of men descending
Down through the vineyard-slopes, and catch a bayonet gleaming.
Every ten minutes, however, – in this there is no misconception –
Comes a great white pull from behind Michael Angelo's dome and
After a space the report of a real big gun;
not the Frenchman's?
That must be doing some work. And so we watch and conjecture.

from Palestrina, and in the chapel immediately to the left of the high altar is a very rare sixth-century painting on wood of the Madonna.

Villa Farnesina

Via della Lungara 230 (06 6880 1767). Bus to lungotevere Farnesina or piazza Sonnino. **Open** 9am-1pm Mon-Sat. **Admission** €4.13/L8,000; €3.10/L6,000 concessions. **No credit cards. Map** p324 1B.
This pretty villa was built between 1508 and 1511 by Baldassare Peruzzi, as a pleasure palace and holiday home for the rich papal banker and party-giver Agostino Chigi. The powerful Farnese family bought and renamed it in 1577, when the Chigis went bankrupt. Chigi was one of Raphael's principal patrons, and in its day the villa was stuffed with great works of art, although many were later sold to pay off debts. The stunning frescos in the ground-floor Loggia of Psyche were designed by Raphael but executed by his friends and followers, including Giulio Romano; according to local lore the master himself was too busy dallying with his mistress, La Fornarina (*see p111*), to contribute any more than was strictly necessary. The Grace with her back

Early Christians repose eternally in the porch of **Santa Maria in Trastevere**. *See p115.*

turned, to the right of the door, is attributed to him. Around the corner, in the Loggia of Galatea, Raphael took brush in hand to create the victorious goddess in her sea-shell chariot. Up the stairs is the Salone delle Prospettive, painted by Peruzzi with views of 16th-century Rome. Next to it is Agostino Chigi's bedroom, with a fresco of the *Marriage of Alexander the Great and Roxanne* by Raphael's follower Sodoma. Like most of his paintings, this is a rather sordid number showing the couple being relieved of their clothes by vicious little cherubs.

South of viale Trastevere

South of the viale is a quiet, evocative enclave where you will find the highest concentration of genuine locals. The church of **San Francesco a Ripa** contains a startling Bernini statue. The warren of lanes around the church of **Santa Cecilia** is a good place to wander aimlessly, watching local craftsmen at work; behind anonymous doorways are architectural gems such as the **Chiostro dei Genovesi**. This area faces the Tiber Island (Isola Tiberina, *see pp107-109*).

Chiostro dei Genovesi

Via Anicia 12 (no phone). Bus to lungotevere Ripa or viale Trastevere/tram to viale Trastevere. **Open** *Apr-Oct* 3-6pm Tue, Thur. *Nov-Mar* 2-4pm Tue, Thur (ring the bell marked Sposito to get in). **Admission** free. **Map** p324 2A.

To the right of the 16th-century church of Santa Maria dell'Orto – recognisable by its obelisks – is a wooden door opening into a glorious flower-filled cloister with a well at its centre, part of a 15th-century hospice for Genoese sailors designed by Baccio Pontelli. Concealed among the octagonal columns supporting the double loggia is a plaque commemorating Rome's first ever palm tree, planted here in 1588.

San Francesco a Ripa

Piazza San Francesco d'Assisi 88 (06 581 9020). Bus or tram to via Induno or viale Trastevere. **Open** 7.30am-noon, 4-7pm daily. **Map** p325 1B.

In a quiet corner, this 17th-century church stands on the site of the hospice where St Francis of Assisi stayed when he visited Rome in 1219. The original church was built by Rodolfo Anguillara, one of Francis's richer followers, in the 13th century. It was entirely rebuilt in the 1680s, and today its unremarkable baroque interior rings to the guitar-strumming of a thriving parish church. It's most visited for Bernini's sculpture of the Beata Ludovica Albertoni (1674), showing the aristocratic Franciscan nun dying in one of those agonised, sexually ambiguous baroque ecstasies (*see also p137*, Santa Maria della Vittoria). A near-contemporary portrait of St Francis hangs in the cell said to have been occupied by the monk himself; if the sacristan is feeling so inclined, he'll take you in and show you the rock that Francis used as a pillow. The Ripa of the church's name refers to its position a stone's throw from what was Rome's main riverside port area, the Ripa Grande.

Santa Cecilia in Trastevere

*Piazza Santa Cecilia (06 589 9289). Bus to
lungotevere Ripa or viale Trastevere/tram to viale
Trastevere.* **Open** *Church, crypt and excavations*
9.30am-12.30pm, 3.45-6.30pm daily. *Cavallini frescos*
10am-noon Tue, Thur; 11.30am-12.30pm Sun.
Admission *Excavations & crypt* €2.06/L4,000.
Cavallini frescos donation expected. **No credit
cards. Map** p324 2A.

This pretty church stands on the site of a fifth-
century building that was itself built over a Roman
house, the bath and storerooms of which can still
be visited beneath the church. According to legend,
it was the home of Valerio, a Roman patrician
who was so impressed (or perhaps frustrated) by
his Christian wife Cecilia's maintaining her vow of
chastity that he also converted. Valerio was
martyred for his pains, and Cecilia was arrested
while trying to bury his body. Her martyrdom was
something of a botched job – after a failed attempt
to suffocate her in the hot steam baths of her house,
her persecutors tried to behead her with three
strokes of an axe (the maximum permitted). She
took several days to die, which, the legend goes on,
she spent singing. Hence she became the patron
saint of music. Her tomb was opened in 1599,
revealing her still-undecayed body. It rapidly
disintegrated, but not before a sketch had been
made, on which Stefano Maderna based the astonishingly delicate sculpture that lies below the high
altar. Her sarcophagus can be seen in the crypt.

Make sure your visit to this church coincides
with the very short periods when visitors can see
a small remaining fragment of what must have
been one of the world's greatest frescos. Pietro
Cavallini's late 13th-century *Last Judgment* is high
up in the gallery, and miraculously survived later
rebuilding work in the church. While still working
within a Byzantine framework, Cavallini floods the
seated apostles with a totally new kind of light
(note the depth of the faces) – the same light that
was to reappear in Giotto's work, and which has
led a growing number of scholars to believe that
Cavallini, not Giotto, was responsible for the St
Francis fresco cycle in the basilica di San Francesco
in Assisi.

The Gianicolo

Above the Regina Coeli prison, the hillside park
of the **Gianicolo** offers a chance for prisoners'
spouses to shout messages down to their
locked-up loved ones during exercise hour.
Reached by the tortuous via Garibaldi, which
passes by Bramante's exquisite **Tempietto**
and the baroque **Fontana Paola**, the Gianicolo
provides one of Rome's most spectacular views
(*see also p78* **The best sunsets**). The
spreading pine tree and statue-dotted gardens
are dominated by an enormous equestrian
statue of Giuseppe Garibaldi, close to which
a cannon is fired every day at noon.

Fontana Paola

Via Garibaldi. Bus to Gianicolo or via G Carini.
Map p324 2C.

This huge fountain on the Gianicolo hill was originally intended, like the Fontana dell'Acqua Felice
(*see p136*), to resemble a triumphal arch. The
columns came from the original St Peter's basilica.
The fountain was designed in 1612 by Flaminio
Ponzio and Giovanni Fontana for Pope Paul V,
from whom it takes its name. It was built to celebrate the reopening of an ancient aqueduct, built
by Emperor Trajan (AD 98-117) to bring water
from Lake Bracciano.

Gianicolo

Bus to Gianicolo or via G Carini. **Map** p324 2C.

The hill of the Janiculum, as it was known in ancient
times, offers one of the best views over the city and,
on a clear day, to the mountains beyond. In 1849 it
was the scene of one of the fiercest battles in the
struggle for Italian unity, when former sailor
Giuseppe Garibaldi and his makeshift army of
garibaldini, a combination of former papal troops
and young enthusiasts, defended the Roman
Republic against French troops that had been
sent to restore papal rule (*see p18, p115* **Smoke,
from the cannon, white**). There is an equestrian statue of him in the middle of the square, while
the busts that line the wall are those of the thousand martyrs of Italy's Risorgimento. If you carry
on past the equestrian statue of Garibaldi's equally
heroic wife Anita, you will reach a curious light-
house, the patriotic gift of Italian emigrants in
Argentina. The view from this part of the hill
takes in the ochre shades of medieval and baroque
Rome. At the Vatican end of the walk, opposite
the Bambino Gesù children's hospital, there's a
good view over St Peter's basilica and the Castel
Sant'Angelo (*see p144*).

Tempietto di Bramante
& San Pietro in Montorio

*Piazza San Pietro in Montorio 2 (06 581 3940). Bus
to Gianicolo or via G Carini.* **Open** 8am-noon, 4-6pm
daily. **Map** p324 2C.

High up on the Gianicolo, on the spot where St
Peter was believed to have been crucified (*see p132*
Peter & Paul), San Pietro in Montorio commands
the finest view of any church in Rome. It also has
one of Rome's greatest architectural gems in its
courtyard: the **Tempietto**, designed by Bramante
in 1508. This much-copied round construction was
the first modern building to follow exactly the
proportions of the classical orders (in this case,
Doric, *see chapter* **Architecture**). Bernini got his
hands on it in 1628, adding the staircase that leads
down to the crypt. The church itself, founded in the
ninth century and rebuilt in the late 15th, contains
a chapel by Bernini (second on the left) and one by
Vasari (fifth on the right). Paintings include
Sebastiano del Piombo's *Flagellation*, and a
Crucifixion of St Peter by Guido Reni.

The Aventine & Testaccio

The Aventine is leafy and exclusive, Testaccio earthy and low-rent: two extremes nestling to the south of the Capitoline.

Though they nestle into each other to the south of the Capitoline hill (see p61), there's a world of difference between the luxurious calm of the Aventine and salt-of-the-earth, bustling Testaccio. It was ever so: while ancient Rome's writers and thinkers opted for the Aventine (Cicero rented out flats there), Testaccio was a hive of warehouses around a busy river port.

The Aventine

The exclusive, leafy Aventine hill boasts Rome's highest property prices, and hosts a sovereign passport-issuing territory in the headquarters of the Knights of Malta, in the square of the same name (**piazza dei Cavalieri di Malta**). The delightful **Parco Savello** offers spectacular views, particularly at sundown, and the churches are an added bonus: the glorious fifth-century **Santa Sabina**, and **Santa Prisca**. The former stands near the site of a major temple to the godess Diana; the latter (in via di Santa Prisca; open by appointment only, see p59) is on top of Rome's best-restored Mithraic shrine.

There are still elderly people on the Aventine and its sister hill San Saba, just across the busy viale Aventino, who remember farmers herding sheep and goats into the area's *piazze* of an evening before taking them to market the next morning. And, until the debris left by an influx of transvestite prostitutes made it a health hazard, old ladies could until very recently be seen picking *rughetta* (rocket) for salads amid the grass at the foot of the Aurelian Wall (see p148).

Parco Savello

Via di Santa Sabina. Bus to via del Circo Massimo or via di Santa Prisca. **Open** dawn to dusk daily. **Map** p325 1A.
Inside the walled area of the Savello family's 12th-century fortress is a pretty garden, full of orange trees and massive terracotta pots of dark green plants. The garden ends in a terrace beyond which a sweeping view of Rome opens up: west-facing, the sunset here can be spectacular (see also p78 **Sunsets**). Close by, on via di Valle Murcia is the city

roseto (rose garden), which is sweet-smelling – but also very crowded – when it opens its gates briefly to the public in late spring and early summer.

Piazza dei Cavalieri di Malta

Bus to via del Circo Massimo or via di Santa Prisca. **Map** p325 1A.
Designed by the great fantasist Gian Battista Piranesi in the 18th century, this diminutive square with its mysterious reliefs and orderly cypress trees looks like the set for some surrealist drama. It takes its name from the Knights of Malta, whose priory is at No.3. If you look through the little hole in the priory doorway, you'll see one of Piranesi's most spectacular illusions: at the end of a neat avenue of trees sits the dome of St Peter's, apparently only a few metres away. This is probably the only keyhole in the world through which you can see three sovereign territories: Italy, the Vatican, and that of the aristocratic, theocratic Knights of Malta themselves, a sovereign order with extraterritorial rights, has its own head of state, and issues its own number plates (starting SMOM) and passports.

Santa Sabina

Piazza Pietro d'Illiria 1 (06 574 3573). Bus to via del Circo Massimo or via di Santa Prisca. **Open** 6.30am-12.45pm, 3.30-7pm daily. **Map** p325 1A.
This magnificent basilica was built in the fifth century over an early Christian *titulus* (see p125 **Inconspicuous Early Church**). Added to and decorated over the centuries, it was shorn of later accretions in a merciless restoration in the 1930s: what you see today is arguably the closest thing – give or take a 16th-century fresco or two – to an unadulterated ancient church that Rome has to offer. The high nave has towering, elegant Corinthian columns, supporting an arcade decorated with original marble inlay work. The late fifth-century wooden doors are carved with scenes from the New Testament, including one of the earliest renderings of the crucifixion. Selenite (thin, translucent sheets of crystalised gypsum) has been placed in the windows, as it would have been in the ninth century; the choir is the genuine ninth-century article, too. In the floor in the middle of the nave is the mosaic tombstone of Brother Muñoz de Zamora, who died in 1300. Above the entrance door, a fifth-century mosaic recalls that the priest Peter of Illyria built the church while Celestine was pope; two figures

Over crowded Testaccio-dwellers were forced to brave the *ballatoi*.

on either side of the inscription represent the *ecclesia ex gentibus* and the *ecclesia ex circumcisione*, the church members who hailed from the pagan world and those descended from Jews. The later additions remaining in the church include the 16th-century fresco in the apse (said to have been inspired by the original mosaic) by Taddeo Zuccari. A tiny window in the entrance porch looks onto the spot where St Dominic was said to have planted an orange tree. The adjoining monastery contains a cell where the saint stayed, but this is usually closed; a peaceful 13th-century cloister, reached by a sloping corridor near the main door, is sometimes open, on the other hand.

Testaccio

Further south, though still within the ancient Wall, is the wedge-shaped Testaccio district. This is one of the few areas of central Rome where a sense of community is strongly felt, and where the line between courtyard and street is blurred enough to allow old ladies to pop into the local *alimentari* in their dressing-gown and slippers. Elsa Morante chose this as the setting for her sprawling Marxist novel *La Storia* (History).

The best place to begin is in piazza Testaccio, home to one of Rome's best-stocked and liveliest food markets. Once a desperately poor area, Testaccio has reaped the benefits of post-war prosperity without losing either its character or its original residents, who remain resolutely salt-of-the-earth, despite encroaching health-food shops and other trappings of gentrification. Many of the apartment blocks are still publicly owned, and let at controlled rents. At the beginning of the 20th century a quarter of all families here slept in their kitchens, and tenants were forced to brave the suspended walkways (*ballatoi*) connecting the apartments on each floor. For a glimpse of these *ballatoi* venture into the recently restored courtyard of the block at piazza Testaccio 20.

You'll meet few non-residents in Testaccio by day, the only tourist destination being the **Cimitero Acattolico** (Protestant Cemetery). The more obscure **Piramide di Caio Cestio** (Pyramid of Caius Cestius), **Museo di Via Ostiense**, **Emporium** and **Monte Testaccio** draw only a few conoisseurs. By night, however, the area is inundated with outsiders who flock to the cheap pizzerias and myriad clubs burrowed into the flanks of Monte Testaccio (*see chapter* **Nightlife**), opposite the huge bulk of the **Mattatoio**, until 1975 Rome's main abbatoir.

Testaccio pays homage to its trading history at the **Fontana delle Anfore**. *See p120.*

Emporio-Porto Fluviale

Lungotevere Testaccio. Bus or tram to piazza dell'
Emporio. **Open** by prior appointment only, *see p59;*
visible from lungotevere Testaccio. **Map** p325 1A.
From the second century BC, the bank just south of
the modern Ponte Sublicio (built in 1919) was
Rome's Emporium, the ancient wharf area, from
which steps led up to the Porticus Emilia, a huge
covered warehouse 60m (200ft) wide and almost
500m (1,600ft) long. Behind the Porticus were the
horrea, or grain warehouses, built under Tiberius
(AD 14-37) to help control the imperial grain
monopoly; the occasional outcrop of bricks from
these buildings can still be seen among Testaccio's
apartment blocks in *vie* Vespucci and Florio. The
20th-century Fontana delle Anfore on the river bank
is a reminder of Testaccio's commercial past.

Il Mattatoio

Piazza Giustiniani. Bus to via Galvani or lungotevere
Testaccio. **Map** p325 2B.
With its Doric arches and bizarre statuary, the
Mattatoio, the municipal slaughterhouse, was
Europe's most advanced abbatoir when it opened in
1891. It coped with an eightfold increase in the population, and provided Testaccio's residents with
work (not to mention noise and smells) until it was
finally pensioned off in 1975. For decades constant
bickering between politicians, architects and planners over what to do with the structure caused stasis: now, finally, the whole area, including the
Campo Boario cattleyards next door, is destined for
(tasteful) redevelopment, with spaces allotted to the
university architecture department, to multi-media
projects, for exhibition space, and to commercial
activities with an arts bent; areas will also be
reserved for the nightclubs and cultural associations
already functioning inside (*see chapter* **Nightlife**).

Monte Testaccio

Via Zabaglia 24. Metro Piramide/bus to via
Marmorata or via Zabaglia/tram to via Marmorata.
Open visit by prior appointment only, *see p59.*
Map p325 2A.
Known locally as the *Monte dei cocci* – the hill of
shards – Monte Testaccio is just that: although it's
covered by soil and scrubby plants, underneath the
'hill' is nothing but a pile of broken amphorae,
ancient earthenware jars, flung here between AD
140 and 255 after being unloaded at the Porto
Fluviale (*see p121*). Most came from the Roman
province of Betica (Andalusia), and contained olive
oil. In the Middle Ages, Monte Testaccio and the
area below it were famous as the site of the pre-
Lenten *carnevale* celebrations, in which the horse
races and religious pageants of the nobility vied wth
the less refined sports of the people. Pigs, bulls and
wild boar would be packed into carts at the top of
the hill and sent careering down; any survivors of
the impact were finished off at the bottom with
spears. Jews, too, were subjected to indignities of all
kinds, although they were spared the *coup de grâce.*
Today some of Rome's most buzzing clubs and

restaurants have been built into the base of the hill
(*see chapter* **Nightlife**), some with glass walls to
afford glimpses of the amphora mound beyond. (The
district's symbiotic relationship with the amphora
is recalled in a 20th-century statue in piazza
dell'Emporio.)

Museo di Via Ostiense

Via R Persichetti 3 (06 574 3193). Metro
Piramide/bus or tram to piazza San Paolo.
Open 9am-1.30pm Mon, Wed, Fri-Sun; 9am-1.30pm,
2-4.30pm Tue, Thur. **Admission** €2.06/L4,000. **No**
credit cards. Map p325 2A.
This small museum is dauntingly placed in the middle of a frantic traffic roundabout, and just opposite
the station for Ostia Antica. A visit can be handily
combined with one to the excavations of the ancient
port city (*see p270*). The ancient gatehouse, the Porta
di San Paolo, contains artefacts and prints describ-
ing the story of the via Ostiense – the Ostian Way –
built in the third century BC to join Rome to its port
and the vital salt-pans at the mouth of the Tiber. The
museum has two large-scale models, of old Ostia and
the port of Trajan.

Piramide di Caio Cestio

Piazza di Porta San Paolo. Metro Piramide/bus or
tram to piazza di Porta San Paolo. **Open** with prior
permission only, *see p59.* **Map** p325 2A.
Lodged in the brick Aurelian Wall is a miniature
Egyptian pyramid. It was built by Gaius Cestius, an
obscure first-century BC magistrate and tribune
who was so impressed by the tombs of the pharaohs
that he decided he wanted one of his own. He did not
build it with as much technical care as the Egyptians
had used (it's made of brick and only clad in
marble) but nevertheless it has survived remarkably
well since Cestius was buried here in 12 BC.

Cimitero Acattolico

Via Caio Cestio 6 (06 574 1900). Metro
Piramide/bus to via Marmorata/tram to piazza di
Porta San Paolo. **Open** *Oct-Mar* 9am-4.30pm Tue-
Sun. *Apr-Sept* 9am-5.30pm Tue-Sun. **Admission**
free (donation expected). **Map** p325 2A.
'It might make one in love with death to know that
one should be buried in so sweet a place.' So Shelley
described the Protestant Cemetery, final resting place
of his friend Keats, in the preface to his poem *Adonais*,
little knowing that he too would be taking up permanent residence here after a fatal boating accident
just a year later. Miraculously, given that only a wall
divides it from the chaos of piazza di Porta San Paolo,
it remains a haven of peace. The inhabitants of the
cemetery – its official title is Cimitero Acattolico, the
non-Catholic cemetery – are not limited to
Protestants: there are Russian Orthodox, Chinese,
Buddhist and even atheist tombs as well. A detailed
map is available at the entrance, and will help you
discover the graves of other distinguished residents
such as Goethe's son Julius, Joseph Severn, faithful
companion to Keats, and Antonio Gramsci, founder
of the Italian Communist Party.

The Celio & San Giovanni

The original Christian basilica, massive Roman baths, ancient churches and a verdant wilderness on the Celio hill.

The south side of old Rome contains some fascinating, spectacular and unusual remains, including the **Terme di Caracalla** (Baths of Caracalla, *see p126*) and the glimpses of the ancient city to be had beneath the churches of **San Clemente** (*see below*) and **Santi Giovanni e Paolo** (*see p126*). But the churches, too, make this area well worth a visit: **San Giovanni in Laterano** (*see p129*) and **Santa Croce in Gerusalemme** (*see p129*) were two of Christian Rome's first major churches, the former donated by the Emperor Constantine himself, and the latter by his mother.

The Celio

For a taste of what large swathes of Rome must have been like as the Barbarians swept in and sent the locals fleeing to what is now the *centro storico*, head for the wilder areas of the Celio. Approached by the winding street opposite the **Terme di Caracalla** and the sprawling white marble cuboids of the UN's Food and Agricultural Organisation – built to house Mussolini's Colonies Ministry – the Celio is lush and unkempt, containing the false-fronted church of **San Gregorio Magno**, with its picturesquely overgrown vegetable garden. It was from here that St Augustine was dispatched to convert the pagans of far-off Britain in the sixth century. Nearby is the **Antiquarium Comunale**, an endearing collection of ancient artefacts unearthed locally.

An arcaded street leads past the church of **Santi Giovanni e Paolo**, which was built over a street of Roman houses, to **Santa Maria in Domnica**, with its pretty mosaic, and the **Villa Celimontana** park. The grid of narrow streets on the hill's lower slopes contain three ancient churches: **San Clemente**, **Santi Quattro Coronati** and **Santo Stefano Rotondo**.

Antiquarium Comunale

Viale del Parco del Celio 22 (06 700 1569). Bus or tram to piazza del Colosseo or via di San Gregorio. Closed for restoration; due to reopen in 2002. **Map** p327 1C.

There's something charmingly provincial about this quiet museum in a villa on the Celio hill. Like any local museum, it houses the ancient finds of the area; this being Rome, however, the collection is rather better than you would find elsewhere. Many of the exhibits were unearthed when the city was expanding at the end of the 19th century. Big collections took the pick of the finds, but this little museum hung on to a wonderful range of domestic artefacts, tools and kitchen equipment, many of which look surprisingly similar to their modern equivalents. Perhaps most touching is a jointed doll, a sort of ancient (small-busted) Barbie, found in the tomb of a young girl who died shortly before she was due to be married; it's exquisitely carved, even detailing the complicated hairstyle fashionable in the second century AD.

San Clemente

Via San Giovanni in Laterano (06 7045 1018/ www.sanclemente.it). Metro Colosseo/bus to piazza del Colosseo or via Labicana/tram to via Labicana. **Open** 9am-12.30pm, 3-6pm Mon-Sat; 10am-12.30pm, 3-6pm Sun. **Admission** *Excavations* €2.58/L5,000. **No credit cards. Map** p326 2B.

San Clemente is one of the most intriguing of all Rome's buildings: three layers of history one on top of the other, and a narrow first-century alley you can still walk down, thanks to excavations begun in 1857 by the Irish Dominicans who have been in charge of the church since the 17th century. The existing basilica is a smaller 12th-century copy of its fourth-century predecessor, which in turn was built over an early Christian *titulus* (*see p125* **Inconspicuous Early Church**). The original church was burnt down when the Normans sacked Rome in 1084, but the *schola cantorum*, a walled marble choir, survived and was moved upstairs to the new church, where it still stands. The most striking feature, however, is a vivid 12th-century mosaic in the apse, showing the vine of life spiralling around delightful pastoral scenes. Peasants tending flocks and crops are interspersed with saints and prophets, and the whole mosaic centres on the crucified Christ. The chapel of St Catherine of Alexandria (facing the altar) has frescoes by Masolino (possibly helped by Masaccio) showing scenes from the life of the saint, who was tortured to death strapped to a wheel (giving her name, much later, to the firework).

San Giovanni in Laterano: the first Christian basilica. *See p129.*

CHRISTO · SALVATORI

Tens of thousands sweated it out at
the **Terme di Caracalla**. *See p126.*

The inconspicuous early Church

Looked upon as dangerously extremist cranks in a world of peaceful paganism, Rome's earliest Christians soon learned to keep their heads down to avoid persecution. They met as inconspicuously as possible in private houses (*domus ecclesia*): these were mostly in Rome's further-flung districts, well away from prying eyes in the city centre. They belonged, in general, to church members brave enough to risk being rumbled, and wealthy enough to have rooms to hold big groups. (The Christians did not, contrary to popular belief, meet in catacombs.)

By the time the Emperor Constantine legalised the odd eastern cult, the city's Christian community had formed some two dozen parish-like nuclei, each centred on one of these houses, many of which had become linked by name with their saintly or martyred former owners. Now safely able to display an inscription (*titulus*) of the cross which marked them out as places of Christian worship,

these embryonic churches came to be known as *titulus Caeciliae* (*see p117*, Santa Cecilia in Trastevere), *titulus Pudentianae* (*see p134*, Santa Pudenziana), and so on. As confidence, membership and funds mounted, it was over or around these *tituli* that the first real church structures were erected.

At the end of the fifth century, Rome had 25 titular churches; their importance was stressed by the fact that each had a cardinal as its priest.

Nowadays, each cardinal – as a member of the *Curia*, the Vatican powerhouse, and therefore a token Roman – is entitled to a 'titular' parish in the Eternal City. As the Church spread and the number of cardinals grew, churches with no connection to the original *tituli* were given the label 'titular', but the princes of the church have to double or even triple up ignominiously, though: there are only 46 titular churches to be divvied out among more than 100 cardinals.

Steps lead down from the sacristy to the fourth-century basilica, the layout of which is much obscured by walls built to support the church above. Faded frescoes illustrate episodes from St Clement's miracle-packed life. According to legend, Clement, the fourth pope, was exiled to the Crimea by the Emperor Trajan, but continued his proselytising undaunted and was hurled into the sea, tied to an anchor, for his pains. A year later the sea receded, to reveal a tomb containing the saint's body; after that, the sea would recede once a year, and another miracle would occur.

At the end of the underground basilica, past the strange modern Slavic memorial to St Cyril – inventor of Cyrillic script, great figure of the Orthodox churches, and responsible for bringing Clement's body back to Rome – a stairway leads down to an ancient Roman lane. On one side are the remains of a second-century apartment block or *insula*, where the cult of the god Mithras was celebrated. Mithraism, Christianity's main rival in the late Empire, was a complex mystical religion of Persian origin. Three rooms have been excavated: the anteroom, with benches and a stucco ceiling; the sanctuary, with an altar depicting Mithras killing a bull; and a schoolroom. On the other side of the lane, meanwhile, are the ground-floor rooms of a Roman house that was used by early Christians as a *titulus*, or meeting place.

San Gregorio Magno

Piazza di San Gregorio 1 (06 700 8227). Bus to via di San Gregorio or via delle Terme di Caracalla/tram to via di San Gregorio. **Open** 8am-12.30pm, 3-6.30pm daily. **Map** p327 1C.

Now essentially a baroque building, finished by Giovanni Battista Soria in 1633, this church is famous as the starting point for St Augustine's sixth-century mission to convert heathen England to Christianity. It was originally the family home of one of the most remarkable popes, Gregory the Great (*see p12*), who had it converted into a monastery in 575. In the chapel to the right of the altar is a marble chair dating from the first century BC, reputed to have been used by Gregory as his papal throne. Also here is the tomb of Tudor diplomat Sir Edward Carne, who came to Rome several times to persuade the pope to annul the marriage of Henry VIII and Catherine of Aragon, so the king could marry Anne Boleyn. You may need to ring the bell to get in during the week. Across the vegetable garden stand three small chapels and, behind, some remains of Roman shops that lined the Clivus Scauri (*see also* Santi Giovanni e Paolo *p126*). The chapels of Santa Barbara and Sant'Andrea are medieval structures, both heavily restored in the early 17th century, and both popularly said to have been part of the house of Gregory the Great and his mother St Sylvia. The cappella di Sant'Andrea has frescoes by Guido Reni and Domenichino. The chapel of Santa Silvia dates from the 17th century.

Santa Maria in Domnica

Via della Navicella 10 (06 700 1519). Bus to via della Navicella. **Open** 9am-6pm daily. **Map** p327 1B.

Santa Maria dates from the ninth century, but its 16th-century portico and ceiling were added by Pope Leo X. In the apse, behind the modern altar, there is one of the most charming mosaics in Rome. It was commissioned in the ninth century by Pope Paschal I, and shows the Virgin and Child surrounded by a crowd of saints. The pope kneels at their feet, with a square halo to indicate that he was still living at the time. Above their heads, the apostles are apparently skipping through a flower-filled meadow, with Christ in the centre. Opening hours depend on the priest roping in someone to watch over the church: when he finds no one, you'll find it closed from noon to 3.30pm.

Santi Giovanni e Paolo

Piazza Santi Giovanni e Paolo 13 (06 700 5745). Bus to via Claudia or via di San Gregorio/tram to via di San Gregorio. **Open** *Church* 8.30am-noon, 3.30-6.30pm daily. *Excavations* due to reopen mid-2001. **Map** p326 2B.

Goths and Normans did their worst to the original church that was built here in the fourth century, but remains of it can be seen embedded in the 12th-century façade of the current construction, in a square that has scarcely changed since medieval times. The interior, however, suffered from heavy-handed decorating in the 18th century and now looks like a luxury banqueting hall, with creamy stucco work and extravagant chandeliers.

Excavations beneath the church have revealed Roman houses of the first and second centuries that were evidently used as places of Christian worship (*see p125* **Inconspicuous early church**), and a cellar used for secret Christian burials. The site has been identified as the home of Pammachius, a senator who gave all his money to the poor and embraced Christianity, converting his house into the original church; his story was recorded for posterity by his friend St Jerome. In a lengthy restoration due for completion in mid-2001, wall frescoes have been beautifully restored and further Roman areas opened up. Ask the sacristan for permission to view the (separate) remains of the **Temple of Claudius**, which once dominated the Celian hill, and is now hidden under the church, monastery and bell-tower. Down the left of the church runs the Clivio Scauro, a lane which bears the same name as it did in Roman times; it is crossed by buttresses built between the fifth and 14th centuries to shore up the church.

Santi Quattro Coronati

Via dei Santi Quattro Coronati 20 (06 7047 5427). Bus or tram to via Labicana. **Open** *Church* 6.15am-8pm daily (sometimes closes 1-3pm). *Cloister & oratory* 9.30-noon, 4.30-5.45pm daily. **Admission** donation expected at cloister and oratory. **Map** p326 2B.

This basilica dates from the fourth century but, like San Clemente (*see p122*) and Santi Giovanni e Paolo (*see p125*), was burnt down by rampaging Normans in 1084. It was rebuilt as a fortified monastery, with the church itself reduced to half its original size; the outside apse, visible as you look uphill along via dei Santi Quattro, remains from the original church. The early basilica form is still discernible, and the columns that once ran along the aisles are embedded in the walls of the innermost courtyard. The

church has a fine cosmatesque floor. There is also a beautiful cloister, from about 1220, with a 12th-century fountain playing amid its flowerbeds.

In the oratory next to the church (ring the bell and ask the nuns for the key) is a fresco cycle depicting the Donation of Constantine – the legend that for centuries was put forward by the papacy as a primary source of its authority – according to which an early pope, Sylvester, cured the emperor of leprosy (or another similarly unpleasant disease), after which he was so grateful that in return he granted the Bishops of Rome spiritual and worldly authority over the whole Empire. The frescoes, painted in the 13th century as a defence of the popes' temporal powers, show a pox-ridden Constantine being healed by Sylvester, and then crowning him with a tiara and giving him a cap to symbolise the pope's spiritual and earthly authority. Just to make sure there are no lingering doubts about Sylvester's capacity for heroics, he resuscitates a bull killed as a sacrifice, and frees the Romans from a dragon. The monastery is still home to an enclosed order of nuns, who ask visitors to be as silent as possible.

Santo Stefano Rotondo

Via di Santo Stefano Rotondo 7 (06 421 191) Bus to via della Navicella. **Open** 1.50-4.20pm Mon; 9am-1pm, 1.50-4.20pm Tue-Sat. **Map** p327 1B.

One of very few round churches in Rome, Santo Stefano dates from the fifth century. The many mystics whose imaginations have been fired by the place over the centuries believed it to have been modelled on the Holy Sepulchre in Jerusalem; in its measurements, they argued, lies the secret of the Holy Number of God. The church originally had three concentric naves separated by antique columns; the simplicity of the place was disturbed when arches were built to shore it up in the 12th century, and the outer ring was walled in in 1450. The haunting peace diminished in the 16th century when the outer interior wall was frescoed with graphic scenes of ghastly martyrdoms. A mithraeum beneath the church can be visited by appointment only (*see p60*).

Terme di Caracalla

Viale delle Terme di Caracalla 52 (06 575 8626). Metro Circo Massimo/bus to viale Aventino or viale delle Terme di Caracalla. **Open** 9am-2pm Mon; 9am-4.30pm Tue-Sun. **Admission** €4.13/L8,000. **No credit cards.** **Map** p327 2B.

The high-vaulted ruins of the Baths of Caracalla, surrounded by trees and grass, are pleasantly peaceful today, but were anything but tranquil in their heyday, when up to 1,600 Romans could sweat it out at any one time in the baths and gyms (*see p135* **Wash & brush-up**). You can get some idea of the original splendour of the baths from the fragments of mosaic and statuary littering the ground, although the more impressive finds are in the Vatican museums (*see pp141-3*). The baths were built at the beginning of the third century AD, the fifth to be built in Rome, and the largest up to that

San Giovanni's saints dominate wilder areas of the Celio.

Twisted columns in **San Giovanni**'s 13th-century cloister. *See p129.*

time (although the later Baths of Diocletian were even bigger, *see p135* **Terme di Diocleziano**). They remained in use until well into the sixth century. The two large rooms down the sides were gymnasia. After exercising, Romans cleansed themselves in saunas and a series of baths. The baths were usually open from midday until sunset, and were opulent social centres where people came to relax after work. The complex also contained a library (still identifiable on one side of the baths), a garden, shops and stalls.

Villa Celimontana

Via della Navicella (no phone). Bus to via di San Gregorio or via della Navicella/tram to via di San Gregorio. **Open** dawn to dusk daily. **Admission** free. **Map** p327 1B.

A pretty, leafy, walled garden, its swings and climbing frames swarming with local kids and its lawns packed with bits of ancient marble from the collection of the Mattei family, which owned the property from 1553 until 1928 when it became a public park. The best examples from the Mattei collection can now be admired in the Palazzo Altemps (*see p95*).

From San Giovanni to Santa Croce in Gerusalemme

Serried ranks of post-Unification apartment blocks now occupy an area that was, until the late 1800s, a largely rural zone both inside and outside the walls around the Porta di San Giovanni. This was home to those ancient and medieval residents who preferred quiet anonymity (including Christians wishing to keep a low profile), and a patch of land to till, to the hubbub of central Rome by the Forum and along the river banks.

The massive basilica of **San Giovanni in Laterano**, immediately recognisable by the host of gigantic statue-saints partying atop its façade, dominates the cityscape here. This is Rome's cathedral and its first ever basilica church: note that even Emperor Constantine, who donated the land for the basilica, preferred to give the new sect out-of-the-way terrain, rather than upset the pagan powers-that-were in the centre. Constantine's mother, St Helena, turned part of her palace down the road into a church, **Santa Croce in Gerusalemme**.

On the eastern side of piazza San Giovanni are the remaining sections of the former papal residence, the **Lateran Palace**, the recently restored (but, sadly, inaccessible to the public) **Sancta Sanctorum**, formerly the pope's private chapel, and the **Scala Santa**, or Holy Staircase. These 28 steps were once the ceremonial staircase of the old palace, but are traditionally believed to be those Christ climbed on his way to trial at Pontius Pilate's house in Jerusalem. They were supposedly brought to Rome by St Helena. Devout pilgrims ascend on their knees, particularly on Good Friday. In 1510 Martin Luther gave this a go, but halfway up he decided that relics were a theological irrelevance, and walked back down again. Gracing the middle of the piazza to the west of the basilica is Rome's oldest, tallest obelisk, made in the 15th century BC and imported in 357 to be placed in the Circo Massimo (*see p66*). Pope Sixtus V had it moved to its present location in 1588.

Between the basilicas are two of Rome's least-visited museums: the **Museo Storico della Liberazione di Roma**, with its grim reminders of wartime experiences, and the **Museo Nazionale degli Strumenti Musicali**.

Museo Nazionale degli Strumenti Musicali

Piazza Santa Croce in Gerusalemme 9A (06 701 4796). Metro San Giovanni/bus to piazza Santa Croce in Gerusalemme. **Open** 8.30am-7.30pm Tue-Sun. **Admission** €2.06/L4,000; €1.03/L2,000 concessions. **No credit cards**.

In the early 20th century opera singer Evan Gorga put together this collection of over 800 rare and beautiful musical instruments. The collection gives a comprehensive overview of the history of European music since ancient times. Look out for the exquisite, triple-stringed Barberini harp, a 17th-century harpsichord, and elegantly curving lutes and viols.

Museo Storico della Liberazione di Roma

Via Tasso 145 (06 700 3866). Metro Manzoni/bus to piazza San Giovanni in Laterano. **Open** 4-7pm Tue, Thur, Fri; 9.30am-12.30pm Sat, Sun. **Admission** free. **Map** p326 2A.

Prisoners of the Nazis were brought to this grim building for interrogation during the occupation of Rome in 1943-4. This haunting museum is a tribute to them: resistance fighters; civilians taken in reprisal; and members of the Nazis' proscribed groups such as Jews, homosexuals, gypsies and Communists. The walls are covered with pictures and biographies of those who passed through on their way to die, and several cells have been preserved, complete with prisoners' farewell messages to their families. It's a moving and a chilling place, not forgotten in a hurry.

San Giovanni in Laterano

Piazza di San Giovanni in Laterano 4 (06 6988 6433). Metro San Giovanni/bus or tram to piazza San Giovanni. **Open** *Church* 7am-5.45pm daily. *Baptistery* 9am-12.30pm, 3.30-7pm daily. *Cloister & museum* 9am-6pm daily. **Admission** *Cloister & museum* €2.06/L4,000. **No credit cards**. **Map** p327 1A.

San Giovanni was built around 313, on a site given to Pope Melchiades for the purpose by the Emperor Constantine himself. Little remains of the original basilica, which has been sacked, destroyed by fire and earthquake and heavily restored and rebuilt over the centuries. The façade, surmounted by 15 huge statues, dates from the final rebuilding and was designed by

Rome's oldest, tallest **obelisk**. *See p128*.

Alessandro Gallei in 1735. The interior was last transformed in 1646 by Borromini, who encased the original columns in pillars and stucco. The enormous bronze doors in the main entrance came originally from the Senate House in the Foro Romano (*see p71*). A 13th-century mosaic in the apse survived the revamp, as did a fragment of fresco attributed to Giotto (behind the first column on the right); it shows Pope Boniface VIII announcing the first Holy Year in 1300 (*see p14*). Another survivor is the Gothic *baldacchino* over the main altar; the two busts behind the grille were once believed to contain the heads of saints Peter and Paul (*see p132* **Peter & Paul**). Off the left aisle is the 13th-century cloister: the twisted columns, studded with mosaics, were made by the Vassalletto family. Remains from the original basilica also appear around the walls. The central well is ninth century. A small museum off the cloister contains vestments, along with manuscripts of music by Palestrina. The north façade was added in 1586 by Domenico Fontana. On its right is the octagonal baptistery, founded by Constantine and rebuilt in 432 and 1637. Restored after a bomb exploded nearby in 1993, it has fine fifth- and seventh-century mosaics.

Santa Croce in Gerusalemme

Piazza di Santa Croce in Gerusalemme 12 (06 701 4769). Bus or tram to piazza di Santa Croce in Gerusalemme. **Open** 7am-7pm daily.

Founded in 320 by Helena, redoubtable mother of the Emperor Constantine, this church began as a hall in her home, the Palatium Sessorianum. It was rebuilt and extended in the 12th century, and again in 1743-4. The outline of the original building can be seen from the grounds of the Museo Nazionale degli Strumenti Musicali (*above*). It was built to house the fragments of Christ's cross brought back from the Holy Land by St Helena; these are now behind glass in a Fascist-era chapel, with lashings of grey marble, off the left side of the nave. As well as three pieces of the cross and a nail, there are two thorns from Christ's crown, a section of the good thief's cross and the finger of St Thomas – allegedly the very one the doubting saint stuck into Christ's wound; bagfuls of soil from Calvary lie under the tiles in the charming lower chapel beneath the altar. The chapel's mosaics were laid in the fifth century, but were redesigned around 1484 by Melozzo di Forlì. A plaque on the chapel wall states that women are only allowed into the chapel on one day a year, a rule that is now overlooked.

Monti & Esquilino

Among the dismal *palazzi* of Roman bureaucracy are gem-like churches and ancient Rome's biggest baths.

Stretching from the **Fori Imperiali** (Imperial Fora, *see p70*) to **Stazione Termini**, these two *rioni* (districts) are criss-crossed by some of the city's busiest and least interesting streets, dominated by more than their fair share of dismal bureaucratic *palazzi*. This said, there are several unmissable sights, including two sections of the **Museo Nazionale Romano** and some ancient churches, not to mention the nearest thing Rome has to a multicultural zone.

A single *rione* until 1874, Monti and Esquilino were among ancient Rome's most exclusive suburbs, their green heights dotted with patrician villas and temples. Paradoxically, they overlooked one of the city's worst slums: the grimy, thronging **Suburra**.

Barbarian invasions forced Rome's elite down from their hilltop residences to the relative safety of what is now the *centro storico*, close to the Tiber. The hill areas went into decline and, despite being well within the **Aurelian Wall** (*see p146*), remained almost uninhabited until the Middle Ages, when Monti became the battleground of bullish families such as the Conti, Frangipani, Annibali, Caetani and Capocci, who are remembered in the names of local streets. Each clan constructed its own fortress, with a *torre* (tower). At the end of the 13th century, when anarchy reached its peak, Rome bristled with 200 towers; of the dozen that remain, over half are in this area.

In the 16th century, Sixtus V, the great town planner, reincorporated the area into the city. He ordered the building of the great via Felice, which stretches (nowadays changing names several times along its length) from the top of the **Spanish Steps** (Scalinata di Trinità dei Monti, *see p85*) in the north to **Santa Croce in Gerusalemme** (*see p129*) in the south, a dead-straight 3.5km (two-mile) sweep. Until the building of via Nazionale and via Cavour 300 years later, the whole *rione* developed around this axis. However, as late as the 1850s, 70 per cent of Monti and Esquilino was still farmland and classical ruins.

Colle Oppio and the Suburra

The serene, green Colle Oppio was the site of Nero's **Domus Aurea** (Golden House), an all-too-vivid reminder of the hated emperor, which was torn down, filled in, and replaced with Trajan's baths complex (*see p135* **Wash and brush-up**) after his death. Lurking below, in the marshy swamp between the Quirinale, Viminal and Esquiline hills, was the **Suburra**, ancient Rome's nastiest, most crowded slum area.

Nowadays the Colle Oppio park is peopled by Roman mums and their toddlers during the day, and by Rome's far-right youth and a sprinkling of its more foolhardy gays after darkness falls.

The ancient Suburra still has a real life of its own. Here you find via dei Serpenti, the villagey high street that connects via Nazionale and its carbon-copy high-street fashion emporia with dreary via Cavour, and piazza degli Zingari, the pretty site of a medieval gypsy encampment.

Too built-up to receive the swingeing post-Unification urbanisation treatment meted out to the northern half of these two *rioni*, the warren of medieval streets south of **Santa Maria Maggiore** contains a clutch of stunning early churches (**San Pietro in Vincoli**, **Santa Prassede**, **Santa Pudenziana** and **San Martino ai Monti**). The area can, however, lay claim to a handful of bureaucratic monstrosities in the shape of the Sisde secret police headquarters on via Lanza, the Bank of Italy headquarters in Palazzo Koch on via Nazionale, or the lab on undulating via Panisperna where in 1934 Enrico Fermi and Ettore Majorana first split the atom.

On via Merulana, the **Museo d'Arte Orientale** is a good place to head for when you've overdosed on Roman culture. For a glimpse of greenery, try **Villa Aldobrandini** at the western end of via Nazionale.

Domus Aurea

Viale della Domus Aurea (information 06 481 5576/bookings 06 3996 7700). Metro Colosseo/bus or tram to piazza del Colosseo or via Labicana. **Open** 9am-7.45pm Mon, Wed-Sun; *ticket office closes 6.45pm.* **Admission** €6.20/L12,000; €3.10/L6,000 concessions; *see also p60* **Tickets. No credit cards. Map** p326 2B.
Note that visits must be booked in advance. In the summer of AD 64, a fire devastated a large part of central Rome. The ashes of patrician palaces were mingled with those of slums. Afterwards, anything in the area east of the Forum left unsinged was knocked down to make way for a home fit for the sun-god that Nero liked to think he was.

Santa Maria Maggiore. *See p132.*

Work began on the emperor's Domus Aurea (Golden House) immediately after the fire had died down. A three-storey structure, its main, south-facing façade was entirely clad in gold; inside, every inch not faced with mother-of-pearl or inlaid with gems was frescoed by Nero's pet aesthete Fabullus. Fountains squirted rich perfumes, and baths could be filled with sea or mineral water. In one room, wrote Suetonius, an immense ceiling painted with the sun, stars and signs of the zodiac revolved constantly, keeping perfect time with the heavens.

The house stood in parkland. Lakes were dug, forests planted, and a gilded bronze statue of Nero 35m (115ft) high erected. The moment Nero was in his grave in AD 68, however, work began to eradicate every vestige of the hated tyrant. Vespasian drained the lake to build his amphitheatre (the tight-fisted emperor kept Nero's colossus simply putting a new head on it, and so the stadium became known as the Colosseum), and Trajan used the brickwork as a handy foundation for his baths. So thorough was the cover-up job that for decades after the house's frescos were rediscovered, in 1480, no one realised it was the Domus Aurea that they had stumbled across. The frescoed 'grottos' became an obligatory stopover for Renaissance artists, inspiring – among many other things – Raphael's weird and wonderful frescos in the Vatican (and incidentally giving us the word 'grotesque'). The artists' signatures, scratched into the ancient stucco, can still be seen on the ceiling. After years of restoration, some 30 rooms of the Domus Aurea reopened in June 1999. Over 100 rooms remain off-limits, and a further 200-odd still wait to be excavated.

Museo Nazionale d'Arte Orientale

Via Merulana 248 (06 487 4415). Bus to via Merulana. **Open** 8.30am-2pm Mon, Wed, Fri, Sat; 8.30am-7.30pm Tue, Thur, Sun. Closed 1st & 3rd Mon of each month. **Admission** €4.13/L8,000; €2.06/L4,000 concessions. **No credit cards**. **Map** p326 1A.

For a break from unrelenting Roman artefacts try this impressive collection of oriental art, in a gloomy palazzo near Santa Maria Maggiore. It's arranged geographically and roughly chronologically. First are ancient artefacts from the Near East – pottery, gold, votive offerings – some from the third millennium BC. Then come 11th- to 18th-century painted fans from Tibet, sacred sculptures, and some Chinese pottery from the 15th century. Perhaps most unusual are artefacts from the Swat culture, from Italian-funded excavations in Pakistan.

San Pietro in Vincoli

Piazza di San Pietro in Vincoli 4A (06 488 2865). Metro Cavour/bus to via Cavour. **Open** 7am-12.30pm, 3.30-6pm daily. **Map** p326 1B.

Built in the fifth century over an earlier church and third-century BC ruins, St Peter in Chains was touched up in the eighth, 11th and 15th centuries, and baroque-ified in the 18th. Dominating the church is the monument to Pope Julius II and

Sightseeing

Peter and Paul

Rome wasn't kind to saints Peter and Paul; they were both imprisoned here repeatedly, and both executed here in 67. The former was crucified upside down (at his own request: he didn't consider himself good enough to die the same way up as his Lord) and the other was beheaded.

But the Roman misadventures of the founders of the Church gave Rome a claim to overwhelming importance, long after it had ceased to be Caput Mundi. But you can follow their footsteps (literally in one case, according to religious lore) through a host of sights that still draw the faithful today.

Peter and Paul are Rome's patron saints, and their feast day on 29 June is a public holiday in the city.

Peter

St Peter's: one candidate for the spot where Peter was crucified; his grave is in the necropolis beneath the basilica (*see p141*).
Bramante's Tempietto: another contender for the spot where Peter was crucified (*see p117*).
Santa Francesca Romana: Peter's footprints in this church outside the Foro Romano (*see p71*).

Domine Quo Vadis?: footprints of Christ at the spot where he met a fleeing Peter and shamed him into going back to Rome to be crucified (*see p146*).
Mamertine Prison: a print where Peter head-butted the wall (*see p70*).
San Giovanni in Laterano: a portrait bust some believe once held the apostle's head (*see p129*).
San Pietro in Vincoli: the chains in which Peter was held in a Roman prison (*see p131*).
Catacombe di San Sebastiano: Peter's body is thought to have been kept here until burial (*see p148*).

Paul

San Paolo fuori le Mura: Paul's tomb (*see p153*).
Abbazie delle Tre Fontane: spot where Paul's severed head bounced about (*see p153*).
San Giovanni in Laterano: a portrait bust some believe once held the apostle's head (*see p129*).
San Paolo alla Regola: Almost certainly nowhere near a house where Paul stayed, but popular lore prefers to differ. The church is in a street of the same name. **Map** p324 1B.

Michelangelo's imposing *Moses* (1515). Julius wanted a final resting place five times this size, with 40 statues, in the larger and more prestigious St Peter's (*see p139*), but he died too soon to check that Michelangelo had put in the required work (the artist was otherwise engaged in the Sistine Chapel at the time). His successors were less ambitious. As a result, the mighty Moses (his horns prompted by a bad translation of the Old Testament, where the old Hebrew word for 'radiant' was mistaken for 'horned') is wildly out of proportion with everything else, and infinitely better than the offerings of Michelangelo's students who threw together the rest. The master's hand can be seen in the statues of Leah and Rachael either side of the patriarch. He clearly had nothing to do with the statue of poor Julius himself, by Maso del Bosco. Julius was never placed in his tomb, ending up in an unmarked grave across in the Vatican. As this guide went to press, Moses was undergoing a lengthy restoration; the work was going on, however, behind perspex screens in order to keep the statue visible at all times.

If tourists flock here for Michelangelo, believers come for the chains. Eudoxia, wife of Emperor Valentinian III (445-55), was given a set of chains said to have been used to shackle St Peter in Jerusalem; when she gave them to Pope Sixtus III, the story goes, he placed them next to others used

on the saint in the Mamertine Prison and they became miraculously entangled. They are now conserved in a reliquary on the main altar. There are several relics of St Peter in Rome (*see above* **Peter & Paul**) but the chains are the most venerated; they are paraded around Rome every 1 August.

Santa Maria Maggiore

Piazza Santa Maria Maggiore (06 483 195). Bus to piazza Esquilino or piazza Santa Maria Maggiore. **Open** *Church* 7am-7pm daily. *Loggia* (Guided tours) Mar-Oct 9am-6.30pm daily. Nov-Feb 9am-1pm daily. **Admission** *Loggia* €2.58/L5,000. **No credit cards. Map** p326 1B.

Behind this blowsy baroque façade is one of the most striking basilica-form churches in Rome. Local tradition says a church was built on this spot c366; documents place it almost 100 years later. The fifth-century church was first extended in the 13th century, and again prior to the 1750 Holy Year, when Ferdinando Fuga overhauled the interior and attached the façade that we see today.

Inside, a flat-roofed nave shoots between two aisles to a triumphal arch and apse. Above the columns of the nave, heavily restored fifth-century mosaics show scenes from the Old Testament. Thirteenth-century mosaics in the apse by Jacopo Torriti show Mary, dressed as a Byzantine empress, being crowned Queen of Heaven by Christ. The

Virgin theme continues in fifth-century mosaics on the triumphal arch. The ceiling in the main nave is said to have been made from the first shipment of gold extracted from the Americas by Ferdinand and Isabella of Spain, and was presented to the church by the Borgia pope, Alexander VI (*see p12* **Lust, murder & incest**). The Borgias' heraldic device of a bull is very much in evidence. In the 16th and 17th centuries, two incredibly flamboyant chapels were added. The first was the Cappella Sistina (last chapel on the right of the nave), designed by Domenico Fontana for Sixtus V (1585-90), and decorated with multi-coloured marble, gilt and precious stones. Sixtus had ancient buildings ransacked for materials, and employed virtually every sculptor working in the city. Directly opposite is the Cappella Paolina, an even gaudier Greek-cross chapel, designed by Flaminio Ponzio in 1611 for Paul V to house the ninth- (or possibly 12th-) century icon of the Madonna on the altar.

To the right of the main altar a plaque marks the burial place of Rome's great baroque genius Gianlorenzo Bernini, and his father Pietro. In the loggia high up on the front of the church (tours leave the baptistery about every ten minutes; notes are provided in English) are 13th-century mosaics that decorated the façade of the old basilica, showing the legend of the foundation of Santa Maria Maggiore. The lower row shows Mary appearing to Giovanni the Patrician who, with Pope Liberius, then sketches the plan for the basilica. The legend goes that the Virgin told Giovanni to build a church on the spot where snow would fall the next morning. The snow fell on 5 August 352, a miracle that is commemorated on that day every year, when thousands of flower petals are released from the roof of the church, in the Festa della Madonna delle Neve (*see p227*). The Capella Paolina also contains a relief (1612) by Stefano Maderno showing Liberius tracing the plan of the basilica in the snow.

Santa Prassede

Via Santa Prassede 9A (06 488 2456). Bus to piazza Santa Maria Maggiore. **Open** 7.30am-noon, 4-6.30pm daily. **Map** p326 1B.

This church is a scaled-down copy of the old St Peter's, a ninth-century attempt to recreate an early Christian basilica. Unfortunately, as the uneven brickwork shows, the Romans had lost the knack. The home-grown mosaic artists were no better, so Pope Paschal I decided to import mosaicists from Byzantium to decorate the church. The results are exotic and rich, and what the mosaics lack in subtle modelling they make up for in glorious colours, flowing drapery and fluid movement. In the apse, Christ riding on a cloud is being introduced to the martyr St Praxedes by St Paul on the right, while St Peter is doing the

Authorities were shocked by art nouveau nudity in **Piazza della Republica**. *See p135.*

Terme di Diocleziano

Diocletian's baths, built from AD 298-306, were the largest in Rome, covering over a hectare and able to accommodate 3,000 people at a time. For an idea of the immense size of the structure, tour the remaining fragments: the *tepidarium* and part of the central hall are in the church of Santa Maria degli Angeli (piazza della Repubblica, map p323 1A); a circular hall can be seen in the church of **San Bernardo alle Terme** (piazza San Bernardo, map p323 1B); and the beautifully restored **Aula Ottagona** (octagonal hall) – which used to house Rome's planetarium and now has a tasteful sprinkling of large classical sculptures – is in via Romita (open 9am-2pm Tue-Sat, 9am-1pm Sun, admission free).

A convent complex was built around the largest surviving chunk of the baths by Michelangelo in the 1560s: freshly restored and now containing stone inscriptions and other minor items from the Museo Nazionale Romano ancient artefacts collection, the Terme di Diocleziano reopened to the public in 2000. The collection is sufficiently low-key to allow you to concentrate on the massive bath buildings themselves, and on Michelangelo's 16th-century restoration of the place, including its magnificent central cloister.

Via Enrico de Nicola 79 (06 4782 6152). Metro Termini or Repubblica/bus to piazza dei Cinquecento or piazza della Repubblica. **Open** 9am-7.45pm Tue-Sun; ticket office closes 7pm. **Admission** €4.13/L8,000; €2.06/L4,000 concessions; *see also p59* **Tickets**. **No credit cards. Map** p323 1A.

---

honours on the left for her sister Pudenziana. Pope Paschal is there too, holding a model of the church and sporting a square halo because he was alive when the mosaic was made. Beneath, 12 lambs represent the apostles. The triumphal arch shows the heavenly Jerusalem, with palm-frond-toting martyrs heading for glory.

Off the right side of the nave is the chapel of St Zeno, with some of Rome's most spectacular mosaics. Entered beneath a carved architrave pilfered from an ancient site, the chapel is a dazzling swirl of Byzantine blue and gold, punctuated with saints, animals and depictions of Christ and his mother. Wall and ceiling mosaics are ninth-century; the jolly Mary clutching a dwarf-like Jesus and flanked by sister-saints Praxedes and Pudenziana in the niche above the altar is 13th century. In a room to the right is a portion of column, said to be part of the one that Jesus was tied to for scourging.

Santa Pudenziana

Via Urbana 160 (06 481 4622). Metro Cavour/bus to piazza Esquilino. **Open** 8am-6.30pm Mon-Sat; 8.30am-8.30pm Sun. **Map** p326 1B.

The mosaic in the apse of Santa Pudenziana dates from the fourth century (although it was hacked about in a brutal restoration in the 16th), and so pre-dates the arrival in Rome of the stiffer Byzantine style. It is a remarkable example of the continuity between pagan and Christian art, depicting Christ and the apostles as wealthy Roman citizens, framed by very Roman architectural details and wearing togas, against an ancient Roman cityscape and a glorious Turner-esque sunset. Were it not for Christ's halo and symbols of the four evangelists in the sky, it could be taken for a portrait of senators.

Santi Silvestro e Martino ai Monti

Viale del Monte Oppio 28 (06 487 3166). Bus to piazza Santa Maria Maggiore or via Merulana. **Open** 7.30am-1pm, 4-6.30pm Mon-Sat; 8.30am-noon, 4.30-7pm Sun. **Admission** *Excavation* donation expected. **Map** p326 1B.

The main reason to visit here is to see the third-century *titulus* (*see p125* **Inconspicuous early Church**) beneath the ninth-century church; ask the sacristan to unlock the gate for you (groups should book ahead on the phone number given above). It's a spooky and rarely visited place, littered with bits of sculpture, decaying mosaics and frescos. It does not have the usual jungle of newer foundations sunk through Roman brickwork, so it's not difficult to picture this as an ancient dwelling and/or place of worship. The church above the *titulus* is chiefly remarkable for two frescos: one showing San Giovanni in Laterano (*see p129*) as it was before Borromini's changes (by Dughet, to the left of the entrance), and the other portraying the original St Peter's (*see p139*; by Gagliardi, left of the altar).

Villa Aldobrandini

Via Mazzarino 11. Bus to via Nazionale. **Open** 7am-dusk daily. **Map** p326 1C.

This villa was built in the 16th century for the Dukes of Urbino, and later bought by the Aldobrandini Pope Clement VIII. It's now state property and closed to the public, but the gardens remain open. Reached through a gate off via Mazzarino, they are formal, with neat gravel paths and well-tended lawns. During renovations, the gardens were raised some 30m (100ft) above street level, behind the high wall that dominates the southern end of via Nazionale. A picturesque place with splendid views over the city, marred only by the thundering traffic below.

From piazza Vittorio to the Terme di Diocleziano

Relatively unpopulated and hard by Termini railway station, this area of Monti and Esquilino was too good an opportunity for post-Unification property speculators to pass up. Many of the ancient ruins dotting the area were swept away, and a whole new city-within-a-city was built in the grid mode favoured by the ruling Turinese.

The railway had reached **Termini** in the 1860s, but the first station building was demolished in the 1930s to make way for what is one of Italy's most remarkable modern buildings. Architect Angiolo Mazzoni produced a triumph of undulating horizontal geometry, complete with tubular towers of metaphysical grace straight out of a De Chirico painting. Building began in 1938, but was interrupted by the war, and the station was not inaugurated until 1950. In the late '90s the station – and the **piazza dei Cinquecento** in which it stands – underwent a major facelift.

Proximity to the railway terminus made this area particularly interesting to the developers. Architect Gaetano Koch designed a ministerial and administrative district, focusing on the semi-circular, arcaded **piazza della Repubblica**, once the *esedra* (or *exedra*) of the massive **Terme di Diocleziano** complex (Baths of Diocletian, *see p134* **Terme di Diocleziano**), and still frequently referred to as piazza Esedra by locals.

This heavily-trafficked roundabout is the traditional starting point for major demonstrations, and a favourite hangout for the motley overflow from Stazione Termini. The **Fontana delle Naiadi** at its centre was due for unveiling in 1901, but the nudity of the art nouveau nymphs cavorting seductively with sea monsters around them so shocked the authorities that it was boarded up again for years. Locals fed up with the eyesore eventually tore the planks down, in an undignified inauguration. Sculptor Mario Rutelli is said to have returned to Rome once a year for the rest of his life just to take his buxom models out to dinner.

The extraordinary Museo Nazionale Romano collection of ancient artefacts which used to be confined to the Terme di Diocleziano has spilled over into the **Palazzo Massimo alle Terme** on the south-east fringe of the square. To the north-west is the church of **Santa Maria della Vittoria**, containing one of Bernini's most extraordinary sculptures, and

Wash and brush-up

Baths (*balneae*) were already a popular feature of Roman life at the end of the Republic (27 BC). By the late Empire, the city had around 1,000 of them: some were private, expensive, and strictly for society's upper echelons. Many though, were public – convivial places for meeting, debating, wheeler-dealing or pumping iron – and cheap. The Baths of Agrippa – Rome's first public bathing establishment – opened in 25 BC between largo Argentina and the Pantheon and were free.

Far from being simple wash-houses, the larger, livelier *thermae* of Imperial Rome were cultural centres with sauna, swimming and gym facilities attached. Philosophers would deliver lectures there; learned citizens would browse in libraries. But, on the advice of the baths' resident physicians, habitués (and habituées: the baths had separate hours and/or days for women and men) would follow a rigid health-and-beauty programme, passing from the sweltering *sudatorium* to the *caldarium* with its hot tub, to the *tepidarium*, then to the *frigidarium* for an icy plunge in an outdoor pool.

If Agrippa's baths were the first, they were by no means the greatest. In 62 AD Nero built a baths complex (extended by Alexander Severus in 227) west of the Pantheon. Titus built his on the Colle Oppio in 80. Trajan chose the same venue for his, giving the architect Apollodorus of Damascus leave to use Nero's hated Domus Aurea (*see p130*) as foundations in 109; large chunks are still visible. The **Baths of Caracalla** (*see p126*) could accommodate 1,600 people when they were inaugurated in 217. Scant remains of the **Baths of Constantine**, inaugurated in 315, can be seen in the garden behind the Palazzo Rospigliosi near the Palazzo del Quirinale (*see p78*). But the biggest of all were the **Terme di Diocleziano** (*see p134* **Terme di Diocleziano**), where over 3,000 could sweat it out together.

Bathing culture didn't die out: it was cut off in its prime by Barbarian invaders of the fifth and sixth centuries, who destroyed Rome's aqueducts – thus cutting off supplies of drinking and bathing water – in order to hurry its besieged citizens into capitulation.

Sightseeing

the **Fontana dell'Acqua Felice**. Designed by Domenico Fontana in the form of a triumphal arch, this fountain was completed in 1589. It was one of many urban improvements that were commissioned in Rome by Pope Sixtus V, and provided this district with clean water from an ancient aqueduct. The statue of Moses in the central niche of the fountain, by Leonardo Sormani, has been roundly condemned as an atrocity against taste ever since it was unveiled in 1586.

To the south-west of piazza della Repubblica, **via Nazionale** descends to the old centre, passing the American church of **San Paolo entro le Mura**, with its art nouveau mosaics, on the way.

If you've had your fill of the picturesque and need a shot of the Kafkaesque, take a look at such monolithic examples of Italian public architecture as the Interior Ministry in piazza del Viminale or the **Teatro dell'Opera** in via Firenze.

Via Nazionale: a fume-choked retail hub.

The bureaucratic hub was accompanied by a residential zone, centreing on **piazza Vittorio Emanuele**. The neighbourhood around this large square – always abbreviated to piazza Vittorio – was designed to be one of Rome's smartest when it was built at the turn of the 20th century. You'd never know it now. A steady decline into characterless slumhood was halted in the 1980s by the arrival of a multi-ethnic community, which has injected some life and colour into the run-down streets around the square. As this guide went to press a long-running tussle between market stall-holders and local authorities was entering a critical phase; the authorities are keen to shift stall-holders into more salubrious quarters in a revamped army barracks in via Lamarmora. The pretty gardens at the heart of piazza Vittorio offer a cool place to rest in the shade of palm trees. As you do so, have a go at breaking the still-encoded recipe for changing base metal into gold on the Porta Magica; this curious door, with hermetic inscriptions dating from 1688, is all that remains of the Villa Palombara, an estate that once occupied this site. After dark, the area gets seriously sleazy.

Museo Nazionale Romano – Palazzo Massimo alle Terme

Largo di Villa Peretti 1 (06 4890 3501/bookings 06 481 5576). Metro Repubblica/bus to piazza dei Cinquecento or piazza della Repubblica. **Open** 9am-7.45pm Tue-Sun; ticket office closes 7pm. **Admission** €6.20/L12,000; €3.10/L6,000 concessions; *see also p60* **Tickets**. **No credit cards**. **Map** p323 2A.

The Italian state's spectacular collection of ancient art underwent a radical reorganisation in the run-up to 2000. It is now divided between the Baths of Diocletian, (*see p134* **Terme di Diocleziano**), Palazzo Altemps (*see p95*) and here at the Palazzo Massimo alle Terme.

In the basement of Palazzo Massimo is an extensive collection of coins from earliest times, Roman luxuries, descriptions of trade routes, and audiovisual aids (all of which make this floor especially appealing to kids). On the ground and first floors are busts of emperors, their families and lesser mortals, in chronological order (allowing you to track changing fashions in Roman hairstyles). The ground floor covers the period up to AD 69. In Room 5 is a magnificent statue of Augustus as Pontifex Maximus; Room 8 has a very graceful Muse.

The first floor begins from the age of Vespasian (AD 69-79), the first of the Flavians: his pugilistic portrait bust can be seen in Room 1. Room 15 contains statues of Apollo and of a young girl holding a tray, both from Nero's villa south of Rome in Anzio, and a gracefully crouching Aphrodite from Hadrian's Villa at Tivoli (*see p273*). Room 6 has a marble Roman copy of a Greek discus thrower, cast

in bronze in the fifth.....
peacefully sleeping h.....
second-century AD copy....
The real highlight of the.....
lies on the second floor, w.....
from assorted villas have bee.....
be assigned a time for a guide.....
your ticket). The spectacular fr.....an-
ium (dining room) of the villa o..... ...s s wife
Livia in Prima Porta, just north o..... ...ne, shows a
fruit-filled garden bustling with animal life, and displays a use of perspective that was rarely seen again until the Renaissance. A *triclinium* from the Roman Villa Farnesina (in Room 3) has delicate white sketches on a black background, surmounted by scenes of courts handing down sentences that have had experts baffled for centuries. Also in Room 3 is a lively naval battle, from a frescoed corridor in the same villa. The three *cubicoli* (bedrooms) in Room 5 all have decorative stuccoed ceilings. Room 10 contains Botero-like larger-than-life (megalographic) paintings, and Room 11 has dazzlingly bright marble intarsio works. On the ground floor is an excellent gift and bookshop, with many titles in English and a fine range for children.

San Paolo entro le Mura

Via Napoli 58 (06 488 3339). Bus to via Nazionale. **Open** 9am-5pm Mon-Fri; Sun for services. **Map** p323 2B.

The Episcopalian church of St Paul's Within the Walls, fronting on to via Nazionale, is one of English Gothic-revivalist architect GE Street's happier creations: a light, airy space made radiant by graceful, glowing pre-Raphaelite mosaics by Edward Burne-Jones. The Arab-inspired wall tiles may be the work of his Arts & Crafts Society buddy William Morris.

Santa Maria della Vittoria

Via XX Settembre 17 (06 482 6190). Metro Repubblica/bus to via VE Orlando. **Open** 8.30-11am, 3.30-6pm Mon-Sat; 8.30-10am, 3.30-6pm Sun. **Map** p323 1B.

This modest-looking baroque church, its interior cosily candle-lit and lovingly adorned with marble and gilt, holds one of Bernini's most famous works. The *Ecstasy of St Teresa*, in the Cornaro chapel (the fourth on the left), shows the Spanish mystic floating on a cloud in a supposedly spiritual trance after a teasing, androgynous angel has pierced her with a burning arrow. The result is more than a little ambiguous. (Writing of the angel incident in her *Life*, Teresa recalled: 'So intense was the pain I uttered several moans; so great was the sweetness caused by the pain that I never wanted to lose it.') As a former president of France commented wryly after seeing Bernini's work, 'If that is divine love, I know all about it.' When the chapel is seen as a whole, with the heavens painted in the dome, the light filters through a hidden window, reflecting gilded rays and bathing Teresa in a heavenly glow. She is surrounded by a row of witnesses – members of the Cornaro family sitting in a balcony and earnestly discussing the spectacle.

Sightseeing

e Vatican & Prati

When you've exhausted the hub of Catholicism, check out restless souls and Saxon hostels.

Map p140

With Italian Unification in 1870, the pope lost his temporal sway over what had been the Papal States of central Italy, and was confined behind the Vatican's Mura Leonina (Leonine Wall). The fields (*prati*) to the north and east of the Vatican were swallowed up by new apartment blocks. Vatican-bating names (piazza del Risorgimento, or 'square of the fight to rid Italy of reactionary powers like the pope'; via Cola di Rienzo, Rienzo being the freedom fighter who set up a Roman republic in 1347) were given to the new streets and squares. And the Vatican's medieval service area – Borgo – adapted jovially to the business of living with one foot in the secular camp and the other in the pontifical one.

THE VATICAN STATE

The Vatican State was given its current status in 1929 under a treaty with Mussolini known as La Conciliazione, or Lateran Pact. This was the papacy's consolation prize for having lost its temporal and political power. As such prizes go, it wasn't bad. Italy gave the Vatican 750 million lire and the income from a billion lire in state bonds, exempted it from taxes and duty on imported goods, and agreed to adopt canon law in marriage and make Catholic teaching compulsory in all schools.

Since then, Italy has emerged sufficiently from the Vatican shadow to make divorce, contraception and abortion legal and religious education optional. The Vatican is now taxed on profits from the stock market, although its employees are still not taxed on their earnings and it remains a duty-free zone.

The Vatican City occupies a hilly area west of the Tiber. Until Caligula, and then Nero, decided to build a circus there in the middle of the first century AD, the area was mainly used for the execution of religious troublemakers such as the early Christians – the most famous being St Peter (*see p132* **Peter & Paul**).

Several decades on, in AD 90, the first monument was built over what was believed to be the site of Peter's martyrdom, and in the periods when the new faith was tolerated, this became a popular spot for pilgrims. In the mid-fourth century, Constantine built a basilica over Peter's tomb, although he chose San Giovanni in Laterano (*see p129*) as headquarters for the new official religion. Christians, however, preferred Peter's tomb, and dozens of dwellings, hostels and Vatican-servicing shops appeared in what became known as the **Borgo** (village, *see p144*).

After a series of invasions by Saracens and Lombards in the eighth and ninth centuries, Pope Leo IV encircled the area with a 12-metre (40-foot) high defensive wall, the Mura Leonina. This was extended by Nicholas III in the 13th century. Caught up in the battle between Habsburgs and Angevins for control of Sicily, Nicholas wisely had a covered walkway built along the stretch of the wall that joined the Vatican palace to the fortified, impregnable **Castel Sant'Angelo** (*see p144*). In the event, he himself never needed to high-tail it to the papal bolt-hole, but Pope Clement VII must have blessed his predecessor's foresight in 1527 when he made use of this *corridoio* to survive the sacking of Rome by Charles V's troops (*see chapter* **History**).

After the sacking of Rome, the Città Leonina lost its strategic importance for ever. The papacy moved across the Tiber, first to the Lateran Palace, then to the **Palazzo del Quirinale** (*see p78*), where it stayed until ousted by the Piedmontese royals in 1870, when Pius IX scuttled back behind the safety of the Vatican walls.

Apart from the massive sprawl of St Peter's basilica, the papal apartments and the magnificent structure that houses the **Musei Vaticani** (*see p141*), the 44 hectares encompassed by the Vatican walls include smaller churches, foreign seminaries and minor papal residences. On a more mundane level, there are also post offices, a railway station, a heliport, a pharmacy, a supermarket and a petrol station.

Note that dress codes are strictly enforced, in St Peter's and throughout the Vatican, including the museums, gardens and the Sistine Chapel. Ensure that you have something to cover exposed shoulders and/or legs above the knee; if you do not, you will almost certainly be turned away.

The Vatican

(Central switchboard 06 6982). **Credit** cards are not accepted anywhere in the Vatican state. **Map** p321 1C and p140.

Saints keep watch over **St Peter's basilica** and Bernini's colonnade.

Tourist Information Office

Piazza San Pietro (tourist information 06 6988 1662/www.vatican.va). Metro Ottaviano/bus to piazza Pia or piazza del Risorgimento. **Open** 8.30am-6.45pm Mon, Tue, Thur-Sat; 12.30-6.45pm Wed.

The tourist information office in St Peter's square dispenses information, organises guided tours, has a bureau de change and postal and philatelic services, and sells souvenirs and publications.

St Peter's basilica

After 120 years as the world's most elegant building site, the current St Peter's was consecrated on 18 November 1626 by Urban VIII – exactly 1,300 years after the consecration of the first basilica on the site. The earlier building was erected on the orders of the first Christian emperor, Constantine. Records show that it was a five-aisled classical basilica, fronted by a large courtyard and four porticoes. It was steadily enlarged and enriched, becoming the finest church in Christendom.

By the mid-15th century, however, its south wall was on the point of collapse. Pope Nicholas V commissioned new designs and had 2,500 wagonloads of masonry from the Colosseum carted across the Tiber, but never got further than repair work. No one wanted to demolish the most sacred church in Christendom. It took the arrogance of Pope Julius II and his pet architect Bramante to get things moving. In 1506, 2,500 workers tore down the 1,000-year-old basilica, and Julius laid the foundation stone for its replacement.

Following Bramante's death in 1514, Raphael took over the work, and scrapped his predecessor's plan for a basilica with a Greek cross plan (*see p87* **Glossary**), opting for an elongated Latin cross. In 1547, Michelangelo took command and reverted to a Greek design. He died in 1564, aged 87, but not before coming up with the design for a massive dome and supporting drum. This was completed in 1590, the largest brick dome ever constructed.

In 1607 Carlo Maderno won the consent of Pope Paul V to demolish the remaining fragments of the old basilica and put up a new façade, crowned by enormous statues of Christ and the apostles. After Maderno's death Bernini took over, and despite nearly destroying both the façade and his reputation by erecting towers on either end (one of which fell down), he became the hero of the hour with his sumptuous *baldacchino* and famous piazza. This latter was built between 1656 and 1667, its colonnaded arms reaching out towards the Catholic world in a symbolic embrace. The main oval measures 340 by 240 metres (1,115 by 787 feet), and is punctuated by the central Egyptian obelisk (dragged from Nero's Circus in 1586) and two symmetrical fountains, by Maderno and Bernini. The 284-columned, 88-pillared colonnade is topped by 140 statues of saints.

In the portico (1612), opposite the main portal, is a mosaic by Giotto (c1298), a survivor from the original basilica. There are five doors leading into the basilica: the central ones come from the earlier church, while the others are all 20th century. The last door on the right is opened only in Holy Years by the pope himself.

Inside, the basilica's size is emphasised on the marble floor, where a boastful series of brass line inscriptions measure the lengths of other churches around the world that haven't made the grade. But it is Bernini's huge

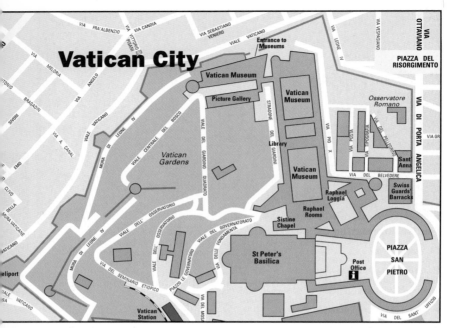

Vatican City

curlicued *baldacchino* (1633), hovering over the
high altar, that is the real focal point. This was
cast from brass purloined from the Pantheon
(prompting local wits to quip *quod non fecerunt
barbari, fecerunt Barberini* – what the
Barbarians didn't do, the Barberini did,
referring to Bernini's patron Pope Urban VII, a
Barberini), and is bathed in light flooding in
from windows in the dome above. The canopy
stands over the traditional site of St Peter's
tomb; two flights of stairs lead beneath the altar
to the *confessio*, where a niche contains a ninth-
century mosaic of Christ, the only thing from
old St Peter's that stayed in the same place
when the new church was built.

Catholic pilgrims head straight for the last
pilaster on the right before the main altar, to
kiss the big toe of Arnolfo da Cambio's brass
statue of St Peter (c1296), worn down by
centuries of pious lips. Tourists, on the other
hand, make a beeline for the first chapel on the
right, where bullet-proof glass now protects
Michelangelo's *Pietà* (1499). This is the only
work that he ever bothered to sign, on the
band across the Virgin's chest. Proceeding
around the basilica in an anti-clockwise
direction, notice Carlo Fontana's highly
flattering monument to the unprepossessing
Queen Christina of Sweden, a convert to

Catholicism in 1655, to the left of the Pietà
chapel. The third chapel has a tabernacle and
two angels by Bernini, plus St Peter's only
remaining painting – a *Trinity* by Pietro da
Cortona – (others have been replaced by mosaic
copies). In the first chapel beyond the right
transept is a tear-jerker of a neo-classical tomb
(of Pope Clement XIII) by Antonio Canova (1792).

Bernini's Throne of St Peter (1665), flanked
by papal tombs, stands at the far end of the
nave beyond the high altar, under an almost
psychedelic stained-glass window. Encased
within Bernini's creation there is a wood-and-
ivory chair, probably dating from the ninth
century but for many years believed to have
belonged to Peter himself. To the right of the
throne is Bernini's 1644 monument to his patron
Urban VIII, who commissioned the bronze
portrait, between statues of *Charity* and *Justice*,
before his death. On the pillars supporting the
main dome there are much-venerated relics,
including a chip off the true cross.

Near the portico end of the left aisle is a
group of monuments to the Old Pretender James
Edward Stuart (the 18th-century claimant to teh
throne of England and Scotland), his wife Maria
Clementina Sobieski and their sons Charles
Edward (Bonnie Prince Charlie) and Henry
Benedict. They are buried in the grottos below.

The **Vatican Grottos** – the Renaissance crypts beneath the basilica, with more papal tombs – are open to visitors. The **Necropolis**, where St Peter is believed to be buried, is beneath these grottos and can be visited with permission. In the treasury off the left nave of the basilica there is a small **treasury museum**, containing some stunning liturgical relics. The **dome** (reached via a cramped lift or hundreds of stairs) offers fabulous views of the **Vatican Gardens**, which can be toured.

Basilica
Open *Oct-Mar* 7am-6pm daily. *Apr-Sept* 7am-7pm daily. **Admission** free.
Free guided tours of the basilica in English set off from the tourist information office at 2.15pm Mon-Sat; 3pm Mon, Wed-Fri; 2.30pm Sun. (Note that these depend on the goodwill of volunteers and do not always take place; phone to check beforehand.)

Dome
Open *Oct-Mar* 8am-4.45pm daily. *Apr-Sept* 8am-5.45pm daily. **Admission** €3.61/L7,000. *With lift* €4.13/L8,000.

Grottos
Open *Oct-Mar* 7am-5pm daily. *Apr-Sept* 7am-6pm daily. **Admission** free.

Necropolis
Apply at the Uffizio degli Scavi (06 6988 5318/ fax 06 6988 5518/uff.scavi@fabricsp.va).
Open *Guided tours* 9am-5pm Mon-Sat.
Admission €7.75/L15,000.
English-language tours must be booked at least 25 days ahead of your visit.

Treasury Museum
Open *Oct-Mar* 9am-5pm daily. *Apr-Sept* 9am-6pm daily. **Admission** €4.13/L8,000; €2.58/L5,000 concessions.

Vatican Gardens
(06 6988 4466). **Guided tours** *High season* 10am Mon, Tue, Thur-Sat (depending on the weather). *Low season* 10am Thur, Sat. **Admission** €8.78/L17,000; €6.71/L13,000 concessions.
Phone the gardens office to book at least three or four days in advance.

Papal audiences
(06 6988 3273/06 6988 3114/fax 06 6988 5863).
Open *Prefettura della Casa Pontificia* 9am-1pm Mon-Sat.
Apply to the Prefettura della Casa Pontificia at the telephone number above. Tickets, which can also be collected on Tuesdays from 3-8pm, are free. Entry is through the bronze door at the basilica end of Bernini's colonnade. For a private audience, your local bishop has to make a written request, which can take between three months and a year to be granted.

Musei Vaticani

It's a brisk ten-minute walk from St Peter's to the entrance of the Vatican Museums. Begun in 1506 by Pope Julius II, this immense, stunning collection represents the accumulated fancies and obsessions of a long line of strong, often contradictory personalities. The popes' unique position allowed them to obtain treasures on favourable terms from other collectors, and artists often had little choice as to whether they accepted papal commissions.

The collections are so vast that it's impossible to take in more than a small portion on one visit. The museum authorities have laid out four colour-coded routes, ranging from a race to the Sistine Chapel, to a conscientious five-hour plod around the lot. The following are selected highlights.

Ancient and modern at **Musei Vaticani**.

Musei Vaticani

Viale del Vaticano (06 6988 3333). Metro Ottaviano/bus to piazza del Risorgimento. **Open** *Mar-Oct* 8.45am-3.30pm Mon-Fri; 8.45am-12.30pm Sat. *Nov-Feb* 8.45am-12.30pm Mon-Sat. *Last Sun of each month* 8.45am-12.45pm. **Admission** €9.30/L18,000; €6.20/L12,000 concessions; free last Sun of month. **No credit cards.**

Note that the Vatican revises its opening times from year to year. If you don't want to be disappointed, phone ahead to check. There are four special itineraries for wheelchair users, with disabled toilets en route; a brochure is available at the ticket office. Wheelchairs can be borrowed at the museum: call ahead (06 6988 3860) to check availability.

Museo Egiziano

Founded by Gregory XVI in 1839, in rooms partly decorated in Egyptian style, this is a representative selection of ancient Egyptian art from 3,000-600 BC. It includes statues of a baboon god, painted mummy cases and a marble statue of Antinous, Emperor Hadrian's lover, who drowned in Egypt and was declared divine by the emperor. A couple of real mummies help make this the most exciting bit of the whole Vatican if you have grisly-minded kids in tow.

Galleria Chiaramonte

Founded by Pius VII in the early 19th century and laid out by the sculptor Canova, this is an eclectic collection of Roman statues, reliefs and busts. Don't miss the replica of a Greek statue by Polyeuctos of stuttering orator Demosthenes, and a copy of a *Resting Satyr* by the Greek sculptor Praxiteles.

Museo Pio-Clementino

In the late 18th century Pope Clement XIV and his successor Pius VI began the world's largest collection of classical statues, which now fills 16 rooms. Don't miss the first-century BC *Belvedere Torso* by Apollonius of Athens; the *Apollo Sauroctonos*, a Roman copy of the bronze *Lizard Killer* by Praxiteles; and, in the octagonal Belvedere Courtyard, the exquisite *Belvedere Apollo*, as well as *Laocoön*, who is being throttled by sea serpents as punishment by the goddess Athena for warning the Trojans that the wooden horse was full of wily Greeks.

Museo Etrusco

Founded in 1837 by Gregory XVI, and enlarged in the 20th century, this collection contains Greek and Roman art as well as Etruscan masterpieces, including the contents of the Regolini-Galassi Tomb from c650 BC, the Greek-inspired fourth-century BC *Mars*, and the fifth-century BC young man and small slave.

Galleria dei Candelabri & Galleria degli Arazzi

Roman marble statues, in a long gallery studded with candelabra. In the next gallery are ten huge tapestries woven by Flemish master Pieter van Aelst from the cartoons by Raphael that are now in London's Victoria and Albert Museum.

Angels preside at **Castel Sant'Angelo.** *See p144.*

Galleria delle Carte Geografiche

Pope Gregory XIII (of the Gregorian calendar, which we use today) had a craze for astronomy, and was responsible for this 120m (394ft) long gallery, with its Tower of the Winds observation point at the north end. Ignazio Danti of Perugia drew the maps showing each Italian region, city and island, with extraordinary precision for the time (1580-3).

Stanza di Raffaello, Loggia di Raffaello, Cappella di Niccolò V

The Raphael Rooms were part of Nicholas V's palace, and were originally decorated by Piero della Francesca. Julius II then let Perugino, Lorenzo Lotto and other Renaissance masters loose on them, until he discovered Raphael, whereupon he gave the young artist *carte blanche* to redesign four rooms of the Papal Suite.

The order of the visit changes from time to time, but it makes sense, if possible, to see the rooms in the order in which they were painted. The Study (Stanza della Segnatura) was Raphael's first bash (1508-11), and features philosophical and spiritual themes – the *Triumph of Truth, Good and Beauty.* Best known is the star-packed *School of Athens* fresco, with contemporary artists as classical figures: Plato is Leonardo; the thinker on the steps – Heraclitus – is Michelangelo; Euclid is Bramante (note the letters RUSM, Raphael's signature, on his gold collar); and Raphael himself stands to the left of a capped man, believed to be his pupil Sodoma. Raphael next turned his hand to the Waiting Room (Stanza di Eliodoro, 1512-14), frescoed with political themes such as *The Expulsion of Heliodorus,* a re-reading of a biblical episode designed to highlight Pope Julius II's supreme political savvy.

The Dining Room (Stanza dell'Incendio, 1514-17) is devoted to the feats of Popes Leo III and IV, including *The Fire in the Borgo,* which Leo IV halted with the sign of the cross. The Reception Room (Sala di Constantino, 1523-5) was completed by Giulio Romano after Raphael's death in 1520, but was based on Raphael's sketches of the Church's triumph over paganism.

The long Loggia di Raffaello (Raphael's Loggia), with a beautiful view over Rome, was started by Bramante in 1513 and finished by Raphael and his assistants. It features 52 small paintings on biblical themes, and leads into the Sala dei Chiaroscuri (Raphael's frescos here were obliterated by Gregory XIII, but the magnificent ceiling remains). The adjacent Cappella di Niccolò V (Chapel of Nicholas V), has outstanding frescos of scenes from the lives of saints Lawrence and Stephen by Fra Angelico (1448-50).

Appartamento Borgia

This six-room suite, known as the Borgia Rooms, was adapted for Pope Alexander VI (1492-1503; *see p12* **Lust, murder & incest**) and decorated by Pinturicchio and his school with a series of frescos on biblical and classical themes. In 1973, some 50 rooms of the Borgia Apartments were renovated to house the Collezione d'Arte Religiosa Moderna, featuring modern religious works.

The Sistine Chapel

The world's most famous frescos cover the ceiling and one wall of the Capella Sistina, built by Sixtus IV in 1473-84. For centuries it has been used for popes' private prayers and papal elections (conclaves, *see p145* **Conclave capers**). In the 1980s and '90s the 930 sq m (10,000sq ft) of *Creation*, on the ceiling, and the *Last Judgment* on the wall behind the altar were subjected to the most controversial restoration job of all time.

In 1508 Michelangelo was commissioned to paint some kind of undemanding decoration on the ceiling of the Sistine Chapel. Julius II may have been egged on to give the job to a sculptor with no experience in fresco by Bramante, who was jealous of the pope's admiration for Michelangelo and desperately wanted to see him fail. Michelangelo responded by offering to do far more than mere decoration, and embarked upon his massive venture alone. He spent the next four years on top of scaffolding on his back, with paint and plaster dripping into his eyes, with his pay arriving so infrequently that he complained to his brother in 1511, 'I could well say that I go naked and barefoot.'

The work, completed in 1512 (so Michelangelo was working a short corridor away from Raphael), was done in the heady days of the high Renaissance when optimistic artists were nobly bent on the pursuit of beauty. Beginning at the *Last Judgment* end, scenes depict the *Separation of Light from Darkness*, the *Creation of Sun, Moon and Planets*, the *Separation of Land and Sea* and the *Creation of Fishes and Birds*, *Creation of Adam*, *Creation of Eve*, *Temptation* and *Expulsion from Paradise*, the *Sacrifice of Noah* (which should come after the *Flood*, but was put here for space reasons), the *Flood*, and the *Drunkenness of Noah*. Michelangelo painted these scenes backwards, beginning with Noah's drunkenness. They are framed by monumental figures of Old Testament prophets and classical sibyls.

Twenty-two years after completing this masterpiece, the aged and embittered artist rolled up his sleeves again and started work on the *Last Judgment* to fill the altar wall. In the interim, Rome had been sacked (1527, *see p15*) – an episode seen by many, including Michelangelo, as the wrath of God descending on the corrupt city – and the atmosphere was altogether gloomier and more pessimistic. It took him seven years to complete the work, in 1541. It is altogether more doom-laden, as befits the subject. Hidden among the larger-than-life figures that stare, leer and cry out from their brilliant blue background, Michelangelo painted his own, frowning, miserable face on the wrinkled human skin held by St Bartholomew, below and to the right of the powerful figure of Christ the Judge. Pius IV objected to so much nudity and wanted to destroy the fresco; thankfully he was persuaded to settle for suitably modest loincloths, most of which were removed in the recent restoration.

Dwarfed by Michelangelo's work, the sorely neglected paintings on the side walls of the chapel are a who's who of Renaissance greats, painted before Michelangelo took up his paintbrush. On the left-hand wall as you look at the *Last Judgment*, are: *The Journey of Moses* by Perugino; *Events from the Life of Moses* by Botticelli; *Crossing the Red Sea* by Cosimo Rosselli; *Moses Receives the Tablets of the Law* by Cosimo Rosselli; *The Testament of Moses* by Luca Signorelli; *The Dispute over Moses' Body* by Matteo da Lecce; *The Resurrection* by Arrigo Paludano; *The Last Supper* by Cosimo Rosselli; *Handing over the Keys* by Perugino; *The Sermon on the Mount* by Cosimo Rosselli; *The Calling of the Apostles* by Ghirlandaio; *The Temptations of Christ* by Botticelli; and *Baptism of Christ* by Perugino. The papal portraits are by the same masters.

Pinacoteca

Founded by Pius VI in the late 18th century, the Pinacoteca (picture gallery) includes many of the pictures that the Vatican hierarchy managed to recover from Napoleon after their forced sojourn in France in the early 19th century. The collection ranges from early paintings of the Byzantine School and Italian primitives to 18th-century Dutch and French old masters, and includes Giotto's *Stefaneschi Triptych*, a *Pietà* by Lucas Cranach the Elder, several delicate Madonnas by Fra Filippo Lippi, Fra Angelico, Raphael and Titian, Raphael's very last work *The Transfiguration*, Caravaggio's *Entombment* and a chiaroscuro *St Jerome* by Leonardo.

Museo Paolino

This collection of Roman and neo-Attic sculpture has been housed since 1970 in the Museo Paolino. Highlights include the beautifully draped statue of Sophocles from Terracina, a *trompe l'œil* mosaic of an unswept floor and the wonderfully elaborate *Altar of Vicomagistri*.

Pio Cristiano Museum

The upper floor of the Museo Paolino is devoted to a collection of early Christian antiquities, mostly sarcophagi carved with reliefs of biblical scenes.

The Vatican Library

Founded by Pope Nicholas V in 1450, this is one of the world's most extraordinary libraries, with 100,000 medieval manuscripts and books and over a million other volumes. It is open to students and specialists on application to the Prefettura (06 6988 3273). *See also p296.*

Borgo & Prati

Leading up to the Vatican is via della Conciliazione, an austere foil to Bernini's elaborate curves. Until the 1930s – when Mussolini did the demolition job that successive popes had been planning to do for centuries – the space occupied by this sweep of road was a fascinating warren of medieval streets, only a few of which now remain in the lively **Borgo** quarter. Here, salt-of-the-earth Romans mingle with off-duty Swiss guards and immaculately robed priests from the Vatican *Curia* (administration). Here, too, is the **Museo Storico Nazionale dell'Arte Sanitaria**, in medieval Rome's British enclave.

Cutting through Borgo is the raised, covered **Passetto** (*see p144*), the 13th-century escape route to **Castel Sant'Angelo**, which saved many a pope's skin through attack and invasion.

Further north, the prosperous **Prati** residential area was largely built in the late 19th century. A spot of retail therapy down Prati's main drag, via Cola di Rienzo, is a good antidote to a surfeit of culture. Otherwise, the area's main features are the Trionfale flower market (*see p215*), the endless military barracks lining viale delle Milizie, some quiet, tree-lined streets close to the river, and the massive, bombastic Palazzo di Giustizia – popularly known as *il palazzaccio*, the big ugly building – sandwiched between piazza Cavour and the Tiber. On the river bank is one of Catholic Rome's truly weird experiences: the **Museo delle Anime dei Defunti**.

Castel Sant'Angelo

Lungotevere Castello 50 (06 681 9111/bookings 06 3996 7600). Bus to lungotevere Vaticano or piazza Cavour. **Open** 9am-8pm Tue-Sun; ticket office closes 7pm. **Admission** €5.16/L10,000; €2.58/L5,000 concessions. **No credit cards. Map** p321 1B.
Begun by the Emperor Hadrian in AD 135 as his own mausoleum, Castel Sant'Angelo has since functioned as a fortress, prison and papal residence. Although it now plays host to temporary art shows (displays of stolen paintings and artefacts recovered by the police are regular choices), the real pleasure

Bernini's **colonnade** embraces the Catholic world. *See p139.*

of a visit to Castel Sant'Angelo lies in wandering from Hadrian's original, spiralling ramp-like entrance to the upper terraces, with their superb views of the city and beyond. In between, there is much to see: the lavish Renaissance salons, decorated with spectacular frescos and *trompe l'œils*; the chapel in the Cortile d'Onore, designed by Michelangelo for Leo X; and, halfway up an easily missed staircase, Clement VII's surprisingly tiny personal bathroom, painted by Giulio Romano. Puccini had Tosca hurl herself from the top of Castel Sant'Angelo in the final tragic, stirring act of the opera of the same name.

The **Passetto** (passageway), built by Pope Nicholas III in the 13th century, connecting the castle to the Vatican, is clearly visible, a reminder of the days when petrified popes, threatened by invading forces, scampered from St Peter's to the relative safety of the castle. There are guided tours (in Italian only) of the Passetto at 3pm every Saturday and Sunday. Booking is advisable though not obligatory, at the number given above. Tours cost €4.13/L8,000 (free under-12s), in addition to the admission fee for the castle.

Museo delle Anime dei Defunti

Lungotevere Prati 12 (06 6880 6517). Bus to piazza Cavour. **Open** 7.30-11am, 4.30-7pm daily. **Admission** free. **Map** p321 1B.

Conclave capers

'May you live a hundred years!' is the Polish greeting that Karol Wojtyla's compatriots use whenever they meet the pope, and close observers say John Paul II is determined not to disappoint. Despite his failing health, the octagenarian former actor and playwright keeps up a punishing schedule, continuing to break records and reach parts no pontiff has reached before.

Yet there is no denying the 'end of an era' atmosphere that has been hanging over the world's smallest state for some time, as potential successors jostle to increase their earthly power base. By the time the College of Cardinals gathers in the Sistine Chapel for its secret ballot, allegiances will have been formed and key decisions made in meetings and over meals in the months and years preceding the conclave itself.

But what exactly happens as the cardinals huddle before Michelangelo's *Last Judgment* and Catholics wait eagerly in St Peter's square for as many days as it takes for a unanimous decision to be reached? Ask any church leader, and he'll tell you the Holy Spirit moves among his modern-day apostles until the best candidate is found. The reality is undoubtedly far murkier: indeed, the Holy Spirit has generally to preside over much frantic politicking and several null ballots before the right man for the job emerges.

Cardinals are kept incommunicado inside the Vatican for the duration of the conclave (albeit in smart guest quarters these days, rather than camping inside the chapel itself). Smoke signals from a particular chimney – black smoke for a null vote, white smoke for a successful one – are the only indication to the outside world of how the election is going. When a unanimous decision is finally made, a handful of straw is placed on the fire to produce white smoke and thus proclaim the good news to the world… or that's the theory. When John Paul II was elected, dirty grey smoke emerged, causing momentary panic and confusion among commentators.

So who are the pundits backing as the most likely man to become the 265th successor of St Peter? With half the world's Catholics concentrated in Latin America, many people are putting their money on *papabili* (papal possibles) from that continent. The powerful Italian lobby, on the other hand, wants one of its own men back in this traditionally Italian job.

Whoever wins, the event will have the kind of coverage no previous papal election has had: for years now, each papal sneeze or tumble has prompted major American networks to fly in camera crews and spend small fortunes in hotel rooms and rooftop accommodation with Vatican views. Record numbers of reporters are preparing to cover the ancient rituals that make up this event. All of which must raise a smile on the lips of John Paul II, who takes pleasure in reminding journalists that they haven't seen the last of him yet!

This macabre collection, attached to the startlingly neo-Gothic church of Sacro Cuore del Suffragio, contains the hand- and fingerprints left on the prayer books and clothes of the living by dead loved ones, reminding those left in the temporal world to say mass to release their souls from purgatory into heaven. Begun just over a century ago, the collection is intended to convince the sceptical of life after death. Among other uncanny exhibits, there's an incandescent hand-print supposedly left by Sister Clara Scholers on the habit of a fellow-nun in Westphalia in 1696, and hand-scorched bank notes left by a dead soul outside a church where he wanted mass to be said.

Museo Storico Nazionale dell'Arte Sanitaria

Lungotevere in Sassia 3 (06 6835 2353). Bus to borgo Santo Spirito or lungotevere in Sassia. **Open** 10am-noon Mon, Wed, Fri. **Admission** €3.61/ L7,000; €2.58/L5,000 concessions. **No credit cards.** **Map** p321 1C.

Anglo-Saxon pilgrims to St Peter's tomb would stay in the *burgus Saxonum*, a hospice established by King Ine of Wessex around 726, which gave its name to this area – in Sassia – south-east of St Peter's. British funds for the hospice were cut off when the Normans invaded in 1066, after which it passed into papal hands, and thence to Templar Guy de Montpellier, who set up a hospital and founded the Order of the Holy Spirit (*Santo Spirito*). A few rooms of the modern(ish) hospital of Santo Spirito house a gruesome collection of medical artefacts, dating from ancient times to the 19th century. As well as the usual collection of skeletons, organs, anatomical charts and surgical instruments, there's a collection of wax votive offerings, left at churches and shrines to encourage God to cure parts of the body conventional medicine could not reach. There are also reconstructions of a 17th-century pharmacy and an alchemist's laboratory. Any rare opportunity to visit the long-closed 15th-century wing of the hospital should be seized.

Sightseeing

The Appian Way

The Queen of Roads had country villas, a race-track and grand tombs that were the only place to be seen dead in.

Map p147

Begun in the late fourth century BC by the statesman, lawmaker and sometime official censor Appius Claudius Caecus, the **via Appia Antica** (old Appian Way, so called to distinguish it from the modern via Appia Nuova to the east) is the oldest Roman military road. Originally stretching from the city centre to Capua near Naples, it was gradually lengthened so troops and supplies could be moved swiftly as Rome extended its control over southern Italy. By 191 BC it had reached Brindisi on the Adriatic coast, making it the Romans' main route to their eastern provinces; so important was it, it was known as the *regina viarum*, the queen of roads.

The via Appia originally began at the Forum Boarium (*see p107*) by the River Tiber, running through the valley where the **Circo Massimo** (*see p66*) and **Terme di Caracalla** (*see p126*) stand. With the construction of the Aurelian Walls around AD 270, its point of departure was considered to be the Porta Appia, now the **Porta San Sebastiano**, where the **Museo delle Mura** (Museum of the Walls, *see p148*) allows access on to a stretch of wall.

Spruced up and made into the centrepiece of an extensive new park, the **Parco della Caffarella-Parco dell'Appia Antica** prior to 2000, the via Appia has become ever more popular as a destination for strolling families, especially on Sundays when the road is closed off to all but local traffic. After dusk, it remains a favoured retreat for lovers, ensconced in parked cars with steamed-up windows; at the Gran Raccordo (ring-road) end, men visit the handful of elderly prostitutes sitting by their braziers. For decades, the Gran Raccordo sliced straight through the ancient road; in 2000 an underpass was completed, and the two truncated stretches of the *regina viarum* were reunited.

Along the Appian Way

The via Appia Antica begins at the Porta di San Sebastiano, the largest and best-preserved of the gates that were built by Aurelian when he walled the city in the third century AD. The gate now houses the **Museo delle Mura** and allows access on to a long stretch of Aurelian's fortifications.

Porta San Sebastiano: the Appia starts here.

Further along on the right, a former paper mill has been transformed into the **Centro Visite Parco Appia Antica** (visitors' centre). On the left is the austere church of **Domine Quo Vadis?** (open 7am-7pm). Inside the door are the imprints of two long flat feet that are supposed to have been left by Christ when he appeared to St Peter (*see p132* **Peter & Paul**), who was running away from Rome and crucifixion. Christ told him that he himself was going back to Rome to be crucified again, and Peter was thus shamed into returning. The painting to the left side of the altar depicts his martyrdom.

A right fork outside the church along the via Ardeatina leads to the **Catacombe di Domitilla** (access from via delle Sette Chiese) and the **Fosse Ardeatine**, a memorial to a more recent act of barbarity. Formerly a quarry, the Fosse is where 335 Italians were shot by the Nazis in 1944 as a reprisal for an attack by the Resistance. They now lie here in an underground mausoleum; a memorial ceremony is held every year on 25 April. A left fork past the Domine Quo Vadis? church along via della Caffarella leads into the **Parco della Caffarella-Parco dell'Appia Antica** proper.

Continuing along the via Appia Antica, the **Catacombe di San Callisto** and the **Catacombe di San Sebastiano** precede three of the road's most famous ancient sites: the **Mausoleo di Romolo**, behind which rise the red brick walls of the **Circo di Massenzio**, which was built by Romulus's father Maxentius for chariot racing; and the **Tomba di Cecilia Metella**.

After the tomb comes a long stretch of road that in parts still retains the original flagstones used by the Romans. The tombs that line it are picturesquely overgrown and have been attracting artists for centuries. Much further on is the site of the second century AD **Villa dei Quintili** (access from via Appia Nuova only). Beyond this point the road is quieter and the landscape wilder, with fragments of aqueduct standing in the fields. Any turning to the left will take you eventually to via Appia Nuova, the main modern route back to the centre of Rome.

Circo di Massenzio & Mausoleo di Romolo

Via Appia Antica 153 (06 780 1324). **Open** 9am-5pm Tue-Sun. **Admission** €2.58/L5,000; €1.55/L3,000 concessions. **No credit cards**.
Built by the Emperor Maxentius in the early years of the fourth century AD, this circus could seat

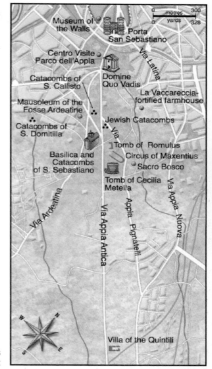

Sightseeing

Popular with runners, strollers and lovers.

Museo delle Mura: access to the walls.

10,000 people. The emperor had his beloved son Romulus buried in the impressive mausoleum near the circus. Between the two are the ruins of Maxentius's vast villa.

Museo delle Mura

Via di Porta San Sebastiano 18 (06 7047 5284). **Open** 9am-7pm Tue-Sat; 9am-5pm Sun. **Admission** €2.58/L5,000; €1.55/L3,000 concessions. **No credit cards.**

Housed in the Porta San Sebastiano, which was built by the Emperor Aurelian (AD 270-75) as the exit-gate from the city on to the Appian Way, the little Museum of the Walls has a smallish collection of artefacts associated with Roman walls and roads, and – best of all – allows its visitors access to the walkway atop a substantial stretch of the Aurelian Wall itself. The wall was built around AD 270 by Emperor Aurelian, at a time when Rome's power was waning and formidable defences were required. It originally had 16 gates around its 20km (12½ mile) length, was 4m (13ft) thick, and stood 7m (23½ft) high. Its top level was later raised to over 10m (32ft). This massive contruction still forms a near-complete circle around central Rome; the best-preserved parts of the ancient construction today are here: at the Muro Torto (crooked wall) section between the Pincio and Villa Borghese (*see p79*); the Porta Ostiense, renamed Porta San Paolo in honour of St Paul, who walked through it on the way to his execution; and the area around the Porta San Giovanni (*see p128*).

Villa dei Quintili

Via Appia Nuova 1092 (06 481 5576). **Open** 9am-4.30pm Tue-Sun. **Admission** €4.13/L8,000; €2.06/L4,000 concessions. **No credit cards.**

Built in the second century AD by the consuls Sextus Quintilius Consianus and Sextrus Quintilius Valerius Maximus (brothers who would later be executed by Emperor Commodus of *Gladiator* fame), this the biggest country villa outside Rome's city walls. Much of the fittings and statuary were removed during digs in the 18th and 19th centuries; what opened up to the public in 2000 was the vast structure itself, set in splendid isolation amid fields strewn with fragments of the many-coloured marble that once faced its mighty halls. At the villa's gate onto the via Appia Antica there is a pretty *nymphaeum*.

Tombs & catacombs

In the fifth century BC, burials were banned within the city walls – in a law enacted for religious reasons that by chance also benefited public health. So the Romans took their dead to the roads leading out of the city. The grandest of ancient Rome's roads, the via Appia, was the chic-est place to end your days.

Flashy overground tombs such as the **Tomba di Cecilia Metella** or the **Mausoleo di**

Romolo – the overgrown remains of the tomb of Emperor Maxentius' son Romulus, near the **Circo di Massenzio** – were too expensive for all but the elite. So, the mortal remains of humbler residents ended up underground.

There are some 300 kilometres (200 miles) of catacombs running through the soft volcanic rock beneath suburban Rome, including three major burial places along the via Appia Antica – the **catacombe di San Sebastiano**, **Domitilla** and **San Callisto**. Most date from between the fourth century BC and the first century AD. Many of the tombs are pagan, including the **Columbarium** (literally, dovecote) of Pomponius Hylas (via di Porta Latina, 10; open with prior permission only, *see p60*), just inside the Porta San Sebastiano; a few are Jewish. The most famous, however, are those of the Christians, for whom the catacombs offered one special advantage: in the underground chambers ceremonies could be carried out, and the dead buried, far from the prying and vindictive eyes of pagan persecutors.

The standard form of burial was in a niche carved in the rock. The body, wrapped in linen and often embalmed, was laid in the niche, which was then sealed with tiles or slabs of marble. The grander, arched niches tend to be the graves of martyrs or other important members of the flock, while some wealthy families had their own crypts where they could all be buried together. Frescos on the walls illustrate the indomitability of faith. Popular symbols include representations of Christ as a fish or a shepherd, while a lamb or a sheep represents humanity.

When Christianity became Rome's official religion and came up to the surface in the fourt century, the catacombs took on a special significance; here were the bones of the heroes of the early Church, including saints Sebastian, Agnes and Cecilia. It is possible that the catacombs of St Sebastian may also have been used to house the relics of St Peter and St Paul during the third century, when worship at their shrines was still strictly forbidden.

Like so many of Rome's ancient monuments, the catacombs were forgotten for long periods, then rediscovered. In the ninth century huge quantities of bones were dug up; it was not until the 16th century, however, that their full extent became apparent.

See also the **Catacombs of Priscilla** *(p150)* and **Sant'Agnese Fuori le Mura** *(p151)*.

Catacombe di Domitilla

Via delle Sette Chiese 282 (06 511 0342). **Open** 8.30am-noon, 2.30-5.30pm Mon, Wed-Sun; ticket office closes 4.50pm. Closed Jan. **Admission** €4.13/L8,000. **No credit cards**.

Catacombe di San Callisto

Via Appia Antica 110 (06 513 0151). **Open** 8.30am-noon, 2.30-5pm Mon, Tue, Thur-Sun. Closed Feb. **Admission** €4.13/L8,000; €2.06/L4,000 concessions. **No credit cards**.

Catacombe di San Sebastiano

Via Appia Antica 136 (06 788 7035). **Open** 9am-noon, 2.30-5pm Mon-Sat. Closed Nov. **Admission** €4.13/L8,000; €2.06/L4,000 concessions. **No credit cards**.

In addition to the catacombs, and overlooked by most visitors, is the basilica San Sebastiano above the catacombs. The church was built in the fourth century and rebuilt in the 17th, and contains an arrow supposedly shot into St Sebastian, and the column he was tied to while the arrows were flying.

Tomba di Cecilia Metella

Via Appia Antica 161 (06 780 2465). **Open** 9am-5pm Tue-Sun; ticket office closes 4pm. **Admission** €2.06/L4,000; €1.03/L2,000 concessions. **No credit cards**.

A squat brick cylinder from the first century BC, this was the final resting place of a woman who had married into the wealthy Metella family; despite being related only by marriage, the family gave her this unusually lavish tomb. During the 14th century the Caetani family, relatives of Pope Boniface VIII, turned the tomb into a fortress, adding the crenellations around its top, and proceeded to extract tolls from passers-by.

Parco dell'Appia Antica
Parco della Caffarella

Painstakingly reclaimed – from property developers, subsistence farmers and drug dealers – over decades, the 25-plus square kilometres (ten square miles) of land between the ancient and modern *vie* Appia have been transformed into a park which, as Rome's closest bit of amenable countryside, has become a popular place for a Sunday stroll.

The Valle della Caffarella – between the via Appia Antica and the via Latina, another ancient road – was the first stretch of *Campagna Romana* (Roman countryside),

lauded by (City in the more dan descend i of Rome' fruit or(reacha' hired ' €2.5ε are a farm for all the wor the local tourist board – and a sacred wood.

The visitors' centre has maps and informa on the ancient road. It also organises tours (for groups of ten or more) and special events for children. Guided tours of the Parco della Caffarella depart each Sunday morning from largo Tacchi Venturi on via Latina; phone 06 789 279 for precise times, and to request an English-speaking guide. On Sunday, the road from Porta San Sebastiano is closed to traffic.

Centro Visite Parco Appia Antica

Via Appia Antica 42 (tollfree 8000 2 8000/ www.parcoappiaantica.org). **Open** 9.30am-5.30pm daily. **Admission** *Park* free. *Guided tours* €5.16/L10,000. **No credit cards**.

The visitors' centre tollfree information line operates from 9am-3.30pm Mon-Fri.

Getting there

The municipal transport company's **Archeobus** (information and bookings 06 4695 4695) is an eco-friendly air-conditioned minibus that departs hourly, on the hour, between 9am and 5pm daily from piazza Venezia, stopping at the Circo Massimo, the Terme di Caracalla, the Museo delle Mura at Porto San Sebastiano, the Parco dell'Appia Antica visitors' centre, the Domine Quo Vadis? church and entrance to the valle della Caffarella, the catacombs of San Callisto and San Sebastiano, the Circo di Massenzio and Tomba di Cecilia Metella, and the Villa dei Quintili. An all-day ticket costs €7.75/ L15,000 (under-11s free; no credit cards) and allows you to hop on and off wherever you like along the route.

Alternatively, the following regular bus services cover some stretches of the Appian Way:

118 (Mon-Sat; minibus) viale Aventino – Terme di Caracalla – Porta San Sebastiano – via Appia Antica to Domine Quo Vadis? and Catacombe di San Callisto – via Appia Pignatelli

218 (daily) piazza San Giovanni in Laterano – Porta San Sebastiano – via Appia Antica to Domine Quo Vadis? – via Ardeatina to Fosse Ardeatine and, with a bit of a hike, the Catacombe di Domitilla

660 (daily) from metro station Colli Albani: via Appia Antica from Circo di Massenzio to Tomba di Cecilia Metella

664 (daily) from metro station Colli Albani: via Appia Nuova to Villa dei Quintili

Suburbs

...'s football stadium to its own little Beverly Hills, the ...ity's suburbs hide a wealth of surprises.

...orth

Flaminia

The dead-straight via Flaminia shoots north from piazza del Popolo, crossing the river at the ancient Ponte Milvio, where the Emperor Constantine had his battle-winning vision (*see p10*). On the way, the road passes through affluent residential areas that contain a host of sports facilities: the Stadio Flaminio and Acqua Acetosa running tracks in the east, and the **Foro Italico** and **Stadio Olimpico** football stadium (*see chapter* **Sport**) to the west.

It also crosses a mushrooming cultural zone, containing Renzo Piano's daring new **Auditorium** and the **Centro per le Arti Contemporanee**, and allows a fleeting glimpse of Paolo Portoghesi's graceful if anomalous **mosque** (for all three, *see p29* **Contemporary**).

Centro per le Arti Contemporanee – Museo del XXI Secolo

Ex-Caserma Montello, via Guido Reni 10 (06 322 981/06 320 2438/www.gnam.arti.beniculturali.it). Bus or tram to piazza Mancini or via Flaminia. **Open** depends on exhibition. **Admission** depends on exhibition. **No credit cards.**
This enormous hangar-like space in a former army barracks is to be transformed – to a design by Anglo-Iranian architect Zaha Hadid, *see p29* **Contemporary** – into the Eternal City's cutting-edge centre for anything to do with the arts of the 21st century. Until Hadid's project is completed (and maybe even after: conservative Rome is unlikely to be able to rival the Tate Modern phenomenon), it will host occasional, low-profile temporary exhibitions.

Parioli

North of the Villa Borghese, this is one of the most expensive but also one of the dullest residential areas of the city, built between the late 19th century and the 1930s on the hilltop estates of some of baroque Rome's finest private villas. When Romans refer to *parioli*, they have in mind the sort of brash rich kids who feel naked without a designer jacket, jeans pressed by the family's *filipina* maid, a cellphone and a four-wheel drive.

Salaria

The via Salaria – the salt road – existed before Rome, when ancient tribes brought vital salt supplies along it from salt pans on the coast. Now home to post-Unification apartment blocks and a bevvy of embassies, it also offers the leafy shade of the **Villa Ada** public gardens, and the **Catacombe di Priscilla**, some of Rome's oldest and most extensive catacombs.

Catacombe di Priscilla

Via Salaria 430 (06 8620 6272). Bus to via Salaria. **Open** 8.30am-noon, 2.30-5pm Tue-Sun. Closed Jan. **Admission** €4.13/L8,000; €2.06/L4,000 concessions. **No credit cards.**
This two-storey burial place, dug out mostly in the second century AD, contains bas reliefs and frescos, including what experts believe to be the first recorded depiction of Mary.

Nomentana

Via Nomentana is the main road leading out of Rome to the north-east, crossed at right angles by the once-majestic via Regina Elena. It's flanked on either side by another middle-class residential area, with some charming art-nouveau buildings. It has its green lung in the **Villa Torlonia** – again with a touch of art nouveau in the **Casina delle Civette** – its art-fest in the **Galleria Comunale d'Arte Moderna**, and perhaps the earliest Christian mosaics in **Santa Costanza**, by the church and catacombs of **Sant'Agnese fuori le Mura**. To the south-east, the area around the via Tiburtina is rather more low-rent.

Casina delle Civette & Villa Torlonia

Via Nomentana 70 (06 4425 0072). Bus to via Nomentana. **Open** 9am-5pm Tue-Sun; ticket office closes 4pm. **Admission** €2.58/L5,000; €1.55/L3,000 concessions. **No credit cards.**
The Villa Torlonia, with its pretty park, was glorified as Mussolini's suburban HQ in the 1930s, trashed by Anglo-American forces when they made it their HQ from 1944-47, and bought by Rome city council in 1978 in a disastrous state, after which the house and its outbuildings disappeared for ages behind the unsightly scaffolding. Unquestionably the best thing to emerge from this long *restauro* is the Casina delle Civette, a wacky Swiss-chalet-meets-faux-medieval-folly garden shed that was bestowed

Mussolini got Italian couch potatoes into their running shoes at the **Foro Italico**. *See p150.*

with all kinds of stupendous stained glass and *boiseries* in 1916-20. The Casina's own art nouveau fittings have been beautifully restored and supplemented with many other works in stained glass from the same period.

Galleria Comunale d'Arte Moderna e Contemporanea (ex-Birreria Peroni)

Via Reggio Emilia 54/via Cagliari 52-54 (06 6710 7900). Bus to piazza Fiume or via Nomentana. **Open** 9am-7pm Tue-Sun. **Admission** €5.16/L10,000; €4.13/L8,000 concessions. **No credit cards.** Map 4/2A.

As well as being a fascinating example of industrial archaeology and the recycling of disused spaces, this refurbished former brewery provides a permanent home for those parts of the Rome council's collection of predominantly Italian modern and contemporary art that no longer fits in the Galleria Comunale in via Crispi (*see p85*). The ex-brewery also hosts temporary and touring contemporary art shows.

Sant'Agnese fuori le Mura & Santa Costanza

Via Nomentana 349 (06 861 0840). Bus to via Nomentana. **Open** *Church* 7am-noon, 4-8pm daily. *Catacombs & Santa Costanza* 9am-noon Mon; 9am-noon, 4-6pm Tue-Sat; 4-6pm Sun. **Admission** *Catacombs* €4.13/L8,000. **No credit cards.**

The circular fourth-century mausoleum of Santa Costanza, 2km (1¼ miles) beyond the beginning of the via Nomentana at Porta Pia, was built for Constantine's daughters, Constance (a saint only by popular tradition, never having been canonised) and Helen, and is decorated with the world's earliest surviving Christian mosaics. They do not look very Christian – simple pastoral scenes with a spiralling vine encircling figures collecting and treading grapes – but historians insist the wine being made represents Christ's blood. In the adjoining church of Sant' Agnese, also dating from Constantine's time, there is a seventh-century apse mosaic showing a diminutive figure of St Agnes standing on the flames of her martyrdom, flanked by two popes. Like the mosaics of San Lorenzo fuori le Mura (*see p152*), there is little of the classical tradition here. St Agnes was almost certainly buried in the catacombs below this church in what is now piazza Navona. The catacombs are among Rome's least-visited and most atmospheric.

East

San Lorenzo

Map p153.

Badly built, densely populated and still showing wounds from World War II, San Lorenzo is scarred like an alley cat. It's also one of Rome's liveliest neighbourhoods, full of restaurants (*see p184*), artists, graffiti and cultural diversity, plus the spillover from the nearby campus of Rome's La Sapienza University. The area has a history of rebellion. It was 'designed' in the 1880s as a working-class ghetto, with few public services or amenities, and soon developed into Rome's most radical area, where anarchist workers bravely resisted the rising tide of fascism. The street battles of the 1920s between *squadracce fasciste* and the *sanlorenzini* form part of Italian left-wing legend. Bordering the district to the north-east is the vast Verano cemetery, at the entrance of which stands the ancient basilica of **San Lorenzo fuori le Mura**.

San Lorenzo fuori le Mura

Piazzale del Verano, 3 (06 491 511). Bus or tram to piazzale del Verano. **Open** 7.30am-12.30pm, 3-7.30pm daily.

This basilica on the ancient via Tiburtina, 1km (½ mile) to the west of Termini station, was donated by Constantine to house the remains of St Lawrence after he met his fiery end on a griddle. Rebuilt in the sixth century by Pope Pelagius II, it was later united with a neighbouring church, using Pelagius's church as the chancel. Successive restorations were undone in the 1860s, when some unfortunate frescos were added. A couple of wayward bombs plunged through the roof in 1943, making San

Lorenzo the only Roman church to suffer war damage, but it was painstakingly reconstructed by 1949. On the right side of the 13th-century portico are frescos from the same period, showing scenes from the life of St Lawrence.

Inside the triumphal arch are sixth-century mosaics reflecting Byzantine influence. The figures are flat, stiff and outlined in black, floating motionless against a gold ground. There is little modelling or play of light and shade, and the colouring is not as subtle as in the earlier mosaics. This is partly due to the Greek-inspired use of marble squares, instead of the glass normally favoured by the Romans.

South

Ostiense, Garbatella & San Paolo

These districts south of Testaccio (*see p119*) are similarly interesting areas of late 19th to early 20th-century workers' housing: many of their apartment blocks are architecturally outstanding. Despite some urban blight, they have a strong community feel.

On via Ostiense lurks the wonderful but undervisited **Centrale Montemartini**, one of Rome's rare examples of innovative museum design. Further down the road is one of Rome's major basilicas, **San Paolo fuori le Mura**.

Heavy industry meets classical statuary at the **Centrale Montemartini**. *See p153*.

Centrale Montemartini

Via Ostiense 106 (06 574 8030). Bus to via Ostiense.
Open 9.30am-7pm Tue-Sun; ticket office closes 6pm.
Admission €4.13/L8,000; €2.58/L5,000 concessions;
see also p60 **Tickets**. **No credit cards.**
It may be true that the Centrale Montemartini
contains the left-over ancient statuary from the
Musei Capitolini (*see p62*), but this being Rome, the
dregs are pretty impressive; moreover, the setting
itself makes this wonderful spot worth a visit. You
enter through the headquarters of Rome's electricity
company, beneath the skeleton of its old gas works.
Inside are fauns and Minervas, bacchic revellers and
Apollos, all starkly white but oddly at home against
the gleaming black machinery of the decommissioned generating station.

San Paolo fuori le Mura

*Via Ostiense, 184 (06 541 0341). Metro San
Paolo/bus to piazzale San Paolo.* **Open** *Basilica* 7am-
6.30pm daily. *Cloister* 9am-1pm, 3-6pm daily.
Constantine founded San Paolo to commemorate the
martyrdom of St Paul at nearby Tre Fontane (*see
p154*). The church, 3km (two miles) beyond the
Porta San Paolo along the via Ostiense, has been
destroyed, rebuilt and restored several times; the
present building is only 150 years old, although a
few details and a wonderful cloister survive from its
ancient beginnings. The greatest damage to the
basilica occurred in a fire in 1823, but subsequent
restorers have also contributed to the destruction of

the older building. Features that have survived
include 11th-century doors decorated with biblical
scenes; a strange 12th-century Easter candlestick,
featuring human-, lion-, and goat-headed beasts
spewing the vine of life from their mouths; and the
elegant 13th-century *ciborio* (painted canopy) above
the altar, by Arnolfo di Cambio. In the *confessio*
beneath the altar is the tomb of St Paul, topped by
a stone slab pierced with two holes through which
devotees stuff bits of cloth to imbue them with the
apostle's holiness.

The cloister is a good example of cosmatesque
work (*see p87* **Glossary**), its twisted columns inlaid
with mosaic, and supporting an elaborate arcade of
sculpted reliefs. In the sacristy are the remnants of
a series of papal portraits that once lined the nave.
The modern church has carried on this tradition,
replacing the originals with mosaic portraits of all
the popes from Peter to the present incumbent.
There are only eight spaces left; once they are filled,
apparently, the world will end.

EUR

Italian fascism managed to be simultaneously
monstrous and absurd, but its delusions of
grandeur helped produce some of the most
interesting European architecture and town
planning of this century.

In the early 1930s, Giuseppe Bottai,
Mussolini's governor of Rome and the leading
arbiter of fascist taste, had the bright idea of
expanding landbound Rome well along the via
Ostiense towards the sea, some 20km (12½
miles) away. He combined this with the notion
of a universal exhibition, pencilled in for 1942
and intended to combine permanent cultural
exhibition spaces with a monument to fascism.

Popular fascist architect Marcello Piacentini
was charged with co-ordinating the vastly
ambitious project, but in the event few of the
original designs were ever built. The planning
committee became so bogged down in argument
that little had been achieved by the outbreak of
World War II, which forced work to be
suspended. After the war, work was resumed,
but with a different spirit. Still known as EUR –
Esposizione universale romana – the project
went ahead disassociated from its fascist
ambitions. Some of Italy's best architects –
Giovanni Muzio, Mario de Renzi, Ludovico
Quaroni and partners Luigi Figini and Gino
Pollini – left their mark on it; many consider the
results an archetype of bombastic modernism,
but EUR is certainly memorable. Fascist-
inspired buildings such as Guerrini's **Palazzo
della Civiltà del Lavoro** (quadrato della
Concordia), popularly known as *il colosseo
quadrato* (the square Colosseum) and Arnaldo
Foschini's toy-town church of **Santi Pietro e
Paolo** (piazzale Santi Pietro e Paolo) can be

seen alongside post-war *palazzi* like Adalberto Libera's highly original **Palazzo dei Congressi** (piazza JF Kennedy) and Studio BBPR's superbly functional Post Office in viale Beethoven.

A slew of fittingly didactic museums (the **Museo dell'Alto Medioevo**, the **Museo della Civiltà Romana**, the **Museo delle Arti e Tradizioni Popolari**, the **Museo Preistorico ed Etnografico**) allows a glimpse inside these grandiose monuments to fascist grandeur.

The 1960 Olympic Games offered another stimulus for filling out the area. The masterpiece is Nervi and Piacentini's flying saucer-like **Palazzo dello Sport** (in piazza dello Sport), hovering over EUR's artificial lake and now often used – despite its abysmal acoustics – for big rock concerts (*see p250*) and political conventions. The area contains several other attractions, such as the LUNEUR Park funfair (*see p231*) and the Piscina delle Rose swimming pool (*see p262*). For a relief from EUR's relentless modernity, head for the leafy charm of the **Abbazie delle Tre Fontane**.

Most Romans never visit EUR except on business or to go to a concert. At night, however, and especially in summer, it becomes the playground of fun-loving, suntanned, wealthy brats. Rome's desire to be a little bit of California finds its most eloquent expression in EUR's relatively unsnarled, tree-lined boulevards, and there's a definite whiff of rich-kid, good-time culture in the air.

Abbazia delle Tre Fontane

Via Acque Salvie 1 (06 540 1655/shop 06 540 2309/tre.fontane@flashnet.it). Bus to via Laurentina. **Open** *San Paolo* 6.45am-12.30pm, 3-8pm daily. *Other churches* 8am-6.30pm daily. *Shop* 9am-1pm, 3.30-6pm daily. **No credit cards.**

To the east of EUR's extensive Tre Fontane sports facilities lies a little haven of ancient, eucalyptus-scented green, dotted with three churches commemorating the three points hereabouts where St Paul's head supposedly bounced after it was severed from his body in 67. (Being a Roman citizen, Paul was eligible for the relatively quick and painless head-chop, as opposed to the long-drawn-out crucifixion.) This is the Trappist monastery of Tre Fontane, where water has gurgled and birds sung since the fifth century. The church of San Paolo delle Tre Fontane is said to be built on the very spot where the apostle was executed (*see p132* **Peter & Paul**); apart from a column in one corner to which Paul is supposed to have been tied, all traces of the fifth-century church were done away with in 1599 by architect Giacomo della Porta, who was also responsible for the two other churches. Monks

Palazzo della Civiltà del Lavoro: memorably fascist. *See p153.*

The vast grounds of the **Villa Pamphili**.

aspirations were, of course, coincidental). The building – vast blank walls and massive straight columns – is fascist-classical at its most grandiloquent. Inside are detailed models of ancient Rome's main buildings. There's also a fascinating cutaway model of the Colosseum's (*see p66*) maze of tunnels and lifts, as well as full-scale casts of the reliefs on the Trajan's Column (*see p70*) in the Imperial Fora which enable you to examine their intricate details. The centrepiece is a giant model of Rome in the fourth century AD, showing the famous buildings in their original state. All in all, this museum manages to put Rome's scattered fragments and artefacts into context very helpfully.

Museo Nazionale delle Arti e Tradizioni Popolari

Piazza G Marconi 8 (06 592 6148). Metro EUR Fermi/bus to piazza dell'Agricultura. **Open** 9am-8pm Tue-Sun. **Admission** €4.13/L8,000; €2.06/L4,000 concessions. **No credit cards**.

An enormous collection dedicated to Italian folk art and rural tradition. Exhibits included elaborately decorated carts and horse tack, as well as craft-related implements, and a bizarre collection of votive offerings left to local saints. Malevolent-looking puppets fill one room; another has costumes and *carnevale* artefacts.

Museo Preistorico ed Etnografico L Pigorini

Piazza G Marconi 14 (06 549 521). Metro EUR Fermi/bus to piazza dell'Agricultura. **Open** 9am-8pm daily. **Admission** €4.13/L8,000; €2.06/L4,000 concessions. **No credit cards**.

This museum displays prehistoric Italian artefacts together with ethnological material from a range of world cultures. The lobby contains a reconstruction of the Guattari cave, with a genuine Neanderthal skull. On the first floor is the ethnological collection, with an all-too-predictable range of spears, pottery, jewellery, masks and a couple of shrunken heads. The second floor has archaeological finds from digs all over Italy, including mammoth tusks and teeth, and some human bones.

planted the gum trees in the 1860s, believing they would drive away the malarial mosquitoes endemic there; they now brew a liqueur from them and sell it in a little shop along with their chocolate and remedies for all ills.

Museo dell'Alto Medioevo

Viale Lincoln 3 (06 5422 8199). Metro EUR Fermi/bus to piazza dell'Agricultura. **Open** 9am-8pm Tue-Sun. **Admission** €2.06/L4,000; €1.03/L2,000 concessions. **No credit cards**.

This museum concentrates on the decorative arts of the period between the fall of the Roman Empire and the Renaissance. Alongside intricately carved gold- and silver-decorated swords, buckles and horse tackle are more mundane objects: painted ceramic bead jewellery, and the metal frames of what may be Europe's earliest folding chairs.

Museo della Civiltà Romana

Piazza G Agnelli 10 (06 592 6135). Metro EUR Fermi/bus to piazza dell'Agricultura. **Open** 9am-7pm Tue-Sat; 9am-1.30pm Sun. **Admission** €4.13/L8,000; €2.58/L5,000 concessions. **No credit cards**.

The exhibits in this museum date from 1937, when Mussolini mounted a massive celebration to mark the bi-millennium of Augustus becoming the first emperor. (Any parallels with his own career or

West

Monteverde

Climbing the steep hill behind Trastevere and the Gianicolo is Monteverde Vecchio, a leafy, well-heeled suburb that is home to the vast, green, tree-filled expanses of the **Villa Pamphili** park (*see p229* **Parks and gardens**), and to the smaller but equally lovely **Villa Sciarra** gardens (*see p229* **Parks and gardens**), with their rose arbours, children's play area and miniature big dipper.

Further west is Monteverde Nuovo, a charmless, more downmarket, predominantly post-war addition.

Sightseeing

Hotel Eden

Restaurant "La Terrazza dell'Eden"
Open Breakfast Lunch & Dinner

HOTEL EDEN

ROMA

VIA LUDOVISI, 49 • 00187 ROMA • ITALIA
TEL. (39) 06 47812752 • 06 4814473
www.hotel-eden.it

Eat, Drink, Shop

Eating Out

Rome's restaurants are resisting the twin threats of BSE and design-over-substance, and simply getting better.

A pavement table beneath a vine-covered pergola. Steaming plates of pasta, a carafe of rustic wine, and the animated buzz of people with something to talk about. Try as we might to update our mental photo archives, this image of the classic Roman trattoria is still as potent as ever.

The good news is that such places can still be found. Mamma is still in the kitchen, aided and abetted by the rest of the family. And you can be fairly sure that she will be cooking up the same traditional Roman dishes, such as *spaghetti all'amatriciana* (with tomato, chilli, onion and sausage) or *saltimbocca* (veal strips and ham), that were on the menu last time you visited. Italian cuisine in general, and the Roman version in particular, is nothing if not conservative.

But although standards are generally high, Rome has never been a city where you can wander into just any restaurant and be sure of a good meal. It has its share of overpriced, under-achieving tourist traps; of starched, expense account restaurants whose decor and cuisine are stuck in a *Dolce Vita* timewarp; of uninspiring pizza emporiums.

For those who value the gastronomic experience over the postcard setting, there are now, however, an increasing number of restaurants in the Eternal City that take their food and wine very seriously. Some of these, like **Antico Arco** (*see p177*) or **Uno e Bino** (*see p185*), are the work of passionate, self-taught amateurs. Others – like **La Pergola** (*see p190*) at the Hilton – are the Roman fiefdoms of ambitious, classically trained chefs.

On the downside, one looming storm cloud is connected to the appearance of the first cases of BSE in Italian cattle at the beginning of 2001. The number of cases is still – at the time of writing – extremely small, and there has not yet been a single human victim. But cattle rearers, butchers and certain sections of the catering industry have started to feel the sting. Traditional Roman restaurants rely heavily on the *quinto quarto*, or 'fifth quarter' – those parts of the beast that were left over after the prime cuts of meat, plus the liver and kidneys, were sold off to the butchers. In other words: brain (*cervello*), spinal marrow (*schienale*), nerves (*nervetti*), stomach and intestines (*trippa* or *pajata*), hooves (*zampi*), the thymus and pancreas glands (*animelle*). Even tails are highly thought of by Roman gourmets – as in the classic slaughterhouse worker's dish, *coda alla vaccinara* (oxtail braised in a celery broth). So far, only *schienale*, *animelle* and *pajata di vitello* (baby calf's intestines with the mother's milk still inside) have been banned outright; and the latter is due to return after a period in the EU cooler. But despite a certain anti-Brussels swagger, Roman gourmands are no longer quite as comfortable as they once were with their offal traditions.

The second mini-epidemic to blow in from across the Alps – with quite as much potential for destruction, in the view of traditionalists – is the restaurant that puts design on an equal par with culinary excellence. The first was **'Gusto** (*see p167*), a multi-functional and multi-level restaurant, pizzeria, wine bar, kitchen shop and bookshop, which opened in 1998. This has now been joined by a clutch of other Conran-style eateries. The most successful have been those – like **Boccondivino** (*see p172*) – which take a softer, Italian approach to fusion cooking. Others, like the brand-new **Reef** in piazza Augusto Imperatore (not listed), offer plenty of style but little substance.

GOING THE COURSE

Most meals consist of *il primo* – usually pasta, occasionally soup; *il secondo* – the meat or fish course; and *il contorno* – the vegetables or salad, served separately. *L'antipasto* – the hors d'œuvre – is supposed to precede the *primo* but can also be ordered as an alternative to it, while *il dolce* – the dessert – is often missed out altogether.

You're under no pressure to order four courses. It's perfectly normal to order a first course followed by a simple salad or *contorno* (often the only option for vegetarians). And, if you choose, you can even invert the usual order by ordering an *antipasto* after the pasta course.

Fixed-price meals are a rarity. Top-flight establishments occasionally offer a *menu degustazione* (taster menu), but any establishment offering a *menu turistico*

More Roman restaurants are taking their food very seriously. **The Bean-Eater**, *see p75*.

should generally be avoided, especially if it is written in several languages. For a full menu vocabulary, *see p188*.

DRINKS

Most top-of-the-range restaurants have respectable wine lists, but more humble *trattorie* and *osterie* tend to have a limited selection (*see p179* **Select your wine**). House wine is usually uninspiring Castelli Romani white, or equally unimpressive Montepulciano d'Abruzzo red, but there are exceptions, especially in more upmarket places, or restaurants which offer, for example, a Campanian wine to complement their Neapolitan cuisine. In pizzerias, the drink of choice is *birra* (beer) or a variety of soft drinks. Mineral water – *acqua minerale* – is either *gassata* (sparkling) or *naturale* (still), and usually comes in litre bottles. If you have a full meal, and they like you, you may be offered free *amaro* or *grappa* with your coffee.

PRICES, TIPPING AND TIMES

In 1995 the city council forced restaurants to abolish the *coperto* (cover) charge, which allowed them to add up to L5,000 a head for providing a tablecloth and a basket of bread. Be warned, though: some restaurants ignore the ban, and others get round it by charging automatically for *pane*.

Service is a grey area. Places that add it to the bill as a fixed item are still in the minority, and it is usually safe to assume that it isn't included. Romans themselves tend not to tip much, especially in pizzerias and family-run places. A good rule of thumb is to leave around five per cent in a pizzeria or humble trattoria, slightly more in more upmarket places – but never more than ten per cent. If service has been slack or rude, don't feel ashamed to leave nothing – or to check the bill in detail, as there is still the very occasional restaurateur who becomes strangely innumerate when dealing with tourists.

Eat, Drink, Shop

Italy is still a cash society, so never assume you can use cards or travellers' cheques without asking first. By law, when you pay the bill (*il conto*) you must be given a detailed receipt (*una ricevuta fiscale*). In theory, if you leave a restaurant without it you can incur a fine; but the law is chiefly aimed at tax-dodging restaurateurs.

Opening times can change according to time of year and the whim of the owners. Times given below are those of the kitchen – in other words, when you can actually turn up and order – but many restaurants stay open for an hour or more after the cook goes home. In the evening, few proper restaurants (as opposed to pizzerias) open before 8pm.

KIDS, WOMEN AND DRESS

Taking children into restaurants – even the smartest – is never a problem in Rome. Waiters will usually produce a high chair (*un seggiolone*) on request, and are generally happy to bring a *mezza porzione* – a half-portion. Also, just about any kitchen in the city will do those two off-menu standbys, pasta *al pomodoro*

(with tomato sauce) or pasta *in bianco* (plain, to be dressed with oil and Parmesan).

Though attitudes are changing, women dining alone may still occasionally attract unwelcome attention – most of it in the form of frank stares. Single diners of either sex can have trouble getting a table in cheaper places at busy times: eating out is a communal experience here. Moreover, no proprietor wants to waste a table that could hold four diners on just one.

Very few places impose a dress code, although shorts and T-shirts go down badly in formal, upmarket restaurants. Some restaurants now ban mobile phones, but no-smoking areas are a rarity. Booking, once unusual, is becoming more of a habit, even in places that might appear to be spit-and-sawdust, and especially on Friday and Saturday evenings.

PIZZA

The city's *pizzaioli* have always been proud of their thinner, flatter *pizza romana*, but recently the fickle public has started to defect to the puffier Neapolitan variety. Whichever you choose, make sure it comes from a wood-fired

The best Restaurants

For all-round dining pleasure at a fair price
Al Presidente, *p163*; Antico Arco, *p180*; Matricianella, *p169*; Uno e Bino, *p185*.

For eating outside
Albistrò, *p175*; Ar Galletto, *p176*; Augusto, *p180*; La Carbonara, *p176*; Checchino dal 1887, *p181*; Monserrato, *p176*; Sahara, *p191*; Santa Lucia, *p173*; San Teodoro, *p161*; La Taverna degli Amici, *p177*.

For a romantic soirée
Albistrò, *p175*; Antico Bottaro, *p165*; Il Dito e la Luna, *p184*; San Teodoro, *p161*; Taverna Angelica, *p188*; La Terrazza dell'Hotel Eden, *p164*.

For seeing and being seen
Fiaschetteria Beltramme, *p167*; for the fashion and entertainment industry 'Gusto, *p167*; Maccheroni, *p167*; Santa Lucia, *p173*; for politicians and journalists Gino in Vicolo Rosini, *p167*.

For creative Italian cooking
Agata e Romeo, *p183*; Antico Arco, *p177*; Ditirambo, *p176*; Uno e Bino, *p185*.

For traditional Roman cooking
Agustarello, *p181*; Checchino dal 1887, *p181*; Osteria dell'Angelo, *p187*; Osteria del Velodromo Vecchio, *p190*.

For Italian regional cooking
Il Dito e la Luna, *p184* (Sicily); L'Ortica, *p189* (Naples); Papà Baccus, *p164* (Tuscany); Siciliainbocca, *p188* (Sicily); Taverna Sottovento, *p183* (Calabria).

For fish & seafood
Alberto Ciarla, *p177*; Crab, *p183*; La Rosetta, *p172*; Sangallo, *p173*.

For pizza
Remo, *p181*; Da Vittorio, *p180*.

For international cuisine
Bishoku Kobu, *p191*.

For wine
Al Bric, *p175*; Albistrò, *p175*; Antico Arco, *p180*; Checchino dal 1887, *p181*; Ditirambo, *p176*; Il Dito e la Luna, *p184*; Food & Wine Testa, *p191*; Sangallo, *p173*; Il Simposio, *p188*; Uno e Bino, *p185*.

For meeting a Swiss Guard
Paninoteca da Guido, *p189*.

brick oven (*forno a legna*); pizzas from electric or gas-fired ovens just don't have the same flavour.

So orthodox is the range of toppings in Roman *pizzerie*, so eyebrow-raising any departure from the norm, that it's worth learning the main varieties by heart. For these, and for the various gap-fillers that it is customary to order while you're waiting for the pizza to be baked, see *p188* **Reading the menu**.

Takeaway pizza – generally referred to as *pizza rustica* or *pizza a taglio* – is not prepared while you wait, but the best outlets (including all those listed) have a fast turnover and take quality seriously; some adhere to the 'slow rising' method pioneered by award-winning Roman *pizzaiolo* Angelo Iezzi, which produces a more digestible base that stays fresh longer.

Note that sit-down pizzerias are usually open in the evenings only, but they generally begin serving early by Roman standards, from 7pm onwards.

WINE BARS
Neighbourhood *enoteche* (wine shops) and *vini e olii* (wine and oil) outlets have been around in Rome since time immemorial, complete with their huddle of old men drinking wine by the glass (*al bicchiere* or *alla mescita*). For a selection of places in which drinking is the main point of the exercise, *see chapter* **Cafés, pubs & gelaterie**. But recently a number of upmarket, international-style wine bars have also sprung up, offering snacks and even full meals to go with their wines. Such is the Roman predilection for eating over drinking that some – **Il Brillo Parlante** *see p171*, **Ferrara** *see p180*, **Il Simposio** *see p188* – are best thought of as restaurants with great cellars.

SNACKS
The Roman habit of sitting down to two full meals each day is fast disappearing, and as a result places designed for eating on the run are mushrooming. Roman snack culture, though, lurks in unlikely places. Few new arrivals, for example, consider stepping into a humble *alimentari* (grocer's) to have their picnic lunch prepared on the spot – and yet for fresh bread and high-quality fillings this is invariably the best option. Favourite casing is the ubiquitous white Roman roll, *la rosetta*, or a slice of *pizza bianca* (plain oiled and salted pizza base, eaten as is or filled); fillings are generally ham, salami or cheese, as *alimentari* do not sell fruit and veg.

The other traditional snack stop is the neighbourhood bar. Some will only have a few uninspiring sandwiches sitting limply on a plate; but others are lunchtime meccas, with full-scale *tavole calde* (buffets).

INTERNATIONAL
If you don't like Italian food, you're in the wrong town: Rome is not a good place to indulge in a gastronomic world tour. True, Chinese restaurants abound, and Indian, Thai, Korean and Mexican food can be tracked down, but the standard is far lower than in London, Paris or New York. The one exception to the rule – a consequence of Italy's murky colonial history – is the range of good Eritrean, Somali and Ethiopian cuisine on offer.

VEGETARIANS
The city has only two bona fide vegetarian restaurants – **Arancia Blu**, *see p184,* and **Margutta RistorArte**, *see p169* – but the number looks set to increase in the wake of the BSE scare. And even in traditional trattorias, waiters will no longer look blank when you say *non mangio la carne* (I don't eat meat). They'll just assume you're a mad cow worrier – and press you to try one of the good range of meatless dishes that Roman cuisine has always specialised in, from *penne all' arrabbiata* (pasta in a tomato and chili sauce), through *tonnarelli cacio e pepe* (thick spaghetti with crumbly sheeps' cheese and plenty of black pepper), to *carciofi alla giudia* (deep-fried artichokes, a Roman Jewish speciality). But never assume that it is enough to tell the waiter that you are vegetarian (*sono vegetariano*); most have only the vaguest concept of what this means, and they may offer seafood, chicken and even ham as an alternative to that T-bone steak. If you are at all unsure about the ingredients of any dish, ask. For vegetarian options on the standard Roman menu, *see p188* **Reading the menu**.

Average restaurant prices listed below are based on three courses, and do not include drinks. For pizzerias, the prices given are for a standard pizza, a beer, and one extra, such as a *bruschetta*. Wine bar and gastropub averages are based on two courses and a glass of wine or beer. No average prices are given for snacks: how much you'll pay depends on how much you consume.

From the Capitoline to the Palatine

Restaurants

San Teodoro
Via dei Fienili 49/51 (06 678 0933). Bus to via del Teatro di Marcello. **Open** 12.30-3.30pm, 7.30-12.30pm Mon-Sat. Closed mid Jan-mid Feb. **Average** €39/L75,000. **Credit** AmEx, DC, MC, V. **Map** p326 2C.

Restaurant • Bar • Boutique • Rock memorabilia

SAVE THE PLANET

Hard Rock CAFE ®

ROME

Rocking the World for 30 years
MUSIC FOR LIFE

Open seven days a week
From 10.00 a.m. to midnight
Friday and Saturday until 1.00 a.m.

Via Vittorio Veneto 62A - 00187 Roma
Tel. 064203051 - Fax 0642030552 - www.hardrock.com

Food with a view: **La Terrazza dell'Hotel Eden**. *See p164.*

In summer this is one of the best places in Rome to eat outside: on a raised terrace amid the medieval houses of a small residential enclave in the shadow of the Forum. Service can be over-cocky; but quality is assured, with fish and seafood taking star billing. *Primi* include *tonnarelli San Teodoro* (pasta with courgettes, king prawns and tomatoes) and *spaghetti fagiolini, triglia e bottarga* (with green beans, red mullet and mullet roe); highlight of the second courses is a succulent roast lamb (*agnello*) from a single herd in Pontremoli, Tuscany. The wine list is selective, and includes some decent regional bottles. But prices have leapt up recently and, overall, San Teodoro is no longer such good value – especially once the fixed 15 per cent service charge is added.

Trevi & the Quirinale

Restaurants

Al Presidente

Via in Arcione 94/95 (06 679 7342). Bus to via del Tritone. **Open** 7pm-midnight Mon, Wed-Fri; 1-3.30pm, 7pm-midnight Sat, Sun. Closed 2wks Aug, 3wks Jan. **Average** €41/L80,000. **Credit** DC, MC, V.
The area around the Trevi Fountain has always been a bit of a culinary desert. But things have started looking up recently, with the slow but steady qualitative metamorphosis of this friendly family trattoria under the walls of the Quirinale palace. In elegant but restrained surroundings, the Petruccioli family offers a balance between creativity and tradition in dishes such as *risotto con ragù di fegatini e cannella* (risotto in a sauce of chicken livers and cinnamon). Fish is a strong point, and desserts such as *tortino al cioccolato con zabaione* come out with all guns blazing. Other bonuses include a good selection of wines by the glass, an intelligent range of taster menus (€33.57-€51.65/L65,000-L100,000), and a pretty summer pergola.

Wine bars & gastropubs

Birreria Fratelli Tempera

Via di San Marcello 19 (06 679 5310). Bus to piazza Venezia. **Open** noon-3.30pm, 7pm-1am Mon-Sat. Closed 2wks Aug. **Average** €18/L35,000. **Credit** AmEx, MC, V. **Map** p323 2C.
Much better known by its traditional name, Birreria Peroni, this is the perfect place for a lunchtime snack. Service is canteen-style, and the food – always with a couple of pasta options – is good and cheap. It still retains its original, beautiful art nouveau decor, featuring slogans like 'drink beer and you'll live 100 years'. Arrive early to avoid the 1.15-2pm lunchtime rush, when you have to push in past the row of regulars eating their pasta standing up at the bar. Evenings are generally quiet.

Vineria Il Chianti

Via del Lavatore 81/82 (06 678 7550). Bus to via del Tritone. **Open** *10am-2.30am Mon-Sat. Meals served 1-3.30pm, 7.30-11pm Mon-Sat. Closed Aug.* **Average** *€26/L50,000.* **Credit** AmEx, MC, V. **Map** p323 2C.

In the middle of the Trevi Fountain souvenir belt, this new wine bar offers welcome relief from the surrounding tack. As the name suggests, there is a definite Tuscan slant – in all except the service, which is young, brisk and Roman. The kitchen does a good line in soups, and there are pizzas in the evening. Bottles dominate the decor; seating is cosy, not to say cramped – especially at lunch when office workers invade and queues form. In summer, tables fill the little *piazzetta* ouside.

Snacks

L'Antico Forno

Via delle Muratte 8 (06 679 2866). Bus to via del Corso or via del Tritone. **Open** *7am-9pm daily.* **Credit** AmEx, DC, MC, V. **Map** p323 2C.

Right opposite the Trevi fountain, this bakery and general store does a good line in fresh filled rolls, plus the usual *tavola calda* fare – rice, seafood salad, and so on. Service is grumpy but efficient.

Ristorante Self-Service del Palazzo delle Esposizioni

Via Milano 9 (06 482 8001). Bus to via Nazionale. **Open** *Bar 10am-8pm Mon, Wed-Sun. Buffet 12.30-3pm Mon, Wed-Sun.* **Credit** AmEx, DC, MC, V. **Map** p323 2B.

The ground-floor bar in this arts complex does standard bar food, with a line in knockout Sicilian pastries. Go up in the glass lift, and you'll find a reasonably priced buffet with a good salad bar – a rarity in Rome.

Via Veneto & Villa Borghese

See also p171 **PizzaRé.**

Restaurants

Cantina Cantarini

Piazza Sallustio 12 (06 485 528). Bus to via XX Settembre. **Open** *12.30-3.30pm, 7.30-10.30pm Mon-Sat. Closed 2 wks Aug, 1wk Christmas.* **Average** *€23/L45,000.* **Credit** AmEx, DC, MC, V. **Map** p323 1A.

A high-quality trattoria in a smart neighbourhood, with extraordinarily reasonable prices. The food is Roman but with influences from the Marches, around Urbino. Meat-based for the first part of the week, it turns fishy from Thursday to Saturday. The atmosphere is as *allegro* as seating is tight, but the excellent *coniglio al cacciatore* (stewed rabbit), *fritto misto di pesce* (fried mixed fish) and *spaghetti al nero di seppia* (squid ink) should quell concerns about comfort.

Papà Baccus

Via Toscana 36 (06 4274 2808). Bus to via Veneto. **Open** *12.30-3pm, 7.30-11.30pm Mon-Fri; 7.30pm-midnight Sat. Closed 1wk Aug; 2wks Christmas/New Year.* **Average** *€41/L80,000.* **Credit** AmEx, DC, MC, V. **Map** p322 2B.

Cucina toscana at its best, in elegant, recently renovated premises just off via Veneto. All the raw materials are imported from owner Italo Cipriani's native valley. Try the *ribollita*, a delicious Tuscan soup made from beans, fresh vegetables and bread; or the *filetto al Brunello* (fillet steak cooked in Brunello di Montalcino wine). Fish is another speciality; and the mark-up on wine is very reasonable. It's open until late, and there is a non-smoking room that really works. There are plans to open on Sundays from autumn 2001 for tastings of wine, fine cheeses and Tuscan *salumi*.

La Terrazza dell'Hotel Eden

Via Ludovisi, 49 (06 478 121). Bus to via Veneto. **Open** *12.30-2.30pm, 7.30-10.30pm daily.* **Average** *€93/L180,000.* **Credit** AmEx, DC, MC, V. **Map** p323 1C.

Cook Enrico Derflingher, formerly of London's Kensington Palace, has imposed his mod-Med approach on this roof-garden hotel restaurant, which boasts a truly spectacular view over the city. The

dishes don't always match up to his ambitions, but he uses the freshest of local ingredients, and is constantly experimenting: on the right day, with dishes such as ricotta and carrot gnocchi with baby squid and *bottarga* (roe) of grey mullet, a meal here can be an unforgettable experience. Since the axeing of the almost affordable business lunch menu, the only alternative to going à la carte remains the macrobiotic menu for lunch and dinner at €77.47/L150,000.

The Tridente

Restaurants

Antico Bottaro
Passeggiata di Ripetta 15 (06 323 6763). Bus to piazza Augusto Imperatore or piazza del Popolo. **Open** 12.30-3pm, 8pm-midnight Tue-Sun. Closed Aug. **Average** €28/L55,000. **Credit** AmEx, DC, MC, V. **Map** p320 2A.
There's a Neapolitan slant to this elegant, relaxed, late-opening restaurant near piazza del Popolo, housed in a warren of pale yellow, vaulted rooms. The food is good, if not outstanding, with fish dominating. The *tagliolini* (flat spaghetti) with rocket pesto and seafood is worth a try; vegetable dishes such as radicchio with gorgonzola are also given

Food with **'Gusto**. *See p167.*

Pralineria

Pizzeria

Enoteca

Restaurant

'Gusto

Bookshop

Wine bar

Live Music

Cigar Club

00187 Roma
Piazza Augusto Imperatore, 9 - Via della Frezza, 23
Tel. 06 3226273

more space here than in many Roman eateries. Desserts can be uninspiring.

Baja

Lungotevere Arnaldo da Brescia (06 3260 0118/ www.bajarome.com). **Open** *Bar* noon-2.30am Tue-Sat. *Restaurant* noon-3.30pm, 8pm-12.30am Tue-Sat. **Average** €34/L65,000. **Credit** AmEx, DC, MC, V. **Map** p320 2B.

In the *Dolce Vita* years, converted Tiber barges were *the* place to eat, drink and party. River pollution and the rise of the seaside soon sent these floating night-clubs into forced retirement; but recently Romans have begun to rediscover their river, and Baja is one of the results. The original barge has been extend-ed upwards with a first-floor restaurant in a steel and glass shell; downstairs, punters sip cocktails to an ambient soundtrack. The food – creative Italian, based on fresh, organic ingredients – varies from the light and tasty (spaghetti with broccoli and prawns) to the competent but uninspiring (*dentice* – a white fish – with a fennel and olive gravy). But in sum-mer, when the action spills on to an outside terrace, this is a great place to play at being Audrey and Gregory in *Roman Holiday*. The barge is moored between ponte Margherita and ponte Nenni; access is by a flight of steps at the ponte Margherita end of lungotevere Arnaldo da Brescia.

La Campana

Vicolo della Campana 18 (06 6867 820). **Bus** to lungotevere Marzio or via Tomacelli. **Open** 12.30-2.50pm, 7.30-11pm Tue-Sun. Closed Aug. **Average** €34/L65,000. **Credit** AmEx, DC, MC, V. **Map** p321 1A.

Some things never change. La Campana, which claims to be the oldest trattoria in Rome, is one of them. Even its younger waiters seem stuck in a 1950s timewarp, and the clientele of journalists, politicos and Gucci wives appear equally unfazed by social or culinary revolutions. The kitchen does conservative but delicious renditions of Roman classics such as *ossobuco, spaghetti con le vongole,* even *vignarola* – a broad bean and ham soup that has become an endangered species.

Edy

Vicolo del Babuino 4 (06 3600 1738). Metro Spagna/bus to via del Babuino. **Open** Oct-Apr noon-3.30pm, 7pm-midnight Mon-Sat. May-Sept 7pm-midnight Mon; noon-3.30pm, 7pm-midnight Tue-Sat. **Closed** 1wk Aug. **Average** €26/L50,000. **Credit** AmEx, DC, MC, V. **Map** p320 2A.

A vaguely arty trattoria with creative but genuine Roman fish and meat cooking at reasonable prices: not bad in an area where the whiff of serious money is all-pervasive. The menu changes with the season, though the house speciality – *spaghetti al cartoccio con frutti di mare,* a spaghetti and seafood creation baked and served in its own silver-foil packet – is always on the menu. Inside can be gloomy in sum-mer; couples might want to angle for one of two tiny outside tables.

Fiaschetteria Beltramme

Via della Croce 39 (no phone). Metro Spagna/bus to piazza San Silvestro. **Open** noon-3pm, 8-11pm Mon-Sat. **Closed** 2wks Aug. **Average** €23/L45,000. **No credit cards. Map** p320 2A.

Don't be fooled by the 'no phone, no credit cards' line and the grandma's front room decor. This historic trattoria is hugely trendy; Madonna once fled a gala dinner to eat here. Specialities include *tonnarelli cacio e pepe* and *pollo con i peperoni* (chicken with peppers). No bookings are taken (unless you're Madonna) – you just join the queue.

Gino in Vicolo Rosini

Vicolo Rosini 4, off piazza del Parlamento (06 687 3434). Bus to largo Chigi or piazza San Silvestro. **Open** 1-2.45pm, 8-10.30pm Mon-Sat. Closed Aug. **Average** €21/L40,000. **No credit cards**. **Map** p321 1A.

In a lane around the back of the main parliament building, and nearly always filled to bursting with MPs, political journos and assorted hangers-on, this unreconstructed traditional trat is a monument unto itself. The cuisine is more varied than usual: the *coniglio al vino bianco* (rabbit in white wine) and *zucchine ripiene* (stuffed courgettes) are both recommended, as is the home-made *tiramisù*. Come early, especially at lunchtime, or be prepared to wait around for one of the hotly contested tables.

'Gusto

Piazza Augusto Imperatore 9 (06 322 6273). Bus to piazza Augusto Imperatore. **Open** *Restaurant* 1-3pm, 8pm-midnight daily. *Pizzeria* 12.30-3pm, 7.30pm-1am daily. *Wine bar* 11am-2am daily. **Average** *restaurant* €39/L75,000; *pizzeria* €15/L30,000. **Credit** AmEx, MC, V. **Map** p321 1A.

One of the most-talked about 1990s dining novel-ties in Rome, 'Gusto is a multi-purpose, split-level pizzeria, restaurant and winebar, with a cook's shop and bookshop next door. The ground floor pizza and salad bar is packed with staff from sur-rounding offices at lunchtime, and with just about everyone in the evening. The wicker-and-beige decor may make you yearn for something more grittily Roman, but the decent pizzas and abun-dant, fresh salads are reasonably priced. Upstairs, the pricier restaurant blends stir-fry with Italian staples, not always convincingly. Perhaps the part that works best is the wine bar out the back – buzzing, stylish, and with a good selection of wines by the glass.

Maccheroni

Piazza delle Coppelle 44 (06 6830 7895). Bus to corso Rinascimento. **Open** 1-3pm, 8pm-midnight Mon-Sat. **Average** €23/L45,000. **Credit** AmEx, DC, MC, V. **Map** p321 1A.

This young, funky eaterie, which opened in 1998, is already an established favourite with locals, office workers and actresses who are just about to make it big. In summer, the tables spill out onto the pretty square. Inside are boathouse-style panelled walls,

Eat, Drink, Shop

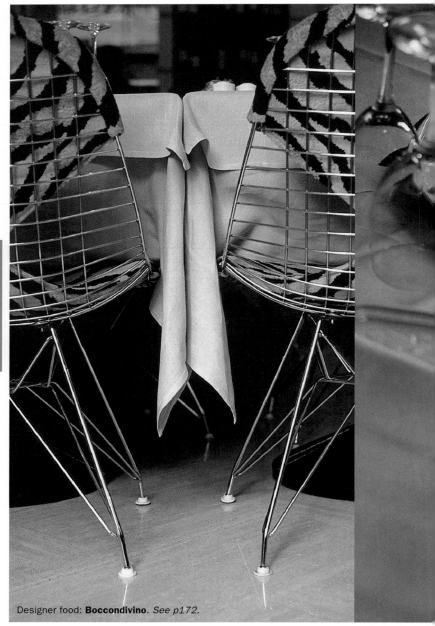

Designer food: **Boccondivino**. *See p172*.

Eat, Drink, Shop

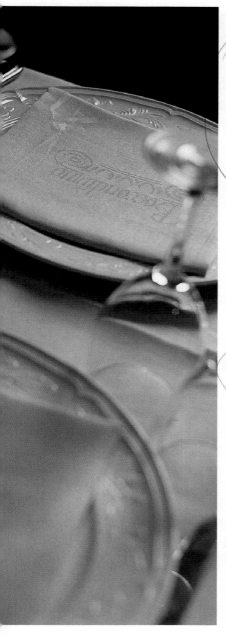

and long marble counters separating the eating area from the open-to-view kitchens. The food is Italian home cooking of variable quality, but mostly reliable.

Margutta Vegetariano – Ristorarte

Via Margutta 118 (06 3265 0577). Metro Flaminio/bus to piazza del Popolo. **Open** 12.30-3.30pm, 7.30-midnight daily. **Average** €26/L50,000. **Credit** MC, V. **Map** p320 2A.

Rome's historic vegetarian diner has expanded into a large plant-filled space on arty, exclusive via Margutta. The decor pays homage to the area, with plenty of modern art; at weekends there is live piano music. For lunch, a set-price all-you-can-eat buffet (€10.33/L20,000, with dessert) is an alternative to the more formal restaurant; on Sunday, this is replaced by a filling €23.24/L45,000 brunch. The menu offers a wide choice: pasta, salads, soufflés, soya rolls and grilled vegetables.

Matricianella

Via del Leone 3/4 (06 683 2100). Bus to lungotevere Marzio. **Open** 12.30-3pm, 7.30-11pm Mon-Sat. Closed Aug. **Average** €26/L50,000. **Credit** AmEx, DC, MC, V. **Map** p321 1A.

An upmarket, central trattoria, spread over three cosy rooms. The Roman imprint is most evident in classics such as *bucatini all'amatriciana*, but there are plenty of lighter, more creative options, including a tasty *risotto mantecato con fiori di zucca* (creamy risotto with courgette flowers). Decor is warm and friendly, service unpretentious and efficient; and the well-chosen wine list is honestly priced. Once you've eaten here, you'll understand why it's almost always packed — so book ahead.

Vic's

Vicolo della Torretta 60 (06 687 1445). Bus to via del Corso. **Open** 12.30-3pm, 7.30-11pm Mon-Sat. Closed 2wks Aug. **Average** €15/L30,000. **No credit cards.** **Map** p321 1A.

This new-but-old wine and salad bar offers a range of creative salads (swordfish, smoked cheese, and so on), *crostini* (toast) with various toppings, and a good selection of crêpes. With its pared-back Roman *osteria* decor, friendly service and excellently-priced wine list (starting from €6.20/L12,000 a bottle), this is a good bet for a cheap, light meal in the heart of the *centro storico*.

International

Hamasei

Via della Mercede 35/36 (06 679 2134). Bus to piazza San Silvestro. **Open** noon-2.30pm, 7-10.30pm Tue-Sun. Closed 1wk Aug. **Average** €23/L45,000. **Credit** AmEx, DC, MC, V. **Map** p323 1C.

A branch of a famous Tokyo eaterie, this is Rome's most traditional Japanese restaurant, oozing oriental elegance and packed with a reassuringly large slice of Rome's Japanese population. Try the sushi, sashimi or sukiyaki, served at candle-lit tables. Set lunch menus start at €12.91/L25,000.

Eat, Drink, Shop

Food and wine: **Buccone**.

Pizzerie

PizzaRé

*Via di Ripetta 14 (06 321 1468). Metro
Flaminia/bus to piazza del Popolo.* **Open** *12.45-
3.30pm, 7.30pm-12.30am daily. Closed 1wk Aug.*
Average €13/L25,000. **Credit** AmEx, DC, MC, V.
Map p320 2A.
One of the leaders of the Neapolitan invasion.
Formulaic but still lively, it offers 40 varieties of
high-rising Neapolitan pizza, various *antipasti* and
a range of salads. Service in the original pizzeria, just
a few paces from piazza del Popolo, is cheery and
efficient, and there are some acceptable bottles of
wine on offer. The via Lucullo branch occupies a

Belle Epoque villa with a garden pat
dining: getting past the man with the b
and the headset phone is almost as diffic
ting into the American Embassy next door;
though, a quality meal (with one or two asta
options) can be had at a very reasonable price.
Branches: PizzaRé, via Oslavia 39A (06 372 1173).
La Villa di PizzaRé, via Lucullo 22 (06 4201 3075).

Wine bars

Il Brillo Parlante

*Via della Fontanella, 12 (06 323 5017/
www.ilbrilloparlante.com). Bus to via di Ripetta or
piazza del Popolo.* **Open** *11am-2am Tue-Sat; 7.30pm-
1am Sun. Meals served 12.30-3.30pm, 7.30pm-1am
Tue-Sat; 7.30pm-1am Sun. Closed 2wks Aug.*
Average €18/L35,000. **Credit** AmEx, DC, MC, V.
Map p320 2A.
In the entrance bar, you can drink wines by the
glass; downstairs, this wine bar around the corner
from piazza del Popolo opens out into a low, vaulted cellar, with obtrusive ventilation ducts and
heraldic frescos. Unusually for a wine bar, it does
pizzas – not exactly the best – as well as some surprisingly creative pasta dishes, such as asparagus-
filled ravioli served with Castelmagno cheese and
toasted almonds. Good for a one-course gourmet
lunch on the run.

Buccone

*Via di Ripetta 19 (06 361 2154). Bus to piazza del
Popolo.* **Open** *Winebar/shop 9am-8.30pm Mon-Wed;
9am-midnight Thur-Sat; 10am-5pm Sun. Meals
served noon-3pm Mon-Wed, Sun; noon-3pm,
8-10.30pm Thur-Sat. Both Closed 3wks Aug.*
Average €18/L35,000. **Credit** AmEx, DC, MC, V.
Map p320 2A.
This historic *osteria* at the piazza del Popolo end of
via di Ripetta began life in the 18th century as a
covered carriage park for local aristocrats. For years
it operated as a takeaway bottle shop with a few
wines available by the glass at the marble counter;
but recently tables have been arranged among the
high wooden shelves, and in a little room behind, for
full meals. There are always three or four pasta
dishes or soups, followed by a range of meaty
seconds and creative salads. The cooking is more
than competent, the prices extremely reasonable.

Shaki

*Via Mario de' Fiori 29A (06 678 9244). Metro
Spagna/bus to piazza San Silvestro.* **Open** *10am-
10pm Mon-Sat.* **Average** €13/L25,000 (salad and
one glass wine). **Credit** AmEx, DC, MC, V.
Map p323 1C.
In the middle of the fashion triangle, this ultra-
stylish wine bar, which opened in March 2001, looks
like it has landed from some distant planet (ie
Milan). Design is cool, modern, and faintly Japanese;
but the food is unrepentantly Mediterranean. There
are no hot dishes, only a selection of rolls and salads made with good, fresh ingredients. Prices,

Eat, Drink, Shop

though, are on the high side for what's on offer; a glass of fairly ordinary wine will set you back €5.16/L10,000. The same outlet has a food and lifestyle shop at piazza di Spagna 65 (06 678 6605).

Piazza Navona & the Pantheon

See also p177 **L'Insalata Ricca**.

Restaurants

Boccondivino
Piazza Campo Marzio 6 (06 6830 8626). Bus to largo Chigi or piazza San Silvestro. **Open** 1-3pm, 8-11.30pm Mon-Sat. Closed Aug. **Average** €46/L90,000. **Credit** AmEx, DC, MC, V. **Map** p321 1A.
Finally, a really convincing Roman attempt to combine design with culinary excellence. The entrance, flanked by two ancient columns, give onto a jazzy space with faux marble walls, a creeper-forest of high-tech lights, zebra-striped wire bucket chairs, and ever-changing artworks (some of which are for sale). The food's good too, with a mod-Med fusion approach that shines in an *antipasto* of tartare of salmon in soy sauce with ginger, or a main dish of caramelised scallops with Traminer sauce and bonsai vegetables. Dinner is à la carte, but at lunch there's a good-value two-course business menu – more traditional Italian than fusion – that is offered with mineral water and house wine at €18.07/L35,000. Service is warm and professional.

Il Convivio
Vicolo dei Soldati 31 (06 686 9432). Bus to corso Rinascimento. **Open** 8-10.30pm Mon; 1-2.30pm, 8-10.30pm Tue-Sat. Closed 1wk Aug. **Average** €72/L140,000. **Credit** AmEx, DC, MC, V. **Map** p321 1B.
In this temple of foodie excellence the menu changes with the season and the moods of chef Angelo; among his creations are warm *tagliolini* with marinated fish, scampi and vegetables, or salt cod in batter with gooseberry sauce. It ain't strictly Roman (the brothers who run the place come from the Marches), but neither is it out-and-out culinary eclecticism. Be warned, though, that prices have crept up recently, and wine comes with a hefty mark-up.

Myosotis
Vicolo della Vaccarella 3/5 (06 686 5554). Bus to corso Rinascimento. **Open** 12.30-3pm, 7.30-11pm Mon-Sat. Closed 2wks Aug. **Average** €31/L60,000. **Credit** AmEx, DC, MC, V. **Map** p321 1A.
Myosotis was a pioneer when it opened in the early 1990s as the *centro storico* offshoot of a historic culinary mecca in Rome's eastern outskirts, which has since closed. But it is no longer the only creative trattoria in the city centre to offer updated versions of Italian classics using home-grown or home-made ingredients. The pastelly decor and the cuisine are both in need of renovation; but if you stick to house specials such as *antipasto* of mozzarella, ricotta,

Fight for your food: **Fratelli Paladini**. *See p175.*

focaccia and stuffed pimento, or *stracci di basilico e pachino* (pasta strips in basil, tomato and olive sauce), Myosotis is still worth a spin.

Osteria dell'Ingegno
Piazza di Pietra 45 (06 678 0662). Bus to via del Corso or largo Chigi. **Open** 12.30-3pm, 7.30pm-midnight Mon-Sat. Closed 1wk Aug. **Average** €36/L70,000. **Credit** AmEx, DC, MC, V. **Map** p321 2A.
The menu changes monthly in this friendly, arty restaurant, decorated with Chagall-inspired artworks on salmon pink walls. Gnocchi *in salsa di tartufo* (truffle sauce) is good, as are the *involtini di rombo con finocchi e salmone* (turbot rolls stuffed with fennel and salmon); vegetarians have a wide choice. Unfortunately, success has caused prices to take a huge leap over the last couple of years, though the wine list is still reasonably priced.

La Rosetta
Via della Rosetta 8/9 (06 686 1002/ www.larosetta.com). Bus to via del Corso or largo Argentina. **Open** 7.45-11.45pm Mon-Wed, Sat; 12.45-3pm, 7.45-11.45pm Thur, Fri. Closed 2wks Aug. **Average** €88/L170,000. **Credit** AmEx, DC, MC, V. **Map** p321 2A.

A good place to come for dinner, if someone else is paying. It has to be admitted that La Rosetta is one of the best seafood restaurants in town, but the prices are punishing. Even in summer, opt for the elegant, vaguely nautical, air-conditioned interior rather than one of the rather cramped pavement tables. The *gran misto di antipasti* (€43.89/L85,000) – a huge selection of tasters such as *carpaccio* of tuna marinated in thyme – gives one a chance to sample what the Rosetta does best: squeaky fresh, top-quality fish, prepared in a way that makes a virtue of simplicity. It is standard practice to follow this up with a *primo* like spaghetti with scampi and cour-gette flowers – a house speciality, cooked with a good deal of chilli – and skip the main course altogether. What hits the palate is divine; but uncom-fortable seats and over-familiar, over-cocky service are hardly what one expects for this kind of money.

Sangallo

Vicolo della Vaccarella 11A, off via della Scrofa (06 686 5549). Bus to corso Rinascimento. **Open** 7.30-10.30pm Mon-Sat. Closed 3wks Aug. **Average** €44/L85,000. **Credit** AmEx, DC, MC, V. **Map** p321 1A.

The walls are lime yellow, the artwork sub-Dali, the music easy listening. What marks out player-manager Gianfranco Panattoni is his unbridled enthusiasm. This can be overwhelming, especially when you're persuaded into choosing the €43.90/L85,000 seafood menu (the restaurant's *pièce de resistance*) rather than going à la carte. Focused foodies should enjoy such dishes as *garganelli con porcini, gamberi e scorza di limone* (pasta with porci-ni mushrooms, prawns and lemon rind), though recently the chef has lost his infallible touch.

Santa Lucia

Largo Febo 12 (06 6880 2427). Bus to corso Rinascimento. **Open** *Bar* 11am-2am daily. *Meals served* noon-3pm, 8pm-midnight daily. **Average** €23/L45,000. **Credit** MC, V. **Map** p321 2B.

The latest venture of Bartolo Cuomo, founder of Bar della Pace (*see p196*), is this late-opening bar/restaurant in largo Febo, a pretty, shady square next to piazza Navona. The decor is a stylish colli-sion between a Roman antique shop and a Moroccan hotel; outside, when weather permits, tables are arranged in the raised piazza. The food has a Neapolitan slant – antipasti like *pizzelle* (puffy

PLANET HOLLYWOOD

RESTAURANT, BAR & STORE
VIA DEL TRITONE, 118
M METRO A "BARBERINI"
TEL. 06 42818909
FAX 06 42901737

mini-pizzas) and *gattò di patate* (potato flan) are followed by good seafood and vegetable pasta dishes; most clients then skip straight to the succulent desserts. Prices are surprisingly low – which means that the place is always booked out. But a few tables are always reserved for those who just want a drink, and room can always be found for passing film stars.

International

L'Eau Vive

Via Monterone 85 (06 6880 1095). Bus or tram to largo Argentina. **Open** 12.30-2.30pm, 7.45-10.30pm Mon-Sat. Closed 3wks Aug. **Average** €36/L70,000. **Credit** AmEx, DC, MC, V. **Map** p324 1A.

Possibly the oddest culinary experience in Rome: if Fellini had ever directed a James Bond film, he would have set it here. Picture the scene: an obscure order of multi-ethnic Third World nuns runs a sophisticated French *haute cuisine*-inspired restaurant in a 16th-century palazzo, complete with Renaissance frescoes on the ceiling. At 9pm, the diners – many in the ill-fitting brown suits favoured by the international espionage circuit – are interrupted by the tinkle of a silver bell and invited to join in the Ave Maria. The only disappointment is the food: French classics like *quiche lorraine*, done with crushing correctness. L'Eau Vive is also a bargain-price tourist lunch.

Pizzerie

Da Francesco

Piazza del Fico 29 (06 686 4009). Bus to corso Vittorio Emanuele. **Open** 12.30-3pm, 7pm-midnight Mon, Wed-Sun; 7pm-midnight Tue. **Average** €13/L25,000. **No credit cards**. **Map** p321 2B.

Accept no imitations: Da Francesco is the original *centro storico* pizzeria. No bookings are taken: if you get there before 7.30pm, you generally walk right on in; if you get there much after eight, you join the milling throng. The reasons for this popularity are simple: tasty pizzas, a warm, traditional ambience, friendly service, and a range of competent, classic *primi* and *secondi* for those who can't face a doughy disc. You often get the distinct feeling that they are rushing you through to free up the table – but that's the price you pay for such a central bargain diner.

Wine bars

Cul de Sac

Piazza Pasquino 73 (06 6880 1094). Bus to corso Vittorio Emanuele. **Open** 7pm-12.30am Mon; 12.30-3.30pm, 7pm-12.30am daily. **Average** €13/L25,000. **Credit** AmEx, MC, V. **Map** p321 2B.

Rome's original wine bar, founded 1968. It's cramped inside and out, and the wines on the extensive list, once a bargain, have climbed towards the *centro storico* average. But the position – just around the corner from piazza Navona, with a ringside view of talking

statue Pasquino keeps the place packed. Food is standard fare, mainly cold: the Greek salad and the lentil soup stand out from the rest.

Riccioli Café Oyster Wine Bar

Piazza delle Coppelle 10A (06 6821 0313). **Open** 12.30pm-1am Mon-Sat. Closed Aug. **Average** €13/L25,000. **Credit** AmEx, DC, MC, V. **Map** p321 1A.

This new offshoot of the famed La Rosetta fish restaurant (*see p172*), with its Mondrian-ish decor, tries to be all things to all men: wine bar, sushi bar, oyster bar, pizzeria, tea room (from 3-7pm) and cocktail hangout. The naturally wary Roman public is still checking it out; but the ingredients are squeaky fresh – sample them at lunch, when there is a range of fixed-price menus (€9.39-€11.88/L18,000-L23,000). Cocktails include a rather unusual Oyster Martini.

Snacks

Fratelli Paladini

Via del Governo Vecchio 29 (06 686 1237). Bus to corso Vittorio Emanuele. **Open** 9am-7pm Mon-Wed, Fri; 8am-3pm Thur. Closed Aug. **No credit cards**. **Map** p321 2B.

This ancient, family-run bakery looks nothing special, but the crowd spilling outside at peak hours knows different. The *pizza bianca* is outstanding, and is filled to order with a variety of hams, cheeses, ready-made sauces, fresh figs, dried tomatoes and other delights. First pay at the till for a large €1.55/L3,000 piece or larger €2.06/L4,000 piece; then join the ruck to get served. Mineral water is free.

The Ghetto & Campo de' Fiori

Restaurants

Albistrò

Via dei Banchi Vecchi 140A (06 686 5274). Bus to corso Vittorio Emanuele or lungotevere Tebaldi. **Open** 7.30-11pm Mon, Tue, Thur-Sat; 12.30-3pm, 7.30-11pm Sun. Closed mid July-mid Aug. **Average** €26/L50,000. **Credit** AmEx, DC, MC, V. **Map** p321 2B.

The Swiss owner and his Italian wife have carved a bistrot ambience out of this narrow space, which spills out into a pretty courtyard. The cuisine is international and creative: try the nettle-stuffed ravioli or aubergine falafel if they have it – the menu is strictly seasonal. Desserts are exceptional: in winter, try the clementine sorbet. An intelligent wine list is offered at near-*enoteca* prices.

Al Bric

Via del Pellegrino 51 (06 687 9533). Bus to corso Vittorio Emanuele. **Open** *June-Aug* 7.30-11.30pm Tue-Sun. *Sept-May* 7.30-11.30pm Tue-Sat; 11.30am-3.30pm, 7.30-11.30pm Sun. Closed 1wk Aug. **Average** €41/L80,000. **Credit** AmEx, MC, V. **Map** p321 2B.

Eat, Drink, Shop

After some teething problems, this relatively new restaurant has really begun to deliver. Now with an extra room (so it's slightly easier to get a booking), complete with a wine-crate decor that indicates what the place is really about, Al Bric offers creative pasta, fish and meat, based on fresh or home-made ingredients. Some dishes work better than others; especially good are the simple spaghetti with anchovies and pecorino cheese, or the *timbale* (bake) of prawns, pears and gorgonzola. There's no wine list; clients choose their bottle after conferring with sommelier Roberto Marchetti (who speaks some English).

La Carbonara

Campo de' Fiori 23 (06 686 4783). Bus to corso Vittorio Emanuele. **Open** 12.30-3pm, 7.30-11.30pm Mon, Wed-Sun. Closed 3wks Aug. **Average** €28/ L55,000. **Credit** AmEx, MC, V. **Map** p321 2B.

At one end of Rome's most photogenic square, those tables look like they have to be a tourist trap. In fact, this old trooper does surprisingly honest *cucina romana*, with old favourites like spaghetti *alla carbonara* (with bacon, egg and parmesan), from which its name derives. The wine list and desserts are uninspired, but it's the setting that counts here. Keep an eye on your bag at outside tables.

Ditirambo

Piazza della Cancelleria 74 (06 687 1626). Bus to corso Vittorio Emanuele. **Open** 8-11.30pm Mon; 1-3.30pm, 8-11.30pm Tue-Sun. Closed Aug. **Average** €21/L40,000. **Credit** MC, V. **Map** p324 1B.

This funky trattoria around the corner from campo de' Fiori has tasty, good-value food based on fresh, mainly organic ingredients. It's regularly booked out in the evenings, despite the cramped conditions and occasionally hassled service. The cuisine is eclectic, mixing pasta dishes such as *maltagliati con i fiori di zucca* (with courgette flowers) with fish and vegetarian *secondi* and some great salads.

Filetti di Baccalà

Largo Librai 88 (06 686 4018). Bus to largo Argentina/tram to via Arenula. **Open** 5-10.40pm Mon-Sat. Closed Aug. **Average** €10/L20,000. **No credit cards**. **Map** p324 1B.

It's officially known as Dar Filettaro a Santa Barbara, but habitués take their cue from the sign over the door, which promises exactly what you get – salt cod fillets in batter. Alongside the obligatory filetti (€2.58/L5,000) there are other goodies such as fried courgettes. Service is brisk, the ambience spit and sawdust, but it's in a pretty square, and dead cheap.

Ar Galletto

Vicolo del Gallo 1/piazza Farnese 102 (06 686 1714). Bus to corso Vittorio Emanuele. **Open** noon-3.15pm, 7-11.30pm Mon-Sat. Closed 1wk Aug. **Average** €23/L45,000. **Credit** AmEx, DC, MC, V. **Map** p324 1B.

You don't need to pay the inflated prices of overrated Camponeschi for a ringside view of piazza Farnese. Ar Galletto, a far humbler trattoria, has

tables on the square in summer. The food is standard Roman, but dishes like *penne all'arrabbiata* or *spaghetti alle vongole* are appetising and – for the location – well-priced. Service is brisk but friendly.

Monserrato

Via Monserrato 96 (06 687 3386). Bus to corso Vittorio Emanuele. **Open** 12.30-3pm, 7.30pm-midnight Tue-Sun. Closed 3wks Aug. **Average** €28/L55,000. **Credit** AmEx, DC MC, V. **Map** p324 1B.

A reliable trattoria around the corner from piazza Farnese, with summer seating in the charming square of Santa Caterina della Rota. It could get by on setting alone, but the pan-Italian food is not at all bad either. Fish is a strong point, especially grilled; primi such as *bigoli* (fat spaghetti) with asparagus and shrimps are generally spot on.

Da Sergio

Vicolo delle Grotte 27 (06 686 4293). Tram to via Arenula/bus to lungotevere Tebaldi. **Open** 1-3.30pm, 7-11.30pm Mon-Sat. Closed 2wks Aug. **Average** €18/L35,000. **Credit** AmEx, MC, V. **Map** p324 1B.

It's cheap, it's friendly, it does good home cooking and it's always full of locals. Add a central location near campo de' Fiori, honest-to-goodness trattoria ambience and it's not hard to understand why there's often a queue going down the road and round the corner. The 7pm evening opening time is a boon for early eaters.

Sora Lella

Via Ponte Quattro Capi 16 (06 686 1601). Bus to piazza Monte Savello. **Open** 12.50-2.30pm, 7.50-11pm Mon-Sat. Closed Aug. **Average** €36/ L70,000. **Credit** AmEx, DC, MC, V. **Map** p324 2A.

Sora Lella was the plump, homely sister of film star Aldo Fabbrizi. A sort of Roman celebrity Queen Mum, she became a folk idol and a TV star in her own right. Her son set up this authentic Roman trat on Tiber island in her honour after she died in 1993. It avoids the obvious trap of folksy kitsch, and offers excellent Roman cooking, with dishes such as *pasta e patate* (pasta and potatoes) and *abbacchio brodettato* (lamb in broth), with one or two lighter and more creative options. Great on cold winter days.

Sora Margherita

Piazza delle Cinque Scole 30 (06 686 4002). Bus to lungotevere de' Cenci/tram to via Arenula. **Open** 12.10-3pm Mon-Fri. Closed Aug. **Average** €13/L25,000. **No credit cards**. **Map** p324 1A.

Margherita Tomassini and her husband have been running this wonderful *osteria* in the Ghetto for over 20 years, opening only for weekday lunches, and without even a sign over the door. It's not for health freaks, but no one argues with Roman Jewish cooking at these prices. The classic pasta and meat dishes on offer include a superlative *pasta e fagioli*, plus daily-changing fishy treats such as *baccalà al sugo* and *aliciotti con l'indivia* (anchovies with endives). Dessert consists of good, home-made *crostate* (jam or ricotta tarts).

La Taverna degli Amici
Piazza Margana 36 (06 6992 0637). Bus to piazza Venezia. **Open** 12.30-3pm, 7.30pm-midnight Tue-Sun. Closed 1wk Aug. **Average** €31/L60,000. **Credit** AmEx, DC, MC, V. **Map** p324 1A.
The setting is idyllic, in an ivy-draped square on the Ghetto side of piazza Venezia. Over the years, the creative Roman cooking has had its ups and downs; our last visit registered an upswing, with a good risotto of radicchio and pine nuts followed by a textbook *filetto di manzo* (beef fillet) with shallots. Though meaty Roman classics are not lacking, there are also a number of vegetarian options. Service is friendly, the wine list short but adequate. In summer, the outside tables are much sought-after.

Wine bars

L'Angolo Divino
Via dei Balestrari 12 (06 686 4413). Bus or tram to largo Argentina. **Open** 10.30am-3pm, 5.30pm-1am Mon, Tue, Thur-Sun. Closed 2wks Aug. **Credit** MC, V. **Map** p321 2B.
This bar on a quiet street near campo de' Fiori has come up in the world since it opened as a humble *vini e olii* 50 years ago. Fifteen or so wines are available by the glass, many more by the bottle. There's an unusually good range of smoked fish, salami and salads, an ample cheeseboard and, in winter, at least one hot dish.

La Bottega del Vino da Anacleto Bleve
Via Santa Maria del Pianto 9A/11 (06 686 5970). Bus to largo Argentina/tram to via Arenula. **Open** *Enoteca* 9.30am-1.30pm, 5-8pm Mon-Sat. *Wine bar* 1-3pm Mon-Sat. Closed 3wks Aug. **Credit** AmEx, DC, MC, V. **Map** p324 1A.
This wine shop has gradually been swamped with tables. The shop's carefully selected range of bottles by top Italian producers ensures that it is well patronised by locals. The restaurant is equally popular, offering a great selection of salads, smoked fish, cheeses and a few pasta dishes.

Snacks

Da Giovanni
Campo de' Fiori 39 (06 687 7992). Bus to corso Vittorio Emanuele/tram to via Arenula. **Open** *Sept-May* 9am-3pm, 5-9pm Mon-Sat. *May-July* 9am-3pm, 5pm-2am Mon-Sat. Closed Aug. **No credit cards**. **Map** p321 2B.
Giovanni does the best takeaway sliced pizza in the campo de' Fiori area. Check out the one with *fiori di zucca* (courgette flowers).

L'Insalata Ricca
Largo dei Chiavari 85 (06 6880 3656). Bus to corso Vittorio Emanuele. **Open** noon-4pm, 6.30pm-midnight daily. **Average** €10/L20,000. **Credit** AmEx, DC, MC, V. **Map** p321 2A/B.

The nearest Rome has to a fast-food salad bar. Not exclusively vegetarian, but a good cheap alternative to obligatory pasta and/or veggie ghettos (although you can order pasta too). The main branch is geared to fast outdoor eating; the smaller one in piazza di Pasquino is a shade more comfortable and intimate. **Branch** piazza di Pasquino 72 (06 6830 7881).

Le Piramidi
Vicolo del Gallo 11 (06 687 9061). Bus to corso Vittorio Emanuele/tram to via Arenula. **Open** 10.30am-12.30am Tue-Sun. Closed 3wks Aug. **No credit cards**. **Map** p324 1B.
Around the corner from campo de' Fiori, Le Piramidi makes for a welcome change from takeaway pizza. The range of Middle Eastern takeaway fare is small, but it's all fresh, cheap and tasty: the pitta bread with falafel and salad is especially good.

Zi' Fenizia
Via Santa Maria del Pianto 64 (06 689 6976). Bus to largo Argentina/tram to via Arenula. **Open** 9am-9pm Mon-Thur, Sun; 9am-3.30pm Fri. Closed Jewish holidays. **Credit** MC, V. **Map** p324 1A.
Rome's only kosher pizza outlet. Auntie Fenizia does over 40 flavours, including the house speciality, *aliciotti e indivia* (anchovies and endives).

Trastevere & the Gianicolo

Restaurants

Alberto Ciarla
Piazza San Cosimato 40 (06 581 8668). Bus or tram to viale Trastevere. **Open** 8.30-11pm Mon-Sat. **Average** €67/L130,000. **Credit** AmEx, DC, MC, V. **Map** p324 2B.
One of those restaurants that nobody really talks about anymore, as its reputation is stuck in the same 1960s time warp as the decor, which makes the place look like a rather dubious *club privé*. Then you go along, and you discover that these guys really know how to cook. In fact, Alberto Ciarla challenges La Rosetta (*see p172*) for the title of Rome's best fish restaurant – and a meal here is a whole lot more affordable, especially if you opt for one of the taster menus. A trademark dish such as *spigola con le erbe* (sea bass with herbs) strikes the right balance between art and nature; a primo of *pasta e fagioli con le cozze* (pasta and beans with mussels) is strong, decisive and very Roman. The menu is a triumph of *Dolce Vita* typography, the overriding mood one of charmingly courteous camp.

Antico Arco
Piazzale Aurelio 7 (06 581 5274). Bus to via Carini. **Open** 8pm-midnight Mon-Sat. Closed 2wks Aug. **Average** €41/L80,000. **Credit** AmEx, DC, MC, V. **Map** p324 2C.
This relaxed, friendly restaurant on the Gianicolo hill is still one of the best bets in Rome for a really special meal at a relatively contained price. The soothingly modern decor makes up for the lack of a

Eat, Drink, Shop

Select your wine

In parts of Italy known for their fine wines – such as Tuscany or the Veneto – a restaurant's house wine will usually be drinkable, occasionally delicious.

In Roman restaurants, the wine usually comes from the Castelli Romani hills to the east of the city – home to those two rustic DOC appellations, Frascati and Marino. At their best, Castelli Romani wines – especially the whites – are robust and more-ish, with a pleasant dry-but-sweet taste. More often, though, they taste like paint stripper. Lazio – the region of which Rome is the capital – has begun to produce some really fine wines recently, thanks to a new breed of young, dynamic producers. But few of these filter down to the street-corner restaurant.

It's a good idea, therefore, to know your labels. Most neighbourhood *trattorie* have only a limited choice of the most obvious, mass-produced wines, but some of these are not at all bad, and if you scan the list or shelves, there's usually at least one worth drinking. There are still quite a few Roman waiters who have no clue about how wine should be served, so it's wise to check the year and temperature, and ask for an ice bucket (*un secchiello di ghiaccio*) if the wine merits it. Most Italian whites should be drunk within a year of bottling.

One recent phenomenom is *vino novello* – the Italian equivalent of Beaujolais Nouveau, a just-pressed red wine made from any one of a number of grape varieties, and released in the late autumn. Waiters, keen to shift cases of the stuff before Christmas, will sing its praises; but with a few exceptions, it doesn't deserve them.

Chianti

Avoid anything in a straw-covered flask. Reliable names include Rocca delle Macìe, San Felice, Agricoltori del Chianti Geografico, Frescobaldi (Chianti Nipozzano), Fattoria di Felsina, Isola e Olena, Vignamaggio, Macchiavelli and Melini. A good alternative – made from 100 per cent Sangiovese grapes – is **Rosso di Montalcino**, younger cousin of the more famous Brunello. Avignonesi, Banfi and Ruffino make good-value versions.

Corvo Bianco/Rosso

Originating in the Duca di Salaparuta's huge Sicilian estates (now owned by Sicily's regional government), this is Italy's most mass-produced wine, with four million bottles rattling off the production line every year. Both the red and the white wines have improved steadily, and make up in consistency what they lack in character. If it's on the wine list, try the special cru Colomba Platino white.

Frascati Superiore

The Superiore is a notch above standard house Frascati, but it's still bland unless you're lucky enough to find Fontana Candida's Santa Teresa cru. Drink, as a rule, as young as possible. Other good Frascatis include Colle Picchioni, Villa Simone, and Castel De Paolis.

Montepulciano d'Abruzzo

Most of the red house plonk served in Roman *trattorie* is Montepulciano d'Abruzzo, and no great advertisement for its qualities. But if you can find it, Cantina Tollo's Colle Secco or, better still, Colle Secco Rubino should reconcile you to this warm, tannic wine, which goes well with red meat. The legendary Montepulciano d'Abruzzo produced in tiny quantities by Edoardo Valentini is in quite another league, and quite another price range. Recently, Masciarelli has been producing a cru that falls somewhere between the two extremes.

Regaleali Bianco

This Sicilian industrial white is ever reliable and great value. Drink young. Villa Tasca is a pricier (but good value) big brother.

Falanghina

White wines from Campania – the region around Naples – are the latest craze in Roman restaurants. Falanghina is an easy-drinking, fruity white, but there are some dodgy producers around. Look out for the excellent-value version made by Feudi di San Giorgio, and drink it as young as possible.

Vini Bianchi Leggeri

A new generation of slightly sparkling, fresh whites. The best known of these is Galestro Capsula Viola, produced by Tuscan giants Antinori. Another good bet is Cala Viola, made by Sardinian winery Sella & Mosca, and Glicine, by Corvo. Best drunk as young as possible.

Eat, Drink, Shop

view, and the service is attentive and affable. First courses, such as the classic *risotto con castelmagno* (risotto with Castelmagno cheese) or the spaghetti *cacio, pepe e fiori di zucca* (with sheep's cheese, pepper and courgette flowers) are a real strength, but *secondi* such as scampi-filled pheasant breast with poppy seeds can be equally impressive. The menu changes with Darwinian langour – but this is only a problem if the place becomes addictive. Maurizio, the sommelier, can help steer a course through an extensive, well-priced wine list.

Augusto

Piazza de' Renzi 15 (06 580 3798). Bus to lungotevere Sanzio/tram to viale Trastevere. **Open** 12.30-3pm, 8-11pm Mon-Fri; 12.30-3pm Sat. Closed mid Aug-mid Sept. **Average** €18/L35,000. **No credit cards. Map** p324 2B.

Don't miss this: one of the last really cheap *osterie* in Trastevere, serving classics of Roman cuisine such as *rigatoni all'amatriciana, pasta e lenticchie* (pasta with lentils) and *pollo arrosto con patate* (roast chicken with potatoes), at unbeatable prices. In a pretty piazza with tables outside in summer, it's frequented both by older *trasteverini* and youngsters with serious haircuts.

Paris

Piazza San Calisto 7A (06 581 5378). Bus or tram to viale Trastevere. **Open** 12.30pm-3pm, 8-11pm Tue-Sat; noon-3pm Sun. Closed 3wks Aug. **Average** €39/L75,000. **Credit** AmEx, DC, MC, V. **Map** p324 2B.

Recent visits to what was once the best Roman Jewish restaurant in town have been disappointing; but the star dish, *fritto misto con baccalà* (fried vegetables with salt cod) is still worth a spin, and classics like *pasta e ceci* (pasta and chickpea soup) and *minestra d'arzilla* (ray soup) make a decent supporting cast.

Pizzerie

Panattoni – I Marmi

Viale Trastevere 53 (06 580 0919). Bus or tram to viale Trastevere. **Open** 6.30pm-2am Mon, Tue, Thur-Sun. Closed 3wks Aug. **Average** €10/L20,000. **No credit cards. Map** p324 2B.

It's better known as *l'Obitorio* (the Morgue) on account of its marble tables, but there's nothing deathly about Panattoni, one of the liveliest pizzerias in Trastevere, especially in summer when you can sit outside and watch the new super-trams glide past. Its pizzas, though, are not the best in Rome, and service can be ruthless.

Dar Poeta

Vicolo del Bologna 45 (06 588 0516). Bus or tram to viale Trastevere. **Average** €13/L25,000. **Credit** AmEx, MC, V. **Map** p324 2B.

This bustling pizzeria in the heart of Trastevere uses the slow-rise method introduced by *nouvelle pizza* guru Angelo Iezzi. Dar Poeta's offerings have fluffy bases and creative toppings, including *taglialegna* (mixed vegetables, mushrooms, sausage and mozzarella) and *bodrilla* (apples and Gran Marnier). The varied *bruschette* are first-rate, and you can eat till late. No bookings are taken, so come early or wait.

Da Vittorio

Via di San Cosimato 14A (06 580 0353). Bus or tram to viale Trastevere. **Open** 7pm-midnight Tue-Sun. **Average** €13/L25,000. **No credit cards. Map** 6/2B.

Vittorio was here way before Neapolitan pizzas became trendy, and no doubt will still be here when the fad has passed. He's as *napoletano* as they come, and so are his succulent pizzas. He has a couple of inventions of his own – like the self-celebratory *Vittorio* (mozzarella, Parmesan, fresh tomato and basil). The place is minute, but bursts with exuberance.

Wine bars & pubs

Enoteca Ferrara

Via del Moro 1A/piazza Trilussa 41 (06 5833 3920). Bus or tram to viale Trastevere. **Open** 8.30pm-2am Mon, Wed-Sun. **Average** €26/L50,000. **No credit cards. Map** p324 2B.

In a surprisingly big space for Trastevere, the Paolillo sisters run a tasteful imbibery with a well-stocked cellar. The apartheid wine list (one book for whites, one for reds) provides a happy evening's reading. The menu includes a good range of soups, and much use is made of grains, beans, and organic vegetables. Some dishes are too ambitious for their own good; if you hit a miss, console yourself with a dessert like mocha coffee tart in hazelnut and chocolate sauce. From May to September (when the *enoteca* closes on Sunday rather than Tuesday), you can wine and dine in a pretty, quiet garden at the back.

Snacks

La Casa del Tramezzino

Viale Trastevere 81 (06 581 2118). Bus or tram to viale Trastevere. **Open** 7am-2am daily. **No credit cards. Map** p324 2B.

In one of his struggles against foreign influences, Mussolini ordered that foreign words be replaced with newly coined Italian ones – so 'sandwich' became *tramezzino* (literally, little-bit-in-the-middle). La Casa del Tramezzino has the widest choice of them in Rome. Apart from classics like mozzarella and tomato, there is fried aubergine, rocket and Gorgonzola, or cheese and caviar.

Frontoni dal 1921

Viale Trastevere 52 (06 581 2436). Bus or tram to viale Trastevere. **Open** 10am-1am Mon-Sat; 5pm-midnight Sun. **No credit cards. Map** p324 2B.

Eat, Drink, Shop

Frontoni claims to have 60 different fillings for the slabs of *pizza bianca* piled up behind its counter: just point to the ones you fancy. It also operates as a takeaway deli.

Sisini
Via San Francesco a Ripa 137 (06 589 7110).
Bus or tram to viale Trastevere. **Open** 9am-9pm Mon-Sat. Closed 3wks Aug. **No credit cards.**
Map p324 2B.
Probably Trastevere's best *pizza rustica* (takeaway pizza) outfit. The flavours are fairly conservative, but there's a wide range and they're all delicious. Roast chicken is another forte.

The Aventine & Testaccio

Restaurants

Agustarello
Via Giovanni Branca 100 (06 574 6585). Bus to via Marmorata or piazza Santa Maria Liberatrice/tram to via Marmorata. **Open** 12.30-3pm, 7.30-11pm Mon-Sat. Closed 2wks Aug. **Average** €23/L45,000.
No credit cards. Map p325 2B.
The decor in this Testaccio trattoria couldn't be more basic, but what matters here is respect for Roman tradition in all its anatomical detail. The arrival of BSE in Italy has put paid to one of its trademark dishes, *rigatoni con la pajata* (with stomach and intestines); but another classic, *involtino con il sedano* (veal rolls with celery stuffing), has been given the Brussels green flag. Romans pay little attention to such health fads, in any case, and finding a table here at short notice is still a desperate task.

Checchino dal 1887
Via di Monte Testaccio 30 (06 574 6318). Bus to via Marmorata or via Galvani/tram to via Marmorata. **Open** 12.30-3pm, 8-11.30pm Tue-Sat. Closed Aug.
Average €46/L90,000. **Credit** AmEx, DC, MC, V.
Map p325 2A.
Nestling among the trendy bars and clubs opposite Testaccio's former slaughter house is Rome's leading temple of authentic *cucina romana*. Specialities include *insalata di zampetti* (hoof jelly salad) and *coratella con i carciofi* (veal heart with artichokes). Both have been okayed by EU mad cow legislators, who have nixed only the veal intestines that go into *pajata di vitello*. Checchino also has what is generally considered to be Rome's finest wine cellar. There's also an outstanding selection of cheeses, with recommended wine combinations.

Ketumbar
Via Galvani 24 (06 5730 5338). Bus to via Marmorata or via Galvani/tram to via Marmorata. **Open** 8pm-midnight Mon-Sat. Closed Aug.
Average €28/L55,000. **Credit** AmEx, DC, MC, V.
Map p325 2B.
There's an odd kind of culture clash in this brand new, hyper-trendy, very un-Roman Roman venue: the vaulted rooms and back walls of Perspex giving

straight on to the amphorae which make up Monte Testaccio mark it out as uniquely *testaccino*; the decor, on the other hand, has a taste of Indo-China, with lacquered chests and paper-lantern wall lights. It works. As does the fusion fare, which mixes oriental tastes with *gnocchi*, or replaces the usual spaghetti with rice noodles. The staff are effortlessly affable; the fact that you can down a plate of pasta and a glass of wine in the bar (which stays open until around 2am) is a plus. The only pity is that the resident DJs play their very serious music so loud that you can't hear your dinner partner for the din.

Tuttifrutti
Via Luca della Robbia 3A (06 575 7902). Bus or tram to via Marmorata. **Open** 8pm-midnight Tue-Sun. Closed Aug. **Average** €21/L40,000.
Credit AmEx, MC, V. **Map** p325 2A.
Substance counts more than decor in this friendly trat, where the food is very good indeed: based on seasonal ingredients, the menu – pan-Italian with international touches – changes nightly. You'll be talked through it by the earnest, welcoming young crew that run the place; they'll be happy to recommend the right honestly priced wine, too. The kitchen stays open late enough for diners to sashay straight from here to one of Testaccio's many clubs.

Pizzerie

Remo
Piazza Santa Maria Liberatrice 44 (06 574 6270). Bus to via Marmorata or piazza Santa Maria Liberatrice/tram to via Marmorata. **Open** 6.30pm-12.30am Mon-Sat. Closed Aug. **Average** €10/L20,000. **No credit cards. Map** p325 1A.
The best place in town for authentic *pizza romana*, Remo is a Testaccio institution, with a prime location on the district's main piazza. You can sit at wonky tables balanced on the pavement, or in the cavernous interior, overseen by Lazio team photos. The *bruschette al pomodoro* are the finest in Rome.

Wine bars & gastropubs

L'Oasi della Birra
Piazza Testaccio 41 (06 574 6122). Bus or tram to via Marmorata. **Open** 7.30pm-1am Mon-Sat. Closed Sun in July; 2wks Aug. **Average** €15/L30,000.
Credit MC, V. **Map** p325 2A.
A must for beer lovers. In the basement of a modest *enoteca* on Testaccio's market square, the Oasis of Beer has over 500 on offer, from Belgian Trappist brews to Jamaican Red Stripe. It's one of few places where you can track down the products of Italian microbreweries such as the award-winning Menabrea. The accompanying food ranges from snacks (rolls, a well-stocked cheeseboard) to full-scale meals, with an Austro-Hungarian slant (goulash and strudel). Booking is always a good idea, especially at weekends.

Eat, Drink, Shop

At T-BONE STATION eat whatever comes to your mind

Snacks

Il Seme e la Foglia
Via Galvani 18 (06 574 3008). Bus to via Marmorata or via Galvani/tram to via Marmorata. **Open** 7.45am-1.30am Mon-Sat; 6pm-1.30am Sun. Closed 3wks Aug. **No credit cards**. **Map** p325 2A.
Once a po-faced macrobiotic affair, this has become a lively daytime snack bar and evening pre-club stop. At midday there's always a pasta dish, plus salads and exotic filled rolls.

Volpetti Più
Via Alessandro Volta 8/10 (06 574 4306). Bus or tram to via Marmorata. **Open** 10am-10pm Mon-Sat. Closed 2wks Aug. **Credit** AmEx, DC, MC, V. **Map** p325 2A.
Close to the upmarket deli of the same name, this snack bar does excellent *pizza a taglio* and a range of other hot and cold dishes. Unusually for a buffet, it also has a range of good wines, and they're at *enoteca* prices.

The Celio & San Giovanni

Restaurants

Crab
Via Capo d'Africa 2 (06 7720 3636). Metro Colosseo/bus or tram to piazza del Colosseo. **Open** 8-11.30pm Mon; 1-3pm, 8-11.30pm Tue-Sat. Closed 3wks Aug, 10 days Dec-Jan. **Average** €46/L90,000. **Credit** AmEx, DC, MC, V. **Map** p326 2B.
This new though unfortunately rather anonymous design restaurant within roaring distance of the Colosseum has one thing going for it: fresh seafood, prepared with some competence. Oysters and lobster (from a panoramic tank in the entrance corridor) co-star alongside the title mollusc. It's not cheap, but service is efficient (if somewhat cloying), the wine list is reasonably priced, and dishes such as clam soup with *fregola* (a kind of Sardinian couscous), or *tegame di calamari con patate* (squid and potato bake) soar above the fake ferns and sub-Conran decor.

International

Shawerma
Via Ostilia 24 (06 700 8101). Metro Colosseo/bus or tram to piazza del Colosseo. **Open** 8pm-midnight Tue-Sun. Closed 2wks Aug. **Average** €21/L40,000. **Credit** AmEx, DC, V. **Map** p326 2B.
You can sit downstairs on seats, or cross-legged on cushions on a low balcony at this Egyptian eaterie near the Colosseum. The cuisine is first-rate, with great couscous and unusual milk-based desserts; lubrication comes in the form of rose wine. By day it's a café, with exotic beverages such as *hansun* and *erfa* as well as mint tea and Arabic coffee.

Monti & Esquilino

Restaurants

Agata e Romeo
Via Carlo Alberto 45 (06 446 6115). Metro Vittorio/bus to piazza Esquilino. **Open** 12.30-2.30pm, 7.30-10.30pm Mon-Fri. Closed 2wks Aug; 2wks Jan. **Average** €67/L130,000. **Credit** AmEx, DC, MC, V. **Map** p326 1A.
The seedy area between Termini and Santa Maria Maggiore is not where you would expect to find one of Rome's gourmet treats. But here *nouvelle cuisine romana* is overseen by Agata Parisella, while husband Romeo hovers in the dining room. Roman specialities such as *pasta e broccoli in brodo d'arzilla* (pasta with broccoli in skate broth), or a gourmet version of *vignarola*, a traditional vegetable soup, mix with international dishes and in-house creations. There are two taster menus, at €51.65/ L100,000 and €92.96/L180,000. Desserts are fabulous (try the superlative *millefoglie*), but at this price, they should be. For serious foodies, or serious romance.

Taverna Sottovento
Via Ciancaleoni 31 (06 474 2265). Metro Cavour/bus to via Cavour. **Open** noon-2.30pm, 7-11.30pm Mon-Sat. Closed 2wks Aug. **Average** €28/L55,000. **Credit** AmEx, DC, MC, V. **Map** p326 1B.
This Calabrian restaurant between Santa Maria Maggiore and via Nazionale has a wood-panelled dining room done out in a nautical theme. The cuisine is full of southern flavour, based on specially delivered Calabrian products, some of which are available for sale upstairs. Among the *primi*, the *tagliolini* with courgette flowers and scampi stands out; main courses are mainly fish-based, but vegetarians are well-served.

International

Africa
Via Gaeta 26 (06 494 1077). Metro Castro Pretorio or Termini/bus to piazza dell'Indipendenza. **Open** 8am-11.30pm Tue-Sun. **Average** €15/L30,000. **Credit** AmEx, MC, V. **Map** p323 1A.
This long-established Eritrean restaurant offers specialities such as *sambussa*, which is a dish of cigar-shaped meat and spice rolls, and *taita* – a sour, spongy bread served with *zighini* (spicy meat), *spriss* (beef cubes with chilli, onion and spices) and other toppings; the restaurant also serves a vegetarian version. The place opens early in the morning for Eritrean breakfast of yoghurt and *fuul* (beans).

Il Guru
Via Cimarra 4/6 (06 474 4110). Bus to via Nazionale or via Cavour. **Open** 7pm-midnight daily. Closed 2wks Aug. **Average** €23/L45,000. **Credit** AmEx, DC, MC, V. **Map** p326 1B.

San Lorenzo

First a railway workers' ghetto, then a cut-price student hangout, the working-class enclave of San Lorenzo (*see p152*), just east of Termini station, has been attracting a smarter, more artsy Bohemian crowd for the last ten years or so. Galleries and craft shops have opened, particularly in the former Cerere pasta factory, which is the closest Rome comes to the New York loft scene. And, alongside the pubs and bars, a slew of bistrot-style restaurants have arisen to stoke the flame – so that serious Roman foodies now head for San Lorenzo rather than passé Trastevere. The four listed below currently lead the pack. **Map p153.**

Arancia Blu

Via dei Latini 65 (06 445 4105). Bus to porta Tiburtina. **Open** 8pm-midnight daily. **Average** €23/L45,000. **No credit cards**.
A friendly, upmarket vegetarian restaurant that prides itself on its wine list. The enjoyable pasta dishes are mainly southern Italian in conception; the more macrobiotic *secondi* are a tad less convincing, but still satisfying. The owners also organise cooking and wine courses, and have rearranged the premises to provide full disabled access.

Il Dito e la Luna

Via dei Sabelli 51 (06 494 0726). Bus to via Tiburtina. **Open** 8pm-midnight Mon-Sat. Closed 2wks Aug. **Average** €26/L50,000. **No credit cards**.
This softly lit bistrot is a good place to bring that special person without breaking the bank. The owner's Sicilian origins are betrayed in a menu that changes with the season – try the *caponata* (a Sicilian *ratatouille*), if they have it, or the *flan di cipolle di Tropea e fonduta di parmigiano* (onion flan with Parmesan sauce). The desserts are good, especially the *cannoli*. A modest wine list offers bottles at near-cost price. The 'no credit cards' policy is a pain, but debit cards are now accepted.

Tram Tram

Via dei Reti 44/46 (06 490 416). Bus to piazzale Verano/tram to via dei Reti. **Open** 12.30-3.30pm, 7.30-11.30pm Tue-Sun. Closed 2wks Aug. **Average** €23/L45,000. **Credit** AmEx, DC, MC, V.
Taking its name from its proximity to the tram tracks (something you're reminded of more than once during your meal), this good-value nouvelle

trattoria attracts a young crowd, who are not fazed by the waiters' permanently hassled manner, or the lack of elbow room. The menu is mainly southern Italian, and particularly strong on fish and vegetables, as in the *tagliolini calamaretti e pesto* (pasta strips with baby squid and pesto). There are also a few vegetarian main courses. The wine list is small but well-chosen, and has very reasonable mark-ups.

Uno e Bino
Via degli Equi 58 (06 446 0702). Bus to piazzale Verano or via Tiburtina/tram to via dei Reti. **Open** 8.30-11.30pm Tue-Sun. Closed 3wks Aug. **Average** €26/L50,000. **Credit** DC, MC, V.
This creative bistro (*pictured*), with soothingly minimalist decor, keeps getting better – and it's still great value for money. Host Giampaolo Gravina can talk you through his excellent (and fairly priced) wine list in competent English. The food is modern Italian, with no regional bias; pasta courses such as *tortelli* stuffed with *caprino* cheese and cabbage in a spring onion sauce are spot-on; *secondi* might include duck breast with apples and shallots, and there's usually at least one vegetarian option. The desserts are good too, and there's even a 'chocolate board' – a selection of gourmet varieties, each served with the appropriate dessert wine. The restaurant's total no-smoking policy is almost unique in Rome.

If you're dying for an Indian, Il Guru will fill the gap... though certainly not as tastily as your local restaurant at home. There's a tandoori oven; the cuisine is standard pan-Indian, with a vegetarian menu, and the staff are friendly.

Hasekura
Via dei Serpenti 27 (06 483 648). Bus to via Nazionale or via Cavour. **Open** noon-2.30pm, 7-10.30pm Mon-Sat. Closed Aug. **Average** €28/L55,000.**Credit** AmEx, DC, MC, V. **Map** p326 1C.
The best value of Rome's Japanese restaurants, Hasekura is an intimate little place, though at first sight it looks more like a Roman trat than a Japanese sushi joint. You can opt for the generous fixed-price lunch menus (tempura €15.50/L30,000; sushi €19.63/L38,000) or spend considerably more by going à la carte. Beautifully presented specialities can be ordered if you phone ahead.

Maharajah
Via dei Serpenti 124 (06 4747 144). Bus to via Nazionale or via Cavour. **Open** 12.30-2.30pm, 7-11.30pm Mon-Fri; 7-11.30pm Sat, Sun. **Average** €26/L50,000. **Credit** AmEx, DC, MC, V. **Map** p326 1B.
Very near to the Guru (*see p183*), the Maharajah has the culinary edge, but is also more expensive. Classic Punjabi food, with a tandoori oven and a vegetarian menu.

Pizzerie

Est! Est! Est!
Via Genova 32 (06 488 1107). Metro Repubblica/bus to via Nazionale. **Open** 7pm-midnight Tue-Sun. Closed 3wks Aug. **Average** €15/L30,000. **Credit** MC, V. **Map** p323 2B.
Usefully placed between the station and piazza Venezia, Est! Est! Est! (after the wine of the same name) was renovated a few years back, but, with the same dark wood fittings and the same starched, elderly waiters, it hasn't lost its conservative allure. The pizzas and *calzoni ripieni* (folded-over pizzas) are still good, but the general air of tiredness can get to one.

Wine bars

Cavour 313
Via Cavour 313 (06 678 5496). Metro Cavour/bus to via Cavour. **Open** *Mid Oct-June* 12.30-2.30pm, 7.30pm-12.30am Mon-Sat; 7.30pm-12.30am Sun. *Mid June-July, Sept* 12.30-2.30pm, 7.30pm-12.30am Mon-Sat. Closed Aug. **Credit** AmEx, DC, MC, V. **Map** p326 1C.
A friendly atmosphere (despite the gloomy mahogany decor), a serious cellar and good snacks explain the eternal popularity of this wine bar at the Forum end of via Cavour. Prices are reasonable, and there's a big selection of hot and cold snacks; in winter, it's especially strong on soups. With over 500 bottles on the wine list, choice is the only problem.

Trimani Wine Bar
Via Cernaia 37B (06 446 9630). Bus to via Cernaia/via Goito. **Open** noon-3pm, 6pm-12.30am Mon-Sat. Closed Aug. **Average** €23/L45,000. **Credit** AmEx, DC, MC, V. **Map** p323 1A.
This wine bar offshoot of Rome's leading *enoteca* (*see chapter* **Shopping**) is looking a bit shabby, especially upstairs, and the service can be infuriatingly slow. But it still offers an excellent choice of Italian regional wines at reasonable (though not *enoteca*) prices, and a range of decent pasta dishes, quiches, soups and *crostini*. Unquestionably better for a lunchtime snack than an evening meal.

Snacks

Indian Fast Food
Via Mamiani 11 (06 446 0792). Metro Vittorio/bus or tram to piazza Vittorio. **Open** 11am-4pm, 5-10pm Mon-Sat. **No credit cards. Map** p326 1A.
Rome's only Indian takeaway, just off piazza Vittorio. There is space to eat in, if you prefer, accompanied by gloriously kitsch Indian music videos – and even send a moneygram while you consume your vegetable samosa.

Pizzeria Leonina
Via Leonina 84 (06 482 7744). Metro Cavour/bus to via Cavour. **Open** 8am-9pm Mon-Fri. Closed 2wks July, all Aug. **No credit cards. Map** p326 1B.
One of the best *pizzerie a taglio* in Rome. Avoid peak times, as the queue is endless (take a number). Not as cheap as one might hope, but with toppings like spicy beans, tuna salad and even apple strudel, it's still worth it.

Shawerma Express
Via Calatafimi 7 (06 481 8791). Bus to piazza dei Cinquecento or via Goito. **Open** 11am-midnight daily. **No credit cards. Map** p323 1A.
Good-value Arab and Middle Eastern specialities such as falafel, *fuul* (spicy beans), couscous and kebabs, served with pitta bread, to take away or eat in. There are tables outside in summer.

The Vatican & Prati

Restaurants

Osteria dell'Angelo
Via Giovanni Bettolo 24 (06 372 9470). Metro Ottaviano/bus to via Ottaviano. **Open** 8pm-midnight Mon, Wed, Thur-Sat; 1-2.30pm, 8pm-midnight Tue, Fri. Closed Aug. **Average** €18/L35,000. **No credit cards. Map** p320 2C.
Angelo Croce's neighbourhood trattoria five minute's walk north of the Vatican is a real one-off, just like the man himself. The decor consists of photos of boxers and rugby players – the two sporting passions of Angelo and his culinary helpmates, who have cauliflower ears but hearts of gold

Reading the menu

Pasti – meals
prima colazione breakfast; **pranzo** lunch; **cena** supper; **uno spuntino** a snack.

Materie prime – basic ingredients
aceto vinegar; **latte** milk; **limone** lemon; **olio d'oliva** olive oil; **pane** bread; **pepe** pepper; **sale** salt; **zucchero** sugar.

Modi di cottura
– cooking techniques
al dente cooked, but still firm; **al forno** baked; **al sangue** rare (for steaks); **al vapore** steamed; **alla griglia, grigliato, alla piastra** grilled; **bollito** boiled; **cotto** cooked; **crudo** raw; **fritto** fried; **in bianco** plain, just with oil or butter (rice, pasta), or no tomato (pizza); **in brodo** in clear meat broth; **all'acqua pazza** (of fish) in thin broth; **ripassato in padella** (of vegetables) fried with garlic and chilli after boiling or steaming; **in umido** poached; **stufato** stewed; **brastato** braised.

Antipasti – hors d'oeuvre
alici marinati marinated anchovies; **antipasto di mare** seafood hors d'oeuvre; **antipasto misto** mixed hors d'oeuvre (usually marinated

vegetables and cold cuts); **bresaola** dry-cured beef; **bruschetta** toast with garlic, oil and optional tomatoes; **fiori di zucca** fried courgette flowers stuffed with mozzarella and anchovy; **olive ascolane** olives in breadcrumb-and-mincemeat coats; **prosciutto cotto/crudo/con melone** cured ham/ raw (Parma) ham/ham with melon.

Pasta, sughi e condimenti –
pasta, sauces and toppings
spaghetti alle vongole spaghetti with clams (usually in bianco, without tomatoes); **ravioli, ricotta e spinacci** ravioli stuffed with cottage cheese and spinach, often served with *burro e salvia* (butter and sage); **agnolotti, tortellini** similar to ravioli but usually meat-filled; **fettucine** long flat past a strips; **tonnarelli** like large spaghetti, square in cross-section; **cannelloni** long pasta rolls, designed for filling; **rigatoni** short pasta tubes; **orecchiette** ear-or hat-shaped pasta discs, often served with a broccoli sauce; **al pesto** with a sauce of pine nuts, pecorino and basil; **al pomodoro fresco** with fresh, raw tomatoes; **al ragù** 'bolognese' (a term not used by Italians), ie with minced meat and tomatoes; **al sugo** with

(you hope). The menu – which, in the evening, comes at a fixed price of €18.07/L35,000, rough-and-ready house wine included – celebrates the Roman tradition in dishes like *tonnarelli cacio e pepe* (among the best in town) and meatballs flavoured with nutmeg, pine nuts and sultanas. Dessert consists of a glass of *romanella* (sweet wine) and *ciambelline* (aniseed biscuits). Non-Italian speakers may have a hard time, and should bring their own boxing gloves.

Siciliainbocca
Via Faà di Bruno 26 (06 3735 8400). Metro Ottaviano/bus to viale Angelico. **Open** 1-3pm, 8-11.30pm Mon-Sat. Closed 2wks Aug. **Average** €34/L65,000. **Credit** AmEx, DC, MC, V. **Map** p320 1C.
This new Sicilian restaurant north of the Vatican proved a huge hit with locals almost from day one. And it's easy to see why: the ambience is *allegro*, the premises include a garden patio that is closed off and heated in winter, and decor has a lemon theme throughout – even on the waiters' uniforms. The mixed *sfizi dell'isola* starter (aubergines, sun-dried tomatoes, olives) is good, and first courses are competent – one of the best being the *conchiglie Vecchia Taormina* (pasta shells with peas, broad beans and pecorino cheese). Among the desserts, the *cassata* –

a classic Sicilian ricotta and candied fruit concoction – stands out. The exclusively Sicilian wine list carries a hefty mark-up.

Taverna Angelica
Piazza delle Vaschette 14A (06 687 4514). Bus to piazza Pia or piazza Risorgimento. **Open** 7.30pm-midnight Mon; 12.30-2.30pm, 7.30pm-midnight Tue-Sat. Closed 3wks Aug. **Average** €36/L70,000. **Credit** AmEx, MC, V. **Map** p321 1C.
The decor is minimalist-modern, the cuisine creative and fish-based. Dishes like nettle *tagliatelle* with curry sauce and *petto di pollo all'aceto e nero di seppia* (vinegared chicken breast with squid ink) establish the joint's modish credentials. Service is attentive, and a well-selected wine list includes *mescita* (by-the-glass) options.

Wine bars

Il Simposio di Piero Costantini
Piazza Cavour 16 (06 321 1502). Bus to piazza Cavour. **Open** 11am-2.30pm, 8-11.30pm Mon-Fri; 6.30pm-12.30am Sat. Closed Aug. **Average** €31/ L60,000. **Credit** AmEx, DC, MC, V. **Map** p321 1B.
This glorious art nouveau *enoteca* – with a huge bottle shop downstairs in the cellar – has recently

puréed cooked tomatoes; **all'amatriciana** with tomato, chilli, onion and sausage; **alla gricia** the same without the tomato; **all'arrabbiata** with tomato and chilli; **alla carbonara** with bacon, egg, Parmesan; **alla puttanesca** with olives, capers, garlic in hot oil; **cacio e pepe** with sheep's cheese and black pepper.

Carne – meat

abbacchio, agnello lamb; **capra, capretto** goat, kid; **coniglio** rabbit; **maiale, maialino** pork, piglet; **manzo** beef; **pancetta** similar to bacon; **pollo** chicken; **prosciutto cotto, prosciutto crudo** 'cooked' ham, Parma ham; **tacchino** turkey; **vitello, vitella, vitellone** veal.

Roman offal specialities

See also p158.

coda alla vaccinara oxtail braised in a celery broth; **pajata** calf's intestines with the mother's milk still inside; **fagioli con le cotiche** beans with pork scratchings; **insalata di zampi** hoof jelly salad; **animelle** the spongy white pancreas and thymus glands, generally fried; **tripa** tripe; **cervello** brain; **lingua** tongue; **guanciale** pig's cheek cured in salt and pepper; **nervetti** strips of cartilage.

Piatti di carne – meat dishes

bollito con salsa verde boiled meat with parsley in vinegar sauce; **carpaccio, bresaola** very thinly sliced types of cured beef; **ossobuco** beef shins with marrow jelly inside; **polpette, polpettine** meatballs; **porchetta** roast piglet; **rognoni trifolati** stir-fried chopped kidneys, usually with mushrooms; **salsicce** sausages; **saltimbocca** veal strips and ham; **spezzatino** casseroled meat; **spiedini** anything on a spit; **straccetti** strips of beef or veal, stir-fried.

Formaggi – cheeses

cacio, caciotta young, coarse-tasting cheese; **gorgonzola** strong blue cheese, in creamy (*dolce*) or crumbly (*piccante*) varieties; **parmigiano** Parmesan; **pecorino** hard, tangy Roman cheese used instead of Parmesan; **ricotta** crumbly white cheese, often used in desserts; **stracchino** creamy, soft white cheese.

Pesce – fish

Sarago, dentice, marmora, orata, fragolino all bream of various kinds; **alici, acciughe** anchovies; **baccalà** salt cod; **branzino, spigola** sea bass; **cernia** grouper; **merluzzo** cod; **pesce San Pietro** John Dory; **pesce spada** swordfish; **razza, arzilla** skate or thornback ray; **rombo** turbot; **salmone** salmon; **sarde, sardine** sardines; **sogliola** sole; **tonno** tuna; **trota** trout.

▶

added a wine bar that is so upmarket as to count as a *bona fide* restaurant. Prices are top-range, but then so is the quality. The wine list includes 2,000 Italian wines by the bottle, with a daily selection of around 20 wine sby the glass; it has to be said that the mark-ups are on the high side for a place that still calls itself an *enoteca*. Food ranges from an excellent cheese board to gourmet delights such as *tagliatelle* in lemon and ginger with giant prawns and ham, prepared by the young chef, Gabriele Bonci.

Snacks

Paninoteca da Guido

Borgo Pio 13 (06 687 5491). Bus to piazza Pia or piazza Risorgimento. **Open** 8.30am-8pm Mon-Sat. Closed Aug. **No credit cards.** **Map** p321 1C.

Where do hungry Swiss Guards eat? In this lunchtime-only hole in the wall no distance from St Peter's, which offers a range of pasta, meat and vegetable dishes with a real home cooking feel to them. This must be one of few places in Rome where you can still eat a full meal for €7.75/L15,000; or staff can just run you up a sandwich. Get there early, or be ready to be very patient, if you want to grab the single outside table.

The Suburbs

See also **PizzaRé** *p177.*

Restaurants

L'Ortica

Via Flaminia Vecchia 573L (06 333 8709). Bus to corso Francia. **Open** 8pm-11pm Mon-Sat. Closed 2wks Aug. **Average** €44/L85,000. **Credit** AmEx, DC, MC, V.

If there were a prize for the oddest gourmet restaurant location, L'Ortica would win it hands down. To get there, head north across Mussolini's still-fascist-after-all-these-years Ponte Flaminio into busy corso Francia, and locate the Standa supermarket on your right. On the terrace above it – next to a billiard parlour – stands Vittorio Virno's oasis of culinary excellence. The accent is Neapolitan – militantly so, with all the ingredients brought in fresh from trusted suppliers; they are put to excellent use in dishes such as squid stuffed with endive, sultanas and pine-nuts. Virno is a discerning collector, and his collection of copper pans, irons, wicker baskets and other domestic antiques adorns a series of elegant, spacious rooms. Outside, a verdant terrace is screened from the surrounding suburban chaos.

Reading the menu (continued)

Frutti di mare – seafood
astice, aragosta lobster, spiny lobster; **calamari, calamaretti** squid, baby squid; **cozze** mussels; **crostacei** shellfish; **gamberi, gamberetti** shrimps, prawns; **granchio** crab; **mazzancolle** king prawns; **moscardini** baby curled octopus; **ostriche** oysters; **polipo, polpo** octopus; **seppie, seppiette, seppioline** cuttlefish; **telline** wedge shells (small clams); **totani** baby flying squid; **vongole** clams.

Verdura/il contorno – vegetables/the side dish
aglio garlic; **asparagi** asparagus; **basilico** basil; **broccoli siciliani** broccoli; **broccolo** green cauliflower; **broccoletti** tiny broccoli sprigs, cooked with the leaves; **carciofi** artichokes; **carote** carrots; **cavolfiore** cauliflower; **cetriolo** cucumber; **cicoria** green leaf vegetable, resembling dandelion; **cipolle** onions; **fagioli** haricot or borlotti beans; **fagiolini** green beans; **fave** broad beans; **funghi** mushrooms; **funghi porcini** boletus mushrooms; **indivia** endive; **insalata** salad; **lattuga** lettuce; **melanzane** aubergine; **patate** potatoes; **peperoncino** chilli; **peperoni** peppers; **piselli** peas; **pomodori** tomatoes; **porri** leeks; **prezzemolo** parsley; **puntarelle** bitter Roman salad usually dressed with an anchovy sauce; **radicchio** bitter purple lettuce; **rughetta, rucola** rocket; **scalogna** shallots; **sedano** celery; **spinaci** spinach; **verza** cabbage; **zucchine** courgettes.

Frutta – fruit
albicocche apricots; **ananas** pineapple; **arance** oranges; **cachi** persimmons; **ciliege** cherries; **coccomero, anguria** water melon; **fichi** figs; **fragole, fragoline** strawberries, wild strawberries; **frutti di bosco** woodland berries; **mele** apples; **nespole** loquats; **pere** pears; **pesche** peaches; **prugne, susine** plums; **uva** grapes

Dolci/il dessert – desserts
gelato ice cream; **montebianco** cream, meringue and *maron glacé*; **pannacotta** 'cooked cream', a very thick, blancmange-like cream, often served with chocolate (*cioccolata*) or wild berry (*frutti di bosco*) sauce; **sorbetto** sorbet; **tiramisù** mascarpone and coffee sponge; **torta della nonna** flan of patisserie cream and pine nuts; **torta di mele** apple flan; **millefoglie** flaky pastry cake

Osteria del Rione
Via Basento 20 (06 855 1057). Bus or tram to via Po or viale Regina Margherita. **Open** noon-2.30pm, 7.30-11pm Mon-Fri; 7.30-11pm Sat. Closed 3wks Aug; 1wk Dec. **Average** €15/L30,000. **No credit cards.** **Map** p322 1A.
Had a hard morning in the quest for culture? This is the place for you: a cheap and cheerful *osteria* of one small room with seven tables, within striking distance of Villa Borghese. You'll find all the old Roman faves – *fiori di zucca*, *pasta e ceci* – plus some more creative dishes such as *penne con provola e crema di zucchine* (pasta with smoked cheese and courgette purée) and some unassuming house wine, all for a risible outlay. For once, don't be put off by the *menu turistico* in six languages outside – the €15.49/ L30,000 fixed-price outlay is money well spent.

Osteria del Velodromo Vecchio
Via Genzano 139 (06 7886 793). Metro Colli Albani/bus to via Genzano. **Open** 12.30-3pm, 8-11pm Mon-Sat. Closed Aug. **Average** €21/L40,000. **Credit** MC, V.
A really friendly, good-value *osteria* in the via Appia Nuova area, near the site of a former cycling stadium – hence the name. Inside is one small room with eight tables; in summer, a few more are arranged outside on a sheltered patio. The cooking represents the lighter end of the Roman tradition, with Jewish influences in dishes such as *alicotti e indivia* (anchovies and endives); there are also a few more creative pasta dishes. Desserts consist of homemade *crostate* (pastry tarts), or aniseed *ciambelline* biscuits with a glass of sweet wine. The wine list is small but surprisingly adventurous. This places provides a great introduction to the best of the local culinary tradition.

La Pergola dell'Hotel Hilton
Via Cadlolo 101 (06 3509 2211). Bus to piazza Medaglie d'Oro. **Open** 7.30-11.30pm Tue-Sat. Closed Jan. **Average** €77/L150,000. **Credit** AmEx, DC, MC, V.
Who wants to eat in a hotel restaurant miles from the city centre? The management of the Hilton-bunker on Monte Mario in the northern suburbs must have asked themselves this when they brought in young German chef Heinz Beck to revitalise their uninspiring rooftop restaurant. His cooking deserves the plaudits Italy's food critics have heaped on it, but some still find the luxury-hotel atmosphere stifling, despite the breathtaking views. The cuisine is international, with almost no pasta; Beck handles fresh fish, meat and vegetables with great finesse, and desserts are out of this world. Service, though, is pompous and

Pizza

calzone a doubled-over pizza, usually filled with cheese, tomato and ham; **capricciosa** ham, hard-boiled or fried egg, artichokes and olives; **funghi** mushrooms; **marinara** plain tomato, sometimes with anchovies; **margherita** tomato and mozzarella; **napoli, napoletana** tomato, anchovy and sometimes mozzarella; **quattro formaggi** four cheeses (in theory); **quattro stagioni** mozzarella, artichoke, egg, mushrooms.

Pizzeria extras

bruschetta coarse toast with raw garlic rubbed into it and oil on top, and usually diced raw tomatoes; **crochette** potato croquettes, often with a cheesy centre; **crostini** slices of toast, usually with a grilled cheese and anchovy topping; **filetto di baccalà** deep-fried salt cod in batter; **olive ascolane** deep-fried battered olives stuffed with sausage meat; **supplì** deep-fried rice balls held together by tomato sauce, with fresh mozzarella inside; may also contain mincemeat.

Veggie options

orechiette ai broccoletti/cima di rape ear-shaped pasta with broccoli sprigs/green turnip-tops; **pasta e ceci** soup with pasta and chick-peas; **pasta e fagioli** soup with pasta and borlotti beans; **pasta alla puttanesca or alla checca** (literally 'là la whore' or 'à la raging queen') based on olives, capers and tomatoes, though anchovies (*alici*) are sometimes slipped into the former; **penne all'arrabbiata** pasta with tomato sauce and lots of chilli; **ravioli** OK if filled with *ricotta e spinacci* (soft cheese and spinach) and served *con burro e salvia* (with butter and sage) or a simple *sugo di pomodoro* (tomato sauce); **risotto ai quattro formaggi** risotto made with four types of cheese; **spaghetti aglio, olio e peperoncino** with garlic, olive oil; **spaghetti cacio e pepe** with crumbled salty ewe-milk cheese and lots of black pepper.

Veggie main courses (*secondi*)

Second courses are more of a problem; often, you'll have to make do with an unispiring. Among the standard options are: **carciofi alla giudia** deep-fried artichokes; **fagioli all'uccelletto** haricot beans with tomato, garlic and olive oil (strictly speaking a *contorno*, but substantial enough to take the place of a main course); **melanzane alla parmigiana** aubergine with Parmesan (this occasionally has meat in the topping); **scamorza** grilled cheese – specify without ham (*senza prosciutto*) or anchovies (*senza alici*).

oddly slow, and the 300 per cent mark-up on wine is difficult to justify. For dedicated foodies with understanding bank managers.

International

Bishoku Kobo

Via Ostiense 110B (06 574 4190) Bus to via Ostiense. **Open** 7.30-10.30pm Mon-Sat. Closed Aug. **Average** €21/L40,000. **No credit cards.**
This new Japanese restaurant is well placed for visitors to the collection of antique statues in the adjacent Centrale Montemartini (*see page 153*). Though the food is classic Japanese, the ambience is that of a neighbourhood trattoria – except for a few details, such as a gloriously kitsch sushi clock. The sashimi, sushi and stuffed vegetables are all good, and the tempura is well worth the extra wait. Prices are low, and it's always packed with locals – so book ahead.

Sahara

Viale Ippocrate 43 (06 4424 2583). Metro Bologna/ bus to viale Ippocrate. **Open** 12.30-2.30pm, 7.30-10.30pm, Mon, Tue, Thur-Sun. Closed 2wks Aug. **Average** €18/L35,000. **Credit** AmEx, MC, V.
Try out Eritrean delicacies while sitting on a delightful and very un-Roman (if equally un-African) patio north-east of Termini station. The dishes – spicy, and mostly meat-based – include *zighinì* (spicy beef or lamb) and *zil zil tibsi* (veal, prepared at your table in a terracotta burner). All are served with *ingera* – spongey Eritrean bread – and can be accompnied by a glass of *mies*, or honey wine. There's a vegetarian menu as well.

Wine bars

Food & Wine Testa

Via Tirso 30 (06 8530 0692). Bus to piazza Buenos Aires or via Salaria/tram to piazza Buenos Aires. **Open** noon-3pm, 8-11.30pm Mon-Sat. Closed 3wks Aug. **Average** €34/L65,000. **Credit** AmEx, DC, MC, V.
This new foodie wine bar in the northern Salaria area has already attracted a loyal local following – which makes booking essential. The seasonal menu offers a light, fresh alternative to the traditional Roman meal, with creative salads and much use of gourmet ingredients such as *formaggio di fossa* (cheese from the Marches, matured in straw-line pits) and *lardo di Colonnata* (fatty ham from a village near the Carrara marble quarries). The succulent desserts include the house speciality, a warm apple tart with mascarpone ice cream. There is also a two-course lunchtime business menu at €18.07/ L35,000.

Eat, Drink, Shop

Cafés, Pubs & *Gelaterie*

Globalisation is forcing the Roman bar to take on new roles.

The neighbourhood bar where Romans take their breakfast shot of espresso with a *cornetto* (croissant), putting out their cigarette on a sawdust-covered floor, still exists, but it's a vanishing breed. In these days of globalisation, the humble Roman bar has taken on new roles, especially in the favourite tourist spots. Piazza Navona has nine establishments on the east side alone, each of which is a pizzeria, *gelateria* and/or restaurant as well as bar – all pleasant, expensive and generally indistinguishable from each other. The din from some 15 bar/pub/pizza joints rings around the statue of Giordano Bruno in campo de' Fiori, much to the dismay of local residents. Surrounding the obelisk in front of the Pantheon is everything from bar-*gelaterie* to a branch of McDonald's with café-style pavement tables: as long as you don't think you're getting a taste of the real Rome, they can be wonderful places for a rest and a look at life in the square.

But whether a bar (or café – there's no difference in Roman terms) is multi-functional or unreconstructed, the etiquette is the same: non-regulars are expected to pay at the *cassa* (cash desk) before consuming, so take a look and identify what you want before you pay. When you order at the bar, adding a L100 or L200 (five or ten cent) coin with your *scontrino* (receipt) will get the bartender's attention. If you sit down, you will be served by a waiter and charged at least double for the privilege.

Besides coffee, which comes in many different forms (*see p196* **Caffè variations**), every bar will have *cornetti* (croissants), which vary widely in quality. It'll also have *tramezzini* (triangle-shaped sandwiches which are good if fresh, but usually to be avoided by the afternoon) and *pizza romana* (ham and cheese inside two slices of pizza). Sandwiches and pizza can be toasted (ask *me lo può scaldare, per favore?*).

To accompany your snack, bars generally offer *spremute* (freshly squeezed juice), and some have *frullati* (fruit shakes) and *centrifughe* (juiced carrots or apples). Water from the tap is free; a glass of mineral water costs around €0.25-€0.50/L500-L1,000.

By law, all bars must have a *bagno* (lavatory) which can be used by anyone, whether or not they buy anything in the bar. The *bagno* may be locked; ask the cashier for the key (*la chiave per il bagno*). Bars must also provide gasping passers-by with a glass of tap water (*acqua dal rubinetto*), again with no obligation to buy.

WINE BARS AND PUBS

Rome's *enoteche* and *vini e oli* (bottle shops) have always been meccas and meeting places for – mostly – old men in hats who like to down a glass or two straight from the barrel before wending their way home with their bottles filled from the hosepipe. Some of these places have developed into fully fledged eateries: for these, *see chapter* **Eating Out**. The ones we list below have remained predominantly watering holes.

Rome's pubs are divided between a handful of long-standing institutions and a host of pub-kit establishments. The best of both categories have been listed in this chapter.

BAR-*PASTICCERIE*

Every neighbourhood has its own *pasticcerie* (cake shops); most (but not all, *see chapter* **Shopping: confectionery & cakes**) are bars where freshly baked goodies can be consumed *in situ* with a coffee or drink.

The range of items on offer rarely varies: choux pastry *bigne* with creamy fillings, *semifreddi* ice-cream cakes, fruit tarts and a large assortment of biscuits. There are huge variations, however, in quality and freshness: the *pasticcerie* listed below are always reliable.

For a change from the usual sweet-tooth offerings, choose feast-day-linked seasonal delicacies. *Panettoni* – sponge cakes with raisins and candied fruit – are ubiquitous around Christmas. The Easter variation is vaguely bird-shaped and called a *colomba* (dove). Around the feast of San Giuseppe (19 March), *pasticcerie* fill up with fried batter-balls filled with custard. During *carnevale* – in the run-up to Lent – you'll find small, compact balls of fried dough called *castagnole* and crispy strips of pastry (generally fried too) dusted with powdered sugar, called *frappe*.

BAR-*GELATERIE*

Many bars in Rome boast a well-stocked freezer cabinet with a sign promising *produzione artigianale* (home-made ice-creams). Generally speaking, this is a con. The contents may have been whipped up on the premises, but the lurid colours and chemical flavours come straight out of a tin. And while this doesn't necessarily

Eternally trendy: the **Bar della Pace**. *See p196.*

mean the ice-cream will be bad – indeed, in some cases this not-so-genuine-article can be very good indeed – it's good to be selective if you're seeking a truly unique *gelato* experience.

Ices to take away are served in a *cono* (cone) or *coppetta* (tub) of varying sizes, usually costing from €1-€3.10/L2,000-6,000. As well as the two main kinds, *frutta* or *crema*, there's also *granita* (a rougher version of the *sorbetto*).

As a general rule, ice-creams kept in aluminium tubs are a safer bet than those in plastic ones. True *gelato* artistes don't have their products on show at all: they are hidden away in closed tubs behind the counter.

When you've exhausted the *gelato*, sample a *grattachecca*, the Roman version of water-ice, consisting of grated ice with flavoured syrup on top. Rome was once full of kiosks selling this treat, but now only a handful remain. They are almost always on street corners (hence *angolo* in the addresses below), and most are closed in winter. Opening hours are erratic.

The Trevi Fountain & the Quirinale

Cafés

Bar del Palazzo delle Esposizioni
Via Milano 9 (06 482 8001/06 482 8540). Bus to via Nazionale. **Open** 10am-9pm Mon, Wed-Sun. **No credit cards. Map** p323 2B.
The excellent bar at this major arts centre (*see also p78 and p195*) is a mecca for local office staff, who also flock to eat at the smart buffet restaurant upstairs. The bar entrance is on the left of the palazzo, halfway up the stairs. Knockout fresh cakes.

Caffè Traforo
Via del Traforo 135 (06 482 2946). Bus to via del Tritone. **Open** 6am-9pm Mon-Sat. **Credit** MC, V. **Map** p323 2C.

The Ruiti brothers have renovated this spot dear to the hearts of clerks from local banks and journalists, but the cherry wood panelling and green Brazilian marble have remained the same. Their *caffè Traforo* and *cappuccino Traforo* – creamy concoctions with secret ingredients – are legendary. It's a crowded, lively spot at noon, when there's a cold buffet and a good assortment of sandwiches and fruit shakes.

Gelaterie

Il Gelato di San Crispino
Via della Panetteria, 42 (06 679 3924). Metro Barberini/bus to via del Tritone. **Open** noon-12.30am Mon, Wed, Sun; noon-1.30am Fri, Sat. Closed 2wks Jan. **No credit cards. Map** p323 2C.
Far and away the best ice-cream in Rome – some would say the world. The secret is an obsessive control over the whole process. Flavours change according to what's in season – in summer the *lampone* (raspberry) and *susine* (yellow plum) are fabulous. Don't even think of asking for a cone: only tubs are allowed. True devotees shun the upstart Trevi fountain branch and head out into the suburbs, where the miracle of San Crispino first occurred. The product is equally exceptional in both places. The central branch has the advantage – over and above its location – of offering exquisite Jamaican coffee too.
Branch: Via Acaia, 56 (06 7045 0412).

Via Veneto & the Villa Borghese

Cafés

Café de Paris
Via Veneto 90 (06 488 5284). Metro Barberini/bus to via Veneto. **Open** 8am-1am Mon, Wed-Sun. **Credit** AmEx, DC, MC, V. **Map** p323 1B.
In via Veneto's *Dolce Vita* heyday Café Doney (*not listed*) was definitely for the nobs, and Café de Paris across the road was for those with street-cred. Here

Eat, Drink, Shop

you could be served in your jeans (quite something in those days), and listen to the *paparazzi* (*see p81*) badmouth their prey. There's little cred about it now: American-style breakfast is served in the morning, and Italian-style meals can be eaten outside. There's an English tea hour, and an international-type wine bar for evenings in the newly refurbished interior.

Il Tridente

Cafés

Antico Caffè Greco
Via Condotti 86 (06 679 1700). Metro Spagna/bus to piazza San Silvestro. **Open** 8am-9pm daily. **Credit** AmEx, DC, MC, V. **Map** p323 1C.
Founded in 1760, this venerable café was the one-time hangout of Casanova, Goethe, Wagner, Stendhal, Baudelaire, Shelley and Byron. Opposition to the French Occupation of 1849-70 was planned here. Today it has its sofas packed with tourists, while locals cram the foyer. Literary and musical evenings with a light dinner hark back to its artistic past; programmes in English are planned.

Babington's
Piazza di Spagna 23 (06 678 6027). Metro Spagna/bus to piazza San Silvestro. **Open** *Sept-June* 9am-8.15pm Mon, Wed-Sun. *July, Aug* 9am-8.15pm Mon-Sat. **Credit** AmEx, DC, MC, V. **Map** p323 1C.
Britons may not consider visiting tearooms abroad a priority, but will often be directed here by well-meaning Romans, convinced that they cannot

survive without an overpriced pot of tea and plate of cakes. Still, if you need a fix of pancakes and bacon, breakfast here can be the answer. Founded by two British spinsters, it has occupied this prime location at the foot of the Spanish Steps for over a century.

La Buvette
Via Vittoria 44 (06 679 0383). Metro Spagna/bus to piazza San Silvestro. **Open** 7.30am-8pm Mon-Sat. Closed 2wks Aug. **Credit** AmEx, DC, MC, V. **Map** p320 2A.
All polished wood and mirrors, the Buvette serves OK coffee with great cakes in a plush, cosy atmosphere. A couple of pasta dishes and a range of salads are also served, for lunch only, from June to September, and for lunch and dinner the rest of the year.

Café Notegen
Via del Babuino 159 (06 320 0855). Metro Spagna/bus to piazza del Popolo or piazza San Silvestro. **Open** 7.30am-1am daily. **Credit** DC, MC, V. **Map** p320 2A.
An historic gathering spot for theatre people, artists and intellectuals, this century-old café prides itself on being a 'café in the French sense', serving hot and cold dishes and great cakes at any hour to sophisticated customers seated in velvet booths. Downstairs, live cabaret, music and the odd play are performed on a rather irregular basis.

Caffeteria La Barcaccia
Piazza di Spagna 71 (06 679 7497). Metro Spagna/bus to piazza San Silvestro. **Open** *Oct-Mar* 7am-9pm daily. *Apr-Sept* 8am-midnight daily. **Credit** AmEx, DC, MC, V. **Map** p323 1C.

Slurp out your froth at **Bar Sant'Eustachio**. *See p196.*

A *caffè* with your culture

Romans have long treated their museums and cafés in similar fashion: dash in, remain on your feet, drink deeply and appreciatively, then rush out again. Perhaps for this reason, it has taken the city a while to latch on to the joys of having an enjoyable spot to rest after a hard day's art-gazing.

The **Palazzo delle Esposizioni** (*see p78 and p193*) set the ball rolling, opening a bar and good rooftop buffet restaurant that immediately become the lunch or snack place of choice for shop and office workers in the area around busy via Nazionale: be prepared to fight off the regulars to get a seat.

Other museums and galleries soon followed suit, and the number of culture-cafés has grown steadily.

You're spoilt for choice during your full-cultural-immersion day around Villa Borghese. The café at the **Galleria Borghese** (*see p81*) is a sleek, modern indoor spot with soothing cream and yellow walls that is sure to take your mind off Caravaggio and Canova as you munch sandwiches, cakes and salads. Across the park, the restaurant at the **Museo di Villa Giulia** (*see p83*) has tables outside under orange trees in summer; in winter, watch the

garden through the dining room's picture windows. At the **Galleria Nazionale d'Arte Moderna** (*see p82*), the big windows and heavy curtains of the Caffè delle Arti make the place look like a 19th-century artist's studio; tables under the trees on the patio make this a popular spot on warm evenings.

The new rooftop bar and restaurant at the **Musei Capitolini** (*see p62*) offers one of Rome's most stunning views, across the rooftops to the dome of St Peter's. Make up for the expensive fare and surly service by using the flower-filled terrace as a foreground for your panoramic snapshots.

Another good view – across the piazza to the Palazzo del Quirinale (*see p78*) – can be had while consuming a plate of *nouvelle* pasta or a salad at the pleasant bar and restaurant at the newly renovated **Scuderie Papali** (*see p78*).

The prize for design has to go to the bar at the **Centrale Montemartini** (*see p153*), which is perched strikingly on an indoor terrace overlooking the classical statues and a generating plant. The choice of food, however, can be spartan.

Right up the street from Prada, Bulgari and Gucci, this is a good place to recover after an exhausting day's shopping. Upstairs, there's a pleasant, airy tea room for relaxing over a sandwich or slice of cake.

Canova
Piazza del Popolo 16 (06 361 2231). Metro Flaminio/bus to piazzale Flaminio or piazza del Popolo. **Open** *8am-midnight daily.* **Credit** *AmEx, DC, MC, V.* **Map** *p320 2A.*
According to tradition, Canova's clientele has always been right-wing, and at daggers drawn with the left-wing rabble at Rosati (*see p196*) across the square. There is little evidence of this now. But this characterless, all-purpose spot (it even sells kitschy souvenirs) catches the late afternoon sun. On summer evenings, it stays open into the small hours, until the last night owl heads home.

Ciampini al Café du Jardin
Viale Trinità dei Monti (06 678 5678). Metro Spagna/bus to piazza San Silvestro or piazza del Popolo. **Open** *Mid Mar-mid May, mid Sept-mid Oct 8am-8pm daily. Mid May-mid Sept 8am-1am Mon, Tue, Thur-Sun. Closed mid Oct-mid Mar.* **Credit** *AmEx, MC, V.* **Map** *p323 1C.*
An open-air café near the top of the Spanish Steps, surrounded by creeper-curtained trellises, with a pond in the centre. There's a selection of tasty

sandwiches, pastas, cocktails, ices and snack lunches, and it also serves a good breakfast. And to make your pre-dinner *aperitivi* slip down every better, there's a stunning view, especially at sunset.

Dolci e Doni
Via delle Carrozze 85B (06 6992 5001). Metro Spagna/bus to piazza San Silvestro. **Open** *8am-8.30pm Tue-Sat. Closed 2wks Aug.* **Credit** *AmEx, DC, MC, V.* **Map** *p321 1A.*
This tiny, bijou tearoom, renowned for its cakes and chocolates, also specialises in breakfasts, brunches and quick quiche-and-salad lunches. There are cakes to take away, and catering can be arranged.

Elen Bar
Via Capo le Case 27 (06 679 3987). Bus to piazza San Silvestro. **Open** *6am-7.30pm Mon-Sat.* **No credit cards.** **Map** *p323 1/C.*
This tiny daytime bar makes a great breakfast or lunch stop. The rolls and salads are fresh and tasty, and Elen's specialises in *centrifughe* – juiced shakes of carrot, apple, pineapple and so on. Desserts consist of home-made *crostate* and fruit salads. The family that run it extend the kind of warm welcome that's rare in central Rome, and there's no extra charge for table service – not even for the single outside table, which is keenly contested by local office workers.

Eat, Drink, Shop

Gran Caffè La Caffettiera
Via Margutta 61A (06 321 3344). Metro Spagna/bus to piazza San Silvestro. **Open** *Sept-Apr* 9am-9pm Tue, Wed, Sun; 9am-midnight Thur-Sat. *May-Aug* 9am-9pm Tue-Sun. **Credit** AmEx, MC, V. **Map** p320 2A.
This huge café occupies the 17th-century Teatro Alibert. A warren of rooms, with decor ranging from 18th century (including original frescos on the cross-beamed ceilings) to art nouveau. No crush at the counter: just understated (if a trifle over-priced) waiter service.

Rosati
Piazza del Popolo 5 (06 322 5859). Metro Flaminio/bus to piazzale Flaminio or via Ripetta. **Open** 7.30am-11.30pm daily. **Credit** AmEx, DC, MC, V. **Map** p320 2A.
Rosati is the traditional haunt of Rome's intellectual left: Calvino, Moravia and Pasolini were regulars. The art nouveau interior has remained unchanged since its opening in 1922. Try the *Sogni romani* cocktail: orange juice with four kinds of liqueur in red and yellow – the colours of the city. *Cornetti* and sandwiches are fresh and good; an ample brunch is served from 1 to 4pm on Sundays.

Caffè variations

To get a short, thick espresso ask for *un caffè*. A cappuccino is an espresso with steamed frothy milk added: it is rarely consumed after 11am; Romans wouldn't be caught dead drinking it after a meal.

Variations on the espresso
caffè americano with a lot more water, in a teacup.
caffè corretto with a dash of liqueur or spirits (indicate which).
caffè freddo iced espresso, sugared unless you ask for a *caffè freddo amaro*.
caffè Hag espresso decaf.
caffè lungo a bit more water than usual.
caffè macchiato with a dash of milk.
caffè monichella with whipped cream.
caffè ristretto tooth-enamel removing coffee essence lining the bottom of the cup.
caffè al vetro in a glass.

Variations on the cappuccino
caffè latte more hot milk and less coffee
cappuccino freddo iced coffee with cold milk; sugared unless you ask specifically for a *cappuccino freddo amaro*.
cappuccino senza schiuma without froth.
latte macchiato hot milk with a dash of coffee.

Piazza Navona & the Pantheon

Cafés

Bar della Pace
Via della Pace 3/7 (06 686 1216). Bus to corso Rinascimento. **Open** 9am-2am daily. **Credit** MC, V. **Map** p321 2B.
Rome's eternally trendy Antico Caffè della Pace (but never known as such) continues to be a great (though expensive) place from which to survey passing fashion victims from pavement tables. On summer evenings the square outside overflows with trendy revellers.

Dolce Vita
Piazza Navona 70A (06 6880 6221). Bus to corso Rinascimento or corso Vittorio Emanuele. **Open** 8am-midnight daily. **Credit** AmEx, MC, V. **Map** p321 2A.
Tiny inside, but with plenty of tables outside, Dolce Vita is a pleasant alternative to other more touristy bars on the piazza. Great for catching the afternoon sun and watching the fascinating parade of piazza Navona life; in summer you can ogle till 2am.

Panico Biondo
Via di Panico 12 (06 686 9583). Bus to corso Vittorio Emanuele. **Open** noon-2am Tue-Sat; noon-8pm Sun. Closed Aug. **Credit** AmEx, MC, V. **Map** p321 2B.
A tearoom with pasta, salads and sweets by day, this becomes a piano bar by night. The singing doesn't drown out conversation in this cosy spot.

Pascucci
Via di Torre Argentina 20 (06 686 4816). Bus or tram to largo Argentina. **Open** 6.30am-midnight Mon-Sat. Closed 3wks Aug. **No credit cards**. **Map** p324 1A.
This very modest bar in the centre of town has earned itself a reputation as milkshake heaven. Milk, though, isn't obligatory: no combination of fresh fruit froth (*frullato*) is too exotic here.

Sant'Eustachio
Piazza Sant'Eustachio 82 (06 6880 2048). Bus to corso Rinascimento. **Open** 8.30am-1am daily. **No credit cards**. **Map** p321 2A.
This may be the most famous coffee bar in the city, and its walls are plastered with celebrity testimonials. The coffee is quite extraordinary – if very expensive. Try the Gran Caffe: the *schiuma* (froth) can be slurped out afterwards with spoon or fingers. Unless you specify *caffè amaro*, it comes heavily sugared.

La Tazza d'Oro
Via degli Orfani 84 (06 678 9792). Bus to via del Corso. **Open** 7am-8pm Mon-Sat. Closed 1wk Aug. **Credit** AmEx, DC, MC, V. **Map** p321 2A.
The powerful aroma wafting from this ancient *torrefazione* overlooking the Pantheon is a siren call to coffee lovers. It's packed with coffee sacks,

All roads lead to **La Vineria**. *See p198.*

tourists and regulars who flock for *granita di caffè* (coffee sorbet), and *cioccolata calda con panna* (hot chocolate with whipped cream) in winter.

Pubs

Trinity College
Via del Collegio Romano 6 (06 678 6472). Bus to via del Corso. **Open** noon-3am daily. **Credit** AmEx, DC, MC, V. **Map** p321 2A.
City-centre pub that is much frequented by thirsty employees of the Cultural Heritage Ministry opposite. It has a more authentic feel (though 'tis all illusion) than many of the capital's Irish pubs, and good-value light meals are served upstairs at lunch and dinner.

Pasticcerie

La Caffettiera
Piazza di Pietra 65 (06 679 8147). Bus to via del Corso. **Open** *Oct-May* 7am-9pm daily. *June-Sept* 7am-9pm Mon-Sat. **Credit** AmEx, MC, V. **Map** p321 2A.
A temple of Neapolitan food. Politicians and mandarins from the nearby parliament buildings lounge in the sumptuous tea room, while lesser mortals – such as parliamentary hacks – bolt down coffee at the bar. The *rum baba* reigns supreme, but many ricotta-lovers rave over the crunchy *sfogliatella*, delicately flavoured with cinnamon and orange peel, and the *pastiera*, a rich tart filled with ricotta, orange-flower water, citrus peel and whole grains of wheat.

Gelaterie

Cremeria Monforte
Via della Rotonda 22 (06 686 7720). Bus or tram to largo Argentina. **Open** 10am-11pm Tue-Sun. **No credit cards**. **Map** p321 2A.
This *gelateria* handily situated around the corner from the Pantheon is a cut above the many others in the area. The white and orange chocolate flavours have lumps of chocolate in them, and are delicious.

I Tre Scalini
Piazza Navona 28-32 (06 6880 1996). Bus to corso Rinascimento or corso Vittorio Emanuele. **Open** 9am-12.30am Mon, Tue, Thur-Sun. Closed Jan. **No credit cards**. **Map** p321 2AB.
This bar is above all famous for its speciality ice cream, the *tartufo* – a calorie-bomb chocolate ice cream with big lumps of chocolate inside. There are tables outside at which to enjoy your ice-cream (or anything else) with a massive price mark-up, and a tearoom on the first floor. Otherwise, take your ice away and enjoy it next to Bernini's fountain.

The Ghetto & campo de' Fiori

Cafés

Caffè Farnese
Via dei Baullari 106 (06 6880 2125). Bus to corso Vittorio Emanuele or largo Argentina. **Open** 7am-2am daily. **Credit** AmEx, MC, V. **Map** p324 1B.

This bar-*gelateria/pasticceria* is a popular meeting-place, offering a fine people-watching vista. It's close to the noisy campo de' Fiori but its outside tables open up to the quieter, more harmonious piazza Farnese. The coffee, *cornetti* and *pizza romana* are all excellent.

Da Vezio

Via dei Delfini, 23 (06 678 6036). Bus or tram to largo Argentina. **Open** 7am-8.30pm Mon-Sat. Closed 3wks Aug. **No credit cards. Map** p324 1A.

Vezio Bagazzini is a legendary figure in the Ghetto area, on account of his extraordinary bar/*latteria* behind the former Communist Party HQ. Every square centimetre is filled with Communist icons and trophies – Italian, Soviet and Cuban. Every Italian leftist leader worth his or her salt arrives here for a photo with Vezio, as you'll see from the walls.

Latteria del Gallo

Vicolo del Gallo 4 (06 686 5091). Bus to corso Vittorio Emanuele. **Open** 8.30am-2pm, 5pm-midnight daily. Closed 2wks Aug. **No credit cards. Map** p324 1B.

With its marble slab tables, this café in a side road between campo de' Fiori and piazza Farnese has remained impervious to passing fashions. Behind the bar, Signora Anna serves up her *cappuccione* – a double, frothy cappucino – as she has done for decades. A *centro storico* institution, it's still popular with Rome's hippies and foreign residents.

Pubs & wine bars

The Drunken Ship

Campo de' Fiori, 20/21 (06 6830 0535). Bus to corso Vittorio Emanuele. **Open** 5pm-2am daily. **Credit** AmEx, MC, V. **Map** p321 2B.

The most popular meeting place on the Campo after the Vineria, the Ship has become a place to go if, like more and more trendy young Romans, you would not be seen dead drinking wine. Oddly, though, the main act – beer – is limited to three varieties. Great location (with tables on the square) and slick design distinguish it from nearby rivals. Student discounts, and DJs in the evening; happy hour 5pm to 8pm.

Il Goccetto

Via dei Banchi Vecchi 14 (06 686 4268). Bus to corso Vittorio Emanuele. **Open** 11.30am-2pm, 5.30-11pm Mon-Sat. Closed 3wks Aug. **Credit** AmEx, MC, V. **Map** p321 2B.

One of the more serious *centro storico* wine bars, occupying part of a medieval bishop's house, with original painted ceilings and a cosy, private-club feel. Wine is the main point, with a satisfying range by the glass from €2.32/L4,500, but there's a choice of cheeses, salami and salads, too. Closes early afternoon on Saturday in July.

La Vineria

Campo de' Fiori 15 (06 6880 3268). Bus to corso Vittorio Emanuele. **Open** 9am-1am Mon-Sat; 5pm-1am Sun. **Credit** AmEx, DC, MC, V. **Map** p321 2B.

Everyone calls in here sooner or later: this is an authentic local wine bar, with a great position on the Campo and decent wine by the glass from €1/L2,000 – cheaper than most. By day and in the early evening it throngs with lived-in locals and historic expatriates; by night, it's a seriously hip hang-out for bright young things (and some slightly tarnished older ones) who crowd its pavement tables.

Pasticcerie

Antica Pasticceria Bella Napoli

Corso Vittorio Emanuele 246 (06 687 7048). Bus to corso Vittorio Emanuele. **Open** 7.30am-9pm Mon-Fri, Sun. Closed 3wks Aug. **Credit** MC, V. **Map** p321 1B.

Best known for its Neapolitan *dolci* such as *sfogliatelle ricce* (pastry with ricotta filling) and *rum babà*, to take away or eat on the spot with a *caffè*. Have your *sfogliatella* heated for a real treat. One of the few cafés to have resisted renovation, its rather dingy walls and light fixtures take you back to 1965.

Bernasconi

Piazza Cairoli 16 (06 6880 6264). Tram to via Arenula. **Open** 7am-8.30pm Tue-Sun. Closed Aug. **No credit cards. Map** p324 1B.

Cramped and inconspicuous like so many of Rome's best cake shops, it's well worth fighting your way inside for *lieviti* (breakfast yeast buns). Bernasconi's *cornetti* are unbeatable, the real vintage variety. Close to the synagogue, this spot straddles Rome's Jewish and Catholic worlds, with kosher sweets and Lenten *quaresimale* cookies.

Gelaterie

Alberto Pica

Via della Seggiola 12 (06 686 8405). Bus to largo Argentina/tram to via Arenula. **Open** *Oct-Apr* 8am-2am Mon-Sat. *May-Sept* 8am-2am Mon-Sat; 4pm-3am Sun. **No credit cards. Map** p324 1B.

Next to the regular bar is an excellent selection of ice-cream flavours, among which the rice specialities stand out: imagine eating frozen, partially cooked rice pudding and you'll get the picture. *Riso alla cannella* (cinnamon rice) is particularly delicious.

Trastevere & Gianicolo

Cafés

Bar Gianicolo

Piazzale Aurelio 5 (06 580 6275). Bus to via G Carini. **Open** 6am-1am Tue-Sun. **No credit cards. Map** p324 2C.

Wooden panels and benches lend this tiny bar on the hill above Trastevere at the site of Garibaldi's doomed battle with the French (*see p18*) an intimate, chatty feel that is unusual in Rome. Fresh carrots and apples juiced on the spot, a range of exotic sandwiches and light meals and outside tables

overlooking the Porta di San Pancrazio city gate
make it a good spot for a drink, a snack or lunch after
a walk at the nearby Villa Pamphili (*see p155*).

Bar San Calisto

*Piazza San Calisto (06 589 5678). Bus or tram to
viale Trastevere.* **Open** 5.30am-2am Mon-Sat. **No
credit cards**. **Map** p324 2B.
Green tourists get their coffee or beer on piazza
Santa Maria in Trastevere; locals who know better
go to this bar, known locally as Marcello's.
Unassuming and inexpensive, it's the haunt of arty
and fringe types (plus a few questionable characters
after sundown) downing beers or spooning an
affogato (ice-cream swamped with liqueur).

Cecere

*Via San Francesco a Ripa 152 (06 5833 2404). Bus
or tram to viale Trastevere.* **Open** 6am-2am daily.
No credit cards. **Map** p324 2B.
A great selection of fresh, hot *cornetti* is turned out
non-stop. Late-nighter revellers throng the place
after midnight. The ice-cream's great too.

Di Marzio

*Piazza Santa Maria in Trastevere 15 (06 581 6095).
Bus or tram to viale Trastevere.* **Open** 7am-2am
Tue-Sun. **Credit** MC, V. **Map** p324 2B.
Piazza Santa Maria is not the cheapest place in Rome
to sit out and have a drink, but if you do want to
admire this square with a drink in your hand, Di
Marzio, facing the church, is where the locals go, and
trasteverini know a good deal when they see one.

Sacchetti

*Piazza San Cosimato 61/2 (06 581 5374). Bus or
tram to viale Trastevere.* **Open** 5.30am-10pm Tue-
Sun. **No credit cards**. **Map** p324 2B.
The Sacchetti family runs one of the least touristy
bars in Trastevere, with tables outside all year round
and a big tearoom upstairs. Everything is home-
made; *cornetti* and ricotta-filled *sfogliatelle romane*
are memorable. The ice-creams, hidden behind
the bar, are delicious, too. Shutters stay up until
around 1am on hot summer evenings.

Wine bars & pubs

Della Scala

*Via della Scala 4 (06 580 3610). Bus or tram to viale
Trastevere.* **Open** 4pm-2am daily. **No credit cards**.
Map p324 2B.
A dark, smoky dive with a selection of wines by the
glass, beers, and cocktails. The crowds that spill out
from the few tables on via della Scala testify to its
popularity with late-night frequenters of Trastevere.

Ombre Rosse

*Piazza Sant'Egidio 12 (06 588 4155). Tram to viale
Trastevere.* **Open** 7am-2am Mon-Sat; 5pm-2am Sun.
Credit AmEx, MC, V. **Map** p324 2B.
A choice spot with tables outdoors on a charming,
carless square. Young *trasteverini* come in the
evening, but at breakfast it's full of locals of every

Garibaldi *chez* **Bar Gianicolo**. *See p198.*

age. Light meals, salads, sandwiches and American sweets: cheesecake, apple pie, brownies. Live music on Wednesday and Sunday evenings.

Gelaterie

See also p199 **Cecere**, **Sacchetti** and **San Calisto**.

Sora Mirella

Lungotevere degli Anguillara, angolo Ponte Cestio (no phone). Bus to lungotevere degli Anguillara. **Open** *Mar-Sept* 10am-3am daily. **No credit cards**. **Map** p324 2A.

Mirella styles herself la *regina della grattacheccha* (the queen of water ices), and there seems no reason to disagree. Sit on the Tiber embankment wall as you tuck into the speciale *superfrutta* – fresh melon, kiwi fruit and strawberry (or whatever's in season) with syrups served in a special glass.

Aventine & Testaccio

Cafés

Bar del Mattatoio

Piazza O Giustiniani 3 (06 574 6017). Bus to via Galvani or via Marmorata/tram to via Marmorata. **Open** 6am-9pm Mon-Sat. **Closed** 2wks Aug. **No credit cards**. **Map** p325 2B.

A brick doll's house of a bar, with Gothic recesses in the front. One of the earliest-opening bars in Rome, it once catered for workers from the slaughterhouse opposite; nowadays it serves dawn revellers from Testaccio's clubs (*see chapter* **Nightlife**).

Gelaterie

Chiosco Testaccio

Via G Branca, angolo via Beniamino Franklin (no phone). Bus to via Marmorata or via Zabaglia/tram to via Marmorata. **Open** *May-mid Sept* noon-1.30am daily. **No credit cards**. **Map** p325 2B.

Still going strong after over 80 years in this working class neighbourhood. The kiosk is painted a different colour each year. Tamarind and limoncocco (lemon and coconut) are it's specialities.

Celio & San Giovanni

Cafés

Café Café

Via dei Santi Quattro 44 (06 700 8743). Bus or tram to piazza del Colosseo. **Open** 10am-1am daily. **Credit** AmEx, MC, V. **Map** p326 2B.

A pleasant change from the usual chrome and glass counters, this attractive place offers teas, wines, salads and sandwiches for travellers weary after a romp around the Colosseum. There's a brunch buffet from 11.30am to 4pm on Sundays.

Monti & Esquilino

Cafés

Antico Caffè del Brasile

Via dei Serpenti, 23 (06 488 2319). Bus to via Nazionale. **Open** *Sept-June* 5.30am-8.30pm Mon-Sat; 7am-2pm Sun. *July & Aug* 5.30am-8.30pm Mon-Sat. **Closed** 2wks Aug. **No credit cards**. **Map** p326 1C.

It's giant coffee-roaster no longer functions but this bar on the characterful main street of Monti still retains its traditional atmosphere. Among its clientele was the current Pope, while he was still humble Cardinal Wojtyla.

Pubs

The Druid's Den

Via San Martino ai Monti 28 (06 4890 4781). Bus to piazza Santa Maria Maggiore. **Open** 6pm-1.30am daily. **No credit cards**. **Map** p326 1C.

Like its rival the Fiddler's Elbow (*see below*), this is a pub that was already well established before the current craze for all things Irish. A decent pint of Liffey water, plus football beamed in from the British Isles.

The Fiddler's Elbow

Via dell'Olmata 43 (06 487 2110). Bus to piazza Santa Maria Maggiore. **Open** 5pm-1.15am daily. **No credit cards**. **Map** p326 1B.

One of the oldest, best-known pubs in Rome, unchanged for years. Its narrow, basic wood-and-bench interior is smoky as ever, with the alternative feel that has long made it popular with students.

Pasticcerie

Dagnino

Galleria Esedra, via VE Orlando 75 (06 481 8660). Metro Repubblica/bus to piazza della Repubblica. **Open** 7am-10.30pm daily. **Credit** AmEx, MC, V. **Map** p323 1B.

Stunning 1950s decor and a chronic oversupply of tables set the scene for this corner of Sicily in the heart of Rome. If you it's Sicilian and edible, it's here: ice-cream in buns, life-like marzipan fruits. Regulars come for crisp *cannoli siciliani* filled with ricotta and, above all, the splendour of shiny green-iced *cassata*, uniting all the flavours of the south: the perfume of citrus, almond paste and the saltiness of ricotta.

Gelaterie

Il Palazzo del Freddo di Giovanni Fassi

Via Principe Eugenio 65/7 (06 446 4740). Metro Vittorio/bus to piazza Vittorio. **Open** noon-midnight Tue-Thur; noon-1am Fri, Sat; 10am-midnight Sun. **No credit cards**. **Map** p324 1A.

With its pompous name, breathtakingly kitsch interior and splendid ices, Fassi is an historic Roman institution. It was founded in 1880 by Giovanni Fassi, and its walls are adorned with Edwardian adverts and fascist-era posters extolling the virtues of the shop's wares. Service is unfailingly irascible, and the crowds can be difficult to elbow your way through, but the ices are sublime: best of all are *riso* – rice pudding – and the Palazzo's own invention, *la caterinetta*, a mysterious concoction of whipped honey and vanilla.

The Vatican & Prati

Cafés

Antonini
Via Sabotino 19/29 (06 3751 7845). Bus to piazza Mazzini. **Open** 7am-9.30pm daily. **Credit** MC, V. **Map** p320 1C.
In winter you can't move for fur coats in this high-class *pasticceria* that's the place to come to buy cakes to take to that important lunch or dinner party. Alternatively, eat them *in situ*: one *montebianco* (meringue, marron glacé spaghetti and cream) is a meal in itself. They also do a great line in *tartine* – cânapés topped with pâté, and caviar. Sitting outside is a good way to observe life in high-rent residential Rome.

Faggiani
Via G Ferrari 23/9 (06 3973 9742). Bus to piazza Mazzini. **Closed** 3 wks Aug. **Credit** AmEx, DC, MC, V. **Map** p320 1C.
As pleasant for breakfast as for an evening *aperitivo*, this classic family bar with excellent coffee has one of northern Rome's finest *pasticcerie* attached. It's worth making the trip up to Prati simply to sample the *cornetti* and *budino di riso* (rice dessert), probably the best in Rome.

Gelaterie

Pellacchia
Via Cola di Rienzo 103 (06 321 0807). Bus to via Cola di Rienzo. **Open** 6.30am-1am Tue-Sun. Closed 1wk Aug. **No credit cards. Map** p320 2B.
This bar on Prati's busiest street produces some of the best ice-cream north of the river. The perfect place to recover after slogging round the Vatican.

The Suburbs

Cafés

Palombini
Piazzale Adenauer 12 (06 591 1700). Metro Magliana/bus to piazza G Marconi. **Open** 7am-midnight daily. Closed 2wks Aug. **Credit** AmEx, DC, MC, V.

In the imposing shadow of the EUR district's Palazzo del Civiltà del Lavoro (*see p154*) stands this airy pavilion, surrounded by sweeping gardens. Its huge patio area, covered by a steel and plastic tent, is a favourite meeting point for young Romans – the nearest Rome gets to Beverly Hills, and a it's not at all bad as imitations go. As a *gelateria*, *pasticceria* and snack supplier, it's also first-rate.

Pasticcerie

Mondi
Via Flaminia 468A (06 333 6466). Bus or tram to via Flaminia. **Open** 7am-10pm Tue-Sun. **Credit** MC, V.
Residents of the Cassia-Flaminia area swear this is the best bar-*pasticceria* in town. Its cakes and luscious *semifreddi* (frozen ice-cream-baseddesserts) are true works of art.

Gelaterie

See also p193 **Il Gelato di San Crispino.**

Duse
Via Eleonora Duse 1E (06 807 9300). Bus or tram to piazza Ungheria. **Open** 8am-midnight Mon-Sat. Closed 1wk Aug. **No credit cards.**
In this otherwise entirely uneventful residential neighbourhood, Duse attracts well-off young *parioli* (for which read Chelsea/Valley girls and boys) on their motorbikes and in their 4WDs. Late at night, the sceneoutside looks like a well-brushed street party. Inside, big metal ice-cream drums are stacked three deep behind the counter. Try out the *cioccolato fondente* (dark chocolate) or *cioccolato bianco* (white chocolate).

Petrini dal 1926
Piazza dell'Alberone 16A (06 786 307). Metro Furio Camillo/bus to via Appia Nuova. **Open** 10.30am-2am Tue-Sun. **No credit cards.**
As its name implies, this *gelateria* a fair hike to the south of the city centre has been purveying ice-cream for decades, and many still consider its product one of the best in Rome. All its creamy flavours are delicious, but the *zabaione* and *nocciola* are particularly mouthwatering.

San Filippo
Via di Villa San Filippo 2/10 (06 807 9314). Bus or tram to piazza Ungheria. **Open** *Jan-Apr* 7am-10pm Tue-Thur; 7am-midnight Fri-Sun. *May-Dec* 7am-midnight Tue-Sun. Closed 3wks Aug. **No credit cards.**
From the outside, this seems like just another modest local bar-*latteria* in the Parioli district, but don't pass it by, as it is the home of some wicked ice-creams. Sample the *nocciola* (hazelnut) and the *cioccolato* – always the *gelato* conoisseur's litmus-test flavours – or one of the big range of seasonal fruit flavours: watermelon (*anguria*), peach (*pesca*) or maybe melon (*melone*).

Eat, Drink, Shop

Shops & Services

From the fashion triangle to suburban *alimentari*, shopping in Rome is best approached with a vagabond spirit.

Shopping in Rome can be a delightful experience, if you hit the sprawling labyrinth of ancient streets with the right, vagabond spirit. Discover your inner-shopping-self. Stroll aimlessly round Rome's maze of streets: you never know what gems you'll discover tucked away off the beaten track. Stop to observe the local artisans at work; enter a delicatessen and savour the vast selection of meats and cheeses; absorb the atmosphere and clock the breadth of produce in the open-air markets; and ogle jewellery designs like you've never seen before. The posh, high-rent **piazza di Spagna** area is home to the city's most-trodden shopping streets; but the hidden oases, the characteristic back alleyways of the Eternal City, offer deeper satisfaction for the shopper's soul.

Rome may lack the pzzazz of the fashion centre Milan, or even of Florence, but it is home to some great fashion houses, including home-grown designers Laura Biagiotti, Roberto Capucci, the Fendi sisters and Valentino. Lesser-known Roman designers have begun congregating in **via del Governo Vecchio** (*see p 221* **Runway success**). Mid-range high-street fashion is generally uninspired and limited to major arteries, including **via Nazionale**, **via del Corso** and **via Cola di Rienzo**. More offbeat upper-mid-range offerings can be found around **Trastevere** and **campo de' Fiori**.

In many Rome shops you'll find assistants who like to pretend that customers don't exist: in others, they think their vocation in life is to intimidate. Don't be put off. Perfect the essential lines *mi può aiutare, per favore?* (can you help me please) and *volevo solo dare un'occhiata* (I just wanted to have a look around): you're ready for any eventuality.

When you've found what you want, don't try bargaining: prices are fixed (unless you are buying at a flea market, in bulk from a small-scale outlet, or from an acquaintance). If ever you are not offered a *scontrino* (receipt) in any shop, ask for it: shops are required by law to provide one, and they and you are liable for a fine in the (unlikely) event of your being caught without it. And though shops are legally bound to accept unused goods returned within days of purchase, they'll do all in their power to refuse.

TAX REBATES

If you are not an EU resident, keep your *scontrino*, as you are entitled to a VAT (*IVA* in Italian) tax rebate on purchases of personal goods over €154.97/L300,000, providing they are exported unused and bought from a shop with the Europe Tax Free sticker. The shop will give you a form to show to customs when leaving Italy.

PAYING

Most food shops will not accept credit cards; most other shops will. When you're handing over cash, it's normal to put it down in the little tray by the till, rather than placing it in the shop assistant's hand; she or he will do the same when giving you your change.

OPENING TIMES

An increasing number of city-centre shops are open non-stop from 9.30am to around 7.30pm, from Monday to Saturday. Even among shops that still shut for lunch, the traditional 1-4.30pm closedown is growing rarer, and shops are more likely to close just for an hour or so, 1-2pm or thereabouts. Times given below are winter opening hours: in summer (approximately June-October), shops that still opt for long lunches tend to reopen later, at 5pm or 5.30pm, staying open until 8-8.30pm. Most food stores close on Thursday afternoons in winter, and on Saturday afternoons in summer. Many non-food shops will be closed on Monday mornings; many very central ones open on Sundays.

Note that many shops close for at least two weeks each summer (generally in August), with no guarantee that any one shop will opt for the same weeks every year. Where no holiday closing is indicated below, the shop stays open all year; where dates are given, they should be taken as approximate only. If you plan to go out of your way to visit a shop in summer try ringing first, to avoid finding it *chiuso per ferie* (closed for holidays).

One-stop shopping

A handful of department stores has existed in central Rome for decades, but malls and giant hypermarkets are a relative novelty and, for obvious space reasons, tend to be confined to the outskirts of the city.

Centro Commerciale Cinecittà Due
Viale Palmiro Togliatti 2, suburbs: east (06 722 0910). Metro Cinecittà. **Open** 9.30am-8pm Mon-Fri; 9.30am-8.30pm Sat; 10am-8.30pm Sun. **Credit** varies.
Rome's biggest shopping mall, a glass and steel structure in the eastern suburbs, houses 100 shops and eateries, including branches of many smart fashion stores and a COIN department store.

COIN
Piazzale Appio 7, San Giovanni (06 708 0020). Metro San Giovanni/bus to piazzale Appio or piazza San Giovanni. **Open** 9.30am-8pm Mon-Sat. **Credit** AmEx, DC, MC, V.
A reliable department store, with some bargains – especially at the make-up counter. Romans go there for sensible skirts, or sheets that last. Excellent houseware department, and sturdy kids' clothes. The Cola di Rienzo branch has a supermarket.
Branches: via Mantova 1B (06 841 6279); via Cola di Rienzo 173 (06 3600 4298); viale Libia 61 (06 8621 4660); Centro Commerciale Cinecittà Due, viale Palmiro Togliatti 2 (06 722 1724).

GS Dí per Dí
Via Monte della Farina 51, Ghetto & campo de' Fiori (06 6813 1373). Bus to largo Argentina. **Open** 8.30am-8pm Mon-Sat. **Credit** AmEx, DC, MC, V. **Map** p321 2A.
There's a distinct lack of supermarkets in the *centro storico*, but this mini-market in the campo de' Fiori neighbourhood has all the picnic fare essentials.

M.A.S.
Via dello Statuto 11, Esquilino (06 446 8078). Metro Vittorio/bus to piazza Vittorio Emanuele. **Open** 9am-12.45pm, 3.45-7.45pm Mon-Sat; 10am-1pm, 3.45-7.30pm Sun. **Credit** MC, V. **Map** p326 1A.
At this bargain-basement wonderland warehouse, you'll find a mind-boggling assortment of clothing, shoes, luggage, jewellery and household linens. There are some great finds if you've got the patience to rummage through four floors of bins, and racks.

Oviesse
Viale Trastevere 62/64, Trastevere (06 5833 3633). Bus or tram to viale Trastevere. **Open** 9am-7.30pm Mon-Sat; 9.30am-1.30pm, 3.30-7.30pm Sun. **Credit** AmEx, DC, MC, V. **Map** p325 1B.
Run-of-the-mill department store clothes, with some cheap and cheerful children's wear. Located in Trastevere's main drag, the store has a good selection of cosmetics and perfume, as well as a basement supermarket, Standa (06 589 5342).
Branches: via Candia 74 (06 3974 3518); piazzale della Radio (06 556 0607).

La Rinascente
Largo Chigi 20, Trastevere (06 679 7691). Bus to largo Chigi or piazza San Silvestro. **Open** 9.30am-10pm Mon-Sat; 10.30am-8pm Sun. **Credit** AmEx, DC, MC, V. **Map** p321 1A.
Leading large-scale store, good for classy jewellery and accessories, designer and off-the-peg clothing; there's also an extensive selection of lingerie. The

La Rinascente: loads of lingerie.

piazza Fiume branch has an excellent basement household department, and English-language desks at both shops give advice on tax-free shopping and shipping home.
Branch: piazza Fiume (06 884 1231).

Termini Drugstore
Below Termini Station, Esquilino (06 8740 6055). Metro Termini/bus to Termini. **Open** 6am-midnight daily. **Credit** AmEx, MC, V. **Map** p323 2A.
Handy for last-minute snacks before train journeys, this underground mall has had a facelift and moved upmarket. The sheltering crowds of transsexuals, backpackers and homeless are no doubt impressed.

UPIM
Piazza Santa Maria Maggiore, Esquilino (06 446 5579). Bus to piazza Esquilino or piazza Santa Maria Maggiore. **Open** noon-8pm Mon; 9am-8pm Tue-Sat. **Credit** AmEx, DC, MC, V. **Map** p323 2A.
Lower-end-of-the-line fashion, plus cosmetics, toiletries and household goods.
Branches: via del Tritone 172 (06 678 3336); via Nazionale 211 (06 484 502).

Antiques

See also **Marmi Line** *p217.*
Some of the best areas to look for (pricey) antiques include **via del Babuino, via Giulia** and around **via de' Coronari**, where dealers

organise antiques fairs in May and October (see p225). The dealers-cum-restorers who picturesquely clutter up **via del Pellegrino** may be cheaper, but quality dips in proportion to prices. Occasionally, a bargain can be picked up in flea markets (see p204).

La Sinopia

Via dei Banchi Vecchi 21C, Pantheon & piazza Navona (06 687 2869). Bus to corso Vittorio Emanuele. **Open** 10.30am-1pm, 4.30-7.30pm Mon-Sat. Closed Aug. **Credit** MC, V. **Map** p321 2B.

Flea markets

Most Italians have little interest in second-hand clothes and bric-a-brac. Objects long considered design classics in the UK and US are regarded as rubbish here, and consequently there are good bargains to be had. In larger markets, such as **Porta Portese** and **via Sannio**, it's *de rigueur* to haggle. This doesn't necessarily require a great level of Italian. Broken English and/or gestures will suffice for most deals. **No credit cards.**

Atelier Ritz

Hotel Parco dei Principi, via Frescobaldi 5, suburbs: north (06 807 8189/ www.romagrandieventi.com). Bus to via Mercadante. **Open** (first weekend of month) 11am-7pm Sat; 10am-8pm Sun. **Admission** €1.81/L3,500. **Map** p322 1B.
Second-hand clothes, hats, shoes and other wearables, all, as befits this elegant end of town, by big-name designers.

Borghetto Flaminio

Piazza della Marina 32, suburbs: north (06 588 0517). Tram to piazza della Marina. **Open** Sept-mid June 10am-7pm Sun. *Mid June-mid July* 5pm-midnight Sun. **Admission** €1.55/L3,000. **Map** p320 1A.
Although this garage sale is held in a well-heeled part of the city, stallholders are required to keep prices relatively low. You can often find interesting trinkets and curios from the fascist period.

Mercato delle Stampe

Largo Fontanella Borghese, Tridente. Bus to piazza Augusto Imperatore. **Open** 7am-1pm Mon-Sat. **Map** p321 1A.
At this market you'll find second-hand and antiquarian books, as well as a great selection of prints.

Porta Portese

Via Portuense from Porta Portese to via Ettore Rolli, Trastevere (no phone). Bus to piazza Ippolito Nievo or lungotevere Ripa/tram to piazza Ippolito Nievo. **Open** 5am-2pm Sun. **Map** p3251-2B.

It's said that if your camera or *motorino* is stolen, it's a good idea to look for it in Porta Portese, Rome's most famous flea market. On Sundays, on the streets between Porta Portese, Ponte Testaccio and viale Trastevere, you'll find dealers in antique furniture, carpets, canework and mirrors; carry on southwards down via Ettore Rolli for clothes, pirated cassettes, glass and china and more antiques. Via Portuense is the market's main thoroughfare: at the Ponte Sublicio end, stalls sell mostly CDs, tapes, kitchenware, jeans, fake Lacoste shirts and leather goods. There's a very good chance that somebody will try and pick your bag or pocket as you rummage, so be extra careful.

La Soffitta Sotto i Portici

Oct-Mar *via F Crispi 96, via Veneto & Villa Borghese (06 3600 5345). Bus to via del Tritone or piazza San Silvestro.* **Open** (first weekend of month) 10am-8pm Sat; 10.30am-7.30pm Sun. **Admission** €1.55/L3,000. **Map** p323 1C.
Apr-July, Sept *piazza Augusto Imperatore, Tridente (06 3600 5345). Bus to piazza Augusto Imperatore.* **Open** 10am-sunset third Sun of month. **Map** p321 1A.
For two days a month a vast underground car park near via Veneto is cleared of vehicles and filled with antiques, junk, and collectors' items of all kinds. In the warmer months the market moves outdoors. A useful multilingual help desk is provided.

Via Sannio

Via Sannio, San Giovanni (no phone). Metro San Giovanni/bus or tram to piazzale Appio. **Open** May-Oct 10am-1.30pm Mon-Fri; 10am-2pm Sat. Nov-Apr 10am-1.30pm Mon-Fri; 10am-6pm Sat. **Map** p327 1A.
Via Sannio is less frenetic than Porta Portese (*above*), and a better place for good second-hand clothes. The main section consists of three covered corridors, a bit like an Arab bazaar, offering new clothing at reasonable prices; behind them are used and retro clothing sections.

La Sinopia is much more than an antiques shop, offering advice, valuations and design hints, plus courses in restoration, gilding and so on. The *objets* on show are not cheap, but prices are reliable.

Artists' supplies & stationery

Il Papiro

Via del Pantheon 50, Pantheon & piazza Navona (06 679 5597). Bus or tram to largo Argentina. **Open** 10am-8pm daily. **Credit** AmEx, DC, MC, V. **Map** p321 2A.

Stunning Florentine writing paper in numerous formats, paper-covered jewellery boxes, tissue boxes, picture frames, photo albums and more.
Branch: via dei Crociferi 17 (06 6992 0537).

Officina della Carta

Via Benedetta 26B, Trastevere (06 589 5557). Bus or tram to piazza Sonnino. **Open** 9.30am-1pm, 3.30-7pm Mon-Sat. Closed 1wk Aug. **Credit** AmEx, DC, MC, V. **Map** p324 2B.

Beautiful hand-made paper is incorporated into albums, gift boxes, notebooks and a host of other items by the ladies of this hole-in-the-wall in Trastevere.

Vertecchi

Via della Croce 70, Tridente (06 679 0155). Metro Spagna/bus to piazza Augusto Imperatore. **Open** 3.30-7.30pm Mon; 9.30am-7.30pm Tue-Sat. **Credit** AmEx, DC, MC, V. **Map** p320 2A.

This large outlet sells an assortment of stationery, leather goods, desk sets, business accessories, paints and wrapping paper; it also stocks a big line in colourful paper plates and party trappings. The newly opened Vertecchi annexe specialises in writing instruments: prices range from €15.50/L30,000 to €6,197.50/L12,000,000 for a solid gold pen.

Bookshops

Amore e Psiche

Via Santa Caterina da Siena 61, Pantheon & piazza Navona (06 678 3908). Bus or tram to largo Arenula. **Open** 9am-2pm, 3-8pm Mon-Fri; 10am-8pm Sat, Sun. Closed 1wk Aug. **Credit** AmEx, MC, V. **Map** p321 2A.

Centrally located store with a good range on psychology, poetry and the arts, and some English and French classics.

Bibli

Via dei Fienaroli 28, Trastevere (06 588 4097/ www.bibli.it). Bus or tram to piazza Sonnino. **Open** 5.30pm-midnight Mon; 11am-midnight Tue-Sun. **Credit** AmEx, DC, MC, V. **Map** p324 2B.

A bookshop that also functions as a cinema, music venue and tea room. Over 30,000 books (some in English), and computers for surfing. The café offers brunch for late-risers, in a lovely courtyard, on Saturday and Sunday from noon-4pm.

Fahrenheit 451

Campo de' Fiori 44, Ghetto & campo de' Fiori (06 687 5930). Bus or tram to largo Argentina. **Open** 4pm-midnight Mon; 10am-1.30pm, 4pm-midnight Tue-Sat; 10.30am-1.30pm, 6pm-midnight Sun. **Credit** AmEx, DC, MC, V. **Map** p321 2B.

Named after Bradbury's masterpiece about a future without books, this shop specialises in art, cinema and theatre, but offers some novels in English as well.

Feltrinelli

Largo Argentina 5A, Ghetto & campo de' Fiori (06 6880 3248). Bus or tram to largo Argentina. **Open** 9am-8pm Mon-Sat; 10am-1.30pm, 4-7.30pm Sun. **Credit** AmEx, DC, MC, V. **Map** p324 1A.

Excellent bookshops with large selections of art, photography, history and comic books, and titles in English. Also magazines, maps, postcards, posters, arty T-shirts and creative toys.
Branches: via del Babuino 39/41 (06 3600 1899); via VE Orlando 78/81 (06 487 0171).

Rinascita

Via delle Botteghe Oscure 1/2, Ghetto (06 679 7637). Bus to piazza Venezia. **Open** 10am-8pm Mon-Sat; 10am-2pm, 4-8pm Sun. **Credit** AmEx, DC, MC, V. **Map** p324 1A.

A temple of left-wing culture, Rinascita offers a good selection of modern literature, art and comic books, with one floor devoted to videos, many in the original language. The record department is next door (*see p220*).

English-language

Anglo American Book Co

Via della Vite 102, Tridente (06 679 5222). Bus to piazza San Silvestro. **Open** 3.30-7.30pm Mon; 9am-1pm, 3.30-7.30pm Tue-Sat. Closed 1wk Aug. **Credit** AmEx, DC, MC, V. **Map** p323 1C.

A good selection of books in English, and a vast range of scientific and technical texts aimed at university students. What isn't in stock, staff will order.

The Corner Bookshop

Via del Moro 48, Trastevere (06 583 6942). Bus or tram to viale Trastevere. **Open** 10am-1.30pm, 3.30-8pm Mon-Sat; 11am-1.30pm, 3.30-8pm Sun. Closed Sun in Aug. **Credit** AmEx, DC, MC, V. **Map** p324 2B.

This minute store carries fiction, non-fiction and general interest books – in all, 25,000 titles – in an incredibly small space at non-rip-off prices.

Economy Book & Video Center

Via Torino 136, Esquilino (06 474 6877/ books@booksitaly.com). Bus to via Nazionale. **Open** 9am-8pm Mon-Sat. Closed 1wk Aug. **Credit** AmEx, DC, MC, V. **Map** p323 2B.

It's not particularly economical, but this bookshop imports the latest from London and New York, and deals in second-hand books (check there's no used copy in stock before buying anything new). There's also a good noticeboard for those seeking work, shelter or Italian lessons.

Eat, Drink, Shop

ONYX
FASHION
ST♥RE

VIA DEL CORSO, 132 TEL. 0669932211
VIA FRATTINA, 92 TEL. 066791509
VIA COLA DI RIENZO, 225 TEL. 0636006073
VIALE MARCONI, 59 TEL. 0655301634

The English Bookshop

Via di Ripetta 248, Tridente (06 320 3301). Metro Flaminio/bus to piazzale Flaminia. **Open** 10am-7.30pm Mon-Sat. Closed 2wks Aug. **Credit** AmEx, DC, MC, V. **Map** p324 2B

A general bookshop with plenty of non-fiction and a good children's selection; there's a tearoom, too.

Feltrinelli International

Via VE Orlando 84, Esquilino (06 482 7878). Metro Repubblica/bus to piazza della Repubblica. **Open** 9am-8pm Mon-Sat; 10am-1.30pm, 4-7.30pm Sun. **Credit** AmEx, DC, MC, V. **Map** p323 1B.

Try Feltrinelli before subsidising other, overpriced English-language bookshops. This attractive store offers fiction, magazines and guidebooks.

Italica Books

Via della Pietà 25, Calcata (333 354 4994/ www.abebooks.com/home/italicabooks). **Open** by appointment only. **Credit** MC ,V.

Once a fixture of Rome's antiquarian book scene, Louise McDermott has shifted her activities to the hilltop village of Calcata, north of Rome. She'll still, however, help you find the rare, second-hand or anti-quarian book in English about any Italian topic you want, and will mail your orders to you.

The Lion Bookshop

Via dei Greci 33, Tridente (06 3265 4007). Metro Spagna/bus to piazza San Silvestro. **Open** 4.30-7.30pm Mon; 10am-7.30pm Tue-Sat. **Credit** AmEx, DC, MC, V. **Map** p320 2A.

The Lion has long been a point of reference for Rome's ex-pats. Recently installed in a new location, it also offers a reading room where customers can browse while sipping tea or coffee.

Cosmetics & perfumes

Antica Erboristeria Romana

Via di Torre Argentina 15, Pantheon & piazza Navona (06 687 9493). Bus or tram to largo Argentina. **Open** 8.30am-1.30pm, 2.30-7.30pm Mon-Sat. Closed 2wks Aug. **Credit** AmEx, DC, MC, V. **Map** p324 1A.

A curiosity shop founded in the 18th century, with banks of tiny wooden drawers, some marked with skull and cross-bones. Herbal remedies, scented paper, liquorice and hellbane are all in stock.

Dorotea

Via Roma Libera 11, Trastevere (06 588 0497). Bus or tram to viale Trastevere. **Open** 9.30am-8.30pm Mon-Sat. **Credit** AmEx, MC, V. **Map** p324 2B.

Crystal-, phyto- and aromatherapy, Bach Flowers, healing stones and Dorotea's own line of natural face to keep your mind and body in balance.

Lush

Via dei Baullari 112, Ghetto & campo de' Fiori (06 6830 1810). Bus or tram to largo Argentina. **Open** 11.30am-10pm Mon-Sat; 2.30-10pm Sun. **Credit** MC, V. **Map** p324 1B.

Mountains of fresh, handmade cosmetics and body products inspired by ancient recipes. Try the karma soap, massage bars and ballistic bath bombs that made this English chain a favourite with rock and film stars. Products are suitable for vegans.

Profumeria Materozzoli

Piazza San Lorenzo in Lucina 5, Tridente (06 6889 2686). Bus to largo Chigi or piazza San Silvestro. **Open** 3-7.30pm Mon; 10am-1.30pm, 3-7.30pm Tue-Sat. Closed 2wks Aug. **Credit** AmEx, DC, MC, V. **Map** p321 1A.

Founded in 1870, this elegant *profumeria* stocks the sought-after Acqua di Parma line, the nearly impossible to find Kiehl's face, hair and body products (their rarity is reflected in the prices), and also has a vast range of bristle shaving brushes.

Roma – Store

Via della Lungaretta 63, Trastevere (06 581 8789). Bus or tram to viale Trastevere. **Open** 10am-8pm Mon-Thur; 10am-midnight Fri, Sat; 11am-8pm Sun. **Credit** AmEx, DC, MC, V. **Map** p324 2B.

Don't let the less-than-inspired name deter you from this heavenly temple of lotions and potions, specialising in the most sophisticated French and English scents by Diptyque, L'Occitane, Crabtree & Evelyn, Penhaligon's and Creed, to name just a few. Tucked away in the corner you'll be surprised to find Crest toothpaste and Listerene mouthwash.

Design & household

Arte

Piazza Rondanini 32, Pantheon & piazza Navona (06 683 3907). Bus to corso Rinascimento. **Open** 3.30-7.30pm Mon; 9.30-7.30pm Tue-Sat. **Credit** AmEx, DC, MC, V. **Map** p321 2A.

Situated in a stunning 18th-century palazzo near the Pantheon, ultra-modern Italian design meets all of your essential and not-so-essential household appliance needs.

C.U.C.I.N.A.

Via del Babuino 118A, Tridente (06 679 1275). Metro Spagna/bus to piazza San Silvestro. **Open** 3.30-7.30pm Mon; 10am-7.30pm Tue-Sat. **Credit** AmEx, DC, MC, V. **Map** p320 2A.

A kasbah for cooks, this store stocks everything you might need or miss from home, including turkey basters, bamboo rice steamers, and a selection of eccentric baking moulds.

Branch: via Mario de' Fiori 65 (06 679 1275).

Frette

Via del Corso 381, Tridente (06 678 6862). Bus to largo Chigi or piazza San Silvestro. **Open** 12.30-7.30pm Mon; 9.30am-7.30pm Tue-Sat. **Credit** AmEx, DC, MC, V. **Map** p321 1A.

The most luxurious (and costliest) custom-made bed and table linens, as well as household accessories, with initials on anything you desire.

Branches: via Nazionale 84 (06 488 2641); piazza di Spagna 11 (06 679 0673).

Eat, Drink, Shop

'Gusto

Piazza Augusto Imperatore 7, Tridente (06 323 6363). Bus to piazza Augusto Imperatore.
Open 10.30am-2am daily. **Credit** AmEx, DC, MC, V. **Map** p320 2A.

Attached to the popular fusion cuisine restaurant of the same name (*see p165*), this *enoteca*/culinary store sells a wide range of excellent wines from around the world and boasts a gastronomic library offering more than 3,000 cookbooks in English, French, Spanish, German, Arabic, and Italian. Gadget-lovers will have a field day amid the reasonably priced wine and kitchen accessories.

Ikea

Via Anagnina 81, suburbs: east (06 723 2098). Metro Anagnina, then Ikea shuttle bus.
Open 10am-10pm Mon-Fri; 10am-8pm Sat, Sun. **Credit** DC, MC, V.

The Ikea phenomenon hit Rome in 2000, since when the Scandinavian megastore has been doing a roaring trade with Roman DIY bargain fiends. Swedish delicacies are served in the store's restaurant if you need to take a break from your shop-a-thon.

Leone Limentani

Via del Portico d'Ottavia 47, Ghetto (06 6880 6949). Bus to largo Argentina/tram to largo Agentina or via Arenula. **Open** 4-8pm Mon; 9am-1pm, 3.30-7.30pm Tue-Sat. Closed 2wks Aug. **Credit** AmEx, DC, MC, V. **Map** p324 1-2A.

Rush to the Ghetto, take a number, and get a guide to lead you through this subterranean Aladdin's cave of high-piled crockery. If you can't match up your broken plate, cup or vase here, chances are you won't find it anywhere. Many brand names are discounted about 10 per cent below market price.

Linn-Sui

Via dei Banchi Nuovi 37/38, Pantheon & piazza Navona (06 683 3406). Bus to corso Vittorio Emanuele. **Open** 4-7.30pm Mon; 10am-1pm, 4-7.30pm Tue-Sat. **Credit** MC, V. **Map** p321 2B.

This Japanese home design store sells its own line of bio-ecological futons and furniture designed for a healthy rest, as well as wall hangings and articles made from traditional Japanese tatami.

Ornamentum

Via de' Coronari 227, Pantheon & piazza Navona (06 687 6849). Bus to corso Rinascimento. **Open** 4-7.30pm Mon; 9am-12.30pm, 4-7.30pm Tue-Fri; 9am-1pm Sat. Closed Aug. **Credit** AmEx, DC, MC, V. **Map** p321 1B.

A temple to fabrics: silks, brocades and indescribably beautiful colours in furnishing fabrics. If you can't find what you want in Franco Inciocchi's vast selection, he'll look it out or have it made for you.

Spazio Sette

Via dei Barbieri 7, Ghetto & campo de' Fiori (06 686 9708). Bus or tram to largo Argentina. **Open** 3.30-7.30pm Mon; 9.30am-1pm, 3.30-7.30pm Tue-Sat. Closed 1wk Aug. **Credit** AmEx, DC, MC, V. **Map** p324 1A-B.

This slick furniture and design store occupies all three floors of a 17th-century cardinal's palace. Admire the latest in interior design beneath frescoed ceilings, with a lush garden courtyard outside.

Stock Market

Via dei Banchi Vecchi 51/52, Ghetto & campo de' Fiori (06 686 4238). Bus to corso Vittorio Emanuele. **Open** 3.30-8pm Mon; 10am-8pm Tue-Sat. Closed 10 days Aug. **Credit** AmEx, DC, MC, V. **Map** p321 2B.

This curious emporium shifts end-of-line kitchen goods, quirky light fittings and odd articles of Indian furniture that no one else can – or wants to – sell. Film directors have been known to slouch in looking for props.
Branches: via Appia Nuova 147 (06 7030 5305); via EQ Visconti 96 (06 3600 2343).

Fashion

Bags, shoes, ties, leatherwear

AVC by Adriana V Campanile

Piazza di Spagna 88, Tridente (06 678 0095). Metro Spagna/bus to piazza San Silvestro. **Open** 10am-2pm, 3-7pm Tue-Fri; 10am-7pm Sat; 10.30am-2pm, 3pm-7pm Sun. **Credit** AmEx, DC, MC, V. **Map** p323 1C.

Adriana Campanile has created an inspired collection of footwear and handbags in a rainbow of colours, which, if you're lucky enough to get the attention of one of the snotty sales assistants, could prove just the match you were looking for.

Borini

Via dei Pettinari 86, Ghetto & campo de' Fiori (06 687 5670). Bus to lungotevere dei Tebaldi or corso Vittorio Emanuele/tram to via Arenula. **Open** 3.30-7.30pm Mon; 9am-1pm, 3.30-7.30pm Tue-Sat. Closed 1wk Aug. **Credit** AmEx, MC, V. **Map** p324 1B.

Borini's shoes – all made in the family workshop – are elegant, created with an eye on current fashion trends and very, very durable. In view of which, the price tags are surprisingly restrained.

Francesco Biasia

Via dei Due Macelli 62, Tridente (06 679 2727). Metro Spagna/bus to piazza San Silvestro. **Open** 2-7.30pm Mon; 10am-7.30pm Tue-Sat. **Credit** AmEx, MC, V. **Map** p323 1C.

Biasia creates what today's handbags and wallets should be: stylish, functional and high quality, with lots of inside pockets to boot. The bags are made from Italy's finest calfskins and reptile-grained leathers, as well as innovative techno fabrics from Biasia's Evolution line.

Loco

Via dei Baullari 22, Ghetto & campo de' Fiori (06 6880 8216). Bus to corso Vittorio Emanuele or largo Argentina/tram to largo Argentina. **Open** 3-8pm Mon; 10.30am-8pm Tue-Sat. **Credit** AmEx, DC, MC, V. **Map** p321 2B.

High style, low style

Big-name designers (*see p213* **Big guns**) flaunt their wares in the classic window-shopping area at the foot of the Spanish Steps. But they aren't the last word in Roman fashion. Over recent years, trendy bijou-boutiques have muscled in among the second-hand clothes stores on via del Governo Vecchio. Their designs are fresh, innovative... and to be found refreshingly far away from the retail crush and whizzing *motorini* of the fashion centre. And if their price tags bring on an attack of vertigo, you can give your credit card a rest in the second-hand emporia.

Starting from the piazza Navona end of the road, the first shop to strike you will be **Maga Morgana**, one of two boutiques of this name (the other is further down the road) presided over by designer Luciana Iannace. One of the first in Rome to stray from the pack, Luciana has acquired a faithful clientele of actors, artists and theatre types. She began her career 20 years ago making jumpers; she now makes one-of-a-kind clothes for women, including hand-knitted sweaters, skirts and dresses as well as woollen coats. Wedding dresses embroidered with antique lace are made to order. Stop in around 5pm to chat and relax when tea is served to clients and passers-by.

Further down the street, Patrizia Pieroni's designs at **Arsenale** make great window displays and party conversation pieces. In silk and latex sandals fit for the nymph Daphne, stellar formations make feet into body art. Take note of the dressing rooms, created by a set designer, made of Meccano.

Most of the shops along via del Governo Vecchio tend towards the expensive. **Antologia** – about halfway along the street – offers lovely sequined evening bags at reasonable prices. (The bags jar noticeably with the 'Age of Aquarius' threads on display.)

But if even this is beyond your credit limit, make for the street's lower-budget establishments. Dust and allergy sufferers beware: take precautions or you'll flee sneezing from the dusty and musky.

If your nose can take it, you'll find a huge selection of army fatigues, jeans, leather jackets, shoes and all the other clutter you'd expect in second-hand shops, along with some real finds hidden among the mounds of garb.

Boutiques on via del Governo Vecchio are open 3.30-7.30pm on Monday, and 10am-7.30pm from Tuesday to Saturday. The second-hand stores are open 10am-2pm, 3.30-7.30pm Monday to Saturday. In all cases, bus to corso Vittorio Emanuele. **Map** p321 B2.

The High

Antologia
via del Governo Vecchio 49 (06 6880 6837). **Credit** AmEx, DC, MC, V.

Arsenale
via del Governo Vecchio 64 (06 686 1380). **Credit** AmEx, DC, MC, V.

Maga Morgana
via del Governo Vecchio 27 (06 687 9995); via del Governo Vecchio, 98 (06 687 8095). **Credit** AmEx, DC, MC, V.

The Low

Abiti Usati
via del Governo Vecchio 35 (06 6830 7105). **Credit** AmEx, DC, MC, V.

Omero & Cecilia
via del Governo Vecchio 110 (06 683 3506). **Credit** MC, V.

Vestiti Usati Cinzia
via del Governo Vecchio 45 (06 686 1791). **Credit** AmEx, DC, MC, V.

This shoe-box size store stocks some of the funkiest shoes around. If you're looking for that perfect pair of hot pink faux-fur heels, you've come to exactly the right place.

Sermoneta Ties
Piazza di Spagna 78A, Tridente (06 678 3879). Metro Spagna/bus to piazza San Silvestro. **Open** 10am-8pm Mon-Sat; 10.30am-7.30pm Sun. **Credit** AmEx, DC, MC, V. **Map** p323 1C.

An incredible selection of Giorgio Sermoneta's ties and scarves as well as many by other top-name designers. Stop by Sermoneta Gloves just a few doors down at piazza di Spagna 61 (06 679 1960).

Tod's
Via Borgognona 45, Tridente (06 678 6828). Metro Spagna/bus to piazza San Silvestro. **Open** 3.30-7.30pm Mon; 10am-7.30pm Tue-Sat. **Credit** AmEx, DC, MC, V. **Map** p323 1C.

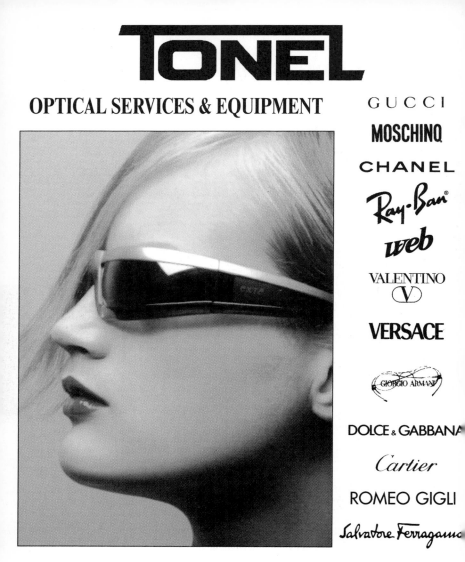

Francesco Biasia: classy bags. *See p208.*

Diego Della Valle has put his trademark leisure-time Tod's shoes on some of the most famous feet in the world, including supermodel Cindy Crawford and Princess Diana. He makes some of the best deck shoes around; the sportier line, Hogan, complements the selection.

Yamila 2000 Shop

Via E Morosini 11, Trastevere (06 5833 4920). Bus or tram to viale Trastevere. **Open** 3.30-7.30pm Mon; 10am-1pm, 3.30-7.30pm Tue-Sat. **No credit cards.** **Map** p325 1B.
For just €23.70/L45,900 you can slip your toes into any pair of shoes at this neighbourhood outlet that sells men's and women's shoes previously worn on Italian catwalks (so they say), as well as some samples.

Mid-range

Eventi

Via della Fontanella 8, Tridente (06 3600 2533). Bus to via del Corso or piazza del Popolo. **Open** 3.30-8pm Mon; 10am-1pm, 3.30-8pm Tue-Sat. Closed 2wks Aug. **Credit** AmEx, MC, V. **Map** p320 2A.
The 1970s revisited. One of few places in Rome to have lurid synthetic tops that clash superbly with tulip-embellished five-inch platforms. Even if the clothes don't grab you, it's worth a visit just for the decor: you change in shower units, and try on shoes sitting on the loo.

Iron G

Via Frattina 101/102, Tridente (06 699 1617). Metro Spagna/bus to piazza San Silvestro. **Open** 2.30-7.30pm Mon; 10am-7.30pm Tue-Sat. Closed 1wk Aug. **Credit** AmEx, MC, V. **Map** p323 1C.
This trend-setter features some of the hippest labels, including DAY Birger et Mikkelsen, Michiko Koshino, John Richmond and Two Flowers, and retro garb in eye-shocking colours.

Il Portone

Via delle Carrozze 71, Tridente (06 679 0265). Metro Spagna/bus to piazza Augusto Imperatore. **Open** 3.30-7.30pm Mon; 10am-7.30pm Tue-Sat. **Credit** AmEx, DC, MC, V. **Map** p321 1A.
Classy, reasonably priced emporium offering all the essentials from boxers, PJs and ties to a vast collection of shirts in every imaginable colour.

Boutiques

Baco della Seta

Via Vittoria 55, Tridente (06 679 3907). Metro Spagna/bus to piazza Augusto Imperatore. **Open** 3.30-7.30pm Mon; 10am-2pm, 3.30-7.30pm Tue-Sat. Closed 2 wks Aug. **Credit** AmEx, DC, MC, V. **Map** p320 2A.
Beautiful, elegant women's day and evening wear, all in pure silks of glorious hues. Prices, given the fabrics, are not exorbitant.

Best Seller

Via dei Giubbonari 96, Ghetto & campo de' Fiori (06 6813 6040). Bus or tram to largo Argentina. **Open** 3.30-7.30pm Mon; 10am-2pm, 3.30-7.30pm Tue-Sat. **Credit** AmEx, DC, MC, V. **Map** p324 1B.
Best sellers are what you'll find here, with ready-to-wear lines by Italian designers such as Moschino, Roberto Cavalli, Dolce & Gabbana and Miss Sixty. Owner Aldo, or his son Fabio, will fit you out for your Roman nights in the best threads that the 'made in Italy' tag has to offer. Decent sales are often to be found in the back room.
Branch: piazzale della Radio 1/4 (06 559 1358).

Degli Effetti

Piazza Capranica 93/4, Pantheon & piazza Navona (06 679 0202). Bus to via del Corso. **Open** 3.30-7.30pm Mon; 10am-2pm, 3.30-7.30pm Tue-Sat. **Credit** AmEx, DC, MC, V. **Map** p321 2A.
Stunning clothes by hotshot designers at horrendous prices.
Branch: piazza Capranica 75/9 (06 679 1650).

O Testa

Via Frattina 42, Tridente (06 679 1296). Metro Spagna/bus to piazza San Silvestro. **Open** 4-7.30pm Mon; 10am-1.30pm, 3.30-7.30pmTue-Thur; 10am-2pm, 3-7.30pm Fri, Sat. Closed Aug. **Credit** AmEx, DC, MC, V. **Map** p323 1C.
Classic men's knitwear and suits, off-the-peg (at lower than big-name-designer prices), or entirely made to order.
Branch: via Borgognona 13 (06 679 6174).

Eat, Drink, Shop

Scala Quattordici

Via della Scala 13, Trastevere (06 588 3580).
Bus or tram to piazza Sonnino. **Open** 4-8pm Mon;
10am-1.30pm, 4-8pm Tue-Sat. Closed 3wks Aug.
Credit AmEx, MC, V. **Map** p324 2B.
If you can't find a style, size or colour on the racks
here, Letterio and Maria Attanasio will invite you to
view a selection of multi-hued silks and other fine
fabrics in their studio, then create the made-to-measure dress or suit of your dreams. Womenswear
only, and at a price.

Victory

*Via San Francesco a Ripa 19, Trastevere (06 581
2437).* Bus or tram to viale Trastevere. **Open** 4-8pm
Mon; 9.30am-1.30pm, 4-8pm Tue-Sat. **Credit** AmEx,
DC, MC, V. **Map** p324 2B.
For Italian and French boutique-chic designs that
will take you from thank-God-it's-Friday to Monday,
the goods make it worth tolerating the aloof staff.
Victory menswear store is located nearby at piazza
San Calisto 10 (06 583 5935).

Lingerie

Lingerie stores are found all over town, but
particularly in the area around **via Condotti**.
Most markets have at least one *bancarella*
selling inexpensive underwear. The large
Rinascente department store (*see p203*) is a
good bet for middle-range items.

Brighenti

Via Frattina 7, Tridente (06 679 1484). Metro
Spagna/bus to piazza San Silvestro. **Open** 3.30-
7.30pm Mon; 9.30am-1.30pm, 3.30-7.30pm Tue-Thur;
9.30am-7.30pm Fri, Sat. Closed 2 wks Aug. **Credit**
AmEx, DC, MC, V. **Map** p323 1C.
Lingerie in glorious, silky shades by Dior, Nina
Ricci, Ferrè and other major names, in a beautiful,
pastel-hued temple to luxury. Their own-name
brand offers similarly opulent things at slightly
lower (a relative concept here) prices.
Branch: via Borgognona, 27 (06 678 3898).

Marisa Padovan

Via delle Carrozze 81, Tridente (06 679 3946).
Metro Spagna/bus to piazza San Silvestro.
Open 3.30-7.30pm Mon; 9.30am-7.30pm Tue-Sat.
Credit AmEx, DC, MC, V. **Map** p321 1A.
One-of-a-kind 'Isadora Duncan-inspired' lingerie in
a rainbow range of colours, made-to-measure bras
and swimsuits, all at astronomical prices.

Simona

Via del Corso 82/83, Tridente (06 361 3742). Bus to
via del Corso. **Open** 3.30-7.30pm Mon; 10am-7.30pm
Tue-Sat. **Credit** AmEx, DC, MC, V. **Map** p320 2A.
This is *the* shop for well-endowed women who have
always longed for sexy, lacy bras: here they'll
alter bra straps and bands till you go home singing
Barry White bedroom tunes. Good selection of
undies, sleepwear and 'non-sleepwear' at prices that
aren't too painful.

Iron G: hippest labels. *See p211.*

Food & drink

With supermarkets a rarity in central Rome,
food shopping is generally a marathon: markets
(*see p215*) are best for fruit and vegetables,
while your corner *alimentari* (grocery store)
will provide other basic necessities, from pasta
and cheese to stock cubes and yoghurt. If
you hanker for something more adventurous
and/or exotic, head for stores like **Volpetti** or
Castroni. For fresh (as opposed to long-life)
milk or cream, your best bet is not a shop at
all, but any bar labelled *latteria*.

Most deli products are sold by the *etto* (100g)
rather than the kilo; when ordering ask for
un'etto, due etti, and so on.

Many *enoteche* (wine shops) sell wine from
large barrels by the litre (bring your own
container); cheap this may be, but unless you're
very lucky, what comes out of the pipe may
bear more than a passing resemblance to paint-
stripper. *See also p179* **Select your wine**; for
cakes, *see p215*.

Castroni

Via Cola di Rienzo 196, Prati (06 687 4383). Metro
Ottaviano/bus to piazza Risorgimento. **Open** 8am-
8pm Mon-Sat. **Credit** MC, V. **Map** p320 2C.
A wonderful shop near the Vatican, Castroni has
lots of Italian regional specialities and imported
international foodstuffs: everything from Chinese
noodles to Vegemite.

Il Cavalletto

Via del Teatro Pace 37, Pantheon & piazza Navona (06 6889 1260). Bus to corso Vittorio Emanuele. **Open** 10.30am-1pm, 3.30-7.30pm Tue-Sat. **No credit cards.** **Map** p321 2B.

This new gourmet shop, located in an alley behind piazza Navona, sells a vast array of tempting Italian delicacies from every region of the boot. Downstairs there's also a well-stocked wine cellar. Group tasting dinners can be arranged on Friday and Saturday evenings. Advance reservation required.

La Corte

Via della Gatta 1, Pantheon & piazza Navona (06 678 3842). Bus to piazza Venezia or via del Plebiscito. **Open** 9am-1pm, 5-7.30pm Mon-Fri; 9am-1pm Sat. Closed Aug. **Credit** MC, V. **Map** p321 2A.

Brit John Fort and his charming wife sell wonderful smoked fishy things in this tiny shop off piazza del Collegio Romano. The place to go for smoked swordfish or (excellent) salmon.

Innocenzi

Piazza San Cosimato 66, Trastevere (06 581 2725). Bus or tram to viale Trastevere. **Open** 7.30am-1.30pm, 4.30-8pm Mon-Wed, Fri, Sat; 4.30-8pm Thur. Closed 2wks Aug. **No credit cards.** **Map** p324 2B.

Pulses spill from great sacks stacked around this treasure trove of foodie specialities from all over the world. If you're seeking currents for your Christmas pud or crunchy peanut butter, look no further.

Viola

Campo de' Fiori 44, Ghetto & campo de' Fiori (06 6880 6114). Bus or tram to largo Argentina. **Open** 8am-1.30pm, 4.30-8pm Mon-Wed, Fri, Sat; 4.30-8pm Thur. **Credit** AmEx, DC, MC, V. **Map** p324 1B.

This 19th-century establishment is dedicated exclusively to the production and sale of pork products; connoisseurs say they're the best in all of Rome. Lovers swear by the aphrodisiac effect of the dried, spicy *coppiette di maiale*.

Big guns

All crowded cosily together in the grid of streets at the bottom of the Spanish Steps, the emporia of the big guns of Italian fashion can be reached from the Spagna metro station, or by buses to piazza San Silvestro. They all take all major credit cards.

DKNY

Via Frattina 44 (06 6992 3472). **Open** 2-8pm Mon; 10am-8pm Tue-Sat. **Map** p321 1A.

Dolce e Gabbana

Via Borgognona 7D (06 678 2990). **Open** 1-7.30pm Mon; 10am-7.30pm Tue-Sat. **Map** p323 1C. **Branch**: D&G, piazza di Spagna 82/83 (06 679 2294).

Fendi

Via Borgognona 36A-38B, 39-40 (06 696 661). **Open** 10am-7.30pm Mon-Sat; 11am-7pm Sun. **Map** p323 1C.

Gianfranco Ferrè

Via Borgognona 5B, 6, 6A (06 679 7445). **Open** 1pm-7.30pm Mon; 10am-7pm Tue-Sat. **Map** p323 1C.

Gianni Versace

Via Borgognona 24/25 (06 679 5037). **Open** 10am-7.30pm Mon-Sat. **Map** p323 1C. **Branches**: Versus, via Borgognona 33/4 (06 67 83 977); via Bocca di Leone 26 (06 67 80 521).

Giorgio Armani

Via Condotti 77 (06 699 1460). **Open** 3-7pm Mon; 10am-7pm Tue-Sat. **Map** p321 A1. **Branches**: Emporio Armani, via del Babuino, 140 (06 3600 2197); Armani Jeans, via del Babuino 70 (06 3600 1848).

Max Mara

Via Condotti 17-19A (06 6992 2104). **Open** 10am-7.30pm Mon-Sat. **Map** p321 A1. **Branches**: via Frattina 28 (06 679 3638); Max&Co, via Condotti 46 (06 678 7946); via del Corso 488 (06 322 7266).

Prada

Via Condotti 92/95 (06 679 0897). **Open** 3-7pm Mon; 10am-7pm Tue-Sat; 1.30-7.30pm Sun. **Map** p321 A1.

Valentino

Via Condotti 13 (06 679 5862). **Open** 3-7pm Mon; 10am-7pmTue-Sat. **Map** p321 A1. **Branch**: via del Babuino 61 (06 3600 1906); menswear, via Bocca di Leone 15 (06 678 3656); haute couture, piazza Mignanelli 22 (06 67 391).

Davide Cenci

Via Campo Marzio 1/8, Tridente (06 699 0681). Bus to via del Corso. **Open** 3.30-7.30pm Mon; 9.30am-1.30pm, 3.30-7.30pm Tue-Fri; 10am-7.30pm Sat. **Map** p321 A1.

Out on a geographical limb (on the Tiber side of via del Corso) to show that it's a cut above the rabble.

Volpetti

Via Marmorata 47, Testaccio (06 574 2352/ www.fooditaly.com/www.volpetti.com). Bus or tram to via Marmorata. **Open** 8am-2pm, 5-8pm Mon, Wed-Sat; 8am-2pm Tue. **Credit** AmEx, DC, MC, V. **Map** p325 2A.

Volpetti is one of the best delis in Rome, with an exceptional choice of cheese, hams and salamis. Once inside, it's hard to get away without one of the jolly assistants loading you up with samples of their wares – and persuading you to buy twice as much as you want: pleasant, but painful on the wallet. If you can't get to Testaccio, check their website: they will despatch all over the world.

Confectionery & cakes

See also **Pasticcerie** *in chapter* **Cafés, Pubs & Gelaterie.**

Cinque Lune

Corso Rinascimento 89, Pantheon & piazza Navona (06 6880 1005). Bus to corso Rinascimento. **Open** 8am-9.30pm Tue-Sun. **Closed** Aug. **Credit** AmEx, MC, V. **Map** p321 2A.

One of the smallest cake shops in Rome, but packed with goodies to take away with you. A front-runner for the title of the best cream cakes in the city, with

unbeatable choux pastry; they also do a great line in traditional Easter and Christmas cakes, including *pangiallo,* a luscious slab of dried fruit.

Confetteria Moriondo e Gariglio

Via del Pie' di Marmo 21/22, Pantheon & piazza Navona (06 699 0856). Bus to via del Corso or largo Argentina/tram to largo Argentina. **Open** 9.30am-7.30pm Mon-Sat. Closed Aug. **No credit cards.** **Map** p321 2A.

A family-run chocolatiers that moulds and sells dark, liqueur-filled confections, all on the premises. At Easter and before Valentine's Day, Romans queue to have their gifts or jewels sealed inside beautifully-packaged chocolate eggs and hearts for a special personalised present. Home deliveries are made anywhere within Italy. When trade is slack, the shop may close from 1.30pm until 3.30pm.

Dolceroma

Via del Portico D'Ottavia 20B, Ghetto (06 689 2196). Bus to lungotevere Cenci/tram to via Arenula. **Open** 9.30am-1.30pm, 3.30-8pm Tue-Sat; 10am-1pm Sun. **Closed** Aug. **No credit cards. Map** p324 1A.

Though it specialises in Viennese cakes, this is also the place for American-style carrot cake and chocolate chip cookies – ideal as presents, or if you are feeling homesick/bingey. Don't get hooked: prices are high.

Produce markets

When peckishness strikes as you make your way along the tourist trail, steer clear of the rip-off fruit stalls lurking around every well-known monument. Head, instead, for a genuine food market.

Handiest for the *centro storico* sights is **campo de' Fiori** (Map p324 1B), a bustling, colourful food and flower market in one of Rome's most picturesque squares. This is the most central, but definitely not the cheapest market in the city. If you're exploring Monti and Esquilino, plunge into the chaotic jumble around **piazza Vittorio** (aka piazza Vittorio Emanuele, Map p326 1A), where the usual Italian fresh produce, cheese and meats are supplemented by pulses, halal meat and sumptuous spices (as this guide went to press this market was due to be moved to more salubrious but less picturesque quarters in a former barracks round the corner). In Trastevere, the market in **piazza San Cosimato** (Map p324 2B) retains some of its neighbourhood feel despite the tourist hordes. Even further from the beaten track is the covered market in **piazza Testaccio** (Map p325 2A), where prices are considerably lower.

A handful of tiny central(-ish) street markets also just manage to keep their heads above water. They can be found in **via dei Santi Quattro** (Map p326 2B) a stone's throw from the Colosseum, **via Milazzo** (Map p323 2A) near Termini station, and **piazza Bernini** (Map p327 2C) on the San Saba side of the Aventine hill. Near the Vatican is the **piazza dell'Unità** (Map p320 2C) covered market on via Cola di Rienzo.

Market hours

Food markets are open from around 6am until 2pm, Monday to Saturday. Some stay open on Tuesday and Thursday afternoons, but how open they are depends on the whims of individual stallholders. None accepts credit cards.

Via Trionfale

North-west of the Vatican at via Trionfale, 45 (bus to via Giuliana or via Andrea Doria, open 10am-1pm Tue) is Rome's wholesale flower market, open to the trade only. Except, that is, on Tuesday morning, when the uninitiated can plunge into this leafy, sweet-smelling haven to buy plants or cut flowers.

Eat, Drink, Shop

Forno del Ghetto

Via Portico d'Ottavia 1, Ghetto (06 687 8637). Bus to largo Argentina/tram to via Arenula. **Open** 8am-8pm Mon-Fri, Sun. **Closed** 2wks Aug & Jewish holidays. **No credit cards. Map** p324 1A.

This tiny shop (officially Pasticceria Il Boccione, though no one knows it as such) run by three unwelcoming women, has no sign over the door, but is immediately recognisable by the line of slavering regulars outside. Unforgettable damson and ricotta (or chocolate and ricotta) pies, and unique *pizze*, solid bricks of moist dough and dried fruit.

Gay-Odin

Via Stoppani 9, suburbs: Parioli (06 8069 3023). Bus or tram to piazza Ungheria. **Open** 10am-1.30pm Mon-Sat; 10.30am-1pm Sun. **No credit cards.**

A myth in Naples for over a century (Oscar Wilde was an enthusiastic patron), the Gay-Odin company has opened a Rome branch. It's well worth the trek to the north-of-centre Parioli district to savour the firm's trademark *foresta di cioccolata* (chocolate in the form of tree bark).

Valzani

Via del Moro 37B, Trastevere (06 580 3792). Bus or tram to piazza Sonnino. **Open** 10am-8.30pm daily. Closed June-Aug. **No credit cards. Map** p324 2B.

A Trastevere institution, having survived numerous eviction orders and the vissicitudes of sweet-eating fashion. Sachertorte and spicy, nutty *pangiallo* are specialities, but form just the tip of an iceberg of cakey, chocolatey delights. The shop opens daily prior to Christmas and Easter, when it's full of out-of-this-world chocolate eggs.

Ethnic foods

The best place to search for Indian, Korean, Chinese or African foodstuffs is the area around **piazza Vittorio**, now home to a large slice of Rome's recent-immigrant population. The piazza Vittorio market (*see p215* **Produce Markets**) has stalls selling halal and kosher meat, and many other products. Kosher products can also be found in shops in the **Ghetto** (*see p104*).

Korean Market

Via Cavour 84, Monti (06 488 5060). Bus to via Cavour or piazza Esquilino. **Open** 9am-1pm, 4-8pm Mon-Sat. **Credit** MC, V. **Map** p326 1B.

An up-market emporium selling everything you'll need for your Korean culinary creations, together with exotic snacks and sweets.

Pacific Trading Co

Viale Principe Eugenio 17-21, Esquilino (06 4468 406). Metro Vittorio/bus to piazza Vittorio. **Open** 9am-1.30pm, 3.30-8pm Mon-Sat. **No credit cards. Map** p326 1A.

An enormous variety of Asian foodstuffs.

Health foods

Il Canestro

Via Luca della Robbia 12, Testaccio (06 574 6287). Bus or tram to via Marmorata. **Open** 9am-8pm Mon-Sat. **No credit cards. Map** p325 2A.

Viola: *coppiette* for lovers. *See p213.*

Eat, Drink, Shop

A piece of Eternity

If you've been captivated by the spellbinding beauty and old-world charm of the Eternal City, you may feel that a pope-on-a-rope or a plaster model of St Peter's fails to evoke the right holiday memories when nostalgia sets in. Dig slightly deeper into your pockets, and a range of more dignified souvenirs becomes available: marble bits and pieces, both ancient and modern; jewellery inspired by the classical world; and even ancient artefacts themselves – or at least, fragments of them small enough not to come under the national heritage export ban.

La Bottega del Marmoraro

Via Margutta 53B, Tridente (06 320 7660). Metro Spagna/bus to piazza San Silvestro or piazza del Popolo. **Open** 9am-1pm, 3.30-7.30pm Mon-Sat. **No credit cards.** **Map** p320 2A.
A treasure trove of things marble, from small pseudo-Roman inscriptions (can be made to order) to full-sized headless statues both modern and ancient.

Maria Favilli

Via della Scrofa 93, Tridente (06 689 2895). Bus to piazza Augusto Imperatore. **Open** 10am-7pm Mon-Sat. Closed 2wks Aug. **Credit** AmEx, MC, V. **Map** p321 1A.
Maria Favilli designs rings, earrings and necklaces in the shape of amphorae, capitals and columns, using a combination of marble and gold. These original pieces don't require pocket-emptying.

Marmi Line

Via dei Coronari 113 & 141/145, Pantheon & piazza Navona (06 689 3795). Bus to lungotevere Tor di Nona or corso Vittorio Emanuele. **Open** 9.30am-8pm Mon-Sat. Closed 1wk Aug. **Credit** AmEx, MC, V. **Map** p321 1B.
Antique and ancient busts, columns, vases and tables as well as reproductions in Numidian and rosso antico marble and more. Well-hidden among some serious tack, look for the wooden crates filled with painted marble fruit that look sumptuous enough to eat. Worldwide shipping.

Siragusa

Via delle Carrozze 64, Tridente (06 679 7085). Bus to piazza San Silvestro. **Open** 9.30am-1pm, 3.30-7.30pm Mon-Fri. Closed mid July-first wk Sept. **Credit** AmEx, DC, MC, V. **Map** p321 1A.
Original Greek, Roman and Etruscan coins, stones and tiny artefacts, in modern gold and oxidised silver settings, based on models from antiquity.

Studio Massoni

Via Canova 23, Tridente (06 322 7207). Bus to piazza Augusto Imperatore. **Open** 9am-1pm, 3-7pm Mon-Fri. **Credit** AmEx, DC, MC, V. **Map** p320 2A.
Made-to-order plaster casts of just about any well-known statue or *objet* you care to have copied. A lot lighter to carry home than the real thing.

Il Canestro offers a huge range of natural health foods, cosmetics and medicines, mostly from within Italy, including some organic versions of regional specialities. The Trastevere branch also has courses on nutrition-related themes and fields, and alternative medicine.
Branch: via San Francesco a Ripa 106 (06 581 2621).

Drink

See also p179 **Select your wine.** *For wine bars, see chapters* **Eating Out** *and* **Cafés, Pubs & Gelaterie.**

Buccone

Via di Ripetta 19/20, Tridente (06 361 2154). Bus to piazza Augusto Imperatore. **Open** 9am-8.30pm Mon, Tue, Wed; 9am-midnight Thur-Sat; 10am-5pm Sun. **Closed** 3wks Aug. **Credit** AmEx, DC, MC, V. **Map** p320 2A.

In a 17th-century palazzo, this *enoteca* is filled from floor to arched ceiling with wines and spirits, all subdivided by region – from cheap Valpolicella to Brunello Riserva at over a million lire.

Costantini

Piazza Cavour 16, Esquilino (06 321 3210). Bus to piazza Cavour. **Open** *Shop* 4.30-8pm Mon; 9am-1pm, 4.30-8pm Tue-Sat. *Wine bar* 11am-3pm, 6.30pm-midnight Mon-Fri; 6.30pm-midnight Sat. *Both* Closed Aug. **Credit** AmEx, DC, MC, V. **Map** p321 1B.
One of the city's most extensive selections of what Bacchus has to offer, this vast, cavernous cellar contains just about any Italian wine you want, divided by region.

Enoteca Vinicolo Angelini

Via Viminale 62, Esquilino (06 488 1028). Metro Termini/bus to Termini. **Open** 9.30am-2pm, 4.30-11pm daily. **Closed** 2wks Aug. **Credit** AmEx, MC, V. **Map** p323 2B.

Eat, Drink, Shop

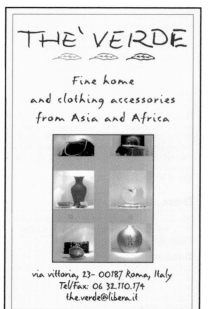

Wines and spirits from all over Italy and the world. A 1964 Barolo or Chianti Classico, for example, runs from €25.80/L50,000 upwards, and there's also real Frascati (not the bleached stuff they put in bottles) from the barrel.

Trimani

Via Goito 20, Esquilino (06 446 9661). Bus to piazza Indipendenza. **Open** 8.30am-1.30pm, 3.30-8pm Mon-Sat. **Credit** AmEx, DC, MC, V. **Map** p323 1A.

The oldest, best wine shop in Rome, founded in 1821 by Francesco Trimani, whose descendent Marco still presides. Purchases can be shipped anywhere in the world.

Gifts

See also p217 **A piece of Eternity**.

L'Impronta

Via del Teatro Valle 53, Pantheon & piazza Navona (06 686 7821). Bus to corso Vittorio Emanuele. **Open** 10am-1.30pm, 3.30-7.30pm Mon-Sat. **Credit** AmEx, DC, MC, V. **Map** p324 1B.

Souvenir prints, posters, calendars and *objets* to remember your Roman holiday by. All at very reasonable prices.

Pandora

Piazza Santa Maria in Trastevere 6, Trastevere (06 581 7145). Bus or tram to viale Trastevere. **Open** 10am-10pm daily. **Credit** AmEx, DC, MC, V. **Map** p324 2B.

If you're not travelling as far north as Venice, then pop into this treasure chest for gorgeous Murano glass clocks, picture frames, lamps and vases. The store also sells a unique array of jewellery items and Japanese tea sets.

Pineider

Via dei Due Macelli 68, Tridente (06 679 5884). Metro Spagna/bus to piazza San Silvestro. **Open** 3-7pm Mon; 9.30am-7pm Tue-Sat. Closed 1wk Aug. **Credit** AmEx, MC, V. **Map** p323 1C.

Francesco Pineider opened his custom stationery shop in Florence, fast becoming the stationer of choice for princes and poets. The finest papers, writing sets, and handsome leather goods, designed by Italy's master craftsmen make wonderful gifts for the most discriminating people in your life. Prices, as you would expect for such *raffinatezza*, are royally high.

Branch: via della Fontanella di Borghese 22 (06 687 8369).

Polvere di tempo

Via del Moro 59, Trastevere (06 588 0704). Bus or tram to viale Trastevere. **Open** 10am-8pm Mon-Sat. **Credit** AmEx, DC, MC, V. **Map** p324 2B.

In the back of his Trastevere shop, talented artisan Adrian Rodriguez creates an unparalleled selection of old-fashioned hour-glasses, sundials, solar watches and other timeless objects. The sun rings are sure to capture your attention.

Pineider: princely products, royal prices.

Jewellery & watches

See also **Siragusa**, *p217*; **Maria Favilli**, *p217*.

Federico Buccellati

Via Condotti 31, Tridente (06 679 0329). Metro Spagna/bus to piazza San Silvestro. **Open** 3.15-7pm Mon; 10am-7pm Tue-Fri; 10am-6pm Sat. **Credit** AmEx, DC, MC, V. **Map** p323 1C.

Buccellati is one of the most talented gold- and silversmiths in Italy, and his design creations speak for themselves.

Bulgari

Via Condotti 10, Tridente (06 679 3876). Metro Spagna/bus to piazza San Silvestro. **Open** 3-7pm Mon; 10am-7pm Tue-Sat. **Credit** AmEx, DC, MC, V. **Map** p323 1C.

Sweep past the unfriendly security to drool over the fantastically expensive creations in Rome's most traditional citadel of extravagant jewellery. The glittering watches are arranged in splendid isolation; browsing clients admire them from straight-backed antique chairs.

Gioielli in Movimento

Via della Stelletta 22B, Tridente (06 686 7431). Bus to via del Corso. **Open** 10.30am-7.30pm Tue-Sat. **Credit** AmEx, DC, MC, V. **Map** p321 1A.

One-of-a-kind jewellery objects designed as kinetic mini-sculptures. Wonderful cufflinks, too, with changeable disks in different colours.

Eat, Drink, Shop

Hedy Martinelli

Via Mario de' Fiori 59B, Tridente (06 679 7733). Metro Spagna/bus to piazza San Silvestro. **Open** 3.30-7pm Mon by appointment; 10am-1pm, 3.30-7pm Tue-Sat. Closed 2wks Aug. **Credit** AmEx, DC, MC, V. **Map** p323 1C.

Modern designs, inspired by art deco styles, by Ms Martinelli, who works with her daughters Alessandra and Francesca. Consult your bank manager before considering a purchase.

Pomellato

Via del Babuino 63, Tridente (06 324 1623). Metro Spagna. **Open** 4-7.20pm Mon; 10.30am-7.20pm Tue-Sat. **Credit** AmEx, DC, MC, V. **Map** p320 2A.

Just a stone's throw from piazza di Spagna, here you'll find some of the most exquisitely designed pieces of jewellery and talismans as well as a dodo bird collection.

Music: CDs, records & instruments

Disfunzioni Musicali

Via degli Etruschi 4-14, suburbs: San Lorenzo (06 446 1984). Bus to via Tiburtina. **Open** 3.30-7.30pm Mon; 10.30am-7.30pm Tue-Sat. **Credit** AmEx, DC, MC, V. **Map** p153.

One of the best places in Rome to buy underground and rare records, new and second-hand, including recent US and British indie releases.

Goody Music

Via Cesare Beccaria 2, suburbs: San Lorenzo (06 361 0959). Metro Flaminio/bus to piazzale Flaminio. **Open** 9.30am-2pm, 3.30-8pm Mon-Sat. Closed 2wks Aug. **Credit** AmEx, DC, MC, V. **Map** p320 1A.

Loads of dance, house, underground and rap vinyl mixes, plus equipment. DJs from all over Italy come here to find the latest tracks.

Jacarandà

Via del Teatro Pace 2A, Pantheon & piazza Navona (06 687 2253). Bus to corso Vittorio Emanuele. **Open** times vary; call first. **No credit cards**. **Map** p321 2B.

Tucked away on a tiny *via* near piazza Navona, this minute musical haven sells instruments from around the world, ranging from Chinese gongs and *kalimbe* (finger pianos) to Caribbean steel drums and didgeridoos. Repairs and modifications are done in-house for certain instruments, and introductory lessons are given.

Ricordi

Via Cesare Battisti 120, Capitoline to Palatine (06 679 8022). Bus to piazza Venezia. **Open** 9am-7.30pm Mon-Sat; 3.30-8pm Sun. **Credit** AmEx, DC, MC, V. **Map** p324 1A.

Rome's best-known music store, for everything from classical to pop. Ricordi also stocks videos, books, scores, instruments and sound equipment, for sale or hire, as well as selling concert tickets.

Rinascita

Via delle Botteghe Oscure 5/6, Ghetto (06 6992 2436). Bus to piazza Venezia. **Open** 10am-8pm Mon-Sat; 10am-2pm, 4-8pm Sun. **Credit** AmEx, DC, MC, V. **Map** p324 1A.

Stocks all the basics, plus a good collection of CD singles and the latest trends. Next door is an also-excellent bookshop (*see p205*).

Services

Dry-cleaning & laundries

The city is bristling with *tintorie monoprezzo* (one-price dry cleaners) – which don't, despite the name, charge the same for all items: tariffs generally start at €1.81-€2.06/L3,500-L4,000, then rise stiffly if there's a pleat to be ironed in. Most laundries take your washing and do it for you, charged by the kilo. The following are self-service.

Onda Blu

Via Lamarmora 12, Esquilino (06 446 4172). Metro Vittorio/bus to piazza Vittorio Emanuele. **Open** 8am-10pm daily. **No credit cards**. **Map** p326 1A.

Six kilos (13lb) of clothes can be washed for €4.00/L6,000; it's the same again to dry them. Bright and friendly.

Wash and Dry

Via della Pelliccia 35, Trastevere (800 231 172). Bus or tram to piazza Sonnino. **Open** 8am-9pm daily. **No credit cards**. **Map** p324 2B.

A spanking-clean self-service launderette: L6,000 for an 8kg (17lb) wash, L6,000 to tumble dry.

Branch: via della Chiesa Nuova 15.

Hairdressers & beauticians

Most Rome hairdressers are closed on Mondays. Appointments are not usually necessary, but you must be prepared to wait if you don't book.

Aveda Day Spa

Rampa Mignanelli 9, Tridente (06 6992 4257) Metro Spagna/bus to piazza San Silvestro. **Open** 3.30-8pm Mon; 10am-8pm Tue-Sat. Closed 1wk Aug. **Credit** AmEx, DC, MC, V. **Map** p323 1C.

Breathe new life into your body and mind at this temple of tranquility. Soothing music and waterfalls cascading down the wall create the perfect setting for those seeking solace, great cuts, plant-derived products, and skin and body treatments.

Femme Sistina

Via Sistina 75A, Tridente (06 678 0260). Metro Spagna/bus to piazza San Silvestro. **Open** 10am-7pm Tue-Sat; 11am- 6pm Sun. **Credit** AmEx, DC, MC, V. **Map** p323 1C.

Don't be put off by the frozen-in-the-'60s-look in the upstairs shop: go downstairs and entrust yourself to one of the hairdressers who have styled the locks

Runway success

Terminally bored? Flight already flown? Not to worry. You could do a lot worse than spend a few unexpected hours at Rome's main airport. One of the beneficiaries of the Rome 2000 Holy Year projects, Fiumicino (aka Leonardo da Vinci, see p284) has just emerged from a complete makeover and now boasts three terminals. Its bright and airy atmosphere puts some of Europe's larger airports to shame. Co-ordinated planning and an ordered licensing of outlets also means that there is no Heathrow-esque claustrophobia or deregularised madness, where departure becomes synonymous with negotiating an obstacle course of fast-food and fresh-juice stalls in a frustrated attempt to get to the gate on time.

Not that there's any lack of shopping opportunities at Fiumicino. If you want to splash out before passport control then Terminal A (domestic flights) is your best option, with its various shops which range from the extravagance of **Bulgari** (don't forget the gold credit card) to the more down-to-earth sports emporia for an impress-them-at-home Roma or Lazio football shirt. And if you have a few lire left, then why not treat

yourself to a well-shaken cocktail at the airport branch of **Harry's Bar**?

Any airport is a good source of the ersatz and Rome is no exception: sympathisers of the synthetic should head straight for the new Piazza di Spagna complex of eateries in Terminal B, with its sleek runway-viewing cappuccino terrace and consciously kitsch gigantic photo-murals of the famous square and steps. Warhol would have approved.

Once through customs, the recently opened Sky Bridge monorail provides a link with the new Terminal C satellite. This is definitely a haven for shopaholics, with top designer boutiques such as **Valentino**, **Bruno Magli** and **Gucci** selling a decent range of bags, shoes and slick accessories (at pretty indecent prices). Just the thing if you're gasping for some serious last-minute retail therapy. There is also an excellently stocked bookshop and a food outlet with a neat selection of Alessi designs.

And as you stuff your purchases into that regulation single piece of hand luggage, you can thank your lucky stars that you ended up at Fiumicino rather than the God-forsaken airport at Ciampino (see p284).

---

of such notables as Anna Maria of Greece, Nicole Kidman and Audrey Hepburn. Also a great place for facials, leg waxing or lash tinting.

Metamorfosi

Via Giovanni Branca 94, Testaccio (06 574 7576). Bus or tram to via Marmorata. **Open** 9am-7.30pm Mon-Fri. Closed 3wks Aug. **No credit cards.** **Map** p325 2B.
This friendly no-frills neighbourhood beautician will do you one of Rome's cheapest leg-waxes, plus massages, make-up and pampering of all sorts.

Sergio Valente Beauty Center

Via Condotti 11, Tridente (06 679 4515). Metro Spagna/bus to piazza San Silvestro. **Open** 9.30am-6.30pm Tue-Sat. **No credit cards. Map** p323 1C.
Roman socialites rely on Sergio for an impeccable 'do', and he knows just how roll out the red carpet for his demanding clientele. Catch up on the latest fashions in the salon's library/video centre.

Opticians

Replacement lenses can usually be fitted overnight. Most opticians will replace a missing screw on the spot; though they will generally do it gracelessly, they'll nearly always do it for

free. If you're having prescription lenses fitted, it is normal to receive a discount on advertised frame prices; if you don't, ask for one. See also *ottica* in the Yellow Pages.

Mondello Ottica

Via del Pellegrino 97/98, Ghetto & campo de' Fiori (06 686 1955). Bus to corso Vittorio Emanuele. **Open** 4-7.30pm Mon; 9.30am-1pm, 4-7.30pm Tue-Sat. **Credit** AmEx, DC, MC, V. **Map** p324 1B.
The friendly couple Giancarlo and Rosaria will frame your face with the most prestigious international designer eyewear. It's worth a visit to this gallery-like store just to goggle at the clever window installations by local artists. Lenses are often replaced on the spot. Adjustments and repairs are free and executed with a smile.

Ottica Efrati

Piazza di Spagna 91, Tridente (06 679 5361). Metro Spagna/bus to piazza San Silvestro. **Open** 1.30-7.30pm Mon; 10am-7.30pm Tue-Sat. **Credit** AmEx, DC, MC, V. **Map** p323 1C.
To appreciate fully all there is to see in Rome, stop by this store for specs that make a statement, with eyewear by Prada, Gucci, Chanel, Versace, Dior, Oakley and Persol, among others.
Branch: via del Corso 161 (06 679 2263).

Eat, Drink, Shop

Photocopying

As well as specialised shops, some *tabacchi* and stationers (*cartolerie*) do photocopies. As a rule, however, give them a miss if you need crisp, clear copies. In the streets around the university, many copy centres offer discounts to students.

Xeromania
Viale Trastevere 119, Trastevere (06 581 4433). Bus to viale Trastevere. **Open** 9am-2pm, 3-7.30pm Mon-Fri; 9am-2pm Sat. **No credit cards.** **Map** p325 1B.
An excellent general copy shop in Trastevere, which also has a reliable fax sending and receiving service.

Photo developers

Film can be bought in specialist camera shops or opticians'.

Cocacolor
Via del Mascherino 4-10, Vatican & Prati (06 687 9498). Bus to piazza Pia or piazza Risorgimento. **Open** 8am-8pm Mon-Sat; 9am-7pm Sun. **Credit** AmEx, DC, MC, V. **Map** p321 1C.
Two minutes' walk from St Peter's, Cocacolor prepares large, glossy prints in an hour or two. It's more expensive, but better, than most same-day services.

Fotocolor Lab
Piazza Buenos Aires 20, suburbs: north (06 884 0670). Bus to via Po or viale Regina Margherita. **Open** 8.30am-1pm, 3.30-7pm Mon-Fri. Closed 2wks Aug. **Credit** MC, V. **Map** p322 1A.
A professional developer, Fotocolor Lab specialises in slides but does a good job on colour prints too.

Foto-Cine di Pennetta
Via Dandolo 2, Trastevere (06 589 6648). Bus or tram to viale Trastevere. **Open** 8.30am-1pm, 4-7.30pm Sat. Closed 1wk Aug. **Credit** MC, V. **Map** p325 1B.
High quality photo shop with one-day developing; digital processing is offered. Cameras repaired too.

Foto Express
Via Quattro Fontane 7, Trevi Fountain & Quirinale (06 474 4278). Metro Barberini/bus to piazza Barberini. **Open** 8am-7.30pm daily. **Credit** AmEx, DC, MC, V. **Map** p323 1B.
This shop just off piazza Barberini produces high-quality colour prints in one hour as promised.

Repairs

F Pratesi (Clinica della Borsa)
Piazza Firenze 22, Tridente (06 6880 3720). Bus to via del Corso or piazza San Silvestro. **Open** 9.30am-1pm, 3.30-7.30pm Mon-Fri; 9.30am-1pm Sat. Closed Aug. **No credit cards.** **Map** p321 1A.
Specialises in repairing bags slit open by thieves. Repairs take up to three days, and cost from L10,000.

Vecchia Sartoria
Via dei Banchi Vecchi 19, Ghetto & campo de' Fiori (06 6830 7180). Bus to corso Vittorio Emanuele. **Open** 8am-1pm, 3-7pm Mon-Fri; 8am-1pm Sat. Closed 3wks Aug. **No credit cards.** **Map** p321 2B.
Run by a skilled traditional tailor and a seamstress, the Vecchia Sartoria does clothing repairs quickly and at reasonable prices.

Ticket agencies

Expect to pay *diritti di prevendita* (pre-sales supplement) on tickets bought anywhere but at the venue on the night. **Ricordi** (*see p220*) sells tickets for classical concerts and for many rock, jazz and other events.

Orbis
Piazza Esquilino 37, Esquilino (06 482 7403). Bus to via Cavour or piazza Esquilino. **Open** 9.30am-1pm, 4-7.30pm Mon-Sat. **No credit cards.** **Map** p323 2A
Tickets are sold here for most concerts, theatre and sporting events.

Travel agencies

Centro Turistico Studentesco (CTS Student Travel Centre)
Via Genova 16, Monti (06 462 0431). Bus to via Nazionale. **Open** 9.30am-1pm, 2.30-6.30pm Mon-Fri; 9.30am-1pm Sat. **Credit** MC, V. **Map** p323 2B.
This student travel agency offers discounts on air, rail and coach tickets for all those in full-time education. CTS services can also be used by non-students.
Branches: corso Vittorio Emanuele 297 (06 687 2672/3/4); via degli Ausoni 5 (06 445 0141).

Viaggi e Vacanze
Via Laurina 23, Tridente (06 321 9541/ www.ginalmi.it). Metro Spagna/bus to via del Babuino. **Open** 9am-1pm, 2-6pm Mon-Fri; 9am-1pm Sat. **Credit** AmEx, MC, V. **Map** p320 2A.
Also known as American-Italian Lloyd, this agency accepts credit cards for some rail tickets as well as air tickets.

Video rental

The **Economy Book & Video Center** (*see p205*) has over 2,000 English-language titles for rent. Membership costs €25.82/L50,000 a year.

Videoteca Navona
Corso Rinascimento 13/15, Pantheon & piazza Navona (06 686 9823). Bus to corso Rinascimento. **Open** 9am-8.30pm Mon-Sat. **Credit** AmEx, MC, V. **Map** p321 2A.
A huge selection of Italian- and English-language films. Lifetime membership costs €25.82/L50,000 (or leave a L50,000 deposit); a two-day rental costs €2.58/L5,000.

Arts & Entertainment

By Season

Stay in town for anything from limp bunting to days of feasting...
or head out for a *ponte* by the sea.

Ancient Rome had over 150 public holidays a year, which may have contributed to its decline and fall. Today there are only ten – well within the EU average. Romans are still very fond of their breaks, often extending them by taking an additional day or two off between the end of an official holiday and the preceding or following weekend, a practice known as *fare il ponte* (doing the bridge). At the faintest hint of sun, citizens will brave hours of fumes at an *autostrada* tollbooth for a glimpse of sea or mountain to help forget the stress of city life.

Different districts of Rome celebrate their own patron saints with anything from a bit of limp bunting on a church to days of parading and feasting. For really special events, makeshift stages are erected in squares, and occupied far into the night by lusty crooners.

Spring

Festa di San Giuseppe
Around via Trionfale. Metro Ottaviano/bus to piazza Risorgimento. **Date** 19 Mar. **Map** p320 2C.
Although no longer an official public holiday, the feast of St Joseph remains popular, especially in the Trionfale district. Only carpenters and woodworkers still get the day off. In the run-up to the feast, the city's cafés and *pasticcerie* are piled high with deep-fried batter-balls called *bigne di San Giuseppe*.

Maratona della Città di Roma
Information 06 406 5064/fax 06 406 5063/ www.maratonadiroma.com. **Date** 3rd Sun in March.
Rome's annual marathon may not be at the level of London's or New York's, but it has a growing reputation and now attracts big-name runners. The serious race begins and ends in the via dei Fori Imperiali.

Festa di Primavera – Mostra delle Azalee
Piazza di Spagna. Metro Spagna/bus to piazza San Silvestro. **Dates** end Mar, early Apr. **Map** p323 1C.
Spring arrives early in Rome, bringing masses of flowers. When the azaleas come out, some 3,000 vases of them are arranged on the Spanish Steps, displacing the resident army of tourists.

Settimana Santa & Pasqua
Vatican: bus to piazza Risorgimento or piazza Pia. **Map** p321 1C. *Colosseum: Metro Colosseo/bus to piazza del Colosseo.* **Map** p326 2B-C. **Dates** Mar, Apr.

On the Saturday before Palm Sunday the city is flooded with tour groups from around the world, here to attend the open-air Mass in St Peter's Square. During the Holy Week that follows, Rome offers Christendom's nearest equivalent to the collective fervour of Mecca, with non-stop services. Events culminate in the Pope's Stations of the Cross (*Via Crucis*) and Mass at the Colosseum late on the evening of Good Friday. On Pasquetta (Easter Monday) the city empties again, as Romans traditionally have their first picnic *fuori le porte* (outside the city gates), of *porchetta* (roast suckling pig) and *torta pasqualina* (cheesey bread, with salami and hard-boiled eggs).

Natale di Roma
Campidoglio. Bus to piazza Venezia. **Date** 21 Apr. **Map** p324 1A.
It may seem odd for a city to have a birthday, but it's not funny to Romans, whose city was 'born' in 753 BC (*see p7*). The spectacular main celebrations take place at the Campidoglio (Capitoline, *see p61*). The City Hall and the other *palazzi* on the Capitoline are illuminated, and enormous quantities of fireworks are set off.

Settimana dei Beni Culturali
Information 06 589 9844/www.beniculturali.it. **Dates** vary, usually early spring.
During this week, which translates as Cultural Heritage Week, all public museums and monuments are open to the public without charge. Many museums and sites that are usually closed are opened up for the occasion. *See p226* **Open day**.

Fiera d'Arte di via Margutta
Via Margutta (06 812 3340). Metro Spagna/bus to piazza del Popolo or piazzale Flaminio. **Dates** end Apr; late Oct-early Nov. **Map** p320 2A.
If via Veneto was where the *Dolce vita* set hung out at night, via Margutta was where they did their daubing. Few active painters still live here, but the street is still chock-full of art galleries. High points of their year are the two art fairs, each four days long. The paintings range from so-so to downright terrible.

> ► See also **When to Go: public holidays**, *in chapter* **Directory** *(p304)*.
> ► For rock, roots and jazz festivals, *see p258*; for classical music and opera festivals, *see p248*; for theatre and dance festivals, *see p265*.

Ensure your pet a place in heaven at **Sant'Eusebio**. *See p227.*

Concorso Ippico Internazionale di Piazza di Siena

Piazza di Siena, Villa Borghese (06 3685 8494/ www.fise.it). Metro Spagna or Flaminio/bus or tram to piazzale Flaminio or via Veneto. **Dates** end Aprbeginning May. **Map** p322 2C.

This international show-jumping event in held in the piazza di Siena in Villa Borghese is one of few truly jet-set occasions Rome still has to offer; it's as smart and self-consciously *all'inglese* as can be imagined.

Primo Maggio

Piazza San Giovanni (06 847 6235). Metro San Giovanni/bus or tram to piazza San Giovanni or piazzale Appio. **Date** 1 May. **Map** p327 1A.

Trades unions celebrate May Day by organising a huge free rock concert, traditionally held in front of the basilica of San Giovanni (*see p129*). Top Italian, and some international, acts perform from mid-afternoon into the night. In recent years, however, organisers have faced an uphill struggle to avoid having the gig transferred to a soulless field in the suburbs.

Campionato Internazionale di Tennis (Italian Open)

Foro Italico, viale dei Gladiatori (06 328 371/ www.tennismastersseries-roma.com). Bus to lungotevere Maresciallo Cadorna or piazza Mancini. **Dates** 10 days in May.

Italy's annual tennis championships, the Italian Open, is one of the first big events in the European tennis season.

Mostra dell'Antiquariato

Via de' Coronari (06 6880 1041). Bus to corso Rinascimento, corso Vittorio Emanuele or lungotevere Tor di Nona. **Dates** mid-end May; mid-end Oct. **Map** p321 1B.

Via de' Coronari is the hub of Rome's antiques trade. During its annual 20-day antiques fair, the shops stay open late, allowing you to browse to your heart's content.

Summer

Estate Romana

Various locations (www.estateromana.caltanet.it). **Dates** June-Sept.

The Estate Romana (Roman Summer) festival brings an embarrassment of cultural riches to the city. *Piazze, palazzi*, parks and courtyards come alive with music from local jazz and pop bands, and films are shown on outdoor screens late into the night.

Festa di San Giovanni

San Giovanni in Laterano. Metro San Giovanni/ bus or tram to piazza San Giovanni. **Date** 23 June. **Map** p326 2A.

This saint's day has lost its resonance except in the San Giovanni district, where singing, dancing and games go on all night. It's *de rigueur* to eat *lumache in umido* (stewed snails) and *porchetta* (roast suckling pig). The religious highlight is a candlelit procession, usually led by the Pope, to San Giovanni in Laterano (*see p129*).

Santi Pietro e San Paolo

San Paolo fuori le Mura. Metro San Paolo/bus to piazzale San Paolo or via Ostiense. **Date** 29 June.

The two founders of Catholicism share the honours as the twin patron saints of Rome, and each is duly honoured in his own basilica. At St Peter's (*see p139*) a special, solemn Mass is the highlight; at San Paolo fuori le Mura (*see p153*), celebrations are centred outside the church, with an all-night street fair along the via Ostiense. (*See also p132* **Peter & Paul.**)

Roma Alta Moda

Piazza di Spagna (02 777 1081). Metro Spagna/ bus to piazza San Silvestro. **Dates** mid-July. **Map** p323 1C.

Rome's fashion community has long been overshadowed by trendier Milan, but it strikes back with Alta Moda, when the coming year's collections are sneakpreviewed in piazza di Spagna and major hotels.

Festa di Noantri

Piazza Santa Maria in Trastevere, piazza Mastai.
Bus or tram to viale Trastevere. **Dates** mid-July.
Map p324 2B.

Roughly translatable as 'a knees-up for us plebs', and theoretically in honour of the Madonna del Carmine, whose procession kicks things off, the Festa di Noantri is one of the last surviving glimmers of Trastevere's old working-class culture. For two weeks, sections of Trastevere are closed to traffic and filled with stalls, open into the small hours. Spectacular fireworks round off the closing night.

Open day

As steeped as they are in the relics of history, Romans still leap at the chance to get a look at the bits that are usually closed off to them, and so they flock in excited droves to open days and special events. There's a cluster of such opportunities in spring, with the **Settimana dei Beni Culturali** (*see p224*), and the **Giornate FAI**, when the non-profit Fondo per L'Ambiente Italiano (*see below*) persuades institutional and private owners of historic properties to open their doors for a weekend.

But besides these national events, there are some very particularly Roman ones, too. In particular, **9 March** is the **feast of Santa Francesca Romana**. During this event the Tor de' Specchi convent – set up in the 15th century by a charitable Roman matron whose good works eventually brought her sainthood – can be visited (parts of the convent are also open every Sunday in March).

The battered wife of a Trastevere gang leader, Francesca (1384-1440) sublimated her frustrations in tending to the bodies and souls of the poor and sick. In 1433 she founded the Oblate di Maria, an order of nuns who never took final vows and could come and go from the convent as they wished. (Their unusual status so confused Napoleon that he failed to close the convent down along with Italy's other religious orders, making it the only one with an uninterrupted history.) Francesca's magnificent medieval palazzo of Tor de' Specchi became the order's headquarters. It was spectacularly frescoed immediately after her death by Antoniazzo Romano with scenes from her miraculous devil-and-disaster-plagued life; part of the palazzo was later given a lovely baroque courtyard.

Francesca was believed to have the gift of dislocation – being in several places at the same time – which endeared her to Italy's pioneer motorists, who adopted her as their patron saint in the early 1900s. Motor vehicles of all descriptions are blessed on 9 March at her church, in the Foro Romano (Roman Forum, *see p71*).

On **16 March** it is the turn of one of Rome's most august dwellings, **Palazzo Massimo alle Colonne** (*see p93*), to open its gates.

The Massimo family is one of the oldest in Rome: its name is recorded as early as the beginning of the 11th century. This family palazzo dates from 1532. In one of its rooms – now the family church (church, note, not chapel: this is Rome's only privately owned church) – San Filippo Neri performed one of his most celebrated miracles. Called to administer the last rites to the young Paolo Massimo, the saint found the boy already dead; nothing daunted, he brought him back to life, chatted for a while, and then – when Paolo declared he was finally ready to die – commended him to God.

With its heavy silk wall coverings, reliquary cases and Gothic paintings, this is one of the best examples of a private family chapel-church in Rome. On the anniversary, after a private Mass, a procession of family, servants and altar boys escorts the presiding cardinal or archbishop to a room – off-limits to visiting plebs – where the remnants of Rome's nobility are treated to a buffet lunch. To see the spectacle in all its Felliniesque glory, turn up around 11.30am, just as Mass is ending.

Fondo per l'Ambiente Italiano (FAI)

Via delle Botteghe Oscure, 32 (06 6880 4789/www.fondoambiente.it). Bus to via della Botteghe Oscure or largo Argentina. **Open** 9.30am-1pm Mon, Wed, Fri; 4-6pm Tue, Thur. **Map** p324 1A.

Monastero Oblate di Santa Francesca Romana

Via del Teatro di Marcello, 32 & 40. Bus to via del Teatro di Marcello or piazza Venezia. **Open** 9 March 8.30-11.45am, 3-5pm. Sundays in Mar, times vary. **Map** p324 1A.

Palazzo Massimo alle Colonne

Corso Vittorio Emanuele, 141 (06 6880 1545). Bus to corso Vittorio Emanuele. **Open** 8am-1pm 16 Mar only. **Map** p321 2A-B.

Festa delle Catene

Chiesa di San Pietro in Vincoli, piazza di San Pietro in Vincoli (06 488 2865). Metro Cavour/bus to via Cavour. **Date** 1 Aug. **Map** p326 1B.

Chains alleged to be those in which St Peter was clapped in prison in Jerusalem, and those with which he was shackled in a Roman prison, are displayed in a special Mass at San Pietro in Vincoli (*see p131*).

Festa della Madonna della Neve

Basilica di Santa Maria Maggiore (06 483 195). Bus to piazza dell'Esquilino. **Date** 5 Aug. **Map** p323 2A.

For Romans sweating through a sticky August, snow is an enticing thought. Perhaps that's why the legend of the snowfall over the Esquiline Hill on 5 August 352 still has such resonance. It is commemorated when a deluge of rose petals flutters down on to Mass-goers in Santa Maria Maggiore (*see p132*).

Ferragosto – Feast of the Assumption

Date 15 Aug.

The Feast of the Assumption is the high point of summer; even the few people who haven't actually fled Rome for August go away for a long weekend, and practically everything is closed. The very few restaurants that stay open serve the traditional Ferragosto dish of *pollo con i peperoni*: chicken with peppers.

Autumn

See also **Mostra dell'Antiquariato** *p225*, **Fiera d'Arte di via Margutta** *p224*.

Ognissanti/Giornata dei Defunti

Cimitero del Verano, piazzale del Verano. Bus or tram to piazzale Verano. **Dates** 1, 2 Nov. **Map** p153.

Otherwise known as Tutti Santi, All Saints' Day (Ognissanti) is followed by La Commemorazioni dei Defunti (or Tutti i Morti), when the Pope celebrates Mass at the vast Verano cemetery. Romans travel en masse to visit family graves.

Winter

Immacolata Concezione

Piazza di Spagna Metro Spagna/bus to piazza San Silvestro or via del Tritone. **Date** 8 Dec. **Map** p323 1C.

The statue of the Madonna in piazza di Spagna is the day's focal point, when, with the Pope looking on, the fire brigade runs a ladder up Mary's column, and a lucky fireman gets to place a wreath over her outstretched arm (in times past, popes themselves did the climbing). At the base of the column locals and dignitaries deposit immense mounds of flowers.

Natale and Santo Stefano

Dates 25, 26 Dec.

Oddly enough, the world centre of Catholicism is no great shakes at Christmas. The trappings of northern Yuletide consumerism have asserted themselves strongly in recent years. Stores now feature extra-long opening hours, Sunday shopping and classy

street decorations. All this is a recent import: until a few years ago it was Epiphany (*see below*) that really counted. For a taste of a more traditional Roman Christmas, get tickets to the papal midnight Mass in St Peter's (from the Prefettura, 06 6988 4631/06 6988 3865, open 9am-1pm Mon-Sat; put your request in months ahead), or visit the cribs: you'll find one in most churches. There's a good example halfway up the Spanish Steps; but piazza San Pietro has the biggest crib of all, plus a huge Christmas tree.

San Silvestro/Capodanno

Dates 31 Dec, 1 Jan.

New Year's Eve is a night to stay inside, and not only because most restaurants are shut: the firework mayhem that builds to a crescendo in the minutes around midnight is unforgettable from a hotel window, but reminiscent of a war zone if you're caught up in it at street level. It's best experienced in down-home areas such as Testaccio or San Lorenzo, but beware: some older residents still honour the tradition of chucking unwanted consumer durables off their balconies. Alternatively, there's a free concert, disco and fireworks in piazza del Popolo.

Epifania – La Befana

Piazza Navona. Bus to corso Rinascimento. **Date** 6 Jan. **Map** p321 2A-B.

Reflecting Rome's pagan spirit, the Feast of the Epiphany is better known by the name of a very un-Christian character, La Befana, the old witch. As the legend goes, this Mother Christmas only brought presents to good children; bad ones found their shoes filled with bits of coal. Today, all Roman *bambini* get their presents anyway, as 'coal' comes in the form of an intense and cloying black sweet. From mid-December to 6 January, piazza Navona fills with market stalls, selling sweets and cheap tat. The climax comes late on 5 January, when La Befana herself touches down in the piazza.

Sant'Eusebio

Via Napoleone III. Metro Vittorio/bus to piazza Vittorio Emanuele. **Date** 17 Jan. **Map** p326 1A.

Animal lovers keen to ensure their pets a place in heaven have them blessed at the little church of Sant'Eusebio, in a ceremony that used to go on for days and was loved by tourists, who used to cause traffic jams as they cooed over this rare example of Italian devotion to animal welfare.

Carnevale

Date week before Lent (usually late Feb-Mar).

In the Middle Ages, this riotous pagan farewell to winter before the rigours of Lent was celebrated with lurid abandon outside the city walls on Monte Testaccio. Anxious to keep a check on their libidinous subjects, Renaissance popes brought the ceremony back within the walls to via del Corso. Nowadays, an array of diminutive princesses and characters from Disney's latest release swarm about the city with their proud parents by day, while older kids shower the streets with shaving foam and confetti by night.

Children

With a little forward planning, and lashings of *gelato*, they'll love Rome.

To the average non-Italian eye, Roman kids are sassy, spoilt and over-dressed. This is perhaps a result of being plunged into an adult world from an early age: they are dragged into family discussions, fed a solid diet of turgid purple prose in school text books… and given their first *telefonino* (cellphone) round about the age of ten.

This all has a positive flip side: Roman kids show no bashful reticence when expected to take part in grown-up discussions, enjoy easy relationships with the cronies of aged grandparents with whom they were dumped for most of their infancy, and care – a little at least – about their appearance.

For the visitor to Rome, this state of affairs has repercussions both positive and negative. As they are considered part of the family unit, rather than annoying excrescences, kids can be taken anywhere – to the smartest restaurant or the grandest opera – and no one will bat an eyelid. But with the family the focus of all leisure-time activities, authorities have never been forced to lay on child-friendly facilities. And though amenable parks – some with swings and climbing frames – have mushroomed in recent years, museums and galleries still tend to be of the hands-off variety.

For all that, there is no reason why your children should not have the time of their life in Rome. The key to their (and your) enjoyment is careful preparation: a children's guidebook to ancient Rome (see *p231*) will bring those ruins to life; a quick parental refresher course on Roman myths or religious iconography will turn paintings and sculptures into material for stories and guessing-games galore. If all else fails, you can always resort to gardens (see *p229* **Top five parks and gardens**) or some of the world's most glorious ice-cream (see chapter **Cafés, Pubs & Gelaterie**).

For further information on child-oriented events, look in the kids' sections of *Time Out Roma*, *Roma C'è*, or the Trovaroma supplement with Thursday's *La Repubblica* (see *p297*). They're all in Italian, but you'll find them quite easy to follow.

TRANSPORT

Most of the city centre is walkable with kids, which is just as well, as other transport options can be tricky. Buses are often crowded, so moving kids and/or a pushchair can be a major

hassle. The No.3 tram route, which covers a long and winding route from viale Trastevere to the **Villa Borghese** (see *p79*) via the **Piramide** (see *p121*), can be made into quite an adventure if trams are a novelty, and ends up conveniently close to the **zoo** (see *p81*). The stuffy Metro is limited in scope, and best avoided during rush hours.

It's rare for an obviously pregnant woman or anyone travelling with babies and toddlers not to be offered a seat on a crowded bus. If you are left standing, feel free to motion to any able-bodied young thing that you need to sit down; they will usually oblige with good grace.

On all city transport, children under the age of ten travel free. Above that, you need to get a full-price ticket for them, unless you're staying for a long time, in which case child-rate season tickets are available.

Sightseeing

Careful planning is the secret to successful sightseeing with children in Rome, and all the more so if you have a demanding cultural wish-list. Before you set out each day, it pays to identify the park/pizzeria/*gelateria* nearest to your selected destination.

If you're craving an hour or two of Renaissance art at the **Palazzo Barberini** (see *p76*) or **Galleria Borghese** (see *p81*), you should meet with little resistance: both are well-situated for a picnic in **Villa Borghese** (see *p79*), where you can while away the non-cultural part of your day by hiring bikes or a rowing boat on the artificial lake. Remember, too, that on the northern side of Villa Borghese is the **Bioparco-Zoo** (see *p81*) and a bells-and-whistles **Museo Zoologico** (see *p83*), complete with a mock-up of a bear cave which will scare your little kids silly if they venture into the depths.

Situated half a kilometre from the Villa Borghese, Rome's long-awaited Children's Museum (**Explora – Museo dei Bambini di Roma**, see *p81*) opened its doors in May 2001. Here, kids up to the age of 12 will be able to explore all the workings of a realistic play-city, with activities from plumbing and car maintenance to commerce and communications. Also nearby, in the lower reaches of via Veneto, is the **Immacolata Concezione** church (see p84), where the bones of some 4,000 late lamented Capuchin monks have been tastefully arranged on the walls of five chapels.

Other churches might also appeal to your kids' sense of the macabre and weird. Frescos in **Santo Stefano Rotondo** (see p126) depict martyrs being boiled in oil, devoured by dogs and suffering other occupational hazards of the early Church. Just down the road, you can admire the frescos and mosaics in **San Clemente** (see p122), while junior travellers revel in the mystery of the place. Dark stairs descend through several layers of civilisation, until you get a glimpse of the Cloaca Maxima, Rome's first sewer system, where the water still rushes noisily down to the Tiber.

San Clemente is a short walk from the **Colosseum** (see p66) where even the most culture-weary of youngsters will love tales of gladiatorial gore. To make the visit memorable, there are legions of self-styled centurions wandering about in full regalia, happy to pose with kids for a couple of thousand lire.

Next door in the **Foro Romano** (Roman Forum, see p71), there's a high risk of kids' refusing point blank to waste time looking at heaps of stone. You could do worse than invest in one of the 'then and now' guidebooks on sale from the many souvenir stalls around the area: they may seem unbearably tacky to you, but they could help bring the place to life for your children. Finish your visit with a picnic on the **Palatino** (see p66) and maybe a game of hide-and-seek among the remains of walls and aqueducts.

The **Vatican** (see p138) will be high on the list of adult priorities. Spice things up for children with a trip up the dome of St Peter's,

from where you can peer down into the basilica or take in the sweeping views over the city outside. Note that carrying a toddler up into the dome is only recommended for the very fit. In the **Vatican Museums**, children may prefer the huge painted 16th-century maps and globes to the overwhelming crowds in the Sistine Chapel. The Egyptian Museum is full of grisly mummies and lush sarcophagi.

A surprise in each itinerary goes down well: the giant marble hands and feet in the courtyard of the **Musei Capitolini** (see p62); the single huge marble foot at the beginning of via Santo Stefano di Cacco, just off piazza del Collegio Romano; the obelisk-bearing **elephant** in piazza della Minerva (see p99); and the charming **Fontana delle Tartarughe** (see p106) in the Ghetto. And there's always coin-throwing at the **Fontana di Trevi** (Trevi Fountain, see p74).

Though most of Rome's museums take a dim view of kids' tactile explorations, there are a few that have enticing bits for youngsters. **Castel Sant'Angelo** (see p144) is a historic pope-bunker full of passageways, turrets and dungeons, and the **Crypta Balbi** (see p103) supplements its fascinating displays on Rome in the Dark Ages with computer games to show how the ancient was gradually incorporated into the modern. The **Centrale Montemartini** (see p153) often holds Sunday morning drawing workshops for kids among its gleaming machinery and classical statues. When real antiquities bore your children, show them plaster versions of how it all looked before the rot set in: the **Museo della Civiltà Romana** (see p155) in EUR contains huge scale models of ancient Rome. It's also conveniently close to

Top five — Parks and gardens

Circo Massimo
The grass is a bit thin, and there are no swings; but inspire them with Ben-Hur ambitions and get them running around the ancient race track, and they'll wear off that excess energy in no time. Bring a hat: there's no shade. See p66.

Villa Borghese
Grass, ancient trees, ponds (with boats for hire) and paths just made for roller blades or bicycles (ditto). See p79.

Villa Celimontana
Swings, a cycle/skating track for tinies and a fishpond that can double (against all rules) as

a paddling pool – in lush green shade dotted with classical marble fragments. See p128.

Villa Pamphili
Rome's biggest park, replete with swings, exercise contraptions, lakes, woods, pony rides: you name it, they've provided it. The problem is finding it, though – not always an easy task in 1.8 square kilometres (one square mile) of parkland. See p155.

Villa Sciarra
A little gem of a park, with lots of swings and climbing frames, a mini-big dipper, rides, fountains, manicured lawns and a pigeon-filled aviary. See p155.

the **Luna Park (LUNEUR)** funpark and the **Piscina delle Rose** swimming pool (*see p262*), a good place to cool off on hot days.

Martially inclined kids will enjoy playing at ancient Roman soldiers along the stretch of Aurelian Wall accessed from the **Museo delle Mura** (*see p148*). And if air traffic controllers turn your homewards trip into a nightmare, try taking a ten-minute walk from Fiumicino airport to the nearby **Museo delle Navi Romane** (*see p269*), where kids can see what Roman ships were really like.

Out of town

The best child-oriented sights within reasonable distance of Rome are the bizarre Renaissance **Sacro Bosco** at Bomarzo (also known as Parco dei Mostri, Monster Park, *see p275*), with its huge scary sculptures that kids can climb in and on; and the fountains and cascades of Tivoli's **Villa D'Este** (*see p274*) and nearby **Villa Adriana** (*see p273*) for picnics. In Bracciano, the **Castello Orsini-Odescalchi** (*see p279*) makes an interesting trip, with its many suits of armour and 16th-century loos. **Lago di Bracciano** (*see p277*) and its smaller neighbour **Lago di Martignano** both have decent beaches and

fairly clean water. The water on the coast near Rome is not the cleanest, but is, they say, improving each year; there are many beach clubs at **Ostia** or **Fregene**, and miles of sand at **Castelporziano**. The Roman remains at **Ostia Antica** (*see p269*) are a perfect (and easily reached) place for sandwiches and hide-and-seek amid the ruins; aspiring thespians can stage impromptu performances of *Julius Caesar* in the Roman theatre.

Entertainment

For the **Bioparco-Zoo** *see p81*; for the **Museo di Zoologia** *see p83*; for **Explora-Museo dei Bambini di Roma** *see p81*.

Biblioteca Centrale per i Ragazzi

Via San Paolo alla Regola 16, Ghetto & campo de' Fiori (06 686 5116). Bus to lungotevere dei Vallati or largo Argentina/tram to via Arenula. **Open** 9am-7pm Tue-Fri; 9am-1pm Sat. **Map** p324 1B.

The Central Children's Library has a selection of English, French, German and Spanish books for tinies, and plans to offer an international range for older kids, too. Non-residents can use the library, but not borrow books. From mid-June, and for most of the summer, the library usually moves to a tent in a park: call for information.

Luna Park (LUNEUR)

Via delle Tre Fontane, EUR (06 592 5933). Metro Magliana/bus to via delle Tre Fontane or piazza dell'Agricultura. **Open** *3-7pm Mon, Wed-Fri; 3pm-1am Sat; 10am-1pm, 3-10pm Sun.* **Admission** *free; rides €0.52-€2.58/L1,000-L5,000.* **No credit cards.**
Rome's funfair is 30 years old, and it shows, but it's saved by the sheer theatricality of the rides and exhibits. There's a very respectable roller-coaster, two haunted houses, a hall of mirrors, and boat, car and pony rides for smaller children.

Acquapiper

Via Maremmana Inferiore, km 29.3, Guidonia (0774 326 538). Metro to Ponte Mammolo, then COTRAL bus to Palombara/by car SS5 (Tivoli road) then SS5ter to Guidonia. **Open** *mid May-mid Sept* 9am-5.30pm Mon-Fri; 9am-6.30pm Sat, Sun. Closed mid Sept-mid May. **Admission** €7.75/L15,000 before 2pm Mon-Fri; €10.33/L20,000 after 2pm Mon-Fri; €10.33/L20,000 before 2pm Sat, Sun; €9.04/L17,500 after 2pm Sat, Sun. €7.75/L15,000 4-10s; free under-4s. **Credit** AmEx, DC, MC, V.
This water park is off the road from Rome to Tivoli, and so can be combined with a trip to Villa Adriana (*see p273*) or the Villa D'Este (*see p274*). It boasts a small children's pool with a tortoise waterslide, plus kamikaze slides and a wave machine for older kids. There are picnic areas, a restaurant and banks of video games, too.

Ancient Rome will keep your kids busy.

Puppeteers & theatre

Italy's long and glorious puppet tradition centres on Sicily and Naples, but Rome also offers decent shows. Two stalwarts claim to be the only real *burattinai* (puppeteers) left. One show is set up on the Gianicolo, run by Mr Piantadosi and identifiable by the sign *Non Tirate Sassi!* (Don't throw Stones!). The other is in Largo K Ataturk, EUR, near a Giolitti ice-cream emporium. Both serve up Pulcinella, just as violent and misogynist as his English descendant Mr Punch, delivered in a Neapolitan accent so thick that most local kids understand it no better than foreigners do: it's the whacks on the head that count, anyway.

For theatre, see also **Teatro Vittoria** (*p264*), which frequently stages variety-cum-acrobatic acts popular with children.

Teatro Verde

Circonvallazione Gianicolense 10, Trastevere (06 588 2034). Bus or tram to Stazione Trastevere. **Box office** *Nov-Apr* 8.30am-6pm Mon-Sat; 2-6pm Sun. Closed May-Oct. **Shows** *Nov-Apr* 5pm Sat, Sun. Closed May-Oct. **Tickets** €6.20/L12.000. **No credit cards.**
The best-known children's theatre in Rome, Teatro Verde offers puppet shows and acted plays in Italian. Visit the costume and prop workshop half an hour before the curtain goes up.

Books

The English-language *Ancient Rome for Kids* (ed. Fratelli Palombi) on sale in Feltrinelli bookshops (*see p205*), gives succinct explanations of major sites, illustrated with drawings of Roman kids doing what kids did in ancient Rome.

The Libreria Mel-Giannino Stoppani (piazza Santi Apostoli, 65, 06 6994 1045) children's bookshop has a small selection of books in English, as do many of the English-language bookshops listed on *p205*.

Babysitters/childcare

Higher-range hotels have their own babysitting services, and all but the most basic hotels will arrange a babysitter for you.

Angels

Via Quattro Fontane 16, Quirinale (06 678 2877/06 4201 3083/0338 667 9718/rebeccaharden@hotmail.com). **Babysitting rates** €15.49/L30,000 agency fee plus €7.75/L15,000 per hour. **No credit cards.**
Tried and tested English-speaking babysitters are provided by Brit Rebecca Harden, who will also find nannies and domestic staff for longer-term visitors in Rome and all over Italy.

Arts & Entertainment

Contemporary Art

Rome may not be the centre of Italian contemporary art, but new exhibition spaces are taking shape.

Rome is not the centre of the Italian modern and contemporary art scene; for that you'll have to go to Milan. The Eternal City is, however, making an ever-increasing commitment to contemporary art, most notably with the development of the **Galleria Communale d'Arte Moderna e Contemporanea** (*see p151*) in a revamped brewery, and, more recently, with the opening of the ambitious **Centro per le Arti Contemporanee di Roma** (*see p150*).

The Centro per Le Arti had already started its exhibition programme as this guide went to press, though it will take another four years to complete the ultra-modern centre, to a design by Anglo-Iranian architect Zaha Hadid (*see p29* **Contemporary**).

The starting-point for checking out the artistic produce of recent decades still remains the **Galleria Nazionale d'Arte Moderna** (*see p82*) on the northern fringe of villa Borghese: this houses the national collection of modern art. Major temporary shows of modern and contemporary art and photography are held at the **Palazzo delle Esposizioni** (*see p78*) in via Nazionale.

Rome's private galleries are numerous and patchy, quality-wise. Only the most renowned and/or most reliable are listed below. For the most part they show a mix of international and Italian contemporary art.

To find out what's going on at any given time, pick up a copy of 'The Art Guide' (www.artguide.it), a free hand-out available in most art galleries. It provides not only listings of exhibitions, but also information about openings, so you can invite yourself along to mingle with the Italian artsy set. Watch out in particular for events at the foreign academies (the British School, Goethe Institut, Accademia di Spagna, and so on); they often show top-class international artists with wonderful opening nights.

Art Gallery Banchi Nuovi

Via Margutta 29, Tridente (06 3265 0316). Metro Spagna or Flaminio/bus to piazza del Popolo. **Open** 4-8pm Mon; 10.30am-1pm, 4-8pm Tue-Sat. Closed mid July-Aug. **Credit** MC, V. **Map** p320 2A.
This gallery consistently shows new artists, although its often hectic programme reveals a predilection for metaphysically inspired magic realism that is not to everybody's taste.

Associazione Culturale L'Attico

Via del Paradiso 41, Ghetto & campo de' Fiori (06 686 9846). Bus to corso Vittorio Emanuele. **Open** 5-8pm Mon-Sat. Closed Aug. **No credit cards. Map** p324 1B.
One of the most innovative galleries in Rome, a starting-point for new artists and a place for known names to introduce new directions in their work.

Associazione Culturale Sala 1

Piazza di Porta San Giovanni 10, San Giovanni (06 700 8691). Metro San Giovanni/bus to piazza San Giovanni in Laterano. **Open** 5-8pm Tue-Sat. Closed July, Aug. **No credit cards. Map** p326 2A.
Sala 1 specialises in the international avant-garde.

Associazione Culturale Valentina Moncada

Via Margutta 54, Tridente (06 320 7956). Metro Spagna/bus to piazza del Popolo. **Open** 4-8pm Mon-Fri. Closed 2 wks July; all Aug; 1 wk Sept. **No credit cards. Map** p320 2A.
This picturesque garden conceals a series of purpose-built 19th-century artists' studios: Wagner, Liszt and Fortuny visited. It now specialises in the work of radical young artists.

Galleria Emanuela Oddi Baglioni

Via Gregoriana 34, Tridente (06 679 7906). Metro Spagna/bus to via del Tritone. **Open** 10am-1pm, 4-7.30pm Mon-Fri; by appointment 10am-1pm Sat. Closed Aug. **No credit cards. Map** p323 1C.
Shows mostly non-figurative Italian sculpture, dating from 1960 onwards; the owners act as agents for young sculptors.

Galleria Gian Enzo Sperone

Via di Pallacorda 15, Tridente (06 689 3525). Bus to piazza San Silvestro. **Open** *Oct-Apr* 4-8pm Mon; 10am-1pm, 4-8pm Tue-Sat. *June-Sept* 4-8pm Mon; 10am-1pm, 4-8pm Tue-Fri. Closed Aug. **No credit cards. Map** p321 1A.
Sperone is one of Rome's most prestigious art promoters, with a gallery in New York. He now frequently holds unusual, experimental shows.
Branch: via dell'Orso, 27 (06 689 3525).

Galleria Giulia

Via Giulia 148, Ghetto & campo de' Fiori (06 6880 2061). Bus to lungotevere dei Tebaldi. **Open** 4-7.30pm Mon; 11am-1pm, 4-7.30pm Tue-Sat. Closed July-mid Sept. **No credit cards. Map** p321 2B.
This gallery on art-packed via Giulia has carved a niche for itself with shows by New Pop artists, German Expressionists and Italian contemporary artists. Strong in graphic arts and sculpture.

Young radicals show at
Valentina Moncada.
See p232.

Galleria Ugo Ferranti

Via dei Soldati 25A, Piazza Navona & Pantheon (06 6880 2146). Bus to corso Vittorio Emanuele or corso del Rinascimento. **Open** *Nov-Mar* 11am-1pm, 5-8pm Tue-Sat. *Apr-Oct* 10am-1pm, 4-8pm Mon-Fri. Closed Aug. **No credit cards. Map** p321 1B.

A showcase for conceptual art: the owner is constantly on the lookout for new artists.

Nove Via della Vetrina Contemporanea

Via della Vetrina 9, Piazza Navona & Pantheon (06 6819 2277). Bus to corso Vittorio Emanuele. **Open** 11am-1pm, 4-7.30pm Tue-Sat. Closed Aug. **No credit cards. Map** p321 2B.

A cute new gallery run by Elisabetta Giovagnoni, showing young painters and sculptors from Italy and the rest of Europe.

Il Ponte Contemporanea

Via di Montoro 10, Ghetto & campo de' Fiori (06 6880 1351). Bus to corso Vittorio Emanuele. **Open** noon-7pm Mon-Sat. Closed Aug. **No credit cards. Map** p321 2B.

This stylish gallery shows mostly photography and installation art. Also check out the gallery's smaller experimental space on the same street at No.3.

Stefania Miscetti

Via delle Mantellate 14, Trastevere (06 6880 5880). Bus to lungotevere della Farnesina. **Open** *Oct-Apr* 4-8pm Tue-Sat. *May, June* 4-8pm Mon-Fri. Closed July-Sept. **No credit cards. Map** p324 1C.

In a warehouse in Trastevere, this gallery holds unusual shows of sculpture and installations.

Studio d'Arte Contemporanea Pino Casagrande

Via degli Ausoni 7A, suburbs: south (06 446 3480). Bus or tram to via dei Reti or piazza del Verano. **Open** 5-8pm Mon-Fri. Closed mid July-mid Sept. **No credit cards. Map** p153.

In the hip area of San Lorenzo, Casagrande's loft-like exhibition space hosts some of Rome's most challenging exhibitions.

Studio Casoli in collaborazione con Caterina Pazzi

Via della Vetrina 21, Piazza Navona & Pantheon (06 6889 2700). Bus to corso Vittorio Emanuele. **Open** 11.30am-7.30pm Tue-Sat. Closed Aug. **No credit cards. Map** p321 2B.

The Studio Casoli shows some of the big names in Italian and international contemporary art.

Film

Movie cameras are whirring again in Rome.

Rome is back in fashion as a place to make films. Long gone are the days when Elizabeth Taylor and Richard Burton launched inflammable looks at each other on the set of *Cleopatra* while director William Wyler went over budget in truly epic style. But the city's historic Cinecittà studios have been staging a small comeback after the slump of the 1980s and early '90s, thanks largely to the return of a few big US productions, attracted by the weak lira and the recently updated studio facilities.

Some of these new films have nothing whatsoever to do with Rome itself. The Sylvester Stallone action vehicles *Cliffhanger* and *Daylight* were both shot here; and for six months between autumn 2000 and spring 2001, the studio backlot was turned into a replica of 1860s New York for Martin Scorsese's period epic *Gangs of New York* – much to the joy of local paparazzi, who kept their telephoto lenses trained on the film's stars, Leonardo DiCaprio and Cameron Diaz.

Other directors, though, are more interested in the city itself as a backdrop. Recent international location shoots in Rome include Jane Campion's *Portrait of a Lady* and Anthony Minghella's *The Talented Mr Ripley*. Minghella shot here in the middle of August, when the city was half empty. Locations included piazza Navona and piazza di Spagna, where a re-creation of the 1950s American Express office was so accurate that tourists queued outside, waiting for it to open.

It's not just foreign directors whose cameras are rolling in Rome. Though it's not always obvious abroad, Italians are still making films – around a hundred a year. The recent huge success of Roberto Benigni's Holocaust tearjerker-comedy *La vita è bella* (*Life is Beautiful*) has not been matched by a general upturn in the international fortunes of Italian cinema; but at the more independent end of the market, there are signs of a return to health. Distinctly Roman talents to have emerged in recent years include Gabriele Muccino, whose thirtysomething comedy drama *L'ultimo bacio* (*One Last Kiss*) was a huge domestic hit in the spring of 2001. Wonder-boy Muccino was recently signed up by Miramax to direct two English-language films.

The Talented Mr Ripley confused tourists in piazza di Spagna.

But the spaghetti Westerns and B-movie horror flicks that used to tide cinema professionals over until the next 'serious' project are – alas – a thing of the past. It is worth remembering that the most successful Italian film of all time was not a classic like *La Dolce Vita* or *Mamma Roma*, but the spaghetti western *They Call Me Trinity* (1970) by EB Clucher – pseudonym of director Enzo Barboni – which was seen in no less than 220 countries.

MOVIEGOING IN ROME

Italians are enthusiastic moviegoers. Rome especially has seen a picture palace renaissance in recent years: between 1993 and 1998 the number of screens in the city more than doubled, and audiences have kept pace. This has been due partly to the conversion of older cinemas into two- or three-screen miniplexes, but also to the creation of new, modern cinemas, especially in the outer suburbs. At the beginning of 1999 the city's first true multiplex opened – the 18-screen Warner Village in Parco de' Medici – followed a year later by the 14-screen Cineland in Ostia.

Arthouse fans are well served by the Circuito Cinema chain, which controls six first-run outlets around the city, plus the long-established **Pasquino** English-language cinema, recently spruced up and given two extra screens. Then there's always the **Nuovo Sacher** in Trastevere. Owned by cult director Nanni Moretti (*see p238* **Nanni Moretti**), this first-run independent wears its cineaste credentials on its sleeve. The most recent addition to the arthouse scene is the **Filmstudio** in Trastevere – the two-screen reincarnation of the club that launched a thousand cineastes in the 1960s and 1970s.

The downside is the dubbing. Italian dubbers are widely recognised to be the best in the world, but that's no consolation for anyone who likes to hear films in the original language (*versione originale* – abbreviated as VO in newspaper listings). Anything that moves is dubbed, and subtitles are virtually unheard of. There are now two permanent English-language cinemas: the Pasquino and the Cecchi Gori-owned **Quirinetta**. Only two other cinemas – the **Alcazar** and **Nuovo Sacher** – have a regular policy of showing current-release films in *lingua originale* – the former on Monday, the latter on Thursday. In addition, one of the screens of the **Warner Village Moderno** – a five-screen miniplex carved out of a former porn palace – often shows big Hollywood films in English.

For a standard 90-minute film, the four daily screenings will generally be at 4.30pm, 6.30pm, 8.30pm and 10.30pm; the box office generally opens half an hour before the first showing. Some screens now accept payment by credit card, but this is still a rarity.

Summer is the time when all Rome closes, and cinemas have traditionally been no exception. Nowadays, most larger cinemas stay open all year, but many cinemas and most cineclubs still close completely in July and August. Compensation is found in the open-air cinemas and festivals around the city (*see p237*).

The best source for information on what's on at any of the cinemas in Rome, including summer venues, is the local section of the daily newspapers *La Repubblica* and *Il Messaggero*. There is also a useful Internet site, www.trovacinema.it, which provides programme details for almost all first-run cinemas in Italy.

First-run cinemas

All first-run cinemas offer lower prices for the first two screenings – generally at 4.30pm and 6.30pm – on Monday, Tuesday, Thursday and Friday, and all day Wednesday. Programmes generally change on Friday.

Alcazar

Via Cardinal Merry del Val 14, Trastevere (06 588 0099). Bus or tram to viale Trastevere. **Tickets** €6.71/L13,000; €4.13/L8,000 reductions. **No credit cards. Map** p324 2B.
A red plush jewel, and one of the first major Rome cinemas to screen its films in the original language (generally English) on Mondays. For the last two showings it's wise to book ahead (tickets must be picked up 30 minutes beforehand).

Dei Piccoli

Viale della Pineta 15, Via Veneto & Villa Borghese (06 855 3485). Metro Spagna/bus to Porta Pinciana. **Tickets** €4.13/L8,000. **No credit cards. Map** p322 2B.
Built in 1934 as a children's theatre in the Villa Borghese park, the tiny, beautifully restored Dei Piccoli now presents a selection of children's films (in Italian only) each afternoon. In the evening it shows independent first- and second-run films; it also stages occasional themed seasons with offerings from the Italian Film Archives.

Filmstudio

Via degli Orti di Alibert 1C, Trastevere (06 6830 1173). Bus to lungotevere Gianicolense. **Tickets** €6.71/L13,000; reductions €4.13/L8,000. **No credit cards. Map** p324 1C.
This historic Rome film club returned from oblivion to its old home at the end of 2000, with new, comfortable seats and state-of-the-art screening facilities. It alternates first-run arthouse films with more *recherché* treats and themed seasons.

Nuovo Sacher

Largo Ascianghi 1, Trastevere (06 581 8116).
Bus or tram to viale Trastevere or viale Induno.
Tickets €6.71/L13,000; €4.13/L8,000 reductions.
No credit cards. Map p325 1B.

The Nuovo Sacher is owned and run by film director Nanni Moretti (*see p238* **Nanni Moretti**), who
bought it out of irritation at the poor state of film
distribution in Rome. It has become a meeting place
for local cinematic talent, and makes an effort to
support independent Italian filmmakers – with
initiatives such as a short-film festival in July, in
the open-air arena alongside the cinema – as well
as presenting strong arthouse titles from abroad on
long runs. If it's by Abbas Kiarostami, Ken Loach,
just about any French indie director or – of course
– Nanni Moretti, you can be sure to find it here.
Films are usually shown in VO on Thursdays.

Pasquino

Piazza Sant'Egidio 10, Trastevere (06 5833 3310).
Bus or tram to viale Trastevere. **Tickets** €6.20/
L12,000; €4.13/L8,000 reductions. **No credit cards.**
Map p324 2B.

Rome's historic English-language cinema – a point
of reference for all English-speaking newcomers –
used to be a fleapit with dodgy sound, but a 1998
refurbishment has turned it into a three-screen modern cinema with dodgy sound. Since it was taken
over by the Circuito Cinema group, programming
has become more adventurous – though arthouse
films are generally relegated to Screen 3, which is
little more than a cupboard. There are occasional
themed seasons of VO films in other languages.

Quattro Fontane

Via Quattro Fontane 23, Trevi Fountain & Quirinale
(06 474 1515). Bus to via Nazionale. **Tickets**
€6.71/L13,000; €4.13/L8,000 reductions. **No credit
cards. Map** p323 2B.

The showcase miniplex of new indie distribution
cartel Circuito Cinema, the Quattro Fontane is a
design cinema with state-of-the-art sound system
and a small bar in the foyer. Small domestic indies
often get their only Italian outing in Sala 4.

Quirinetta

Via M Minghetti 4, Trevi Fountain & Quirinale
(06 679 0012). Bus to via del Corso. **Tickets**
€5.16/L10,000; €4.13/L8,000 reductions. **No credit
cards. Map** p323 2C.

A cavernous, threadbare, pungent single-screen
movie house that the Cecchi Gori group has offered
up as an English-language cinema, in competition
with the historic Pasquino (*see above*). The schedule
depends on what American titles Cecchi Gori happen to be distributing at the time.

Warner Village Moderno

Piazza della Repubblica 45/46, Esquilino
(reservations 06 477 7911/information 06 4777
9202). Metro Repubblica/bus to piazza della
Repubblica. **Tickets** €7.23/L14,000; €5.16/L10,000
reductions. **Credit** AmEx, DC, MC, V. **Map** p323 2B.

The full-on American Moviegoing Experience; it's
enough to make you nostalgic for the grubby but
venerable porn palace that used to stand here.
Warner Village now has two Rome outposts; the
other is a huge 18-screen multiplex at Parco de'
Medici, just off the Fiumicino airport road. The more
restrained five-screen central branch is remarkable
only for occasionally dedicating a screen to original-
language prints of Hollywood blockbusters.

Cinema d'essai & cineclubs

Cinema d'essai are generally small and cheap,
and feature mainly classics or contemporary
arthouse cinema, occasionally in *versione*
originale. It is in these cinemas and the still
smaller cineclubs that the full range of
international cinema and the best of the Italian
cinema heritage can be seen. All are private
ventures, except the Palazzo delle Esposizioni
(*see p78*), the municipal arts centre. Some clubs
also re-screen films that suffered from truncated
first releases. Some *centri sociali* (*see chapter*
Nightlife) also offer screenings of alternative
or difficult-to-see films. A membership card
(*tessera*) is required by many clubs, but they
can be bought at the door for a minimal charge.

Azzurro Scipioni

Via degli Scipioni 8, Vatican & Prati (06 3973
7161). Metro Lepanto/bus to via Marcantonio
Colonna. **Tickets** *Sala Chaplin* €5.16/L10,000 per
film. *Sala Lumière* €6.20/L12,000 per day. **No
credit cards. Map** p320 2C.

Best-known of the *d'essai* cinemas, with two screens:
the Sala Chaplin, showing more recent art-house successes, and Sala Lumière, with a video projector,
devoted to cinema classics and themed seasons. Run
by director Silvio Agosti. By a house rule,
streetsweepers get in free.

Detour

Via Urbana 47A, Monti (06 487 2368). Metro
Cavour/bus to piazza Santa Maria Maggiore.
Tickets €3.10/L6,000 with membership card
(€1.02/L2,000). **No credit cards. Map** p323 2B.

A small but committed cineclub near Santa Maria
Maggiore, with an eclectic programme alternating
cinema classics, world cinema, shorts, and more.
Workshops and debates are also organised.

Grauco Film Ricerca

Via Perugia 34, suburbs: south (06 782 4167).
Bus or tram to piazzale Prenestino. **Tickets** €2.58-
€4.65/L5,000-L9,000 (obligatory yearly membership
€5.16/L10,000; includes one ticket). **No credit cards.**
The tiny Grauco concentrates on powerful
independent cinema from around the world, sometimes in *versione originale*, with a particular day of
the week often devoted to one country. On
Saturday and Sunday afternoons, kids' classics are
screened (in Italian). Films are usually shown at
7pm and 9pm.

Festivals & summer programmes

Around the beginning of July, as cinemas are closing and box-office figures take a nosedive, Rome becomes a great place to take in a movie. A raft of second-run or arthouse open-air cinema feasts is launched as part of the Estate Romana (Roman Summer) festivities (*see p225*), many in breathtaking settings. In addition, there are several *arene* (open-air screens) that provide a chance to catch up with that blockbuster you missed, or take in obscure underground classics.

There are also two regular mini-festivals, **Cannes a Roma** and **Venezia a Roma**, which show a selection of original-language films from the Cannes and Venice film festivals a few days after they close (in May and September respectively). Venues change annually: check local press for details. Festivals and *arene* come and go, but the following two are regular summer fixtures.

Cineporto

Parco della Farnesina, suburbs: north (06 3600 5556/www.cineporto.com). Bus to lungotevere Maresciallo Cadorna. **Dates** July, Aug. **Tickets** €5.16/L10,000. **No credit cards**.

One of the most successful and popular summer festivals is in the park by the Stadio Olimpico. There are two separate screens, each showing two dubbed films a night, often recent releases. Live concerts are presented between shows on many nights. Check local press before setting out for this northern suburb: there was talk in 2001 of shifting the festival.

Massenzio

(Information 06 4423 8002/06 4281 5714/ 06 4281 4962/www.massenzio.it). **Dates** July, Aug. **Tickets** €5.16/L10,000. **No credit cards**.

The biggest and most politically correct of Rome's open-air film festivals, featuring about 200 films each year. The venue changes annually; check local press for details. The imaginative programmes are organised around directors, actors, countries, genres or themes; there is usually one large viewing area with more commercial programming, and a smaller arthouse space. Films are usually dubbed.

Long-established **Pasquino**. *See p236.*

Nanni Moretti

Imagine Woody Allen crossed with Ken Loach, and you come close (but not that close) to the flavour of Roman director Nanni Moretti's work. Moretti has directed, written and taken a starring role in nine feature films to date, beginning in 1976 with the aptly named *Io sono un autarchico* (*I Am an Autarch*). Career highlights include the marvelous *Ecce bombo* (1978), with perhaps the highest 'do you remember that scene...?' count of any of his movies; *La messa è finita* (1985), where he plays a left-leaning Catholic priest; and *Caro diario* (1994), in which he proves that it is possible to film a man riding around Rome on a Vespa for 20 minutes without boring your audience.

Moretti is a hero for a whole generation of radical-ish left-ish Italians, who are often rather narrowly identified as *i sessantottini* – products of the 1968 student protest generation. But it is not only his fans who can recite key Morettian scenes off by heart; certain lines of dialogue have become common cultural references, entering upon an afterlife of quotes and misquotes. The following are some of the most famous.

Va be', continuiamo così, facciamoci del male – OK, fine, let's just go on hurting each other. (*Bianca*, 1983. The infuriated hero's unbalanced response to his father's revelation that he has never tried a Viennese *sacher torte*, Moretti's favourite cake. Note that Moretti's production company is called Sacher Film).

Chi parla male, pensa male e vive male – He who talks badly, thinks and lives badly. (*Palombella Rossa*, 1989. From what must be the only film ever to have mixed water polo with the crisis of Euro-communism).

Voi gridavate cose orrende e violentissime e voi siete imbruttiti. Io gridavo cose giuste, ed ora sono uno splendido quarantenne – The things you shouted were horrible and ultra-violent, and you have grown ugly. The things I shouted were right and just, and now I'm a splendid forty-year-old. (*Caro Diario*, 1994. Moretti is taking issue with former revolutionary comrades who feel that it was all a waste of time).

Cos'è questo film? E la storia di un pasticciere troskista nell'Italia degli anni '50. E un film musicale – What's the film about? It's the story of a Trotskyite pastry chef in 1950s Italy. It's a musical. (*Caro Diario*, 1994. In order to gain entry to houses he is curious to see, Moretti pretends he is scouting for locations for a film).

D'Alema, dì una cosa di sinistra! – D'Alema, say something a little bit Left! (*Aprile*, 1998. Watching a televised debate between right-wing media magnate turned political leader Silvio Berlusconi and the former leader of the Italian left, Massimo D'Alema, Moretti is infuriated by D'Alema's refusal to say anything that could be construed as socialist).

Gay & Lesbian

2000's World Pride brought a rude awakening, and a fresh start.

The year 2000 was a watershed for the city's lesbians and gay men. Those who thought that Rome was slowly catching up with other European capitals in terms of tolerance and opportunities had a rude awakening in the run-up to the summer's World Pride event.

When the Vatican realised that the Eternal City was about to be invaded by legions of pilgrims of a rather different ilk from the usual pious Holy Year hordes, all hell broke loose. Ever eager to curry Church favour, then-Mayor Francesco Rutelli turned his back on his gay-friendly credentials (he had led a previous Pride) and withdrew council support for the event. The controversy polarised public opinion: press and political parties took predictable stands, but inadvertently gave such publicity to Pride 2000 that, when it came to the event's Saturday march (by then reduced by city authorities to a stroll from the Pyramid to the Colosseum), hundreds of thousands of gay and straight men and women joined the national and international contingents on the rainbow parade.

The next day, the Pope spoke of the great 'offence' that the sacred city of Rome had suffered, but by then the success of the march was undeniable. Now Rome's Mario Mieli (*see p242*) association even speaks of making 8 July – the date of the march – a national alternative to the traditional Stonewall anniversary. Imma Battaglia, MM's charismatic leader, reckons that July 2000 did wonders for the city's gay men and women. Much of the closetry that once characterised gay life in the city is now being replaced by openness and a weakening of the 'us and them' divide. Hallelujah indeed.

OUTDOORS, INDOORS

For the sweltering summer months, Rome's gay scene moves outside (*see p240* **Let's go outside**) and even out of town.

During the colder months, life continues indoors and a whole gamut of venues has emerged to cater for various tastes: the appearance of self-styled sex clubs and the proliferation of dark rooms are quite recent trends; moreover, the city now boasts two leather groups. There are still few places, however, where gay men and lesbians can meet during the day: the gay terrace café has yet to hit the Eternal City.

PERSONAL SAFETY

Discretion is the keyword. Although Romans pride themselves on their worldly acceptance of human variety, public effusions are best avoided. The police are as likely to protect you as they are to harass.

TRANSVESTITES, TRANSSEXUALS, TRANSGENDER

When gay pioneer Mario Mieli published *Homosexuality and Liberation* in 1977 (English edition published by Gay Men's Press, 1980), transvestites were seen as the cutting edge of gay politics. These days in Rome the vast army of South American *viados*, and some home-grown transsexuals, do little more than satisfy the needs of the sex industry.

The Circolo Mario Mieli has given more and more space to transgender issues, and its cultural programmer and ringmaster/mistress Vladimir Luxuria is a constant presence on TV, not always to the liking of more hard-line gay campaigners.

Bars, clubs & restaurants

Rome's gay venues open and close at an alarming rate, so a phone call to check the establishment still exists is a good idea before you slip into something sexy. Some bars charge no entrance fee but oblige you to buy a drink. A growing number of venues ask for an **Arci Uno Club card**. This costs €12.90/L25,000 for annual membership, can be bought in any venue that requires it, and gives admission to many venues throughout Italy. Some places, though, have their own membership cards, valid only in the individual venue. In most bars you are given a printed slip on which the barman ticks off what you consume; you pay the total amount on leaving. Be careful not to lose your slip, or you'll have to pay a stiff penalty on leaving.

Rome now has one restaurant sporting a couple of gay rainbow flags outside its portals. At the **Asinocotto** – literally 'cooked ass' – (via dei Vascellari 48, 06 589 8985, closed Mon, average €31/L60,000) cook Giuliano Brenna has impressed Italian foodie columnists as much with his right-on political stance as with his culinary skills; what's on the plate, though undeniably competent, doesn't always live up to its pretensions.

Let's go outside

Once upon a time the gay scene in Rome was synonymous with outdoor cruising. Older Romans talk about the hedonistic delights available at the **Circo Massimo** (before bushes were uprooted) or inside the **Colosseum** (before railings were put up). In recent years, popular outdoor sites have included the **Monte Caprino** side of the Capitoline hill (pictured), **piazzale Gramsci** by the British Academy and the *galoppatoio* (yes, horse-riding) section of the **Villa Borghese** gardens. Even in these hallowed places, however, lighting has been improved, *pissoirs* demolished and the slash-and-burn deforestation of cruising spots has continued apace.

The exception that proves the rule is Rome's nudist beach, which survives as one of the community's *al fresco* glories. **Il Buco** (the hole) is a short stretch of beach nestling unexpectedly between the family-fun resorts of Ostia and Torvaianica (*see p270*). Gay men and women of all ages flock to the Buco from June to September, to enjoy sun and sand (though unfortunately not the less than crystal-clear sea). Nudism was once the order of the day, but bathing suits are now tolerated. To get there by car take via

Cristoforo Colombo to Ostia, turn left at the coast and drive for about eight kilometres (five miles – an '8km' milestone marks the spot). Alternatively, take the train from the Roma-Ostia Lido station (Metro Piramide) to Lido di Ostia-Cristoforo Colombo, then the 061 bus (summer months only), from outside the station to the last stop. From here it's a 10-15 minute walk.

Alcatraz

Via Aureliana 39, Via Veneto & Villa Borghese (06 482 3650). Metro Repubblica/bus to via XX Settembre. **Open** 10pm-2am Thur-Sun. **Admission** free with Arci Uno Club card (*see p239*). **No credit cards. Map** p323 1B.

Smallish disco cum sex-bar, situated next to the Europa sauna for those who like to go from sweat and steam to, erm, sweat and steam – in one easy move. Neat prison theme (with a mini-labyrinth in the cellar) and a youngish crowd. Hosts Rome Leather Club parties on the last Saturday of the month (October-May), though as this guide went to press, there were plans afoot to shift these events to Qube (*see p257*).

L'Alibi

Via di Monte Testaccio 39/44, Testaccio (06 574 3448). Bus to via Marmorata, via Galvani or lungotevere Testaccio. **Open** 11pm-4.30am Wed-Sun. **Admission** free Wed, Thur, Sun; €7.50/L15,000 Fri (includes one drink); €13/L25,000 Sat (includes one drink). **No credit cards. Map** p325 2B.

The Alibi paved the way for Testaccio's boom as a quarter with an alternative feel (*see p256*) and is still one of Rome's few full-time gay discos. Just as well it's good. Two floors in winter, three in summer;

the roof garden is its best feature. There's a well-oiled sound system, occasional floor shows and a noticeably competitive atmosphere.

L'Apeiron

Via dei Quattro Cantoni 5, Monti (06 482 8820/ apeironclub@tiscalinet.it). Metro Cavour/bus to via Cavour. **Open** 10.30pm-3am Mon-Sat. **Admission** free with Arci Uno Club card (*see p239*). Compulsory first drink. **No credit cards. Map** p326 1B.

A fuzzy mega-screen, offering everything from MTV to Discovery Channel highlights, dominates the bar and lounge area, though Apeiron's *raison d'être* is downstairs, where a dank ante-room shows porn videos to get punters in the mood for the delights of the darkroom. There are striptease specials most Fridays. A clientele of timid suburbanites and hardened darkroom devotees.

Edoardo II

Vicolo Margana 14, Ghetto (06 6994 2419). Bus to piazza Venezia. **Open** 10.30pm-3am Tue-Sun. **Admission** free, with compulsory first drink. **No credit cards. Map** p324 1A.

This venue relies on the unfortunate Plantagenet king both for its name and its image. The split-level venue, draped in *ersatz* medieval chains, armour and

the like, is popular with a youngish crowd. The bar's one unbeatable attraction, however, is its *centralissimo* location.

Hangar

*Via in Selci 69A, Monti (06 488 1397/
hangaroma@hotmail.com). Metro Cavour/bus to
via Cavour.* **Open** 10.30pm-2am Mon, Wed-Sun.
Closed 3wks Aug. **Admission** free with Arci
Uno Club card (*see p239*). **No credit cards.**
Map p326 1B.

American John Moss has been at the helm of Rome's oldest gay bar since it opened in 1983 (breaking the monotony with his foray into food at the Asinocotto, *see p239*). Hangar maintains its friendly but sexy atmosphere whether it's half full (occasionally midweek) or packed (weekends and for the Monday porn shows). Two bars are linked by a long, dark passage, designed for cruising before consuming. A small dark area is the bar's latest addition.

K Men's Club

*Via Amato Amati 6/8, Suburbs: south (347 622
0462/06 2780 0292). Bus to via Casilina.*
Open 10pm-4am Mon-Thur, Sun; 10pm-5am Fri,
Sat. **Admission** €5.15/L10,000 with annual
membership card (costs €5.15/L10,000).
No credit cards.

Kappa blazed the trail as Rome's first sex and SM cellar, though these days you'd be hard-pushed to find much leather or rubber in this far-flung den of iniquity. The main attraction is still its variety of well-equipped dark areas and the occasional midweek 'total naked' party. If you're after raunch'n'sleaze, then look no further.

Max's Bar

*Via A Grandi 7A, Monti (06 7030 1599). Metro
Manzoni/bus to piazza di Porta Maggiore.* **Open**
10.30pm-3.30am Mon, Tue, Thur, Fri; 10.30pm-5am
Sat, Sun. **Admission** free Mon; €5.16/L10,000 Tue,
Thur, Sun; €7.75/L15,000 Fri; €10.33/L20,000 Sat
(prices include one drink). **No credit cards.**

A stone's throw from one of the city's liveliest transvestite prostitution areas by piazza Vittorio (map p326 1A). Its dancefloor (disco-commercial) and bars are popular with all ages and walks of life, which may explain its bluff, chummy charm, and why it attracts its fair share of Roman bears.

Shelter

*Via dei Vascellari 35, Trastevere (no phone).
Bus to lungotevere Ripa/tram to viale Trastevere.*
Open 9pm-3am daily. **Admission** free, with
free membership card. **No credit cards.**
Map p324 2A.

The atmosphere in this relaxed venue tends towards coffee and chat rather than cruise and choose. One of the few places where gay men and women get together and enjoy company, cocktails and desserts.

Skyline

Via degli Aurunci 26/28, Suburbs: south (06 444 0817/skylineclub@tin.it/www.skylineclub.it). Bus to via Tiburtina. **Open** 10.30pm-2am Tue-Thur; 10.30pm-3am Fri, Sat; 6.30pm-2am Sun. **Admission** free with Arci Uno Club card *(see p239)*. **No credit cards. Map** p153.

A compact club in San Lorenzo. The decor is a strange hybrid, somewhere between military fatigues and stainless steel slick. The crowd is relaxed and mixed, with constant to-ing and fro-ing between the bar and the cruisy balcony and tiny dark areas. The Rome Eagles organises the occasional Saturday leather/bear event while Sunday evenings are dedicated to film shows.

Residencies/one-nighters

Mucca Assassina (Killer Cow), the DJ crew based at the Mario Mieli gay centre, run the largest and best one-nighters around Rome. On Fridays from October to June they're usually at the Qube *(see p257)*, after which they often transfer outdoors to the Buco *(see p240* **Let's go outside)**, although it's worth calling the Mario Mieli centre *(see below)* to check on summer locations and programmes.

The crew mixes a standard disco diet with novelty theme evenings. The success of the Mucca with Roman youth of all sexual orientations has inspired a series of otherwise straight clubs (from the traditional Piper, *see p257,* and the trendy Goa, *see p256,* to the terminally tedious Gilda, *see p256)* to indulge in 'gay' one-nighters. Check local listings for latest bandwagon jumpers.

Saunas

Europa Multiclub

Via Aureliana 40, Via Veneto & Villa Borghese (06 482 3650). Bus to via XX Settembre. **Open** 1pm-2am daily. **Admission** (with Arci Uno Club card, *see p239)* €12.95/L25,000; €10.33/L20,000 after 11pm Fri, Sat. **No credit cards. Map** p323 1B.

Rome's largest and smartest sauna boasts 1,300sq m (4,335sq ft) of gym facilities and pools complete with waterfall features. Leave your togs in the multi-coloured lockers and cruise on down to the steam, sweat, and romantically star-lit booths.

Mediterraneo Sauna

Via Villari 3, Esquilino (06 7720 5934). Metro Manzoni/bus to via Merulana. **Open** 2pm-midnight daily. **Admission** (with Arci Uno Club card, *see p239)* €10.33/L20,000 Mon-Fri; €12.91/L25,000 Sat, Sun. **No credit cards. Map** p326 2A.

Tasteful decor and an emphasis on hygiene distinguish this sauna from many others. The steam room and Jacuzzi provide repose prior to the exertions of the 'relax rooms' on the upper and lower levels.

Information/organisations

There are about 30 gay activist organisations in Italy, mostly in the north. Foremost is the Bologna-based Arcigay network.

Arcigay

Piazza di Porta Saragozza 2, 40123 Bologna (051 644 7054).

Circolo Mario Mieli di Cultura Omosessuale

Via Efeso 2A, Suburbs: south (06 541 3985/fax 06 541 3971/www.mariomieli.it). Metro San Paolo/bus to via Ostiense. **Open** 10am-6.30pm Mon-Fri.

This is the most important gay, lesbian and transgender group in Rome, and a base for debates and events. Its one-nighters, run by Mucca Assassina *(see above)*, are highly popular. The centre also offers a counselling and HIV testing and care facilities.

Leather Club Roma

(338 423 0118 after 6pm daily/www.lcroma.com).

This new group devoted to leather and fetish lifestyles meets on Tuesday at 9.30pm at the Alcatraz *(see p240)* and organises special end-of-month parties. As this guide went to press, plans were afoot to move events to Qube *(see p257)*.

Websites, publications & outlets

For up-to-date information on happenings and events, www.gay.it is the website to consult. Click on 'Lazio' for listings, news and chatrooms in Rome and its surrounding region.

Edicole (newsstands) are often good for gay books and videos. If porn's your bag, try the *edicole* in piazza dei Cinquecento (map p323 1-2A) or at piazza Colonna (map p321 1A). There's a discreet amount of material on display by day; by night, however, piles of the stuff come out.

Aut

A monthly magazine published by the Circolo Mario Mieli *(see above)*. Interesting articles and an up-to-date listings page; available free at many gay venues.

Edizioni Babilonia

Via Astura 8 20141, Milan (02 569 6468/ babilonia@iol.it/www.babilonia.net).

Italy's principal gay publishing house, responsible for a fairly lively monthly magazine, *Babilonia* (€5.16/L10,000 at selected newsstands) which contains a detailed listings guide for the whole of Italy.

Europa 92
*Via Vitelleschi 38/40, Vatican & Prati (06 687
1210). Bus to piazza del Risorgimento.* **Open** 2.30-
7.30pm Mon; 9.30am-1pm, 2.30-7.30pm Tue-Sat.
No credit cards. **Map** p321 1C.
Hard by the Vatican (and the subject of recent controversy), this predominantly gay video shop also
sells magazines and a variety of gadgets.

Libreria Babele
*Via dei Banchi Vecchi 116, Ghetto & campo de'
Fiori (06 687 6628/babelecla@tiscalinet.it). Bus to
corso Vittorio Emanuele.* **Open** 3-7.30pm Mon;
10am-2pm, 3-7.30pm Tue-Sat. **Credit** AmEx, MC, V.
Map p321 2B.
The largest exclusively gay and lesbian bookshop
in Rome. The small space contains a big selection of
books, videos, guides and magazines.

Queer
*Via del Boschetto 25, Monti (06 474 0691/
queer@itelcad.it). Metro Cavour/bus to via Nazionale.*
Open 2.30-7.30pm Mon; 9.30am-7.30pm Tue-Sat.
Credit MC, V. **Map** p326 1B.
This aptly named outlet stocks all manner of books,
magazines, posters, T-shirts and various *objets
d'art.* Also a good place to catch up on last-minute
listings. Well-situated in the increasingly gay
enclave of downtown Monti, with friendly staff.

Lesbian Rome

There are two distinct factions in Roma lesbica.
The older lesbian groups meet at the Buon
Pastore centre (see below), have their roots
in the feminist movement of the 1970s, and
continue to claim separate identity from men,
gay or straight.

Younger lesbians, on the other hand, tend to
join with the less separatist-oriented Arci-Lesbica
association or meet up with the lads at the
Circolo Mario Mieli. Joint ventures like
Mucca Assassina get good turn-outs from
both gay men and lesbians, and the **Shelter**
café is also popular with women.

Although Rome has yet to host a permanent
lesbian club or disco, there are one-nighters and
events for an occasional good night out. Check
the noticeboards at the city's gay and women's
bookshops, stop by the Buon Pastore, or ring
Arci-Lesbica or Circolo Mario Mieli for the
latest happenings.

See also p241 **Shelter** .

Discos, bars & one-nighters

Jolie Cœur
*Via Sirte 5, Suburbs: north (06 8621 5827). Bus to
viale Eritrea.* **Open** 10pm-5am Fri. **Admission**
€10.33/L20,000. **No credit cards.**

Saturday is women's night at this club in the northern suburbs, which now has a karaoke room and billiard table. On the dancefloor, it's strictly techno. A
friendly atmosphere, and no men allowed.

La Stanza dei Frutti Rubini
*Via Efeso 2A, Suburbs: south (06 541 3985). Metro
San Paolo/bus to via Ostiense.* **Open** from 9.30pm
Thur. **Admission** free. **No credit cards.**
Laid-back women-only event at Circolo Mario Mieli.

Le Sorellastre
*Via San Francesco di Sales 1B, Trastevere
(06 686 4201). Bus to lungotevere della Farnesina.*
Open 7pm-midnight Tue-Sat. **No credit cards.**
Map p324 1C.
Bar and small restaurant within the walls of the his-
toric Buon Pastore women's centre. No men.

Organisations & outlets

Arci-Lesbica Roma
*Via dei Monti di Pietralata 16, Suburbs: north
(06 4180211/www.women.it/arcils/roma). Metro
Tiburtina/bus to via Tiburtina.* **Open** for events.
Often working in close association with the Mario
Mieli group (*see p242*), Arci-Lesbica offers a helpline
and organises midweek get-togethers, country
walks, pub evenings and occasional residencies at
local nightspots: phone for information.

Collegamento tra le lesbiche italiane (CLI)
*Buon Pastore, via San Francesco di Sales 1B,
Trastevere (06 686 4201/cli_network@iol.it). Bus
to lungotevere della Farnesina.* **Open** 7.30-11pm Tue.
Map p324 1C.
Formed in 1981, this separatist group meets in the
Buon Pastore women's centre in Trastevere once
a week to discuss politics. It's strictly women-only,
but you don't need to be a member to take part.
Organises conferences, literary evenings, concerts,
dances, holidays and an annual masqued ball. The
Coordinamento Lesbiche Romane, little sister of the
CLI, meets here on Wednesdays (7-9pm).

Libreria delle Donne: Al Tempo Ritrovato
*Via dei Fienaroli 31D, Trastevere (06 581 7724/
libreriadelledonne@libero.it). Bus or tram to viale
Trastevere.* **Open** 3.30-8pm Mon; 10am-1.30pm, 3.30-
8pm Tue-Sat. **Credit** MC,V. **Map** p324 2B.
Bookshop with a well-stocked lesbian section
(including some titles in English) and a helpful,
information-packed noticeboard. Also organises
debates, meetings and book presentations.

Zipper Travel Association
*Via Castelfidardo 18, Monti (06 488 2730/
www.zippertravel.it). Metro Castro Pretorio/bus to
piazza Indipendenza.* **Open** 9.30am-6.30pm Mon-Fri.
Credit MC, V. **Map** p323 1A.
The only travel agency in Italy offering customised
travel for gay women.

Music: Classical & Opera

Fresh springs of energy make classical music better every year.

In many ways, Rome is a victim of its own extraordinary range of attractions: it just doesn't work hard enough to sell itself. Nowhere is this more true than in its music scene, where fresh springs of energy bubble so quietly to the surface that few people seem to know or notice that classical music in Rome is getting better every year.

Yes, it's true that Renzo Piano's state-of-the-art auditorium (*see p29, p246*) – to be called, perhaps, **Spazio** – was still, as this guide went to press, a massive building site, and unlikely, realistically speaking, to be ringing to the sound of music before 2003-2004 at the very earliest. But new-millennium pride – and precious extra funding – have prodded previously semi-conscious institutions into action, and there's every chance of catching top-class international events at Rome's (relatively) modest prices.

THE SCENE

The top job in the city's musical scene is the directorship of the Accademia Nazionale di Santa Cecilia, Italy's most prestigious academy, founded in the 16th century by no less a personage than Palestrina. Composer Luciano Berio is the current chairman of the academy and although he is known for being rather inflexible and rigorous in his pursuit of perfection (he is a true contemporary composer), more and more often these days the doors of the Accademia's Auditorio Pio are being flung open to 'non-classical' music.

In recent cross-current happenings, it has hosted the likes of Richard Galliano and Michael Nyman. Meanwhile, in-house conductor Myung-Whung Chung has drilled his orchestra mercilessly, elevating it to world standards. He has recently signed a number of prestigious recording contracts.

Arts & Entertainment

RomaEuropa Festival

From its humble, if stylish, origins in 1986 as a small summer happening at the Villa Medici – the French academy, see p81 – the RomaEuropa Festival has mushroomed to become Rome's trendiest, most prestigious performing arts festival, offering a packed programme of major international dates through the late summer and autumn.

Its impact on Rome's staid, stuffy theatre- and concert-going public has been dramatic: far from rejecting the ever-more-daring programme as too avant-garde, *romani* en masse have come round to the idea that the place to be seen is amid the contemporary cutting edge. So it's on with the high heels and designer togs, and off for a bit of cross-cultural contamination.

Globalisation is the philosophy behind this slew of ethnic events and multimedia performances: East meets West and old meets new in dance and dance/theatre happenings, and in events where the concept of 'music' is pushed to its limits. So high has the Festival's profile become, that big names are drawn to the Eternal City: Peter Sellars, Bob Wilson and Heiner Goebbels are just a few of the recent highlights. But the Festival also caters to hedge-sitters – those music-lovers who like loads of atmosphere and tunes they can sink their teeth into. Because of that, there are ancient music concert cycles and a host of events staged against backdrops of some of Rome's most beautiful sights and monuments.

Tickets can be purchase by credit card on the tollfree number, or directly at the individual venues. Check local press or the festival's website for programme details.

RomaEuropa Festival
Via XX Settembre 3 (06 4890 4024/tollfree 800 795 525/fax 06 4890 4030/ www.romaeuropa.net). **Box office** at individual venues. **Credit** AmEx, MC, V.

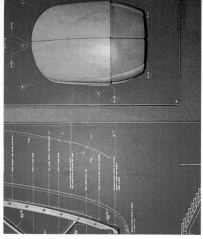

Plans for **Spazio**. *See p246.*

Santa Cecilia also continues to attract some of the world's greatest conductors for its symphonic season. World-class musicians such as Mstislav Rostropovich and Vladimir Ashkenazy come back repeatedly. Wonderful chamber music orchestras such as Philip Pickett's English Consort and Gidon Kremer and his Kremerata Baltica are also frequent guests in the Eternal City, although most Romans are unaware they've passed through.

Berio has also embraced and injected fresh energy into a pre-existing initiative to organise brief monothematic festivals dedicated to individual artists, and has pulled off extravagant successes like getting the entire Berliner Philarmonisches Orchester – conducted by Claudio Abbado – over for an intense week in mid-season. (Note that for world-class events such as this, prices rise to international levels accordingly.)

Besides Santa Cecilia, many other institutions, large and small, make their voices heard to those attentive enough to listen. One of those voices comes from the **Accademia Filarmonica Romana** (information 06 320 1572; www.filarmonicaromana.org), founded in 1821. It's smaller and newer than Santa Cecilia (in Roman terms being nearly 200 years old is practically adolescent), but boasts composers like Rossini, Donizetti, Paganini and Verdi among its founders. It offers a varied programme of chamber music, ancient music, ballet and chamber opera. It is also particularly active in co-producing large multi-media events with big-name stage directors such as Bob Wilson and modern composers like Philip Glass, who has become a habitué on the stage of the Accademia's own venue: the **Teatro Olimpico**.

Another major concert provider is the **Istituzione Universitaria dei Concerti** (information 06 361 0051; www.concertiiuc.it/bigliet.htm), founded after World War II to inject some life into Rome's then culturally dead campus. Today the IUC offers a varied season with a core programme of often outstanding – and often experimental – international and Italian recitals and chamber music at Rome University's main auditorium, the rather stark **Aula Magna**. IUC serves a mixed audience with a series of afternoon and evening concerts, the former mostly attracting a faithful audience of long-time subscribers, the latter most popular with astute music lovers.

The newly restored 16th-century **Oratorio del Gonfalone** (information 06 687 5952), with its glorious late-Renaissance and early-baroque frescos, hosts a chamber music season that reflects the joyful personality of its director, Angelo Persichilli. Each and every concert and recital on the programme, which runs from October to June, seems to have been lovingly chosen to fit the beautiful surroundings, and to show off the magnificent 18th-century organ.

Of course, Rome's contemporary music scene also is worthy of mention. Many contemporary Italian composers are highly regarded on an international level. And although many of their performances take place in Milan and Turin, Rome also holds its own. The **Centro Ricerche Musicali** (information 06 446 4161; www.crm-music-org), headed by eclectic composer Michelangelo Lupone, is at the forefront of scientific research into electronic sound. Lupone and his technical team are not only the brains behind the sophisticated new computers that generate elaborate sound, they are also the most daring in organising highly intellectual events and conferences.

Then there's Rome's **Teatro dell'Opera**. Acoustically, it is close to perfect and singers claim to love it. But the state-run institution is still struggling to overcome decades of scandalously poor administration and political misdeeds that have left it with a staggering financial deficit and an even worse reputation. Though lately the foundering facility seems to have achieved a less perilous position, its situation is nonetheless shaky, and conductors come and go, leaving the orchestra constantly rebuilding, but never seeming to get ahead. As this guide went to press, Gianluigi Gelmetti was at the helm. Working hand-in-hand with super-bureaucrat Francesco Ernani, Gelmetti is managing to serve up a dignified bill of fare. Belt-tightening forced Ernani to cut down on opulent new opera productions, so he has opted to fill the house with many smaller – often contemporary – offerings such as opera

Myung-Whung Chung conducts. *See p244.*

tryptichs, ballets and concerts as well as some larger co-productions with other Italian opera houses. The season, from January to July, includes about five full-fledged operas plus a host of other events. Top-name singers rarely stay around after the opening night, so keep an eye on cast lists for second-rate substitutes, and check the reviews before committing yourself by buying tickets.

Auditoria

Auditorio Pio – Santa Cecilia

Via della Conciliazione 4, Vatican & Prati (06 6880 1044/www.santacecilia.it). Bus to piazza Pia. **Concerts** Oct-June. **Box office** *Oct-June* 11am-6pm Mon, Tue, Thur-Sun; until interval on concert days. *July-Sept* 11am-6pm Mon-Fri. **Credit** MC, V. **Map** p321 1C.

Since it was first rented from the Vatican in 1958, this has been the 'temporary' home of the Accademia Nazionale di Santa Cecilia concert series. Bearing more resemblance to an oversized school hall than a concert hall, its acoustics have been tinkered with and greatly improved over the years, but few will be sorry to leave when the new auditorium (*see below*) is complete. It's worth spending more for good seats: tickets for single concerts are sold in two phases: from mid-October (Oct-Jan concerts) and from February (Feb-June concerts), and can be booked online.

Aula Magna dell'Università la Sapienza

Piazzale Aldo Moro, Esquilino (information 06 361 0051/fax 06 3600 1511/segreteria.iuc@concertiiuc.it/www.concertiiuc.it/bigliet.htm). Metro

Policlinico/bus or tram to viale Regina Elena. **Concerts** Oct-Apr. **Box office** up to one hour before concerts. **Credit** MC, V.

With its kitsch Fascist decor, but reasonable acoustics, the Aula Magna is the principal auditorium for the IUC season (*see p245*). Tickets can be purchased at the Aula Magna up to one hour before concerts, at agencies (*see p222*) or online.

Spazio

Via P de Coubertin, Suburbs: north (information 06 8069 2295). Bus to piazza Euclide.

Spazio was to be (as this guide went to press) the name of the new concert venue that keeps on promising to become the city's pride and joy, though endless construction delays have given the three-hall auditorium a phantom-like quality. The official date for the opening night currently hovers somewhere between the end of 2002 and the beginning of 2003. If all goes to plan, architect Renzo Piano's baby (*see p29*) should be Rome's greatest architectural and cultural triumph since the 1960s, and – at 55,000sq m (591,397sq ft) – the largest complex of its kind in Europe. Spazio will host Santa Cecilia's (*see above*) symphonic and chamber music seasons as well as the numerous other concerts, performances, multimedia events, ballets, musicals, film festivals and exhibitions that up until now have struggled to find a worthy space. The structure also comprises an open-air central piazza intended – among other things – for rock concerts. Spazio will also house a library, an historical archive with audio and video documents, a Museum of Instruments plus cafés, restaurants, museum shops and music stores.

Teatro Olimpico

Piazza Gentile da Fabriano, Suburbs: north (06 326 5991). Bus or tram to piazza Mancini. **Concerts** Oct-May. **Box office** 11am-7pm daily; from 8pm on concert days. **No credit cards.** **Map** p320 1B.

A very successful cinema conversion has created one of the most functional venues in Rome for all types of performances. It has good acoustics, even in cheaper seats, especially the first central rows of the circle. Owned by the Accademia Filarmonica (*see p245*), it's used for their Thursday concerts and hosts many RomaEuropa Festival (*see p244*) events.

Teatro dell'Opera di Roma

Piazza B Gigli 1, Esquilino (06 481 601/06 4816 0255/www.opera.roma.it). Bus to via Nazionale. **Box office** 9am-5pm Tue-Sat; 9am-1.30pm Sun; until 15 minutes after the beginning of performances. **Credit** AmEx, DC, MC, V. **Map** p323 2B.

The lavish late 19th-century *teatro all'italiana* interior comes as quite a surprise after Mussolini's angular façade and the accompanying tacky potted palms. There are towering rows of boxes, loads of stucco, frescos and gilded everything. Acoustics vary greatly – the higher (and cheaper) seats are unsatisfactory – so splash out on a box; it's part of the experience. Bookings can be made online at www.chartanet.it.

Churches

There is nothing in Rome to compare with the church music tradition of cities like Vienna and London. But not all venues are the same, and some of the city's most famous, and beautiful, churches are dreadful places to hear concerts. Take, for example, **St Peter's** basilica (*see p139*) which has the acoustics of a football stadium and lousy choirs to match. In fact, many of the offerings from the city's churches are less than stellar. Among the city's monasteries and convents, only **Sant' Anselmo** (piazza dei Cavalieri di Malta 5, 06 57 911) manages decent plainchant. Kitsch amplification in places like **San Giovanni in Laterano** (*see p129*) completely destroys the effect. The only truly outstanding church choir is that of the **Russicum** (via Carlo Alberto 2, 06 446 5609), the Eastern Rite church opposite Santa Maria Maggiore, but **Santa Maria degli Angeli** (piazza della Repubblica, 06 488 0812) has become a popular venue for concerts and sacred representations, thanks to its sprawling interior and recently restored ancient organ.

The Festival di Pasqua (*see p248*) often makes use of this interesting church where you can sometimes catch singers like José Carreras or Montserrat Caballé on important church holidays. The church hierarchy does not allow paying concerts in consecrated churches so

events are free and very popular. Make sure you arrive early, or ring ahead to find out if booking is possible. There are also occasional free performances by visiting choirs, so it's worth keeping an eye on posters at church entrances all over the city.

Organ buffs should make a beeline for the splendidly restored 1670s instrument in the church of **San Giovanni de' Fiorentini** (via Acciaioli 2, 06 6889 2059), played for mass at noon on Sundays; and the Luca Blasi organ in **San Giovanni in Laterano** (*see p129*), which is played after 10am mass. There are organ concerts at **San Marcello al Corso** (piazza San Marcello 5, 06 699 301) and **San Carlo ai Catinari** (piazza Cairoli 117, 06 6880 3554).

Minor musical associations

A host of small associations, many of which produce good, solid programmes, are indicative of the wealth of energy and vitality that underlie the official city scene.

See also **Oratorio del Gonfalone** *p245*, **Centro Ricerche Musicali** *p245*, **Concerti nel Tempietto** *p248*.

Associazione Musicale Romana

(Information 06 686 8441/06 3936 6322/ fax 06 3936 6229/amr.it@agora.stm.it/ www.agora.stm.it/amr/). **Concerts** July. **Box office** at venues before concerts. **No credit cards.**

Claudio Abbado had an intense week at **Santa Cecilia**. *See p246.*

Arts & Entertainment

The AMR presents an interesting summer season in the Orto Botanico (see p115). Programmes include Gershwin and Piazzola as well as mainstream chamber music.

Associazione Nuova Consonanza

(Information 06 3741277/fax 06 372 0026/ info@nuovaconsonanza.it/www.nuovaconsonanza.it. **Concerts** Apr-June, Oct-Dec. **Box office** at individual venues before concerts. **No credit cards**.
The ANC organises the prestigious autumn Festival di Nuova Consonanza, presenting the best in contemporary music. There is also a short spring season, plus lectures and seminars.

Teatro Ghione

Via delle Fornaci 37, Vatican & Prati (06 637 2294/www.ghione.it). Bus to via Gregorio VII. **Box office** 10.30am-9pm daily. **Credit** MC, V.
This plush little red and gold theatre regales its faithful public with extraordinary recitals by legendary – and mostly ancient – perfomers, as part of the Eurmusica Master Series. You can catch the likes of Gyorgy Sandor (Bela Bartok's pupil), Mikhail Pletnov and Fou Ts'Ong, just to name a few. (Just round the corner at Santa Cecilia, see p246, a ticket for the same recital would cost triple the price).

Festivals

Accademia di Santa Cecilia

(Information 06 328 171/toll free 800 907 080/ credit card sales 06 6880 1044/www.santacecilia.it). **Concerts** end June-end July. **Credit** MC, V.
As this is being written, the Accademia's summer venue hung in the balance: it was a toss-up between the Terme di Caracalla (see p126) and its old residence at Villa Giulia (see p83). Both are spectacular venues, the former grandiose and breathtaking, the latter an exquisite Renaissance courtyard. Check local media or the Accademia's website for developments. The series includes international orchestras, along with classical/popular cross-overs, gypsy bands and gospel choirs.

Concerti del Tempietto

(Information 06 8713 1590/fax 06 2332 26360/ tempietto@tiscalinet.it/www.tempietto.com/www.temp ietto.it). **Box office** at venue from 1hr before concerts. **No credit cards**. **Map** p324 2A.
From November to July, Associazione Il Tempietto organises concerts in various city venues, mainly the Complesso del Vittoriano (see p62), the church of San Nicola in Carcere (see p109), or the Aula Adrianea in the ancient Horti Sallustiani (piazza Sallustio 21, see p84) which opens to the public for these events only. In the summer, concerts and recitals move to the Teatro di Marcello (see p109), which was being restored as this guide went to press, and to the lovely art nouveau Casina delle Civette (see p150). It's rather low-level musically, but the season offers a concert or recital practically every evening and the venues are beautiful. Tickets can be booked online.

Festival di Pasqua

(Information 06 6880 9107/8/9/fax 06 6880 9111/ www.festivaldipasqua.it). **Box office** at individual venues before performances. **Season** around Easter. **No credit cards.**
The Easter Festival is an annual event organised by the city council in conjunction with the Associazione Arte in Comune. As part of its offerings, free concerts take place in churches and theatres across Rome over the Easter holidays.

Teatro dell'Opera

Piazza B Gigli 1, Esquilino (06 481 601/ www.opera.roma.it). Bus to via Nazionale. **Box office** 9am-5pm Tue-Sat; 9am-1.30pm Sun. **Season** July-Aug. **Credit cards** AmEx, DC, MC, V. **Map** p323 2B.
Since 1997, when the it was banished from its traditional summer home in the Terme di Caracalla (see p126), the opera's outdoor season has never really settled, as it keeps trying out different – and generally unsatisfactory – venues around the city. The Stadio Olimpico football stadium (see p259) continues to host opera productions, but it is sadly uninspiring; the field in the far-flung eastern suburb of Tor Vergata that has been assigned to the Opera for 2001 may work better. Check local media or the Teatro's website for performance details.

Out of town festivals

Festival dei Due Mondi

Piazza Duomo 8, 06049 Spoleto (0743 44 700/06 808 8352/tollfree bookings 800 907 080/tollfree information 800 565 600/www.spoletofestival.it). **Season** end June-mid July. **Credit** AmEx, MC, V.
Perhaps Italy's most famous performing arts festival, and certainly its most international, Spoleto is now recovering some of the dynamism of its early years. Founded over 40 years ago by Gian Carlo Menotti, and now under the direction of his son Francis, it has always showcased modern opera, theatre, film and music, but now includes almost everything from gypsy horse shows to grand opera, visual art and even science. Check the highly informative and efficient website for programmes and booking.

Festival Pontino

Castello Caetani, Sermoneta/Abbazia di Fossanova, Priverno (information 0773 605 551/bookings 0773 480 672/fax 0773 605 548/www.festivalpontino.it). **Season** end June-early July. **No credit cards**.
Composer Goffredo Petrassi always draws excellent musicians from all over Europe to his small-scale festival of orchestral and chamber music in two outstandingly beautiful venues: the medieval Castello Caetani in the pretty hill town of Sermoneta south of Rome, and the abbey of Fossanova, one of central Italy's few 'real' Gothic churches. A contemporary music festival also takes place in June. Ticket sales are at the door only.

Nightlife & Music

Take a step back in time… but not too far.

If you've just flown in from New York or London, you may feel you've stepped back in time… by a year or so, at least. But with patience (a necessary virtue in dealing with most things Roman) and a little insider information, you'll find everything you need for a lively night out. When it comes right down to it, Rome might not be the world's party capital, but its venues – down age-old alleys and in any number of odd locations – are truly unique.

For details of upcoming events, check out weekly magazines such as *Trovaroma* (out Thursday with the *La Repubblica* daily), *Roma C'e'* (out Friday on newsstands) or the monthly *Time Out Roma*.

NIGHTLIFE

The Roman night out is a sedately paced thing. First, there's the long, slow pizza; then at 11pm, it's time to head off to a disco bar; only after that will Romans take in a club or two. Around 1am a happy crowd forms to see the night through and finish it up in the early hours at a bar serving hot *cornetti* (croissants) and sandwiches to bed-bound clubbers.

As in most countries, Fridays and Saturdays are the busiest nights, with clubs and bars churning out commercial and Eurodisco sounds. For something a bit alternative, head for **Agatha** at **Brancaleone** (Friday), or **Bluecheese** at **Ex-Bocciodromo** (Saturday).

Feeling more transgressive? The **Mucca Assassina** crew, accompanied by stunning drag queens, take over one of Rome's biggest clubs – **Qube** – each Friday. To get off the beaten track, head for one of Rome's *centri sociali*: highly recommended during the summer when drinking cheap, cold beer while listening to music out under the stars can be a real treat.

LIVE MUSIC

Rome has always lacked proper venues for big musical events; consequently many big stars never make it south of Milan. Sport stadiums do host large-scale concerts, but sadly, these are marred by bad sound quality and tight noise restrictions; the only exception is the **Palacisalfa**, where bands like the Beastie Boys have played recently with satisfactory results. Smaller bands fare much better, thanks to *centri sociali* and clubs committed to promoting new sounds.

Winter is the season for local bands. Watch out for Almamegretta with their mixture of Neapolitan dialect and Afro-Arab influences; Tiromancino for melodic rock; clever, ironic songwriter Daniele Silvestri; indie-rockers Marlene Kuntz who recently worked with Skin from Skunk Anansie; Snafu, an energetic dub trip-hop band; and Ikebana with their sophisticated electro sound.

Jazz has few, but excellent, icons, including Antonello Salis and Roberto Gatto who performs weekly at the **Big Mama**.

The long hot Roman summer has more to offer. Clubs close their winter quarters and move to open-air spaces; festivals take off and international stars are more likely to play in the Eternal City. Keep an eye on wall posters and on the local press for events information. For where to buy concert tickets, *see p222*.

WHERE TO GO

Testaccio (*see p119 and p256*) is one of Rome's liveliest quarters: you'll be spoilt for choice. Just take a walk around and you'll find the vibe you're looking for.

The fashionable crowd heads for the *centro storico*: an evening sipping wine in **campo de' Fiori** (*see p101*) or the **triangolo della Pace** (*see p92*), and you're part of trendy Roman life.

San Lorenzo (*see p152*) is less pretentious: in this university quarter drinks are cheap, and there's always something new going on.

Trastevere (*see p110*) has lovely alleys packed with friendly, crowded bars. If you're longing for company and your Italian's weak, then this is the place for you: English is the *lingua franca*.

GETTING THROUGH THE DOOR

Romans love saving money on entrance fees, and make a point of cosying up to PR people or door staff to get their names on guest/discount lists. Many clubs admit women free before midnight.

Admission tickets include usually one 'free' drink. Subsequent drinks are generally quite pricey, presumably to compensate for the Roman habit of making one drink last all evening.

Often you will have to pay for a *tessera* (membership card) on top of the entrance fee: this is the law, and *tessere* can be valid for a season or even for a few years.

Live music venues: large events

Palacisalfa

Viale dell'Oceano Atlantico 271, suburbs: EUR (06 5728 8024/www.palacisalfa.com). Bus to viale dell'Oceano Atlantico. **Open** depends on event. **Admission** depends on event. **No credit cards.**
This large new venue on the very southern edge of EUR (*see p153*) is an indoor sports hall. It has better acoustics than Palaeur (*see below*), its older rival as a sports-cum-concerts venue, and is slightly less cavernous. Now a major venue for big-name acts.

Palaeur

Piazzale dello Sport, suburbs: EUR (See local press for information). Metro EUR Palasport/bus to Palazzo dello Sport. **Open** varies with event. **Admission** varies with event. **No credit cards.**
Until recently, Nervi and Piacentini's saucer-shaped Palaeur (built for the 1960 Olympics, and also known as the Palazzo dello Sport) was the only megastar-sized venue in town – which never stopped (and still doesn't stop) smaller acts playing it, often with disastrous results. The acoustics are appalling, and it's slightly less atmospheric than an empty aircraft hangar.

Live music venues: small-to-medium events

Akab/Cave

Via di Monte Testaccio 68/69, Testaccio (06 575 7494). Bus to via Marmorata or via Galvani/tram to via Marmorata. **Open** 10pm-4am Wed-Sat. **Admission** €7.76-€12.90/L15,000-L25,000 (incl 1 drink). **No credit cards. Map** p325 2A.
Situated near the Mattatoio (*see p121*), this club has two levels with the underground Cave featuring music from black to R&B, commercial and house. Very busy Saturdays. Avoid the long queue by making friends with the English-speaking bouncers.

Alpheus

Via del Commercio 36, Testaccio (06 574 7826). Metro Piramide/ bus to via Ostiense. **Open** Sept-June 10.30pm-4am Tue-Sun. *July, Aug* 10pm-4.30am Fri, Sat. **Admission** free Tue; €5.16/L10,000Wed, Thur, Sun; €7.75/L15,000 Fri, Sat. **Credit** AmEx.
Once a cheese factory, the Alpheus has three big halls (Mississippi, Momotombo and Red River) featuring live gigs, music festivals, theatre and cabaret followed by disco. The music varies every night: rock, Latin, world music, revival, happy trash and black. Women get in free till midnight.

Circolo degli Artisti

Via Casilina Vecchia 42, suburbs: south (06 7030 5684). Bus to via Casilina or piazza D Pigneto. **Open** 9pm-3am Tue-Sun. **Admission** varies with event; 6-month membership €5.17/L10,000. **No credit cards.**

A huge exhibition hall hosts live music, disco and more in a club that is much-loved by the university crowd. Killa night, Shampista night and Movie night are just a few of the events that attract swarms of eager punters into the Circolo's large garden during the heat of the Roman summer; dancing under the stars makes everything (and everybody) look surreal.

Frontiera

Via Aurelia 1051, suburbs: west (06 6618 0110). **Open** 9pm-late Thur-Sun. **Admission** varies with event. **No credit cards.**
This is one of the few places where big names play their gigs. After live bands there's always a DJ set. You'll need a car to get there; it's beyond the Grand Raccordo (ring road) on the via Aurelia.

Horus Club

Corso Sempione 21, suburbs: north (06 8689 9181). Bus to piazza Sempione. **Open** 9pm-3am Wed-Sat. **Admission** from €10.33/L20,000, depending on event. **Credit** AmEx, DC, MC, V.
Once a cinema, this big venue in the north of Rome features good concerts, and parties with famous DJs. The schedule is eclectic and the style varies: check it out for big names.

Il Locale

Vicolo del Fico 3, Pantheon & piazza Navona (06 687 9075). Bus to corso Vittorio Emanuele or corso Rinascimento. **Open** Oct-May 10pm-4am Tue-Sat. Closed June-Sept. **Admission** €3.61-€5.16/L7,000-L10,000. **No credit cards. Map** p321 2B.
This is the place to go to for the most interesting local bands and theatre performances. Its goal is to promote original songwriting. Many famous bands and singers started their careers here; once in a while they come back, attracting more-than-capacity audiences to this small club.

Palladium

Piazza Bartolomeo Romano 8, suburbs: south (06 5160 1077). Metro Garbatella. **Open** varies with event. **Admission** varies with event. **No credit cards.**
In the heart of the down-home Garbatella quarter (*see p152*), the Palladium has excellent sound quality and is favoured by big-name bands when they call in on Rome: Blur played here recently. It is also the venue for festivals and special parties (including a great New Year's Eve bash) too: check the local press or phone for details.

La Palma

Via Giuseppe Mirri 35, suburbs: south (06 4359 9029). Metro Tiburtina/bus to via Tiburtina. **Open** 10pm-2am daily. **Admission** varies with event; one-year membership €1.55/L3,000. **Credit** MC, V.
This beautifully located club is like an oasis in the desert. Live bands are selected according to La Palma's strict taste criteria: new jazz, avant-garde rock and ethnic music, followed by a DJ set.

Il Locale: a launchpad for musical talent. *See p250.*

Live music venues: *centri sociali*

These throw-backs to a hippier age blossomed two decades ago when a few committed people occupied abandoned, publicly owned buildings in order to create spaces that would be open to anyone interested in making art and music, or organising cultural events, all without spending a fortune.

A small donation (usually €2.58/L5,000) gives you access to this world, where some of Rome's best and cheapest night-time entertainment is to be had. Once secret and illegal, *centri sociali* are now tolerated thanks to a special law which stopped police breaking in every now and again. Neighbours, however, remain hostile.

Brancaleone

Via Levanna 11, suburbs: north (06 8200 0959/www.brancaleone.it). Bus to piazza Sempione. **Open** 10.30pm-5am Wed-Sat. **Admission** donation of €2.51-€5.16/L5,000-L10,000 expected; concerts may cost more. **No credit cards**.

This is the best-run of the *centri sociali*, with a cinema, recording studio and courses in photography, yoga and shiatsu, to mention but a few. The big club

section hosts one of Rome's most exciting nights on Friday with Agatha, now legendary for its innovative music selection and famous guests, including Goldie, Sonic Youth and Roni Size.

Forte Prenestino

Via Delpino, suburbs: east (06 2180 7855/ www.forteprenestino.net). Bus/tram to via Prenestina. **Open** Most nights; times vary, call to check. **Admission** donation of €2.51/L5,000 expected. **No credit cards**.

This 19th-century fortress is a labyrinth of different atmospheres. Weekends are for dancing, with reggae, drum 'n' bass and two-step. In summer, the big courtyard hosts festivals and open-air DJ sets.

Villaggio Globale

Ex Mattatoio, lungotevere Testaccio (06 5730 0329/www.ecn.org/villaggioglobale). Bus to lungotevere Testaccio or piazza dell'Emporio. **Open** *Concerts* times vary. *Restaurant* 8pm-1am daily. **Admission** €2.51-€5.16/L5,000-L15,000 depending on event. **No credit cards**. **Map** p325 2B.

Rome's former slaughterhouse is currently due for redevelopment (*see p121*) but, after bitter battles – some of them violent and out on the streets – the Villaggio Globale has been assured that it will be able to continue its activities inside the new-look structure. The huge cattleyard occupied by the Villaggio hosts concerts and courses, and also has a

second-hand bookshop, a tearoom, a darkroom, an Internet service and much more. The *centro* is very attentive to immigrants, and people with little money for cultural pastimes.

Live music venues: jazz

Alexanderplatz

Via Ostia 9, Vatican & Prati (06 3974 2171). Metro Ottaviano/bus to piazza Risorgimento. **Open** *Mid Sept-mid June* 9pm-2am Mon-Sat. Closed mid June-mid Sept. **Admission** 1-month membership €5.16/ L10,000; tourists €2.58/L5,000 with passport. **Credit** AmEx, DC, MC, V.

Highly regarded jazz club offering nightly concerts with famous names from the Italian and foreign jazz scene. Artists like George Coleman and Lionel Hampton are regulars. Dinner is served from 9pm; live music starts at 10.30pm. Reservations recommended.

Big Mama

Vicolo San Francesco a Ripa 18, Trastevere (06 581 2551/www.bigmama.it). Bus/tram to viale Trastevere. **Open** *Oct-June* 9.30pm-1.30am Tue-Sat. Closed July-Sept. **Admission** annual membership €10.33/ L20,000; 1-month membership €5.16/L10,000; extra charge for star acts. **Credit** AmEx, MC, V. **Map** p325 1B.

This is the blues heart of Trastevere where great guitarist Roberto Ciotti plays at least once a week. American songwriters and more international live acts play regularly, guaranteeing a quality night out.

Live music venues: Latin American

Rome has hosted an energetic Latin American colony since the 1970s, and Romans can often be found dancing the night away together with the South American crowd. Salsa and merengue are both very popular. In summer, check out the **Fiesta di Capannelle** (*see p258*): it has only been in existence since the mid-1990s but its fame is growing, and crowds throng there nightly throughout the hottest months.

Caruso

Via di Monte Testaccio 36, Testaccio (06 574 5019). Bus to via Marmorata or via Galvani. **Open** *Sept-May* 10pm-3am Tue-Sun. *June* 10pm-3am Thur-Sat. Closed July, Aug. **Admission** €7.75/L15,000 Tue-Thur, Sun; €10.33/L20,000 Fri, Sat. **No credit cards. Map** p325 2A.

A must for lovers of Latin sounds. From Tuesday to Saturday there's live music with La Banda du Pelo, followed by salsa and merengue. On Sunday, Arab night makes for an exotic atmosphere.

No Stress Brasil

Via degli Stradivari 35, Trastevere (06 5833 5015). Bus/tram to viale Trastevere. **Open** 8.30pm-2am Mon-Sat. **Admission** free Mon-Wed; €7.75/L15,000 Thur, Fri (incl 1 drink); €10.33/L20,000 Sat (incl 1 drink). **Credit** MC, V. **Map** p325 2B.

This restaurant and disco is full of Brazilian tastes and colours. There's live music every night, with Brazilian bands and dancers. After the live acts move off-stage, well-known DJs often entertain the crowd until dawn.

Discobars & clubs

See also *p250* **Akab/Cave**; *p250* **Alpheus**; *p251* **Brancaleone**; *p250* **Circolo degli Artisti** ; *p251* **Forte Prenestino**; *p251* **Villaggio Globale**.

L'Alibi

Via di Monte Testaccio 40/47, Testaccio (06 574 3448). Bus to via Marmorata or via Galvani. **Open** 11pm-4am Wed-Sun. **Admission** free Wed, Thur, Sun; €7.75/L15,000 Fri, Sat. **No credit cards. Map** p325 2B.

This gay club becomes more hetero-tolerant during the summer months, when the glorious roof terrace is opened up. There's live music upstairs, and generally a more mixed crowd: the basement has a great sound system, thumping out house hits and '70s and '80s classics. *See also chapter* **Gay**.

Alien

Via Velletri 13-19, suburbs: north (06 841 2212). Bus to piazza Fiume. **Open** *Sept-May* 11pm-4am Tue,Thur-Sun. *June, July* 11pm-4am Fri, Sat. Closed Aug. **Admission** €10.33-€15.49/ L20,000-L30,000. **Credit** AmEx, DC, MC, V. **Map** p322 2A.

This popular clubs keeps crowds of under-25s happy with a solid diet of house and revival. Saturday is gay night, with separate rooms for men and women and fashion shows.

Anima

Via dell'Anima 57, Pantheon & piazza Navona (06 686 4021). Bus to corso Vittorio Emanuele or corso del Rinascimento. **Open** *Sept-June* 11pm-4am Tue-Sun. Closed July, Aug. **Admission** free Tue; €5.16/L10,000 Wed, Thur, Sun (incl 1 drink); €7.75/ L15,000 Fri, Sat (incl 1 drink). **No credit cards. Map** p321 2B.

Heavy on the funk and house, this is more bar than disco. It's very close to piazza Navona, and often so crowded that you'll be lucky if you've got space enough to raise a drink to your lips. You'll be glad if you can, however, as it offers an excellent selection of cocktails.

Black Out

Via Saturnia 18, suburbs: south (06 7049 6791/ www.blackoutrockclub.com). Metro Re di Roma/bus to piazza Tuscolo. **Open** *Sept-June* 10pm-3am Thur-Sat. Closed July, Aug. **Admission** €7.75/L15,000. **No credit cards. Map** p327 2A.

Coldly post-industrial, the Black Out nonetheless keeps its crowd warm with rock, indie and a bit of goth, plus the punk and heavy metal that was its mainstay through the 1980s and '90s. A visit here can be a trip down memory lane.

Arts & Entertainment

The eclectic **Classico Village**.

Classico Village
Via Libetta 3, suburbs: south (06 5728 8857/
06 5728 8793) Bus to via Ostiense. **Open** *Oct-May*
10pm-2am. *June, July, Sept* 10pm-2am Fri, Sat.
Closed Aug. **Admission** varies with event.
No credit cards.
This eclectic club has theatre, music, short-movie
festivals, poetry and exhibitions. It has a number of
rooms: the biggest with a stage for live acts, the
groove room for house and garage, and the loft with
an exotic atmosphere and a strong whiff of incense.

Il Controlocale
Via dei Santi Quattro103, Celio (347 447 8167).
Metro Colosseo/bus or tram to piazza del Colosseo.
Open 10.30pm-3am daily. Closed Aug. **Admission**
€2.58-€5.16/ L5,000-L10,000. **No credit cards**.
Map p326 2B.
Music's the thing in this bar where a bright red stage
hosts an eclectic choice of quality bands. Bio-snacks
can be washed down with good Italian wines.

Dome Rock Café
Via D Fontana 18, Celio & San Giovanni (06 7045
2436). Bus or tram to piazza San Giovanni. **Open**
Sept-mid July 10pm-3am daily. Closed mid July-Aug.
Admission free. **No credit cards**. **Map** p326 2A.

Great pub with live acts three times a week, and DJ
sets playing funky jungle, Brit pop, black and ska
on Wednesday. Nicely crowded over the weekends.

Ex-Bocciodromo
Via di Monte Testaccio 23, Testaccio (06 5728
8312/www.bluecheese.it). Bus to via Galvani/
tram to via Marmorata. **Open** 11pm-4am Thur-
Sat. **Admission** €2.58-€3.61/L5,000-L7,000.
No credit cards. **Map** p325 2B.
Open on Fridays for electronic vibes, the Ex-
Bocciodromo really comes into its own on Saturdays
with the gem of Roman nightlife: Bluecheese. This
club took shape in 1998 with an open-air dancefloor
and two or three DJs experimenting with new styles.
It now boasts two rooms: the bigger one has brakes,
drum & bass and visual effects; the smaller one is
for funk and rare grooves. But there's more: once a
month Bluecheese plays host to independent labels
from London and what are usually excellent DJ sets.
Guests have included Orb, DJ Food, Aphrodite,
Aquasky and Apachi 61. And it all comes dead
cheap, as the Blue Cheese mission is to spread good
sounds at rock-bottom prices… but the word is out,
so expect long, long queues. Once you do get in, have
a few drinks at the iron-cage bar.

Testaccio

A small village within the big city, Testaccio (*see also p119*) is a homely place where everyone knows everyone else, where the covered fruit and vegetable market is a lively, noisy community centre, and where local traditions are strong.

But beyond this salt-of-the-earth façade lies another Testaccio: an after-dark Testaccio packed with restaurants, pulsating with nightlife, where wine bars and clubs stay open until the small hours and where venues are truly unique.

This working-class district was constructed between 1873 and 1883 around an odd protruberance known as the Monte dei Cocci (Shard Hill). Locals dug deep into the base of that hill – an accumulation of broken fragments of amphorae unloaded at the Roman port nearby – to create cellars for storing wine. It's here, in this ancient rubbish dump, that the bulk of Testaccio's clubs are concealed.

From the dump to the slaughterhouse: Testaccio's *mattatoio* was fully operational until 1975, after which it went into a decline. But the western side of this abbatoir now hosts the **Villaggio Globale** (*see p251*), as well as horses that draw Rome's tourist carriages; the eastern part plays host to the twice-yearly Biennale dei giovani artisti europei, with photographs, paintings, videos and installations by young artists from all around Europe.

For a perfect night out in this ever-exciting neighbourhood, start with a glass of wine in the **Enoteca Palombi** (piazza Testaccio 38/42, 06 574 6122, closed Sun) where excellent vintages are served by the glass at fair prices. When hunger sets in, head for **Da Oio a Casa Mia** (via Galvani 43/45, 06 578 2680, closed Sun, average €23.24/ L45,000) which serves Roman dishes in a relaxed atmosphere (*see also chapter* **Eating Out**).

Ready to dance? It's an arduous choice: **Akab/Cave** (*see p250*) is a trendy venue; **Caruso** (*see p253*) serves up Latin sounds; **Radio Londra** (*see p257*) offers table dancers; and the **Ex-Bocciodromo** (pictured, *see p255*) provides a cool alternative scene. If you can't decide, just settle for a walk, and get closer to the soul of Rome through the warm colours, the peeling façades and the friendly residents of Testaccio.

Ex-Magazzini

Via Magazzini Generali 8 bis, Testaccio (06 575 8040). Bus to via Ostiense. **Open** 9pm-4.30am daily. Closed June-Aug. **Admission** €5.16-€7.75/L10,000-L15,000. **No credit cards.**
This is a trendy disco bar, that frequently produces new events. Downstairs it offers live music three times a week, theatre, disco and a vintage market on Sundays; upstairs are drinks and drummers.

The Gallery

Via della Maddalena 12, Pantheon & piazza Navona (06 687 2316/www.thegallery.it). Bus to via del Corso. **Open** 7.30pm-3am Tue-Sun. **Admission** free Tue-Thur, Sun; €5.16/L10,000 Fri, Sat. **Credit** AmEx, MC, V. **Map** p321 1A.
Electric blue and orange dominate this English-style disco bar. Tuesdays are great for trip hop and lounge music; the rest of the week is more commercial, ending with salsa and merengue on Saturdays and Sundays. Excellent cocktails and a huge variety of draught and bottled beers.

Gilda

Via Mario de' Fiori 97, Tridente (06 678 4838/ www.gildabar.com). Metro Spagna/bus to piazza San Silvestro. **Open** 11pm-4am Tue-Sun. Closed June-mid Sept. **Admission** €20.66/L40,000 (incl 1 drink). **Credit** AmEx, DC, MC, V. **Map** p323 1C.
The hangout *per excellenza* of ageing film stars, slimy politicians and would-be groovers with more money than style, Gilda's *habitués* are all there to be photographed for the celebrity gossip rags. All silicone and no soul, this is an extraordinarily Roman experience.

Goa

Via Libetta 13, suburbs: south (06 574 8277).Metro Garbatella/bus to via Ostiense. **Open** 11pm-4am Tue, Thur-Sat. Closed June-Sept. **Admission** €10.33-€15.49/L20,000-L30,000. **Credit** AmEx, DC, MC, V.
In this garage-turned-loft decorated with drapes and ethnic detail, the best Italian and international DJs choose the best music. Goldie has been here a few times, enchanting the trendy crowd. It is sometimes closed on Sundays, so call ahead.

Hang-out

Via Ostiense 131, suburbs: south (06 578 3146). Metro Garbatella/bus to via Ostiense. **Open** 9pm-2am Thur-Sun. **Admission** €7.75/L15,000. **No credit cards.**
One of the busiest places around via Ostiense, this club is one big hall with different areas to dine, have a drink and dance. Commercial, funky and revival after your pizza must be good for the digestion.

Piper

Via Tagliamento 9, suburbs: north (06 841 4459). Bus to via Tagliamento or corso Trieste. **Open** 11pm-4am Thur-Sat. **Admission** €10.33/L20,000 Thur, Fri; €8.26/L16,000 Sat before 8pm, Sun; €15.49/L30,000 Sat after 8pm. **Credit** AmEx, DC, MC, V. **Map** p322 1A.

The Piper has been popular since the 1960s, when it was the coolest place to be for wannabes and pop-stars. Still trading on its glorious past, it's far from trendy now, but still manages to draw a big crowd on Saturdays for its gay-friendly Stomp Night with street rhythms.

Qube

Via di Portonaccio 212, suburbs: east (06 438 5445). Metro Tiburtina/bus to via Tiburtina or via di Portonaccio. **Open** 11pm-4am Thur-Sat. **Admission** €5.16-€10.33/L10,000-L20,000. **No credit cards.**
One of Rome's biggest club venues, Qube's week climaxes on Fridays when the Mucca Assassina (Killer Cow) crew – with its art director, drag queen Vladimir Luxuria – stages another outrageous night. Each week there are new set pieces; light-hearted transgression for a multi-sexual, multi-musical and multi-ethnic crowd.

Radio Londra

Via di Monte Testaccio 65B, Testaccio (06 575 0044). Bus to via Marmorata or via Galvani/tram to via Marmorata. **Open** 9pm-3am Mon, Wed-Sun. **Admission** free Mon, Wed; €5.16/L10,000 Thur, Sun; €7.75/L15,000 Fri; €10.33/L20,000 Sat. **No credit cards. Map** p325 2A.
Listen to rock, blues and dance music while you eat your chips and sandwiches. There are occasional live acts, too.

Late bars

Bars in the centre, especially around via della Pace, tend to stay open well into the morning.

Bar del Fico

Piazza del Fico 26/8, Pantheon & piazza Navona (06 686 5205). Bus to corso Rinascimento or corso Vittorio Emanuele. **Open** 8am-2am Mon-Sat; 6pm-2am Sun. **Credit** AmEx, MC, V. **Map** p321 2B.
Round the corner from Bar della Pace (*see below*), the Fico (the name means fig tree, in honour of an ancient tree in front of the bar) serves good food and drinks, but at a price. Still, the *torte salate* (flans) make a filling brunch.

Bar della Pace

Via della Pace 4, 5, 7, Pantheon & piazza Navona (06 686 1216). Bus to corso Rinascimento or corso Vittorio Emanuele. **Open** 3pm-3am Mon; 9am-3am Tue-Sun. **Credit** AmEx, MC, V. **Map** p321 2B.
A legend of the *centro storico*, the Bar della Pace's pavement tables are the place to see and to be seen, particularly if you wish to establish your credentials as an exclusive, arty type. The drinks are pricey, but the position is unique, and the age-worn building is a perfect background for stylish holiday snaps.

Hemingway

Piazza delle Coppelle 10, Pantheon & piazza Navona (06 686 4490). Bus to via del Corso or corso Rinascimento. **Open** 8.30pm-2am daily. **Credit** AmEx, MC, V. **Map** p321 1A.

This is simply a great bar, and a great place to observe the nightlife scene around the Pantheon. Come back Sunday morning for brunch in a relaxing environment.

Jonathan's Angels

Via della Fossa 16, Panettheon & Piazza Navona (06 689 3426). Bus to corso Rinascimento or corso Vittorio Emanuele. **Open** 8pm-2am Mon; 5.30pm-2am Tue-Sat; 2pm-2am Sun. **No credit cards.** **Map** p321 2B.

The surroundings in this long-established fixture of *centro storico* are astonishing: colours, decorations, paintings of all kinds in happy balance. The owner, an ex-acrobat and stuntman, adds his own magic touch. Every evening after 11pm there's live music.

La Vineria

Campo de' Fiori 15, Ghetto & campo de' Fiori (06 6880 3268). Tram to via Arenula/bus to corso Vittorio Emanuele. **Open** *Mid Oct-mid June* 9.30am-3pm, 5pm-1.30am Mon-Sat. *Mid June-mid Oct* 9am-1am Mon-Sat; 5pm-1am Sun. Closed 10 days Aug. **Credit** AmEx, MC, V. **Map** p324 1B.

Campo de' Fiori is the centre of Roman social life during the summer, and La Vineria (officially Vineria Reggio, and known to old hands as Giorgio's) is the centre, socially speaking, of campo de' Fiori. Any night out might well start off with a glass or two of wine at the Vineria's outside tables, surveying the goings-on of the Campo while making plans for the evening. Winter is less busy outside, but the crowd inside La Vineria will help keep the chill away.

Festivals

The first big event of the outdoor season takes place on 1st May, when Italy's trade unions organise a free concert (*see also p225*) played by any number of Italian – and a sprinkling of international – stars. Traditionally held in piazza San Giovanni (*see p129*), the event moved to a field in the eastern suburbs in 2000, only to return again to its former home in 2001.

The **Estate Romana** (Roman Summer; 06 3600 4399/www.estateromana.caltanet.it), the mother of all Roman festivals, runs from the end of June until the end of September. Music, theatre and movies are on offer outdoors, often in astonishingly beautiful settings. See local media for details. *See also p244* **RomaEuropa Festival**, and **Festa di Noiantri** (*p225*).

Along Came Jazz

Various venues in Tivoli (0774 313 755/0774 331 597/www.alongcamejazz.org). Cotral bus (see p268) from Ponte Mammolo. **Dates** last wk June, first wk July. **Admission** €1.55-€9.30/L3,000-L18,000, varies with event. **No credit cards.**

This jazz festival runs for several days at the beginning of July in Tivoli, 30km (20 miles) to the east of Rome (*see p273*); it features mainly Italian

musicians, such as Antonello Salis, Pino Minafra or Mauro Orselli, with a few international guests like Evan Parker.

Fiesta Capannelle

Via Appia Nuova 1,245, suburbs: east (06 7129 9855/06 7834 6587/06 718 2139/www.fiesta.it). Metro Colli Albani/ bus along via Appia Nuova to Ippodromo Capannelle. **Dates** Mid June-Aug. **Admission** €6.71/L13,000. **No credit cards.**

This huge Latin American-themed festival regularly attracts more than a million people with a mix of performances by names like Khaled, Ziggy Marley, Compay Segundo and Lou Reed; it features four dancefloors, 40 restaurants and 120 stalls selling exotic bits and bobs. There's an exhibition hall with works by South Americans artists and, of course, plenty of salsa and merengue.

Jazz & Image Festival

Villa Celimontana, Celio & San Giovanni (06 7049 5005/06 589 7807). Bus to piazza della Navicella or Colosseum. **Dates** Mid June-Aug. **Admission** from €7.75/L15,000, varies with event. **No credit cards.** **Map** p327 1B.

Organised by the Alexanderplatz jazz club (*see p253*), this festival takes place in the glorious, leafy Villa Celimontana park (*see p128*) on the Celio hill. It's Rome's best outside venue to hear jazz in the summertime: the formal garden is dotted with ancient rubble and trickling fountains, and international and local bands play under the trees. There are also film and video showings.

Roma Incontra il Mondo

Villa Ada, via di Ponte Salario, suburbs: north (06 418 0369). Bus to via Salaria. **Dates** end June-Sept. **Admission** €2.58-€5.16/L5,000-L10,000. **No credit cards.**

Music from around the world echoes through the beautiful Villa Ada park, not far from Villa Borghese (*see p79*), in this truly magical festival.

Roma Estate al Foro Italico

Viale Olimpiadi, largo de Bosis, suburbs: north (06 807 4560/06 8072 625). Bus to lungotevere Maresciallo Cadorna. **Dates** June-mid Aug. **Admission** €5.16/L10,000. **No credit cards.**

Music, theatre and sport all take place in the big concert hall by the tennis stadium. Traditional music pairs up with experimental new bands. Features include food stalls and a kids' area.

Testaccio Village

Viale del Campo Boario, Testaccio (No phone). Bus to piazza dell'Emporio or via Galvani. **Dates** June-Sept. **Admission** €5.16/L10,000. **No credit cards.** **Map** p325 2B.

Many of Testaccio's clubs move outside for the summer season to this quiet area behind Rome's former slaughterhouse. Concerts, which begin at 10pm, include international and Italian rock, jazz, Latin and funk. But come early for food, markets, stalls and bars, and then stay late for the DJs.

Sport & Fitness

If you like to take your sport sitting down, you've come to the right place.

For the average Roman, the idea of personal exercise doesn't arouse much excitement. Even the suggestion of walking, say, from piazza Venezia to the Colosseum causes consternation: distances like that (500 metres, a quarter of a mile) are unthinkable without a scooter. There is a growing gym culture in the city, but this is limited mainly to Italian males seeking to beef up their Latin stud image with appropriate musculature. Romans who exercise with any regularity are few and far between. Workout methods such as yoga and pilates have yet to come in from the extreme fringes of fitness-dom.

This state of affairs is nothing new. Vexed at his fellow countrymen's layabout attitude, Mussolini went all out to promote athleticism in the 1920s and '30s. The concrete results of his campaign are best seen at the sports complexes of the **Foro Italico** in the northern suburbs. However, these facilities are reserved almost exclusively for professional athletes. Sports clubs and gyms in the centre of the city are predominantly private, expensive and not very friendly. Unless you're staying in a top-end hotel with gym facilities, you may find it hard to keep up an exercise regime while visiting Rome.

However, if watching, rather than participating, sounds appealing, you've come to the right place. Rome boasts two first-class football teams, one of which plays at home almost every Sunday from September to June. Going to a match at the **Stadio Olimpico** is a great way to do sport as most Romans do: sitting down.

Football

Like most of their fellow countrymen, Romans are passionate about soccer. A few people play it; many, many more opt for a role as spectator-pontificator. Though any day of the week is good for wild football-related gesticulating and agitated debate, most energy is expended on Sunday, when the 18 teams of Italy's Serie A (Premier League) meet. Two hundred or so players break a sweat, and about 50 million Italians watch them, either at the stadium or on the box, burning off calories in violent physical reactions to referees' bad calls and players' faked injuries.

Rome's two football clubs, AS Roma (www.asromacalcio.it) and SS Lazio (www.sslazio.it), both compete in Serie A. The teams share the Stadio Olimpico, in the Foro Italico complex. City derbies are hotly contested.

Lazio owner Sergio Cragnotti has poured bucketloads of money into his club over recent years, and his investment has paid off. Lazio has emerged as a dominant force in Serie A, putting up such a good fight for the national title, that it became *campione d'Italia* in 2000.

Founded in 1927, Roma has made its touchingly faithful supporters suffer over the years. Since winning the league in 1983, it has managed to clock up a couple of seconds, a third and a fourth place, but the longed-for *scudetto* continued to illude them. As this guide went to press, however, Roma was top of the league and looking set to make its fans very happy indeed.

As with almost everything else in Italy, Roman soccer is politicised: Roma supporters traditionally hail from the left – be it working class or intellectual – while Lazio is seen as the team of the right, drawing support from the wealthy Parioli and Prati districts and the countryside around the city. In the city centre, *romanisti* outnumber *laziali*. And despite their team's two-decade run of bad luck, *romanisti* have no qualms about reminding gloating *laziali* of the 12 years their team spent in Serie B prior to their recent successes.

Tickets can be bought directly from the Stadio Olimpico box office, from the club merchandising outlets listed below, and from Orbis (*see p222*). Once inside the stadium, Lazio fans fill the *curva nord* (north end) with sky blue and white, while the Roma faithful occupy the *curva sud* (south end) red and yellow. The *curve* have the best pyrotechnics and cheapest tickets. For better (and more expensive) seats, ask for the *Tribuna Tevere* or *Tribuna Monte Mario*.

Stadio Olimpico

Viale dello Stadio Olimpico, suburbs: north (06 323 7333). Bus to piazza Mancini or lungotevere Maresciallo Cadorna/tram to piazza Mancini.
If you get off the bus or tram in piazza Mancini, follow the crowds over the Duca d'Aosta bridge across the Tiber to reach the stadium. Tickets cost around €15.49-€61.97/L30,000-L120,000; even the cheap seats have a reasonable view.

Essential accessories

These shops stock a wide range of official club merchandise and sell tickets for matches (cash only) up to seven days in advance:

AS Roma Store

Piazza Colonna 360, Tridente (06 678 6514/06 6920 0642). Bus to piazza Colonna or via del Corso. **Open** 10am-7.30pm Mon-Sat; 10.30am-7pm Sun. **Credit** AmEx, DC, MC, V. **Map** p321 1A.

Lazio Point

Via Farini 34, Esquilino (06 482 6768). Metro Vittorio/bus to piazza Vittorio Emanuele or via Principe Amedeo. **Open** 9am-7pm Mon-Sat. **Credit** AmEx, MC, V. **Map** p323 2A.

Golf

Golf is an exclusive game in Italy. In most clubs, you have to produce a membership card from your home club and proof of your handicap, before being allowed to play. It is not normally necessary to be introduced by a member. Green fees, including those quoted below, are normally charged per day rather than per round.

Circolo del Golf di Roma

Via Appia Nuova 716, suburbs: east (06 780 3407). Metro Colli Albani, then bus 663 or 664. **Open** 8am-sunset Tue-Sun. **Rates** €41.32/L80,000 Tue-Fri; €56.81/L110,000 Sat, Sun. *Driving range* €9.30/L18,000 Tue-Fri; €18.08/L35,000 Sat, Sun (use of range included in green fees). *Club hire* €18.08/ L35,000. **No credit cards.**

At this friendly club in the green belt to the east of the city non-members can take part in competitions on Sundays.

Country Club Castelgandolfo

Via Santo Spirito 13, località Pavona Laghetto (06 931 2301). Metro Anagnina, then taxi/train to Pavona from Termini, then taxi. **Open** 8am-8pm daily. **Rates** €36.15/L70,000 Mon-Fri; €46.48/L90,000 Sat, Sun. *Electric cart hire* €30.99/L60,000 Mon-Fri; €36.15/L70,000 Sat, Sun. *Trolley hire* €5.16/L10,000. *Club hire* €18.08/ L35,000. *Driving range* €5.16/L10,000 (use of range included in green fees). **Credit** AmEx, DC, MC, V.

This course near the Pope's summer residence in the Alban hills to the east of Rome was designed by leading American golf architect Robert Trent Jones inside a (dormant) volcanic crater, and is overlooked by its very distinguished 16th-century clubhouse.

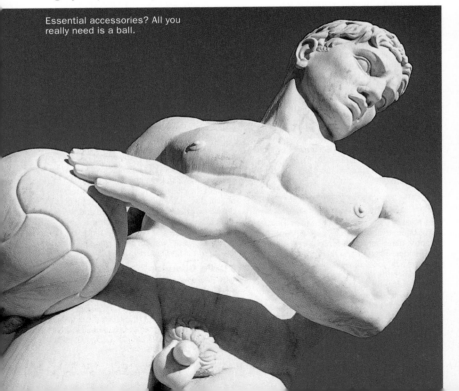

Essential accessories? All you really need is a ball.

The best # Jogging

Crowds of people and omnipresent cars make a jog through the streets of central Rome a decidedly unpleasant experience. So head for a park for your jog or stroll.

Villa Borghese
The dirt tracks and leafy avenues of Rome's most central park welcome joggers of all shapes and sizes, but can be crowded at weekends. **Map** p322.

Villa Pamphili
Popular with locals, this sprawling park just west of the Gianicolo has broad paths and workout stations along the way. **Map** p319.

Villa Ada
Running paths around ponds and lakes make this large park north-east of the centre a haven from the chaos of the city. **Map** p319.

Circo Massimo
Get a taste of ancient Rome while you work up a sweat. The sunken, grassy area of Rome's old chariot track is now a popular place for dog-walkers, frisbee throwers and joggers. **Map** pp326-7.

Terme di Caracalla
Serious runners congregate down the road from the Circo Massimo on the stretches of lawn along via delle Terme di Caracalla, opposite the ancient baths of the same name. **Map** p327.

Gyms

You will need lots of Lycra, a taut, well-exercised and an unseasonably dark tan to blend in at the average Roman gym. You can expect a snobby atmosphere and high prices. The private clubs listed below are slightly more human.

Big Gym
Stadio dei Marmi, Foro Italico, suburbs: north (06 3200712/www.biggym.it). Bus to piazza Mancini or lungotevere Maresciallo Cadorna/tram to piazza Mancini. **Open** *June, July* 9am-midnight . **Rates** €5.16/L10,000; additional charge for some facilities or classes €7.75/L15,000. **No credit cards.**
Through June and July, this venue in the fascist-era Foro Italico is transformed into an outdoor play-ground with all kinds of sports facilities: there's a ski ramp, climbing wall, mountain bike track, volleyball courts, and spinning classes.

Fitness Express by Linda Foster
Via de' Coronari 46, Pantheon & Piazza Navona (06 686 4989/06 686 5248). Bus to via Zanardelli. **Open** 9am-9pm Mon-Fri; 10am-4pm Sat. **Rates** €15.49/L30,000. **No credit cards.** **Map** p321 1B.
Founded by an American, this small, hip, friendly gym (for men and women) near piazza Navona is one of the few in Rome that caters to foreigners. The rate given above allows all-day use of the gym, or attendance at a single fitness class, including yoga, t'ai chi, and pilates.

Roman Sports Center
Viale del Galoppatoio 33, Via Veneto & Villa Borghese (06 320 1667/06 321 8096/06 322 3665). Metro Spagna/bus to via Veneto. **Open** *Nov-May* 9am-3pm daily. Closed June-Oct. **Membership** €1,084.56/L2,100,000 for 15 months; €25.82/L50,000 per day. **Credit** AmEx, DC, MC, V. **Map** p322 2C.
Strictly speaking, you need to be introduced by a member to use the club, but the rules are often waived, and one-day membership is available. 'La Roman' has 8,000 sq m (86,000 sq ft) of facilities, including aerobics studios, saunas, hydromassage pools, weights, cardiovascular machines, squash courts, two Olympic-size swimming pools, and of course, sun beds.

Sporting Palace
Via Carlo Sigonio 21, suburbs: east (06 785 6391/06 788 7910/06 788 7918). Metro Furio Camillo. **Open** 9.30am-10.30pm Mon-Fri, Sun; 9.30am-6.30pm Sat. **Rates** €12.91/L25,000 per day. **No credit cards.**
A bit of a hike from the centre, but easily accessible by metro, this gym has four levels and a full range of equipment and services. Men without spiky, gel-intensive hairdos may feel out of place.

Jogging & running

(*See also p261* **Jogging**).
The Rome City Marathon (*see p224*), held each spring, is slowly making a name for itself in international running circles, although it remains an essentially Roman event. Though a far cry from the London or New York marathons, the race is slowly being adopted by Romans who are recognising its entertainment potential (as opposed to considering it as a totally unwarranted occupation by pesky runners of perfectly good driving space).

Riding

Italy's annual showjumping Grand Prix takes place in one of horse riding's most beautiful arenas, the piazza di Siena, in the leafy surroundings of Villa Borghese (*see p79*). The Concorso Salto Ostacoli (CSIO – international showjumping competition) takes place in May (information 06 3685 8494/www.fise.it).

Arts & Entertainment

Il Galoppatoio

Via del Galoppatoio 25, Via Veneto & Villa Borghese (06 322 6797). Metro Spagna/bus to via Veneto. **Open** 8.30am-6pm Tue-Sat; 8.30am-2pm Sun. Closed Aug. **Rates** sign-up fee €206.58/L400,000 per year; under-18s sign-up fee €51.65/L100,000 per year; ten lessons €154.94/L300,000, plus €18.08/L35,000 insurance; . **No credit cards. Map** p322 2C.
Galloping is not actually allowed at Il Galoppatoio, the only facility for *equitazione* in the city centre. Located deep in the Villa Borghese, the predictably snooty atmosphere is matched by high prices.

Rugby

Rugby in Rome is a subculture, ignored by the mainstream. Those who do play, however, take it seriously. Since 2000, the national side has been competing in the Six Nations Championship; home games are played at the Stadio Flaminio. Rome also boasts a first-class rugby side in RDS Roma, who play their league matches at the Stadio Tre Fontane.

Stadio Flaminio

Viale Tiziano, Suburbs: north (06 3685 7309/06 3685 7848). Bus or tram to via Flaminia.

Stadio Tre Fontane

Via delle Tre Fontane, Suburbs: EUR (06 5922 485/06 592 6610). Metro Magliana/bus to via delle Tre Fontane or piazza dell'Agricultura.

Swimming

Pools are not numerous in the city and, apart from a few far-flung exceptions, those that do exist are privately run. The beaches near Rome are not particularly inviting; you're better off making a day of it and exploring parts of the coast a little further afield (*see p270*).

Alternatively, for relief from the summer heat, make your way to one of the following private pools:

Oasi della Pace

Via degli Eugenii 2, Suburbs: east (06 718 4550). Metro Arco di Travertino, then bus 765. **Open** *Mid June-Sept* 9.30am-6pm daily. Closed Oct-mid June. **Admission** €7.75/L15,000 Mon-Fri; €9.30/L18,000 Sat, Sun. **No credit cards.**
A pleasant open-air pool off the ancient via Appia Antica (*see p146*), surrounded by tall hedges and cypresses. Facilities are fairly simple.

La Piscina delle Rose

Viale America 20, Suburbs: EUR (06 5425 2185). Metro EUR-Palasport/bus to Palasport. **Open** *June-Sept* 9am-7pm daily. Closed Oct-May. **Admission** €9.30/L18,000 full day; €6.71/L13,000 half-day (9am-2pm; 2-7pm); €3.61/L7,000 1-4pm; free for children under 1m tall; 10-day ticket €61.97/L120,000. **No credit cards.**

Rome's largest public pool, in the heart of the EUR district (*see p153*). This outdoor facility has deck-chairs and shady gardens, and often gets crowded.

Hotel pools

Cramped spaces in central Rome mean there are no hotels in the heart of the city with swimming pools. In leafier areas around the outskirts of town, though, there are several hotels, most of them part of international chains, that have pools that can be used by non-residents.

Cavalieri Hilton

Via Cadlolo 101, suburbs: north (06 3509 2950). Bus to piazzale Medaglie D'Oro. **Open** *May-Sept* 9am-7pm daily. Closed Oct-Apr. **Admission** €36.16/L70,000, €18.08/L35,000 under-12s, Mon-Fri; €51.66/L100,000, €25.83/50,000 under-12s, Sat, Sun. **Credit** AmEx, DC, MC, V.
Luxurious hotel pool on the north side of the city with fabulous views down the Monte Mario hill across Rome. Prices include a towel and use of showers; there is one Olympic-size swimming pool, and a smaller pool for children, with hydromassage.

Parco dei Principi

Via Frescobaldi 5, suburbs: north (06 854 421). Bus to via Paisiello or via Mercadante/tram to viale Rossini. **Open** *May-Sept* 9.30am-6pm daily. Closed Oct-Apr. **Admission** €23.24/L45,000 Mon-Fri; €30.99/L60,000 Sat, Sun. **Credit** AmEx, DC, MC, V.
A more centrally located outdoor pool, set in its own gardens on the edge of the Villa Borghese, and much favoured by local swimmers (especially at weekends). There's a 20% discount for children.

Tennis

Every May, Rome hosts the Italian Open tennis tournament, one of the most important European clay court tournaments outside the Grand Slam (*see p225*). It's worth a visit just to see the venue: the fascist-era Foro Italico, a vast sports complex set in the shadow of the Stadio Olimpico and filled with giant (and camp) marble statues of Roman athletes.

Foro Italico

Viale dei Gladiatori 31, suburbs: north (06 3685 8218). Bus to piazza Mancini or lungotevere Maresciallo Cadorna/tram to piazza Mancini.

Circolo della Stampa

Piazza Mancini 19, suburbs: north (06 323 2452). Bus or tram to piazza Mancini. **Open** 9am-11pm Mon-Fri; 9am-8pm Sat, Sun. **Court hire** (for 50mins) *Singles* €9.30/L18,000. *Doubles* €12.40/24,000. *Floodlight fee* (for 50mins) singles €11.37/L22,000; doubles €14.47/L28,000. **No credit cards.**
Owned by the Italian journalists' association, but friendly and open to non-members, the Circolo offers both clay and synthetic grass courts. There's no dress code, but studded trainers are not allowed.

Theatre & Dance

Unique venues, patchy productions.

Rome's theatre and dance scene, while not exactly pushing back any dramatic frontiers, is lively and varied.

The Eternal City has no theatre district like London's West End or New York's Broadway, but the uniqueness of the city's performing halls amply makes up for any lack of geographical concentration: from the opera house-like **Teatro Valle**, with its frescoed ceiling and red velvet boxes, to the **Teatro XX Secolo**, a small space perched above the great Fontanone fountain that splashes mightily atop one of Rome's most magnificent viewpoints on the Gianicolo (see p117).

Watching theatre-frequenting Romans is a treat in itself: at all but the most offbeat productions (of which there are lamentably few) people dress up to the nines for a night at the theatre, especially for the *prima* (première) when stars of stage, screen and politics roll ostentatiously up to claim their freebie tickets.

THEATRE

One recent attempt – by wonder-boy Mario Martone – to break the stodgy trend of 'official' theatre in Rome suffered a set-back when politics raised its ugly head: with right-wing bigwigs baying for his blood, the innovative Neapolitan was forced to quit his post as director of the city-owned **Teatro Argentina** and its offspring, the **Teatro India**.

Outside the 'official' circuit, some 80 theatres provide more stages than any other Italian city where untried actors, directors, and writers can do their (not always top-quality) thing. Some venues can, however, be relied upon to produce fare worth savouring: the **Teatro Ghione** (see p248) has its own, highly respected company; something off the beaten track can usually be found at the **Cometa**, **Vascello** or **Orologio**. And the Ambra-Jovinelli (see p265 **Teatro Ambra Jovinelli**), a mainstay of Rome's riotous pre-war variety scene, has been spruced up and is back in business.

DANCE

Classical ballet can be seen at the **Teatro dell'Opera** (see p246) and its satellite spaces the *teatri* **Nazionale** and **Brancaccio**.

However, fans of contemporary dance will have to look hard for something to sink their teeth into. The best bets are the **Teatro Olimpico** in the northern suburbs where international companies are regular visitors, and the **Teatro Greco**, which has its own dance school.

PROGRAMME INFORMATION

Rome dailies such as *La Repubblica* and *Il Messaggero* carry theatre and dance listings, as do the monthly *Time Out Roma* and weekly *Roma C'è* and *Trovaroma* magazines (see also p297). There's also a useful (though Italian-only) theatre website at www.tuttoteatro.com. Tickets can be bought at theatres themselves, or at agencies (see p222).

Main public theatres

See also **Teatro dell'Opera** p246.

Palazzo delle Esposizioni

Via Nazionale 194, Trevi Fountain & Quirinale (06 474 5903). Bus to via Nazionale. **Open** 10am-9pm Mon, Wed-Sun. **Shows** depends on event. **No credit cards. Map** p323 2B.
Rome's only multicultural arts centre has a cinema, lecture hall and a dance space as well as extensive exhibition spaces. The occasional productions are often linked to art shows. See also p78.

Teatro Brancaccio

Via Merulana 244, Monti (06 487 4566). Bus to via Merulana. **Box office** 11am-1pm, 3-7pm daily. **Shows** 9pm Tue-Sat; 5pm or 6pm Sun. **No credit cards. Map** p326 1A.
This theatre, which traditionally stages the overflow from the Teatro dell'Opera (see p246), is planning to shift away from music and towards prose drama.

Teatro Nazionale

Via del Viminale 51, Esquilino (06 4782 5140). Metro Termini/bus to via Nazionale. **Box office** at Teatro dell'Opera (see p246). **Shows** depends on event. **Credit** AmEx, DC, MC, V. **Map** p323 2B.
This is the venue for the less prestigious productions of the Teatro dell'Opera.

Teatro di Roma – Argentina

Largo Argentina 52, Ghetto & Campo de' Fiori (06 6880 4601). Bus or tram to largo Argentina. **Box office** 10am-2pm, 3-7pm Tue-Sun. **Shows** *Oct-June* 9pm Tue, Wed, Fri, Sat; 5pm Thur, Sun. **Credit** AmEx, DC, MC, V. **Map** p324 1A.
Rome's plush flagship theatre has a wide-open range of offerings, from Shakespeare to Yehoshua, with some dance and poetry. The Teatro di Roma occasionally uses interesting alternative spaces for more avant-garde productions.

Teatro di Roma – India

Lungotevere Papareschi/via Pierantoni 6, Suburbs: south (06 6880 4601). Bus to piazzale della Radio. **Box office** tickets from Teatro Argentina (*see above*) or at Teatro India half an hour before shows. **No credit cards** at Teatro India.

Opened in late 1999, the India is Rome's newest and most modern space for performances of all kinds. Situated in a former soap factory, it aims to make high-profile international experimental theatre and dance a regular feature in this otherwise tradition-orientated city.

Teatro Valle

Via del Teatro Valle 23A, Pantheon & Piazza Navona (06 6880 3794). Bus to corso Vittorio Emanuele or largo Argentina. **Box office** 10am-7pm Tue-Sat; 10am-1pm Sun. **Shows** 9pm Tue, Fri, Sat; 5pm Wed, Thur, Sun. **Credit** AmEx, DC, MC, V. **Map** p321 2A.

This gem of a theatre is part of the state-owned ETI circuit. It hosts an increasingly interesting choice of performances, with pieces by many contemporary Italian authors interspersed, and the occasional concert featuring some of Italy's most eclectic singer-songwriters.

Teatro Quirino

Via Mario Minghetti 1, Trevi Fountain & Quirinale (0679 4585) Bus to piazza Venezia or via del Corso. **Box office** 10am-7pm Tue-Sat. **Shows** 9pm Tue-Sat; 5pm Sun. **No credit cards. Map** p323 2C.

Part of the state-owned ETI circuit, the Quirino features mainly household-name playwrights such as Luigi Pirandello and Samuel Beckett.

Private & smaller venues

See also **Teatro Olimpico** *p246*; **Teatro Ghione** *p248*.

Salone Margherita

Via Due Macelli 75, Tridente (06 679 1439/06 679 8269). Metro Spagna/bus to piazza San Silvestro or via del Tritone. **Box office** 10am-9pm Tue-Sun. **Shows** 9.30pm Tue-Fri; 6pm Sat, Sun. **No credit cards. Map** p323 1C.

Cabaret and political satire, with cocktails and pasta in between: a Roman tradition.

Teatro Belli

Piazza Sant'Apollonia 11A, Trastevere (06 589 4875). Bus to lungotevere Sanzio or piazza Sonnino/tram to viale Trastevere. **Box office** 10am-1pm, 4.30-9pmTue-Sat; 4-6pm Sun. **Shows** *Sept-May* 9pm Tue-Sat; 5.30pm Sun. **No credit cards. Map** p324 2B.

Small, private theatre with an emphasis on Italian plays and dialect theatre, with a new cycle dedicated to British drama (in Italian, of course).

Teatro Colosseo

Via Capo d'Africa 5, Celio & San Giovanni (06 700 4932). Metro Colosseo/bus or tram to piazza del Colosseo. **Box office** 10am-1pm, 6.30-10.30pm

Tue-Sat. **Shows** *Sala Grande* 8.30, 10.30pm Tue-Sat; 5.30, 7.30pm Sun; *Ridotto Sala A* 8.30pm Tue-Sat, 5.30pm Sun; *Ridotto Sala B* 10.30pm Tue-Sat, 7pm Sun. **No credit cards. Map** p326 2B.

The Colosseo provides a showcase for young Italian directors and actors in two spaces frequented by Rome's young and theatre-savvy.

Teatro della Cometa

Via del Teatro di Marcello 4, Ghetto & Campo de' Fiori (06 678 4380). Bus to piazza Venezia or via del Teatro di Marcello. **Box office** 11am-7pm Tue-Sat; 10am-1pm, 4-5pm Sun. **Shows** 9.15pm Tue-Sat; 5pm Sun. **Credit** AmEx, DC, MC, V. **Map** p324 1A.

This fringe theatre near piazza Venezia has a faithful following, intimate atmosphere and thoughtful productions. Credit cards are accepted for phone bookings only.

Teatro Eliseo–Piccolo Eliseo

Via Nazionale 183, Trevi Fountain & Quirinale (06 488 2114). Bus to via Nazionale. **Shows** 9.30am-2.30pm, 3.30-7pm Tue-Sun. **Shows** 8.45pm Tue, Wed, Sun; 5pm Wed, Sat; 4.30pm, 8.45pm Sun. **Credit** DC, MC, V. **Map** p326 1C.

This huge, fairly modern theatre is an important venue for productions of classic Italian and international playwrights. The Piccolo Eliseo serves up similar fare in smaller productions. Italian favourites such as Eduardo De Filippo and Carlo Goldoni frequently take the stage, as do Shakespearean and Greek dramas.

Teatro Flaiano

Via Santo Stefano del Cacco 15, Pantheon & Piazza Navona (06 679 5696/06 678 7424). Bus or tram to largo Argentina. **Box office** 10.30am-1.30pm, 3-7pm Tue-Sun. **Shows** 9pm Tue,Thu-Sat; 5pm Wed; 7pm Sun. **Credit** AmEx, MC, V. **Map** p321 2A.

A cosy theatre decorated in blue velvet, the Flaiano intersperses its regular Italian prose repertory with opera evenings throughout the season. Adjacent is a delightfully camp dinner-theatre (9.30pm Wed-Sat) with quality cabaret.

Teatro Greco

Via R Leoncavallo 16, Suburbs: north (06 860 7513). Bus to largo Somalia. **Box office** 10am-1pm, 4-7pm Tue-Sun. **Shows** 9pm daily. **No credit cards.**

A well-designed performance venue in north-east Rome, with some dance performances at international level, and a penchant for little-tried writers, both domestic and international.

Teatro dell'Orologio

Via de' Filippini 17A, Pantheon & Piazza Navona (06 6830 8735/06 6830 8330). Bus to corso Vittorio Emanuele. **Box office** *Sept-June* 4-8pm Tue-Sat; 4-6pm Sun. **Shows** Sala Grande 9pm Tue-Sat; 5.30pm Sun; Sala Artaud 9.30pm Tue-Sat, 6.30pm Sun; Sala Gassman 9.30pm Tue-Sat, 6.30pm Sun. **No credit cards. Map** p321 2B.

The offbeat and experimental are given a stage in the four separate theatre spaces at this venue.

Arts & Entertainment

Teatro Rossini

Piazza Santa Chiara 14, Pantheon & Piazza Navona (06 6880 2770). Bus or tram to largo Argentina. **Box office** 10.30am-1pm, 3pm-7pm daily. **Shows** 9pm Tue, Thur-Sat; 5pm Wed, Sat, Sun. **No credit cards. Map** p321 2A.

A cosy old theatre with a programme dedicated to original dramas and Roman dialect reworkings.

Teatro Sistina

Via Sistina 129, Via Veneto & Villa Borghese (06 420 0711). Metro Barberini or Spagna/bus to piazza Barberini. **Box office** 10am-1pm, 3.30-7pm daily. **Shows** 9pm Tue-Sat; 5pm Sun. **Credit** MC, V. **Map** p323 1C.

Glitzy Italian musicals and even glitzier international variety hits make up the fare of this old trooper; evenings with major – and sometimes even interesting – Italian singer-songwriters.

Teatro XX Secolo

Via Garibaldi 30, Gianicolo (06 588 1444). Bus to via G Carini. **Box office** 10.30am-1.30pm, 3.30-7pm Mon-Fri; 5-7pm Sat; 3-5pm Sun. **Shows** 9pm Tue-Sat; 5.30pm Sun. **Credit** DC, MC, V. **Map** p324 2C.

This smallish theatre in an improbable location above a gushing fountain stages offerings by 20th-century playwrights, and tries to give a chance to 21st-century newcomers too.

Teatro Vascello

Via G Carini 72, Suburbs: west (06 588 1021). Bus to via G Carini. **Box office** 5-8pm Tue-Sat; 3-5pm Sun. **Shows** 9pm Tue-Sat; 5pm Sun. **No credit cards. Map** p325 1C.

Independent theatre that presents some fairly decent experimental theatre and dance productions, plus conferences and workshops.

Teatro Vittoria

Piazza Santa Maria Liberatrice 8, Testaccio (06 574 0170/06 574 0598). Bus to via Marmorata or piazza Santa Maria in Liberatrice/tram to via Marmorata. **Box office** 10am-1pm, 4-7pm Mon; 10am-7pm Tue-Sat; 10am-1pm Sun. **Shows** 9pm Tue-Sat; 5pm Sun. **Credit** MC, V. **Map** p325 2A.

This cavernous venue in the Testaccio district specialises in translated texts and international variety. It also features a special programme specifically for children.

Summer venues

See also **RomaEuropa Festival** *p244.*

Anfiteatro della Quercia del Tasso

Passeggiata del Gianicolo, Gianicolo (06 575 0827). Bus or tram to viale Trastevere. **Box office** from 7pm before shows. **Shows** *July-Sept* 9.15pm Mon-Sat; occasional afternoon matinées. **No credit cards. Map** p324 1C.

An ancient amphitheatre on the Gianicolo, specialising in classical Greek and Latin theatre and 18th-century Venetian comedy.

Teatro Romano di Ostia Antica

Scavi di Ostia Antica, viale dei Romagnoli 117, Ostia Antica (06 6880 4601). **Box office** from 6pm daily; also at Teatro Argentina (*see p263*). **Shows** *Mid July-mid Aug* 8.30pm daily. **Credit** at Teatro Argentina.

This wonderfully preserved Roman theatre, set amid the ruins of ancient Rome's main port (*see p250*), hosts prestigious productions of Roman and Greek classics, plus a host of concerts. The seats are stone: bring your own cushion.

Arts & Entertainment

Teatro Ambra Jovinelli

In the early years of the 20th century, Italy's best-loved comedians got their early breaks by raising the roof at Rome's high church of variety, the Teatro Ambra Jovinelli.

But as variety went into decline, so did that venerable institution: comedy gave way to strip shows, strip shows were replaced by x-rated movies. The ever-more-run-down building – in the heart of the seedy, squalid area around Termini station – was even slated for demolition.

How things change. In 2000 the theatre reopened, restored to its former glory. The stucco columns and swirls of its art-nouveau façade have been cleaned, the original cast-iron decorations salvaged and cheery orange paint applied, while a massive overhaul brought the theatre acoustically up to date.

In its first year of activity, full houses flocked back to the Ambra Jovinelli to see stars of Italian political and social satire tread the boards which were once the stomping ground of Italy's favourite postwar comedian Antonio De Curtis – better known as Totò – and, before him, the comic legend Ettore Petrolini. The new complex aims to become a shrine to Italy's comedy heritage, with a school for comic writing and acting, and a video and research library to record this country's funniest moments.

Via Guglielmo Pepe 41/45, Esquilino (06 4434 0262). Metro Vittorio/bus to piazza dei Cinquecento or piazza Vittorio. **Box office** 10am-6pm Mon-Sat; 11am-1.30pm Sun. **Shows** varies. **No credit cards. Map** p326 1A.

The **Time Out City Guides** spectrum

Available from all good bookshops and at www.timeout.com/shop

www.timeout.com

www.penguin.com

Trips Out of Town

Trips Out of Town

Beaches, villas and more archaeology are a stone's throw from central Rome.

Maps p316 and p317

Much of the ruin-strewn *campagna romana* (Roman countryside) so beloved of the Grand Tourists of the 18th and 19th centuries has disappeared under a welter of hypermarkets and high-rise dwellings. But even today it's not difficult to reach a bit of rural green, for a rest from Rome's unrelenting urban-ness. Nor is it hard to reach smaller, more manageable outcrops of ancient history.

Getting around

By car

Rome is surrounded by the Grande Raccordo Anulare (GRA) ring road, which links up with the network of well-kept and generally quick motorways (*autostrade*) and slower *strade statali* (SS). Traffic on the GRA and approach roads to the city can be intense in rush hours and on Friday and Sunday evenings, when long queues form at motorway tollbooths.

You can save on time (but not money) at tollbooths by using a Viacard, a debit card costing €25.82/L50,000, €51.65/L100,000, or €77.47/L150,000, available from all *tabacchi* (*see p302*), and most motorway service stations. Many tollbooths at major points of entry accept credit cards (AmEx, DC, MC, V), too.

The *strade statali* that fan out from Rome are known by their ancient names – Aurelia, Salaria, Tiburtina etc – as well as numbers.

The www.autostrade.it website has regularly updated information on motorway traffic flow. Isoradio (103.3 FM, occasional English-language bulletins in summer) gives regular traffic updates for all major roads. For information on driving in Italy and car hire, *see p287*.

By train

The network of local railways around Rome, the Ferrovie Metropolitane (FM) is handy for reaching destinations around the city. FM trains can be picked up at the following mainline stations: Ostiense (FM1, FM5, FM3), Tiburtina (FM1, FM2), Termini (FM4, FM6, FM7), Trastevere (FM1, FM3, FM5).

Mainline trains, for further-flung destinations, are operated by Ferrovie dello Stato (FS). Tickets can be bought at stations or

travel agents with an FS sign, or online by credit card on the FS website. There is a 20 per cent discount on tickets (not supplements) for those aged under 26 with the Carta Verde card, which costs €23.24/L45,000 per year and can be purchased at stations; there are reductions, too, for family groups of three or more, but only the most tuned-in ticket-seller will have heard of these. Children under 12 pay half fare; children under four travel free. For information on taking wheelchairs on trains, *see p292*.

Train timetables can be purchased at any *edicola* (newsstand), or checked on the website (www.fs-on-line). The number listed below also provides information, but there's no guarantee you'll find anyone who speaks English.

Slower trains (*diretti, espressi, regionali* and *interregionali*) are very cheap; a system of supplements means that faster services – InterCity (IC), EuroCity (EC), Eurostar Italia (ES) – are closer to the European norm. The first two cost up to 50 per cent more than slower trains, Eurostar (not to be confused with Channel tunnel trains of the same name) more than double.

Advance reservation is obligatory and free on ES trains on Fridays and Sundays, and all week at certain peak times of year. An R inside a square on train timetables indicates this; check when purchasing your ticket. Booking a seat on IC and internal EC routes costs €2.58/L5,000, and is well worth it even when not obligatory, to avoid standing in a packed corridor at peak times. If your ES, IC or EC train arrives more than 30 minutes late – it rarely will – and you have a seat booking, you can have the supplement reimbursed at the booth marked *rimborsi*.

You must stamp your ticket and supplements in the yellow machines at the head of each platform before boarding the train. You will be fined if you don't.

Rome's larger stations, including Termini, Tiburtina and Ostiense (*see p287*), accept all major credit cards. Most travel agents persist in accepting cash only for train tickets.

Ferrovie Metropolitane (FM)

(*tollfree information 800 431 784*). **Open** 8am-6pm Mon-Fri.

Ferrovie dello Stato (FS)

(*Information 848 888 088*). **Open** 7am-9pm daily.

Interesting discoveries at **Ostia Antica**.

By bus

The Lazio transport authority COTRAL
(formerly ACOTRAL/Li.La.) covers the region
fairly efficiently. Buses leave from several city
termini, each of which serves a different
direction; most services ply *strade statali*
(SS; state roads).

The tollfree information line listed below can
be difficult to get through to, but persevere and
you will find English speakers on the other end.
Fares mount according to the number of
kilometres travelled, and range from
€0.77/L1,500 for a 20km (12½ mile) hop to
€4.39/L8,500 for 125km (78 miles).

COTRAL
*Via Volturno 65, Monti (06 57 531/tollfree 800 431
784). Metro Termini/bus to piazza del Cinquecento.*
Open *Office* 8am-1.40pm, 2.10-4.40pm Mon-Fri; 8am-
1.40pm Sat. *Information line* 8am-6pm Mon-Fri.
Map p323 1A.
COTRAL termini
Lepanto
Metro Lepanto/bus to viale G Cesare. Map p320 2B.
Saxa Rubra
Train from Roma Nord-Flaminio (map p320 1A)
to Saxa Rubra.
Stazione Tiburtina
Metro Tiburtina.
Ponte Mammolo
Metro Ponte Mammolo.
Anagnina
Metro Anagnina.
EUR Fermi
Metro EUR Fermi/bus to viale America.

Archaeology near Rome

If it weren't for the lack of a backdrop like
Vesuvius, the ruins of **Ostia Antica** would be
as famous as Pompeii: it certainly conveys just

as uncannily what everyday life was like in a
working Roman town. Ostia was Rome's main
port for over 600 years, until its decline in the
fourth century AD. Thereafter, river mud and
sand gradually buried the town. Visit on a
sunny weekday, and bring a picnic
to eat under the pines or on the steps of the
theatre: it's a place that deserves to be taken
at a leisurely pace.

The Decumanus Maximus (high street) runs
from the Porta Romana for almost a kilometre,
past the theatre and forum, before forking left
to reach what used to be the seashore (which
is now three kilometres – two miles – away at
Ostia, *see p270*). The right fork, via delle Foce,
leads to the Tiber. On either side of these main
arteries there is a network of intersecting
lanes, and it's here that the most interesting
discoveries can be made.

Behind the theatre is the Forum of the
Corporations, ringed by offices and shops with
mosaics referring to the trades practised by the
ancient guilds. The Thermopilium is an ancient
Roman bar, complete with marble counter,
a fresco advertising the house fare and a garden
with fountain out the back; the House of Cupid
and Psyche is an elegant fourth-century
construction; the House of the Dioscuri has
beautiful mosaics. In the site's museum is a
good collection of artefacts from the site itself,
including bas-reliefs of scenes of ordinary life.

The medieval fortified village of Ostia
Antica, five minutes' walk from the entrance to
the excavations, has a brick **castle** built in
1483-6 for the future Pope Julius II, and some
picturesque cottages that were once inhabited
by workers in the nearby salt pans.

As Rome's population grew to around a
million at the height of the Empire, its port
activities overflowed from Ostia to the ports
of Claudius (AD 42) and Trajan (AD106); the

latter can be visited on guided tours (booking and own transport essential) which leave from the **Museo delle Navi**, a charming museum in the shadow of Fiumicino airport with genuine Roman ships and displays on ancient trade. The **Porto di Traiano** was scheduled to open regularly as a sight, but as this guide went to press, a tour was still the only way to see the hexagonal harbour where up to 200 ships could tie up at any time.

Castello di Giulio II
Piazza della Rocca, Ostia Antica (06 5635 8024). **Open** 9am-1pm, 2.30-4.30pm Tue, Thur; 9am-1pm Wed, Fri, Sat, Sun;. **Admission** free.

Museo delle Navi
Via A Guidoni 35, Fiumicino Aeroporto (06 652 9192). **Open** 9am-1pm, 2.30-4.30pm Tue, Thur; 9am-1.30pm Wed, Fri, Sat, Sun;. **Admission** €2.06/L4,000. **No credit cards.**

Porto di Traiano
(06 652 9192). **Open** (guided tours only) 9.30am first Sat, last Sun of month. Tours leave from the Museo delle Navi; own transport essential. **Admission** included in Museo delle Navi ticket.

Scavi di Ostia Antica
Viale dei Romagnoli 117, Ostia Antica (06 5635 2830/bookings 06 32 810). **Open** *Apr-Oct* 9am-7pm Tue-Sun. *Nov-Mar* 9am-5pm Tue-Sun. Ticket office closes one hour earlier. **Admission** €4.13/L8,000; concessions €2.07/L4,000. **No credit cards.**

Getting there

By car
For Ostia Antica, take the via del Mare or via Ostiense (SS8). For Museo delle Navi and Porto di Traiano, take the Autostrada Roma-Fiumicino.

By train
For Ostia Antica, trains run from Roma-Lido station next to Piramide metro (map 7/2A). For Museo delle Navi and Porto di Traiano, take the FM1 to Fiumicino Aeroporto.

Tourist information

See p303.

Beaches

The local riviera for Romans is at **Ostia**, with its murky sea, and dark sandy beaches lined by private, pay-on-entry beach clubs that fill to bursting every summer. If you're desperate for a swim, head towards **Torvaianica**, 11 kilometres (seven miles) further south, where the water is a bit cleaner and laudable efforts have been made of late to keep the sand rubbish-free. The **Castelporziano/Capocotta**

beach between Ostia and Torvaianica is also acceptable, and free, with a sprinkling of beach-hut bars; it has a Gay section (*see p240*) and a nudist stretch at around nine kilometres south of Ostia (signposted on the road).

If you're looking for discos and *racchettone* (beach tennis), the resorts north of Ostia – such as **Fregene** and **Ladispoli** – will not disappoint. Romans flock here, but for secluded beaches and clean sea you must travel further afield. For details of how to reach these beaches, see **Getting there**, *p272*.

The northern coast

In **Santa Severa**, 54km (33½ miles) north-west of Rome, the four-square Castello Orsini squats like an outsized sandcastle on the sandy beach, where the swimming is fine if you're not too fussy about the colour of the water. Inside the castle is a little village, with a chapel with 14th-century frescos, and a fountain. Next door are the remains of the Etruscan port of Pyrgi, the main sea outlet of **Cerveteri** (*see p280*) and the site of an important sanctuary to the Etruscan goddess Uni (Roman Juno). There's a small museum of finds from the excavations, the **Antiquarium di Pyrgi**.

Continuing northward, past the family resort of **Santa Marinella**, the power stations and industrial waste of **Civitavecchia** scupper the theory that the further from Rome, the cleaner it gets. It's not until you reach the border with Tuscany that things start to improve again. Just across the boundary, **Chiarone** has the first clean sea and sandy beach this side of Rome.

You can walk along the beach from here all the way (12 kilometres/7½ miles) to the upmarket holiday destination of **Ansedonia**, site of the Etruscan town of Cosa. Halfway along, just beyond **Lago di Burano** – a WWF bird sanctuary – is the **Marina di Capalbio**, marked by the incongruous bulk of the Casale di Macchiatonda, a former hunting lodge. For many years this has been the beach resort for Rome's monied Left. The beautiful walled village of **Capalbio** itself stands seven kilometres (four miles) inland.

Antiquarium di Pyrgi
Castello di Santa Severa (0766 570 194). **Open** 8.30am-7.30pm Tue-Sun. **Admission** free.

The southern coast

The first cleanish sea south of Rome is at **Sabaudia**, the fascist answer to Bournemouth. The town stands in the Parco Nazionale del Circeo, next to a large artificial lake. The beaches (around a kilometre from town) are clean and

San Felice Circeo becomes a poseurs' paradise in summer.

sandy. Looming to the south is **Monte Circeo**, where Odysseus was waylaid by the enchantress Circe, who turned his men into pigs. On the other side of the rock, a road leads up to **San Felice Circeo**, a pretty little town that becomes a poseurs' paradise in summer.

Terracina is a port town with two centres. The pleasant modern part is down by the sea, and along the via Flacca. The medieval town above lies on top of the forum of the Roman port of Anxur. Its cathedral was built out of the main hall of a Roman temple to Augustus; above the portico is a 12th-century mosaic frieze, while below it is a big basin that was reputedly used for boiling Christians. The paving slabs in the piazza are those of the old forum, and just beyond is a gate and stretch of the ancient via Appia (*see also p146*). Bombing during World War II uncovered these ancient remains and made space for the modern town hall and **Museo Civico di Terracina**. Above the town, and spectacularly lit at night, is the first-century BC Tempio di Giove (Temple of Jupiter), which offers views along the coast from Circeo to Gaeta.

Between Terracina and Sperlonga the beaches are almost all sewn up by private beach facilities. **Sperlonga** itself is a pretty seaside resort. The whitewashed medieval town on the spur overlooking the two beaches – its narrow lanes lined with potted geraniums, boutiques, bars and

restaurants – fills up with well-heeled Romans in the summer months. The **Museo Archeologico di Sperlonga**, at the end of the sandy beach to the south of the town, contains some important second-century BC sculptures depicting scenes from the story of Odysseus; the ticket includes a tour of Tiberius's Villa and Grotto.

There are some pretty sandy coves between Sperlonga and Gaeta, but you will often have to pay to park on the road (around €2.58/L5,000) and to use the steps down to beaches, even if the beaches themselves are *spiagge libere* (free-access beaches).

The last resort along this stretch of coast is **Gaeta**, a town of great strategic and historical importance. It was the last stronghold of King Francesco II of Naples against Garibaldi's Piedmontese troops (*see chapter* **History**), falling on 13 February 1861 to end 130 years of Bourbon rule in southern Italy. The modern lower town clusters around the harbour; the old medieval walled town has more tackily adorned Madonnas in wall-niches than Naples, and an impressive 12th-century castle. Serapo beach, to the north, is long, wide and very crowded in summer.

Museo Archeologico di Sperlonga & Villa di Tiberio

Via Flacca km16.6, Sperlonga (0771 548 028).
Open 8.30am-7.30pm daily. **Admission** €2.06/L4,000. **No credit cards.**

Tiberius's villa at **Sperlonga**. *See p271.*

Museo Civico di Terracina

Piazza Municipio, Terracina (0773 707 313).
Open *May-Sept* 9.30am-1.30pm Mon; 9.30am-
1.30pm, 3-9pm Tue-Sat; 10am-1pm, 5-9pm Sun.
Oct-Apr 9am-1pm Mon; 9am-1pm, 3-7pm Tue-Sat,
9am-1pm, 3-6pm Sun. **Admission** €1.55/L3,000.
No credit cards.

Where to eat

On the beach in Chiarone is the bar/trattoria
L'Ultima Spiaggia (0564 890 295, closed
Sept-Mar & weekdays Apr, May) where a
sit-down fish meal costs €36.15/ L70,000 and
bar snacks a lot less. The Bar della Stazione
inside Capalbio station is a front for a trattoria
(0564 898 424, closed Tue in low season,
average €25.80/L50,000) serving excellent
fresh fish. You can also snack or eat fish
meals on Capalbio beach at the oh-so-chic
Carmen Bay (0564 893 196, closed Nov-
Easter & weekdays Easter-end May, Oct,
average €36.15/L70,000).

In Terracina, the **Bottega Sarra 1932**
(via Villafranca 34, 0773 702 045, closed Mon,
average €23.25/L45,000), not far from the
cathedral, serves excellent renditions of
simple local fare. In Sperlonga head for the
family-run **La Bisaccia** (via Romita 25,
0771 548 576, closed Tue & Nov, average
€25.80/L50,000), in the modern lower town,
for great fish. In the old quarter of Gaeta
the **Antico Vico** (vico II del Cavallo 2,

0771 465 116, closed Wed & 2wks Nov, average
€25.80/L50,000) is also a reliable place for a
well-priced seafood meal.

Getting there

By car
Ostia: Via Cristoforo Colombo or via del Mare
(SS8), then coast road (SS601).
Ladispoli, Santa Severa & Santa Marinella:
Via Aurelia (SS1).
Chiarone, Capalbio & Monte Argentario:
Via Aurelia (SS1).
Sabaudia, Terracina & Sperlonga: Via Appia
(SS7) or via Pontina (SS148) to Sabaudia (93km/58
miles), Terracina (105km/65 miles), or Sperlonga
(123km/76 miles).

By train
Ostia: from Roma-Lido station (metro Piramide);
for full-on beach umbrellas, get out at Lido Centro;
for Capocotta and Torvaianica go to the end of the
line (Cristoforo Colombo) and take bus 061 (Mar-Oct).
Fregene: FM5 from Ostiense or Trastevere.
Ladispoli, Santa Severa & Santa Marinella:
FM5 from Ostiense or Trastevere.
Chiarone, Capalbio & Monte Argentario: FS
train from Termini, Ostiense or Trastevere to
Chiarone and Capalbio (for both, there's a 3km/2 mile
walk or hitch to the beach).
Sabaudia, Terracina & Sperlonga: FS train
from Termini, Tiburtina or Ostiense to Priverno (for
buses to Sabaudia and buses/trains to Terracina),
Fondi (for buses to Sperlonga), and Formia (for
buses to Gaeta).

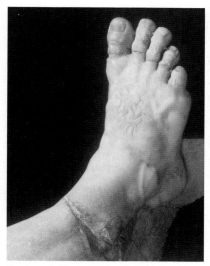

Sperlonga's **Museo Archeologico**. See p271.

By bus
Fregene and Ladispoli: COTRAL from Lepanto.
Santa Severa & Santa Marinella: COTRAL from Lepanto.
Sabaudia, Terracina & Sperlonga: COTRAL from EUR Fermi; for Gaeta bus to Latina and change.

South from Rome

The town of **Tivoli**, founded by an Italic tribe, was conquered by the Romans in 338 BC. The surrounding area became a popular location for country villas, and Tivoli itself was littered with temples. A favourite destination for day trips from Rome, its greatest attractions are the largest of the Roman Imperial villas, the **Villa Adriana** and the Renaissance **Villa d'Este**.

Also worth looking at are the Villa Gregoriana (closed indefinitely for restoration but visible from outside), a wild park in a rocky gorge, next to two waterfalls; the cathedral of San Lorenzo, which contains a 13th-century wood-carving of the Descent from the Cross; and a very well preserved circular Roman Temple of Sybil. At the top of the town is a 15th-century castle built by Pope Pius II, the Rocca Pia.

Nearby **Palestrina** was built over a huge temple, parts of which date back to the sixth century BC, dedicated to the oracle Fortuna Primegenia. The ancient Etruscan town here, Praeneste, fought many wars with the Romans before it was defeated in 87 BC. The temple was rebuilt on a grander scale, and Praeneste became

a favourite holiday resort. Pliny the Younger had a villa here. After the oracle shut up shop in the fourth century AD, the medieval town was built on top. Bombing during World War II exposed the huge extent of the remains. The town's **Museo Archeologico** contains a spectacular mosaic of the Nile in flood. Palestrina's most famous son was Giovanni da Palestrina, the 16th-century composer.

Museo Archeologico Prenestino
Piazza della Cortina, Palestrina (06 953 8100).
Open 9am-7.30pm daily. **Admission** *Museum & excavations* €2.06/L4,000. **No credit cards**.
A circular temple with a statue of the goddess Palestrina originally stood where the 17th-century Palazzo Colonna-Barberini is now; today it houses the museum. Its star exhibit is the second-century BC Nile mosaic: a work admired by Pliny, which came from the most sacred part of the temple, where the cathedral now stands. It is an intricately detailed, brightly coloured representation of the Nile in flood from Ethiopia to Alexandria, showing warriors hunting exotic animals, people dining, goddesses preaching and birds galore.

Villa Adriana
Via di Villa Adriana, Tivoli (0774 382 733). **Open** *Apr-Sept* 9am-6.30pm daily. *Oct-Mar* 9am-3.30pm daily. **Admission** €6.20/L12,000; €3.10/L6,000 concessions. **No credit cards**.
Hadrian started work on his grandiose country retreat in the mountains near Tibur (ancient Tivoli) in AD 118. It was completed in 134, and later used by several other emperors. In the centuries following the fall of the Empire it became a luxury quarry for later builders, but was never destroyed completely; the restored remains, lying between olive groves and cypresses, are still impressive (the model in the pavilion gives an idea of the villa's original size).

Hadrian was a great traveller, and in his old age built himself replicas of some of his favourite buildings. After dinner he could stroll in the shade of the arcaded *stoa poikile* (painted porch), with its huge pool, and feel he was back in Athens; or he could recline around the pool in the *canopus* (a replica of the sanctuary of Serapis near Alexandria), surrounded by Egyptian statues – a reminder of the emperor's favourite, a Greek boy called Antinous, who had drowned in Egypt. If he was feeling particularly miserable, he could take a trip through his reconstruction of Hades, the underworld – a series of underground passages to the east of the *odeion* or Greek theatre. And for moments of private reflection there was the *teatro marittimo* (naval theatre), a charming circular study in the middle of an artificial pool. The complex also included extensive guest and staff apartments, dining rooms, assembly halls and libraries, baths and a stadium. The whole villa complex was connected by underground passages (*cryptoportici*), a private subway that gave welcome relief from the beating sun.

Trips Out of Town

Villa d'Este

Piazza Trento 1, Tivoli (0774 312 070). **Open** *May-Sept* 9am-6.15pm Tue-Sun. *Oct-Apr* 8.30am-4pm Tue-Sun. **Admission** €6.20/L12,000; €3.10/L6,000 concessions. **No credit cards**.

This lavish pleasure palace was built over a Benedictine monastery in 1550 for Cardinal Ippolito d'Este, son of Lucrezia Borgia (*see p12* **Lust, Murder & Incest**). Inside the villa – by Mannerist architect Pirro Ligorio – there are frescos and paintings by Correggio, da Volterra and Perrin del Vaga. The main attraction, though, is the garden, with huge, elaborate and ingenious fountains. The Fontana dell'Organo Idraulico used water pressure to compress air and play tunes; the Owl Fountain imitated an owl's song. The villa has become frayed at the edges over the centuries, and restoration is a struggle: the musical fountains have not made a sound for years, but others have regained their original splendour. Note too the *Rometta* – a miniature model of the Tiber Island in Rome.

The Castelli Romani

The tame volcanoes that make up the Alban Hills have long provided refuge for Romans on *scampagnate* (Sunday outings). The 16 small towns dotted around the hills that make up the Castelli Romani are not all equally worth a visit, but there is plenty of good eating and walking, and some wonderful sights.

Most of the modern-day Castelli are creations of the struggle for power and influence between Rome's noble families. In pre-classical times this area was the centre of the Latin League, whose capital, Alba Longa, above Lake Albano, has now made way for **Castelgandolfo**, summer residence of the Pope. Subjugated by Rome, the Castelli became a favourite summer haunt of Roman patricians. Their Renaissance successors also built a string of villas.

Frascati is the closest of the Castelli to the city, and offers perhaps the most satisfying balance of food, wine and culture. Of the numerous Renaissance villas sprinkled over the hillside behind the town, only the garden of the 17th-century **Villa Aldobrandini** (via Massaia, open Mar-Oct 9am-1pm, 3pm-6pm Mon-Fri, admission free) is visitable. The villa was built in 1598-1603 by Giacomo della Porta for Cardinal Pietro Aldobrandini. In nearby **Villa Torlonia** – a public park – Carlo Maderno's 16th-century Teatro delle Acque fountain has been restored to its original glory. There is also an elegant smaller fountain by Bernini.

The name 'Frascati' is synonymous with uninspiring Italian table wine, but you'd do well to give it another try here. Local topers claim that it has to be drunk *sul posto* – on site – and, quaffing it fresh from the barrel in a cool cellar, you may well agree.

Grottaferrata is a small, lively town whose main street leads down to the tenth-century **Abbazia di San Nilo** (Corso del Popolo, open 6.30am-12.30pm, 3.30-7pm daily), a mainly Romanesque monastery fortified in the 15th century. The abbey church of Santa Maria has a fine 12th-century campanile, and an even finer carved marble portal. Inside, the cappella di San Nilo contains frescos by Domenichino.

Of all the Castelli, **Nemi** is definitely the most picturesque – so try to avoid visiting on a Sunday, when it fills up with Roman strollers. Perched on the edge of Lake Nemi's

Hadrian hankered after his lost love at **Villa Adriana**. *See p273.*

Villas and gardens

Northern Lazio's villas were commissioned by families raised to pre-eminence through the lottery of ecclesiastical power. They were personal and political statements. Villa Farnese, Villa Lante and the Sacro Bosco at Bomarzo were all built in the 16th century for patrons related to one other. They used the same artists and architects – chiefly those busy Mannerists Sangallo and Vignola.

The park of **Il Sacro Bosco**, also known as the *Parco dei Mostri* or 'Monster Park', is situated just below the town of Bomarzo, and was built by Duke Vicino Orsini (1523-84) shortly after his wife died. This, though, is more a bizarre Renaissance theme park than a dignified retreat for a bereaved husband. Using the volcanic *peperino* stone that dotted his estate, Orsini spent years filling the park with surreal, sometimes grotesque sculptures, which were completely at odds with the conventional tastes of his day. Lurking in the undergrowth are a skewed, leaning house and enormous, absurd beasts. The park was much appreciated by Salvador Dalì, who played a part in publicising it.

The little town of Caprarola is dwarfed by the imposing **Villa Farnese**. It began as a castle, designed by Sangallo the Younger and Peruzzi, but was taken over by Vignola in the 1560s. As you approach the villa it appears to be only two storeys high, but climb the semi-circular ramps and the ground floor appears. Vignola raised and extended the approach road, burying the lower storeys of the existing houses to provide an optimum view of the villa. Inside, a wide spiral staircase, which the villa's owner, Cardinal Alessandro Farnese, used to climb on horseback, leads up to the *piano nobile*, the only part open to the public. In the Salone dei Fasti Farnese are frescos depicting the heroic deeds of the Farnese family: note the Farnese Pope Paul III in the act of excommunicating Henry VIII of England. The Sala dei Sogni has bizarre allegorical scenes intended to induce sweet dreams. There is also a room with frescoed maps of the world from 1500, and another in which whispers (including the menacing ones of John Malkovich to Nicole Kidman in *Portrait of a Lady*) rebound from wall to wall. Behind the villa are two formal gardens (included in the tour) and the *barchino*, a steep, wooded park that leads up to the fountains of the Giardino Grande and the Palazzina del Piacere summer house.

The town of Bagnaia lies beneath the gardens and park of **Villa Lante**. The villa was built in the 1570s for Cardinal Gambara. The two identical palaces are surrounded by a geometrically perfect formal Italian garden, punctuated with fountains and pools, fed by a spring at the top of the garden. Water cascades down over five terraces, performing spectacular water-games to impress and surprise guests. Not all are still working, but the ropework cascade and stone dining table with central wine-cooling rivulet can still be admired.

Sacro Bosco
Località Giardino, Bomarzo (0761 924 029). **Open** *May-Sept* 8.30am-7.30pm daily. *Oct-Apr* 9am-4.30pm daily. **Admission** €7.75/ L15,000 adults; €6.71/L13,000 concessions. **No credit cards**.

Villa Farnese
Caprarola (0761 646 052). **Open** *Villa* 8.30am-6.45pm daily. *Tours of villa & park* half-hourly 8.30am-5.30pm Mon-Sat; 10am, 11am, noon, 3pm, 4pm, 5pm Sun. **Admission** €2.06/ L4,000; €1.03/L2,000 concessions. **No credit cards**.

Villa Lante
Bagnaia (0761 288 008). **Open** *Gardens only Apr-Sept* 8.30am-7.30pm Tue-Sun. *Oct-Mar* 8.30am-4.30pm Tue-Sun. **Admission** €2.06/ L4,000; €1.03/L2,000 concessions. **No credit cards**.

Getting there

By car
Bomarzo: A1 to Attigliano exit, then minor road to Bomarzo.
Caprarola: Via Cassia (SS2), then road to Ronciglione/Caprarola.
Bagnaia: A1 to Orte exit, then SS204.

By train
Bomarzo: FM1 to Orte, then FS train to Attigliano-Bomarzo (5km from park).
Bagnaia: From Roma-Nord/Piazzale Flaminio to Bagnaia, change at Viterbo.

By bus
Bomarzo: COTRAL from Saxa Rubra, change at Viterbo.
Caprarola: COTRAL from Saxa Rubra.
Bagnaia: COTRAL from Saxa Rubra, change at Viterbo.

tree-covered crater is a site once used for worship by the cult of Diana. For Romans, the medieval village is synonymous with strawberries, grown under glass by the lake. Across the lake, **Genzano** holds an annual flower festival (early June), when the town's streets are decorated with elaborate carpets of flowers.

In the plain south-east of Rome, **Ninfa** – local legend says – was named after a nymph who was so devastated at the loss of her lover that she cried copiously enough to form a stream. Today, a stream still flows though some of Italy's most beautiful gardens, which ramble through the ruins of a medieval town.

Oasi di Ninfa
Doganella di Ninfa (06 687 3056). **Open** *Apr-Oct* 9am-noon, 3-6.30pm first Sat, Sun of each month. **Admission** €7.23/L14,000; under-10s free. **No credit cards.**
The origins of the ruined town of Ninfa are obscure. That it existed in the eighth century is certain. In the 12th century it made the mistake of supporting a rival to the then pope, and was sacked by the pontiff's defender, Holy Roman Emperor Frederick Barbarossa. It rallied, though, and by the early 1380s it had 150 large *palazzi*. Shortly afterwards, however, the town came definitively to grief in an inter-clan war. What warfare did not destroy, malaria finished off, and Ninfa was gradually left as a deserted ruin.

The Caetani family acquired it in the 14th century, but showed little interest in their ghost estate until the 1920s, when Don Gelasio Caetani decided

to plant his vast collection of exotic species here. The result of his botanical dabbling is pure magic: catch it in late spring to see it at its romantic best. Only a limited number of visitors are allowed, so tickets are best purchased in advance in Rome from the Fondazione Caetani (via delle Botteghe Oscure 32, open 9am-1.20pm, 3.30-7.30pm Mon-Fri). The Fondazione also provides information on occasional extra openings from April to June.

Where to eat

On the approach road to Villa Adriana is the **Adriano** (via di Villa Adriana 194, 0774 535 028, closed dinner Sun, average €25.40/ L55,000), a surprisingly untouristy restaurant that's great for al fresco eating in summer.

In Frascati you're spoiled for choice. Among the crowd, **Cacciani** (via Armando Diaz 13, 06 942 0378, closed Mon, average €36.15/ L70,000), is one of the best restaurants in the Castelli (with prices to match). For something simpler, try **Zarazà** (viale Regina Margherita 45, 06 942 2053, closed Mon & 2wks Aug, average €20.65/ L40,000).

In Grottaferrata, **La Briciola** (via G D'Annunzio 12, 06 945 9338, closed dinner Sun, all Mon & 3wks Aug, average €28.40/L55,000) uses the freshest of local ingredients.

In Nemi, the **Specchio di Diana** (corso Vittorio Emanuele 13, 06 936 8805, average €23.25/L45,000) serves its vast pizzas on a terrace overlooking the lake.

More than an uninspiring wine: Frascati's Renaissance **Villa Aldobrandini**. *See p275.*

An Englishman in Lazio

Landscape architect Russell Page (1906-1985) may have been British by birth and upbringing, but his many delightful designs dotted around France (where he studied), Italy, the United States, Middle East and South America show the extent to which he succeeded in blending his own particular garden tastes with the surrounding native countryside and vegetation.

The best Italian example of this is the lush, rocky garden of La Mortella, on Ischia, an island off Naples. But Lazio, too, boasts its Page masterpieces, at **La Landriana** to the south of Rome, and **San Liberato** on the south-west shore of Lake Bracciano (*see p277*).

Looking at its perfect progression from trimly clipped box parterres through some 30 softer-edged garden 'rooms' to faux-wilderness, you'd never guess that La Landriana was the result of a battle of very strong wills: Lavinia Taverna, a member of Rome's nobility, had been working on her oasis in the middle of the swampy flatlands south of Rome for a decade before Page arrived in the late 1970s to announce, 'When I got there, there was no garden at all, there was absolutely nothing.' But what the *marchesa* and the landscapist went on to create through their odd symbiosis is simply delightful.

At San Liberato, Page tinkered for ten years with his creation on a property sloping in graceful terraces down towards the Lago di Bracciano: around the house and the fourth-century chapel which gives the property its name are a garden of simples and sweet-smelling rose gardens; beyond, sweeping lawns dotted with trees from exotic climes provide welcome shade in summer and dramatic colour schemes through the autumn.

Information on special open days and events at these two and many other Italian gardens can be found by consulting www.grandigiardini.it, the website of the Grandi Giardini Italiani organisation (031 756 211/fax 031 765 768).

Giardino della Landriana
Via Campo di Carne 51, località Tor San Lorenzo, Ardea (06 687 6333/06 9101 0350/fax 06 687 2839). **Open** *Apr-mid June* 10am-noon, 3-6pm Sat, Sun. *Mid June-Sept* 3-6pm Sun. **Admission** €5.16/L10,000; €2.58/L5,000 concessions. **No credit cards**.

Tenuta di San Liberato
Via Settevene Palo 33, Bracciano (06 998 8384/fax 06 9980 2506). **Open** *guided tours only* 4.30pm first and last Sun of month. **Closed** Aug. **Admission** €5.16/L10,000; €2.58/L5,000 concessions. **No credit cards**.

Getting there

By car
Tivoli & Villa Adriana: A24 (exit Tivoli) or via Tiburtina (SS5).
Palestrina: Via Prenestina (SS155).
Castelli Romani: Via Tuscolana (SS215) to Grottaferrata and Frascati; via Appia (SS7) to Genzano, Castelgandolfo and Nemi.
Ninfa: Via Appia (SS7) to Tor Tre Ponti, then follow signs to Latina Scalo then Ninfa (65km/40 miles).

By bus
Tivoli & Villa Adriana: COTRAL from Ponte Mammolo; note that the autostrada bus makes the journey more quickly. Not all services stop at Villa Adriana; check before boarding.
Palestrina: COTRAL from Ponte Mammolo or Anagnina.
Castelli Romani: COTRAL from Anagnina.

By train
Castelli Romani: FM4 to Frascati and Castelgandolfo.

Ninfa: From Termini to Latina Scalo, then haggle with waiting taxi drivers for the 9km/5½ mile ride to the gardens.

Tourist information

APT Tivoli
Largo Garibaldi (0774 311 249/fax 0774 331 294). **Open** 9am-1pm, 3-6pm Mon-Sat.

APT Frascati
Piazzale Marconi 1 (06 942 0331/fax 06 942 5498). **Open** *Oct-May* 9am-1.10pm, 3-6pm Mon-Sat. *June-Sept* 9am-1.10pm, 4-7pm Mon-Sat.

North from Rome

Lago di Bracciano, about 40km (24 miles) north of Rome, in the crater of an extinct volcano, is surrounded by picturesque villages and sailing, windsurfing and canoeing clubs. Swimming is possible all around the generally clean lake, but the best spots are just north of

The **Castello Orsini-Odescalchi** dominates Bracciano.

Bracciano town on the western shore, and on the east side near Trevignano. **Anguillara**, the nearest lakeside town to Rome, is a medieval town perched on a rocky crag, and especially beautiful at sunset.

Bracciano, the main town on the lake, is dominated by the **Castello Orsini-Odescalchi**, built in 1470, with fine apartments decorated by Antoniazzo Romano and the Zuccari brothers. Close by is **Lago di Martignano**, a quieter, smaller, offshoot of the Bracciano crater. There's a small beach, where you can rent sailing boats, pedalos and canoes. You need a car to get there: turn sharp right at the little chapel before Anguillara, follow the road past a drinking trough and go left on a track (signposted 'lago') for three kilometres (two miles).

Trevignano is a medieval town with a pleasant *lungolago* (lakeside promenade). It's best reached on the via Cassia, which leads past the ruins of **Veio**, Rome's great Etruscan rival in the fifth century BC (*see also p280*).

If you turn right instead of left at the Trevignano junction on the Cassia you will come to **Calcata**, isolated on a volcanic spur above the verdant Valle del Treja. This picturesque village is a mecca for ageing hippies, and there's no shortage of wholefood snack bars and ethnic jewellery shops. It's also the hub for several spectacular walks, some of which are marked.

Viterbo was an important Etruscan town and an insignificant Roman one; it was fortified in the eighth century by the Lombard King Desiderius as a launching pad for sacking Rome. Viterbo was caught up in the medieval quarrels between the Holy Roman Empire and

the Church: the town played host to popes and anti-popes, several of whom relocated here when things got too hot in Rome. Gregory X was elected pope in Viterbo and lasted a month; Hadrian V died on arriving in town; John XXI was killed a year after his election when his bedroom floor in the Papal Palace collapsed.

Viterbo was badly bombed in World War II, but has been meticulously restored. In its narrow streets you will stumble across medieval laundries, ancient porticos, imposing towers and crenellated buildings. There are lions (the symbol of Viterbo) and fountains everywhere.

The medieval quarter of San Pellegrino lies at the southern edge of the city, flanked by piazza della Morte. Across the bridge is the elegant 12th-century – but much altered and restored – cathedral of San Lorenzo. Next door to it is the Palazzo Papale, built for the popes in the 13th century and restored in the 19th. The pretty 12th-century church of Santa Maria Nuova has an ancient head of Jupiter on the façade, and a pulpit from where St Thomas Aquinas preached. Behind the church are the remains of a small Lombard cloister (always open).

Piazza del Plebiscito is dominated by the **Palazzo Comunale** town hall (1500), where the lovely courtyard has a 17th-century fountain; a staircase leads to the Senate rooms, which are usually open to the public in the morning. At the top of the stairs is the Chapel of the Commune with two huge canvases by Sebastiano del Piombo and a *Visitation* by Bartolomeo Cavarozzi. From the piazza, via Roma leads past the Fontana dei Leoni into Corso d'Italia; at number 11 is the Caffè

Schenardi, a 15th-century hotel that has been a café since 1818. Mussolini had breakfast here in 1938, at the third table on the right.

Taking via Cavour out of piazza del Plebiscito, past the 13th-century Fontana Grande, via Garibaldi leads up to the Porta Romana. Just inside the gate on the left is the church of **San Sisto**, parts of which date from the ninth century. It has a chancel raised 15 steps above the nave, and two curious twisting columns.

Outside the walls, opposite Porta della Verità, is the 12th century **Santa Maria della Verità**, with some of the most Tuscan frescos outside of Tuscany in the Gothic Cappella Mazzatosta, painted by local boy Lorenzo di Viterbo in 1469. The charming 'Marriage of the Virgin' panel was badly damaged in the war, and reconstructed from 16,000 pieces. The chapel pavement has remains of majolica decoration. In the old convent next door is the renovated **Museo Civico**, with Etruscan finds and works of art from local churches, and two canvases by Sebastiano del Piombo.

Within a seven-kilometre (4½-mile) radius of the city (accessible by car only), there are several bubbling pools of sulphurous water. Local residents like to sit around in them, smeared in greeny-white clay. The best place to wallow is the Bagnaccio, where four basins of varying degrees of heat are scooped out of the clay. To get there, leave Viterbo on the Montefiascone road, and after five kilometres (three miles) turn left on to the road to Marta. After another kilometre you'll see a ruin on your left. Just before this, an unpaved road branches off to the Bagnaccio.

Castello Orsini-Odescalchi

Piazza Mazzini 14, Bracciano (06 9980 4348). **Open** 10am-1pm, 3-6pm Tue-Sun. **Admission** €5.68/ L11,000; €4.65/L9,000 concessions. **No credit cards.**

Museo Civico

Piazza Crispi 2, Viterbo (0761 348 275). **Open** *Apr-Oct* 9am-7pm Tue-Sun. *Nov-Mar* 9am-6pm Tue-Sun. **Admission** €3.10/L6,000. **No credit cards.**

Where to eat

In Bracciano, **Vino e Camino** (piazza Mazzini 11, 06 9980 3433, closed Mon, 1wk Aug, average €18.10/L35,000) is an excellent wine bar with tables outside right beneath the Castello Odescalchi. In Viterbo, the **Porta Romana** (via della Bontà 12, 0761 307 118, closed Sun & 2wks Aug, average €18.10/L35,000) serves good food in a friendly, family atmosphere. More upmarket but equally good value is the **Enoteca La Torre** (via della Torre 5, 0761 226 467, closed Sun, average €23.25/L45,000), which serves creative versions of local dishes.

Getting there

By car

Lago di Bracciano & around: Via Braccianense (SS493) to Anguillara (32km/20 miles), Bracciano (40km/25 miles); via Cassia (SS2) to Trevignano (43km/26.5 miles), Calcata (45km/28 miles). **Viterbo**: A1 or Via Cassia (SS2) to Viterbo (85km/53 miles).

By train

Lago di Bracciano & around: From Termini, Tiburtina, Ostiense to Anguillara or Bracciano. **Viterbo**: FS hourly services from Ostiense or Trastevere to Viterbo.

By bus

Lago di Bracciano & around: COTRAL from Lepanto. **Viterbo**: COTRAL from Saxa Rubra.

Tourist information

APT Viterbo

Piazza San Carluccio (0761 304 795/fax 0761 220 957). **Open** 9am-1pm Mon-Sat.

Into the mountains

When the city gets too hot and the sea too crowded, smart Romans head for the hills. There are some serious mountains within an hour and a half of the capital. The nearest range is the **Monti Lucretili**, only 40 kilometres (25 miles) north-east of Rome (you can see them on a clear day from the Gianicolo, *see p117*). A good base is the pretty hill town of **Licenza**, with the remains of Horace's country retreat, the Sabine Farm, close by. From **Civitella di Licenza**, a tiny hamlet just outside the town, it's possible to climb **Monte Pellecchia** (1,368 metres/4,490 feet), the highest peak in the Lucretili, in about two and a half hours. Another good walk is the hour-long trek to the upland plain of **Il Pratone**, from the end of the Monte Morra road above the village of **Marcellina**.

Getting there

By car

A24 then minor roads: exit Tivoli for Marcellina, exit Vicovaro-Mandela for Licenza; via Tuscolana (SS5) then well-signposted minor roads.

By bus

COTRAL services from Ponte Mammolo.

Tourist information

See p303.

Etruscan Lazio

Comparatively little is known about the Etruscans, and their language has not been deciphered. They were undoubtedly more sophisticated than the early Romans, and passed on to them many of their engineering techniques before falling prey to Rome's brutal territorial expansion campaign in the late fourth century BC.

The territory occupied by the Etruscan League stretched across central Italy, but Etruscan Lazio can be considered as the strip of land stretching from just north of Rome to the Tuscan border, with most of the important towns (Cerveteri, Tarquinia and Vulci) set on hills a few kilometres from the coast.

For an overview of the Etruscans' talents, have a look at the Etruscan Museum at Villa Giulia in Rome (see p83) before setting out for the sites. The contents of many tombs have ended up here or in the Vatican's Museo Gregoriano (see p141). The only on-site museum with exhibits of the same quality is at Tarquinia. Etruscan houses were built of wood; only their tombs, dug down into volcanic rock, have survived.

Cerveteri

Etruscan Kysry, romanised as Caere, was a vast, prosperous town with three ports, one of the great trading centres of the Mediterranean between the seventh and fifth centuries BC. It was situated further along the same volcanic spur that is occupied by the modern town, but covered an area 20 times greater. In the modern town, the 16th-century Orsini castle is home to the small **Museo Cerite**, with local finds.

Much more interesting than the town itself is the **Necropoli di Banditaccia**, one kilometre (half a mile) from the piazza. The necropolis has plenty of atmosphere. Beneath the pines, this town of the dead – with streets, *piazze* and tidy little houses – is one of the most touching archaeological sites in Italy. The area that is visitable today represents only a small part of its total extent. The earliest tombs here date from the seventh century BC; the latest are from the third, by which time there had been a progressive impoverishment of tomb size and decoration. Don't miss the well-preserved sixth-century BC Tomba dei Capitelli, the fourth-century BC Tomba dei Rilievi, with bas-reliefs of weapons and domestic utensils, and the three parallel streets of fifth- and sixth-century BC cube-shaped tombs between the via degli Inferni

and via delle Serpi. Outside the main gate, the Tomba degli Scudi e delle Sedie has chairs carved out of tufa rock and bas reliefs of shields adorning the walls.

Museo Cerite

Piazza Santa Maria, Cerveteri (06 994 1354). **Open** 8.30am-7.30pm Tue-Sun. **Admission** free.

Necropoli di Banditaccia

Via della Necropoli, Cerveteri (06 994 0001). **Open** *Oct-Apr* 8.30am-4.30pm Tue-Sun. *May-Sept* 8.30am-7.30pm Tue-Sun. Ticket office closes one hour earlier. **Admission** €4.13/L8,000; €2.06/L4,000 concessions. **No credit cards**.

Tarquinia

Tarquinia's tombs are hidden beneath a grassy hill about two kilometres (1¼ miles) out of town. (Though the necropolis can be visited separately, it's worthwhile to call for information and tickets at the **Museo Nazionale**). The necropolis has the art that Cerveteri lacks: over a hundred vividly painted tombs that provide an insight into Etruscan life. There are scenes of work and social life, athletic contests, mysterious rituals and erotic encounters. In order to limit atmospheric pollution, only a handful of tombs are open at a time. The Tomba della Caccia e della Pesca has delightful fishing and hunting scenes; in the Tomba dei Leopardi, couples recline in a banqueting scene (note the man passing his partner an egg – a recurrent symbol, though experts have not been able to agree what it represents). There is a similar scene with dancers in the elegant Tomba delle Leonesse. The Tomba dei Tori, one of the oldest, has a scene of Achilles waiting to ambush Troilus, and another containing *un po' di pornografico*, as Etruscan fan DH Lawrence gleefully (but ungrammatically) described it.

The town of Tarquinia bristles with medieval defensive towers, and its 12th-century church of Santa Maria di Castello dominates the plain below. The **Museo Nazionale** has one of the best Etruscan collections outside Rome. Its chief exhibit is a pair of fourth-century terracotta winged horses from a temple, proof that the Etruscans could model with as much finesse as the Greeks.

Museo Nazionale & Necropolis

Palazzo Vitelleschi, piazza Cavour, Tarquinia (0766 856 036). **Open** *Museum* 8.30am-7.30pm Tue-Sun. *Necropolis* 8.30am-1hr before sunset Tue-Sun. **Admission** *Museum & necropolis* €6.20/L12,000; €3.10/L6,000 concessions. *Museum or necropolis* €4.13/L8,000; €2.06/L4,000 concessions. **No credit cards**.

Cerveteri's **Necropoli di Banditaccia**: dead interesting. *See p280.*

Tuscania

In Tuscania it's the post-Etruscan bits that
really stand out – even though the town itself
was dealt a devastating blow by a major
earthquake in 1971.

The town boasts two Romanesque-Lombard
churches, San Pietro and Santa Maria
Maggiore. The Colle San Pietro, on which they
stand, was the site of an Etruscan and then
a Roman settlement; fragments of the
pre-Christian acropolis are incorporated into
the apse of **San Pietro**.

Founded in the eighth century, the church
was reworked from the 11th to the 13th
centuries, when the adjacent bishop's palace
and towers were added. The façade is startling:
three-faced trifrons, snakes and dancers owe
more to pagan culture than Christian
iconography. The interior has a cosmatesque
(*see p87* **Glossary**) pavement and 12th-century
frescos. **Santa Maria Maggiore** (Strada Santa
Maria) was built at the same time, with
tamer beasts on its marble façade, and a
more harmonious interior.

The main Etruscan sight in the town is in
the small **Museo Archaeologico**, in the
cloisters of the Santa Maria del Riposo
convent. Inside, four generations of the same
Etrusco-Roman family gaze from the lids of
their sarcophagi.

Museo Archeologico

*Via Madonna del Riposo 36, Tuscania (0761
436 209).* **Open** 8.30am-7.30pm Tue-Sun.
Admission free.

Where to eat

A plate of home-made pasta or fresh fish on
the square-side tables of Cerveteri's **Antica
Locanda Le Ginestre** (piazza Santa Maria
5, 06 994 0672, closed Mon & 2wks Nov,
average €41.30/L80,000) is a perfect end to
a tomb-hopping day.

Tuscania has one of northern Lazio's best
restaurants, **Al Gallo** (via del Gallo 22, 0761
443 388, closed Mon & 3wks Jan-Feb, average
€41.30/L80,000); gourmet dishes and an
extensive wine list raise it above the usual
trattoria di campagna.

Getting there

By car

Cerveteri: 44km (27 miles) by A12 or Via Aurelia
(SS1).
Tarquinia: 91km/56.5 miles, by A12 and Via
Aurelia (SS1).
Tuscania: 85km/53 miles, Via Cassia (SS2) to
Vetralla, then local road.

By train

Cerveteri: From Termini, Tuscolana, Ostiense or
Trastevere to Cerveteri-Ladispoli station (6km/3½
miles out of town), then local bus.
Tarquinia: (irregular) from Termini or Ostiense to
Tarquinia.

By bus

Cerveteri: COTRAL from Lepanto.
Tarquinia: COTRAL from Lepanto, change at
Civitavecchia.
Tuscania: COTRAL from Saxa Rubra (summer
only; in winter bus to Viterbo, then change).

Directory

Directory

Getting Around

By air

Aeroporto Leonardo Da Vinci, Fiumicino

Via dell'Aeroporto di Fiumicino 320 (switchboard 06 65951/information 06 6595 3640/06 6595 4455/ www.adr.it). **Open** 24 hrs daily.
Rome's main airport is about 30km (18 miles) from the city, and handles all scheduled flights.

Aeroporto GB Pastine, Ciampino

Via Appia Nuova 1650 (information 06 794 941/www.adr.it). **Open** 24hrs daily.
Ciampino, about 15 km (9 miles) south-east of the city, is mainly a military airbase, but is also used by charter flights to Rome.

On from Fiumicino

By train

There is an express rail service between the airport and Termini station, which takes 32 minutes and runs every 30 minutes from 6.51am until 9.51pm daily. Tickets in either direction cost €8.78/L17,000. The regular service from Fiumicino takes 25-40 minutes, and stops at Trastevere, Ostiense, Tuscolana and Tiburtina stations. Trains leave about every 15 minutes (less often on Sundays) between 5.57am-11.27pm (5.06am-10.36pm to Fiumicino). Tickets cost €4.65/L9,000 (BIRG tickets also valid, *see p286*).

You can buy tickets for both these services from automatic machines in the main airport lobby and rail stations, from the Alitalia office in front of the central platforms, from the ticket office (open 7am-9.30pm daily), and the airport *tabacchi*. Some carriages have access for

wheelchair users (*see also p292*). Stamp your ticket in the machines on the station platform before boarding.

By bus

During the night, a bus service (information 800 431 784) runs between Fiumicino (from outside Terminal C) and Tiburtina in Rome. Tickets cost €3.62/L7,000 from automatic machines or on the bus. Buses leave Tiburtina at 12.30am, 1.15am, 2.30am and 3.45am, stopping at Termini 10 minutes later. Departures from Fiumicino are at 1.15am, 2.15am, 3.30am and 5am. Neither Termini or Tiburtina station are attractive places at night, and it's advisable to get a taxi directly from there to your final destination. Metro line B, which passes through Tiburtina, closes at midnight, and buses are scarce.

By taxi

A taxi into Rome from Fiumicino will cost at least €41.32/L80,000, including a surcharge for the airport trip (€6.20/L12,000 from Fiumicino, €7.23/L14,000 to Fiumicino from Rome, with an added €2.58/L5,000 for night service between 10pm and 7am) . Use only yellow or white officially licensed cabs lined up at ranks (ignore all touts). *See also p287*.

On from Ciampino

The best way into town is by COTRAL bus to Anagnina metro station. Buses for Anagnina leave from in front of the arrivals hall every 30-40 mins, 6.50am-11.40pm daily (6.10am-11pm, Anagnina to Ciampino). The fare is

€1.03/L2,000. Tickets can be bought from an automatic machine in the arrivals hall and at the newsstand in the departures hall. A taxi to the centre of town will set you back about €36.15/L70,000; the supplement from town to Ciampino is €5.16/L10,000.

By bus

There is no central long-distance bus station in Rome. Most international and national coach services terminate outside the following metro stations: Lepanto, Ponte Mammolo and Tiburtina (routes north); Anagnina and EUR Fermi (routes south). For further information, *see p268*.

By train

Most long-distance trains arrive at Termini station, which is also the centre of the metro and city bus networks. The station is a pickpocket's paradise, so watch your wallets and luggage carefully. Trains arriving at night stop at either Tiburtina or Ostiense, both some way from the centre of Rome. The metro, bus routes 649 and 492, or night bus 40N, run from Tiburtina into the city centre. If you arrive at Ostiense after midnight, it's advisable to take a taxi to your final destination.

Some trains also bypass Termini during the day, while some others stop at more than one station in Rome; it may be more convenient to get off at one of the smaller stations rather than go all the way into Termini.

For information on buying train tickets, *see p268*.

Airlines

Alitalia

*Via L Bissolati 11, Via Veneto &
Villa Borghese (06 6562 8222/
domestic flights 06 65 641/
international flights 06 65 642/
www.alitalia.it). Metro Barberini/bus
to via Bissolati.* **Open** 9am-6pm
Mon-Fri. **Credit** AmEx, DC, MC, V.
Map p323 1B.
*Fiumicino Airport (domestic flights
06 6563 4590/international flights
06 6563 4951).* **Open** 24hrs daily.

British Airways

*Via L Bissolati 54, Via Veneto &
Villa Borghese (848 812 266/
www.britishairways.com/italy). Metro
Barberini/bus to via Bissolati.* **Open
Office** 9am-5pm Mon-Fri. *Phone
reservations* 8am-8pm Mon-Fri; 8am-
5pm Sat. **Credit** AmEx, DC, MC, V.
Map p323 1B.
Fiumicino airport (06 6501 1513).
Open 6am-10pm daily.
BA's downtown office in via
Bissolati was due to close down in
July 2001, after which bookings must
be made by phone or online.

Qantas

Reservations 06 5248 2725. **Open**
8am-8pm Mon-Fri; 8am-2pm Sat.
Credit AmEx, DC, MC, V.

Getting around

See transport map pp328-9.

City-centre transport

City-centre and inner suburb
destinations are covered by the
buses and trams of the ATAC
transport authority.

The municipal transport
system is increasingly efficient
and easy to use once you've
got the hang of it. Moreover,
it's fairly safe, even at night.
Gropers and pickpockets tend
to limit their activities to
packed tourist buses along major
tourist routes, most
notoriously the 64 and 40
Express between Termini
station and the Vatican.

ATAC **buses** are mainly
orange (though some, to fool
you, are green, including the
zippy new supertrams and
bendy-buses).

Routes are added or
suspended, and numbers

Useful routes

See also p149 for buses
serving the via Appia Antica;
Colosseum 60 Express, 75,
85, 87, 117, 175, 186,
204, 810, 850, 29N, 40N,
tram 3, J4, J5, metro B
(Colosseo).

Foro Romano, Fori Imperiali
60 Express, 84, 85, 87,
175, 186, 810, 850, J2,
J4, J5.

**Largo Argentina (for campo
de' Fiori, Pantheon, Ghetto)**
30 Express, 40 Express,
46, 62, 63, 64, 70, 81, 87,
186, 204, 492, 628, 780,
810, 916, 45N, 72N, 78N,
96N, 98N, 99N, tram 8,
J4, J5.

Piazza Navona 46, 62, 64,
70, 81, 87, 116, 116T,
186, 492, 628, 45N,
78N, 98N.

**Piazza San Silvestro (for
the Spanish Steps and
central shopping streets)**
52, 53, 61, 71, 80 Express,
85, 160, 850, J7.

**Via del Tritone (for Spanish
Steps, central shopping
streets and the Trevi
Fountain)** 52, 53, 61, 62,
63, 95, 116, 119, 175,
492, 590, 630, 25N,
45N, 60N.

Piazza Venezia H, 40
Express, 44, 46, 60
Express, 62, 63, 64, 70,
81, 84, 85, 87, 95, 117,
119, 160, 170, 175, 186,
204, 492, 628, 630, 780,

781, 810, 850, 916, 25N,
44N, 45N, 60N, 72N, 78N,
90N, 91N, 96N, 98N, 99N,
J2, J4, J5.

Trastevere H, tram 8, 23,
280, 780.

Vatican, St Peter's 23, 32,
34, 40 Express, 62, 64, 81,
280, 916, 29N, 30N, tram
19, metro A (Ottaviano), J4,
J5, J6, J9.

Villa Borghese tram 3, tram
19, 88, 95, 116, 116T,
204, 490, 491, 495, 910
25N, 55N, metro A
(Spagna), J6, J7.

**Termini station (also for
Terme di Diocleziano, and
Palazzo Massimo alle
Terme)** C, 16, 36, 38, 75,
84, 86, 90 Express, 92,
105, 157, 170, 175, 204,
217, 310, 360, 590, 591,
649, 714, 6N, 12N, 40N,
45N, 55N, 78N, 91N, metro
A (Termini), metro B
(Termini), J2, J3, J6.

Tiburtina station C, 71,
111, 163, 168, 204, 211,
309, 409, 443, 448, 490,
491, 492, 495, 545, 40N,
metro B (Tiburtina), J5.

Ostiense station 30
Express, 95, 175, 280,
715, 719, 91N, metro B
(Piramide), J4.

Trastevere station H,170,
228, 766, 773, 774, 780,
781, 786, 871, 72N, 96N,
tram 3, tram 8.

change, with some regularity:
if you plan to use public
transport, it's a good idea to
pick up a copy of the latest city
bus map, available free from
ATAC HQ (*below*).

All ATAC routes – except
night services – run between
about 5.30am and midnight
daily, with a frequency of
between 10 to 45 minutes,
depending on the route. The

doors for boarding (usually
front and rear) and alighting
(usually centre) are clearly
marked. Each bus stop shows
the lines that stop there, and
lists the stops each line makes
along its route.

Note that the new 'Express'
buses are so-called because
they make few stops along
their route: check before
boarding that you aren't going

Directory

to be whisked helplessly past your destination.

A small fleet of electric mini-buses also plies the centre. The 116, 116T, 117 and 119 connect places such as the piazza di Spagna, campo de' Fiori, and piazza Venezia with via Veneto and Termini. It's a bit like trundling around on a milk float, but they're handy when it's too hot to walk.

Tram routes mainly serve suburban areas, and an express tram service – No.8 – links largo Argentina to Trastevere and the western suburbs.

Metroferro is responsible for Rome's two **metro** lines, which form a rough cross, with the hub at Termini station. Line A runs from the south-east to the north-west, line B from EUR in the south to the north-eastern suburbs. Both lines are open from 5.30am to 11.30pm daily (12.30am on Saturday). Plans for Line C, to cross the city centre, are moving forward at a snail's pace.

TICKETS

The same tickets are valid on all city bus (except J lines, *see below*), tram and metro lines, whether operated by ATAC, Metroferro, or the regional transport authority COTRAL (*see p287*). They must be bought before boarding, and are available from ATAC automatic ticket machines, information centres, some bars and newsstands and all *tabacchi* shops (*see p302*).

When you board, you must stamp tickets in the machines by the rear and/or front doors. As this guide went to press, the ticket-issuing system was being changed: old-style orange tickets must be stamped in the orange machines; new-style tickets must be stamped in the yellow machines.

Children under ten travel free, after which they pay the adult fare for single, daily and weekly tickets, as do

pensioners. Students, pensioners and the disabled pay lower rates for monthly and yearly tickets.

If travelling without paying looks an easy option, bear in mind that there are ticket inspectors around: if you are caught you will be fined €51.65/L100,000 on the spot.

Tickets can be bought on board night buses, where they cost €1.03/L2,000 (exact money only accepted).

ATAC & Metroferro

Via Volturno 65, Esquilino (06 46 951/06 57 531/tollfree information line 800 431 784). Metro Termini/ bus to piazza dei Cinquecento. **Open** *Office 6.30am-5pm Mon-Fri. Phone line 8am-6pm Mon-Fri.* **Map** *p323 2B.* This is ATAC's HQ: the friendly porter hands out free bus maps. The phone line is Italian-speaking only.

Timed ticket

The *biglietto integro a tempo* (BIT) is valid for 75mins, during which you can use an unlimited number of ATAC buses, plus one trip on the metro; €0.77/L1,500.

Integrated ticket

The *biglietto integrato giornaliero* (BIG) is valid for one day; covers the whole urban network except express services from Termini station to Fiumicino airport; €3.10/L6,000.

Weekly ticket

The *carta integrata settimanale* (CIS) is valid seven days; covers all bus routes and the metro system, including the lines to Ostia; €12.39/L24,000.

Monthly ticket

The *abbonamento mensile* is valid one calendar month for unlimited travel on the entire metropolitan transport system; €25.82/L50,000.

Regional Ticket (BIRG)

The *biglietto integrato regionale giornaliero* (BIRG) is a one-day ticket covering rail travel within the Lazio region. The price varies according to the zone of your destination. The BIRG is valid on the metro, buses, the FS (second class only) and the rail link to and from Fiumicino, but not on the Fiumicino Express line from Termini station.

TOUR BUSES

ATAC's 110 city tour bus leaves Termini station every 30 minutes from 10am to 8pm

(Mar-Sept 9am-8pm), taking in sights such as the Colosseum, Circo Massimo, piazza Venezia, St Peter's, piazza del Popolo and via Veneto, before returning to Termini. The two-hour tour costs €7.75/ L15,000 non-stop or €12.90/ L25,000 for an all-day stop'n'go ticket.

ATAC also offers a three-hour tour of Rome's major basilicas, costing €7.75/ L15,000. It leaves Termini at 10.30am and 3pm, stopping at St Peter's, San Paolo fuori le Mura, San Giovanni in Laterano and Santa Maria Maggiore, stopping at each for 30 minutes.

Tickets for tours can be bought at booths in front of Termini station. For bookings or information, phone 06 4695 2252 (open Oct-Mar 9am-7pm daily, Apr-Sept 9am-8pm daily).

J-BUSES

A special privately operated network of buses was put in place to ferry pilgrims to major tourist sights and churches during the Holy Year in 2000. Blue and orange, with air-conditioning and wheelchair facilities, the future of these 'J' lines, run by the SITA company, was under review as this guide went to press.

Tickets for J buses can be bought in the normal places or from the driver. Normal ATAC tickets are not valid for J buses, although ATAC monthly and yearly passes are. A ticket valid for 75 minutes costs €0.98/ L1,900; a one-day ticket costs €2.43/L4,700; a weekly pass costs €9.30/ L18,000.

SITA (Linea J)

Tollfree information line 800 076 287. **Open** *9am-6pm Mon-Fri.*

Suburban transport

See transport map p317. Metroferro (*see above*) operates three **suburban railway lines** from Termini, Porta San

Paolo and Roma Nord stations. Local lines of the Ferrovie dello Stato (FS), the state railway, are also integrated into the city transport network. Regular bus/tram/metro tickets are valid on trains as far as the stations marked in red on the map on p317.

The coaches of the regional transport company COTRAL (formerly Li.La. or ACOTRAL) cover further-flung destinations (*see p268*).

Taxis

Licensed taxis are painted white (a few old yellow ones remain), and have a meter. If anyone approaches you at Termini or any of the other major tourist magnets, muttering 'taxi?' always refuse, as they are likely to charge you up to 400 per cent more than the normal rate.

FARES & SURCHARGES

When you pick up a taxi at a rank or hail one in the street, the meter should read zero. As you set off, it will begin to indicate the minimum fare – €2.32/L4,500 at the time of writing – for the first 200 metres (700 feet), after which the charge goes up according to time and distance. There are surcharges on Sundays, public holidays and for trips to and from the airport (*see p284*), plus €1.03/L2,000 for each item of luggage placed in the boot; €2.58/L5,000 is also added to the basic fare between 10pm and 7am.

Most of Rome's taxi drivers are honest workers; but if you suspect you're being ripped off, make a note of the driver's name and number from the metal plaque inside the car's rear door. The more ostentatiously you do this, the more likely you are to find the fare returning to its proper level. Report complaints to the drivers' co-operative (its

phone number is shown on the outside of each car) or, in serious cases, the police (*see p299*).

TAXI RANKS

Ranks are indicated by a blue sign with *Taxi* written in white. In the central area there are ranks at largo Argentina, the Pantheon, piazza Venezia, piazza San Silvestro, piazza Sonnino (Trastevere), piazza di Spagna and Termini station.

PHONE CABS

You can phone for a taxi from any of the following companies. When your call is answered, name the street and number, or the name and location of a bar, club or restaurant where you wish to be picked up. You will then be given the taxi code-name (which is always a location followed by a number) and a time, as in *Bahama 69, in tre minuti* (Bahamas 69, in three minutes). A radio taxi will start the meter from the moment your phone call is answered.

Cooperativa Samarcanda 06 55 51.
Cosmos Radio Taxi 06 88 177/ 06 88 22
Società Cooperativa Autoradio Taxi Roma 06 35 70
Società la Capitale Radio Taxi 06 49 94

Trains

For information on train travel to destinations around Rome, *see p268*.

For timetable and general information on rail services anywhere in Italy, call the central information line on 848 888 088 (7am-9pm daily) or consult the state railway's website on www.fs-on-line.it.

Rome's principal stations are:

Stazione Ostiense
Piazzale dei Partigiani, Testaccio (06 4730 5123/06 4730 5066). Metro Piramide/bus to piazzale Porta San Paolo. **Map** p325 2A.

Stazione Piazzale Flaminio (Roma Nord)
Piazzale Flaminio, suburbs: north (06 5753 3115/tollfree 800 431 784). Metro Flaminio/bus to piazzale Flaminio. **Map** p320 1A.

Stazione Termini
Piazza dei Cinquecento, Esquilino (06 4730 6599). Metro Termini/bus to Termini. **Map** p323 2A.

Stazione Tiburtina
Circonvallazione Nomentana, suburbs: south (06 4730 7220/06 4730 7184). Metro Tiburtina/bus to piazza Stazione Tiburtina.

Stazione Trastevere
Piazzale Biondo, Trastevere (06 4730 5034). Bus or tram to circonvallazione Gianicolense.

Cars

Having a car in Rome can be great fun, or a huge liability. At first glance, Roman driving resembles the chariot race in *Ben Hur*, until you realise that it's like a high-speed conversation, with its own language of glances, light flashing and ostentatious acceleration, all carried out with panache.

If you do use a car in the city, some tips to be borne in mind are listed below. Short-term visitors should have no trouble driving with their home licences, although if they are written in different scripts or less common languages an international licence can be useful. EU citizens are obliged to take out an Italian driving licence after being resident for one year.

Remember the following:
• You are required by law to wear a seat belt at all times, and to carry a warning triangle in your car.
• Keep your driving licence, Green Card, vehicle registration and personal ID documents on you at all times.
• Do not leave anything of value (including a car radio) in your car. Take all your luggage into your hotel when you park.

•Flashing your lights in Italy means that you will *not* slow down (contrary to British practice).
•If traffic lights flash amber, you should *stop* and give way to the right.
•Watch out for death-defying mopeds and pedestrians. By local convention, pedestrians usually assume they have the right of way in the older, quieter streets without clearly designated pavements.

RESTRICTED AREAS

Large sections of the city centre are closed to non-resident traffic during business hours, and sometimes in the evening. The municipal police and electronically activated video cameras stand guard over these areas.

You may be fined if you are caught trying to get in; your vehicle may be wheel-clamped if you do manage to slip through the net and park, in which case you'll have to pay a fine and a charge to have the clamp removed. If you are in a hired car or have foreign plates and are stopped, you can sometimes get through by unscrupulous means. Just mention the name of a hotel in the area you want to enter, and you will often be waved on. The first Sunday of most months is designated a no-car day: this is rigidly enforced in the city centre.

BREAKDOWN SERVICES

It is advisable to join a national motoring organisation, like the AA or RAC in Britain or the AAA in the US, before taking a car to Italy. They have reciprocal arrangements with the Automobile Club d'Italia (ACI), which offers assistance in the case of a breakdown, and can provide useful general information. Even for non-members, ACI is the best number to call if you have any kind of breakdown.

If you require extensive repairs and do not know a mechanic, pay a bit more and go to a manufacturer's official dealer, as the reliability of any garage depends on long years of building up a good client-mechanic relationship. Dealers are listed in the *Yellow Pages* under *auto*, along with specialist repairers such as *gommista* (tyre repairs), *marmitte* (exhaust repairs) and *carrozzerie* (bodywork repairs). The *English Yellow Pages*, available from most English bookshops (*see p205*) has a list of garages where English is spoken.

Automobile Club d'Italia (ACI)

(06 49 981/24hr emergency line 116/24hr information line 166 664 477/traffic report in Italian 1518). The ACI has English-speaking staff and provides a range of services for all foreign drivers, which are either free or at low prices. Members of associated organisations are entitled to basic repairs free, and to other services at preferential rates. Non-members will be charged, but prices are generally reasonable.

Touring Club Italiano (TCI)

Via del Babuino 20, Tridente (information 06 3609 5801/24hr members' emergency line 800 337 744/touring@iol.it). Metro Spagna/ bus to piazza del Popolo. **Open** *Office* 9am-9pm Mon-Fri; 9am-noon Sat. *Bookshop* 9am-7.30pm Mon-Sat. **Map** p320 A2.
The Rome office has a bookshop with an English-language section and a travel agency with agreements with national and international tour operators. English is spoken and there's a 20% discount on official prices for all members, including those from international sister clubs.

PARKING

A system in which residents park free and visitors pay has recently been introduced to many areas of the city, and is efficiently policed: watch out for tell-tale blue lines. Parking fees are paid at pay-and-display ticket dispensers, at the rate of €1.03/L2,000 per hour. In some areas you can park free after a certain time at night (usually after 11pm), or at weekends, so check the instructions on the machine before feeding it with coins.

For longer stays, a €25.82/L50,000 parking card, available from *tabacchi*, allows you to deduct parking fees gradually, and saves having to search your pockets for small change.

Elsewhere, anything resembling a parking place is up for grabs, with some exceptions: watch out for signs by entrances saying Passo carrabile (access at all times), Sosta vietata (no parking), and disabled parking spaces marked by yellow stripes on the road. The sign Zona rimozione (tow-away area) means no parking, and is valid for the length of the street, or until the next tow-away sign with a red line through it denoting the end of the restricted area. If a street or square has no cars parked in it, you can safely assume that it's a seriously enforced no-parking zone. In some areas, self-appointed *parcheggiatori* will 'look after' your car for a small fee; though it is illegal and a ridiculous imposition, it's worth coughing up to ensure that your tyres remain intact.

Although cars are fairly safe in most central areas, you may prefer to pay the hefty rates charged by underground car parks to ensure the vehicle is not tampered with. The following are centrally located.

ParkSi Villa Borghese Società Italinpa

Viale del Galoppatoio 33, Via Veneto & Villa Borghese (06 322 5934/06 322 7972). Metro Spagna/bus to via Veneto. **Open** 24hrs daily. **Rates** *Cars* €1.14/L2,200 per hr for up to 3hrs; €0.93/L1,800 per hr for 4-24hrs; €14.46/L28,000 for 24hrs. *Scooters & motorbikes* €1.29/L2,500 for 24hrs. **Credit** AmEx, MC, V. **Map** p322 2C. Vehicle entrances are on via del Muro Torto (from both sides of the road). The car park is linked to the Spagna metro station, with 24hr pedestrian access to piazza di Spagna.

Valentino
*Via Sistina 75E, Via Veneto & Villa
Borghese (06 678 2597). Metro
Spagna/bus to piazza Barberini.*
Open 7am-1am Mon-Sat; 7am-
12.30pm, 6pm-1am Sun. **Rates**
€18,08-€25.82/L35,000-L50,000 for
24hrs. **Credit** AmEx, MC, V.
Map p323 1C.

CAR POUNDS
If you do not find your car
where you left it, it has
probably been towed away.
Phone the municipal police
(Vigili Urbani) on 06 67 691 and
quote your number plate to find
out which of the various car
pounds it has been taken to.

PETROL
Petrol stations sell unleaded
petrol (*senza piombo* or *verde*)
and regular (*super*), though
this latter will be phased out
under EU regulations. Diesel is
gasolio. Liquid propane gas is
GPL. Most stations offer full
service on weekdays; pump
attendants do not expect tips.
At night and on Sundays
many stations have automatic
self-service pumps that accept
L10,000 or L50,000 notes, in
good condition; this will
probably change to €5 and
€10 notes after February
2002. Sometimes unofficial
'assistants' will do the job
for you for a small tip
(€0.50/L1,000).

VEHICLE HIRE
To hire a car you must be
over 21 – in some cases 23 –
and have held a licence for at
least a year. You will be
required to leave a credit card
number or a substantial cash
deposit. It's advisable to take
out collision damage waiver
(CDW) and personal accident
insurance (PAI) on top of basic
third party insurance.
Companies that do not offer
CDW are best avoided.

Avis
*Via Sardegna 38A, Via Veneto &
Villa Borghese (06 4282 4728).
Metro Spagna/bus to via Veneto.*
Open 8am-8pm Mon-Fri; 8am-5pm
Sat; 8am-1pm Sun. **Credit** AmEx,
DC, MC, V. **Map** p322 2B.

*Fiumicino Airport (06 6595
4146/06 6501 1531).* **Open** 7am-
midnight daily.

Ciampino Airport (06 7934 0195).
Open 8am-1.30pm, 3-8pm Mon-Fri;
8.30am-1pm Sat; 8am-1pm, 4pm-
8pm Sun.

*Termini station, Esquilino (06 481
4373). Metro Termini/bus to piazza
dei Cinquecento.* **Open** 7am-8pm
Mon-Fri; 8am-6pm Sat; 8am-1pm
Sun. **Map** p323 2A.

Maggiore
*Fiumicino Airport (06 6501
0678/tollfree 848 867 067).* **Open**
7am-midnight daily. **Credit** AmEx,
DC, MC, V.

*Termini station, Esquilino (06 488
0049). Metro Termini/bus to piazza
dei Cinquecento.* **Open** 7am-8pm
Mon-Fri; 8am-6pm Sat; 8.30am-
12.30am Sun.

Ciampino Airport (06 7934 0368).
Open 8.30am-1pm, 2.30-8pm Mon-
Fri; 8.30am-1pm Sat. Booking
required for Sundays.

MOPED, SCOOTER & CYCLE HIRE
To hire a scooter or moped
(*motorino*) you need a credit
card, an identity document
and/or a cash deposit. Helmets
are required on all motorbikes,
scooters or mopeds, and the
police are very strict about
this. For mopeds up to 50cc
you need to be over 14; a
driver's licence is required for
anything over 50cc. For
bicycles, you can normally
leave an identity document
rather than pay a deposit.

Apart from the companies
listed below, there are useful
pay-and-ride bike hire stands
with similar rates outside
Spagna metro; in piazza del
Popolo; by the car park under
Villa Borghese; and at the tiny
bar in piazza di Ponte Milvio, at
the start of the cycle path that
takes you out of central Rome
along the banks of the Tiber.

Happy Rent
*Via Farini 3, Monti (06 481 8185/
www.happyrent.com). Metro Termini/
bus to piazza Santa Maria Maggiore.*
Open 9am-7pm daily. Credit AmEx,
DC, MC, V. **Map** p323 2A.
Friendly outlet with special offers
and tourist advice. Also rent out
Smart cars and electric Ligier models
for which no driving licence is
required. Daily rates: mopeds 50cc

€30.99/L60,000; scooters 250cc
€51.65/L100,000; motorbikes
€103.29/L200,000; cars from
€51.65/ L100,000.

Romarent
*Vicolo dei Bovari 7A, Ghetto &
campo de' Fiori (phone/fax 06 689
6555). Bus to corso Vittorio
Emanuele.* **Open** 8.30am-7pm daily.
Credit AmEx, DC, MC, V.
Map p321 2A.
As well as bike, moped and
motorbike hire, Romarent also offers
guided bike and scooter tours in
English, French and Spanish. Bike
rental for one day costs €7.75/
L15,000 or €10.33/ L20,000 for a
mountain bike. Mopeds range from
€18.08-€46.48/L35,000-L90,000 per
day. A 650cc motorbike costs
€103.29/L200,000 per day.

Scoot a Long
*Via Cavour 302, Monti (06 678
0206). Metro Cavour/bus to via
Cavour.* **Open** 9am-8pm daily.
Credit AmEx, MC, V. **Map** p326 1C.
Based near the Colosseum, this
company offers student discounts.
Daily and weekend rates for 50cc
mopeds are from €25.82-€30.99/
L50,000-L60,000; 125cc scooters cost
€41.32/L80,000 per day. Motorbikes
are also available for €77.47/L150,00
a day. A deposit of €103.29/L200,000
plus a passport is required.

Scooters for Rent
*Via della Purificazione 84, Via
Veneto & Villa Borghese (06 488
5485). Metro Barberini/bus to piazza
Barberini.* **Open** 9am-7pm daily.
Credit AmEx, DC, MC, V.
Map p323 1C.
Daily rentals of motorini cost
€25.82/L50,000; smaller HondaSkis
are €30.99/L60,000, 125cc scooters
€41.32/L80,000 and 250cc scooters
€103.29/L 200,000. Special weekly
rates are also available. A deposit of
€154.94/L300,000 is required.

Treno e Scooter Rent
*Piazza dei Cinquecento, Esquilino
(06 4890 5823/fax 06 4891 9539).
Metro Termini/bus to piazza dei
Cinquecento.* **Open** 8.30am-7.30pm
daily. **Credit** AmEx, MC. V.
Map p323 2A.
Located on Termini station forecourt
near the taxi rank, this is a joint
venture between the railway and
Piaggio, suppliers of bikes and
motorini to around half of Italy. A
scooter can be rented for €30.99-
€59.39/L60,000-L115,000 a day, or
from €165.27/L320,000 for a week.
Treno e Scooter Rent also has
bicycles for hire. Daily hire costs
€5.16-€9.30/L10,000-L18,000;
weekly hire is €18.08-€27.89/
L35,000-L54,000.

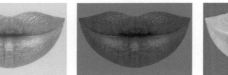

Resources A-Z

Accommodation

The **Enjoy Rome** agency (*see p304*) offers a free hotel reservation service. The **Hotel Reservation** agency (*see p37*) also offers free booking, with a shuttle service to or from Fiumicino airport.

Age restrictions

Cigarettes and alcohol cannot legally be sold to under-16s. Anyone over 14 can ride a moped or scooter of 50cc; no licence is required.

Business

If you're doing business in Rome, a stopover at your embassy's commercial section (*see p293*) is always a good first move. There you will find trade publications, reports, databases of fairs, buyers, sellers and distributors, and helpful initial advice.

As ever in Italy, any personal recommendations will smooth your way immensely. Use them shamelessly.

Business centres

Finding temporary office space and services can be difficult. The following provide basic facilities, including conference and secretarial services.

Centro Uffici Parioli
Via Lima 41, suburbs: north (06 8530 1350/fax 06 8449 8332/ parioliofice@mclink.it).

Pick Center
Via Attilio Regolo 19, Vatican & Prati (06 328 031/fax 06 3280 3227/www.pickcenter.com).

Conference organisers

Rome offers superb facilities for conferences in magnificent *palazzi* and castles. Most of the major hotels can cater for events of all sizes (*see chapter* **Accommodation**). If you don't wish to handle the details yourself, a number of agencies will smooth the way for you.

Rome At Your Service
Via VE Orlando 75, Esquilino (06 484 583/06 482 5589/fax 06 484 429/www.romeatyourservice.it).

Studio Ega
Viale Tiziano 19, suburbs: north (06 328 121/fax 06 324 0143).

Tecnoconference Europe srl
Via A Luzio 66, suburbs: east (06 7835 9617/fax 06 7835 9385/ www.tecnoconference-europe.com.

Triumph Congressi
Via Proba Petronio 3, suburbs: west (06 3972 7707/fax 06 3973 5195/ www.triumphpr.it).

Interpreters

CRIC
Via dei Fienili 65, Capitoline to Palatine (06 678 7 950/fax 06 679 1208/www.linet.it/cric).

Couriers (international)

DHL *06 790 821/tollfree 800 345 345/www.dhl.it*
Federal Express *tollfree 800 123 800/www.fedex.com*
TNT *06 232 908/06 232 909/fax 06 2326 7929/06 2326 7930/ www.tntitaly.it*
UPS – United Parcel Service *tollfree 800 877 877/www.ups.com*

Couriers (local)

Boy Express/DHL *06 474 5696*
Presto *06 3974 1111/ www.prestoexpress.it*
Speedy Boys *06 39 888/ www.speedyboys.it*

Customs

EU citizens do not have to declare goods imported into or exported from Italy for personal use, as long as they arrive from another EU country.

For non-EU citizens, the following limits apply: 400 cigarettes or 200 small cigars or 100 cigars or 500 grams (17.64oz) of tobacco; one litre of spirits (over 22 per cent alcohol) or 2 litres of fortified wine (under 22 per cent alcohol); 50 grams (1.76oz) of perfume. There are no restrictions on the import of cameras, watches or electrical goods. Visitors are also allowed to carry up to €10,329.14/L20,000 000 in cash.

Disabled travellers

There's no denying that Rome is a difficult city for disabled people, especially for anybody in a wheelchair. You'll almost certainly have to depend on other people more than you would at home.

Narrow streets make life difficult for those who can't flatten themselves against a wall to let passing vehicles by, while the cobblestones turn even wheelchairs with excellent suspension into bone-rattlers. Getting on to pavements is made well-nigh impossible by bumper-to-bumper parked cars. Once off the streets, you're faced with the problems of old buildings with narrow corridors, lifts that, if they're there at all, are too small.

Blind and partially sighted people often find that there's no curb at all between the road proper and that bit of street that pedestrians are entitled to walk along (the one exception is a smooth brick walkway laid into the cobblestones leading from the Trevi Fountain to piazza Navona, along which braille notes on bronze plaques give historical explanations of landmarks en route).

The Enjoy Rome agency (*see p304*) and the official APT tourist office (*see p303*), have a selection of information for disabled people.

Directory

Information

CO.IN

(06 712 9011/coin@coinsociale.it/
www.coinsociale.it). **Open** 9am-6pm
Mon-Fri.
CO.IN (short for Cooperative
Integrate Onlus) has no information
office as such, but publishes a
multilingual guide, *Roma Accessibile*,
which should be available (but often
is not) at the APT *(see p303)*. It lists
disabled facilities at museums,
restaurants, stores, theatres, stations,
hotels and so on, and has a map of
Rome showing disabled parking
places. It was fully revised for 2000.
To obtain a copy, phone or write to
CO.IN directly (via Enrico Giglioli
54A/via Torricola 87); the guide is
free and CO.IN will pay for it to be
sent anywhere in Europe. The group
will also organise transport equipped
for disabled people with up to eight
places. Bookings for this service need
to be made several days in advance –
it can cover airport journeys as well
as travel within Rome.

Roma per Tutti

(06 7128 9676/turismo@
coinsociale.it/www.coinsociale.it).
Open 9am-5pm Mon-Fri.
A phone information line run by
CO.IN *(see above)* and Rome city
council. Staff speak Italian and
English and answer queries on
accessibility in hotels, buildings and
monuments. CO.IN also has a separate
information service in Italian and
English. The tollfree number (800
271 027; open 9am-5pm Mon-Fri,
9am-1pm Sat) can only be dialled
from within Italy; it offers up-to-date
information for the whole country.

Sol.Co.Roma (Consorzio della Cooperazione Sociale)

Piazza Vittorio 31, Esquilino (06 490
821/fax 06 491 623/
www.solcoroma.net). Metro Vittorio/
bus or tram to piazza Vittorio. **Open**
9am-7pm Mon-Fri. **Map** p326 A1.
Sol.Co's free guide (with CD-Rom)
was published in 2000, and contains
information and itineraries for the
disabled. It's in Italian, but simple
symbols makes it easy to follow. Staff
will deliver the guide to your hotel or
you can collect it from their office.

Transport

Rome is in the process of
making the whole of its bus
network accessible to
wheelchairs. Orange-red and
silver buses, and green bendy
buses are adapted for

wheelchairs, as are the newest-
generation trams: they have
extra-large central doors and
an access ramp. As this guide
went to press, these buses
served the routes listed below.
Nine hundred new air-
conditioned, wheelchair-
friendly buses were due to go
into operation in 2001,
gradually replacing all the
city's older buses.
H, 23, 40 Express, 44, 64, 30 Express,
36, 60 Express, 75, 80 Express, 86, 90
Express, 105, 170, 280, 310, 492, 660,
714, 719, 780, 791, 913, 04. The
electric buses (116, 117, 118, 119) that
serve the *centro storico*, tram 8 and
some trams on Line 3 can also take
wheelchairs.

On the metro, Line A is
something of a no-go area. All
stations on Line B have lifts,
disabled WCs and special
parking spaces, with the
exception of Circo Massimo,
Colosseo and Cavour
(southbound).

Most taxi drivers will carry
wheelchairs (they have to be
folded); if possible, phone and
book a cab rather than hail one
in the street *(see p287)*.

To ascertain which trains
have wheelchair facilities, call
(or visit) the *Ufficio disabili*
(office for the disabled) at the
station from which you plan to
depart (Termini, beside
platform 1, 06 488 1726;
Ostiense 06 4730 5123;
Tiburtina 06 4730 7220), or
consult the official timetable,
which shows a wheelchair
symbol next to accessible
trains. Twenty-four hours
prior to departure, the disabled
traveller or someone
representing him/her must go
to the *Ufficio disabili* in the
appropriate station to fill in a
form requesting assistance.
Reserve a place, also, when
buying a ticket, and make sure
you arrive three quarters of an
hour before departure time.

This procedure also applies
to all train services to and from
Fiumicino airport. In theory,
you should call or send a fax to
Fiumicino Airport station (06

6501 1821) to arrange for help
the day before your arrival; in
practice, you'll be helped on to
the train anyway.
Both Rome's airports have
facilities such as adapted
toilets. Inform your airline of
your needs: they will contact
the office at Fiumicino or
Ciampino, where you will be
able to use special facilities
and waiting rooms on arrival
and departure.

Sightseeing

Well-designed ramps, lifts and
toilets have been installed in
many museums. Among sites
with full facilities are the
Vatican Museums and Castel
Sant'Angelo, Galleria Doria
Pamphili, Palazzo delle
Esposizioni and Palazzo
Venezia, the Galleria Nazionale
d'Arte Moderna and Galleria
Borghese, and the Bioparco-
Zoo. CO.IN's Roma per Tutti
service *(see above)* provides
up-to-date information on
disabled facilities.

Museum

Fax 06 540 2762/
www.assmuseum.it.
This volunteer group offers tours of
some galleries and catacombs for
individuals or groups with mobility,
or, especially, visual problems. A
small voluntary donation to cover
costs is requested. Museum guides –
some of whom speak English, and
when they don't, an interpreter can
be arranged – have braille notes,
copies of some of the main paintings
in relief, and permission to touch
sculptures and other artefacts in the
museums. Guides also seek to make
works of art comprehensible to the
non-sighted with music cassettes and
recorded text. For general
information or bookings contact the
association at the above fax number.
English is spoken.

Where to stay & eat

Financial incentives from the
2000 Holy Year committee
mean the number of accessible
hotels has increased: CO.IN
(see above) has details. Cheaper
hotels and *pensioni*, often on
upper floors of old *palazzi*, can

Directory

be a problem. If you have special needs, make them known when you book.

Local by-laws now require restaurants to have disabled access and toilets; in practice, few have made the necessary alterations. But if you phone ahead and ask for an appropriate table, most will do their best to help. In summer, the range of outdoor restaurants makes things easier. Getting to toilets, though, can be difficult or impossible.

Most bars open on to the street at ground level, and/or have tables outside in summer. Again, though, most bar toilets are tiny dark holes down long flights of steps.

Toilets

Public toilets accessible to wheelchair users are very scarce. However ATAC, in collaboration with the city council, is equipping various bus termini with adapted loos.

Wheelchair hire

Ortopedia Colosseo

Via dei Santi Quattro 60, Celio & San Giovanni (06 700 5709). Bus to via di San Giovanni in Laterano. **Open** 8am-1pm, 3-7pm Mon-Fri; 8am-1pm Sat. **No credit cards**. Ortopedia Colosseo rents wheelchairs of all kinds – including antiques – starting at €20.66/L40,000 per day. The shop can have any item delivered by taxi: you pay the fare unless you are in one of the larger hotels with which the shop has an agreement.

Drugs

If you are caught in possession of drugs of any type, you will be taken before a magistrate. If you can convince him or her that the tiny quantity you were carrying was for purely personal use, you will be let off with a fine or ordered to leave the country.

Habitual offenders will be offered rehab. Anything more than a tiny amount will push

you into the criminal category: couriering or dealing can land you in prison for up to 20 years. It is an offence to buy or sell drugs, or even to give them away. Sniffer dogs are a fixture at most ports of entry into Italy; the customs police take a dim view of visitors entering with even the smallest quantities of narcotics, and those caught are nearly always refused entry.

Electricity

Most wiring systems work on 220v, which is compatible with British-bought appliances. With US 110v equipment you will need a current transformer. Adaptors can be bought at any electrical shop (look for *casalinghi* or *elettricità*).

Embassies & consulates

Listed below are embassies of the larger English-speaking countries. A full list can be found under *Ambasciate* in the telephone directory. Except where indicated, consular offices, which provide most services of use to tourists and the general public, share the same address as embassies.

Australia

Via Alessandria 215, suburbs: north (06 852 721). Bus to via Nomentana. **Map** p322 2A.

Britain

Via XX Settembre 80A, Esquilino (06 482 5551/06 482 5441/fax 06 4220 2334/www.ukinitalia.it). Bus to piazzale Porta Pia. **Map** p323 1A.

Canada

Embassy: via GB de Rossi 27, suburbs: north (06 445 981). Consulate: via Zara 30, suburbs: north (06 445 981). Bus to Viale Regina Margherita.

Ireland

Piazza Campitelli 3, Ghetto (06 697 9121). Bus to via del Teatro di Marcello or piazza Venezia. **Map** p324 1A.

New Zealand

Via Zara 28, suburbs: north (06 441 7171). Bus to viale Regina Margherita.

South Africa

Via Tanaro 14, suburbs: north (06 852 541). Bus to piazza Buenos Aires or via Tagliamento. **Map** p322 1A.

USA

Via Vittorio Veneto 119, Via Veneto & Villa Borghese (06 46 741). Metro Barberini/bus to piazza Barberini or via Veneto. **Map** p323 1B.

Emergencies

See also **Safety & security** *p301*, **Health** *pp294-5*, **Police** *p299*, **Money** *p298-9*. Thefts or losses should be reported immediately at the nearest police station (*see p299*). You should report the loss of your passport to your consulate or embassy (*see above*). Report the loss of a credit card or travellers' cheques immediately to your credit card company (*see p298*).

National emergency numbers

Police *Carabinieri* (English speaking helpline) 112; *Polizia di stato* 113
Fire service *Vigili del Fuoco* 115
Ambulance *Ambulanza* 118
Car breakdown *Automobile Club d'Italia* (*ACI*) 116

Domestic emergencies

If you need to report a malfunction in any of the main services, the following emergency lines are open 24 hours a day. Which of the two Rome electricity companies (ACEA or ENEL) you should call will be indicated on your electricity meter.
Electricity ACEA 06 57 991/ emergency tollfree 800 130 332. ENEL 16 441.
Gas (Italgas) 06 57 391/ tollfree 800 900 999.
Telephone (Telecom Italia) 188.
Water ACEA tollfree 800 130 335.

Directory

Health

Emergency health care is available for all travellers through the Italian national health system and, by law, hospital accident and emergency departments (*see below*) must treat all emergency cases free.

If you are an EU citizen, obtain an E111 form from your local health authority before leaving home: this entitles you to a free consultation with any doctor. Non-EU citizens should consider taking out private health insurance (*see p295*).

Accident & emergency

If you need urgent medical care, go to the *pronto soccorso* (casualty department) of one of the hospitals listed below, all of which offer 24-hour casualty services. If you have a child needing emergency treatment, head only for the excellent casualty department at the Ospedale Bambino Gesù.

Ospedale Fatebenefratelli

Isola Tiberina, Ghetto (06 683 7299). Bus to piazza di Monte Savello, lungotevere degli Anguillara or piazza Sonnino. **Map** *p324 2A.*

Ospedale Pediatrico Bambino Gesù

Piazza Sant'Onofrio 4, Gianicolo (06 68 591/www.opbg.net). Bus to via del Gianicolo or via G Carini. **Map** *p321 2C.*

Ospedale San Camillo-Forlanini

Via Portuense 332, suburbs: west (06 551 801). Bus to via Portuense or circonvallazione Gianicolense.

Ospedale San Giacomo

Via Canova 29, Tridente (06 36 261). Metro Spagna/bus to via del Corso. **Map** *p320 2A.*

Ospedale San Giovanni

Via Amba Aradam 8, Celio & San Giovanni (06 77 051). Metro San Giovanni/bus to piazza San Giovanni. **Map** *p327 1A.*

Policlinico Umberto I

Viale Policlinico 155, suburbs: north (06 49 971/06 446 2341). Metro Policlinico/bus or tram to viale Regina Elena.

Complementary medicine

Homeopathic remedies are available from most chemists'.

Contraception & abortion

Condoms are on sale near check-outs in supermarkets, or over the counter in pharmacies. They are relatively expensive.

The contraceptive pill is available on prescription. Abortion is available on financial hardship or health grounds, and is legal only when performed in public hospitals.

Each district has a *consultorio familiare* (family-planning clinic), run by the local health authority, and EU citizens with an E111 form are entitled to use them, paying the same low charges as locals.

The most centrally located *consultori* are:

Via Arco del Monte 99A, Ghetto & campo di Fiori (06 6880 3545). Bus to largo Argentina/tram to largo Agentina or via Arenula. **Open** 9am-noon, 3-5pm Mon, Wed; 9am-noon Tue, Thur, Fri. **Map** *p324 1B.*

Via San Martino della Battaglia 16, Esquilino (06 7730 5515). Metro Termini/bus to piazza dei Cinquecento. **Open** 2-6pm Mon; 8am-1pm Tue, Wed, Fri; 10am-1pm, 2-6pm Thur. **Map** *p323 1A.*

The following privately run gynaecological clinics are also recommended:

AIED

Via Toscana 30, Via Veneto & Villa Borghese (06 4282 5314). Metro Barberini/bus to via Boncompagni. **Open** 9am-7pm Mon-Fri; 9am-1pm Sat. **Credit** MC, V. **Map** *p322 2B.* These private family-planning clinics offer check-ups, contraceptive advice, menopause counselling and smear tests. Once you buy a membership card (*tessera*) for €5.16/L10,000, check-ups cost €36.16/L70,000. Smear tests are €15.50/L30,000; follow-up visits are free.

Artemide

Via Sannio 61, Celio & San Giovanni (06 7047 6220). Metro San Giovanni. **Open** 10am-7pm Mon-Fri; 10am-1pm Sat. **No credit cards**. **Map** *p327 1A.* This private clinic offers gynaecological check-ups (€51.65/L100,000) and smear tests (€20.66/L40,000), together with a wide range of other tests and services. Appointments can be made at 24 hours' notice, and emergencies are invariably dealt with immediately.

Dentists

Most dentists (see *Dentisti* in the *Yellow Pages*) in Italy work privately. You may wait for months for a dental appointment in a national health service hospital; children are somewhat better served at the out-patients department of the Ospedale Bambino Gesù (*see above*). Dental treatment in Italy is not cheap and may not be covered by your health insurance. For serious dental emergencies, make for the hospital casualty departments listed above.

Doctors

EU nationals with an E111 form (obtain this before leaving home from your local health authority) can consult a national health service doctor free of charge. Drugs that he or she prescribes can be bought at chemists at prices set by the Health Ministry. If you need tests or specialist out-patient treatment, this, too, will be charged at fixed rates.

Non-EU nationals who need to consult health service doctors will be charged a small fee at the doctor's discretion.

Hospitals

Rome's public hospitals (*see above* **Accident & emergency**) offer good-to-excellent treatment for most ills, though nursing standards can appear slack to anyone used to Anglo-Saxon hospitals.

Many facilities have undergone facelifts in recent years, but waiting lists for treatment can be very long.

Opticians

See p221.

Pharmacies

Pharmacies (*farmacia*, identified by a red or green cross) will give informal medical advice for straightforward ailments, as well as making up prescriptions from a doctor. Most pharmacies also sell homeopathic and veterinary medicines, and all will check your height/weight/blood pressure on request. Anyone who requires regular medication should bring adequate supplies of drugs with them. Also, take care to know the chemical (generic) rather than brand name of medicines you need. They may only be available in Italy under different names.

Normal opening hours are from 8.30am to 1pm, 4pm to 8pm Monday to Saturday. The best-stocked pharmacy in the city is the one in the Vatican, which always has a range of medicines not found on Italian territory.

Outside of normal hours, a duty rota system operates. A list by the door of any pharmacy indicates the nearest ones that will be open at any time. The daily rota is also published in local papers. At duty pharmacies there is a surcharge of €3.87/L7,500 per client (not per item) when the main shop is shut and only the special duty counter is open.

Farmacia della Stazione

Piazza dei Cinquecento, corner of via Cavour, Esquilino (06 488 0019). Metro Termini/bus to piazza dei Cinquecento. **Open** 24hrs daily. **Credit** AmEx, DC, MC, V. **Map** p323 2A.

Farmacia del Vaticano

Porta Sant'Anna entrance, Vatican (06 6988 3422). Metro Ottaviano/bus to piazza del Risorgimento. **Open** 8.30am-6pm Mon-Fri; 7.30am-1pm Sat. **Credit** MC, V. **Map** p321 1C.

Piram

Via Nazionale 228, Esquilino (06 488 0754). Metro Repubblica/bus to via Nazionale. **Open** 24hrs daily. **Credit** AmEx, DC, MC, V. **Map** p323 2B.

Helplines & agencies

Alcoholics Anonymous

06 474 2913.
An active English-speaking support group holds meetings at the church of St Paul's Within the Walls at via Napoli 56. Phone for meeting times.

Associazione Differenza Donna

Via delle Tre Cannelle 15, Trevi Fountain & Quirinale (24hr emergency line 06 2326 9049). **Map** p326 1C.
A helpline for victims of sexual violence. The women-only volunteers offer legal assistance and psychological support. Some are English-speaking.

Drogatel

(Tollfree 800 016600). **Open** 9am-9pm daily.
A state-run drug helpline in Italian only, unless you're lucky enough to find someone on the other end who happens to speak English.

Samaritans

06 7045 4444/06 7045 4445.
Staffed by native English speakers, this confidential help and counselling line was set up for the diplomatic and expatriate community.

Telefono Azzurro

(19 696). **Open** 24hrs daily.
A freephone helpline for children and young people with abuse problems (normally Italian-speaking only).

Telefono Rosa

(06 3751 8261). **Open** 10am-1pm, 4-7pm Mon-Fri.
Provides sympathetic counselling and sound legal advice to women who have been victims of either sexual abuse or sexual harassment.

ID

You are required by law to carry photo ID with you at all times. You will be asked to produce this if you are stopped by traffic police (who will demand your driving licence, which you must have on you whenever you are in charge of a motor vehicle). ID will also be required when you check into a hotel.

Insurance

See also **Health** *p294* and **Police** *p299.*

EU nationals are entitled to reciprocal medical care in Italy, provided they have an E111 form, available in the UK from health centres, post offices and Social Security offices. This will cover you for emergencies, but using an E111 naturally involves having to deal with the intricacies of the Italian state health system, and for short-term visitors it's better to take out health cover under private travel insurance. Non-EU citizens should take out private medical insurance for all eventualities before setting out from home.

Visitors should also take out adequate property insurance before setting off for Italy. If you rent a vehicle, motorcycle or moped, make sure you pay the extra charge for full insurance cover, and sign the collision damage waiver when hiring a car.

Internet & email

Most budget hotels will allow you to plug your modem into their phone system; more upmarket establishments should all have PC points in bedrooms. You can caper in cyberspace or check email at ever more Internet points around the city.

A number of Italian providers offer free Internet access, including Caltanet (www.caltanet.it), Libero (www.libero.it), Tiscali (www.tiscalinet.it), Kataweb (www.kataweb.com), Telecom Italia (www.tin.it) and Wind (www.inwind.it).

Directory

EasyEverything

Via Barberini 2, Trevi Fountain & Quirinale (06 4290 3388/www. easyeverything.com). Metro Barberini/bus to piazza Barberini. **Open** 24hrs daily. **Rates** €1.55/L3,000 for 30mins at peak times (usually 4-7pm); €1.55/L3,000 for 3hrs off-peak. **No credit cards**. **Map** p323 1B.
This Internet café has 350 computer terminals on three floors. All have webcam, scanner, fax and printer service. There's also a coffee bar.

Bibli

Via dei Fienaroli 28, Trastevere (06 588 4097/www.bibli.it). Bus or tram to piazza Sonnino. **Open** 5.30pm-midnight Mon; 11am-midnight Tue-Sun. **Rates** €6.20/L12,000 per hour; €30.99/L60,000 for 10hrs. **Credit** MC, V. **Map** p324 2B.
Bookshop, cultural centre, restaurant and Internet point in a quiet Trastevere backstreet (*see also p205*).

The Netgate

Piazza Firenze 25, Tridente (06 689 3445/www.thenetgate.it). Bus to via del Corso. **Open** 10.30am-9pm Mon-Sat; 4-8pm Sun. **Rates** €3.87/L7,500 per hour; €0.98/L1,900 for 10min mail check; €25.83/L50,000 for 10hrs. **Credit** AmEx, MC, V. **Map** p321 1A.
This clinical but very functional Internet point has 35 work stations, and offers laser printing, fax, scanning and digital photo services. Special rates for students.

Left luggage

The left luggage office by platform 24 of **Termini** station is open from 7am until midnight daily; lockers can be found on platforms 1 and 24. **Fiumicino** airport has left-luggage offices in its international (24 hours daily) and domestic (7.15am-11.15pm daily) terminals. If you're staying in a hotel, staff are generally willing to look after your luggage for you during the day, even after you have checked out. *See also* **Enjoy Rome** *p304*.

Legal help

The first stop if you need legal advice should be your embassy or consulate; *see p293*, or look under *Ambasciate* in the telephone directory.

If you expect to use Rome's libraries for research, be ready for red tape, restricted hours and patchy organisation. Many libraries do not have computer catalogues, so finding a book can be a frustrating experience. All libraries listed below are open to the public. Other specialist libraries can be found under *biblioteche* in the phone book. It is always useful to take an identity document with you; in some cases, a letter from your college or tutor stating the purpose of your research will also be required.

Archivio Centrale dello Stato (State archives)

Piazzale Archivi 27, EUR (06 545 481/fax 06 541 3620). Metro EUR Fermi/bus to piazza G Marconi. **Open** 9am-7pm Mon-Fri; 9am-1pm Sat.
This efficiently run archive has original documents, historical correspondence and many other items. Get there before noon to order the ones you want, which must be consulted in situ. Most can be photocopied.

Biblioteca Alessandrina

Piazzale Aldo Moro 5, Esquilino (06 447 4021). Metro Policlinico/bus to viale dell'Università. **Open** 8.30am-7.30pm Mon-Fri; 8.30am-1.30pm Sat.
La Sapienza's (*see p301*) main library is grossly inefficient for the needs of a huge university.

Biblioteca Nazionale

Viale Castro Pretorio 105, Esquilino (06 49 891). Metro Castro Pretorio/bus to viale Castro Pretorio. **Open** 8.30am-6.50pm Mon-Fri, 8.30am-1.30pm Sat.
The Biblioteca Nazionale holds 80% of everything that is in print in Italy, as well as books in other languages. A computerised system was installed in 2001, and will hopefully facilitate research.

Biblioteca dell'Università Gregoriana

Piazza della Pilotta 4, Trevi Fountain & Quirinale (06 67 011). Bus to piazza Venezia. **Open** 8am-6.30pm Mon-Fri; 8am-noon Sat. **Map** p323 2C.

Much better organised than La Sapienza's Biblioteca Alessandrina (*see above*), but books are not allowed off the premises.

Biblioteca Vaticana

Via di Porta Angelica, Vatican (06 6987 9411). Metro Ottaviano/bus to piazza Risorgimento. **Open** 9am-5.30pm Mon-Fri. Closed mid July-mid Sept. **Map** p321 1C.
To consult the Vatican tomes, students need a letter on headed notepaper signed by a professor stating the purpose of their research. This must be presented between 9am and noon to gain an entrance card. Postgraduate students only are admitted.

British Council Library

Via Quattro Fontane 20, Trevi Fountain & Quirinale (06 478 141). Metro Barberini/bus to piazza Barberini or via Nazionale. **Open** 10am-1pm Mon, Fri; 2-5pm Wed. **Map** p323 2B.
A good English-teaching resource centre.

The British School at Rome

Via Gramsci 61, Via Veneto & Villa Borghese (06 321 3454/06 326 4931). Bus or tram to viale delle Belle Arti. **Map** p322 1C.
Closed for refurbishment until 2002. The reading room of the British School contains English and Italian books on every aspect of Rome, especially archaeology, art history and topography. To be admitted, students need two photos and a letter from a museum or university. No lending facilities.

Lost property

Anything mislaid on public transport, or stolen and subsequently discarded, may turn up at one of the lost propery offices (*ufficio oggetti rinvenuti*) below.

ATAC

Via Bettoni 8, Trastevere (06 581 6040/tollfree 800 431 784/www.atac.roma.it). Bus or tram to viale Trastevere. **Open** 8.30am-1pm Mon, Tue, Thur; 8.30am-1pm, 2.30-5.30pm Wed, Fri. **Map** p325 2B.
Anything found on the city bus and tram network may turn up here.

Metroferro

(Line A 06 487 4309/Line B 06 5753 2264/COTRAL buses 06 57 531). **Open** 9.30am-12.30pm Mon, Wed, Fri.

Ferrovie dello Stato/ Stazione Termini

Termini station, platform 1, Esquilino (06 4730 6682). Metro Termini/bus to piazza dei Cinquecento. **Open** 7am-midnight daily. **Map** p323 2A.

Articles found on FS trains anywhere in the Rome area are sent here; the office is halfway along platform one.

Media

Magazines

With the naked, glistening female form emblazoned across their covers most weeks, Italy's serious news magazines are not always immediately distinguishable from the large selection of soft porn on newsstands. But *Panorama* and *L'Espresso* provide a generally high-standard roundup of the week's news, while *Sette* and *Venerdì* – respectively the colour supplements of *Corriere della Sera* (Thursday) and *La Repubblica* (Friday) – have nice photos, though the text often leaves much to be desired.

For tabloid-style scandal, try *Gente* and *Oggi* with their weird mix of sex, glamour and religion, or the execrable *Eva 3000*, *Novella 2000* and *Cronaca Vera*.

Internazionale (www. internazionale.it) provides an excellent and readable digest of interesting bits and pieces gleaned from the world's press over the previous week. *Diario della Settimana* (www.diario.it), is informed, urbane and has a flair for investigative journalism.

But the biggest-selling magazine of them all is *Famiglia Cristiana* – available from newsstands or in most churches – which alternates Vatican line-toeing with Vatican-baiting, depending on the state of relations between the Holy See and the idiosyncratic Paoline monks who produce it.

National dailies

Italian newspapers can be a frustrating read. Long, indigestible political stories with very little background explanation predominate. On the plus side, Italian papers are delightfully unsnobbish and happily blend serious news, leaders by internationally known commentators, and well-written, often surreal, crime and human-interest stories. Sports coverage in the dailies is extensive and thorough, but if you're not sated there are the mass-circulation sports papers *Corriere dello Sport*, *La Gazzetta dello Sport* and *Tuttosport*.

Corriere della Sera

www.rcs.it
To the centre of centre-left, the solid, serious but often dull Milan-based *Corriere della Sera* is good on crime and foreign news.

Il Manifesto

www.ilmanifesto.it
A reminder that, though the Berlin Wall is a distant memory, there is still some corner of central Rome where hearts beat Red.

La Repubblica

www.repubblica.it
The centre-ish, left-ish *La Repubblica* is good on the Mafia and the Vatican, and comes up with the occasional major scoop on its business pages.

La Stampa

www.lastampa.it
Part of the massive empire of Turin's Agnelli family – for which read Fiat – *La Stampa* has good (though inevitably pro-Agnelli) business reporting.

Local dailies

Both the Rome-based *La Repubblica* and *Corriere della Sera* (*see above*) have large Rome sections every day.

Il Messaggero

www.messaggero.it
A fixture on top of the ice-cream cabinet of every Roman bar, *Il Messaggero* is the Roman daily *per excellenza*. Particularly useful for classified ads – with many flat rents – on Saturdays.

L'Osservatore Romano

www.vatican.va
The Vatican's official newspaper was an organ for liberal Catholic thought during the 1960s and '70s, but now, under the guiding hand of Opus Dei, it reflects the conservative orthodoxies issuing from the top. Weekly edition in English on Wednesday.

Il Tempo

www.iltempo.it
A high-circulation right-wing paper.

Foreign press

The *Financial Times*, *Wall Street Journal*, *USA Today*, *International Herald Tribune* (with its Italy Daily supplement) and most European dailies can be found on the day of issue at most central newsstands; US dailies can take 24 hours to appear.

Listings & small ads

Porta Portese

www.porta-portese.it
Essential reading for anyone looking for a place in Rome (to rent or buy). Published twice a week, on Tuesday and Friday, it also has sections on household goods and cars. Place ads free on 06 598 304.

Roma C'è

www.romace.it
A weekly guide with comprehensive listings for theatre, music venues, dance, film and nightlife. On newsstands on Friday. English-language section.

Solocase

www.solocase.it
Houses for sale and to rent. On newsstands every Saturday.

Time Out Roma

Same format as the London version, but monthly and in Italian, with an English section. Features on events and unusual facets of Roman life.

Wanted in Rome

www.wantedinrome.com
Essential information and upmarket housing ads for ex-pats.

Radio

The three state-owned stations (**RAI 1**, 89.7 MHz FM, 1332 KHz AM; **RAI 2**, 91.7 MHz FM, 846 KHz AM; **RAI 3**, 93.7 MHz

Directory

FM, 1107KHz AM) play classical and light music, and have chat shows and regular, excellent news bulletins.

For UK and US chart hits, mixed with home-grown offerings, try the following:

Radio Capital 95.8 MHz FM
Radio 105 96.1 MHz FM
Radio Centro Suono
101.3 MHz FM
Radio Città Futura 97.7 MHz FM
Italy's most PC 24hr station
Radio Kiss Kiss Network
97.25 MHz FM
Radio Subasio 94.5 MHz FM
Vatican Radio 105 MHz FM,
1260 KHz AM
World events as seen by the Catholic Church can be heard in English and Italian in a live news-and-music session from 8.30am to 2pm daily; there's a news update at 6.15pm. A features programme in English is broadcast at 5.10pm and 9.50pm daily.

Television

Italy has six major networks (three owned by state broadcaster RAI, three belonging to Silvio Berlusconi's Mediaset group), together with two channels operated across most of the country by third-ranking Telemontecarlo. When these have bored you, there are any number of local stations to provide hours of compulsively awful channel-zapping fun.

The standard of television news and current affairs programmes varies; most, however, offer a breadth of international coverage that makes British TV news look like a parish magazine.

RAI 3 supplements its 2pm, 7pm and 10.30pm news programmes with regional round-ups. There's also an international news programme that begins at 1.15am and has an English section.

Money

See also p302 **Tax**.
The Italian currency is the lira (plural *lire*). Italian banknotes come in denominations of L1,000, L2,000, L5,000,

L10,000, L50,000, L100,000 and L500,000, though this last is rarely seen. There are coins for L50, L100, L200, L500 and L1,000.

If all goes to plan, the euro will become legal tender on 1 January 2002, and the lira will go out of circulation on 28 February 2002. There will be euro banknotes of €5, €10, €20, €100, €200 and €500, and coins worth €1 and €2 plus 1, 2, 5, 10, 20 and 50 cents.

ATMs

Most banks have 24-hour cashpoint (Bancomat) machines, and the vast majority of these accept cards with the Maestro and Cirrus symbols. Most cashpoint machines will dispense the daily limit of €258.23/ L500,000; older ones may only let you have €154.94/L300,000.

Banking hours

Most banks are open from 8.30am to 1.45pm and 2.45pm to 4.30pm, Monday to Friday. Some central branches now have extended hours, opening until 6pm on Thursdays and from 8.30am to 12.30pm on Saturdays. All banks are closed on public holidays, and staff work reduced hours the day before a holiday, usually closing around 11am.

Bureaux de change

Banks usually offer better exchange rates than private bureaux de change (*cambio*). It's a good idea to take a passport or other identity document whenever you're dealing with money, particularly to change travellers' cheques or withdraw money on a credit card. Commission rates vary considerably: you can pay from nothing to €5.16/L10,000 for each transaction. Watch out for 'no commission' signs,

as the rate of exchange will almost certainly be terrible.

Many city-centre bank branches have automatic cash exchange machines, which accept notes in most currencies. Notes need to be in good condition.

Main post offices also have exchange bureaux. Commission is €2.58/L5,000 for all cash transactions, with a maximum of €1,032.91/ L2,000,000. Travellers' cheques are not accepted. *See p299* **Postal services**.

American Express

Piazza di Spagna 38, Tridente (06 67 641). Metro Spagna/bus to piazza San Silvestro. **Open** 9am-5.30pm Mon-Fri; 9am-12.30pm Sat. **Map** p323 1C.
Travellers' cheque refund service, card replacement, poste restante, and a cash machine that can be used with AmEx cards. Money can be transferred from any American Express office in the world within 24 hours.

Thomas Cook

Piazza Barberini 21, Via Veneto & Villa Borghese (06 4202 0150/fax 06 482 8085). Metro Barberini/bus to piazza Barberini. **Open** 9am-7pm Mon-Sat; 9.30am-5pm Sun. **Map** p323 1B.
The three branches of Thomas Cook are among the very few exchange offices open on Sunday. A 2.5% commission is charged on all transactions apart from Thomas Cook, MasterCard and travellers' cheques, which are cashed free of charge. MasterCard holders can also withdraw money here. Money can be transferred to the Rome branches from any Thomas Cook branch in the UK. A fourth branch was due to open inside the Colosseo metro station sometime in 2001.
Branches: via della Conciliazione 23/25 (06 6830 0435); via del Corso 23 (06 320 0224).

Credit cards

Italians have an enduring fondness for cash, but persuading them to take to plastic has become considerably easier in the last few years. Nearly all hotels of two stars and above now accept at least some of the major credit cards.

If you lose a credit or charge card, phone one of the emergency numbers listed below. All lines have English-speaking staff and are open 24 hours daily.

American Express 06 7228 0371
Diner's Club 800 864 064
Eurocard/CartaSi (including MasterCard and Visa) 800 018 548
MasterCard 800 870 866
Visa 800 877 232

Police

The principal Polizia di Stato station, the Questura Centrale, is at via Genova 2 (06 46 861). The addresses of others, and of the Carabinieri's Commissariati (police stations), are listed in the telephone directory under *Polizia* and *Carabinieri* respectively. Incidents can be reported to either force.

Postal services

Big improvements have been made recently in Italy's notoriously unreliable postal service (www.poste.it) and you can now be more or less sure than your letter will arrive in reasonable time.

Italy's new equivalent to first-class post, *posta prioritaria*, generally works very well: it promises delivery within 24 hours in Italy, three days for EU countries and four or five for the rest of the world; more often than not, it succeeds. A letter of 20g or less to Italy or any EU country costs €0.62/L1,200 by *posta prioritaria*; outside the EU the cost is €0.77/L1,500; special stamps can be bought at post offices and *tabacchi*; letters can be posted in any box.

Stamps for slower regular mail are also sold at post offices and *tabacchi* shops. A 20g or lighter letter costs €0.41/L800 to EU countries and €0.52/L1,000 to non-EU European countries, the US, Canada, Australia and New Zealand.

If you harbour lingering doubts about the Italian system, there's always the Vatican Post Office (*see below*), which is run in association with the Swiss postal service.

Most postboxes are red and have two slots, *per la città* (for Rome) and *tutte le altre destinazioni* (for everywhere else). The **CAI-Posta Celere** service (available only in main post offices) costs somewhat more than *posta prioritaria* and delivers at the same speed, the only advantage being that you can track the progress of your letter on their website (www.poste.it) or by phone (800 009 966).

Registered mail (*raccomandata*) costs €2.17/L4,200 over the normal rate.

There are local post offices (*ufficio postale*) in each district, which are open from 8.25am to 6pm, Monday to Friday (8.25am-2pm in August), and from 8.25am to 1.30pm on Saturday and any day preceding a public holiday. They close two hours earlier than normal on the last day of each month. Main post offices in the centre of town have longer opening hours and a range of additional services, including fax facilities.

For postal information of any kind, phone the central information office on 160.

Centro Pacchi (Parcels Office)

Via Monterone 1C, Piazza Navona & Pantheon (information 160). Bus to largo Argentina or corso Rinascimento. **Open** 9am-6pm Mon-Fri; 9am-2pm Sat. **Map** p321 2A. Parcels can be sent from any post office, but the Parcels Office is the only branch where they can be sent insured. It is advisable to send any package worth more than €51.65/L100,000 from this office.

Posta Centrale

Piazza San Silvestro 18/20, Tridente (06 6788 0788/information 160). Bus to piazza San Silvestro. **Open** 8.30am-6.30pm Mon-Fri; 8.30am-1pm Sat; 9am-noon last Sat of month. **Map** p323 2C.

The central post office is the hub of Rome's postal system, although the other main post offices offer many of the same services. Letters sent poste restante/general delivery (*fermo posta*) to Rome should be addressed to Roma Centro Corrispondenza, Posta Centrale, piazza San Silvestro, 00186 Roma. You will need your passport to collect letters, and you have to pay a small charge. The fax service remains open until 8.30pm.

Other main offices

Piazza Bologna 39, suburbs: east (06 4423 8115). Metro Bologna/bus to piazza Bologna.

Via Marmorata 4, Testaccio (06 574 3809). Metro Piramide/bus to Via Marmorata. **Map** p325 2A.

Viale Mazzini 101, suburbs: north (06 3770 9211). Bus to viale Mazzini. **Map** p320 1B.

Via Taranto 19, suburbs: south (06 772 791). Metro San Giovanni.

Via Terme di Diocleziano 30, Esquilino (06 4745602). Bus to piazza dei Cinquecento. **Map** p323 2A.

Poste Vaticane

Piazza San Pietro, Vatican (06 6988 3406). Bus to piazza Pia or piazza del Risorgimento. **Open** 8.30am-7pm Mon-Fri; 8.30am-6pm Sat. **Map** p321 1C.

Queuing

Lining up one behind the other doesn't come easy to Romans, but, despite the apparent chaos, queue-jumpers are usually given short shrift. Hanging back deferentially, on the other hand, is taken as a clear sign of stupidity, and if you're not careful the tide will sweep contemptuously past you. In busy shops and bars, be aware of who is in front of and behind you and, when it's your turn, assert your rights emphatically.

Religion

There are over 400 Catholic churches in the city: several hold Mass in English. The main British Catholic church is San Silvestro at piazza San Silvestro 17A (06 679 7775). San Patrizio, at via Boncompagni 31 (06 488 5716), is the principal Irish church in

Directory

Rome, and the American Catholic church is Santa Susanna, at via XX Settembre 14 (06 4201 3734).

For information on papal audiences *see p141*. Some of the non-Catholic denominations and religions represented in Rome are listed below, with the times of their main services or prayers.

Anglican

All Saints, via del Babuino 153B, Tridente (06 3600 1881). Metro Spagna/bus to piazza del Popolo. **Services** 8.30am, 10.30am, 6.30pm Sun. **Map** p320 2A.
The church was opened in 1887, but the Rome chaplaincy dates from 1816, when services were held in the chaplain's rooms in piazza di Spagna. Today the church hosts an active programme of cultural events, including regular, high-quality concerts. Times are liable to change, so phone ahead.

Episcopal

Saint Paul's-within-the Walls, via Napoli 58, Esquilino (06 474 3596). Metro Repubblica/bus to via Nazionale. **Services** 8.30am, 10.30am Sun. **Map** p323 2B.

Jewish

Comunità Israelitica di Roma, lungotevere Cenci, Ghetto (06 684 0061). Bus to piazza di Monte Savello. **Map** p324 2A.
There are services every day but times vary throughout the year. Guided tours of the synagogue are offered from the museum, the Museo d'Arte Ebraica (*see p106*).

Methodist

Ponte Sant'Angelo Church, via del Banco di Santo Spirito, Piazza Navona & Pantheon (06 686 8314). Bus to corso Vittorio Emanuele. **Services** 10.30am Sun. **Map** p321 1B.

Moslem

La Moschea di Roma, viale della Moschea, suburbs: north (06 808 2167). Train to Campi Sportivi. Paolo Portoghesi's masterpiece (*see also p29*) is always open to Moslems for prayer. It can be visited by non-Moslems from 9-11.30am on Wednesday and Saturday.

Presbyterian (Church of Scotland)

Saint Andrew's, via XX Settembre 7, Via Veneto & Villa Borghese (06 482 7627). Bus to via XX Settembre. **Services** 11am Sun. **Map** p323 1B.

Relocation

To help newcomers get started, Welcome Neighbor (06 3036 6936) is a group of English-speaking ex-pats who organise talks on various aspects of living in Rome.

Anyone staying here is obliged by the Italian state to pick up a whole series of forms and permits. The basic set is described below. EU citizens should have no difficulty getting their documentation once they are in Italy, but non-EU citizens are advised to enquire at an Italian embassy or consulate in their own country before travelling. There are agencies that specialise in obtaining documents for you if you can't face the procedures yourself – for a price (see *Pratiche e certificati – agenzie* in the Yellow Pages).

Carta d'Identità (Identity card)

Foreigners resident in Rome should have an ID card. You'll need three passport photographs, a *permesso di soggiorno*, and a special form that will be given you at your *circoscrizione* – the local branch of the central records office, which will eventually issue the card. To find the office for your area, look in the phone book under *Comune di Roma: Circoscrizioni*.

Codice Fiscale (tax code) & Partita IVA

Anyone working in Italy needs a codice fiscale. It is essential for opening a bank account or setting up utilities contracts. Take your passport and *permesso di soggiorno* to the tax office (*ufficio delle entrate*) listed below, fill in a form and return a few days later to pick up the card. It can be posted on request.

The self-employed or anyone doing business in Italy may also need a Partita IVA. It costs €129.11/L250,000, and most people pay an accountant to handle the formalities. Take your passport and *codice fiscale* (tax code) to your nearest tax office (*ufficio delle entrate*) and be prepared for a long wait. Make sure you cancel your VAT number when you no longer need it: failure to do so may result in a visit from tax inspectors years later.

New *uffici delle entrate* (revenue offices) have been opened to

streamline fiscal affairs. Further information can be found by calling the Ministry of Finance's information line (848 800 333) or consulting its website at www.finanze.it. Which office you should go to depends on the circoscrizione (city district) in which you live; they are open 9am-1pm Mon, Wed, Fri; 9am-1.15pm, 2.50-4.50pm Tue, Thur. Their location can be found in the phone book under Ministero delle Finanze.

Permesso di Soggiorno Carta di Soggiorno (permit to stay)

EU citizens need a *permesso di soggiorno* if they're staying in Italy for over three months; non-EU citizens should (but usually don't) apply for one within eight days of their arrival in Italy. Take three passport photographs, your passport, and proof that you have some means of supporting yourself and reason to be in Italy (preferably a letter from an employer or certificate of registration at a school or university) to the nearest Commissariato (police station; see the phone book under Polizia di Stato), or the Questura Centrale (main police station), via Genova, 2 (06 46 861) between 8am and 2pm (people start queuing before 7am). For information call 06 4686 2928.
The *carta di soggiorno* (card) is similar to the permesso but allows you to stay in Italy indefinitely, though it has to be renewed every ten years. EU Citizens who have been in Italy for at least five years and who also have a renewable *permesso di soggiorno* can request the card. Those married to a foreigner whof already has a card can request one for themselves at the Questura Centrale.

Permesso di Lavoro (work permit)

In theory, all non-Italians employed in Italy need a work permit. Application forms can be obtained from the Ispettorato del Lavoro, via Cesare de Lollis 6 (06 444 931/06 445 0669/fax 06 445 0334; open 9am-noon, 2.15-4.30pm Mon-Thur; 9am-noon Fri). The form must be signed by your employer; you then need to take it with your *permesso di soggiorno* and a photocopy back to the Ispettorato. Don't rush: often the requirement is waived, or employers arrange it for you.

Residenza (residency)

This is your registered address in Italy, and you'll need it to buy a car, get customs clearance on goods brought from abroad, and many other transactions. Take your *permesso di soggiorno* (which must be valid for at least another year) and your passport to your local circoscrizione office (*see p300, carta d'identità*). Staff will check that rubbish collection tax (*nettezza urbana*) for your address has been paid (ask your landlord about this) before issuing the certificate.

Bank accounts

To open an account you'll need a valid *permesso di soggiorno* or *certificato di residenza*, your *codice fiscale* (*see p300*), proof of regular income from an employer (or a fairly substantial sum to deposit) and your passport.

Work

Casual employment can be hard to come by, so try to sort out work before you arrive. English-language schools and translation agencies are mobbed with applicants, so qualifications and experience count.

The classified ads paper *Porta Portese* has lots of job advertisements. Other good places to look are *Wanted in Rome* (for both, *see p297*) and noticeboards in English-language bookshops (*see p205*). You can also place an ad in any of the media above. For serious jobs, try *Il Messaggero* and *La Repubblica*, or try the following agencies.

Manpower
Via Barberini 58, Trevi Fountain & Quirinale (06 4287 1339/ fax 06 4287 0833/www.manpower.it). Metro Barberini/bus to via Barberini. **Open** 9am-6pm Mon-Fri. **Map** p323 1B. **Branch**: via Molajoni 70 (06 4353 5349/fax 06 4353 5357).

Adecco
Via Cavour 275, Monti (06 4782 4134/ fax 06 4788 2114/www. adecco.it). Metro Cavour/bus to via Cavour. **Open** 9am-7pm Mon-Fri. **Map** p326 1B. **Branch**: via Ostiense 93 (06 574 0100).

Accommodation

Best places to look for accommodation are again *Porta Portese, Wanted in Rome* and English-language bookshops. Look out for

affittasi (for rent) notices on buildings, and check classifieds in *Il Messaggero* on Thursday and Saturday.

When you move into an apartment, it's normal to pay a month's rent in advance plus two months' deposit, which should be refunded when you move out, although some landlords create problems over this. You'll probably get a year's contract, normally renewable. If you rent through an agency, expect to pay the equivalent of two months' rent in commission.

Safety & security

Muggings are fairly rare in Rome, but pickpockets and bag snatchers are particularly active in the main tourist areas. You will find that a few basic precautions greatly reduce a street thief's chances:
• Don't carry wallets in back pockets, particularly on buses. If you have a bag or camera with a long strap, wear it across the chest and not dangling from one shoulder.
• Keep bags closed, with your hand on them. If you stop at a pavement café or restaurant, do not leave bags or coats on the ground or the back of a chair where you cannot keep an eye on them.
• When walking down a street, hold cameras and bags on the side of you towards the wall, so you're less likely to become the prey of a motorcycle thief or *scippatore*.
• Avoid groups of ragged children brandishing pieces of cardboard, or walk by quickly, keeping hold of your valuables. They'll wave the cardboard to confuse you while accomplices pick pockets or bags.

If you are the victim of crime call the police helpline (*see p293*) or go to the nearest police station and say you want to report a *furto* (theft). A *denuncia* (written statement) of the incident will be made by or

for you. It is unlikely that your things will be found, but you will need the *denuncia* for making an insurance claim.

Smoking

Smoking is not permitted in public offices (including post offices, police stations, etc) or on public transport. For where to buy cigarettes, *see p302* **Tabacchi**.

Study

See also p296 **Libraries**. The three state universities, La Sapienza, Tor Vergata and Roma Tre, and the private LUISS (Libera Università Internazionale degli Studi Sociali) offer exchanges with other European universities through the EU's Erasmus programme. Several American universities also have campuses in Rome, which students attend on exchange programmes.

There are also private Catholic universities, which run some of Italy's most highly respected faculties of medicine. The student scene, however, is dominated by La Sapienza. Specialist bookshops are mostly found in neighbouring San Lorenzo and viale Ippocrate.

Bureaucracy & services

Foreigners studying on any type of course in Italy must obtain a student's permit to stay (*see p300*). Apart from student offices in the universities themselves, there are private agencies that will take care of enrolment formalities.

Centro Turistico Studentesco (CTS)
Via Genova 16, Monti (06 462 0431). Bus to via Nazionale. **Open** 9am-1pm, 2.30-6.30pm Mon-Fri; 9.30am-1pm Sat. **Credit** MC, V. **Map** p323 2B.
The CTS student travel centre issues student cards giving discount travel tickets, hostels or language courses.

Directory

Nuovo Centro Servizi Universitari

Viale Ippocrate 160, Esquilino (06 4470 2330/www.cstonline.it). Metro Policlinico/bus to viale Ippocrate. **Open** 9am-1pm, 4-7pm Mon-Fri. **Credit** AmEx, MC, V.
This private agency takes charge of enrolment, registration for exams and all other time-consuming details. A €10.33/L20,000 membership fee entitles you to travel offers and discounts to concerts and cinemas.

Tabacchi

Tabacchi or *tabaccherie* (identified by signs with a white T on a black or blue background) are the only places where you can legally buy tobacco products. They also sell stamps, telephone cards, tickets for public transport, lottery tickets and the stationery required when dealing with Italian bureaucracy.

Most *tabacchi* keep proper shop hours; many, however, are attached to bars and, through that outlet, can satisfy your nicotine cravings well into the night.

Tax

Sales tax (IVA) is charged at varying rates on most goods and services, and is almost invariably quoted as an integral part of prices. Occasionally top-end hotels will quote prices without IVA. Some trades people will also offer you rates without IVA, the implication being that if you are prepared to hand over cash and not demand a receipt in return, then you'll be paying around 19 per cent (the amount you would have spent on IVA) less than the whole fee. For tax-free shopping, *see p202.*

Telephones

Dialling & codes

All normal Rome numbers begin with the area code 06, and this must be used whether you call from within or outside

the city. Phone numbers within Rome generally have eight digits, although some of the older numbers may have seven or fewer. If you try a number and cannot get through, it may have been changed to an eight-digit number. If you have difficulties, check the directory or ring enquiries (12).

All numbers beginning with 800 are freephone lines (until recently, these began 176; you will still find old-style numbers listed, in which case replace the prefix with 800). For numbers beginning 840 and 848 (147 and 148 until recently) you will be charged one unit only, regardless of where you're calling from or how long the call lasts. These numbers can be called from within Italy only; some only function within one phone district.

Rates

Telecom Italia operates one of the most expensive systems in Europe, particularly for international calls. The minimum charge, which covers a local call from a private phone, is about €0.08/L153.2 (€0.10/L200 from a public phone); the normal rate for a minute to northern Europe, the UK and the US is €0.31/L600 on reply and then €0.25/L480 per minute; to Australia and New Zealand it's €0.31/L600 on reply and then €0.87/L1,680 per minute. In all cases it costs more if you use a public phone.

One way to keep costs down is to phone during off-peak hours (6.30pm to 8am Mon-Sat, all day Sun). Another is to avoid using phones in hotels, which may carry extortionate surcharges.

Public phones

Rome has no shortage of public phone boxes and many bars have payphones. Most public phones only accept

phone cards (*schede telefoniche*); a few also accept major credit cards. Telephone cards cost €2.58/L5,000, €5.16/L10,000, €7.75/L15,000, and €12.91/L25,000 and are available from *tabacchi* (*see p302*), some newspaper stands and some bars. Beware: phone cards have expiry dates (usually 31 December or 30 June), after which you won't be able to use them. The Vatican City has its own special phone cards, obtainable from the Vatican post offices (*see p299*) and usable only within the City State. To use public coin phones you will need L100, L200 and L500 coins. The minimum charge for a local call is L200.

International calls

To make an international call from Rome, dial 00, then the appropriate country code: Australia 61; Canada 1; Irish Republic 353; New Zealand 64; United Kingdom 44; United States 1. Then dial the area code (for calls to the UK, omit the initial zero of the area code) and the number.

To phone Rome from abroad, dial the international code (00 in the UK), then 39 for Italy and 06 for Rome, followed by the individual number.

Operator services

To make a reverse charge (collect) call, dial 170 for the international operator in Italy. Alternatively, to be connected to the operator in the country you want to call, dial 172 followed by a four-digit code for the country and telephone company you want to use (for the UK and Ireland this is the same as the country code; for other countries see the phone book). If you are placing a collect call from a phone box, you will need to insert a L200 coin, which will be refunded after your call.

The following services operate 24 hours daily:
Operator and **Italian Directory Enquiries** 12
International Operator 170
International Directory Enquiries 176
Communication problems on national calls 182
Communication problems on international calls 176
Wake-up calls 114; an automatic message will ask you to dial in the time you want your call, with four figures on a 24hr clock, followed by your phone number.

Mobile phones

Italian cellphone numbers begin with 3. Note that until mid-2001 they began 03.

Owners of GSM phones can use them on both 900 and 1800 bands; British, Australian and New Zealand mobiles work without problems. US mobiles work on a different frequency and cannot be used in Italy.

Nolitel

Via Sicilia 54, Via Veneto & Villa Borghese (06 4200 7001/ www.nolitel.it). Bus to piazza Fiume or via Boncompagni. **Credit** AmEx, DC, MC, V. **Map** p322 B.
Nolitel rents dual-band mobile phone at €4.15/L8,000 per day, plus a €103.29/L200,000 deposit.
Branch: Fiumicino airport, international arrivals (06 6501 1257).

Fax

Faxes can be sent from most large post offices (*see p299*), which will charge you for the number of sheets sent. Rates are €1.29/L2,500 per page in Italy or €5.09/L9,860 for Europe. Faxes can also be sent from some photocopying outlets. In all cases, the surcharge will be hefty. Do-it-yourself fax/phones can be found in main stations and at Fiumicino airport.

Telegrams & telexes

These can be sent from main post offices. The telegraph office at the Posta Centrale on piazza San Silvestro (entrance 18; *see p299*) is open 8.30am-

8.30pm Monday to Friday and 8.30am-1pm Saturday. Alternatively, you can dictate telegrams over the phone. Dial 186 from a private phone and a message in Italian will tell you to dial the number of the phone you're phoning from. You will then be passed to a telephonist who will take your message.

Time

Italy is one hour ahead of London, six ahead of New York, eight behind Sydney and 12 behind Wellington. Clocks are moved forward by one hour in early spring and back in late autumn, in line with other EU countries.

Tipping

Foreigners are expected to tip more than Italians, but the ten per cent customary in many countries is considered generous even for the richest-looking tourist. Most locals leave €0.05/L100 or €0.10/ L200 on the counter when buying drinks at the bar and, depending on the standard of the restaurant, €1/L2,000 to €5/L10,000 for the waiter. Many larger restaurants now include a 10-15 per cent service charge. Tips are not expected in family-run restaurants, although even here a couple of thousand is always appreciated. Taxi drivers will be happy if you round the fare up to the nearest whole €0.5/L1,000.

Toilets

If you need a toilet, the easiest thing is usually to go to a bar (which won't necessarily be clean or provide toilet paper). There are modern lavatories at or near most of the major tourist sites; most have attendants, and you must pay a nominal fee to use them. Fast food joints and department stores also come in handy.

Tourist information

The offices of Rome's tourist board, APT, and the state tourist board, ENIT, have English-speaking staff, but a surprisingly limited amount of information. For more personal service, the private agency Enjoy Rome can be recommended (*see p304*).

The Rome city council now has well-stocked green-painted tourist information kiosks PIT (Punti Informativi Turistici) in:
Piazza Pia, Vatican & Prati (06 6880 9707). Bus to piazza Pia. **Map** p321 1C.
Largo Goldoni, Tridente (06 6813 6061). Bus to via del Corso. **Map** p321 1A.
Piazza delle Cinque Lune, Piazza Navono & Pantheon (06 6880 9240). Bus to corso Rinascimento. **Map** p321 1A.
Piazza San Giovanni in Laterano, Celio & San Giovanni (06 7720 3535). Metro San Giovanni/bus to piazza San Giovanni in Laterano. **Map** p326 2A.
Via dell Olmata, Monti (06 4788 0294). Bus to piazza Santa Maria Maggiore. **Map** p3261B.
Piazza dei Cinquecento, Esquilino (06 4782 5194). Metro Termini/bus to piazza dei Cinquecento. **Map** p323 2A.
Piazza del Tempio della Pace, Capitoline to Palatine (06 6992 4307). Bus to via dei Fori Imperiali. **Map** p326 1C.
Via Nazionale (06 4782 4525). Bus to via Nazionale. **Map** p323 2B.
Piazza Sonnino, Trastevere (06 5833 3457). Bus or tram to viale Trastevere. **Map** p324 2B.
Via Minghetti, Tridente (06 6782 988). Bus to via del Corso. **Map** p323 2C.
Termini station, platform 4, Esquilino (06 4890 6300). Metro Termini/bus to piazza dei Cinquecento. **Map** p323 2A.
Fiumicino airport, terminal C (06 6595 6074).

APT (Azienda per il Turismo di Roma)

Via Parigi 5, Esquilino (06 3600 4399/www.romaturismo.com). Metro Repubblica/bus to piazza della Repubblica. **Open** *Office* 8.30am-7pm Mon-Sat. *Phoneline* 9am-7pm daily. **Map** p323 1B.
Branches: Termini station (06 3600 4399). Fiumicino Airport (06 6595 6074/06 6595 4471).

Directory

Enjoy Rome

Via Marghera 8A, Esquilino (06 445 1843/ fax 06 445 0734/ www. enjoyrome.com). Metro Termini/bus to piazza dei Cinquecento or viale Castro Pretorio. **Open** 8.30am-6.30pm Mon-Fri; 8.30am-2pm Sat. **No credit cards. Map** p323 2A.

This friendly English-speaking company is a handy place for information (on Rome and further afield) and advice. The office provides an accommodation-booking service and left luggage facilities, both for free. It also arranges walking and cycling tours.

Centro Servizi Pellegrini e Turisti

Piazza San Pietro, Vatican (06 6988 1662). Bus to piazza Pia or piazza Risorgimento. **Open** 8.30am-7pm Mon-Sat. **Map** p321 1C.

The Vatican's own tourist office.

Water & drinking

Most of Rome's water comes from a vast underground lake to the north of the city and is completely safe for drinking. In some areas of the *centro storico* water is still carried along ancient aqueducts from springs in the countryside: this is so good that locals will come from outside the centre to fill up their plastic containers with the stuff. (*See also p113* **Big Nose**).

When to go

See also chapter **By Season**.

Climate

Rome can sizzle at close to 40°C in July and August, when humidity levels can also be high. Spring and autumn are usually warm and pleasant, although there may be occasional heavy showers, particularly in March, April and September. Between November and February you cannot rely on good weather, and might either come across a week of rain, or crisp, bright (sometimes even warm) sunshine. The compensation is the comparative scarcity of fellow tourists.

Public holidays

On public holidays (*giorni festivi*) virtually all shops, banks and businesses are closed, although (with the exception of May Day, 15 August and Christmas Day) bars and restaurants tend to stay open.

Limited public transport runs on 1 May and Christmas afternoon. Holidays falling on a Saturday or Sunday are not celebrated the following Monday; however, if a holiday falls on a Thursday or a Tuesday, many people will take the Friday or Monday off as well. Public holidays are:

New Year's Day (Capo d'anno) 1 January
Epiphany (La Befana) 6 January
Easter Monday (Pasquetta)
Liberation Day 25 April
May Day 1 May
Patron Saints' Day (San Pietro e San Paolo) 29 June
Feast of the Assumption (Ferragosto) 15 August
All Saints' (Tutti santi) 1 November
Immaculate Conception (Festa dell'Immacolata) 8 December
Christmas Day (Natale) 25 December
Boxing Day (Santo Stefano) 26 December

Women

Compared with many others in Europe, Rome is a safe city for women, and as long as you stick to central areas you can walk alone late at night without wishing you'd brought your mace. If you *do* find yourself being hassled, take comfort in the fact that Italian men are generally all mouth and no trousers.

For women on their own, common sense will usually be enough to keep potential harassers at bay. If you're not interested, ignore them and they'll probably go away. Or duck into the nearest bar: they'll give you up as a lost cause and look for a new victim.

Young Roman blades head for piazza Navona, piazza di Spagna and Fontana di Trevi to pick up foreign talent. If you'd rather enjoy Rome's nocturnal charm in peace, you're better off in the areas around campo de' Fiori, Testaccio and Trastevere. The Termini station area gets seriously seedy after sundown.

Accommodation

The vast majority of Rome's hotels and pensions are perfectly suitable for women, but if you're uneasy about walking around at night, avoid those near Termini station and around via Nazionale, a major shopping artery that becomes pretty deserted once the shops are shut. Stick to the more populated areas in the centro storico where you can still get good prices and enjoy the nightlife without too much fret.

Health

See also p294 **Health**.

Women suffering gynaecological emergencies should head for the nearest pronto soccorso (accident & emergency department, *see p294*). Tampons (*assorbenti interni*) and sanitary towels (*assorbenti esterni*) are cheaper in supermarkets, but you can also get them in pharmacies and *tabacchi*.

Visas

EU nationals and citizens of the US, Canada, Australia and New Zealand do not need visas for stays of up to three months. For EU citizens, a passport or national identity card valid for travel abroad is sufficient, but all non-EU citizens must have full passports. In theory, all visitors have to declare their presence to the local police within eight days of arrival. If you're staying in a hotel, this will be done for you. If not, contact the Questura Centrale, the main police station, for advice (*see p299*).

Directory

Vocabulary

Romans always appreciate attempts at spoken Italian, no matter how incompetent. In hotels, and all but the most spit-and-sawdust restaurants, you're likely to find someone with at least a basic grasp of English.

There are two forms of address in the second person singular: *lei*, which is formal and should be used with strangers and older people; and *tu*, which is informal. The personal pronoun is usually omitted.

Italian is pronounced as it is spelt.

Pronunciation

a – as in **a**sk.
e – like a in **a**ge or e in s**e**ll.
i – like ea in **ea**st.
o – as in h**o**tel or in h**o**t.
u – as in b**oo**t.

Romans have a lot of trouble with their consonants. C often comes out nearer g; n, if in close proximity to an r, disappears. Remember that **c** and **g** both go soft in front of e and i (becoming like the initial sounds of **ch**eck and **gi**raffe respectively). An h after any consonant makes it hard. Before a vowel, it is silent.
c before a, i and u: as in **c**at.
g before a, i and u: as in **g**et.
gl like lli in mi**lli**on.
gn like ny in ca**ny**on.
qu as in **qu**ick.
r always rolled.
s has two sounds, as in **s**oap or ro**s**e.
sc like the sh in **sh**ame.
sch like the **sc** in **sc**out.
z can be sounded **ts** or **dz**.

Useful phrases

hello and goodbye (informal) *ciao, salve*
good morning *buon giorno*
good evening *buona sera*
good night *buona notte*
please *per favore, per piacere*
thank you *grazie*
you're welcome *prego*
excuse me, sorry *mi scusi* (formal), *scusa* (informal)
I'm sorry, but... *mi dispiace...*
I don't speak Italian (very well) *non parlo (molto bene) l'italiano*
can I use/where's the toilet? *posso usare/dov'è il bagno/la toilette?*
open *aperto*
closed *chiuso*
entrance *entrata*
exit *uscita*

Female self-defence

no thank you, I can find my way by myself *no grazie, non ho bisogna di una guida*
can you leave me alone? *mi vuole* (or *vuoi* – informal – if you want to make it clear you feel very superior) *lasciare in pace?*

Times & timetables

could you tell me the time? *mi sa* (formal)/*sai* (informal) *dire l'ora?*
it's – o'clock *sono le* (number)
it's half past *sono le* (number) *e mezza*
when does it (re-)open? *a che ora (ri)apre?*
does it close for lunch? *chiude per pranzo?*

Directions

(turn) left *(giri a) sinistra*
(it's on the) right *(è a/sulla) destra*
straight on *sempre diritto*
where is...? *dov'è...?*
could you show me the way to the Pantheon? *mi potrebbe indicare la strada per il Pantheon?*
is it near/far? *è vicino/lontano?*

Transport

car *macchina*
bus *autobus, auto*
coach *pullman*
taxi *tassì, taxi*
train *treno*
tram *tram*
plane *aereo*
bus stop *fermata (d'autobus)*
station *stazione*
platform *binario*
ticket/s *biglietto/biglietti*
one way *solo andata*
return *andata e ritorno*
(I'd like) a ticket for *(vorrei) un biglietto per...*
where can I buy tickets? *dove si comprono i biglietti?*
are you getting off at the next stop? *(ie get out of my way if you're not) che, scende alla prossima?*
I'm sorry, I didn't know I had to stamp it *mi dispiace, non sapevo che lo dovevo timbrare*

Communications

phone *telefono*
fax *fax*
stamp *francobollo*
how much is a stamp for England/Australia/the US? *quanto viene un francobollo per l'Inghilterra/ l'Australia/ gli Stati Uniti?*
can I send a fax? *posso mandare un fax?*
can I make a phone call? *posso telefonare?*
letter *lettera*
postcard *cartolina*
courier *corriere, pony*

Shopping

I'd like to try the blue sandals/black shoes/brown boots *vorrei provare i sandali blu/le scarpe negre/gli stivali marroni*
do you have it/them in other colours? *ce l'ha in altri colori?*
I take (shoe) size... *porto il numero...*
I take (dress) size... *porto la taglia...*
it's too loose/too tight/just right *mi sta largo/stretto/bene*
can you give me a little more/less? *mi dia un po' di più/meno*
100 grams of ... *un etto di...*
300 grams of ... *tre etti di...*
one kilo of ... *un kilo/chilo di...*
five kilos of... *cinque chili di...*
a litre/two litres of... *un litro/due litri di...*

Accommodation

a reservation *una prenotazione*
I'd like to book a single/twin/double room *vorrei prenotare una camera singola/doppia/ matrimoniale*
I'd prefer a room with a bath/shower/window over the courtyard *preferirei una camera con vasca da bagno/doccia/finestra sul cortile*
can you bring me breakfast in bed? *mi porti la colazione al letto?*

Eating & drinking

I'd like to book a table for four at eight *vorrei prenotare una tavola per quattro alle otto*
that was poor/good/delicious *era mediocre/buono/ottimo*
the bill *il conto*
is service included? *è incluso il servizio?*
I think there's a mistake in this bill *credo che il conto sia sbagliato*
See also p188 Reading the menu.

Days & nights

Monday *lunedì*; **Tuesday** *martedì*; **Wednesday** *mercoledì*; **Thursday** *giovedì*; **Friday** *venerdì*; **Saturday** *sabato*; **Sunday** *domenica*; **yesterday** *ieri*; **today** *oggi*; **tomorrow** *domani*; **morning** *mattina*; **afternoon** *pomeriggio*; **evening** *sera*; **night** *notte*; **weekend** *fine settimana, weekend*

Numbers & money

0 *zero*; **1** *uno*; **2** *due*; **3** *tre*; **4** *quattro*; **5** *cinque*; **6** *sei*; **7** *sette*; **8** *otto*; **9** *nove*; **10** *dieci*; **11** *undici*; **12** *dodici*; **13** *tredici*; **14** *quattordici*; **15** *quindici*; **16** *sedici*; **17** *diciasette*; **18** *diciotto*; **19** *dicianove*; **20** *venti*; **30** *trenta*; **40** *quaranta*; **50** *cinquanta*; **60** *sessanta*; **70** *settanta*; **80** *ottanta*; **90** *novanta*; **100** *cento*; **200** *duecento*; **1,000** *mille*; **2,000** *duemila*; **1,000,000** *un milione*.
how much is it/does it cost? *quanto costa/quant'è/quanto viene?*
do you take credit cards? *si accettano le carte di credito?*
Can I pay in pounds/dollars/travellers' cheques *posso pagare in sterline/dollari/con i travellers*

Further Reference

Books

Classics

Catullus *The Poems*
Sometimes malicious, sometimes pornographic; well worth a read

Juvenal *Satires*
A contemporary view of ancient Rome's seedy underbelly

Ovid *The Erotic Poems*
Ovid's handbook for cynical lovers got him banished from Rome

Suetonius *The Twelve Caesars*
Salacious biographies of rulers from Julius Caesar to Domitian

Virgil *The Aeneid*
Rome's foundation myth is a great yarn

Fiction & literature

AH Clough *Amours de Voyage*
A whimsical poem of love and war in mid 19th-century Rome

Michael Dibdin *Vendetta*
Thriller set in contemporary Rome

George Eliot *Middlemarch*
Dorothea's big honeymoon let-down takes place in 19th-century Rome

Nathaniel Hawthorn *The Marble Faun*
A quaint, moralising novel about two female artists in Rome

Henry James *The Portrait of a Lady*
Besides *Portrait*, try *Daisy Miller* and a couple of essays in *Italian Hours*

Elsa Morante *History*
A compelling evocation of life for the very poor in wartime Rome

Shakespeare *Julius Caesar, Antony & Cleopatra, Titus Andronicus, Coriolanus*
The Bard's take on ancient Rome

Non-fiction

Luigi Barzini *The Italians*
Insightful look into the Italians and how they run their lives and country

Donald Dudley *Roman Society*
Culture, politics and economics from the 9th century BC to 4th century AD

Edward Gibbon *The Decline and Fall of the Roman Empire*
The definitive low-down on where they went wrong

Paul Ginsborg *A History of Contemporary Italy*
Excellent introduction to the ups and downs of post-war Italy

Michael Grant *History of Rome*
Highly readable and full of facts

Peter Hebblethwaite *In the Vatican*
Opinionated insight into the inner workings of the Vatican

Christopher Hibbert *Biography of a City*
Engaging account of Rome's history

John Kelly *The Oxford Dictionary of Popes*
The life stories of the various occupants of the Throne of St Peter's

DH Lawrence *Etruscan Places*
Lawrence frolics through the territory of the sensual Etruscans

Georgina Masson *Queen Christina*
Biography of the Catholic church's illustrious Protestant convert gives great insights into 17th century Rome

Rudolf Wittkower *Art & Architecture in Italy 1600-1750*
Everything you ever wanted to know about the baroque

Film

Accattone
(Pier Paolo Pasolini, 1961)
Sub-proletarian no-hoper Franco Citti careers from bad, to worse, to ignominious early death in Testaccio in this devastating portrait of the lowest of Rome's low

The Agony & the Ecstasy
(Carol Reed, 1965)
Charlton Heston – looking much like a muscly Michelangelo statue if not like the artist himself – daubs the Sistine ceiling as Pope Rex Harrison looks on

Bellissima
(Luchino Visconti, 1951)
Screen-struck mamma Anna Magnani pushes her plain and ungifted daughter through the agony of the film studio casting circuit

Ben-Hur
(William Wilder, 1959)
Charlton Heston pushes sexual ambivalence to its limits in this epic, with religion and a chariot race chucked in for good measure

Caro Diario (Dear Diary)
(Nanni Moretti, 1994)
As much a wry love-letter to the lesser-known parts of Moretti's home town as a diary (*see chapter* **Film**)

La Dolce Vita
(Federico Fellini, 1960)
The late, great Fellini's unforgettable portrait of the fast-lane, paparazzo-fuelled life in 1950s and '60s Rome

Fellini's Roma
(Federico Fellini, 1972)
Patchwork of cameos with the kind of visual gems that only the master could pull off

Mamma Roma
(Pier Paolo Pasolini, 1962)
Anna Magnani in a gut-wrenching performance as a mother striving, and failing, to keep her son from a bad end in the mean streets of Rome's outskirts

The Portrait of a Lady
(Jane Campion, 1996)
Nicole Kidman sniffs through her miserable stay in and around Rome in Campion's laboured adaption of Henry James's novel

Roma, Città Aperta
(Roberto Rossellini, 1945)
This semi-documentary on the war-time resistance is considered the foundation stone of neo-realism

Roman Holiday
(William Wyler, 1953)
Endlessly endearing story of bored Princess Audrey Hepburn on the lam in Rome. Uniquely for its time, it was filmed on location

The Roman Spring of Mrs Stone
(Jose Quintero, 1961)
Fading, widowed Vivien Leigh tries to spice up her Roman holiday with an affair with gigolo Warren Beatty

Quo Vadis?
(Mervyn Le Roy, 1951)
Blood, sand, and love in the lions' den. A huge – and hugely long – epic

Spartacus
(Stanley Kubrick, 1960)
Kirk Douglas does his best to get the slaves revolting in another marathon

The Talented Mr Ripley
(Anthony Minghella, 1999)
Jude and Matt play out part of their tortuous relationship against a Roman background

Three Coins in the Fountain
(Jean Negulesco, 1954)
Rome looks like one big, luscious postcard, and the three American tourist lasses get their Latin lovers

Websites

The first port of call for information on museums, archaeological sites is the Cultural Heritage Ministry's excellent (but alas Italian-only; English pending as this guide went to press) site at www.beniculturali.it.

Also useful is the city council's site at www.comune.roma.it.

Other informative sites include:
www.atac.roma.it
Transport in and around the city (English)

www.enjoyrome.it
The informative site of the ever-reliable Enjoy Rome agency (*see p304*; English)

www.museionline.it
Constantly updated guide to museums and exhibitions (English)

www.romaturismo.com
The APT's (*see p303*) site has information on exhibitions, theatres and what to do with your kids (English)

Index

Priscilla 150
San Callisto 147, **149**
San Sebastiano 132, 147, **149**
Sant'Agnese fuori le Mura 151
Catanei, Vanozza 12-13, 65
cats 108
Cavallini, Pietro 33, 65, 115, 117
Celio 122-128
  hotels **51**, 53
  restaurants & cafés 183, 200
cemetery 121
Centrale Montemartini 71, *152*, 152, **153**, 229
  bar 195
centri sociali 251
Centro per le Arti Contemporanee di Roma **150**, 232
Centro Ricerche Musicali 245
Centro Servizi Pellegrini e Turisti 304
Centro Servizi per L'Archeologia 60
Centro Turistico Studentesco 301
Cerveteri 270, **280**, 281
Chapel of Nicholas V 33, **142-143**
Chiarone **270**, 272
Chiesa Nuova/Santa Maria in Vallicella 28, **92**
children's Rome 228-231
  abuse helpline 295
  amusement parks 231
  babysitters 231
  cinema (Dei Piccoli) 235
  eating out 160
  guidebooks 231
  hospital 294
  library 230
  theatre **231**, 265
  see also Bioparco; Explora
Chiostro dei Genovesi 116
Christians, early 10-11, 125, 144
Christmas 65, **227**
churches 58-59
  architecture 26-29
  art 32, 33, 34
  concerts 247
  English-speaking 85, 299-300
  mosaics **32**, 115, 122, 125-126

non-Catholic 300
opening times 60
out of town 279, 281
see also specific churches
Cimitero Acattolico 121
cinemas 235-236
Cineporto 237
Circo di Massenzio **147**, 148
Circo Massimo **66**, 229, 261
Circolo degli Artisti 250
Circolo Mario Mieli di Cultura Omosessuale 239, **242**
Cloaca Maxima 11, 70, 107, **109**
clubs 121, 249, **253-257**
  admission 249
  gay 239-242
  lesbian 243
  live music 250-253
coffee 196
Colle Oppio 130-134
Colonna di Marco Aurelio 86, **87**
Colosseum 10, 25, 30, **66**, 229
Columbiarium 148
comedy 265
Commodus, emperor 63
concerts, classical 245-248
conference facilities 291
Constantine, Emperor 10-11, 66, 126, 128, 129, 139, 150, 151, 152
contraception 294
corso Vittorio Emanuele 92
Cortona, Pietro da **26**, 29, 63, 65, 76-77, 84, 92, 93, 140
Counter-Reformation 15-16, 28
couriers 291
credit cards 298-299
crime 301
Crypta Balbi **103**, 104, 229
Cryptoporticus 69
CTS *see* Centro Turistico Studentesco
currency 298
customs 291

d

dance **263**, 264, 265
delicatessens 215
dentists 294

Diocletian, emperor 10
disabled access 291-293
  Vatican Museums 142
doctors 294
Dolce Vita, La 74, 81, 84
Domine Quo Vadis? 132, 146
Domus Aurea 65, 66, 69, **130-131**
Domus Flavia 69
Domus Livia 69
driving *see* cars & driving
drugs 293
  helpline 295
dry cleaners 220
Dying Gaul, The 32, 63, 84

e

Easter and Holy Week **224**, 248
Eden hotel 38
  restaurant 164
electricity 293
email 295-296
embassies & consulates 293
  French 103
  US 84, 293
emergencies 293, 294
Emporio-Porto Fluviale 121
Enjoy Rome 291, **304**
Epiphany 227
Esquilino *see* Monti & Esquilino
Estate Romana 225, 237, 258
Etruscans 7-8, 11, 32, 270, 273, 278, **280-281**
  museums 83, 100, 142, 270, 279, 280, 281
EUR 19, 30, **153-155**, 231
Explora – Museo dei Bambini di Roma **81**, 228

f

FAI *see* Fondo per l'Ambiente Italiano
fashion 208-212
  accessories 208-211
  boutiques 209, 211-212
  designer 213
  lingerie 212
  Roma Alta Moda 225
faxes 303

Fellini, Federico 74, 81, 84, 85
Ferragosto 227
festivals & events **224-227**, 237
  Genzano flower festival 276
  music 225, 244, 248, 258
film festivals 237
film industry 81, 84, 234-235, 238
film locations 74, 109, 234, 275
fire service 293
Flaminia 150
Fondazione Memmo *see* Palazzo Ruspoli
Fondo per l'Ambiente Italiano 226
Fontana, Domenico **26**, 129, 133, 135
Fontana dei Quattro Fiumi 96
Fontana del Moro 96
Fontana del Tritone 76
Fontana dell'Acqua Felice 135
Fontana delle Api 84
Fontana delle Tartarughe **106**, 229
Fontana di Trevi *see* Trevi Fountain
Fontana Paola 117
football 259-260
fora 69-73
  Fori Imperiali 65, *69*, **70-71**
  Foro Romano 32, 69-70, **71-73**, 229
Foro Italico (sports complex) 19, 30, *151*, 258, 259, **262**
Fosse Ardeatine 146-147
fountains, drinking 113
Frascati **274**, 276
Fregene 230, **270**
Frontiera 250
Fuksas, Massimiliano 29

g

Gaeta 271, 272
Galleria Borghese 34, **81-82**
  café 195
Galleria Chiaramonte 142
Galleria Colonna 74, **75**
Galleria Comunale d'Arte Moderna e Contemporanea 34, **85**, 232

Advertisers' Index

Please refer to the relevant sections for
addresses and telephone numbers.

Maps

Railways Around Rome

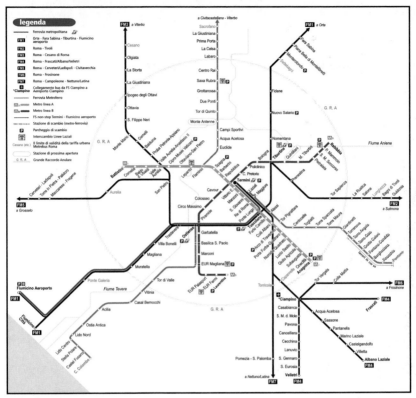

© Copyright ATAC S.p.A. By kind permission.

Targasys.

A world of services.

Targasys is always with you, ready to assure you all the tranquillity and serenity that you desire for your journeys, 24 hours a day 365 days a year.

Roadside assistance always and everywhere, infomobility so not to have surprises, insurance... and lots more.

To get to know us better contact us at the toll-free number **00-800-55555555**.

...and to discover Targa Connect's exclusive and innovative integrated infotelematic services onboard system visit us at:

www.targaconnect.com

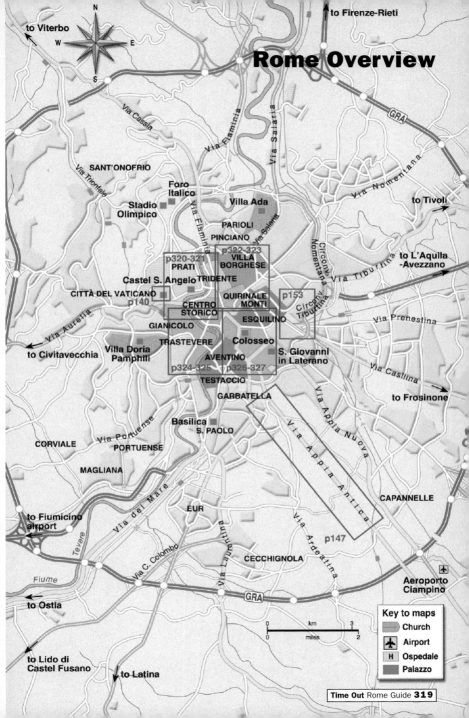

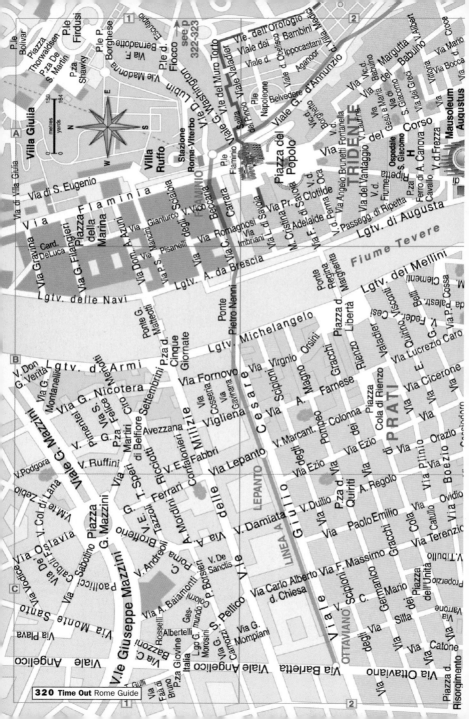

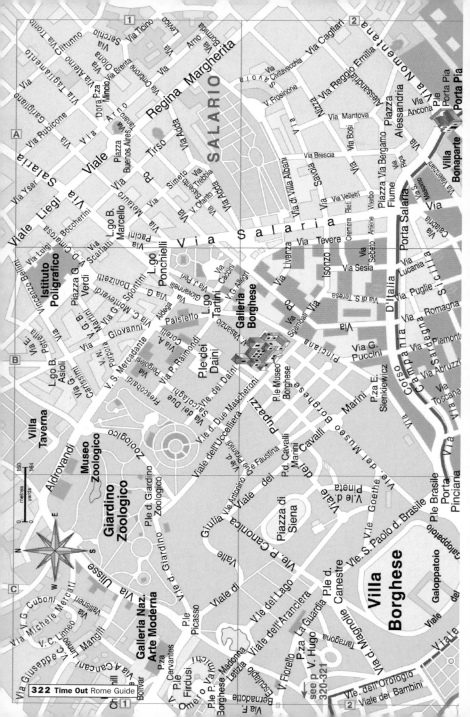

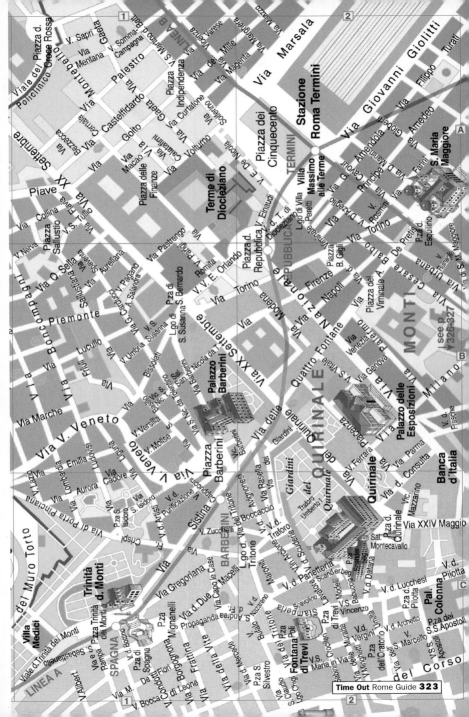

see p. 326-327

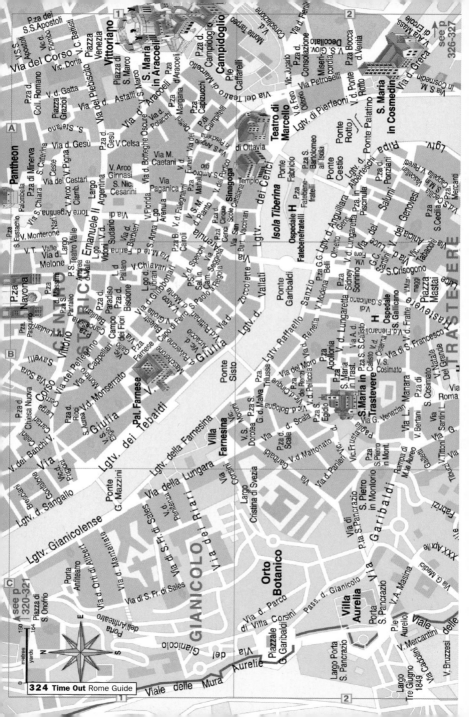

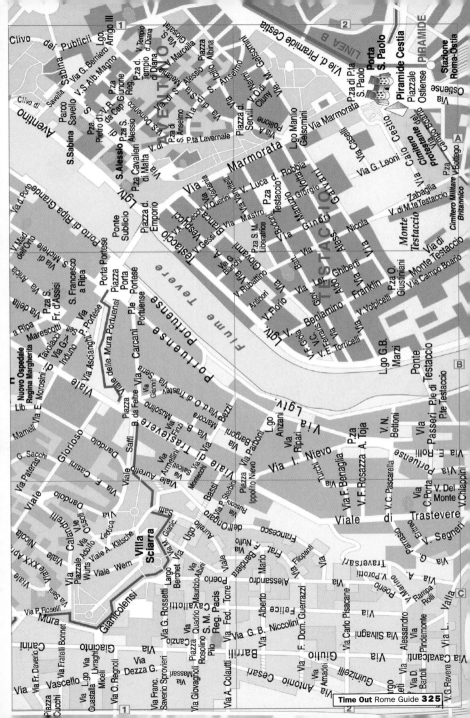

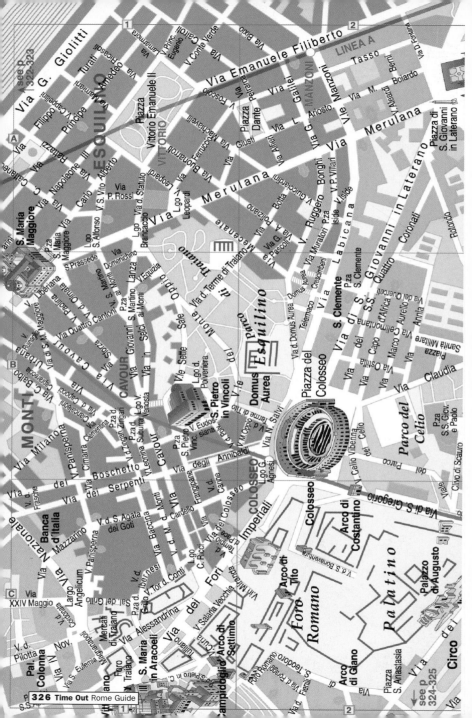

see p. 322-323

see p 324-325

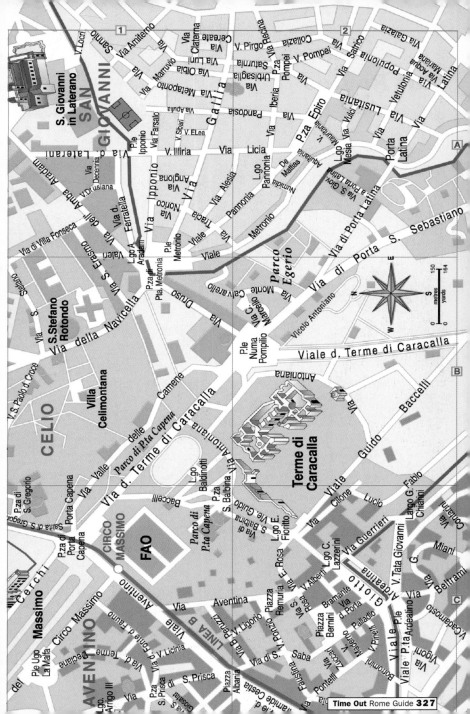

Bus Routes

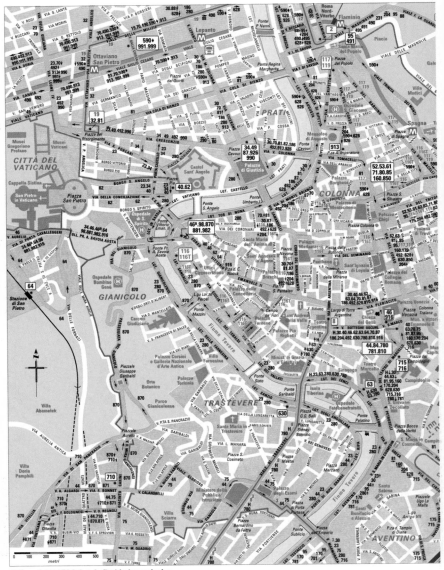

© Copyright ATAC S.p.A. By kind permission.

Street Index